FIFTH EDITION

MW01196888

Introduction to Human Services

Through the Eyes of Practice Settings

Michelle E. Martin
California State University, Fullerton

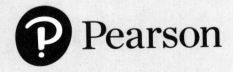

Content Development: Curtis Vickers
Content Management: Rebecca Fox-Gieg
Content Production: Neha Sharma
Product Management: Drew Bennett
Product Marketing: Rachele Strober
Rights and Permissions: Lavkush Sharma

Please contact https://support.pearson.com/getsupport/s/ with any queries on this content

Cover Image by Oxygen/Moment/Getty Images

Copyright © 2022, 2018, 2014 by Pearson Education, Inc. or its affiliates, 221 River Street, Hoboken, NJ 07030. All Rights Reserved. Manufactured in the United States of America. This publication is protected by copyright, and permission should be obtained from the publisher prior to any prohibited reproduction, storage in a retrieval system, or transmission in any form or by any means, electronic, mechanical, photocopying, recording, or otherwise. For information regarding permissions, request forms, and the appropriate contacts within the Pearson Education Global Rights and Permissions department, please visit www.pearsoned.com/permissions/.

PEARSON, ALWAYS LEARNING REVEL, and MYLAB are exclusive trademarks owned by Pearson Education, Inc. or its affiliates in the U.S. and/or other countries.

Unless otherwise indicated herein, any third-party trademarks, logos, or icons that may appear in this work are the property of their respective owners, and any references to third-party trademarks, logos, icons, or other trade dress are for demonstrative or descriptive purposes only. Such references are not intended to imply any sponsorship, endorsement, authorization, or promotion of Pearson's products by the owners of such marks, or any relationship between the owner and Pearson Education, Inc., or its affiliates, authors, licensees, or distributors.

Library of Congress Cataloging-in-Publication Data

Names: Martin, Michelle E., author.
Title: Introduction to human services : through the eyes of practice
    settings / Michelle E. Martin, California State University, Fullerton.
Description: Fifth Edition. | Hoboken : PEARSON, [2022] | Includes
    bibliographical references and index.
Identifiers: LCCN 2020048482 | ISBN 9780136801771 (Paperback) | ISBN
    9780136802044 (ePub)
Subjects: LCSH: Human services—Vocational guidance—United States.
Classification: LCC HV10.5 .M37 2021 | DDC 362.973023—dc23
LC record available at https://lccn.loc.gov/2020048482

ISBN-10:   0-13-680177-3
ISBN-13: 978-0-13-680177-1

2   2021

About the Author

Dr. Michelle Martin is an Assistant Professor in the Department of Social Work at California State University, Fullerton (CSUF), where she teaches courses in social welfare policy, research, and community practice. Her current research interests are focused on the politicization of immigration, human rights of displaced populations, and how social media is used by diaspora and migrant populations to express a range of narratives. She also researches how social media is used for social justice advocacy purposes and the dissemination of propaganda that influences political identity and ideology. Dr. Martin is the author of three textbooks in social work, human services, and global advocacy policy practice, as well as other publications. Dr. Martin is on the board of the United Nations Association of the United States, San Diego Chapter—a nonprofit grassroots organization dedicated to promoting political and public support for the United Nations on a local level, including garnering support for the UN Sustainable Development Goals. Dr. Martin has practiced in the field of human services and social work for approximately 25 years, working in a range of practice settings, most recently in global policy practice. Dr. Martin is an active blogger and writes about current events and political dynamics related to immigration as well as women and well-being.

Preface

The fifth edition of *Introduction to Human Services: Through the Eyes of Practice Settings* includes many important updates and additions reflecting the many changes that have occurred in the world since the first edition was written, and particularly since 2016. I was motivated to write this book after teaching my very first human services class back in 2002. I didn't know (way back then) that most professors adopted one or two textbooks and then developed a class based on their content. I developed a course curriculum based on what I knew from having worked in the field for more than a decade. Imagine my surprise when I couldn't find a single book that matched the way I thought the course should be taught! Rather than teaching through the lens of populations (e.g., working with children, working with families), I believed an introductory course should be taught from the perspective of the practice settings we work in, which often reflects a range of major social problems within society.

You see, I had worked with children in schools, in foster care, and in hospice, and I was confident that each setting involved distinctly different approaches. Yes, children are children, regardless of the practice setting, but the way a human services provider works with them is wholly dependent on the practice context. Why? Because the human services is one of the few helping professions that is focused as much on social problems as it is on human behavior. With roots in social justice movements, human services professionals evaluate clients within the context of their environments, considering structural dynamics and social problems such as poverty, homelessness, violence, food insecurity, and a range of human rights violations and intolerance, bias, and prejudice against people of color, immigrants, LBGTQ people, women, and other at-risk populations. So I essentially flipped the script, using practice settings (and social problems) as the lens through which to evaluate the nature, functions, and roles of human services agencies and the professionals who work there.

There have been several major changes in society since the first edition of this book, most notably the evolution of technology and social media. Social media has changed just about everything in the world—from how we relate to others on a personal level (including dating), to how politics is perceived and discussed, and more recently to the dramatic increase in polarization on most social problems in the world. These shifts have significantly impacted the human services field, and I've done my best to reflect the range of these changes and how they have impacted the evolution of various social problems, the perceptions of those who struggle in society, and how assistance is structured and delivered.

Another shift includes increased globalization, also influenced by the internet and social media, and this book, particularly the fifth edition, includes the range of ways that the shrinking world has impacted the most vulnerable members of society and challenged service provision. Social problems are dynamic, as are the people most impacted by them; so the profession of human services must be equally dynamic in helping to address social problems on micro and macro levels. Thus, in addition to exploring the traditional aspects of human services provision, I have also touched on a wide range of emerging issues as well. For instance, the climate crisis has exacerbated a range of existing challenges, increasing the struggles experienced by many populations and warranting creative and effective responses on the part of helping professions, including the human services. Consider the dramatic increase of wildfires, particularly in California and Colorado, and the impact of forced displacement and trauma on communities and the human services providers who work in those communities. In that sense, this book, and this edition in particular, provides a comprehensive up-to-date exploration of what it means to be a human services professional, in all its various forms, in the 21st century.

NEW TO THIS EDITION

The fifth edition of this textbook includes a comprehensive updating of the entire book, with a particular focus on emerging issues related to the current political condition in the United States, the state of **poverty** and its impact on **at-risk populations,** and issues often not included in other human services textbooks such as **immigration, environmental injustice,** the growth of **tent encampments,** shifts in approaches to social policy and the impact of **technology** and **social media** on the everyday lives of Americans, and our political systems. In addition, all of the research and statistics have been updated, the impact of social media has been integrated throughout the book, and relevant current events, such as **escalating racial tensions,** have been updated, as has legislation impacting those in the human services and the populations they serve. I have made a distinct effort to incorporate suggestions from professors and students from around the country (and globe) who use my text and were kind enough to take the time to reach out to me.

Here are some of the major updates in this text:

- **Updated research,** policy, and statistics.
- Increased content on **trauma-informed approaches.**
- **Opening vignettes** in all chapters for easier application of challenging concepts and theories.
- Increased infusion of **multicultural and diversity issues** throughout each chapter related to a range of experiences, strengths, and challenges facing members of the Black community, Latinos, Native Americans, Native Alaskans, and Native Hawaiians and Pacific Islanders, which will help students recognize the varied way social problems impact diverse populations.
- New content on the **role of technology and social media** in social problems and intervention strategies.
- Increased content on **mandated child abuse reporting** requirements with current legal reporting requirements.
- Increased infusion of issues related to **LGBTQ+ populations,** including content on the current climate related to a range of sexual and gender expressions.
- Updated content on military personnel and their family members, and **veteran populations** (Chapter 6), which will better prepare students who wish to work with these populations and their growing needs.

- Updated content on **interfamily violence and campus rapes** (Chapter 11) to better reflect the current state of gender inequity and the state of rape culture.
- New content on **immigrants and refugees** related to recent presidential Executive Orders that will provide students with increased awareness about current dynamics surrounding global conflict, migration flow, and the ongoing politicization of immigration in the United States.
- Chapter 12: Updated content on **rural human services,** with increased exploration of dynamics and social problems impacting rural communities and rural enclaves, including economic challenges related to deindustrialization, the **opioid crisis,** and increased **food insecurity.**
- Chapter 13: New content on **natural disasters**, the **climate crisis,** and **environmental injustice.**
- Updated content on **global human services** (Chapter 13) provides students with increased global awareness necessary for an increasingly globalized world, including content on global pandemics such as **COVID-19.**

Key Content Updates by Chapter

All chapters have undergone a thorough update, with a particular focus on research, statistics, and issues related to racial diversity. The following reflect the updates and new content within each chapter:

- Chapter 1: Updated information on **ethical standards** and **educational requirements.** A new section on **multicultural and diversity perspectives** and a new section on the **importance of terminology,** particularly in relation to people of color.
- Chapter 2: Updated content on the **history of social welfare** in the United States. New content on **contributions of Black social justice reformer**s. New content on **global comparisons of social welfare models** and on **the impact of Trump administration policies** on at-risk populations and social welfare programs and provision.
- Chapter 3: New case studies highlighting **multicultural and diversity perspectives in ethical practice.** Updated content on generalist skills. New content on the **impact of technology** on practice, including an exploration of opportunities and challenges.
- Chapter 4: Updated content on the **historic treatment of children, particularly children of color.** Updated research and **child welfare statistics.** Updated content on **child welfare legislation,** and generalist practice with children in substitute care. New content on **disparities in the treatment of families in the child welfare system,** particularly Black and Native American families. Content on working with the adolescent population integrated meaningfully into Chapter 4, with **increased focus on psychosocial developmental transitions.** New content on **multicultural and diversity issues within the child welfare system.**
- Chapter 5: Updated **research and statistics on the aging of America,** and successful and active aging. New content on **opportunities and challenges facing LGBTQ older adults.** Updated content on **housing insecurity among the older adult population** and on grandparents parenting. New content on **legislation impacting the older adult population.**

- Chapter 6: New content on the state of **behavioral health care in the United States,** including updated incident rates, demographics, and disparities. New content on **trauma-informed care, dual diagnoses,** and the **harm reduction model.** Updated content on **working with the military and their family members, LGBTQ people,** and **ethnic minority populations.**
- Chapter 7: Updated content on **homeless definitions and counts.** Updated content on perceptions of the poor and homelessness, including the **NIMBY phenomenon.** Updated content on **single parent homelessness** and the **myth of the welfare queen.** New content on the current state of homelessness and the significant increase on tented encampments in larger U.S. cities. Updated content on **runaway and homeless youth.**
- Chapter 8: Updated research and statistics on the state of the **U.S. healthcare system.** New content on the global **coronavirus pandemic,** including the **disparate impact of COVID-19 on communities of color.** New content on the status of the Affordable Care Act.
- Chapter 9: Updated content on **ethical dilemmas common in school-based human services,** including new content on ethical mindfulness. Updated content on the state of **teen pregnancy** in the United States. New content on **multiculturalism,** including working with diverse populations. New content on decolonizing **human services practice in the public school system.** New content on working with **LGBTQ students.** New content on working with **Muslim students.**
- Chapter 10: New content on **faith-based human services,** including updated content on **the role and benefit of religion and spirituality in practice.** Updated content on the **federal government's approach to supporting faith-based human services agencies,** including a comparison between the Obama and Trump administrations. An updated case study of a human services agency using a **contemplative and mindfulness approach.**
- Chapter 11: New content on **violence in America,** including new content on **police brutality against Black people, particularly unarmed black men, and the role of Black Lives Matter in advocating for police reform.** Updated content on **IPV and the Violence Against Women Act** and **hate crimes legislation.** New content on **sexual assault on college campuses,** the **rape myth,** the **#MeToo campaign,** and **hate crimes against LGBTQ people.**
- Chapter 12: Updated content on the state of **rural America.** New content on **persistent poverty** and **areas of recovery** in rural communities.
- Chapter 13: Updated content on **globalization, global poverty,** and the **UN Sustainable Development Goals.** New content on **international human services organizations.** New content on the **climate crisis** and the impact on human populations, **extreme weather events, and environmental injustice.** New content on the impact of **COVID-19** on Least-Developed Countries. Updated content on the state of **HIV** infections and impacts. Updated content on **gender-based violence** and **human sex trafficking.** New content on the **mistreatment of the world's displaced populations.**

PEDAGOGICAL FEATURES

This text offers numerous pedagogical features that enhance learning of important concepts and theories. For instance, each chapter includes an opening vignette that illustrates the roles and functions of human services providers working in various practice settings. Several chapters also include boxed features that draw attention to important issues and concepts. Each chapter also includes end-of-chapter summaries and end-of-chapter reflection questions.

Pearson eText (9780136801993)

The Pearson eText is a simple-to-use, mobile-optimized, personalized reading experience. It allows you to easily highlight, take notes, and review key vocabulary all in one place—even when offline. Seamlessly integrated videos and other rich media will engage you and give you access to the help you need, when you need it. To gain access or to sign into your Pearson eText, visit https://www.pearson.com/pearson-etext. Features include the following:

- **Video Examples:** Each chapter includes *Video Examples* that illustrate principles or concepts aligned pedagogically with the chapter. These clips illuminate practice scenarios and examples of dynamics explored in the chapter. Each video clip includes reflective questions that facilitate deeper learning as students reflect on the ways a range of dynamics impact clients and client communities, the application of concepts and theories, and how experts respond in given situations.

  With this edition, we are excited to feature a series of human services videos filmed on the campus of California State University, Fullerton, as well as other Pearson video clips featuring experts in the field responding to various client situations. Each chapter is also supported by video clips from media outlets, nongovernmental organizations, and other professional sources. These are some examples:

  Chapter 3.3: The Impact of Racism and Microaggressions on Practice
  Chapter 5.3: Advocating for LGBTQ Older Adults
  Chapter 7.3: Single Parent Homelessness and Shelter Living

- **Interactive Glossary:** All key terms in the eText are bolded and provide instant access to full glossary definitions, allowing you to quickly build your professional vocabulary as you are reading.

LMS-Compatible Assessment Bank

With this new edition, all assessment types—quizzes, application exercises, and chapter tests—are included in LMS-compatible banks for the following learning management systems: Blackboard (**9780136801887**), Canvas (**9780136802105**), D2L (**9780136801863**), and Moodle (**9780136801597**). These packaged files allow maximum flexibility to instructors when it comes to importing, assigning, and grading. Assessment types include the following:

- **Learning Outcome Quizzes:** Each chapter learning outcome is the focus of a *Learning Outcome Quiz* that is available for instructors to assign through their Learning Management System. Learning outcomes identify chapter content that is most important for learners and serve as the organizational framework for each chapter. The higher-order, multiple-choice questions in each quiz will measure your understanding of chapter content, guide the expectations for your learning, and inform the accountability and the applications of your new knowledge. When used in the LMS environment, these multiple-choice questions are automatically graded and include feedback for the correct answer and for each distractor to help guide students' learning.

- **Application Exercises:** Each chapter provides opportunities to apply what you have learned through *Application Exercises*. These exercises are usually short-answer format and can be based on Pearson eText Video Examples, written cases, or scenarios modeled by pedagogical text features with reflective questions (e.g., "How do professional ethics drive social workers' responses to clients' challenges?"). When used in the LMS environment, a model response written by experts is provided after you submit the exercise. This feedback helps guide your learning and can assist your instructor in grading.

- **Chapter Tests:** Suggested test items are provided for each chapter and include questions in various formats: true/false, multiple choice, and short answer/essay. When used in the LMS environment, true/false and multiple-choice questions are automatically graded, and model responses are provided for short answer and essay questions.

Instructor's Resource Manual and Test Bank (9780136802136)

The Instructor's Resource Manual and Test Bank includes an overview of chapter content and related instructional activities for the college classroom and for practice in the field as well as a robust collection of chapter-by-chapter test items.

PowerPoint® Slides (9780136801924)

PowerPoint® slides are provided for each chapter and highlight key concepts and summarize the content of the text to make it more meaningful for students.

Note: All instructor resources—LMS-compatible assessment bank, instructor's manual, and PowerPoint slides—are available for download at www.pearsonhighered.com. Use one of the following methods:

- From the main page, use the search function to look up the lead author (i.e., Martin) or the title (i.e., Introduction to Human Services: Through the Eyes of Practice Settings). Select the desired search result, then access the "Resources" tab to view and download all available resources.
- From the main page, use the search function to look up the ISBN (provided above) of the specific instructor resource you would like to download. When the product page loads, access the "Downloadable Resources" tab.

Acknowledgments

I would like to thank several people who helped make this edition possible. First and foremost, I would like to thank my family and friends—my son Xander, who was only 9 when I started writing the first edition of this book, and who is now 25 and living and thriving in Boulder, Colorado. I'd like to thank my dear friend Gail Watts Burkholder, who helped me more times than I can count through the writing of this edition. I would like to thank my colleagues and students at the California State University, Fullerton for their support and for challenging me to remain up-to-date and consider people and their challenges in new ways, and various faculty and students from other institutions who cared enough to reach out and provide important feedback, particularly about race, diversity, and indigenous issues. I would also like to thank everyone who reviewed this book. This edition is far stronger because of their insights and recommendations. And finally, I would like to thank the editors who provided valuable input for revising this edition, including my developmental editor, Curtis Vickers; Pearson editors, Rebecca Fox-Gieg and Jenifer Niles; and the production team, Vigneshwar Kanagasabapathy and Neha Sharma.

Brief Contents

Contents

PART II: GENERALIST PRACTICE AND THE ROLE OF THE HUMAN SERVICES PROFESSIONAL

4. Child and Youth Services   106

7. Housing and Homelessness   225

8. Medical, Health Care, and Hospice   248

1

Introduction to the Human Services Profession

Purpose, Preparation, Practice, and Theoretical Frameworks

© KOMKRIT SUWANWELA / 123 RF

Sara is a bereavement counselor at a hospice agency where she spends about an hour or so per week with clients who have received a terminal diagnosis. Steve, one of Sara's clients, has terminal liver cancer and has approximately 6 months to live. He has been estranged from his adult daughter for 4 years, and Sara is helping him develop a plan for reunification. Sara helps Steve deal with his terminal diagnosis by helping him talk through his feelings about his illness and impending death. Steve talks a lot about his fear of being in pain and his overwhelming regret for many of his life choices. Sara listens, reflects, and reframes where appropriate. She is also helping Steve develop a plan for talking to his family members and saying everything he wants to say before he dies. For instance, during a recent session, Sara helped Steve write a list of what he would like to say to his estranged daughter, his ex-wife, and other family members. She is also helping him make important end-of-life decisions, including planning his own funeral. Sara and Steve will continue to meet until his death, and if possible, she will be with him and his family when he passes away.

Gary is an academic counselor at a public middle school, where he meets with sixth- and seventh-graders every Monday to talk about their feelings. The goal for the group is to help the students learn how to develop prosocial behaviors, such as empathy and respect for others. He also helps them learn better ways of expressing their feelings of anger and frustration so they can focus on their academics. Gary also works with students on organizational and time management skills, and helps them develop new learning strategies to help with their academic and social–emotional development. Gary works closely with other school staff, including the administration, as well as community professionals and students' family members

Lauren works as a case manager in the child welfare division of a county social services agency. Lauren just began working with Chloe, whose three young children were recently removed from her home due to physical abuse and emotional neglect. Lauren has arranged for Chloe to have parenting classes and individual counseling so that she can learn how to better manage her frustrations with her children. Lauren has also arranged to have Chloe admitted to a drug rehabilitation program to address her opioid addiction. Lauren and Chloe meet once a week to talk about her progress. Lauren also monitors Chloe's weekly visitation with her children and provides her with guidance on more positive ways to engage her children. Lauren is required to attend court once per month to update the judge on Chloe's progress on her parenting plan. Successful completion of this plan will enable Chloe to regain custody of her children. Chloe's children have been placed in a relative foster care placement ("kinship care") with their paternal grandmother, and Lauren also monitors their progress. Lauren will continue to work with the family even after the children return home, providing support when needed to prevent another family crisis.

José is currently lobbying several legislators in support of a bill that would increase funding for indigenous health programs. As the social policy advocate for a local grassroots organization serving several Native American reservations in Arizona, José is responsible for writing position statements and contacting local lawmakers to educate them on the importance of legislation aimed at increasing Native American access to a range of health-related services, both on and off the reservations. José also writes grants for federal, state, and private funding and does outreach in Native American communities to increase awareness about available public health services.

What do all these professionals have in common? They are all working within the interdisciplinary field of human services, each possessing a broad range of generalist skills and having a wide range of responsibilities related to their respective roles in helping people overcome a variety of **social problems**. The National Organization for Human Services (NOHS), a national professional association of human services practitioners and educators, describes the human services profession as an interdisciplinary field that exists to meet the needs of clients through prevention efforts and direct practice, with the goal of significantly improving their lives. Human services professionals are also committed to improving the ways in which services are provided (service delivery systems), as well as improving the quality of those services (Bureau of Labor Statistics, 2011).

WHAT IS THE HUMAN SERVICES PROFESSION?

Learning Outcome 1.1 **Develop a working definition of human services that identifies key reasons why people may need to use these services**

The *human services* profession is broad, covering a number of careers, all having one thing in common—helping people meet their basic needs that for whatever reason cannot be met without outside assistance. The primary goal of human services is to assist people and communities function at an optimum level across a number of life domains. According to the NOHS, the profession is concerned with improving access to services (often called delivery systems), as well as ensuring accountability for professionals. The profession is also committed to increasing the coordination of providers since interprofessional cooperation improves the effectiveness of services provided (NOHS, n.d.). The human services profession can include a variety of job titles and levels of responsibilities, such as caseworker, program coordinator, outreach counselor, crisis counselor, and victim advocate. However, increasingly those working in the human services fields with a degree in human services are identified as human services providers, workers, practitioners, and generalists.

The human services profession is relatively young, and thus is still developing a professional identity, which includes distinguishing human services from its close "cousin," social work. Many human services educational programs were developed in the 1970s by social workers, and thus there was considerable overlap with bachelor of social work (BSW) programs (Topuzova, 2006). But in recent years, human services educational programs have become far more distinct with the development of a unique professional identity. With regard to similarities, both human services and social work disciplines are interdisciplinary in nature, and both focus on meeting the needs of marginalized and historically oppressed populations. Both are committed to social justice and advocacy on micro and macro levels. Additionally, both disciplines require students to engage in a field experience, which is perceived as a foundational component of the respective programs' pedagogy.

With regard to differences, the human services profession is multidisciplinary in nature, including professionals in psychology, counseling, and other mental health fields in further developing the human services profession from a practice perspective. Further, many grassroots professionals with associate degrees may be included under the umbrella of human services professionals. Many human services programs also tend to be more interdisciplinary in hiring practices, including hiring instructors from a variety of helping fields, whereas social work programs place an emphasis on hiring faculty with social work degrees from Council on Social Work Education (CSWE)-accredited programs (Topuzova, 2006). Social workers also have state licensing requirements to become licensed to practice, whereas currently there are no state licensing requirements for human services graduates. This does not mean that human services professionals can engage in therapy services, but rather that they need to complete graduate educations in social work, psychology, or counseling.

An important question then is, are the differences between human services and other helping professions solely educational ones or are there actual differences in the field that makes human services a distinct discipline? And if the former is true, why did the field of human services evolve at all as a specific discipline? The answers to these questions are complex, and while there remains no prevailing consensus many believe that with regard to social work specifically, human services evolved to fill gaps left by social work's increasing professionalization. In other words, as the requirements to become a social worker continued to increase, professional social workers tended to move out of paraprofessional and/or grassroots roles and into more highly trained direct service and administration roles.

Prior to the professionalization of the social work field, anyone who worked with those in need could identify as a social worker. Yet, licensing requirements mean that only professionals who have a BSW or Master of Social Work (MSW) and hold a state license (Licensed Social Worker [LSW] or Licensed Clinical Social Worker [LCSW]) can refer to themselves as social workers. So, what about everyone else? What about those professionals working in homeless or domestic violence shelters, those who are court advocates working with victims of violent crime, or those who manage the cases of recently arrived refugees? Well, if they have completed an associate, baccalaureate, or master's program in human services, we call them *human services professionals, providers, practitioners,* or *generalists.* Thus, human services professionals fill a very important role in society, and while there is some overlap with social work with regard to the professions' roots, educational philosophies, and professional missions, human services professionals are unique in their scope and in some respects, their focus.

Because of the overlap between human services and social work, I use the title *human services professional, practitioner, provider,* or *generalist* to refer to all professionals working within the human services fields; however, if I use the term *social worker,* then I am referring to the legal definition and professional distinction of a licensed social worker, indicating either a BSW or MSW level of education. Also, I use the terms *human services* and *human services agency* rather than *social services* and *social service agency,* although these terms tend to be used interchangeably in the professional literature.

Why Is Human Services Needed?

Human services will always be needed because all human beings have basic needs that at times cannot be met without outside assistance. Some basic human needs include the need for food, health care, shelter, and safety. People also have social needs, such as the need for interpersonal connection, love, and community. People have psychological needs as well, such as the need to heal past trauma, or the need to address the psychological ramifications of enduring a disaster, such as a tornado, hurricane, or wildfire. People can get their needs met in a variety of ways. For instance, family, friends, and places of worship can meet many social and psychological needs. Needs related to food, shelter, childcare, housing, and health care can be met through paid employment, assistance from family and friends, and employer-sponsored health care benefits. The path toward meeting many needs is education, which increases access to good jobs and increased consumer awareness.

But sometimes people experience crises that are beyond their ability to manage with their available resources. Examples include a natural disaster or a health care crisis. There are also many people in society who are unable to meet even their most basic needs. Perhaps they do not have a supportive family or have no family at all; they may have no friends or have friends who are either unsupportive or unable to provide assistance. They may have no social support network of any kind—no faith community, no family, no friends, no supportive neighbors. They may lack the skills or education to gain sufficient employment, and thus they may not have health insurance and may live paycheck to paycheck and not have a "rainy day" savings account. Perhaps they've spent the majority of their lives dealing with an abusive and chaotic childhood and are now suffering from the manifestation of that experience in the form of psychological problems and substance abuse, and as a consequence cannot focus on meeting their basic needs until they are able to deal with their childhood psychological trauma. Or perhaps they are older adults and their savings accounts and pensions are exhausted.

Pearson eText

Video Example 1.1

This video highlights the mass devastation of the 2018 Camp Fire in Paradise, California, which wiped out the entire community, killing 85 people and displacing all of its residents. What are some issues a human services professional might deal with when providing counseling to survivors?

https://www.
youtube.com/
watch?v=kAGXSLUn9RY

People who have always had good support systems and have not experienced challenges requiring extensive resources may mistakenly believe that those who cannot meet their most basic needs of shelter, food, health care, and emotional and social needs must be doing something wrong. This belief is often mistaken because numerous barriers exist that prevent some people from meeting their needs. These barriers may or may not be apparent to others, but they do exist, and they often have nothing to do with personal choices. Rather, such barriers are often systemic in nature.

Many people experience challenges that push them beyond their level of self-sufficiency.

This leads to another reason why human services are needed—the existence of structural and systemic forms of oppression and social injustice that impacts certain populations. For instance, in the United States many people of color, such as members of the Black community, Latina/os, and indigenous people, have been targets of racial discrimination, oppression, and marginalization. This disparate treatment has led to intergenerational poverty and a number of other social problems, including higher rates of mental illness, substance abuse, housing insecurity, and unemployment compared to the general population. Intergenerational human rights violations against members of a population have long-term consequences, and human services professionals are often the frontline workers addressing these issues on a micro and macro level.

Essentially, human services agencies come into the picture when people find themselves confronting barriers to getting their basic needs met and their own resources for overcoming these obstacles are insufficient. Some of these barriers include the following:

- Lack of family (or supportive family)
- Lack of a healthy support system of friends
- Mental illness
- Poverty (particularly chronic poverty)
- Marginalization (e.g., due to racial discrimination, gender bias)
- Racism
- Oppression (e.g., racial, gender, age, ability)
- Social inequality (such as policies or laws that unfairly target one population while privileging another)
- Trauma
- Natural disasters
- Lack of education
- Lack of employment skills
- Unemployment/underemployment
- Economic recession
- Physical and/or intellectual disability

How best to help people meet their basic needs and increase their well-being is controversial and various philosophies exist regarding what types of services will truly help those in need. For instance, some people believe that social welfare programs foster dependence and thus should be stigmatized to discourage liberal use. Those who adopt this philosophy are most likely to believe that people cause their own problems and society is not to blame.

However, others believe that structural problems within society, such as **White privilege** and income inequality, are primarily responsible for many of the social problems experienced by marginalized populations, and a solid social safety net that ensures a basic level of services will allow people to function at their optimal level. Those who adopt this philosophy are most likely to believe that while people do make choices, most social problems are caused by inequities on a societal level. The NOHS Ethical Standards for Human Services Professionals' emphasis on social injustice reflects the profession's commitment to the latter position—the belief that many of the social problems people experience that may appear to be of a personal nature, actually exist on a societal level. This is one reason why human services professionals are trained to work on a macro level as well as a micro level, advocating for social change within communities and governments.

The primary goal of human services is to assist people in achieving self-sufficiency and reaching their optimal level of functioning. This means that human services professionals are committed to helping people develop the necessary skills to become self-sufficient and fully functioning (to the best of their ability), personally and within society. Thus, although an agency may subsidize a family's rent for a few months when they are in a crisis, human services professionals will then work with the family members to remove any barriers that may be keeping them from meeting their housing needs in the future. Examples of such barriers are substance abuse disorders, a lack of education or vocational skills, health problems, mental illness, or needing self-advocacy skills necessary for combating prejudice and discrimination in the workplace, to the greatest extent possible.

Human services professionals are committed to working on **micro (individual)** and **mezzo (group) levels** with a broad range of populations, including high-needs and **disenfranchised populations**, as well as members of **historically oppressed and marginalized groups**, providing them with the necessary resources to get their basic needs met. Human services professionals are also committed to working on a **macro (societal) level** to remove barriers to optimal functioning that affect large groups of people. They do this by advocating for oppressed and marginalized populations to have a voice in society, which increases their political and social power within society. For instance, by advocating for changes in laws and various policies, human services professionals, in coordination with other helping professions, have contributed to making great strides in confronting prejudice and discrimination based on race, gender, sexual orientation, socioeconomic status, or any of a number of characterizations that may lead to marginalization within society.

EDUCATIONAL REQUIREMENTS AND PROFESSIONAL STANDARDS FOR THE HELPING PROFESSIONS

Learning Outcome 1.2   **Describe the role of the Council on Standards for Human Service Education (CSHSE) and the National Organization for Human Services (NOHS)**

The human services field is generalist and interdisciplinary in nature, and thus includes different professions with varying functions, levels of education, and requirements for

Table 1.1   Multiple Discipline Degree Requirements

Degree	Academic Area/Major	License/Credential	Possible Careers
BA/BS	Human Services	BS-BCP	Caseworker, youth worker, residential counselor, behavioral management aide, case management aide, alcohol counselor, adult day care worker, drug abuse counselor, life skills instructor, social service aide, probation officer, child advocate, gerontology aide, juvenile court liaison, group home worker, child abuse worker, crisis intervention counselor, community organizer, social work assistant, psychological aide
BA/BS	Psychology, Sociology	N/A	Same as above, depends on state requirements
BSW	Social Work (program accredited by CSWE)	Licensing (LSW, LCSW) depends on state requirements	Same as above, depends on state requirements
MA/MS 30–60 credit hours	Counseling Psychology	LCP (Licensed Clinical Professional—on graduation); LCPC (Licensed Clinical Professional Counselor—3,000 postgrad supervised hours)	Private practice, some governmental and social service agencies
MSW 60 credit hours	Social Work (program accredited by CSWE)	LSW (on graduation, depending on state); LCSW (Licensed Clinical Social Worker—3,200 postgrad supervised hours)	Private practice, not-for-profit social service agencies, for-profit agencies, governmental agencies (some requiring licensure)
PsyD 120 credit hours	Doctor of Psychology	PSY# (Licensed Clinical Psychologist—~3,500 postgrad supervised hours)	Private practice, many governmental and social service agencies, teaching in some higher education institutions
PhD (Psychology) 120 credit hours	Doctor of Philosophy in Psychology	PSY# (Licensed Clinical Psychologist—3,500 postgrad supervised hours)	Private practice, many governmental and social service agencies, teaching in higher education institutions

state licensure. Understanding the specific requirements for the various careers within the broader human services profession helps human services students better understand the requirements for their careers of interest.

Table 1.1 reflects a very general breakdown of degrees in the helping fields, their corresponding certifications and licenses, as well as commonly associated careers. Some states may have different requirements.

Human Services Educational Standards

The Council for Standards in Human Service Education (CSHSE) was established in 1979 for the purposes of ensuring excellence in human services education at the associate, baccalaureate, and master's levels, through the guidance and direction of educational programs offering degrees specifically in human services. The CSHSE developed a set of research-based national standards for curriculum and subject area competencies for human services education degree programs at colleges and universities and provides guidance and oversight to educational programs during the accreditation process.

The CSHSE requires that the curriculum in a human services program cover the following standard content areas: *knowledge* of the human services field through the understanding of relevant *theory, skills, and values* of the profession, within the context of the *history* of the profession; the interaction of *human systems*; the range and scope of *human services delivery systems; information literacy*; common *program planning and evaluation* methods; appropriate *client interventions and strategies*; the development of students' skills in *interpersonal communication; client-related values and attitudes*; and students' *self-development*.

The curriculum must also meet the minimum requirements for *field experience* in a human services agency, as well as illustrate that students are receiving appropriate *supervision* within their field placement sites (CSHSE, 2019). The CSHSE is the only organization that accredits human services educational programs and also offers continuing education opportunities for human services professionals and educators, networking opportunities, an informational website, and various professional publications.

Human Services Professional Certification

In 2010, the CSHSE and the NOHS in collaboration with the Center for Credentialing & Education (CCE) took a significant step toward the continuing professionalization of the human services profession by developing a voluntary professional certification called the Human Services Board Certified Practitioner (HS-BCP). Human services professionals who hold at least an associate degree in human services (or related field) from a regionally accredited college or university and have 350 hours of post-graduate work in the human services field may be qualified to take the HS-BCP exam (pending an evaluation by the CCE).

The implementation of the HS-BCP certification has moved both the discipline and the profession of human services toward increased professional identity and recognition within the broader helping professional fields by verifying human services practitioners' attainment of relevant education and practice knowledge. Credentials are maintained through a recertification process that requires 60 hours of continuing education every 5 years, including 6 hours of ethics (CCE, n.d.).

DUTIES AND FUNCTIONS OF A HUMAN SERVICES PROFESSIONAL

Learning Outcome 1.3   Describe the rationale for the scope and parameters of human services functions and competencies

The NOHS, as the primary professional organization for human services students, educators, and practitioners, provides a range of benefits to members, including opportunities for professional development as well as networking, advocacy of a human services agenda, and the promotion of professional and organizational identity. The NOHS has also been influential in developing the scope and parameters of human services professional functions and competencies, some of which include the following:

- Understanding the nature of human systems, including individuals, groups, organizations, communities, and society, and how each system interacts with others.
- Understanding conditions that promote or limit optimal functioning of human systems.
- Selecting, implementing, and evaluating intervention strategies that promote growth and optimal functioning, and that are consistent with the values of the practitioner, client, agency, and human services profession.
- Developing process skills that enable human services professionals to plan and implement services, including the development of verbal and oral communication skills, interpersonal relationship skills, self-discipline, and time management skills.

The reason why these competencies are so important is because in the human services profession the human services practitioner is the primary tool used to effect change in people's lives. Thus, to be effective, they must develop a comprehensive and **generalist skill set** that enables them to work with a wide range of clients, with diverse backgrounds, many of whom are experiencing a wide range of challenges, within varying contexts. For instance, imagine that you have a 40-year-old White mother of two young girls as a client. She has recently left a violent relationship and is currently residing in a transitional housing shelter. Now imagine that you have another client who is a 75-year-old Black veteran with an alcohol addiction who is grieving the recent death of his wife. And finally, imagine that you have a client who is a young Native American teen who was living in foster care and recently ran away from home and is now living on the streets, hasn't attended school in weeks, and is refusing to return home.

Each of these cases will require that you develop the ability to understand and assess these clients through the lenses of their generational cohort, gender, race and ethnicity, socioeconomic status, the systems within which each client is operating (e.g., educational, legal, family, vocational), and how each system interacts with the others. You will also need to develop an understanding of and ability to assess conditions that support or limit functioning, such as histories of trauma and abuse, mental and physical health status, educational and employment backgrounds, prior losses, coping styles, and available resources. You will need to become familiar with a range of intervention strategies, including the ability to evaluate what interventions would be appropriate for each client, and then learn how to engage in an ongoing evaluation of the selected interventions' effectiveness.

Finally, you will need some additional skills to pull all this off, such as good interpersonal skills that enable you to connect with clients who are likely very different from you, who may be resistant to change, or who are emotionally guarded. You will also need to have excellent writing skills so you can succinctly write process notes and enter them on your agency's electronic records system using your excellent technical skills. Whew! If you can accomplish all of this, you'll be a true generalist human services professional!

Of course, you won't be flying by the seat of your pants and making things up as you go. Rather, you will have access to a set of guiding principles, also called *theoretical orientations,* to guide your decision making and interactions with clients and client systems. The human services discipline is built on theoretical foundations that reflect the values of the profession. Understanding the underlying assumptions of any theoretical framework is important because such assumptions guide practice decisions about the people we work with and society as a whole. For instance, theoretical orientations and frameworks (also called *theoretical models*) make assumptions about human nature and what motivates people to behave in certain ways under certain conditions.

We rely on theories every day when coming to conclusions about people and events, and why people behave as they do. So if you have ever expressed an opinion about why people don't work (they are lazy, or they don't have sufficient opportunities), or why some people commit crimes (they are evil, or they are socialized during a bad childhood), you are espousing a theory and may not even realize it!

THEORETICAL FRAMEWORKS AND APPROACHES USED IN HUMAN SERVICES

Learning Outcome 1.4   Apply key theoretical frameworks used in the human services discipline to real scenarios

Theoretical frameworks can serve as the foundational underpinnings of a profession, reflecting its overarching values and guiding principles (such as human services' commitment to social justice and a belief in a person's natural capacity for growth). They can also extend into the clinical realm by outlining the most effective ways to help people become emotionally healthy based on some presumptions about what caused them to become emotionally unhealthy in the first place. For instance, if a practitioner embraces a psychoanalytic perspective that holds to the assumption that early childhood experiences influence adult motivation to behave in certain ways, then counseling sessions will likely focus on the client's childhood. But if the practitioner embraces a cognitive behavioral approach, which focuses on behavioral reinforcements and thinking patterns, then the focus of counseling will likely be on how the client frames and interprets their life experiences.

All of this information about theoretical frameworks and approaches raises the question of what theories tend to be used the most in the human services discipline—both as theoretical foundations (or underpinnings) for the profession, as well as those that guide practice. When considering the various theories of human behavior and social dynamics, it is important to note that theories can be either descriptive (e.g., describing a range of child behaviors), or prescriptive (e.g., determining which behaviors in children are normative and healthy, and which ones are not). A theory may begin by merely describing certain phenomena related to how people think, feel, and behave, but in time, as the theory develops, it may become more prescriptive in the sense that certain determinations are made by the theorists with regard to what is normative and healthy versus what is maladaptive.

It is also important to remember that culture and history often affect what is considered normative thinking and behavior. For instance, 100 years ago if a woman chose to remain single and not have children so she could focus on her career goals, she likely would have been considered mentally ill. A common criticism of the major theories of human behavior is that they are based on Western cultural values, and thus the behaviors deemed normative and healthy are often culturally prescribed and not necessarily representative or reflective of non-Western cultures. For instance, is it appropriate to apply Freud's psychoanalytic theory of human behavior, which was developed from his work with high-society women in the Victorian era, to individuals of a Masai tribe in Kenya? What about using a Western-based theory of parenting with parents from an indigenous culture in South America?

Theories of human behavior used in the human services must reflect the values and guiding principles of the profession and also the range of human experiences, which supports the evaluation and assessment of clients *in context*. Important areas of context include personal characteristics, such as age, race and ethnicity, national origin, sexual orientation, gender and gender identity, geographical region, health status, socioeconomic status, and religion. Context involving social characteristics is important as well, such as the economy, political culture, various laws, the educational system, the health care system, racial oppression, privilege, gender bias, and any other broader social dynamic that may have an impact (even a distant one) on an individual's life.

The theoretical frameworks and approaches most commonly used within the human services discipline evaluate and assess clients in the context of their various personal and environmental systems, while also considering the transactional relationship between clients and their various systems. Consider this case example:

> A woman in her 40s is feeling rather depressed. She spends her first counseling session describing a fear that her children will be killed. She explains how she is so afraid of bullets coming through her walls and windows that she doesn't allow her children to watch television in the living room. She never allows her children to play outside and worries constantly when they are at school. She admits that she has not slept well in weeks, and she has difficulty feeling anything other than sadness and despair.

Would you consider this woman mentally ill? Paranoid, perhaps? Correctly assessing her mental state does not depend solely on her thinking patterns and behavior, but on the *context* of her thinking and behavioral patterns, including her various experiences within her environment. If this woman lived in an extremely safe, gate-guarded community where no crimes had been reported in decades, then an assessment of some form of paranoia might be appropriate. But what if she lived in a high-crime neighborhood, where "drive-by" shootings were a daily occurrence? What if you learned that her neighbor's children were recently shot and killed while watching television in their living room? What about her economic level, the relationship between her, her neighborhood, and local law enforcement? What about the relationship between her children and their school? Her thinking and behavioral patterns do not seem as bizarre when considered within the context of the various systems in which she is operating; rather, it appears as though she is responding and adapting to her various social systems in quite adaptive ways!

Theoretical Frameworks Based on General Systems Theory

General systems theory is a foundational framework used in the human services discipline because it reflects these systemic interactions. General systems theory is based on the premise that various elements in an environment interact with one another, and that this interaction (or transaction) has an impact on all elements or components involved. This presumption has certain implications for the hard sciences such as ecology and physics, but when applied to the social environment, its implications involve the dynamic and interactive relationship between environmental elements (such as one's family, friends, neighborhood, and gender, as well as broader social elements, such as religion, culture, one's ethnic background, politics, and the economy) and an individual's thoughts, attitudes, beliefs, and behavior.

The systems within which we operate influence not just our thoughts, attitudes, beliefs, and behaviors, but our sense of identity as well. Consider how you might respond if someone asked you who you were. You might describe yourself as a female college student who is married, who has two high school-aged children, and who attends church on a regular basis. You might further describe yourself as an active online blogger from a second-generation Italian Catholic family who loves to run. On further questioning you might explain that your parents are older, and you have been attempting to help them find alternate housing that can assist them with their extensive medical needs. You might describe the current problems you're having with your teenage daughter, who was recently caught with drugs by her high school's police officer and has been referred to drug court.

Whether you realize it or not, you have shared that you are interacting with the following environmental and social systems: family, friends, neighborhood, social media, Italian American culture, Catholicism, gender, marriage, adolescence, the sports community, the medical community, the school system, and the criminal justice system. Your interactions with each of these systems is influenced by your expectations of these systems and their expectations of you. For instance, what are your expectations of your college professors? Your family? The Catholic Church? And what about what is expected of you as a college student? What is expected of you as a woman? As a wife? As a Catholic? What about the expectations of you as a married woman who is Catholic? What about the expectations of your family within the Italian American Catholic community? As you attempt to focus on your academic studies, do these various systems offer support or added pressure? If you went to counseling, would it be helpful for the practitioner to understand what it means to be a member of a large, Catholic, Italian American family? Would it be helpful for your therapist to understand what it means to be in college when married with teen daughters and aging parents?

The focus on the transactional exchanges between individuals and their social environment is what distinguishes the field of human services from other fields such as psychology and psychiatry (which tend to take a more intrinsic view of clients), although recently systems theory has gained increasing attention in these disciplines as well. Several theoretical frameworks and approaches have evolved in the last several decades that are based on general systems theory and thus capture this reciprocal relationship between individuals and their social environment and broader social systems, including Bronfenbrenner's ecological systems theory, the ecosystems perspective, and a practice orientation called the person-in-environment approach.

Urie Bronfenbrenner (1979) developed the ecological systems theory, which conceptualizes an individual's environment as four expanding spheres, each with increasing levels of interaction with the individual. The **microsystem** includes one's family, the **mesosystem** (or mezzosystem) includes elements such as one's neighborhood and school, the exosystem includes elements such as the government, and the **macrosystem** includes elements such as one's broader culture. The primary principle of Bronfenbrenner's theory is that individuals can best be understood when evaluated in the context of their relationships with the various systems in their lives, and understanding the nature of these reciprocal relationships will aid in understanding the individual holistically.

Pearson eText

Video Example 1.2

In this video a human services provider is facilitating a support group and using the person-in-environment approach. How does this approach shift the perspective of the human services provider?

Similar to Bronfenbrenner's theory is the ecosystems theory, which conceptualizes an individual's various environmental systems as overlapping concentric circles, indicating the reciprocal exchange between a person and various environmental systems. Although there is no official recognition of varying levels of systems in ecosystems theory (from micro to macro), the basic concept is very similar to Bronfenbrenner's theory (see Figure 1.1) (Meyer, 1988).

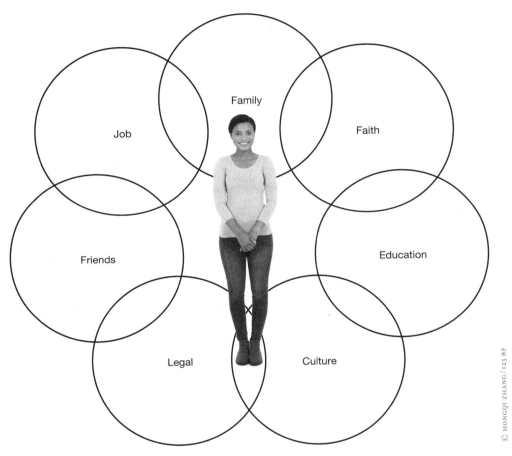

Figure 1.1
Person-in-Environment Model.

© HONGQI ZHANG / 123 RF

The person-in-environment (PIE) approach is often used as a basic orientation in practice because it encourages practitioners to evaluate individuals within the context of their environment. Clients are evaluated on a micro level (i.e., intra- and interpersonal relationships and family dynamics) and on a macro (or societal) level (i.e., the client is a Black male youth who experiences significant cultural and racial oppression). It is important to note that these theories do not presume that individuals are necessarily aware of the various systems they operate within, even if they are actively interacting with them. In fact, effective human services professionals will help their clients increase their personal awareness of the existence of these systems and how they are currently operating within them (i.e., the nature of reciprocity). It is through this awareness that clients increase their level of empowerment within their environment and consequently in all aspects of their life.

Pearson eText

Video Example 1.3

In this video, a human services provider uses a strength-based approach to reframe a client's negative self-perceptions. How might the human services provider's focus on resilience shift the perspective of the client?

Self-Actualization and Strengths-Based Frameworks

Other theories that can help human services professionals better understand why people behave as they do come from the positive psychology movement, which focuses on people's strengths rather than viewing people from a pathological perspective. Abraham Maslow (1954) developed a theoretical model focusing on needs motivation, theorizing that people self-actualize naturally, but are motivated to get their most basic physiological needs met first (e.g., food and oxygen) before they are motivated to meet their higher-level needs.

According to Maslow, most people would find it difficult to focus on higher-level needs related to self-esteem if they were starving or had no place to sleep at night. Maslow's theory suggests that thoughts of self-esteem and self-actualization quickly take a back seat to worries about mere survival. Maslow's Hierarchy of Needs theory can assist human services professionals in recognizing a client's need to prioritize more pressing needs over others and can also explain why clients in crisis may appear to resist attempts to help them gain insight into their situations, choosing instead to focus on more basic needs. Many people were criticized during the 2020 global COVID-19 pandemic for hoarding toilet paper despite no reports of disruptions in the toilet paper supply chain, resulting in shortages lasting for months. And yet, evaluated through the lens of Maslow's Hierarchy of Needs theory, this seemingly irrational behavior may make sense since toilet paper is a very basic need for many Americans and hoarding it may have been reflective of people's fears that the pandemic would prohibit them from getting their basic needs met.

The strengths perspective is another theoretical approach commonly used in the human services field because it encourages the practitioner to recognize and promote a client's strengths rather than focusing on their deficits. The strengths perspective also presumes a client's ability to solve their own problems through the development of self-sufficiency skills and self-determination. Although there are several contributors to the strengths perspective approach, Dennis Saleebey, a social work professor at the University of Chicago, is often attributed with the development of the strengths-based perspective in social work practice. Saleebey (1996) developed several guiding principles for practitioners that promote client empowerment, including recognizing that all clients

1. have resources available to them, both within themselves and their communities;

2. are members of the community and as such are entitled to respect and dignity;

3. are resilient by nature and have the potential to grow and heal in the face of crisis and adversity;

4. need to be in relationships with others in order to self-actualize; and

5. have the right to their own perception of their problems, even if this perception isn't held by the practitioner.

Figure 1.2
Illustration of Maslow's Hierarchy of Need.

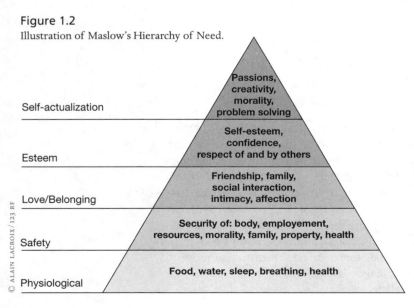

© ALAIN LACROIX / 123 RF

Sullivan (1992) was one of the first theorists to apply a strengths-based approach to practice with clients experiencing chronic mental illness, where practitioners encouraged clients to recognize and develop their own personal strengths and abilities. This was a revolutionary approach since the prevailing approach to working with the chronically mentally ill population was based on a medical model where clients are viewed as sick and in need of a cure. Sullivan asserted that by redefining the problem and focusing on a clients' existing strengths and abilities rather than on their deficits, treatment goals were more consistent with the goals of early mental health reformers who sought to remove treatment barriers by promoting respectful, compassionate, and comprehensive care of the mentally ill.

In the human services field, using strengths-based approaches is empowering for the practitioner and clients because we aren't coming into their lives presuming that they are sick and we are the experts. Rather, we spend as much time looking for strengths as we do problems. Strengths-based approaches also enable us to partner with our clients in a way that encourages them to take more ownership over their journey toward increased self-sufficiency and more optimal functioning.

MULTICULTURAL AND DIVERSITY PERSPECTIVES

Learning Outcome 1.5   Explore the human services profession from multicultural and diversity perspectives

The United States is racially diverse, particularly in the more highly populated cities in the country, such as New York, Chicago, and Los Angeles. Such diversity offers many advantages, particularly in the areas of an interesting blend of cultural activities and food. But racial diversity can also lead to conflict, oppression, marginalization, and social injustice, particularly when various cultural traditions conflict with or are misunderstood by the majority culture. Research on why so many White working-class men voted for Donald Trump for president in 2016, when many had previously identified as Democrats, found that many expressed concerns about increasing multiculturalism and they worried that they were losing their place in the social hierarchy—a phenomenon called *cultural backlash* (Cox et al. 2017; Inglehart & Norris, 2016).

Multicultural human services practice emphasizes the importance of seeing people and communities as having unique cultures, ideologies, worldviews, and life experiences (Sue et al. 2015). Human services practitioners understand the unique experiences of their clients and the communities within which they live, particularly clients who are members of historically marginalized groups. From an educational perspective, multicultural human services focuses on cross-cultural training, cultural competence, cultural sensitivity, and ethnic relations, including teaching about the nature and impact of White privilege (Akintayo et al. 2018).

But, why do we need to use a multicultural lens? Aren't we all human? Aren't we all "one"? I mean, shouldn't we be striving to be "color blind" and equal? The "we're all members of the human race" and the "I don't see color" narratives may sound good on the surface, but they're actually quite dangerous because they negate the histories of oppression, discrimination, and disenfranchisement of many groups of people in the United States. These narratives are also often based on the premise that everyone in the country has an equal chance for success. The reality is that we do not have a 'level playing field' in the United States. Some subpopulations—racial and ethnic minorities; indigenous people; religious minorities; immigrants; sexual minorities; women, particularly women of color; people with physical and intellectual disabilities; and other disadvantaged populations—have a long history of disparate treatment. Some examples include overt and covert racial discrimination, gender bias, ageism, ableism, disparate criminal justice laws, forced displacement, and environmental injustice.

I have integrated multicultural perspectives and theories throughout this book, using them as lenses to explore the roles and functions of human services professionals and the clients they serve. I've also included special sections within each chapter to highlight and more deeply explore social problems and the populations they impact, such as how White privilege (individual and systemic) has impacted diverse populations, or how people of color have figured prominently among leaders in the fight for social justice, reflecting the resiliency and strength of various marginalized populations. I do both — infuse and highlight content—as a way of calling attention to historic and current systemic injustice and the impact these injustices have on diverse populations. My goal is also to highlight the resiliency and many other strengths of historically marginalized people who have far too often been portrayed solely from a deficit perspective.

A WORD ABOUT TERMINOLOGY

Word are important because they reflect meaning and intent. For this reason, I have taken a lot of care in the selection of terminology used in this book. For instance, when selecting labels to describe various populations, I have deferred to the preferences of the populations themselves. When exploring lesbian, gay, bisexual, transgender, and queer/questioning (LGBTQ) issues, I've used terminology recommended in GLAAD's Media Reference Guide (GLAAD, 2016). I've also consulted surveys of target populations to ensure I am using their preferred terminology, such as a a recent poll that found that only 2% of the U.S. Hispanic population preferred the term *Latinx* (ThinkNow, 2020). Thus, despite the popularity of this label in academic circles, based on the growing controversy surrounding its use, I will be using either *Hispanic* or *Latina/o* depending on use and context.

I use the term *people of color* when my goal is to use inclusive language in reference to a broad range of racial and ethnic minority populations, but I use more specific terminology when I am referring to a particular group. Throughout the book I use the term *Black* rather than African American in response to the longtime push by Black scholars and advocates (Tharps, 2014). Additionally, I am following the lead of the Brookings Institution and capitalizing the "B" in Black as an act of racial respect in response to centuries of White Americans refusing to capitalize any reference to the Black population out of sense of superiority (Lanham & Liu, 2019).

When referencing indigenous populations, I use the most specific terminology possible. I use the term *Native American* in reference to broader indigenous populations in the continental United States, *Alaska Natives* when referencing indigenous populations in the state of Alaska, and *Native Hawaiian and/or other Pacific Islanders* when referencing indigenous populations in Hawaii, Tonga, the Marshall Islands, and Fiji.

Words and terminology are important and meaningful. They can be used to bring people together or divide them. My goal is to be specific and inclusive in my choice of words, respecting the wishes of the populations I am writing about, if there is a consensus and an authoritative reference. Despite my thoughtful approach though, there is bound to be some controversy surrounding the words I and other authors use to describe people, communities, and movements, particularly when so many of the people being written about in books like this one have been subject to labels specifically designed to harm them for so many years. It is important to me that the readers of this book know that I have invested time and energy in being respectful in my choice of words, and yet, if I get it wrong, please reach out and let me know.

CONCLUSION

The human services profession is generalist, meaning that we work with a wide range of people experiencing a wide range of challenges. Human services professionals practice in numerous settings, such as schools, hospitals, advocacy organizations, faith-based agencies, government agencies, hospices, prisons, and police departments, as well as in private practice if they have advanced degrees and an appropriate professional license. The nature of human services interventions is wholly dependent on the specific practice setting delivering the services. In other words, intervention strategies and approaches are contextually driven. For instance, let's assume you work with children in a school setting and your colleague works with children in a hospice setting. Certainly, there will be some similarities, particularly if the children are in a similar age range, but for the most part your jobs will be quite different, utilizing different skill sets and intervention strategies to deal with significantly different psychosocial issues.

It would be difficult to present an exhaustive list of practice settings due to the broad and often very general nature of the human services profession. Sometimes practice settings target specific social issues (i.e., domestic violence, homelessness, child abuse), and sometimes a specific target population is the focus (i.e., older adults, the chronically mentally ill), and sometimes practice settings may target a specific area of specialty (i.e., grief and loss, marriage and family). Regardless of how we choose to categorize the various fields within human services, it is imperative that this career be examined and explored contextually in order to accurately explore the nature of the work performed by human services professionals, the range of psychosocial issues experienced among various client populations, and the career opportunities available to human services professionals, within each practice setting.

For the purposes of this book, the roles, skills, and functions of human services professionals are explored in the context of particular practice settings, as well as areas of specialization within the generalist human services field—general enough to cover as many functions and settings as possible within the field of human services, but narrow enough to be descriptively meaningful. The role of the human services professional is examined by exploring the history of the practice setting, the range of clients served, the psychosocial issues most commonly encountered, the modes of service delivery, the nature of case management, the level of practice (e.g., micro, mezzo, or macro), and the most common generalist intervention strategies used within a particular area. The practice settings explored in this book are child and youth services; aging; mental health; housing; health care and hospice; schools; faith-based agencies and spirituality; violence, victim advocacy, and corrections; and international practice.

SUMMARY

- A working definition of the human services professional is developed that identifies key reasons why people may need to use a human services professional. The nature of the human services profession was explored, providing comparisons and distinctive aspects of the human services profession compared to other helping fields. A range of social problems and individual challenges that may lead to people needing the services of a human services professional is explored. The nature of vulnerability and how social conditions often render some populations more at risk of needing assistance to overcome various challenges are also explored.
- The role of the Council on Standards for Human Service Education (CSHSE) and the National Organization for Human Services (NOHS) is described. The function and purpose of the professional organizations that monitor and support the human services profession, including educational standards, state licensure, and professional certification, are also explored.
- The rationale for the scope and parameters of human services professional functions and competencies is described. The roles, functions, and scope of human services professionals engaging in practice on micro and macro levels are described.
- Key theoretical frameworks used in the human services discipline to real scenarios are applied. The foundational theoretical approaches most often used in the human services discipline, including systems theory, self-actualizing, and strengths-based approaches, are explored.
- An introduction to multicultural and diversity perspectives is provided with a particular focus on the importance of multicultural training and education related to cultural competence, cultural sensitivity, and ethnic relations, including teaching about the nature and impact of White privilege.
- Clarification on terminology used in the book provides an important basis for understanding the importance of words and labels, particularly when they apply to at-risk populations that have been subjected to historic and current marginalization and oppression. Identifying the rationale for terminology used in the book reflects efforts taken by the author to be sensitive to and help diminish the stigmatization associated with certain populations and social problems.

END-OF-CHAPTER QUESTIONS

1. What are some of the unique characteristics of the human services profession compared to other helping professions?
2. Why is it important for human services providers to use a strengths-based framework or approach when working with clients?
3. Why is using a "multicultural lens" when evaluating clients and their situations so important?
4. Why is it important to use respectful terminology and labels when describing at-risk populations?

References

Akintayo, T., Hämäläinen, J., & Rissanen, S. (2018). Global standards and the realities of multiculturalism in social work curricula. *International Social Work*, 61(3), 395–409.

Bronfenbrenner, U. (1979). *The ecology of human development: Experiments by nature and design.* Harvard University Press.

Bureau of Labor Statistics [BLS]. (2011). Helping those in need: Human service workers. *Occupational Outlook Quarterly*, 55(3), 23–32. https://www.bls.gov/careeroutlook/2011/fall/art03.pdf

Center for Credentialing & Education [CCE]. (n.d.). *Human Services–Board Certification Practitioner.* http://www.cce-global.org/hsbcp

Council for Standards in Human Service Education. [CSHSE]. (2019). *Standards.* https://cshse.org/membership-resources/standards/

Cox, D., Lienesch, R., & Jones, R. P. (2017, May 9). *Beyond economics: Fears of cultural displacement pushed the White working class to Trump.* PRRI/The Atlantic Report. https://www.prri.org/research/white-working-class-attitudes-economy-trade-immigration-election-donald-trump/

GLAAD. (2016). *GLAAD media reference guide* (10th ed.). https://www.glaad.org/sites/default/files/GLAAD-Media-Reference-Guide-Tenth-Edition.pdf

Inglehart, R. F., & Norris, P. (2016). *Trump, Brexit, and the rise of populism: Economic have-nots and cultural backlash.* Harvard Kennedy School Faculty Research Working Paper Series RWP16-026. https://www.hks.harvard.edu/publications/trump-brexit-and-rise-populism-economic-have-nots-and-cultural-backlash

Lanham, D., & Liu, A. (2019). *Not just a typographical change: Why Brookings is capitalizing Black.* The Brookings Institution. https://www.brookings.edu/research/brookingscapitalizesblack/

Maslow, A. (1954). *Motivation and personality.* Harper.

Meyer, C. H. (1988). The eco-systems perspective. In R. A. Dorfman (Ed.), *Paradigms of clinical social work* (pp. 275–294). Brunner/Mazel, Inc.

National Organization for Human Services [NOHS]. (n.d.). *What is human services?* http://www.nationalhumanservices.org/what-is-human-services

Saleebey, D. (1996). The strengths perspective in social work practice: Extensions and cautions. *Social Work*, 41(3), 296–305.

Sue, D. W., Rasheed, M. N., & Rasheed, J. M. (2015). *Multicultural social work practice: A competency-based approach to diversity and social justice.* John Wiley & Sons.

Sullivan, W. P. (1992). Reclaiming the community: The strengths perspective and deinstitutionalization. *Social Work*, 37(3), 204–209.

Tharps, L. (2014). The case for Black with a capital "B." *New York Times.* https://www.nytimes.com/2014/11/19/opinion/the-case-for-black-with-a-capital-b.html

ThinkNow. (2020, January). *How do Hispanics prefer to describe their ethnicity? Report brief.* http://campaigns.thinknow.com/downloads/files/thinknow-latinx-report-2-2020.pdf

Topuzova, L. (2006). *Community colleges and the preparation of the U.S. human services workforce.* https://www.cswe.org/CMSPages/GetFile.aspx?guid=5d3d1d46-35ab-4f74-a6ef-47b196586c15

The History and Evolution of Social Welfare Policy

© EVERETT HISTORICAL / SHUTTERSTOCK

Ida B. Wells was born a slave on July 16, 1862 in Holly Springs, Mississippi. The Emancipation Proclamation was signed 6 months later, ending slavery but not the racist system that allowed the legalized ownership and exploitation of Black people. When Wells was 16, she went to visit her grandmother and while there, she received news that her parents and baby brother had died of yellow fever. She dropped out of school and got a job as a teacher, lying to the school and saying she was 18, so she could care for her siblings. When she was 20, she moved with her siblings to Memphis, Tennessee to live with her aunt, and got a job as a teacher at an all-Black school just out of town.

Wells had experienced a tremendous amount of racism throughout her life, and when she was in her early 20s, she began to fight back. For instance, in 1883, when she was about 20 years old, she was riding on a train in a rear, first-class car reserved for women. When the White train conductor came by to collect tickets, he told her he couldn't accept hers because she was in the car that was reserved for White women. He told her she needed to move to the front car, but Wells refused, stating that she had a ticket for the first-class car and therefore she would not be forced to move. Wells later stated that the front coach cars were "rougher," filled with men who were drinking and smoking, and she did not believe it was an appropriate environment for a lady. When Wells refused to move, the conductor attempted to drag her out of her seat, but Wells fought back, holding onto her seat and using her feet as leverage. The conductor was then assisted by two other White men, who successfully and violently tore Wells from her seat and dragged her out of the car, to the applause of the other White passengers. She refused to stay in the front car, though, because of the smoke and drunken men, so she got off at the next station with a torn dress.

Because of an 1881 court case that required public transportation to reserve first-class accommodations for Black women wishing to ride in first-class accommodations, Wells sued the train company for violating the equal accommodation statute. Despite her first attorney being paid off by the train company, she ultimately won her case along with a $500 award for damages. But the train company, knowing that Wells' suit was about far more than a train car, appealed to the Tennessee Supreme Court. They knew that if Wells' suit was allowed to stand, public transportation companies would be forced to either integrate passengers or offer first class accommodations to Black customers, as the local statute required. The Tennessee Supreme Court not only overturned the lower court's decision but ruled that the co-ed coach smoking car was "identical" to the first-class nonsmoking women's car and also attacked Wells' character, stating that her sole intent was to harass the train car company. She was forced to pay back the $500, and also pay $200 in court fees. Wells was devastated by the court's decision but vowed to continue fighting for civil rights.

A few years later, she became co-owner of a Memphis newspaper where she wrote about civil rights issues impacting the Black community. When she wrote an editorial criticizing the poor educational system for Black students, she was fired from her teacher job. When she wrote about the increase in extrajudicial lynching of Black men, particularly Black men who dated White women and politically active Black men, the White community in Memphis became enraged and went to her newspaper office to lynch her; when they were unable to find her, they burned the building down instead. She was in Chicago at the time, so was safe, but White community leaders warned her never to return to Memphis. She ultimately moved to Chicago, where she continued her advocacy work against the lynching of Black men. She also helped found the National Association for the Advancement of Colored People (NAACP) and fought for women's right to vote during the suffrage movement, despite White suffragettes often rejecting her efforts. Wells fought many more battles before her death at 68 years of age, including fighting against films that depicted the Black community in a negative light, for the right of Black people to vote, and for equal access and against segregation in all aspects of civil society (Wells, 2020).

THE ROOTS OF THE AMERICAN SOCIAL WELFARE SYSTEM: POOR CARE IN ENGLAND

Learning Outcome 2.1   Analyze how England's historic system of poor care influenced the development of social welfare policies in the United States

Helping others in need can be traced back to ancient times, but the human services profession in its current context has historic roots dating back to at least the late 1800s. Human services practice is highly influenced by social welfare policy, which is why this chapter is placed so early in the book. The goal of this chapter is to help readers better understand the interconnected nature of social problems and policy responses and how political ideology and prevailing attitudes toward those in need influence how social problems are understood and why certain policy responses are selected over other possible options.

Human services practitioners are most effective when they have social and cultural understanding of what drives certain ideologies and attitudes toward those in need, particularly if the populations being served are historically marginalized due to their race, ethnicity, gender, age, nationality status and immigration status, and other marginalizing characteristics. Current trends in and attitudes about social welfare policy, such as why some people are poor and how society should respond, do not exist in a vacuum; they have roots. Thus, a general understanding of the ideological roots of current social problems and social welfare policy responses is essential to any practicing human services professional, even those with no intention of engaging in policy practice.

Social welfare policy practice is supposed to be evidence based, objective, and free of ideological bias. What this means is that if, as a society, we want to end homelessness, we would conduct empirical research on the causes of housing insecurity and what remedies are likely to be the most successful at reducing homelessness. And yet, significant evidence exists indicating that both historic and current social policy practices are very much interwoven with moral and religious philosophy, reflecting the cultural and social values of the times (Malka et al., 2011; Martin, 2012).

Essentially, social welfare policies, particularly those addressing the well-being and protection of at-risk and marginalized populations, are often driven by dominant ideologies, including religious and societal moral belief systems. The problem is that many of these dominant ideologies are based on negative stereotypes of people struggling with poverty, people of color, sexual minorities, women, and other populations at increased risk for a range of social problems. They are also rooted in belief systems based on social hierarchies, most often involving White privilege (see Box 2.1).

Some of the dominant ideologies that influence social welfare policy include those that perceive the poor as lazy, thus responsible for their economic struggles (Martin, 2012), patriarchal ideologies that presume women who dress scantily are asking to be sexually assaulted (also called rape myth) (Burt, 1980; Calhoun et al., 1976; LeMaire et al., 2016) and anti-immigrant policies that characterize all immigrants as lazy and criminals (Donovan & Redlawsk, 2018). Dominant ideologies that play on the historic stereotypes of certain populations, such as racism, sexism, classism, and xenophobia, are antithetical to the ethical and foundational values of the human services profession. As we explore the history of social welfare policy, first in England and then in the United States, policies

Box 2-1

White privilege is a social phenomenon where Caucasian members of society enjoy a distinct advantage over members of other ethnic groups. White privilege is defined as the institutionalized unearned advantage and associated power of being White in a racially stratified society (Pinterits et al., 2009). It is something that most Caucasians do not necessarily acknowledge, leading many Caucasians to take personal credit for whatever they gain through White privilege (McIntosh, 2007; Neville et al., 2001). Unfortunately, this also means that many Caucasians may blame those from non-Caucasian groups for not being as successful as they are. Yet, due to various forms of racial discrimination, it has typically been White men who have benefited most from White privilege—historically gaining access into the best educational systems (or being the only ones to obtain an education at all), the best jobs, and the best neighborhoods. Although there have been many advances made by racial groups and women in recent years, even if White privilege were to be completely eradicated today, the cumulative benefit of years of advantage enjoyed by White men would continue well into the future. Similarly, the negative consequences of years of **social exclusion** will continue to negatively impact diverse groups who have not benefited from White privilege.

and policy stances that are based on these harmful ideologies will become clear. In later chapters I will explore ways that human services professionals can advocate against ideologically driven policies that foster disparate treatment and increase marginalization, particularly of historically disenfranchised populations.

POOR CARE IN EUROPE

The Feudal System of the Middle Ages

A good place to begin this examination is the Middle Ages, from about the 11th to the 15th centuries, where a sociopolitical system called **feudalism** prevailed as England's primary method of caring for the poor. Under this elitist system, privileged and wealthy landowners would parcel off small sections of their land, which would then be worked by peasants (also called serfs). Many policy experts consider feudalism a governmentally imposed form of slavery or servitude because individuals became serfs through economic discrimination (Trattner, 2007).

Serfs were commonly born into serfdom with little hope of ever escaping, and as such they were considered the legal property of their landowner, or what was commonly called, a lord. Although lords were required to provide for the care and support of serfs in exchange for farming their land, lords had complete control over their serfs and could sell them or give them away as they deemed fit (Stephenson, 1943; Trattner, 2007). Despite the seeming harshness of this system, it did provide insurance against many of the social hazards associated with being poor, a social condition considered an inescapable part of life, particularly for the lower classes. Many economic and environmental conditions led to the eventual decline of the feudal system from the mid-14th century through its legal abolition in 1660. Some of these conditions included several natural disasters that resulted in massive crop failures, the bubonic plague (also called Black Death), various political dynamics, social unrest, and urbanization due to the development of trade and towns.

Officially, poor relief during the Middle Ages was the responsibility of the Catholic Church, primarily facilitated through the monasteries and local parishes. Catholic Bishops administered poor care through the support of mandatory taxes or compulsory tithing. Poverty was not seen as a sin, and, in fact, the poor were perceived as a necessary component of society, in that they gave the rich an opportunity to show their grace and goodwill through the giving of alms to the less fortunate. Thus, caring for the poor was perceived as a noble duty that rested on the shoulders of all those who were able-bodied. Almost in the same way that evil was required to highlight good, according to biblical scripture and Catholic theology, poverty was likewise necessary to highlight charity and goodwill as required by God (Duncan & Moore, 2003; Trattner, 2007).

Poor Laws of England: 1350 to 1550

Many economic and environmental conditions led to the eventual phasing out of the feudal system between 1350 and 1550, including health and natural disasters (such as the bubonic plague and massive crop failures). Increased demand for factory wage labor in the cities led to droves of people moving to growing cities to work in factories. Mass urbanization led to freedom from serfdom for the poorest members of English society, but it also generated a vacuum in how poverty was managed, creating the necessity for the development of England's earliest poor laws (Trattner, 2007).

These gradual shifts in how poverty was managed also led to a shift in how poverty was perceived. During the Middle Ages, poverty was seen as an inescapable condition people were born into. People were either lords or serfs, rich or poor. But after the dismantling of the feudal system, when people were migrating to the cities, the poor were often nameless, faceless strangers living in the city slums or on the streets. They were often from different countries and spoke different languages, ate odd foods, and behaved in very different manners than traditional English societal norms. Thus, it became easier to blame the poor for their lot in life (Martin, 2012; Trattner, 2007).

The increasingly impersonal nature of caring for the poor, as well as the complexities of life in cities, ultimately led to the incorporation of punitive measures into poor relief policy to control begging and vagrancy, and decrease crime in the cities. Also, during this time period about one-third of the English population was poor, prompting the need for a complete overhaul of the social welfare system (Trattner, 2007). England responded to these changing dynamics and the associated problems by passing several relief laws, called *Tudor Poor Laws*, between the mid-1500s and 1601. Tudor Poor Laws placed responsibility for dealing with the poor at the local level and reflected a complete intolerance of idleness. Local police scoured the cities in search of beggars and vagrants, and once found, a determination was made between those who could not work—the **worthy poor**, and those who were able-bodied but refused to work—the **unworthy poor** (Beier, 2003).

Legislative guidelines typically stipulated that only pregnant women, individuals who were extremely ill, or any person over the age of 60 were considered justifiably poor; thus, they were treated more leniently, including receiving government authorization to beg (typically in the form of a letter of authorization). In some cases, the poor were given other forms of sustenance in addition to authorized begging, such as food and medicine. But, if an able-bodied person was found to be unemployed, they were considered vagrant and were punished in a variety of harsh ways, including whippings, being paraded through the streets naked, being returned to the town of their birth, or incarceration. Repeat offenders were often subjected to having an ear cut off or were even put to death (Chambliss, 2017; Trattner, 2007).

Clearly, there was no sympathy to be had for individuals, male or female, who were deemed capable of working but found themselves without a job or any means of support. Additionally, little consideration was given to social or economic dynamics or what is now referred to as the **cycle of poverty**. What's even more surprising is that little sympathy was extended even to children, particularly adolescents who were unparented and found begging in the streets. In fact, district officials often took these children into custody, placing them into apprenticeship programs or **almshouses**, and subjected them to what we would now consider to be child slavery (Trattner, 2007).

The Elizabethan Poor Laws of 1601

The Tudor Poor Laws were replaced by the **Elizabethan Poor Laws of 1601**, a set of laws that established a system of poor relief in England and Wales. The Elizabethan Poor Laws of 1601 reflected an organized merging of England's earlier, sometimes conflicting and erratic, social welfare legislation. The Elizabethan Poor Laws of 1601 formalized many of the driving principles rooted in the Tudor Poor Laws, including the belief that the primary responsibility for provision of the poor resided with one's family, that poor relief should be handled at the local level, that vagrancy was a criminal offense, and that individuals should not be allowed to move to a new community if unable to provide for themselves financially.

It was quite common for community members to bring charges against others if it could be proven that they had moved into the district within the last 40 days and had no means to support themselves. Such individuals would be charged as vagrants by local officials and returned to their home districts. The underlying notion was that local parishes didn't mind supporting individuals who had fallen on hard times after years of paying taxes and contributing to society, but they didn't want to be forced to support strangers who came to their district for the sole purpose of receiving aid. The Elizabethan Poor Laws of 1601 served as the foundation for social welfare legislation in colonial America, and elements of residency requirements can be found in current U.S. welfare policy.

During this time period in England there were generally two types of charitable provision: **indoor relief** and **outdoor relief**. Indoor relief was provided for the unworthy poor—those deemed able-bodied but who did not work (vagrants, indigents, and criminals). Indoor relief consisted of mandatory institutionalization in workhouses or poorhouses, where residents were forced to work. Workhouses were designed to be harsh, with the hope that they served as a deterrent for those individuals who lacked the skill or desire to work and become self-sufficient. Outdoor relief consisted of money, clothing, food baskets, and medicine, provided in the homes of those who were considered the worthy poor, most often widows, the disabled, and the aged (Jones, 1969; Slack, 1990).

THE HISTORY OF POOR CARE DURING THE COLONIAL ERA

Learning Outcome 2.2   Compare and contrast key movements and influences in poor care and social reform in early America

Life in colonial America offered tremendous economic opportunities as well as significant hardship related to life on the frontier. Many immigrants were quite poor to begin with, and the long and difficult ocean voyage to the New World often left them unprepared for the rigors of life in America. Thus, even though colonial America offered many opportunities not available in the "Old World," such as land ownership and numerous vocational opportunities, many of the social ills plaguing new immigrants in their homeland followed them to North America.

Colonial America: 1607 to 1775

English and Scottish colonization of North America began in 1607 in Virginia and continued through most of the 1700s until independence. Because there was no existing infrastructure in the original 13 British colonies, poor relief consisted primarily of mutual kindness, family support, and distant help from England. Self-sufficiency was a must, and life was not easy on the frontier. There was a dramatic increase in the population during the 75 years before independence, increasing from 250,000 settlers in 1700 to an estimated 2.5 million in 1775! And, as the population increased, so did the need for a more formal and organized system of poor care.

Poor Care in the Industrial and Progressive Eras: 1776 to 1920s

After independence in 1776, poor care remained minimal, consisting primarily of free land grants primarily for White settlers, pensions for widows, and aid to disabled veterans. There was very little formal social welfare legislation passed at the state or federal levels until the early 1900s. And even those early laws provided only minimal benefits for some groups of children and the disabled. One of the first federal social welfare efforts was the Civil War Pension Program passed in 1862, which provided aid to Civil War Veterans and their families. Unemployment benefits were offered in most states by about 1929, and a program offering veterans benefits, consisting primarily of medical aid, was instituted after World War I.

World War I Veterans stand in front of a New York City Post Office, to fill out applications for their long promised bonuses.

© EVERETT HISTORICAL / SHUTTERSTOK

The Great Depression in 1929 marked the first time the federal government recognized the need for a national social welfare system, but the nature of provision in the 1800s through the early 1900s was highly influenced by philosophical and religious belief systems that presumed to explain why poverty and other social ills existed. These ideologies in turn influenced how the leaders of early American society believed poverty should be addressed. Two philosophies that have strongly influenced the development of social welfare policy in the United States, and perceptions of those who are in need, are John Calvin's Protestant theology, specifically his doctrine of predestination, and philosopher Herbert Spencer's **social Darwinism** (explored in the next section).

Calvin's doctrine of predestination emanated from the Protestant Reformation in the 16th century. Calvin wrote about the nature of God's control over the world and how this control was exercised, primarily in the form of who God would allow into heaven (the elect) and who he would condemn to hell (the condemned). According to Calvin's doctrine, a person's salvation was predestined by God and based solely on God's grace, not by what people did in their lives (whether they were essentially good or bad). Thus, even though all people were called to faith and repentance, not all people would be allowed into heaven.

Even though many Protestants rejected Calvin's concept of predestination, including Lutherans and Methodists, Calvin's doctrine became embedded into early American society in a number of ways. In his book *The Protestant Ethic and the Spirit of Capitalism,* Max Weber described in detail the vast influence of Calvin's doctrine on European and American society. According to Weber, Calvin theorized that since everyone deserved to go to hell anyway, that was the lot they should accept, and those who were saved from condemnation were blessed by the grace of God. Human action in an attempt to secure their own salvation (through works) was futile since one's eternal fate rested not on human goodness, but on God's mysterious desire and will (Weber, 1905/1958). Roman Catholic theology, which previously influenced poor care, recognized the omnipotence of God in matters of salvation, but also acknowledged that people had free will and choice, and could elect to walk with God and have everlasting life by following his commandments.

According to Weber, the Calvinists accepted the concept of predestination, but did not accept that there was no way to determine who was saved and who was condemned, since privilege and participation in society were based in large part on separating people into two categories: those who were godly and those who were not. For instance, only God's faithful were allowed to become members of the church, receive communion, and enjoy other benefits of salvation, including societal respect. Determining that one was condemned to hell, not because of anything that person necessarily did, but because of God's mysterious determination, became a common form of social exclusion.

In time, particular behaviors and conditions became indicators—or signs—of one's eternal fate. For instance, hard work (what Weber referred to as the **Protestant work ethic**) and good moral conduct (the ability to deny worldly pleasures in pursuit of purity) became signs of the elect since it was believed that God blessed the elect by giving them a vocation, and only the "elect" were granted the ability to be pure (Weber, 1905/1958). In other words, those who could not work for any reason, even through no fault of their own, were perceived in society to be condemned, because they were not bestowed a vocation.

A "catch-22" with regard to living a pure life was that it was the privileged members of society who determined what was considered "pure." For instance, church attendance was a requirement of purity, but only members of the elect were permitted to join the church, and the remainder were excluded, which was then used as an indicator that they were not pure, and thus not a member of the elect. Even if the poor and suffering had a voice and could protest the paradoxical reasoning behind the signs, according to Calvin, everyone deserved to be condemned anyway, thus there was simply nothing to complain about (Hudson & Coukos, 2005; Weber, 1905/1958).

The influence of the Protestant work ethic and Calvin's doctrine of predestination on U.S. society as a whole, and specifically on the poor, were significant, extending well beyond religious communities (Kim, 1977). With hard work, material success, and good moral conduct serving as the best signs of election to salvation, it did not take long for poverty and presumed immoral behavior (remember, it was presumed that only the elect had the spiritual fortitude to behave morally) to become clear indications of one's

Pearson eText

Video Example 2.1

This video highlights the roots of the human services profession. Why is it important for human services professionals to be aware of the history of social welfare?

condemnation (Chunn & Gavigan, 2004; Gettleman, 1963; Hudson & Coukos, 2005; Kim, 1977; Schram et al., 2008; Tropman, 1986; Weber, 1905/1958).

EARLY SOCIAL WORK MOVEMENTS

Charity Organization Societies: 1870 to 1893

The **Charity Organization Society (COS)** is often considered one of the forerunners of the modern social services profession and marked one of the first organized efforts within the United States to provide charity to the poor. The COS movement began in England in 1869, in response to increased urbanization and immigration and common frustration with the current welfare system, which consisted primarily of disorganized and chaotic almsgiving. The COS movement was started by Rev. S. Humphreys Gurteen, who believed that it was the duty of good Christians to provide an organized and systematic way of addressing the plight of the poor in a manner that would increase self-sufficiency and personal responsibility. Gurteen and his colleagues strongly believed that giving alms indiscriminately, and without conditions, encouraged fraud and abuse, as well as encouraged laziness among those receiving the help.

The first COS was founded in Buffalo, New York, in 1877 and served as a sort of umbrella organization for other charities by assisting in the coordination and oversight of relief services to the poor (Schlabach, 1969). The COS concept of organized and systematic provision quickly spread to large cities across the nation, and in 1890 over 100 cities had at least one COS serving the community (Wahab, 2002). The COS philosophy focused on achieving self-sufficiency and reducing dependence. Therefore, outdoor relief, such as cash assistance, was discouraged because it was considered harmful to the beneficiary based upon the belief that material relief would encourage dependence and laziness, thus ultimately increasing poverty (Gettleman, 1963; Kusmer, 1973). In this respect, the COS included concepts of the worthy and unworthy poor.

The COS practiced what was called *scientific charity*, which involved *intelligent giving,* embracing the notion that charity should be natural, not artificial (Gettleman, 1963; Leiby, 1984). Natural giving was both spontaneous and informal, and was drawn from the philosophies advanced by Thomas Chalmers, a Scottish political economist and member of the clergy. Chalmers made a distinction between "natural charity" and "artificial charity," where the former was based on what he called the "four fountains of charity": (1) people's willingness to help themselves, (2) the willingness of families to help, (3) the willingness of neighbors to help, and (4) the willingness of wealthy people to contribute to their community. Chalmers believed that "natural charity" was far less likely to involve fraud, whereas "artificial charity", involving more organized forms of giving by churches and the government, had a far greater likelihood of being abused by both the giver (e.g., politicians) and the beneficiaries.

Based on this ideology, COS leaders were highly suspicious of organized giving, and while they believed in the importance of charity, they wanted to root out fraud, by coordinating the often haphazard and disorganized giving of alms to the poor, as well as create relationships with those in need (typically single women) to determine the individual cause of their poverty (Gettleman, 1963). According to COS philosophy, poverty was almost always caused by laziness, drinking alcohol, and spending too much money (Rauch, 1975). COS directors employed **friendly visitors**, an early version of caseworkers, to visit the homes of aid applicants, diagnose the reasons for their poverty, and, if possible, develop a case plan to alleviate their poverty (Rauch, 1975; Trattner, 2007). Because poverty was defined as an individual problem, and because most aid recipients were women, there was excessive focus placed on sexual morality, with the goal of modeling appropriate moral behavior (O'Neill, 2016). Since material relief was discouraged, most friendly visitors offered only sympathy, encouragement, and guidance on how to seek employment, with minimal financial assistance (Wahab, 2002).

The COS movement was highly influenced by Calvinism, but also by another sociopolitical ideology called *social Darwinism*, which involved the application of Charles Darwin's theory of natural selection to the human social world. Darwin's theory, developed in the mid-19th century, was based on the belief that environmental competition—a process called natural selection—ensured that only the strongest and most fit organisms would survive (allowing the biologically fragile to perish), thus guaranteeing successful survival of a species (Darwin, 1859/2009). Social Darwinists apply Darwin's theory to humans and the social world in an attempt to provide naturalistic explanations for various phenomena in human social life (Weikart, 1998).

One of the most influential social Darwinists was Herbert Spencer, an English sociologist and philosopher who coined the term **"survival of the fittest"** (a term often incorrectly attributed to Darwin) in reference to the importance of human competition for resources in securing the survival of what were considered the fittest members of society (Hofstadter, 1992). Spencer was a fierce opponent of any form of government intervention or charity on behalf of the poor and disadvantaged, arguing that such interventions would interfere with the natural order, thus threatening society as a whole. Although Spencer's theory of social superiority was developed in advance of Darwin's theory, his followers relied on Darwin's theory of natural selection for scientific validity of social Darwinism.

The fatalistic nature of the concept of predestination, the Protestant work ethic, and social Darwinism became deeply imbedded in U.S. religious and secular culture and were used to justify a laissez-faire approach to charity throughout most of the 19th and 20th centuries (Duncan & Moore, 2003; Hofstadter, 1992). Although the specific tenets of these ideologies may have softened over the years, the significance of hard work, good fortune, material success, and living a socially acceptable life have remained associated with special favor and privilege in life, whereas poverty and disadvantage have remained associated with presumed weak character, laziness, and immoral behavior. Leaving the poor and disadvantaged to their own devices was perceived as nothing more than complying with God's (or nature's) grand plan (Duncan & Moore, 2003). Remnants of these doctrines and philosophies can still be seen in contemporary approaches to helping the poor and disadvantaged, and continue to influence the development of legislation in the United States, as well as people's attitudes about poverty and the poor (Chunn & Gavigan, 2004; Duncan & Moore, 2003; Gettleman, 1963; Hudson & Coukos, 2005; Kim, 1977; Schram et al., 2008; Tropman, 1986).

The social hierarchy espoused by social Darwinists was reflected in the philosophical motivation of COS leaders, often the community's wealthiest and most religious members, who agreed to provide charity to the poor as long as the poor remembered their proper place in society (Gettleman, 1963). Yet even the deserving poor did not escape the influence of the Protestant work ethic or the fatalism of social Darwinism, both of which were deeply imbedded in COS culture. For example, friendly visitors often focused excessively on the sexual behavior of the women they helped. The COS viewed immorality as the primary problem in most slums, believing that the women living in the slums (many of whom were single mothers) were weak and fallen, having succumbed to the charms and sexual advances of male suitors (Wahab, 2002). Friendly visitors would often use the guise of friendship to connect to these women, hoping they could influence them through modeling the value of becoming a good Christian woman. Many COS "friendly visitors" even went so far as to ask neighbors to monitor the younger women in the slums and report back on any male visitors (Wahab, 2002).

The principles of the Protestant work ethic and social Darwinism, with their focus on hard work, self-sufficiency, and natural selection, were clearly reflected in various speeches and writings of COS leaders. Common themes included arguments that even widows would become lazy if too much help was given, and life was made too easy for them. Many COS leaders also argued that providing charity to the unemployed, able-bodied poor was actually immoral since, according to natural selection, this population was destined to perish, and providing them charity only prolonged their suffering and was therefore in neither their nor society's best interest (Gettleman, 1963). Despite clear indications that the COS movement was influenced by the ideologies of the Protestant work ethic and social Darwinism, Leiby (1984) points out that many of the early COS leaders and volunteers, while Christians and members of society's upper classes, were committed reformers who perceived charity as a form of much-needed love—a concept that contradicted the social Darwinists' noninterventionist approach.

Mary Richmond, the general secretary of the Baltimore COS, is an example of a committed reformer. Richmond was a fierce advocate for social justice and social reform and believed that charities could employ good economics and engage in compassionate giving at the same time. Richmond became well known for increasing public awareness of the COS movement and for her fundraising efforts. Richmond's compassion for the poor was likely due to her own experience with poverty as a child. Richmond was orphaned at the age of two and then later abandoned by her aunt, who left Richmond to fend for herself in New York when she was only 17 years old. Thus, Richmond no doubt understood the social components of poverty, and how factors outside of peoples' control could have a devastating impact on their lives. Richmond is credited for contributing to the development of the modern case management model through her conceptualization of **social diagnosis**, a process involving friendly visitors assessing clients and their environments. **Social diagnoses** enabled the visitor to identify sources of strength and barriers to self-sufficiency (Kusmer, 1973; Richmond, 1917).

Despite the general success of the COS and the contributions the movement made to professionalizing the helping fields, its adherence to deterministic philosophies that negated social factors of poverty while pathologizing the poor deepened the belief that the poor were to blame for their lot in life. In retrospect, one can recognize the naiveté of believing that poverty could be controlled merely through moral behavior. But the country was about to learn a very hard collective lesson during the Depression era—one that immigrants, many ethnic minority groups, and single mothers had known for years— that sometimes conditions exist that are beyond one's control, creating immovable barriers to economic self-sufficiency.

Jane Addams and the Settlement House Movement: 1889 to 1929

During the same time that the COS "friendly visitors" were addressing poverty in the slums by focusing on personal morality, Jane Addams was confronting poverty in a vastly different way—by focusing on social injustice. Addams was a social justice advocate and a social reformer who started the **settlement house movement** in the United States with the opening of the Hull House in Chicago. Addams considered the more religiously oriented COS movement as being rather heartless because most COS leaders were more concerned with efficiency and controlling fraud than alleviating poverty (Schneiderhan, 2008). Addams used a relational model of poverty alleviation based on the belief that poverty and disadvantage were caused by problems within society, not idleness and moral deficiency (Lundblad, 1995). Addams advocated for changes within the social structure of society in order to remove barriers to self-sufficiency, which she viewed as an essential component of a democracy (Hamington, 2005; Martin, 2012). In fact, the opening of the Hull House, the first settlement house in the United States, was considered the beginning of one of the most significant social movements in U.S. history.

Addams was born in Cedarville, Illinois, in 1860. She was raised in an upper-class home where education and philanthropy were highly valued. Addams greatly admired her father, who encouraged her to pursue an education at a time when most women were destined to solely pursue marriage and motherhood. She graduated from Rockford Female Seminary in 1881, the same year her father died. After her father's death, Addams entered Woman's Medical College in Pennsylvania but dropped out because of chronic illness. Addams had become quite passionate about the plight of immigrants in the United States, but due to her poor health and the societal limitations placed on women during that era, she did not believe she had a role in social advocacy.

Leaders of the American Settlement House movement, Jane Addams of Chicago and Lillian Wald of New York. 1916. Members of the movement often lived in settlement houses in poor urban areas to offer services, education, and public health services to improve the life of the poor.

The United States experienced another significant wave of immigration between 1860 and 1910, with 23 million people emigrating from Europe, including Eastern Europe. Many of these immigrants were from non–English-speaking countries, such as Italy, Poland, Russia, and Serbia, and were very poor. Unable to obtain work in the skilled labor force, many immigrants were forced to work in unsafe urban factories and live in subhuman conditions, crammed together with several other families in tenements. For instance, New York's Lower East Side had approximately 330,000 inhabitants per square mile (Trattner, 2007). With no labor laws for protection, racial discrimination and a variety of employment abuses were common, including extremely low wages, unsafe working conditions, and child labor. Poor families, particularly non–English-speaking families, had little recourse, and their mere survival depended on their coerced cooperation.

Addams was aware of these conditions because of her father's political involvement, but she was unsure of how she could help. Despondent about her father's death and her failure in medical school, as well as her ongoing health problems, Addams and her friend Ellen Gates Starr took an extended trip with friends to Europe where, among other activities, she visited Toynbee Hall settlement house, England's response to poverty and other social problems. Toynbee Hall served as a neighborhood welfare institution in an urban slum area, where trained settlement house volunteers worked to improve social conditions by providing community services and promoting neighborly cooperation.

The concept of addressing poverty at the neighborhood level through social and economic reform was revolutionary. Rather than monitoring the behavior of the poor through intermittent visits, settlement house workers lived right alongside the immigrant families they endeavored to help. In addition to providing a safe, clean home, settlement houses also provided poor immigrants with comprehensive care such as assistance with food, health care, English language lessons, child care, and general advocacy. The settlement house movement had a mission of no longer distinguishing between the worthy and unworthy poor, and instead recognizing the role that society played in the ongoing plight of the poor—a stance that was a departure from the traditional charity organizations.

Addams and Starr returned home from Europe convinced that it was their duty to do something similar in the United States, and with the donation of a building in Chicago, the Hull House became America's first settlement house in 1889. Addams and her colleagues lived in the settlement house, in the middle of what was considered a bad neighborhood in Chicago, offering services targeting the underlying causes of poverty such as unfair labor practices, the exploitation of non–English-speaking immigrants, and child labor. The Hull-House quickly became the social hub for residents who gathered in the Hull-House café, and was also the informal headquarters for many of Addams' social advocacy efforts, which ranged from advocating for women's suffrage to advocating for racial equality (e.g., advocating against the extrajudicial lynching of Black men), to child labor laws, to global peace efforts to end war (Knight, 2010).

Addams' influence on American social welfare policy was significant, in that her work represented a shift away from the fatalistic perspectives of social Darwinism and the religious perspectives of Calvin's Reformed theology. Instead, Addams highlighted the need for social change so that barriers to upward mobility and optimal functioning could be removed (Martin, 2012). Addams and her colleagues were committed to viewing the poor as equal members of society, just as worthy of respect and dignity as anyone else. Addams clearly saw societal conditions and the hardship of immigration as the primary cause of poverty, not necessarily one's personal moral failing. Social inequality was

© CHIPPIX/SHUTTERSTOCK

Vintage Photo of a Workshop With Young Boys Working.

perceived as the manifestation of exploitation, with social egalitarianism perceived as not just a desirable but an achievable outcome (Lundblad, 1995; Martin, 2012). Addams' focus on social inequity was reflected in her tireless lobbying for the passage of child labor laws (despite fierce opposition by corporations and conservative politicians). Addams also advocated on a local and national level for labor laws that would protect the working-class poor, who were often exploited in factories with **sweatshop conditions**. She also worked alongside Ida B. Wells, confronting racial inequality in the United States, such as the extrajudicial lynching of Black men (Addams, 1909).

Although there are no working settlement houses today, the prevailing concepts espoused by this movement, with its focus on social components of poverty and disadvantage, remain foundational to the human services and social work professions, and also serve as the roots of today's urban neighborhood centers. Yet, despite the overall success of the settlement house movement and the particular successes of Addams with regard to achieving social reform in a variety of arenas, the threads of moralistic and deterministic philosophies have remained strongly interwoven into American society, and have continued to influence perceptions of the poor and social welfare policy and legislation.

Ida B. Wells and the Fight Against Racial Oppression

The opening vignette is about one of the greatest social reformers in modern history—Ida B. Wells, a Black reformer and social activist whose campaigns against racial oppression and inequity laid the foundation for the civil rights movement of the 1960s. As referenced in the vignette, although legal slavery ended 6 months after her birth, Wells' life was never free from the crushing effects of severe racial prejudice and discrimination. Her schooling was interrupted when she was orphaned at the age of 16 leaving her responsible for raising her five younger siblings. This experience not only forced her to grow up quickly but also seemed to serve as a springboard for her subsequent advocacy against racial injustice. The newspaper she owned was called *Free Speech*, and she used this platform to write about matters of racial oppression and inequity, including the vast amount of socially sanctioned crimes committed against members of the Black community (Hamington, 2005).

The indiscriminate lynching of Black men was prevalent in the South during Wells' lifetime and was an issue that Wells became quite passionate about. Black men were commonly perceived as a threat on many levels, and there was no protection of their personal, political, or social rights. The Black man's reputation as an "angry rapist" was endemic in White society, and many speeches were given and articles written by White community members (including clergy) about this allegedly growing problem. For example, an article published in the mainstream newspaper in the South, the *Commercial*, entitled "More Rapes More Lynchings," cites the Black man's alleged penchant for raping White women, stating:

> The generation of Negroes which have grown up since the war have lost in large measure the traditional and wholesome awe of the white race which kept the Negroes in subjection. . . . There is no longer a restraint upon the brute passion of the Negro. . . . The facts of the crime appear to appeal more to the Negro's lustful imagination than the facts of the punishment do to his fears. He sets aside all fear of death in any form when opportunity is found for the gratification of his bestial desires. (Davidson, 2008, p. 154)

Wells wrote extensively on the subject of the "myth of the angry Black man," and the myth that all Black men raped White women (a common excuse used to justify the lynching of Black men) (Hamington, 2005). She challenged the growing sentiment in White communities that Black men, as a race, were growing more aggressive and "lustful" of White women, which she believed was prompted in part by the increasing number of biracial couples. The response to Wells' articles was swift and harsh. A group of White men surrounded her newspaper building with the intention of lynching her, but when they could not find her, they burned down her business instead (Davidson, 2008).

Although this act of revenge essentially stopped her newspaper career, what it really did was motivate Wells even further. After the burning down of her business, Wells left the South and moved to Chicago, where she continued to wage a fierce anti-lynching campaign, often coordinating efforts with Jane Addams. She wrote numerous books and articles on racial inequality, challenging socially entrenched notions that all Black men were angry and violent sexual predators (Hamington, 2005). Wells and Addams worked as colleagues, coordinating their social justice advocacy efforts fighting for civil rights. Together, they ran the Chicago Association for the NAACP and worked collectively on a variety of projects, including fighting against racial segregation in schools (Martin, 2012; Wells, 2020).

THE NEW DEAL AND GREAT SOCIETY PROGRAMS

Learning Outcome 2.3   **Describe ways that the New Deal and Great Society programs alleviated poverty after the Great Depression**

In 1929 the stock market crashed, leading to a series of economic crises unprecedented in the United States. For the first time in modern U.S. history, large segments of the middle-class population lost their jobs and all means of income. Within a very short time, thousands of people who had once enjoyed financial security were suddenly without money, homes, and food. This served as a wake-up call for social reformers, many of whom had abandoned their earlier commitment to social activism because of decades of a good economy. In response, many social reformers started pushing President Hoover to develop the country's first comprehensive system of social welfare on a federal level.

Hoover was resistant, though, fearing that a federal system of social welfare would create dependency and displace the role of private and local charities. Hoover wanted to allow time for the economy to self-correct through the capitalist system and the market economy before intervening on a federal level. Hoover was a strong believer in the power of volunteerism, believing that everyday people could be convinced of the power of helping others, without coercion. He wanted to allow time for people to jump into action and help their neighbors, and for democracy and capitalism to self-correct before intervening with broad entitlement programs (McElvaine, 1993). But much of the country apparently did not agree with this plan. In 1933, Hoover lost his bid for reelection, and Franklin D. Roosevelt was elected as the country's 32nd president. Roosevelt immediately set about to create changes in federal policy with regard to social welfare, promising dramatic changes, including sweeping reforms in the form of comprehensive poverty alleviation programs.

From 1933 through 1938, Roosevelt instituted a series of legislative reforms and domestic programs collectively referred to as the **New Deal programs**. In his first

100 days in office, Roosevelt passed 13 legislative acts, including one that created the Civil Works Administration, which provided over a million temporary jobs to the unemployed; the Federal Emergency Relief Act, which provided direct aid and food to the unemployed (and was replaced by the Works Progress Administration in 1935); and one that created the Civilian Conservation Corp (CCC), which put thousands of young men ages 18 to 25 to work in reforestation and other conservation programs. Yet, as progressive as Roosevelt was, and as compassionate as the country had become toward the poor due to the realization that poverty could strike anyone, racism was still rampant, as illustrated by Roosevelt placing a 10% enrollment limit for Black men in the CCC program (Trattner, 2007).

By far the most famous of all programs in the New Deal were those created in response to the Social Security Act of 1935, which among other things created old-age pensions for all workers, unemployment compensation, Aid to Families with Dependent Children (AFDC), and aid to the blind and disabled. Programs such as the Federal Deposit Insurance Corporation (FDIC), which provided insurance for bank deposits, helped to instill a sense of renewed confidence in the banking system, and the development of the Securities and Exchange Commission (SEC), which regulates the stock market, helped to ensure that a crash similar to the one in 1929 would be unlikely to occur again. In total, Roosevelt created 15 federal programs as a part of the New Deal, some of which remain today, and some of which were dismantled once the crisis of the Great Depression subsided. Although some claim that the New Deal was not good for the country in the long run, it did pull the country out of a severe economic decline, providing relief for millions of Americans who could have literally starved had the federal government not intervened.

The United States recovered from the Great Depression and has since experienced several periods of economic growth and decline, but never any as severe as that which was prompted by the 1929 stock market crash. This is likely because of federal programs such as the FDIC and the creation of the SEC (and similar government agencies). In later times, though, the dismantling of some post-Depression financial regulations would contribute to yet another devastating economic downturn in 2007—perhaps not as severe as the Great Depression, but more serious and long lasting than any other recession experienced in the U.S. post-Depression era, particularly because of its global consequences.

The 1940s remained a time of general recovery and the 1950s was a relatively stable time, both economically and socially. Several laws were passed and agencies created that continued to advance the state of social welfare in the United States, including the creation of the U.S. Department of Health, Education, and Welfare in 1953 and the passage of the U.S. Housing Act of 1954 (Ch. 649, 68 Stat. 590).

The 1960s was a time of civil unrest and increasing rates of poverty, which spawned a resurgence of interest in social problems, including poverty and social injustice, particularly related to many at-risk populations, such as ethnic minority populations, older adults, and the mentally ill. For instance, President John F. Kennedy signed into law the Community Mental Health Centers Act (Pub. L. No. 88-164) on October 31, 1963, which transitioned the U.S. mental health-based care system from one of institutionalization to a community model. Kennedy was assassinated less than a month later, on November 22, 1963, and President Lyndon B. Johnson continued the Kennedy legacy with the introduction of the **Great Society programs**—a set of social welfare programs designed to eliminate poverty and racial injustice.

Policy areas within the Great Society programs included civil rights, education, and poverty (later popularly referred to as Johnson's **War on Poverty**). Examples of some of the social welfare legislation and programs included under the umbrella of the Great Society are the Economic Opportunity Act of 1964 (Pub. L. No. 88-452); the Civil Rights Act of 1964 (Pub. L. No. 88-352); the Food Stamp Act of 1964 (Pub. L. No. 88-525); Medicare, Medicaid and the Older Americans Act of 1965 (Pub. L. No. 89-73); the Elementary and Secondary Education Act of 1965 (Pub. L. No. 89-10); the development of the U.S. Department of Housing and Urban Development (HUD); and the Voting Rights Act of 1965 (Pub. L. No. 89-110).

Whether the Great Society and the War on Poverty programs were successful in reducing poverty, racial discrimination, and other social problems continues to be debated to this day. It's no surprise that conclusions tend to fall along party lines, with many conservatives complaining that Johnson's social experiment amounted to nothing more than throwing money at oversimplified problems with disastrous results, and liberals decrying just the opposite—that most of the programs had the potential to be successful, but were grossly underfunded (Zarefsky, 2005). Some point to racism as the reason why many Great Society programs were ultimately dismantled (Quadagno, 1994), while others pointed to the Vietnam War as the reason for government (and societal) shifting priorities (Zarefsky, 2005). Regardless, many of the programs remain and represent a time in history when there was increased recognition of structural barriers in society that can keep many people from functioning at their optimal level and achieving economic self-sufficiency.

SOCIAL WELFARE IN CONTEMPORARY UNITED STATES

Learning Outcome 2.4   Identify key debates surrounding public assistance goals, benefits, and eligibility requirements

A Time of Recovery: 1970 to 1990

The 1970s and 1980s was a time of mixed reviews on welfare and welfare reform. There was considerable conservative backlash in response to what was considered a few decades of liberal social welfare legislation and entitlement programs, but despite President Nixon's opposition to welfare, existing programs continued to grow. The mid-1970s through the 1980s was a boom time economically in the United States, and boom times typically mean that people become less sympathetic toward the plight of the poor. And that's exactly what happened—there was a resurgence of earlier negative sentiments toward the poor beginning in the mid-1970s and peaking in the 1990s.

This increased negative attitude toward the poor was reflected in several studies and national public opinion surveys that indicated a general belief that the poor were to blame for their lot in life. For instance, a national survey conducted in 1975 found that the majority of those living in the United States attributed poverty to personal failures, such as having a poor work ethic, poor money management skills, a lack of any special talent that might translate into a positive contribution to society, and low personal moral values. When asked to rank several causes of poverty, subjects ranked social forces, such as racism, poor schools, and the lack of sufficient employment opportunities the lowest of all possible causes of poverty (Feagin, 1975).

Ronald Reagan capitalized on this negative sentiment toward the poor during his 1976 presidential campaign when he based his platform in large part on welfare reform. In several of his speeches Reagan cited the story of the woman from the South Side of Chicago who was finally arrested after committing egregious welfare fraud. He asserted that she had 80 names, 30 addresses, and 12 Social Security cards, claiming that she was also collecting veteran's benefits on four husbands, none of whom was real. He also alleged that she was getting Social Security payments, Medicaid, and food stamps, and was collecting public assistance under all of her assumed identities (Zucchino, 1999). While Reagan never mentioned the woman's race, the context of the story as well as the reference to the South Side of Chicago (a primarily Black community) made it clear that he was referring to a Black woman—thus playing on the common stereotype of welfare users (and abusers) as being Black (Krugman, 2007). And with that, the enduring "**Myth of the Welfare Queen**" was born.

Journalist David Zucchino (1999) attempted to debunk the myth that women on welfare were lazy and engaged in rampant fraud in his book *The Myth of the Welfare Queen*, where he explored the realities of being a mother on welfare. He noted that despite the availability of ample factual information on public assistance utilization showing very low rates of welfare fraud, the image of the Black woman who drove a Cadillac while illegally collecting welfare under numerous false identities was so imbedded in American culture it was impossible to debunk the myth. Krugman (2007) also cites how politicians and media commentators have used the myth of the welfare queen to reduce sympathy for the poor and gain public support for welfare cuts, arguing that while covert, such images clearly play on negative racial stereotypes. They also play on the common belief in the United States that those who receive welfare benefits are poor because they are lazy, promiscuous, and generally immoral.

More recent surveys conducted in the mid-1990s revealed an increase in the tendency to blame the poor for their poverty (Weaver et al., 1995), even though a considerable body of research points to social and structural dynamics as the primary cause of enduring poverty. Examples of structural causes of poverty include a shortage of affordable housing, recent shifts to a technologically based society requiring a significant increase in educational and training requirements, longstanding institutionalized oppression of and discrimination against certain racial and ethnic groups, and a general increase in the complexity of life (Martin, 2012; Wright, 2000).

The general public's perception of social welfare programs seems to be based in large part on this negative bias against the poor and the stigmas such bias creates. Surveys conducted in the 1980s and 1990s showed support for the general idea of helping the poor, but when asked about specific programs or policies, most respondents became critical of governmental policies, specific welfare programs, and welfare recipients in general. For instance, a 1987 national study found that 74% of those surveyed believed that most welfare recipients were dishonest and collected more benefits than they deserved (Kluegal, 1987).

Welfare Reform and the Emergence of Neoliberal Economic Policies: 1990 to Now

Political discourse in the mid-1990s reflected what is often referred to as economic **neoliberal philosophies**—a political movement embraced by most political conservatives, espousing a belief that capitalism and the free market economy were far better solutions to many social conditions, including poverty, than government programs, which were presumed to be inefficient and poorly run. Advocates of neoliberalism pushed for social programs to be privatized based on the belief that getting social welfare out of the hands of the government and into the hands of private enterprise, where market forces could work their magic, would increase efficiency and lower costs. Market theory can be applied to many areas of the economy, when there is competition among providers, a reliable workforce, clear goals, and known outcomes. Yet research has consistently shown the limits of neoliberalism, particularly in public services, including social welfare services, due to the complexity of human services issues, unknown outcomes, a highly trained workforce, the lack of competition among providers, and other dynamics that make social welfare services so unique (King, 2007; Nelson, 1992; Van Slyke, 2003).

During the 1994 U.S. Congressional campaign, the Republican Party released a document entitled *The New Contract with America,* which included a plan to dramatically reform welfare, and according to its authors, the poor would be reformed as well (Hudson & Coukos, 2005). *The New Contract with America* was introduced just a few weeks prior to Clinton's first mid-term election and was signed by all but two of the Republican members of the House of Representatives, as well as all of the GOP Congressional candidates. In addition to a renewed commitment to smaller government and lower taxes, the contract also pledged a complete overhaul of the welfare system to root out fraud and increase the poor's commitment to work and self-sufficiency.

Hudson and Coukos (2005) note the similarities between this political movement and the movement 100 years before, asserting that the Protestant work ethic served as the driving force behind both. Take, for instance, the common arguments for welfare reform (policies that reduce and restrict social welfare programs and services), which have often been predicated on the belief that (1) hardship is often the result of laziness; (2) providing assistance will increase laziness (and thus dependence), hence increasing hardship, not decreasing it; and (3) those in need often receive services at the expense of the working population. These arguments were cited during the COS era as reasons why material support was ill-advised.

One of the more stark (and relatively recent) examples of this sentiment was expressed by Rep. John Mica, a congressman from Florida, when he stood on the U.S. House floor, holding a sign that read "Don't Feed the Alligators" while delivering an impassioned speech in support of welfare reform. During hearings on the state of public welfare in the United States, Rep. Mica compared people on welfare to alligators in Florida, stating that the reason for such signs is because "unnatural feeding" leads to dependency and will cause the animal to lose its natural desire for self-sufficiency. Mica argued that welfare programs have done the same for people, creating subsequent generations of enslavement and servitude (Lindsey, 2004).

While there may be some merit in debating the most effective way of structuring social welfare programs, arguments such as Mica's negate the complexity of poverty and economic disadvantage, particularly among historically marginalized populations. They also play into longstanding stigmas and negative stereotypes that portray the poor as a homogenous group with different natures and characters than mainstream working society. These types of narratives also reflect the *genderized* and *racialized* nature of poverty, contributing to institutionalized gender bias and racism (Seccombe, 2015).

Whether veiled or overt, negative bias, particularly that which is bestowed on female public welfare recipients of color, negates the disparity in social problems experienced by

Black women and other women of color (El-Bassel et al., 2009; Martin, 2012; Siegel & Williams, 2003). Negative stereotypes and myths also provide a false picture of welfare recipient demographics by implying that the largest demographic of beneficiaries is Black single women with numerous children, which statistics do not support.

PRWORA of 1996, TANF, and Other Programs for Low-Income Families

A Republican Congress may have initiated welfare reform, but it was passed by the Democratic Clinton administration in the form of the **Personal Responsibility and Work Opportunity Reconciliation Act** (PRWORA) of 1996. This bipartisan effort illustrated the wide support for welfare reform as well as for the underlying philosophical beliefs about what causes poverty and what types of poverty alleviation methods are effective.

The social welfare program authorized under PRWORA of 1996 is called the Temporary Assistance for Needy Families (TANF) program, which replaced the **Aid to Families with Dependent Children** (AFDC). TANF is operated at the state level through federal block grants as well as state funding. According to the PRWORA act, TANF has four primary goals: (1) to provide help to needy families and their children; (2) to promote job preparation, employment, and marriage so that families no longer need to depend on government assistance; (3) to reduce out-of-wedlock births, and (4) to encourage two-parent families.

Initially, TANF listed 12 different categories of acceptable work activities, but in 2008 the federal government provided additional clarity in terms of what activities would count toward TANF's work requirement in each category. Among the 12 categories, nine are considered "core," which means they directly count toward the required number of hours per week. Three of the categories are considered "non-core" and count only after the required hours for core activities are met. The nine core work activities include unsubsidized work, subsidized work, work experience, on-the-job training, job searches, job readiness, community service, vocational education, and providing child care to anyone participating in community service. Non-core activities include employment-related education, job skills training, and attendance at a high school or GED program.

TANF benefits include modest cash assistance for basic needs; transitional services focused on

Racial Breakdown of 2,277,663 recipients of TANF in FY 2.18

- ☐ Hispanic*
- ☐ Black
- ☐ Asian
- ■ Multi-Racial
- ☒ White
- ☒ American Indian or Alaska Native
- ☐ NHOPI: Native Hawaiian or Pacific Islander

Source: https://www.acf.hhs.gov/ofa/resource/characteristics-and-financial-circumstances-of-tanf-recipients-fiscal-year-2018

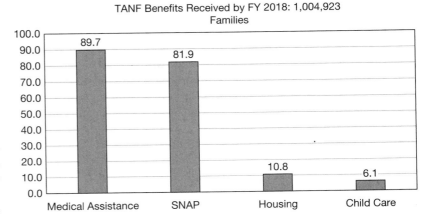

TANF Benefits Received by FY 2018: 1,004,923 Families

Source: https://www.acf.hhs.gov/ofa/resource/characteristics-and-financial-circumstances-of-tanf-recipients-fiscal-year-2018

self-sufficiency, such as vocational training, rehabilitation, and child care; substance abuse, mental health, and domestic violence screening and referrals; medical assistance through a government-funded health insurance program; and Supplemental Nutrition Assistance Program (SNAP) benefits (formerly called food stamps).

States have considerable latitude in how to meet the four goals of TANF as well as how to deliver the benefits, as long as their programs remain within federal guidelines. Guidelines include time limits, which are not to exceed 60 months of lifetime benefits (in most cases); eligibility requirements, which include barring all immigrants who have lived in the United States for less than 5 years; all undocumented immigrants, and work requirements of at least 30–35 hours per week for two-parent families and 20 hours per week for single parents with young children. Parents who fail to comply with the work requirement experience sanctions such as the termination of all family benefits. Approved work activities include subsidized and unsubsidized work at a for-profit or not-for-profit organization and can also include on-the-job training and vocational training (not to exceed 12 months). A significant area of concern among social justice advocates is that educational programs, including programs to assist recipients with earning their high school diplomas, are not included in approved work categories.

According to a 2020 U.S. Department of Health and Human Services (DHHS) report, in fiscal year 2019 there were just over 1.9 million families receiving TANF benefits, with the total individual TANF caseload of about 3.8 million individuals (DHHS, 2019). This represents about 400,000 additional recipients compared to 2013 (DHHS, 2015). About half of all caseloads consisted of small female head-of-household families with one or two children, with the other half consisting of child-only cases. With regard to the racial makeup of recipients, in fiscal year 2018, 37.8% were Hispanic, 28.9% were Black, 27.2% were White, 1.9% were Asian, 1.5% were Native American and Alaska Natives, and 0.6% were Native Hawaiian and other Pacific Islanders (UDHHS, 2018). Among all families receiving TANF benefits, about 90% received medical assistance, 82% received SNAP benefits, 10.8% received housing assistance, and 6.1% received subsidized child care. These percentages have remained relatively stable in the last 5 years, except SNAP benefits have increased by about 2%. The average monthly cash benefit for TANF recipients (per individual based on a family of three) ranges from $56 (Mississippi) to $308 (Alaska), and 35 states haven't raised TANF benefits in over a decade (Burnside & Floyd, 2019).

Many social welfare advocates believe that TANF is too punitive in nature because of its strict time limits for lifetime benefits, stringent work requirements, and other punitive measures designed to control the behavior of recipients. Supporters of welfare reform rely on old arguments, citing the need to control welfare fraud and welfare dependency. They cited a host of other behaviors exhibited by female welfare recipients, including perceived sexual promiscuity and out-of-wedlock childbearing, while focusing very little on the behaviors of the fathers, particularly those who abandon their children (Hudson & Coukos, 2005; Rainford, 2004).

Uluorta (2008) cautions that far too often morality in the United States has been defined in very narrow terms, focusing on select groups of individuals and on very specific behaviors, such as sex and sexuality, marital status, and social standing. (It is interesting to note that rarely do those criticizing the immoral behavior of the poor also frame behaviors such as greed or lacking compassion in moral terms). While individual responsibility is certainly worth achieving, it can also be a code word for philosophies that scapegoat the poor and minimize long-standing social inequalities. Such scapegoating is of great concern to many within the human services fields and others who recognize the wide range of ways that social problems and their causes can be framed, and the danger of focusing too heavily on perceived behavioral flaws of those who are struggling.

The belief that generous social welfare programs will result in increased dependence has deep roots in the United States and has been a powerful influence on social welfare policy development from the country's inception. But is this true? Is there any evidence to support the contention that generous social welfare programs will increase dependence and decrease self-sufficiency? There are a few ways we can answer this question. The first is to explore empirical research on the effectiveness of TANF, specifically whether the punitive nature of the program has the intended result—to increase compliance and decrease dependence. A 2019 study examined this very dynamic and found that TANF's structure, particularly its sanctions mechanisms that punish single mothers for noncompliance (not working enough hours, etc.), actually led to increased dependence and lower levels of self-sufficiency (Hamilton et al., 2019). The other method of assessing the effectiveness of TANF is to compare the U.S. social welfare system with systems in other high-income countries.

The Male Breadwinner Model Versus the Nordic Model

There are two primary social welfare models used in high-income countries, such as the United States and European countries: the male breadwinner model and the 'all adult worker model'. The former is the traditional model, which assumes that men are the wage earners and women stay home and care for the children and are then provided for financially through their husbands' earnings. Western societies have long presumed that this traditional model resulted in stable families (Clark, 2000; Weitzman, 1985). In fact, modern welfare systems have been constructed on the concept of the full engagement of a male workforce, where wages from employment were considered the best form of "welfare provision" (with regard to monthly income, health care benefits, and pensions) (Lewis, 2001), which may be one reason why the United States has been resistant to provide more governmental universal programs

The male breadwinner model has been used by many countries to enforce a social structure that was believed to be the foundation of society. AFDC, the program that preceded TANF, was based on a male breadwinner model because it presumed that men were the wage earners of the family and women stayed home to care for the children, and in the absence of a male provider, the government stepped in until the woman remarried (Moffitt et al., 1994).

U.S. family behaviors have changed significantly since the 1950s, resulting in the general breakdown of the traditional family structure. We now have far more fluidity and flexibility in intimate relationships, a large increase in single-person households, as well as an increase in women entering the labor force (Lewis, 2001). Welfare reform in the mid-1990s was fueled for many reasons, but a primary one was related to these shifting cultural tides in the United States and a building resentment toward AFDC recipients whom many Americans believed should be working (Murray, 2008).

The other social welfare model that has been adopted in most European countries is the "all adult worker model," which assumes that all adults, males and females, are equally involved in the labor market and thus all adults are economically independent. Both TANF and the Nordic Model (the social welfare systems in the Nordic countries of Sweden, Iceland, Finland, Denmark, and Norway) are considered all adult worker models, but their design and impact are dramatically different. While TANF is technically considered an all adult worker model, the philosophical basis of the legislation strongly reflects male breadwinner values, which is captured in the legislative definition of poverty as primarily a result of teen out-of-wedlock births, and the legislative goal of marriage promotion.

The TANF program does expect all beneficiaries to work, which is consistent with the all adult worker model, but research shows that while family behavior in the United States has changed considerably since the 1950s, it hasn't changed as much as the all adult worker model requires to be effective. For instance, women's behavior in the United States has changed pretty substantially with respect to entering the paid workforce, but most women still only work part-time, and most are in far lower-paying fields. Also, the majority of women in the United States still perform the bulk of unpaid care work, whereas men have not changed significantly in their work-related patterns. They still engage primarily in paid work (and are paid on a much higher scale), and as a whole haven't significantly increased their involvement in childcare or other unpaid work (Dush et al., 2018; Lewis, 2001).

Thus, while TANF is considered an all adult worker model because it is a welfare-to-work program, it does not match current behaviors in the United States with regard to labor engagement and unpaid work provision. For instance, TANF expects new mothers to enter the labor force rapidly, yet most enter low-wage service sector jobs that offer little opportunity for advancement (Mitchell et al., 2018; Seefeldt, 2017). Also, because TANF is an income-tested program, it tends to stigmatize beneficiaries, blaming poverty on individual circumstances (primarily women and their sexual behavior) rather than structural problems, such as a poor economy, a lack of jobs offering a living wage, racial oppression, domestic violence, and poor educational systems. The U.S. social welfare model in general also discourages parents from leaving the labor market to care for their children, by failing to provide paid paternity leave on a federal level.

The Nordic Model is also an all adult worker model, but the Nordic countries have a strong commitment to universal care entitlements focusing on children and older adults, thus utilization is far less stigmatized (Lewis, 2001). Temporarily exiting the labor market in the Nordic countries for unpaid care work is encouraged. Men are incentivized to temporarily leave their jobs to care for their children by the availability of generous parental leave (about 480 days) that can be split between the parents. Finally, the United States pays a fraction of what Nordic countries pay for family benefits (Owaza, 2004).

So, what's the answer to our question then? Which program is more effective in reducing poverty without creating dependence? Surprisingly, there aren't many comparative studies, but a set of data we can examine are poverty rates among single mothers between the United States and the Nordic countries, to get an idea of the effectiveness of the two models. In 2018 the poverty rate of single mothers in the United States was 35.1% (U.S. Census Bureau, 2018). This is an improvement over 2007 rates when 50% of single mothers in the U.S. lived below the poverty line (Legal Momentum, 2011), but the U.S. poverty rate for single mothers is still far higher at 35.1% than most Nordic countries, which range from 17% in Denmark to 24% in Sweden.

Poverty is highly complex and is influenced far more by structural factors than individual ones. As long as social welfare policy in the United States is fueled by fears of dependency (that a generous safety net will make us all lazy), chances are many people will continue to believe in the myth of the welfare queen and negate the despair many single mothers feel when faced with challenges of rising out of poverty with minimal support and high levels of stigma (Seccombe, 2015).

The Economic Crisis of 2007–2008

After years of an economic boom, the U.S. economy began faltering in about 2007 and devolved into a full-blown recession by 2008, which lasted until about 2009 or 2010. The economic recession of 2007 consisted of a dramatic and lengthy economic downturn not experienced since the Great Depression. The real estate market bubble burst, the stock market crashed, the banking industry seemed to implode, and many people lost their jobs and their houses as a result (Geithner, 2009).

President Obama and the 111th Congress responded to the economic crisis with several policy and legislative actions, including the passage of the American Recovery and Reinvestment Act of 2009 (often referred to as the Stimulus bill [Pub. L. No. 111-5]). This economic stimulus package, worth over $787 billion, included a combination of federal tax cuts, various social welfare provisions, and increases in domestic spending, and was designed to stimulate the economy and assist Americans who were suffering economically.

As a part of the 2009 Recovery Act, Congress allotted $5 billion in emergency funding to assist states with increased TANF caseloads (expired in September 2010). TANF was reauthorized in 2009 and was up for reauthorization in 2015 but experienced several delays. The National Association of Social Workers (NASW) released a statement regarding reauthorization recommending several changes to the TANF program, some of which include the following:

- Increase the floor for TANF benefits to 100% of the federal poverty line. Currently, many states' benefits are 50% of the federal poverty line, while benefits in several states are only about 30% of the federal poverty line.
- Expand the definitions of employment to include higher education, English and literacy classes, and more expansive vocational training.
- Address common barriers to employment such as physical illness, mental illness, disabilities, substance abuse, domestic violence, and sexual violence.
- Restore benefits for documented immigrants (NASW, 2015).

The stimulus package was considered largely successful and initially had the approval of the majority of Americans (Pew Research Center, 2008). The economy took years to recover, though, and some populations and regions never fully recovered, including many rural communities (Farrigan, 2014). Over time, Americans became increasingly critical of what many now call the "Wall Street Bailout." When the 2008 elections rolled around, many in the United States were ready for a change, reflected in the election of Democrat Barack Obama.

© DONNA VAUGHN / SHUTTERSTOCK

Nashville TN, November 7, 2008 newspapers from around the country announcing the President Elect Barack Obama the first African American President.

The Election of the First Black President

The 2008 presidential election was unprecedented in many respects. The United States had its first Black and first female presidential candidates of a major party. Many people who had historically been relatively apathetic about politics were suddenly passionate about this election for a variety of reasons. Growing discontent with the leadership in the preceding 8 years coupled with a lengthy war in the Persian Gulf region and a struggling economy created a climate where significant social change could take root. Barack Obama's campaign slogans based on hope and change (e.g., "Yes We Can!" and "Change We Can Believe In") seemed to tap into this growing discontent.

Perhaps one of the most significant federal laws to be passed during the Obama administration was the **Patient Protection and Affordable Care Act** of 2010 (ACA) (PPACA, 2010). The ACA (or its more commonly used name, Obamacare) was signed into law by former President Obama in March 2010 after a fierce public relations battle waged by many Republicans and health insurance companies designed to prevent its passage. The ACA, which took effect incrementally between 2010 and 2014, is a comprehensive health care reform bill. Overall, this legislation is designed to make it easier for individuals and families to obtain quality lower-cost health insurance by having people apply for a policy through a central exchange. One of the goals of the legislation was to make it more difficult for health insurance companies to deny coverage, particularly based on preexisting conditions. The ACA also expands Medicare in a variety of ways, including bolstering community and home-based health care services, and providing incentives for preventative, holistic, and wellness care. With respect to behavioral and mental health care, the ACA provides increased incentives for coordinated care and school-based care, including mental health care and substance abuse treatment. It also includes provisions that will require the inclusion of mental health and substance abuse coverage in benefits packages, including prescription drug coverage and wellness and prevention services. Although the Trump administration attempted to weaken the ACA in a variety of ways, it remains an effective piece of legislation as long as states comply with the act's mandates, including providing oversight for unwarranted price increases.

Political speeches and debates leading up to the 2012 presidential elections revealed the same debate about the causes of poverty and effective poverty alleviation strategies. After a brief display of compassion toward the poor at the height of the 2008 economic crisis, harsh sentiments reflecting historic stigmatization of the poor were strongly espoused, particularly among potential Republican primary candidates who continued their campaign against "big government," social welfare programs, and civil liberties in general. One 2012 Republican presidential candidate, Newt Gingrich, even went so far as to challenge current child labor laws, calling them "stupid." In a campaign speech in Iowa in the fall of 2011, Gingrich characterized poor ethnically diverse children living in poor neighborhoods as lazy and having no work ethic. In two different speeches (his initial speech and a subsequent speech where he was asked to clarify his earlier comments), Gingrich suggested that poor children in poor neighborhoods could start work early, perhaps as janitorial staff in their own schools (Dover, 2011). Gingrich's sentiments completely negated the role of racial oppression and White privilege in the poverty experienced by racial and ethnic minorities in the United States.

President Obama significantly advanced social justice during his presidency, including signing into law the Matthew Shepard and James Byrd, Jr. Hate Crimes Prevention Act of 2009, which extended federal protection to victims of a hate crimes based on actual or perceived sexual orientation or gender identity. Obama also signed into law the Fair Sentencing Act of 2010, which addressed the disparity in sentencing laws between powder cocaine and crack cocaine, impacting primarily people of color. In 2012, Obama repealed **Don't Ask, Don't Tell (DADT)** (an official policy of the U.S. government that prohibited the military from discriminating against gay and lesbian military personnel as long as they kept their sexual orientation a secret), which meant that lesbian, gay, and bisexual Americans could serve openly in the U.S. Armed Services without fear of dismissal.

Other advances in social justice legislation and policy include Obama's 2012 Executive Order implementing the Deferred Action for Childhood Arrivals (DACA) policy, providing legal protection for undocumented migrant youth who came to the United States as children with their parents, until federal legislation could be passed to provide them a path to citizenship. Obama also advocated in support of marriage equality for same-sex couples in advance of the 2015 Supreme Court case *Obergefell* v. *Hodges,* which legalized same-sex marriage throughout the United States. And in 2016, the Obama administration increased the annual refugee threshold to 110,000 to accommodate the resettlement of Syrian refugees, among other highly vulnerable populations.

Some of these advances have since been dismantled by President Trump, including the withdrawal of DACA (an action since reversed by the U.S. Supreme Court) and the consistent lowering of the annual refugee threshold to 18,000 in 2020, the lowest number in the history of the United States Refugee program (U. S. Department of State, 2020). Despite these dramatic shifts in values and policy approaches, President Obama remains a key figure in U.S. history, not only because of his race, but because of his social justice legacy and his overall popularity,

The Tea Party Movement

A powerful conservative social movement that sprung up 2009 in a reaction to the Obama presidency is the American Tea Party Movement, a part of the **Christian Right** and a fringe part of the Republican base. Tea Party members advocated for smaller government, lower taxes (the name of the group is a reference to the Boston Tea Party), states' rights, and the literal interpretation of the U.S. Constitution. The Tea Party movement gained a reputation for advocating for very conservative policies that advanced traditional American values such as marriage between a man and a woman, restrictions on abortions, and governance that supported conservative Christian values. For instance, Michele Bachmann, a Tea Party member, former Minnesota congresswoman, and 2012 presidential candidate, asserted in a 2006 speech that religion was supposed to be a part of government, and that the notion of separation of church and state (contained in the First Amendment of the U.S. Constitution) was a myth (Turley, 2011).

The Tea Party has been criticized for many reasons, including being anti-immigrant and racist, accusations the party's leadership strongly denied. And yet, media coverage of Tea Party rallies frequently highlighted their racially charged tone, such as racial slurs on posters, many of which were directed at former President Obama's ethnic background. Although "tea partiers" often denied accusations of bias, a study conducted during the height of the movement showed that about 60% of Tea Party opponents believed that the movement had strong racist and homophobic overtones (Gardner & Thompson, 2010). Most members as of 2019 have shed the Tea Party label but remain an influential core of the Republican party as conservative evangelicals.

The Era of Donald Trump

Learning Outcome 2.5   Examine the impact of the 2016 presidential election on U.S. social welfare policy and programs

Donald Trump, a reality television star and real estate mogul, was elected president in 2016, and took office the following January, surprising many people in the United States and around the globe. Trump's election was also a surprise to political pollsters, many of whom predicted Hillary Clinton had a clear path to the White House (Wright & Wright, 2018). The disappointment and shock many Democrats felt in response to Trump's win was in large part rooted in the contentious nature of the election and the belief that Americans would not vote for someone so mired in scandal and who espoused such controversial rhetoric in speeches and tweets that many believed reflected racism, sexism, and xenophobia (Jacobson, 2017; Tani, 2016). But that's precisely what happened.

Trump's policies, particularly his stance on immigration and his "America First" rhetoric, are consistent with right-wing populism, a far-right political ideology that is rooted in nationalism and protectionism (Dunn, 2015; Mudde, 2013; Wodak, 2015). Right-wing populism is by definition anti-immigrant, since immigrants are perceived as a threat to the country's traditional culture and way of life (Bonikowski, 2017; Ybarra et al., 2016).

Charlotte, North Carolina - 2 March 2020: President Trump concludes his campaign speech at the rally in the Bojangle's Coliseum.

© JEFFERY EDWARDS/SHUTTERSTOCK

A wave of right-wing populism, particularly those fueling anti-immigrant social movements, has swept the globe in recent years (Donovan & Redlawsk, 2018), so from a broader perspective Trump's election is wholly in line with global political trends throughout the second decade of the 21st century.

The dominant narrative in the wake of Trump's 2016 win was that it was economic anxiety that drove support for Trump—the forgotten White working class, those living in rural communities, the former manufacturing states of the upper Midwest (often called the Rust Belt), and coal country. And yet, recent research has revealed that Trump's popularity was rooted not as much in economic anxiety, but in cultural anxiety—a profound concern among White voters, particularly working-class men without a college education, that they were losing their cultural status to ethnic minority populations (Mutz, 2018). This dynamic is referred to by researchers as "out-group anxiety," a response to multicultural changes in the United States, such as increasing acceptance of multiculturalism (Barreto et al., 2011).

In addition to the support of White working-class voters, approximately 80% of White conservative Christians who self-identified as born-again and/or evangelical (Protestants, Catholics, and Mormons) voted for Trump in 2016 (CNN, 2016; Smith & Martinez, 2016). This was also surprising to many Americans, in light of Trump having been married three times, reports of his many extramarital affairs, and his personal admission on an Access Hollywood videotape of his sexual exploits, including grabbing women by their genitals (Fahrenhold, 2016). A 2016 poll by Christianity Today revealed that despite admitting that Trump was difficult to like, the majority of self-described White evangelicals believed that Trump was honest, a good role model, and well qualified to be president (interestingly, the majority of Black evangelicals reported almost the exact opposite sentiments) (Eekhoff-Zylstra & Weber, 2016).

In addition to the unrelenting support of his base, the 2016 election was significantly influenced by social media, particularly propaganda (or "fake news") disseminated via Facebook and Twitter that swayed many people's opinions about both Hillary Clinton and Donald Trump (Allcott & Gentzkow, 2017). Concerns about Russian election meddling and e-mail hacking, allegations that the Trump administration cooperated with the Russian government, and the discovery of Russian "troll farms" that used Facebook and Twitter to influence Americans to vote for Trump rather than Clinton remain controversial topics that will likely take years to fully understand. In the meantime, political polarization remains high, with research showing that most Americans now have little contact with people in the opposing political party (Pew Research Center, 2016).

Social media will no doubt continue to play a pivotal role in the political polarization in the United States. Research indicates that when people are exposed to opposing views on sites like Twitter, they become even more entrenched in their political stances (Bail et al., 2018). Social media is also used for good. For instance, advocacy is increasingly occurring online to affect changes in public policy. A 2017 study found that among advocates and advocacy organizations 70% use Facebook for advocacy purposes and 75% use Twitter. Additionally, over 50% of advocacy organizations now have a professional position designated for social media (Rehr, 2017). Social media is consistently evolving, in both usage and functionality, so it's important that human services professionals remain up to date in all ways social media is being used—both positively and negatively.

The election of Donald Trump has significantly changed the policy priorities of the United States, including social welfare policy. Human services professionals and others in the helping fields applauded Trump's support for criminal justice reform by signing into law the Step Act—a bipartisan bill that addresses racial disparities in sentencing laws—but remain highly concerned about the Trump administration's stances on immigration, including the separation of Central American families seeking political asylum, the increase in expedited deportations without hearings, a dramatic reduction in the refugee resettlement threshold, and rollbacks in environmental protections. The NASW's first statement regarding President Trump, released the day after the 2016 election, encouraged Trump to heal the divisiveness caused by his campaign (NASW, 2016), and yet, according to the Southern Poverty Law Center, hate crimes have risen steadily during the Trump administration (Beirich, 2019).

The NASW has also released statements expressing significant concern about Trump's various policies, particularly those that impact the most vulnerable and marginalized members in U.S. society. Examples include the NASW statements on the Trump administration's travel ban on refugees coming from primarily Muslim nations (NASW, 2017b), its policy to separate migrant families at the border (NASW, 2018), and the administration's economic policies (NASW, 2017a). Trump was also highly criticized by his handling of the 2020 coronavirus pandemic, including concerns that he was slow to respond to the crisis (particularly with regard to testing and quarantining), but the NASW also praised the Trump administration for signing into law two emergency bills, Families First Coronavirus Response Act (H.R. 6201), which among other things expanded unemployment benefits, emergency family leave, and sick leave for those impacted by the coronavirus, and the Coronavirus Preparedness and Response Supplemental Appropriations Act of 2020 (H.R. 6074), which provided emergency funding for public health agencies and major expansions in the use of telehealth,

Despite the controversy surrounding Trump's 2016 election and the values and choices made by his administration, another positive development in response to his election has been the dramatic increase in grassroots social justice advocacy in the form of rallies and protests (e.g., the Women's March, the March for Science), and a significant increase in people of color and women running for political office. Social media played a significant role in these developments as well. For instance, the Women's March was organized primarily on Facebook through shared statuses on timelines, and in pages and groups, as well as the use of the platform's event calendar to organize people globally. The number of women who showed up globally to march for gender equality was unprecedented, and this grassroots coordination could not have occurred without the broad and rapid reach of social media. President Trump lost his 2020 re-election bid to Joe Biden, which many social reformers saw as a positive sign. And yet, it's likely that political and social polarization will continue for quite some time.

CONCLUSION

The United States is often referred to as a reluctant welfare state because throughout its history a battle has been waged between reformers, who advocate for a compassionate, inclusive, less-stigmatized social safety net, and opposing groups, who advocate for a system with less government involvement, more privatization, and increased work incentives based on fears that a generous social safety net will decrease incentives for people to work. Currently it would be more accurate to describe the U.S. social welfare system as a piecemeal welfare-to-work system that focuses more on the behavior of the poor than on structural causes of poverty that act as the barriers to self-sufficiency. But it is also accurate to describe the U.S. social welfare system as ever evolving, reflected in the passage of emergency stimulus bills in response to the 2020 pandemic. Other changes are on the horizon as well, but they will be highly influenced by political leadership and economic constraints.

SUMMARY

- The ways in which England's historic system of poor care influenced the development of social welfare policies in the United States is analyzed. England's early social welfare system, including the development of social welfare policy in the United States, is discussed, tracing aspects of social welfare provision from England's feudal system in the Middle Ages to Elizabethan Poor Laws, to the development of the social welfare system in Colonial America.
- Movements and associated philosophical influences in poor care and social reform in early America are compared and contrasted. Various philosophical and religious movements that have influenced perceptions of the poor and social welfare policy, such as Calvin's Protestant work ethic and the concept of predestination, social Darwinism, and the settlement house movement, are discussed.
- Early leaders in the fight for social justice are explored, including Jane Addams and Ida B. Wells, with a particular focus on how the social justice movement formed the underlying values of the human services profession.
- The ways that the New Deal and Great Society programs alleviated poverty after the Great Depression are discussed. The successes and failures of the post–Depression New Deal programs on poverty alleviation in the United States are explored.
- A summary and analysis of current social welfare approaches and programs are explored, including the 1970s recovery, welfare reform and TANF, the 2008 economic crisis, the Obama administration, and the Trump administration, with a particular focus on the impact of social welfare policy and provision on at-risk populations.

END-OF-CHAPTER QUESTIONS

1. Describe the importance of understanding the history of social welfare policy in the United States when working with historically marginalized and oppressed clients.
2. What impact did Calvinism and social Darwinism have on how people struggling with poverty were viewed and treated in the United States?
3. What is the lasting impact of the work and advocacy of Jane Addams and Ida B. Wells on the human services profession, and how did their approach to human suffering differ from the COS movement?
4. What are the strengths and weaknesses of the TANF program and how does it compare to social welfare in the Nordic Countries?

References

Addams, J. (1909). *The spirit of youth and the city streets* (Vol. 80). University of Illinois Press.

Allcott, H., & Gentzkow, M. (2017). Social media and fake news in the 2016 election. *Journal of Economic Perspectives, 31*(2), 211–236.

Bail, C. A., Argyle, L. P., Brown, T. W., Bumpus, J. P., Chen, H., Fallin Hunzaker, M. B., Lee, J., Mann, M., Merhout, M., & Volfovsky, A. (2018). Exposure to opposing views on social media can increase political polarization. *Proceedings of the National Academy of Sciences, 115*(37), 9216–9221.

Barreto, M. A., Cooper, B. L., Gonzalez, B., Parker, C. S., & Towler, C. (2011). The Tea Party in the age of Obama: Mainstream conservatism or out-group anxiety? In *Rethinking Obama* (pp. 105–137). Emerald Group Publishing Limited.

Beier, A. L. (2003). *The problem of the poor in Tudor and early Stuart England*. Routledge.

Beirich, H. (2019). *The year in hate: Rage against change. White supremacy flourishes amid fears of immigration and nation's shifting demographics*. Southern Poverty Law Center. https://www.splcenter.org/fighting-hate/intelligence-report/2019/year-hate-rage-against-change

Bonikowski, B. (2017). Ethno-nationalist populism and the mobilization of collective resentment. *The British Journal of Sociology, 68*, S181–S213.

Burnside, A., & Floyd, I. (2019). *More states raising TANF benefits to boost families' economic security*. Center on Budget and Policy Priorities. https://www.cbpp.org/research/family-income-support/more-states-raising-tanf-benefits-to-boost-families-economic-security

Burt, M. R. (1980). Cultural myths and supports for rape. *Journal of Personality and Social Psychology, 38*, 217–230.

Calhoun, L. G., Selby, J. W., & Warring, L. J. (1976). Social perception of the victims' causal role in rape: An exploratory examination of four factors. *Human Relations, 29*, 517–526.

Chambliss, W. J. (2017). A sociological analysis of the law of vagrancy. In *Law and Poverty* (pp. 3–13). Routledge.

Chunn, D. E., & Gavigan, S. A. M. (2004). Welfare saw, welfare fraud, and the moral regulation of the 'Never Deserving' Poor. *Social & Legal Studies, 13*(2), 219–243.

Clark, A. (2000). The new poor law and the breadwinner wage: Contrasting assumptions. *Journal of Social History, 34*(2), 261–281.

CNN. (2016). Exit polls. https://www.cnn.com/election/2016/results/exit-polls.

Darwin, C. (2009). *The origin of species: By means of natural selection, or the preservation of favoured races in the struggle for life*. Cambridge University Press. (Original work published in 1859.)

Davidson, J. W. (2008). *They say, Ida B. Wells and the reconstruction of race*. Oxford University Press.

Donovan, T., & Redlawsk, D. (2018). Donald Trump and right-wing populists in comparative perspective. *Journal of Elections, Public Opinion and Parties, 28*(2), 190–207.

Dover, E. (2011). Gingrich says poor children have no work habits. ABC News. http://abcnews.go.com/blogs/politics/2011/12/gingrich-says-poor-children-have-no-work-ethic/

Duncan, C. M., & Moore, D. B. (2003). Catholic and Protestant social discourse and the American welfare state. *Journal of Poverty, 7*(3), 57–83.

Dunn, K. (2015). Preference for radical right-wing populist parties among exclusive-nationalists and authoritarians. *Party Politics, 21*(3), 367–380.

Dush, C. M. K., Yavorsky, J. E., & Schoppe-Sullivan, S. J. (2018). What are men doing while women perform extra unpaid labor? Leisure and specialization at the transitions to parenthood. *Sex Roles, 78*(11–12), 715–730.

Eekhoff-Zylstra, S., & Weber, J. (2016). *Top 10 stats explaining the evangelical vote for Trump or Clinton*. Christianity Today. https://www.christianitytoday.com/news/2016/november/top-10-stats-explaining-evangelical-vote-trump-clinton-2016.html

El-Bassel, N., Caldeira, N. A., Ruglass, L. M., & Gilbert, L. (2009). Addressing the unique needs of African American women in HIV prevention. *American Journal of Public Health, 99*(6), 996–1001.

Fahrenhold, D. (2016). *Trump recorded having extremely lewd conversation about women in 2005*. The Washington Post. https://www.washingtonpost.com/politics/trump-recorded-having-extremely-lewd-conversation-about-women-in-2005/2016/10/07/3b9ce776-8cb4-11e6-bf8a-3d26847eeed4_story.html?utm_term=.fd608fc59e6c

Farrigan, T. (2014). *Poverty and deep poverty increasing in rural America*. United States Department of Agriculture, Economic Research Service. https://www.ers.usda.gov/amber-waves/2014/march/poverty-and-deep-poverty-increasing-in-rural-america/

Feagin, J. R. (1975). *Subordinating the poor: Welfare and American beliefs*. Prentice Hall.

Gardner, A., & Thompson, K. (2010). *Tea Party group battles perceptions of racism*. Washington Post-ABC News Poll. Retrieved from http://www.washingtonpost.com/wp-dyn/content/article/2010/05/04/AR2010050405168.html?hpid=moreheadlines

Geithner, T. F. (2009). *Regulatory perspectives on the Obama administration's financial regulatory reform proposals-Part two*. House Financial Services Committee. Retrieved from http://www.house.gov/apps/list/hearing/financialsvcs_dem/geithner_-_treasury.pdf

Gettleman, M. E. (1963). Charity and social classes in the United States, 1874–1900. *American Journal of Economics & Sociology*, 22(2), 313–329.

Hamilton, L., Wingrove, T., & Woodford, K. (2019). Does generous welfare policy encourage dependence? TANF asset limits and duration of program participation. *Journal of Children and Poverty*, 25(2), 101–113.

Hamington, M. (2005). Public pragmatism: Jane Addams and Ida B. Wells on lynching. *Journal of Speculative Philosophy*, 19(2), 167–174.

Hofstadter, R. (1992). *Social Darwinism in American thought*. Beacon Press.

Hudson, K., & Coukos, A. (2005). The dark side of the Protestant ethic: A comparative analysis of welfare reform. *Sociological Theory*, 23(1), 1–24.

Jacobson, G. C. (2017). The triumph of polarized partisanship in 2016: Donald Trump's improbable victory. *Political Science Quarterly*, 132(1), 9–42.

Jones, G. H. (1969). *History of the law of charity, 1532–1827*. CUP Archive.

Kim, H. C. (1977). The relationship of Protestant ethic beliefs and values to achievement. *Journal for the Scientific Study of Religion*, 16(3), 252–262.

King, L. P. (2007). Does neoliberalism work? Comparing economic and sociological explanations of postcommunist performance. *Economic Sociology_The European Electronic Newsletter*, 8(2), 10–17.

Kluegal, J. R. (1987). Macro-economic problems, beliefs about the poor and attitudes toward welfare spending. *Social Problems*, 34(1), 82–99.

Knight, L. W. (2010). *Jane Addams: Spirit in action*. W. W. Norton & Company.

Krugman, P. (2007). *Conscience of a liberal*. W. W. Norton & Co.

Kusmer, K. (1973). The functions of organized charities in the progressive era: Chicago as a case study. *Journal of American History*, 60(3), 657–678.

LeMaire, K. L., Oswald, D. L., & Russell, B. L. (2016). Labeling sexual victimization experiences: The role of sexism, rape myth acceptance, and tolerance for sexual harassment. *Violence and Victims*, 31(2), 332–346.

Legal Momentum. (2011). Poverty rates for single mothers are higher in the U.S. than in other high income countries. http://www.ncdsv.org/images/LM_PovertyRatesSingleMothersHigherUS_6-2011.pdf

Leiby, J. (1984). Charity organization reconsidered. *Social Service Review*, 58(4), 523–538.

Lewis, J. (2001). The decline of the male breadwinner model: Implications for work and care. *Social Politics: International Studies in Gender, State & Society*, 8(2), 152–169.

Lindsey, D. (2004). *The welfare of children*. Oxford University Press.

Lundblad, K. (1995, September). Jane Addams and social reform: A role model for the 1990s. *Social Work*, 40(5), 661–669.

Malka, A., Soto, C. J., Cohen, A. B., & Miller, D. T. (2011). Religiosity and social welfare: Competing influences of cultural conservatism and prosocial value orientation. *Journal of Personality*, 79(4), 763–792.

Martin, M. E. (2012 January). Philosophical and religious influences on social welfare policy in the United States: The ongoing effect of Reformed theology and social Darwinism on attitudes toward the poor and social welfare policy and practice. *Journal of Social Work*, 12(1), 51–64.

McElvaine, R. S. (1993). *The great depression: America, 1929–1941*. Broadway Books.

McIntosh, P. (2007). White privilege: Unpacking the invisible knapsack. *Race, class, and gender in the United States: An integrated study*, 177–182.

Mitchell, T., Pavetti, L., & Huang, Y. (2018). *Life after TANF in Kansas: For most, unsteady work and earnings below half the poverty line*. Center on Budget and Policy Priorities. https://www.cbpp.org/research/family-income-support/life-after-tanf-in-kansas-for-most-unsteady-work-and-earnings-below

Moffitt, R. A., Reville, R. T., & Winkler, A. E. (1994). State AFDC rules regarding the treatment of cohabitors: 1993. *Social Security Bulletin*, 57, 26.

Mudde, C. (2013). Exclusionary vs. inclusionary populism: Comparing contemporary Europe and Latin America. *Government and Opposition*, 48(2), 147–174.

Murray, C. (2008). *Losing ground: American social policy, 1950–1980*. Basic Books.

Mutz, D. C. (2018). Status threat, not economic hardship, explains the 2016 presidential vote. *Proceedings of the National Academy of Sciences, 115*(19), E4330–E4339.

National Association of Social Workers [NASW]. (2015). *Temporary Assistance to Needy Families (TANF) reauthorization*. Retrieved http://www.naswdc.org/advocacy/issues/tanf/resources/GR-FL-10015.TANF-Flyer.pdf

National Association of Social Workers [NASW]. (2016). NASW statement on Donald J. Trump's election as 45th President. [Press Release]. Available at https://www.socialworkers.org/News/News-Releases/ID/88/NASW-Statement-on-Donald-J-Trump-Election-as-45th-US-President

National Association of Social Workers [NASW]. (2017a). *NASW says President Trump's proposed budget would harm well-being of all Americans*. https://www.socialworkers.org/News/News-Releases/ID/154/NASW-says-President-Trumps-proposed-budget-would-harm-well-being-of-all-Americans

National Association of Social Workers [NASW]. (2017b). *President Trump's immigration executive order is inhumane, de facto ban on Muslim immigrants* [Press Release]. http://www.socialworkblog.org/advocacy/2017/01/nasw-statement-president-trumps-immigration-executive-order-is-inhumane-de-facto-ban-on-muslim-immigrants/

National Association of Social Workers [NASW]. (2018). *NASW says plan to separate undocumented immigrant children from their parents is malicious and unconscionable* [Press Release]. https://www.socialworkers.org/News/News-Releases/ID/1654/NASW-says-plan-to-separate-undocumented-immigrant-children-from-their-parents-is-malicious-and-unconscionable.

Nelson, J. I. (1992). Social welfare and the market economy. *Social Science Quarterly, 73*(4), 815–828.

Neville, H., Worthington, R., & Spanierman, L. (2001). Race, power, and multicultural counseling psychology: Understanding white privilege and color blind racial attitudes. In J. Ponterotto, M. Casas, L. Suzuki, & C. Alexander (Eds.), *Handbook of multicultural counseling* (pp. 257–288). Sage.

O'Neill, E. A. (2016). Guardians of chastity and morality: A century of silence in social work. *Journal of Sociology & Social Welfare, 43*, 67.

Owaza, M. (2004). Social welfare spending on family benefits in the United States and Sweden: A comparative study. *Family Relations, 53*(3), 301–309.

Pace, J., & Sloan, S. (2020, March 23). *Fallout '08 bailout looms over Washington negotiations*. Associated Press. https://apnews.com/e00c645ac9badfeaf4fad-dcffd5d02d6.

Patient Protection and Affordable Care Act, 42 U.S.C. § 18001 et seq. (2010).

Pew Research Center. (2008). *57% of public favor Wall Street bailout*. U.S. Politics & Policy. https://www.people-press.org/2008/09/23/57-of-public-favors-wall-street-bailout/.

Pew Research Center. (2016). *Few Clinton or Trump supporters have close friends in the other camp*. U.S. Politics & Policy. http://www.people-press.org/2016/08/03/few-clinton-or-trump-supporters-have-close-friends-in-the-other-camp/

Pinterits, E. J., Poteat, V. P., & Spanierman, L. B. (2009). The White privilege attitude scale: Development and initial validation. *Journal of Counseling Psychology, 56*(3), 417–429.

Quadagno, J. (1994). *The color of welfare: How racism undermined the war on poverty*. Oxford University Press.

Rainford, W. C. (2004). Paternalistic regulation of women: Exploring punitive sanctions in Temporary Assistance to Needy Families. *Affilia, 19*(3), 289–304.

Rauch, J. B. (1975). Women in social work: Friendly visitors in Philadelphia, 1880. *Social Service Review, 49*(2), 241–259.

Rehr, D. (2017). How is social media being used in advocacy? Huffington Post. https://www.huffpost.com/entry/how-is-social-media-being-used-in-advocacy_b_589a7b12e4b0985224db5bac

Richmond, M. E. (1917). *Social diagnosis*. Russell Sage Foundation.

Schlabach, T. (1969). *Rationality & welfare: Public discussion of poverty and social insurance in the United States 1875–1935*. Social Security Commission, Research Notes and Special Studies. http://www.ssa.gov/history/reports/schlabachpreface.html

Schneiderhan, E. (2008, July). *Jane Addams and the rise and fall of pragmatist social provision at Hull-House, 1871–1896* [Paper presentation]Annual meeting of the American Sociological Association, Sheraton Boston, and the Boston Marriott Copley Place, Boston.

Schram, S. F., Fordingy, R. C., & Sossz, J. (2008). Neo-liberal poverty governance: Race, place and the punitive turn in U.S. welfare policy. *Cambridge Journal of Regions, Economy and Society, 1,* 17–36.

Seccombe, K. (2015). *"So you think I drive a Cadillac?": Welfare recipients' perspectives on the system and its reform.* Pearson.

Seefeldt, K. S. (2017). Serving no one well: TANF nearly twenty years later. *Journal of Society & Social Welfare, 44, 3.*

Siegel, J., & Williams, L. (2003). The relationship between child sexual abuse and female delinquency and crime: A prospective study. *Journal of Research in Crime and Delinquency, 40*(1), 71–94.

Slack, P. (1990). *The English poor law, 1531–1782* (Vol. 9). Cambridge University Press.

Smith, G., & Martínez, J. (2016). *How the faithful voted: A preliminary 2016 analysis.* Pew Research Center. http://www.pewresearch.org/fact-tank/2016/11/09/how-the-faithful-voted-a-preliminary-2016-analysis/

Stephenson, C. (1943). Feudalism and its antecedents in England. *The American Historical Review, 48*(2), 245–265.

Tani, M. (2016). *Trump's win has shattered the Democratic Party.* Business Insider. https://www.businessinsider.com/trump-win-democratic-party-2016-11

Trattner, W. I. (2007). *From poor law to welfare state: A history of social welfare in America* (6th ed.). Simon and Schuster.

Tropman, J. E. (1986). The "Catholic ethic" versus the "Protestant ethic": Catholic social service and the welfare state. *Social Thought, 12*(1), 13–22.

Turley, J. (2011). *Separation of church and state? Not on the 2012 campaign trail.* The Washington Post. https://www.washingtonpost.com/opinions/separation-of-church-and-state-not-on-the-2012-campaign-trail/2011/09/27/gIQA0vT8AL_story.html?utm_term=.4b69a993d4ef

Uluorta, H. M. (2008). Welcome to the "All-American" fun house: Hailing the disciplinary neo-liberal non-subject. *Millennium: Journal of International Studies, 36*(2), 51–75.

U.S. Census Bureau. (2018). *Poverty status in the past 12 months of families.* https://data.census.gov/cedsci/table?q=poverty%20rate%20families&hidePreview=false&tid=ACSST1Y2018.S1702&t=Poverty&vintage=2018.

U.S. Department of Health and Human Services [DHHS]. (2015, July 24). *Characteristics and financial circumstances of TANF recipients, Fiscal year 2013.* Office of Family Assistance, Administration for Children & Families. http://www.acf.hhs.gov/programs/ofa/resource/characteristics-and-financial-circumstances-of-tanf-recipients-fiscal-year-2013

U.S. Department of Health and Human Services [DHHS]. (2018). *Characteristics and financial circumstances of TANF recipients, Fiscal year 2018.* Office of Family Assistance, Administration for Children & Families. https://www.acf.hhs.gov/sites/default/files/ofa/fy18_characteristics_web_508_2.pdf

U.S. Department of Health and Human Services [DHHS]. (2019, October 1). *TANF caseload data 2019.* Office of Family Assistance, Administration for Children & Families. https://www.acf.hhs.gov/sites/default/files/ofa/tanf_recipients_fy19.pdf

U.S. Department of State. (2020), *Proposed refugee admissions for fiscal year 2020.* https://www.politico.com/f/?id=0000016d-bb51-d0d8-af6d-ff79261f0002

Van Slyke, D. M. (2003). The mythology of privatisation in contracting for social services. *Public Administration Review, 63*(3), 296–315.

Wahab, S. (2002). For their own good: Sex work, social control and social workers, a historical perspective. *Journal of Sociology and Social Welfare, 29, 39.*

Weaver, R. K., Shapiro, R. Y., & Jacobs, L. R. (1995). The polls–trends: Welfare. *Public Opinion Quarterly, 59,* 606–627.

Weber, M. (1958). *The Protestant ethic and the spirit of capitalism* (T. Parsons, Trans.). Charles Scribner's Sons. (Original work published in 1905.)

Weikart, R. (1998). Laissez-faire social Darwinism and individualist competition in Darwin and Huxley. *The European Legacy, 3*(1), 17–30.

Weitzman, L. J. (1985). *Divorce revolution.* Collier Macmillan.

Wells, I. B. (2020). *Crusade for justice: The autobiography of Ida B. Wells.* University of Chicago Press.

Wodak, R. (2015). *The politics of fear: What right-wing populist discourses mean.* Sage.

Wright, F. A., & Wright, A. A. (2018). How surprising was Trump's victory? Evaluations of the 2016 US presidential election and a new poll aggregation model. *Electoral Studies, 54,* 81–89.

Wright, T. (2000). Resisting homelessness: Global, national and local solutions. *Contemporary Sociology, 29*(10), 27–43.

Ybarra, V. D., Sanchez, L. M., & Sanchez, G. R. (2016). Anti-immigrant anxieties in state policy: The great recession and punitive immigration policy in the American states, 2005–2012. *State Politics & Policy Quarterly, 16*(3), 313–339.

Zarefsky, D. (2005). *President Johnson's war on poverty: Rhetoric and history.* University of Alabama Press.

Zucchino, D. (1999). The myth of the welfare queen: A Pulitzer-prize winning journalist's portrait of women on the line. Touchstone.

3

Ethical Standards, Generalist Skills, and Intervention Strategies

© LIGHTFIELDSTUDIOS/123 RF

Rocio is a bachelor's-level human services practitioner working in the county child protective services, providing case management services for children in foster care. She recently had a very difficult case where a sibling group of three, ages 10, 11, and 13, were removed from their home on an emergency basis. Rocio was there when the children were taken into county custody and her heart broke as she witnessed the children crying hysterically. The parents apparently had not been home in days; there was evidence of drug use, no food in the home, and trash everywhere. The children were dirty and hungry and reported that they had not been in school in weeks. The children seemed to bond almost immediately with Rocio and begged her not leave them. They also asked whether they could stay with their aunt, with whom they'd apparently lived with before returning home to their biological parents a few months ago. Rocio took the children to the hospital for a checkup, and then back to the county's temporary shelter while she attempted to contact their aunt. By the evening, though, she was still unable to reach the aunt and the only option available was to place the children in a group home for the night and try to reach the aunt again in the morning. The children were very upset, pleading with Rocio to not leave them. She felt terrible and did worry about their safety at the group home, which she'd heard from other children was often filled with delinquents and uncaring staff. Rocio decided that the best thing to do was bring the children home with her for the night, reasoning that the children would be at her home for less than 12 hours. Rocio lived alone in a nearby apartment and she knew they'd be safe at her home. She also reasoned that placing them in a group home would risk increasing their trauma, and that wouldn't be in the children's best interest.

Sean is a licensed master's-level human services practitioner with a local hospice agency, where he provides therapy to the surviving family members of terminally ill patients. One year ago, Sean started counseling Sara and Dan's son, Michael, in relation to Dan's terminal illness from a rare form of brain cancer. Sara and Dan have been married for 21 years and Michael is their only child. During a call with Sean, Sara shared that she felt conflicted because her marriage was not good and she'd been very unhappy for years, but she knew she could not leave her husband when he was dying. She explained that her husband was diagnosed with brain cancer about a year before they had Michael, who was now 10 years old, so they'd been dealing with his illness for over a decade. Sara was concerned for her son, not only because he was about to lose his father, but also because there was so much tension in the home. Sean began seeing Michael weekly and working on issues related to his father's illness and terminal diagnosis, and the tension in the home related to his parents' marital dynamics. Sean checked in with Sara frequently, providing her with updates on Michael's progress. During those calls Sara shared past experiences with Dan, including a history of controlling and manipulative behavior and other examples of unhealthy behavior. Sean felt a strong bond with Sara, and their communication increased to the point where they were texting each other throughout the day and evening—sometimes about Michael and sometimes about what Sara was feeling and experiencing. On several occasions Sara expressed that she didn't know what she would have done without Sean, which made Sean feel good because he liked knowing he was making a difference. Shortly after Dan's death, Sean and Sara began dating, which Sean felt okay with because his identified client was Michael, not Sara. After a few months of dating through, Sean began to believe the relationship did not have much potential because Sara was too dependent on him and didn't seem interested in his problems, only hers and her son's. After dating for about 6 months, Sean broke up with Sara. Sara was devastated, but Sean told her he was looking for a more reciprocal relationship.

THE NATURE OF ETHICAL AND PROFESSIONAL STANDARDS IN THE HUMAN SERVICES

Learning Outcome 3.1   **Describe how professional ethical standards and codes of conduct can assist professionals in resolving ethical dilemmas**

If you were asked to describe ethical violations in the human services profession, you may describe scenarios that involve blatant violations, such as having sex with a current client and then manipulating them, lying to clients, or sharing confidential information about a client with a friend or another client. But both opening vignettes involve good, caring, and generally ethical people who are behaving in very unethical manners and thus have violated their professional ethical standards. So, while some human services practitioners may knowingly engage in overtly unethical behavior, the majority of ethical violations involve practitioners who, with good intentions, "tip-toed" their way into murky waters and at some point crossed the line from poor professional judgment to behavior that definitively violated the Ethical Standards for Human Services Professionals (National Organization for Human Services, 2015).

The opening vignettes are important because they highlight behaviors that may not seem unethical, and in the case of the first scenario, may actually seem heroic. And yet, both scenarios do involve ethical violations. The first vignette involved ethical violations because Rocio became overinvolved with her clients and as a result crossed very important legal and professional boundaries by circumventing important standards. In the second vignette Sean put his emotional and sexual needs before his client's needs (and yes, Sara was still Sean's identified client, even though he was primarily seeing her son), robbing her of an important resource (him) during a time of crisis and adding to her emotional burden when he ended the relationship because she wasn't meeting his needs. Both vignettes involved practitioners allowing their emotions to drive their decision making and in the process damaged their clients.

Ethical standards can help us navigate situations where our emotions get in the way of our logical thinking by providing us with a methodical way of managing ethical dilemmas (situations where there may be no apparent "right" or "wrong" path). So, if you've ever asked yourself why you need a detailed set of professional standards, because you're a good person, now you know! Although it may be true that very few people wake up in the morning and say to themselves, "Hey, I think I'm going to lie, cheat, and steal today!" it is also true that many people become highly emotional in certain situations, which may impact their ability to see a situation in an unbiased and objective manner. People can also act in ways that reflect naiveté or ignorance, and in the process of being so very human, they may behave quite unethically as they make decisions based more on their urges, desires, passions, personal biases, negative stereotypes, or uninformed opinions, than on reasoned processes and sound professional knowledge.

Ethics can be defined in many different ways, with most definitions including references to a set of guiding principles or moral values. In a professional context, ethics often refers to a set of standards that provide guidance to individuals within a particular discipline, with the goal of assisting them in resolving **ethical dilemmas** they may face in the process of engaging in their business practices. A professional set of **ethical standards** is typically based on a set of ethical values that stipulate what behaviors and practices are considered acceptable and which are not, and also provides general guidance in managing ethical dilemmas.

It would be very convenient for many of us if there was one long list of rules in life, and all situations could be perceived in the same manner by everyone. But of course, that is not how life works. Some people believe there are **universal moral principles**, particularly relating to issues such as murder and robbery. But even with these seemingly black-and-white situations, the gray abounds. Consider the case of someone killing in self-defense or stealing bread for a starving child. So, is **morality** universal or relative? Is there an absolute right and wrong in this world? Or is the rightness and wrongness of a decision or action dependent on perspective, culture, or even one's own version of the truth?

This is an age-old philosophical debate and not one that I will attempt to answer definitively in this chapter. But, many moral theorists argue that both are true—there are universal moral principles that exist across almost all cultures (e.g., sexually abusing a child is always considered immoral) and there are **relative moral principles** where one must consider the appropriateness of a certain behavior within situational context (e.g., the example of killing someone in self-defense) or within the situational context of one's culture—shared values among a community of people (e.g., burping in public or eating with one's hands). In this chapter I will address some of the issues that have the great-est potential of "muddying the waters" when it comes to determining how we know whether an action is moral or immoral and ethical or unethical, which in turn helps us determine how we can ensure we're making moral and ethical decisions, not only in our personal lives, but also in our professional lives.

The Nature of Ethical and Moral Behavior

When there is a breakdown in moral behavior, often it is because people get caught up in their emotions, which cloud their judgment. This does not mean that whenever we are emotional, we're bound to behave immorally, but it is both normal and common to at times feel caught in a tug-of-war between our ethical standards (or sense of right and wrong) and our emotional feelings and desires. I used to have a counseling practice, and I often told my clients that feelings and emotions are like the interior design of a house—moving and poignant, even beautiful at times—but useful only if protected by the exte-rior and structure of the house—the walls and roof, which are the framework, similar to our ethical standards, values, and principles. Thus, although humans are by nature emotional beings, individuals with high moral character are not driven to act solely on the basis of their desires and passions, but by their intellect, critical thinking, and logical reasoning.

Certainly, there are times when emotions should lead, and we do not want to become rigid or heartless in our application of rules and standards. When someone is driven to act solely on the basis of their values or rules, they are often deemed to be heartless legalists. But, when someone is driven solely by their feelings and desires, they are often deemed immature, volatile, and impulsive. This is not because their emotions are wrong, or inher-ently evil, but because their values and principles may not be sufficiently defined and/or developed to regulate their emotions. So, they act out impulsively, saying things they don't mean or behaving in ways that are self-or-other destructive. For instance, an employee who has poor **emotional regulation** might become angry with his boss and punch him in the face, even if he doesn't believe in violence, because he acted on his anger before think-ing about the consequences of his actions. A person's ethical values can act as a rudder of behavior, and although there are certainly times when people will be influenced by their passions, typically their emotions should not drive their decision-making processes.

Another reason why it is important to understand the connection between ethical values and emotions is that people often use their emotions to justify their unethical or immoral behavior: cheating on a test is wrong, unless the test is too hard and we hate our teacher; adultery is wrong, unless we're in a loveless marriage, and are extremely lonely, and fall hopelessly in love with someone else; lying is wrong, unless we need the day off from work and will only get paid if we're sick; violence is wrong, unless we're provoked; drinking too much alcohol is wrong, unless we've gone 2 weeks without and we've had a

© ALPHA HISTORICA / ALAMY STOCK PHOTO

really bad day. One of the primary functions of ethical values is to keep us on a good moral track, particularly when we find our ethical values at odds with our emotional desires and urges.

Former slave and Underground Railroad conductor Harriet Tubman (1822-1913), along with her husband, step-daughter, extended family, and former slaves she helped during the Civil War.

Behaving ethically may also be challenging if we experience conflicting values. Employees who shred documents to protect their employers may very well believe they were acting ethically based on their ethical value of loyalty to their employer. Yet, they may later be perceived as unethical and may even be charged criminally for their actions. Perhaps in retrospect these employees will realize that their values were conflicting, which clouded their judgment, or they may forever believe that they were behaving ethically and were treated unfairly. So how do you make choices when your ethical values collide, and when you're on the front end of your decision and don't have the benefit of hindsight?

Consider the case of Harriet Tubman, a "conductor" in the Underground Railroad, a network of people who helped slaves in the South escape to the North. Tubman was born into slavery and escaped to Pennsylvania in 1849. But it wasn't enough for Tubman that she was safe, she decided shortly after crossing the border from slavery to freedom that she had to cross back into the Southern territory to rescue members of her family. This began a 10-year process where Tubman made between 13 and 19 trips back and forth across the border to rescue others from slavery (Clinton, 2004). It is estimated that by 1860, Tubman had rescued over 300 slaves, guiding them to freedom and safety. Were Tubman's activities ethical? She considered herself to be an honest and law-abiding person, but she violated several laws as a conductor in the Underground Railroad, including the Fugitive Slave Act of 1850, passed by Congress as a compromise with the Southern states. This Act required people in the North to return former slaves to their Masters in the South and punished those helping runaway slaves with a hefty fine and 6 months in jail.

So, despite believing herself to be law-abiding, Tubman broke federal law because she had conflicting values. To resolve this ethical dilemma, she had to choose the higher value—the value she believed was more important. What did she value more? Obedience to authority or social justice? In light of what we now know about slavery, Tubman is lauded as a hero for behaving in the highest moral fashion and refusing to sit by and do nothing when people were held captive against their will and tortured for their entire lives. Recognizing Tubman's selflessness and high moral and ethical behavior is made easier with the benefit of retrospective knowledge. But at the time, Tubman's decision to violate one ethic to support another was risky because during that time, helping people escape slavery was considered a betrayal to the country. While it may seem preposterous now that anyone would have ever supported slavery, the reality is that many people during that era did, as they did not perceive owning slaves as unethical or as an immoral act. Rather, they viewed slavery as a vital aspect of the country's economic structure. Ultimately though, we now know with certainty that Tubman was correct in her ethical decision making.

Does this mean though that those who did not rescue slaves acted unethically? What if you had the opportunity to interview someone who was aware of the Underground Railroad, but refused to get involved? What if this person told you that federal authorities used to chase escaping slaves and their guides with vicious dogs and if the dogs didn't kill them, they would be arrested and sentenced to prison? What if this person explained that they believed they behaved morally in not rescuing slaves because their first ethical responsibility was to protect their children? Would you still consider their behavior unethical? Or, what about the ruling authorities' perspective? Tubman and other "conductors" were breaking federal law. From the authorities' perspective, then, their behavior was unethical, as well as illegal, constituting treason.

What makes Tubman's behavior unethical then, and so highly ethical now? Our current belief that slavery is evil? But, does this mean that if you or I believe our government is acting in some evil manner, that we'd be justified in disobeying its laws? Some divorced parents kidnap their children because they strongly believe the family courts will not protect the children from the other parent whom the kidnapping parent believes is abusive. If this is true, is their decision to disappear with their children justified? Many Black men believe that if they are pulled over by the police, it is because they are being racially profiled, and they may be arrested for no legitimate reason. Does this justify an attempt to flee? Would their behavior be any more or less ethical than a slave who escaped prior to President Abraham Lincoln signing the Emancipation Proclamation? Why or why not?

I hope you are beginning to see that evaluating ethical behavior in retrospect, when we have the benefit of perspective and know all the facts, including the outcome, is a far easier task than determining what is ethical in the moment. In fact, the lens that we use to evaluate the ethical nature of a behavior is often determined *by* the outcome—something that we don't have the benefit of knowing (or have any control over)—during our decision-making process. This explains why some people who are initially perceived as highly unethical are later considered heroes, while other people, who truly believe they are behaving ethically, end up going to prison.

The Development of Moral Reasoning Ability

Before adopting a set of ethical and moral values, it is important to understand how most of us develop the ability to think and reason morally. How do we grasp the nature of ethical behavior? How do we distinguish right from wrong? And does everyone have the same ability? Do adolescents have the same ability to understand the implications of behaving immorally or unethically as do adults? Do all adults have this same ability, or are there some people who, for whatever reason, have deficits in their ability to identify various choices and then select the most ethical path by using their cognitive reasoning ability?

Obviously, what people base their values on can vary profoundly. Value systems can be based on the values of one's family of origin, on one's culture, on one's religious beliefs, or on the prevailing societal values of the time. But Lawrence Kohlberg theorized that an individual's ability to reason morally relies on the ability to reason intellectually (Gibbs, 2003). In other words, in order for people to really grasp the nature of moral behavior, they need to first have the cognitive capacity to do so. To test his theory, Kohlberg conducted interviews presenting subjects of all ages with what he called *moral dilemmas*. He then asked for their opinions about the most moral course.

The Heinz dilemma, one of the more popular of Kohlberg's moral dilemmas, involved a woman who had cancer and was close to dying. The dilemma was that there was only one drug that could save her life and the local druggist, who discovered the drug, was charging 10 times what the drug cost him to make, making the drug beyond Heinz's financial ability to pay. Heinz's husband was able to raise half the cost of the drug and pleaded with the druggist to either lower his cost or let him pay the other half later, explaining that his wife would die without the drug. The druggist refused, citing his desire to make money from the drug. To save his wife's life, Heinz broke into the laboratory, stole the drug, and saved his wife's life. Kohlberg then asked the subjects whether Heinz's actions were moral or immoral and why.

Kohlberg discovered that those who had not developed sufficient cognitive reasoning ability (younger children and immature adults) had difficulty considering contextual factors when determining the most ethical course of action. As a result, they often cited external factors, such as the negative consequences of a behavior, as their reasoning for why stealing the drug was morally wrong. They also had difficulty exploring the more nuanced nature of moral behavior. For instance, if you were to ask pre-adolescent children whether hitting someone is wrong, they would likely say yes. When asked why, they would likely tell you that hitting is wrong because they would get in trouble. They would also likely have difficulty identifying the impact of hitting someone on the victim's feelings, or even instances when hitting might be justified (e.g., in self-defense).

Most adolescents and mature adults have developed abstract reasoning abilities and thus have the cognitive ability to grasp the various shades of gray involved in a moral dilemma. When confronted with the Heinz dilemma, these subjects could cite the moral nature of the situation, relying on internal references and contextual factors. For instance, they could cite examples of when stealing might reflect the highest level of moral behavior if it resulted in saving someone's life. Kohlberg also theorized that the capacity for moral reasoning did not necessarily mean that someone would behave morally. Thus, someone may have the cognitive ability to apply moral reasoning but may not act on that ability, deciding to behave immorally instead.

Professional Ethical Standards and Resolving Ethical Dilemmas

Virtually all professions rely on some form of ethical standards to maintain integrity and trust within the profession. Numerous professions espouse basic ethical principles that serve as a foundation for their business practices, but a number of professions are also bound by legally enforced standards, or codes of conduct that if violated can result in punitive consequences ranging from professional or financial sanctions (such as license suspension or fines) to a range of criminal penalties.

Many professions also operate under a professional organization or licensing entity that enforces their ethical codes in some form. Attorneys follow legal ethical standards administered by the American Bar Association. Psychologists must abide by the professional standards set forth by the American Psychological Association (APA). Stockbrokers must abide by the legally binding ethical standards set forth by the Securities

Pearson eText

Video Example 3.1

In this video a human services provider shares how she used social media to dig up dirt on her client. Her colleague suggests a different approach. Why is sleuthing clients on social media unethical?

and Exchange Commission, which if violated can include both professional and financial sanctions or, in extreme cases, even a criminal indictment. And the human services profession is bound by both a set of professional standards set forth by the National Organization for Human Services (NOHS) and applicable state and federal laws pertaining to specific practice settings such as mental health, health care, school, and childcare settings.

Professional codes of ethics are evolving and changing entities, never in final form, and always open for evaluation and debate. The ever-evolving state of professional codes of ethics enables a profession to remain current with contemporary ethical thinking, particularly with regard to matters of social justice and equity. Consider how far U.S. culture has evolved from the time when the American Psychiatric Association once considered homosexuality to be a mental disorder. Their historic stance on same-sex relationships would be considered highly unethical in today's culture.

Once a professional code of ethics has been adopted, the next challenge is to determine how to respond when an ethical breach is believed to have occurred and, if that is deemed to be the case, what action should be taken. Consider a professional who has been cited for breaching an ethical code. Then what? Do we presume that the professional is unethical and must be punished? Keeping Kohlberg's ethical dilemmas in mind, what if the higher moral ground required violating an ethical standard for some greater good? How does a professional ethical board evaluate the ethical and moral nature of a professional's behavior without becoming moral relativists, on the one hand, or too legalist on the other?

Ethical mindfulness is a term often used to describe a professional who behaves in a manner that involves constant awareness of ethical decision making (Greenberg & Mitra, 2015). There are no checklists people can follow that will ensure ethical decision making, no formula or guide we can follow, step by step, that can guarantee we won't cross over an ethical line. Ethical mindfulness requires us to slow down and really think about the situation we're confronting and how we want to respond (Handy & Russell, 2018). Being ethically mindful can guide human services practitioners in a wide range of situations that may not have a clear ethical path. For instance, how would you handle a situation where a female client has no money to take a bus home and therefore must walk five miles in cold weather alone, at night? Your agency has a policy against giving clients cash, but would allowing her to walk home alone and potentially face danger, be ethical? Even if everyone agrees that having high ethical standards is a good thing and that constant evaluation is necessary, not everyone is going to respond to ethical dilemmas in the same way because mental health providers often face paradoxical situations that involve competing ethical values (Handy & Russell, 2018).

Kitchener's (1984) model of ethical decision making can help us navigate many of the ethical dilemmas human services practitioners may face in the field. Kitchener's model is based on five assumptions that Kitchener maintains are at the heart of any ethical evaluation. Kitchener's model can, in a sense, be used as a "litmus test" when attempting to determine whether a certain action or behavior is in fact unethical. The model's assumptions are that all ethical behaviors are presumed to be based on: (1) autonomy, (2) beneficence, (3) nonmaleficence, (4) justice, and (5) fidelity. When evaluating the ethical nature of actions and behaviors using Kitchener's model within the context of the helping professions, the evaluator would examine whether the practitioner permitted clients to act of their own free will (autonomy), whether the practitioner's actions were intended to benefit the client (beneficence), whether the practitioner's actions did harm to the client (nonmaleficence), whether the actions were carried out in a manner that

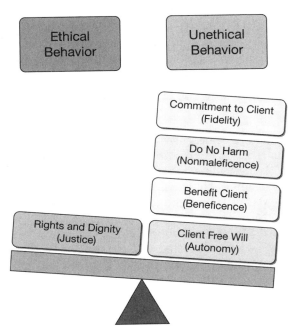

Figure 3.1
Applying Kitchener's Model of Ethical Decision-Making to Kate's Professional Actions.

respected the rights and dignity of all involved parties (justice), and whether the practitioner's actions reflected loyalty and commitment to the client (fidelity).

Let's use Case Study 3.1 as an example of how to apply Kitchener's model of ethical decision making to a common counseling situation:

Case Study 3.1 The Case of An Ethical Dilemma

Kate works for an adoption agency in the Chicago area. Although she has many responsibilities, her primary role is to counsel women experiencing an unplanned pregnancy and help them decide whether they want to place their babies for adoption. Kate counsels the parents (primarily the mothers) about all viable options, and if the parents select adoption, Kate helps to prepare them emotionally and practically for the adoption process. Kate also coordinates services with her co-worker, Sara, who is the caseworker for adoptive families. Kate and Sara work together to prepare both the birth mothers and adoptive parents, ensuring that both know their legal rights and are psychologically and emotionally prepared for what may occur. More specifically, the birth mothers need to be prepared to manage the grief they will experience after placing their babies for adoption, and the adoptive parents must be able to prepare for becoming parents, while understanding that the birth mother has the legal right to change her mind at any time until she signs the adoption papers (and in many states, even for a certain amount of time after that point).

Kate and Sara have been working very hard lately to match a 16-year-old birth mother with an adoptive family. Kate is aware of the plight of this adoptive family, including numerous miscarriages and three failed adoption attempts, so she really hopes this one will work out for them. Kate is an adoptive parent herself, so she knows how emotionally devastating it is when a birth mother changes her mind at the last minute (even though Kate knows they have the legal right to do so). When the birth mother went into labor, Kate could not help but feel elation for the adoptive couple who have waited so long to have a baby. But then the birth mother started expressing doubts, describing how she had no idea of the emotional connection she would feel for her baby once he was placed in her arms. Kate then could not help but feel conflicted by her client's seeming wavering. Kate does not believe her client has the emotional maturity or the resources necessary to be a good parent. Neither the birth father nor the birth mother's extended family is involved, so the birth mother would have very little support. Kate cannot fathom having to break the news to the adoptive parents that they may not be taking this baby home.

After some consideration and based on Kate's belief that her client would likely not be a very good parent, Kate decides to place pressure on the birth mother to go through with the adoption. She does this by being very directive with her client, and by making her feel guilty and selfish for wanting to take her baby home. Kate concludes by telling her client that the best way she can show her love for her baby is by making a sacrifice and placing him with a family who can provide for all of his needs—something that a 16-year-old certainly cannot do. Although Kate knows that her client is emotionally vulnerable and very confused, she continues to push, reminding her client of incidences of abuse she disclosed during counseling sessions—"remember when you told me about how your own teen mother wasn't loving, and neglected you so often? Do you want to do that to your own child?" By the time Kate is done with the session, her client agrees to sign the adoption papers, effectively terminating her parental rights.

Were Kate's actions ethical or unethical? She was, after all, considering the best interest of the baby, wasn't she? Isn't it best for all babies to be raised in a two-parent, financially secure, and emotionally mature home? Do the ends justify Kate's means? Apply Kitchener's model of decision making to this scenario and then you decide. Did Kate's actions (and motivations) support her client's right to act with *autonomy* and independence? Were Kate's actions *beneficent*; was she acting in a way that reflected altruism toward her client and all others involved? Did Kate's action harm her client, or was there *maleficence* involved? Were Kate's actions *just*? Did Kate consider the rights of her client, the birth mother, alongside the rights of the baby and adoptive parents? Could Kate's client, the birth mom, trust that Kate had her best interest in mind, or did Kate violate her *fidelity* and commitment to her?

Can you see now how complicated ethical decision making is, particularly in high-stakes cases? Which, let's face it, include the majority of human services caseloads! While there may be some disagreement about the nature of Kate's actions, my evaluation of this case using Kitchener's model deems Kate's behavior as unethical. Even though she may have been motivated by her desire to ensure the best interest of the child, I believe she was more motivated by her sympathy for the adoptive parents and their plight, and perhaps was even influenced by her own experiences as an adoptive parent.

ETHICAL STANDARDS IN THE HUMAN SERVICES PROFESSION

The ethical standards that govern the human services profession depend on different factors such as the human services professionals' level of education, professional license (including whether they have one), and the state in which they practice. The NOHS website states that its purpose is to connect educators, students, practitioners, and clients within the field of human services. Although it has no enforcement powers, NOHS members agree to abide by a set of ethical standards, which can be used as a guideline for resolving ethical dilemmas they face with clients and within the community at large (NOHS, 2015). Those who can use the NOHS code of ethics include human services practitioners working in community agencies, researchers, administrators, students in academic programs focusing on human services, and faculty in human services programs.

The preamble of the NOHS *Ethical Standards for Human Service Professionals* states that its purpose is to provide human services professionals and educators with guidelines to help them manage ethical dilemmas effectively. The guidelines are broken down into two sections, with Section 1 focusing on standards for human services professionals, and Section 2 focusing on standards for human services educators. In the section on human services professionals, the standards are organized by categories pertaining to *responsibility to clients, responsibility to the public and society, responsibility to colleagues, responsibility to the profession,* and *responsibility to employers, responsibility to self, and responsibility to students.* Overall, the general theme of these ethical standards centers on respect for the dignity of others, doing no harm, honoring the integrity of others, and avoiding exploitation of others, particularly clients and students, by recognizing power differentials within society. This is accomplished by maintaining self-awareness, engaging in all aspects of one's professional and personal life honestly and ethically, and developing an awareness of past and current global dynamics, particularly those involving the marginalization and oppression of others.

Examples of a human services practitioner's duty to clients includes the recognition of the client's strengths (Standard 1); the right to confidentiality, except in cases where this right may be limited, such as cases involving harm to self or others (Standard 3); the obligation to avoid having sexual or romantic relationships with clients (Standard 6); avoiding imposing personal biases and values on clients (Standard 7); and the protection of client records and information electronically (Standard 9).

Examples of a human services practitioner's responsibility to the public and society include an obligation to provide services without discrimination or bias (Standard 10); the awareness of local, state, and federal laws and the advocacy for changes if such laws violate a client's or client group's rights (Standard 12); an awareness of social and political issues that impact clients of diversity (Standard 14); and the advocacy for social justice to eliminate oppression (Standard 16). Examples of a human services practitioner's responsibility to colleagues include avoiding the duplication of services (Standard 19) and responding to the unethical or problematic behavior of another human services professional (Standard 21).

Examples of a human services practitioner's responsibility to the profession include promoting cooperation among related disciplines (such as psychology and social work) (Standard 29) and the promotion of continuing professional development. An example of responsibility to self includes human services practitioners' awareness of their own cultural backgrounds, beliefs, and biases (Standard 34). And finally, a few examples of human services practitioners' commitment to students include high standards of scholarship and pedagogy, staying current in the field (Standard 39) and appropriately monitoring students' field placements (Standard 41).

A Focus on Multicultural Issues and Social Justice

Learning Outcome 3.2   **Analyze how cultural diversity affects ethical perceptions and decision making within the context of the human services profession**

Earlier in this chapter, I discussed how many professions have adopted ethical codes of conduct mandating how practitioners should conduct themselves professionally. There are significant similarities among the ethical standards of the various helping professional

Pearson eText

Video Example 3.2

This video explores how diversity, racism and micro-aggressions can influence perceptions.

© ADAM GREGOR / SHUTTERSTOCK

Active listening skills involve good eye contact.

organizations, such as the NOHS (2015), the American Psychological Association (2016), the American Counseling Association (2014), and the National Association of Social Workers (NASW) (2017). However, a review of each discipline's ethical standards reveals how the disciplines focusing on the human services (NOHS and NASW) tend to focus as much on macro responsibilities (communities and the broader society) as on the individual client. For instance, the human services and social work fields have the added responsibility to advocate for social justice—both on behalf of clients and on a societal level as a whole. *Ethical Principles of Psychologists and Code of Conduct* (APA, 2016), for instance, refers to justice in individual terms as it relates to every individual's right to benefit from the contributions of psychology, but there is no reference to advocacy for social justice on a societal level.

Since the human services profession is rooted in social justice movements, professionals focus as much on the role of society in the lives of clients and client groups as on personal behaviors and functioning levels. Thus, virtually all aspects of the helping relationship will include an evaluation of both the client's personal dynamics (e.g., personal coping strategies, mental health, level of resilience, personal motivation, personality style), and societal dynamics that are potentially impacting the client and the client's environment (e.g., structural racism, historic oppression and marginalization, bias-based treatment, poverty). The focus on social justice in a broader context is important because it highlights the macro focus of human services, with the recognition that society and its social structures play a significant role in the mental and physical health of its members.

Cultural context is another very important factor to consider when evaluating the ethical nature of professional behavior. The normative nature of behaviors is often perceived differently from culture to culture. Thus, cultural context is an important factor to consider when evaluating the ethical nature of behavior, since not all cultures evaluate behaviors in the same way (Garcia et al., 2003; Houser et al., 2006). And while we can't be expected to be experts on every racial and ethnic group, we are expected to practice cultural humility, to embrace multiculturalism, and to recognize that cultural bias is something we must all work hard to acknowledge and challenge within ourselves. So many aspects of our lives—how we choose to parent our children, our faith perspectives, our attitudes about gender roles in society, our perspectives on sexuality and intimate relationships, and even beliefs about how people should treat dying and death—are culturally influenced. So, while human services professionals may not be "experts" on the cultural norms and values of every racial and ethnic group, we can become experts on the nature of culture and how culture influences people's beliefs, attitudes, and perspectives. This process begins with a commitment to cultural awareness, cultural sensitivity, and cultural humility (Barsky, 2018).

Another important consideration is that not all cultures value autonomy in the same way as do human services practitioners in Global North countries. For instance, Garcia et al. (2003) note that many cultures operate on a more interdependent basis, thus encouraging clients from collectivist cultures to make completely autonomous decisions in their personal self-interest, without helping them to consider the broader consequences of their choices, may not be appropriate in some cultural contexts. Human services practitioners in the United States highly value a client's right to self-determination, yet this perceived "right" may conflict with the cultural values of our clients, or our clients' family members.

This type of cultural conflict often arises when working with second-generation immigrants. I used to facilitate a support group for recently resettled refugee female youth from Central Africa (Rwanda, Burundi, the Democratic Republic of the Congo). A consistent theme brought up by the older teen girls in the group was a conflict with their parents around dating and career choices. Adapting to U.S. culture involved a recognition that they had far more choices available to them than in their home countries—they could wear whatever they wanted, date whomever they wanted, go to college if they wished, major in whatever academic disciplines they wanted, and pursue whatever careers they wanted. The sky was the limit! Or so it seemed to these newly arrived refugee teen girls. Most of them adapted very quickly to many aspects of Western culture. They acquired language skills more quickly than their parents, they embraced U.S. cultural norms more readily, and for most of the group members, they wanted to be considered "real Americans." Their rapid cultural adaptation created considerable conflict with most of their parents who wanted them to maintain traditional gender roles.

As a human services professional, I wanted to encourage the girls' sense of autonomy and their right to self-determination. I wanted to encourage them to strike out on their own, to be independent, to embrace gender equality. But I recognized that I needed to tread lightly because I understood that maintaining strong family and cultural ties was important for the girls, even if they didn't recognize it at their stage of development. I engaged the parents in some psychoeducation, I encouraged the group members to be patient with their parents and try to understand the nature of their cultural conflicts. This was not an easy process and I wasn't able to resolve all of their conflicts completely, but I was able to create a climate in which there was increased communication and understanding in the girls' homes—respecting the families' cultural traditions, but also recognizing the validity of girls' feelings and desires.

Regardless of how one goes about determining what is ethical and how ethical decisions are made (or how unethical decisions are made), it is very important to be sensitive to various cultural influences, as well as dynamics such as gender and age cohort. Often what appears clearly unethical in retrospect may have seemed quite ethical when the decision was being made. Thus, taking the time to understand behavior from the actor's perspective is imperative, despite its challenging nature.

GENERALIST HUMAN SERVICES PRACTICE

Learning Outcome 3.3   Examine how the generalist practice model serves as a theoretical foundation for human services practice

Most professionals use tools to accomplish their job duties. A professional baseball player uses a bat, a ball, and a mitt. An accountant uses various computer programs; an airline pilot uses an airplane. What is unique about the human services field is that the professional *is* the tool. Human services practitioners use their instincts, their compassion, their insights, and their training, along with their interpersonal or "people skills" to affect meaningful change in the lives of their clients.

Most people who enter the field of human services already possess many of these skills, which is often what prompts them to pursue this career in the first place. One might question, then, why someone who is naturally inclined toward counseling others needs a college degree to become a human services professional. The answer to that question is that while we can certainly help others by just being a good friend, or by volunteering for a charity or humanitarian organization, in order to work within a professional capacity, even the most naturally talented practitioner needs training to learn theoretical foundations, models, and approaches; the underlying reasons why some people need assistance; the nature of the change process; how multicultural dynamics impact people's lives and the helping relationship; and different intervention strategies and counseling methods that have been shown to be effective in research studies.

Because the human services practitioner is the primary tool for intervention, it is very important that those working in the field gain insight into their own values and belief systems because our values and belief systems influence how we perceive and understand our clients. Without gaining insight into what we believe and how our values evolved, we risk being unfairly biased against some people while giving others the benefit of the doubt. Gaining personal insights into one's own life experiences, whether one was raised with privilege or disadvantage, for instance, will help the human services practitioner consistently address any personal biases in relation to certain groups of people, and social problems.

Throughout this chapter I use the words *counsel* and *counseling* in a general sense in reference to engaging in any type of **direct practice** with clients. This distinction is important because although most human services practitioners engage in some level of counseling, in most states one must have at least a master's degree and hold a clinical license to provide clinical counseling services. In the human services field, though, many practitioners provide some level of generalist counseling services in the course of their professional duties.

Generalist counseling services may include talking with clients about their feelings and experiences, interviewing clients during an intake process, facilitating a support group, and providing emotional support and resources to people who call a crisis hotline. Generalist practice may also include more therapeutic counseling if the human services professional has a license to provide professional counseling services. Since the human services profession includes such a wide range of activities at so many levels of practice (from paraprofessional helpers to professional licensed counselors), the term *counseling* in this chapter should be interpreted broadly.

Before exploring the **generalist practice model** and related skills and competencies, I want to explore the equally important area of confidentiality and related mandates that exist for all of the helping professionals. Understanding the nature of confidentiality in practice, including its limits, as well as understanding our legal and ethical obligations to keep our clients and society safe, are vital components of the professional practice of helping.

Pearson eText

Video Example 3.3

In this video a human services supervisor shares the importance of entering client information correctly in agency databases. What are some steps providers can take to protect the confidentiality of clients' electronic information?

Informed Consent, Confidentiality, and Duty to Protect

When we disclose to our clients the nature and risks of the counseling relationship, and their legal and ethical rights, we are providing our clients with *informed consent*. Before beginning any formal relationship with a client, the client and the human services practitioner must first agree on the purpose, goals, and nature of the helping relationship—in other words, clients must have a clear understanding of what the helping relationship involves, including what it can and cannot do (i.e., the limitations of the helping relationship). The NOHS' ethical standards (2015) state that "clients should be informed that they may withdraw consent at any time except where denied by court order and should be able to ask questions before agreeing to the services" (Standard 2). Clients must also be informed that they have the right to terminate the helping relationship at any time they choose, with the exception of mandated clients (Kenney et al., 2018).

The NOHS (2015) also mandates the client's right to privacy and confidentiality, which is an important aspect of the counselor–client relationship because it assures that whatever clients share with their counselors will not be shared with others. The commitment to maintain confidentiality of **privileged communication** (any private information that does not reflect that the client is a threat to themselves or others) is considered so vital to mental health treatment that confidentiality is a legal mandate in every state in the nation. Thus, most mental health professionals offering counseling services must by law maintain confidentiality or face professional sanctions that could include the loss of their professional license.

The importance of confidentiality is based on the premise that for trust to develop in the counseling relationship, clients must be assured that they have a safe place to discuss their most private thoughts, feelings, and experiences (Lamont-Mills et al., 2018). Without such a guarantee, clients might not be willing to discuss their deepest feelings—their fears that they are not good parents, their intermittent desire to abandon their families because they are so overwhelmed in life, their histories of child sexual abuse, a recent extramarital affair, or a current struggle with drug abuse. Knowing that they have a safe place to share their deepest secrets with a person who is not personally affected by their feelings and choices, and who cannot disclose what they have shared, makes this exploration possible for many individuals, enabling them to become better parents, be less overwhelmed in their lives, be able to turn childhood victimization into a survivor mentality, and gain the strength and insight to work through difficult times in their lives.

There are occasions, though, when privileged communication can be disclosed to others, either with or without the client's consent (voluntarily or involuntarily). Situations involving voluntary disclosure of privileged communication include occasions when a client signs an **authorization to release information**—a legal document that provides all relevant information about what information can be released, how it is to be released, and for what purpose it is being released. Involuntary disclosure of privileged communication generally occurs in three types of situations: (1) when a client is legally mandated to receive mental health treatment and does not comply, (2) when clients pose a danger to themselves or others, and (3) in cases of suspected child abuse, maltreatment, and neglect. Situations involving the involuntary breaking of confidentiality highlight the **limits of confidentiality**—those difficult situations where a counselor (or other mental health professional) is legally required to break confidentiality (Koocher & Keith-Spiegel, 2018).

Mandated Clients and Duty to Warn.

Human services practitioners often have **mandated clients** on their caseload—those clients who are required by some legal entity to seek mental health and/or substance abuse treatment. For instance, some people are mandated to obtain certain types of mental health treatment as a part of a criminal case, such as a batterers' intervention program, a parenting class, or a drug and alcohol treatment program. If a mental health provider works for an agency that has a contract to provide legally mandated services, they are typically required to submit periodic progress reports to the court or governing agency (e.g., department of probation), including whether the client has failed to comply with the requirements of the court.

When clients pose a danger to themselves or others, a counselor has a **duty-to-warn** and a **duty-to-protect**. For instance, if a client tells his counselor that he plans to leave the office and kill himself, the counselor has the legal obligation to protect the client from himself by disclosing this information to the client's family or perhaps even law enforcement. If a client shares that she was recently fired from her job and plans to kill her former boss, the counselor has a legal obligation to warn her former employer, as well as report the disclosure to the proper legal authorities.

Duty-to-warn laws have been greatly influenced by a tragic event that occurred on the University of California, Berkeley campus when a student disclosed his intent to kill his girlfriend to a campus psychologist. Although the psychologist informed various individuals, including the student's supervisor and campus police, he did not inform the intended victim or her family. The client later killed the girlfriend, and the family of the victim sued the university based on the psychologist's failure to warn the victim. The case, *Tarasoff v. Regents of the University of California,* resulted in two decisions by the California Supreme Court in 1974 and 1976 (*Tarasoff I* and *II*, respectively). *Tarasoff I* found that a therapist has a duty to use reasonable care to give threatened persons a warning to prevent foreseeable danger. *Tarasoff II* was more specific in referencing the therapist's duty and obligation to warn intended victims, if necessary, to protect them from serious danger of violence. Virtually every state in the nation now uses the *Tarasoff* decisions as a foundation for duty-to-warn laws (Fulero, 1988; Swerdlow, 2018).

It's not always so clear-cut when and if confidentiality should be broken. There are many occasions when counselors find themselves needing to use their clinical skills to determine whether breaking confidentiality is the appropriate course of action (Pollard et al., 2019). For instance, consider the client who *may* be suicidal and who discloses a level of despair that *may* indicate suicidal ideation. Couple this with a disclosure that the client attempted suicide 4 months before and told no one, that he uses alcohol to make the pain go away, and that although he won't admit to a suicide plan, he doesn't always feel safe.

A client who shares this type of disclosure—denying any outright plan to commit suicide but appearing to manifest many signs of suicidal behavior—can present quite a clinical challenge, because it requires that the counselor take a clinical risk. If the counselor takes no action, the client may indeed commit suicide; however, if the counselor breaks confidentiality and the client was not really at risk for suicide but just expressing feelings of temporary despair, then the counselor–client relationship might be seriously damaged. Because confidentiality laws in most states do not bar professional discussions among practitioners within the same agency, clinical dilemmas such as these are most appropriately explored in clinical supervision, where a team of counselors discusses the risks and benefits involved with each possible response.

Mandated Reporting of Child Abuse.

Human services professionals are **mandated reporters**, and as such they are required by federal and state statute to report all cases of suspected child abuse, maltreatment, and neglect to the appropriate authorities. The requirement to report suspected child abuse is established by federal law, but the circumstances under which a report is made is stipulated by state law. Mandated reporters include any professional who comes into contact with children as a part of their professional duties. Some examples of mandated reporters are social workers, teachers (and other school personnel), health care workers, counselors, therapists, and all other mental health workers, childcare providers, church ministry personnel, and law enforcement officers (Child Welfare Information Gateway, 2016). Other people can certainly report suspected child abuse if they wish (and in most states they can do so anonymously), but they are not legally required to unless they are designated as a mandated reporter.

A counselor or other mental health provider needs not be certain that a child is being abused; rather, if they have a reasonable suspicion of abuse, they are required to make a report, which in most states involves calling a toll-free child abuse hotline facilitated by a county or state child welfare agency. Decisions about whether a situation warrants a hotline call is difficult. A spanking that seems to the counselor to go beyond mere discipline, verbal abuse that might meet the criteria of child maltreatment, a child's disclosure that a babysitter or other supervising adult behaved in a way that made the child uncomfortable and may indicate potential sexual abuse, or any other indication that the child *may* be experiencing abuse at home may each warrant a hotline call.

Determining when the line has been crossed between appropriate caregiving and abuse is an issue best explored within clinical supervision, whenever possible, or even through consultation with child protective services. It is important to note though that it is the counselor who is legally responsible for complying with child abuse reporting laws. It is the counselor's professional license that may be at risk if appropriate actions are not taken in response to cases where it would be reasonable to assume that child abuse, maltreatment, or neglect is likely. In some states a failure to report suspected child abuse can result in professional sanction, loss of the clinician's license, and even criminal charges in extreme cases. Thus, while clinical supervision can be very helpful in making these types of decisions, the counselor must make the final reporting decision.

Clients often forget about the nature and limits of confidentiality during the course of the counseling relationship, so it's a good idea to remind them from time to time. Otherwise, clients who share deeply personal information in counseling that must be disclosed for any of the reasons listed above, may feel betrayed by the counselor who then informs them that the disclosure is not protected information. For instance, it's not uncommon for children to at some point disclose that they're being abused at home. When their counselor then shares that they must make a report to child protective services, the child may be surprised and upset, believing that the information would remain confidential. Thus, periodically reminding clients of the limits of confidentiality may temper their potential feelings of betrayal if shared information must be reported (Gustafson & McNamara, 1987; Lamont-Mills et al., 2018; Lloyd-Hazlett et al., 2018).

HIPAA Laws.

According to federal legislation called the Health Insurance Portability and Accountability Act of 1996 or, more commonly, the **HIPAA Privacy Rule**, patients have the right to have their personally identifiable medical and mental health information remain confidential and protected. The HIPAA Privacy Rule stipulates how patients' electronic health information and records are to be kept private. Covered entities include insurance companies (including contractors and subcontractors), health care providers (including mental health care providers), and health care clearinghouses. Entities that are not covered under HIPAA include life insurers, employers, schools and school districts, and state agencies such as child protective service agencies and law enforcement agencies.

As mental health care providers, many of whom work for state agencies (e.g., child protective services, law enforcement, school counselors), human services professionals are bound by HIPAA; thus, it is important for anyone entering the field of human services to understand HIPAA laws and how they impact work with clients. It's also important for human services professionals to know what information HIPAA laws protect, such as information that is placed in a client's file, conversations we have with our clients, information about clients we keep in electronic format, and billing information.

HIPAA laws also stipulate that client information is to be protected. Human services professionals must employ safeguards to protect client records to ensure that protected information is not disclosed inappropriately or inadvertently. For instance, a file cannot be left unattended in a caseworker's car, but rather it must be contained in a locked filing cabinet. Client information may be kept on an electronic device, such as a tablet or laptop, but those devices must have HIPAA-approved protections in place, such as encryption technology and passwords. If client information is kept on a server or the cloud, agencies must make all necessary efforts to ensure electronic information is protected, including using secure and encrypted online sites and password-protected online access, where only necessary and appropriate employees have access to protected client information.

Protected client information must be shared with others only to the extent that is necessary. For instance, in clinical supervision meetings mental health care providers may elect to not share the names of the clients when discussing clinical situations and dilemmas unless such identifying information is absolutely necessary. Agencies are also required to train their employees on HIPAA laws, including what information is protected, and how to appropriately and effectively protect client information.

Covered entities are required to inform clients of their HIPAA rights in written form, using clear, concise, and easy-to-understand language. There are many templates available for use by covered entities, including a range of acceptable options provided by the U.S. Department of Health and Human Services website. Essentially a HIPAA notification must inform clients that they have the right to see and obtain a copy of their health records, have corrections added to their health information, and receive a notice about how their protected information may be used and shared. Clients also have the right to decide whether to provide permission to providers prior to information being shared (for marketing purposes, for instance), receive a report on when and why protected information was shared, and information on how to file a complaint with a covered entity or the U.S. government if clients (or patients) believe their HIPAA rights were violated.

HIPAA laws may appear relatively straightforward, but in the era of the Internet, this is not always the case. Consider the practitioner who has a frustrating day and posts a status on Facebook without client names, but with enough information that someone may be able to deduce to whom the intern is referring. Or consider a counselor who responds to a client's e-mail from a home computer without encryption capacity and provides answers to personal questions that include protected information. Or consider a human services caseworker whose car is stolen with a stack of client files piled on the backseat. All of these scenarios either are or could be HIPAA violations, depending on the circumstances and the nature of the information involved. Thus, it is very important for practitioners working as sole practitioners or with a covered entity to be educated and aware of HIPAA laws in all respects to avoid overt or inadvertent violations.

The Generalist Practice Model, Skills, and Competencies

According to the National Organization for Human Services (NOHS) the primary role of the human services practitioner is to help people function at their optimal level in the various areas of their life, such as interpersonally with family and friendships, in their work domains, and within their community. Human services practitioners also help communities to function better in much the same way, but by using different techniques on a broader level. The term *generalist practice* refers to a model of working with people in a helping capacity that focuses on basic skills involved in the helping process.

Generalist practice is a theoretical approach used to help individuals, families, groups, organizations, and communities (Hepworth et al., 2016). But before I describe the underpinnings of the generalist practice model, it will be useful to describe what generalist practice is not. Typically, when we reference generalist practice or a *generalist practice model*, we are not referring to specific theoretical modalities, such as psychoanalysis or Adlerian therapy. Rather, we are referring to basic skills and capacities that can be used with a broad range of clients and client systems.

A generalist practice model is based on certain assumptions about the nature of generalist practice. The first assumption is that generalist practice involves a basic skillset and goes beyond our natural inclinations and abilities (although it certainly relies on them). The second assumption is the recognition that all interventions occur within an ethical framework based on adopted ethical guidelines and standards. The third assumption is that clients (individuals, families) and client systems (groups, organizations, and communities) operate within systems, and therefore certain assumptions can be made about the nature of a client's or client system's functioning within their respective environments. Finally, a generalist practice model assumes that human services practitioners use problem-solving approaches and intervention strategies that are well researched, planned, and effective (Kirst-Ashman & Hull, 2015).

The NOHS lists several generic human services professional competencies on its website. Some of these competencies include understanding the nature of human systems and their interactions; understanding conditions that promote or limit optimal functioning; and having skills that allow for the effective identification and selection of interventions that promote personal growth and the ability to reach personal goals and desired outcomes, and that are consistent with the values of the provider, client, organization, and professional ethics of the profession. Other competencies include the ability to plan, implement, and evaluate chosen intervention strategies used with client and client systems, where the provider is considered the primary intervention tool and has a wide range of both interpersonal and generalist skills.

The generalist practice model includes basic skills and competencies that guide human services practitioners in their work with a diverse client population. Among the important foundational values of the generalist model is an emphasis on social justice, which humanizes clients in the process of helping them achieve optimal functioning and well-being (Schatz et al., 1990). Despite the generalist nature of the human services profession, and the fact that in most (if not all) states human services professionals working on a bachelor's level will not be permitted to work in the capacity of a professional licensed mental health provider, some direct practice with clients will occur in various contexts. Thus, it is important for all human services professionals engaging in any type of direct work with clients to become familiar with some basic skills and counseling techniques as well as some of the foundational theories that guide generalist practice.

When referring to direct work with clients, we often use the term **micro practice**, which is defined as working with individuals, whereas **mezzo practice** involves working with groups and **macro practice** involves working on a larger scale, with organizations, communities, and society in general. I will initially explore skills used in micro practice within the context of helping characteristics shared by effective human services providers, including the nature of effective communication skills, and intervention strategies that can be used within generalist practice. Later in this chapter I will explore the nature of macro practice, including various types of practice on a broader scale.

Basic Helping Characteristics

Many of the foundational competencies and skills shared by effective human services professionals could be considered personality characteristics, and while many people who go into the helping fields may be naturally inclined toward empathy, compassion, and caring, these characteristics still need to be developed and honed. For instance, someone can be naturally compassionate and caring, but such traits are learned, not necessarily innate, and must be further developed in a professional capacity. Helping characteristics are important to develop educationally and professionally because generalist skills, such as communication and intervention skills, emanate from foundational helping characteristics. Some of the basic skills we'll be exploring in this section are empathy, boundary-setting, and **active listening skills**.

Empathy.

The ability to authentically walk in the shoes of other human beings and see the world through their eyes is called empathy. Empathy is not the same as sympathy—an important distinction, particularly for human services professionals. Sympathy involves feeling sorrow or concern for another's welfare, whereas empathy involves being absorbed in the feelings of another (Escalas & Stern, 2003). Sympathy is not a difficult emotional response to muster, particularly when in response to those we believe are real victims, but empathy is far more challenging because it requires more of us, particularly when we are working with unsympathetic clients such as batterers or child abusers (Greenberg et al., 2001).

Empathy is also challenging when the issues clients are facing are frightening. Imagine watching the news and hearing about the plight of a young couple whose 5-year-old daughter was recently abducted. Your immediate response would likely be to express feelings of sorrow for this family. You would likely express concern for the welfare of the parents as they search for their missing child and for the safety of the child. But you may stop short of allowing yourself to become absorbed in the parents' feelings of grief and fear because allowing yourself to immerse that deeply into their experiences may hit too close to home, particularly if you have children of your own. In fact, you may even feel compelled to distance yourself emotionally from their situation and to resist putting yourself even slightly in their "shoes."

Human services professionals do not have the luxury of shutting out the world of their clients in this way. They cannot limit their emotional responses to sympathy alone. To be effective counselors and advocates, they must be willing to go on the emotional rollercoaster ride with their clients, extending their responses to empathetic ones, which in a counseling relationship involve the ability and willingness to experience their clients' beliefs, thoughts, and feelings through their clients' personal lenses. Empathy requires emotional maturity, the ability to be honest with oneself, the capacity for immersing one-self in another's emotional crisis without getting lost in the experience. Empathy requires the ability to keep the focus on the client in the counseling process, even if the counselor can strongly relate to a client's experience. Essentially, an empathetic response in a counsel-ing relationship not only requires the counselor to have the emotional capacity to see the world through a client's eyes, but also to have the willingness to walk alongside the client through their difficult times, while maintaining the focus on the client and not on oneself.

This process can be emotionally exhausting. Consider the counselor working with a client who has been sexually assaulted. Counselors must be willing to understand the experience of being sexually violated as best they can, without having gone through the experience themselves. They must be able and willing to understand what it feels like to be traumatized, powerless, and humiliated, and what it feels like to be filled with shame and embarrassment, and stigmatized in response. While the idea of empa-thy might seem appealing on the surface, empathizing with clients is very challenging because it requires that clinicians search their own minds and hearts, to reflect on their own past traumas, and, in this example, times in their lives where they have felt humil-iated, shamed, embarrassed, and/or stigmatized—experiences and feelings many may not want to reexperience.

Another challenge involves responding empathetically to clients who do not seem worthy of our empathy. It is challenging for many within the helping fields, including the human services, to empathize with the feelings of those engaging in violent behaviors—batterers and child abusers, those who have sexually assaulted women, or those who have gotten intoxicated and crashed into a family on the freeway. Since human services practitioners often work with mandated clients, it is quite likely that they will be working with clients who may be generally unsympathetic. Looking at the world through the eyes of a domestic batterer or a chronic alcoholic might be the last thing any sane human being would want to do, but the willingness and ability to do so is a prerequisite for those entering the human services field, at least to some extent.

So how does one accomplish this feat, when the behavior of a client is perceived as morally incomprehensible? The first step in developing the ability to empathize with unsympathetic clients is to understand that to empathize does not mean to condone. Consider the last motion picture that you watched. It was the director's job to help the viewer see the world through each of the characters' eyes. Considering the role of the director, although not a direct parallel, illustrates the concept of the human services pro-fessional essentially sitting alongside those they counsel and seeing the world through their eyes. You do not have to believe their perspective is accurate, and you certainly do not have to agree with their actions, but to be an effective human services professional you must be willing and able to understand what it feels like to be them.

For instance, many perpetrators of abuse were victimized themselves, and it is important that the counselor permit an unsympathetic client to share his or her own experiences of being a victim. While it might not make sense that a victim of abuse goes on to become an abuser, this dynamic does occur. The boy who was sexually abused *may* grow up to be a pedophile, the girl who was beaten *may* grow up to beat her own chil-dren, and the boy who witnessed his father beat his mother *may* grow up to beat his own wife. The nature of this dynamic will be discussed in later chapters but understanding that most abusive behavior is borne out of pain might help you see mandated clients not as monsters, but as very broken human beings in need of assistance.

Boundaries.

Any discussion of empathy and the need for emotional immersion in another's problems must be considered in the context of boundary setting. Although the human services profession is not the sort of career one can leave at the office, it would be imprudent to become so immersed in a client's problems that practitioners cannot distinguish the difference between their problems and the problems of their clients. It is probably easier to discuss good boundary setting by giving examples of poor boundary setting. The practitioner who counsels a victim of domestic violence and spends the majority of the session talking about her own abusive relationships has poor boundaries. The practitioner who becomes so upset about a mother abusing her child that he takes the child home with him is not setting good boundaries. The practitioner who becomes so upset at a client who projects anger in the counseling session that she yells back is not setting good boundaries. Finally, the practitioner who gets so immersed in his clients' problems that he becomes convinced his clients cannot survive without him is not setting good boundaries.

To help understand the nature of personal boundaries, they can be compared to physical boundaries, such as the property line around one's house—porous enough so that someone can enter the property, but solid enough that a neighbor knows not to set up a shed in another neighbor's yard (Cloud & Townsend, 1992). So too must human services professionals establish boundaries in their mental, physical, and emotional lives to determine what falls within their domain of responsibility and what does not.

In the human services field, some boundaries are determined by the ethical standards of the profession. For instance, having a sexual relationship with a client violates an ethical standard because this type of intimacy can exploit the practitioner–client relationship that grants the practitioner a significant measure of control—even authority—over the client. Violating the prohibition against having sexual relations with a client is so serious that it can result in suspension of one's professional license. Violating this ethical boundary might seem like an obviously bad idea to most practitioners, but it occurs more often than one might suspect. Counseling creates a sense of intimacy that can sometimes foster romantic feelings, particularly on the part of the client. A client who is depressed and lonely may experience the counselor's comfort and guidance as intimate love. But a sexual relationship when one party possesses power and some level of control and the other is vulnerable and struggling will always result in emotional and physical exploitation.

A counselor who respects this intimacy boundary will recognize the clinical nature of the client's feelings and will help clients see that experiencing intimacy can be a positive experience without exploitation of their vulnerabilities. This is an example of a clearly marked boundary, and it is difficult to cross this boundary line without knowing one is in dangerous territory. However, other boundaries are not so clear and may be more readily violated (or at least somewhat trampled upon) by human services professionals, including myself.

My first job in human services was as an adolescent counselor at a residential facility. I was 23 years old, fresh out of college, and excited to finally be making a difference in people's lives. I became too involved in my adolescent clients' lives though, and quickly began to overidentify with the teens on my caseload because I had also experienced a difficult adolescence. I was so flattered by my clients' expressed need for me that I was willing to work any hours necessary to make sure they knew how much I cared. If I worked a later shift and one of the girls on my caseload told me that she needed me there in the morning, I would make sure I was there bright and early, even if it meant getting little sleep. If another counselor called me at home because a teen on my caseload was struggling and was insisting that she would only talk to me and no other counselor, I dropped whatever I was doing and rushed down to the facility, feeling good that I was so needed.

This sort of behavior indicated several problems. First, it led to a situation where I almost left the field of human services altogether because after 3 years, I was so burned out that I was no longer sure I could handle the pressure. My behavior also encouraged a sense of dependency among the girls on my caseload. Because it felt good to be needed, I neglected one of the fundamental values of the human services profession: empowering clients to be more self-sufficient. Setting healthy boundaries would not have been uncaring; rather, it would have encouraged my clients to develop positive relationships with other counselors, and it would have also taught them how to rely on themselves and their newly developed coping skills. Finally, had I had better boundaries, I would also have modeled better self-care for my teen clients by kindly setting healthy limits to protect my emotional and physical health.

Since that point in my career I have developed some "rules for the road" for recognizing healthier boundaries with clients that better balance the need to be caring with the need to foster client self-sufficiency and healthy self-care. One rule is that I try to avoid overfunctioning in the counseling relationship. If I start to feel exhausted and burned out, I ask myself whether I am working harder than my client. This does not mean that I do not advocate for my clients, or that I do not assist my clients in performing various tasks, but what it does mean is that I recognize that I am not helping my clients if I am doing the work for them. Overfunctioning is often rooted in impatience and a need to see progress more quickly. However, clients have the right to self-determination, which means they have the right to progress as they wish or are able. So, if I begin to feel exhausted and impatient with a particular client, I recognize these feelings as a sign that it may be time to step back a bit and give my clients more emotional space to grow, and ultimately to decide the best course of action for themselves.

Another "rule" I have for myself is to remember that my clients' lives and all that occurs within them are a part of *their* journey, not mine. I may believe I know what is best for my clients under certain circumstances, but that may not always be the case because ultimately, they need to live their lives in the way they deem best. This conceptualization allows us to view ourselves as one of many individuals who will come alongside clients and help them at some point along their journeys, just as various people have helped and influenced us along our own life journeys. This conceptual framework helps to remind us that our clients have free will to make whatever choices they deem appropriate. Client self-determination means that our clients can accept our assistance and suggestions, or they can reject them.

Another conceptualization that can help establish and maintain healthy boundaries in a counseling relationship is to recognize that people grow and change at varying rates and in their own unique ways. Thus, when we are working with clients early in their journeys, we may be the *seed planter*. This is an important role, but it can also be frustrating if it appears as though nothing we are doing or saying is making a difference. Seed planters do just as it sounds—they plant the seeds of future growth—but oftentimes they do not have the benefit of seeing growth actually come to fruition. It is often this way when working with children and adolescents. Sometimes we see the manifestation of our work with them, but often we do not. We can trust that in most cases, years later, something we said, some kindness we showed, some reframing we did will result in healthy personal growth.

It is equally important to recognize the role of the *fertilizer* and the *harvester* in counseling relationships. These are the counselors who come into the lives of clients after the seeds have already been planted. The fertilizer is the practitioner who helps the client do the hard work of implementing changes using a range of intervention strategies. This is no easy task, but the counselor often has the benefit of seeing the results of the seed planting and intervention strategies. The harvester is often the most gratifying role in direct practice because the client at this stage of their journey is often highly motivated and ready to make the necessary changes for a healthier life. They recognize past negative patterns in relationships and choices, can better navigate challenges they've experienced in their environment, and have the necessary insight and motivation to effect true change.

I recently had a client who was at this point in her life. Fortunately, I was able to recognize that I could not take full credit for helping her to make the significant realizations and changes she was making in counseling. She'd had several prior counseling experiences, and my role was to help her integrate all that she had previously learned so that she could finally make the necessary and enduring changes in herself and her approach to life. She was highly motivated to become a healthier, happier, and more productive individual, recognizing her own right to self-determination and dignity and her responsibilities to herself, her family, and her community. I did not take credit for all of her rapid progress. Instead, I appreciated the work of the previous counselors, recognizing that my client had the benefit of many talented counselors through the years, each of whom had contributed greatly to her personal growth and progress.

If you are working productively with a client but see little to no progress, you may very well be the seed planter. If you are working productively with a client but it seems as though change is still a long way off, then you are probably the fertilizer, and if you are reaping changes left and right with a client, then you may very well be the harvester. If you are all of these things with one client, you have probably been working with your client for a long time! Regardless, envisioning yourself operating as a part of a team, even though you may never meet the counselors who came before you (or those who may come after), helps to ease the sense of responsibility you may feel for a client's growth (and it helps us to resist the temptation to take full credit for the client's progress!).

Active Listening Skills.

Active listening skills involve the ability to attend to the speaker fully, without distraction, without preconceived notions of what the speaker is saying, and without being distracted by thoughts of what one wants to say in response. Active listening in the counseling relationship includes behaviors such as maintaining direct eye contact and observing the client's body language. It also involves considering virtually everything that the client says as relevant.

Active listening involves empathy and acceptance, in that it relies on unconditionally accepting clients and exhibiting unbiased reflection when hearing their stories (Weger et al., 2014). You may have heard the old adage that most people aren't really listening, but instead are preparing what they're going to say in response when the other person has finished talking. When someone is actively listening, they are not thinking about what they're going to say next but are instead concentrating on all aspects of the listener—what they're saying, as well as their facial expressions and body language. Effective active listening involves setting aside our own biases and agendas (Drollinger et al., 2006).

Active listening has several components, including being mindful and present, paying as much attention to clients' nonverbal communication as their verbal communication (e.g., rocking back and forth, fidgety hands, leaning back), and being comfortable with silence. (Empathetic people often want to jump in and fill the space!) Active listening also involves setting aside our biases and any agenda we may have for the session. For instance, you may want to complete a psychosocial assessment in one session, but your client keeps becoming distracted and digressing into side stories. Well, if you were to consistently interrupt him and direct him back to the original question so you can complete your psychosocial assessment on your timetable, imagine the wealth of information you'd be missing! The side stories are every bit as important as the primary story, and when we're actively listening to our clients, we can hear them and value what they tell us about our client's values, concerns, histories, fears, and hopes. In fact, sometimes it's the side stories that yield more information because something may be too scary to address directly.

Observing your own thoughts but from a distance and resisting is also very important. the temptation to engage in them. One of the most important components of active listening is the ability to hear what a client is saying without judging them (Kabat-Zinn, 2014). The desire to be heard and understood is universal, and if a counselor jumps in with an intervention too soon, and a client does not feel heard or understood, resistance is likely. A human services practitioner who is practiced at active listening can listen to a client's story without feeling the need to assess or critique them—they just receive the message.

Activing listening also involves the ability to reflect back what the client has shared, but not in a rote manner. Rather, a skilled counselor is able to paraphrase what the client has said in a way that reflects understanding, empathy, and compassion. Reflecting back what a client has said also helps to create a sense of intimacy in the relationship (Weger et al., 2014). The final step in active listening involves asking questions of the client. These can be clarifying questions (to fill in any gaps, for instance), or questions that encourage more self-disclosure. For instance, if you were working with a Central African client whose parents were pressuring her to break up with her boyfriend, you might ask her how she felt when she was threatened with being cut off by her family, and if she could think of a different way her parents could express their feelings of disappointment. Asking follow-up questions not only provides a way to obtain additional information, they can also lay a foundation for further reflection later on.

INTERVIEWING SKILLS AND ASSESSMENT TOOLS

Learning Outcome 3.4   **Describe how assessment and intervention strategies are used in generalist practice**

After honing our basic helping competencies and skills, we are ready to move onto assessing a client's needs so that effective generalist counseling intervention strategies can be implemented. While we continue to assess clients in some respects throughout the counseling relationship, effective interviewing skills are most often used during the assessment phase of a counseling relationship. Effective interviewing utilizes a combination of skills, such as active listening skills, **observation skills**, and the ability to ask **open-ended questions**, which includes reflecting back the client's answers while summarizing their concerns and needs, in a way that doesn't seem artificial or condescending.

When we use active listening skills during the assessment stage of the counseling relationship, we attend to what our clients are saying fully, without distraction (Fitzgerald & Leudar, 2010). We don't prejudge what they are saying because we want to give them the time and space to express themselves fully. We also don't interrupt, jumping in to give our impressions, before they've had a chance to conclude their comments. Active listening in the counseling relationship includes behaviors such as maintaining direct eye contact (if that is deemed culturally appropriate) and observing the client's body language and nonverbal cues. It also involves considering everything the client says as relevant. It is often the subtle offhand comments that yield the most information about the client's interpersonal dynamics.

Good observation skills are also an important part of the assessment process because individuals communicate as much through their bodies as they do through their words. Practitioners should observe their clients' eye contact, whether they are shifting uncomfortably in their seats when talking about certain subjects, crossing their arms self-protectively, or tapping their feet anxiously. All these behaviors can be clues or indicators of deeper dynamics. Employing good observation skills can also yield information about whether a client is being direct or evasive, genuine or masked, sincere or manipulative, open or guarded.

A good interviewer can obtain very specific information in a way that seems natural and conversational, while at the same time increasing a client's comfort level and openness. Counselors who are uncomfortable may appear contrived or too formal, which may make a client feel equally uncomfortable and therefore reluctant to share sensitive information. I recall a time when I was in college and seeking the services of a counselor. While the counselor was asking all of the right questions, he was awkward and too formal in his delivery, almost as if he were checking boxes off a list. When I began sharing something deeply personal, I shifted my glance, which allowed me to feel safer and more comfortable, and yet he was so determined to maintain eye contact that he moved his head in a way that dramatically and rather artificially attempted to reconnect. I found his insistence that I maintain eye contact intrusive and almost aggressive, and it shut me down emotionally. He also reflected back my answers in a way that seemed artificial:

Me: "Well, I suppose even though all of this occurred years ago, it is still quite painful."
Him: "It sounds like even though all of this occurred years ago, it is still quite painful."
Me: "Yes. This is exactly what I said."

Needless to say, I never went back.

Honing good interviewing skills that allow for us to actively listen, maintain appropriate eye contact, observe our clients holistically, ask open-ended questions, and reflect back and summarize what our clients have shared is difficult. Authenticity cannot be faked. Interest cannot be faked. Genuineness cannot be faked. If you are authentically interested in your client's story, and genuinely care, then this will shine through and compensate for any nervousness or awkwardness you may feel. Studying good interviewing skills and practicing them diligently is important, but so is having trust in oneself and a desire to really hear what clients share by showing genuine interest in and concern for their experiences.

The Psychosocial Assessment

The first session with a client is often spent conducting an intake interview for a **psychosocial assessment**—a report that includes comprehensive information about clients and their needs that will be relied on when developing an intervention and treatment plan. Psychosocial assessments can take many forms depending in large part on the types of services being offered and the client's needs, but generally they include basic demographic information about the client (e.g., age, marital status, number of children, ethnicity), the nature of the identified problem(s), employment status, housing situation, physical health status, current and past medications, history of substance abuse, criminal history, history of trauma, any history of mental health problems (including depression, suicidal thoughts, or other mental illness), and any history of mental health services. Human services psychosocial evaluations use a **strengths-based approach** or perspective, which means that while clients' needs are identified, their strengths are as well. This practice perspective helps the counselor avoid seeing the client from a pathological perspective, focusing solely on their deficits, while viewing clients as having inherent strengths, such as resiliency (Saleebey, 2005). According to Saleebey, the strengths-based approach can be used with other practice theories, particularly those that encourage self-determination and personal growth.

The specific focus of the psychosocial assessment will vary depending on the services being sought. For instance, clients who are seeking services from a domestic violence shelter will be asked more questions related to the clients' relationship histories, histories of family abuse, and levels of functioning, sufficiency, and safety. Clients seeking hospice services will be asked more health-related questions and questions pertaining to their feelings about dying. Clients seeking substance abuse services will be asked more questions about their history of alcohol consumption and their history with prescription and illicit drugs. Finally, some agencies (or grant funders) have specific forms used for psychosocial evaluations; thus, the human services professional won't have much latitude in the questions being asked, whereas at other agencies, the counselor will have much greater autonomy, particularly if the services being provided are of a more general nature.

Even though the psychosocial assessment process will be concentrated in the first few sessions, some level of assessment will continue throughout the counseling process. This is important because often new information will continue to emerge long after the initial assessment period is over. If counselors assume the assessment is complete after the first few sessions, they might overlook important information about the client that emerges later in the counseling relationship.

I recall working with one female client seeking counseling services for depression and parenting issues. In response to my questions regarding her perception of the origins of her struggles she spent a considerable amount of time discussing her troubled marriage and her difficulty making friends. In a much later session, she was sharing a particularly painful story about a difficult interaction with a friend, and in the process made a casual and joking comment about it reminding her of something hurtful her mother always said to her when she was a child. If I had not been actively listening, I could have missed the significance of her comment, but I also noticed her brief pause and a very subtle sadness in her eyes. The entire exchange lasted no more than a few seconds, but it completely turned the course of our counseling. In other words, she shared something months after the psychosocial assessment was completed that altered my assessment of her situation.

Patience, therefore, is imperative in conducting a quality assessment. One reason why people may have entered the field of human services is because they love to figure other people out. But a seasoned professional will not allow this passion to result in a rush to judgment. It is important to hold at bay the desire to exclaim "Aha!" too quickly.

Pearson eText

Video Example 3.4

This video shows how Bowen's Family Systems Theory and a genogram can be used to assess clients.

People are complex beings, with unique communication patterns and perspectives. Gaining a comprehensive picture of our clients' lives involves allowing their stories to unfold slowly at the client's pace. We are not conducting a criminal investigation, which involves seeking the ultimate truth; rather, we are interested in our clients' perspectives and their version of their lives and experiences, which may or may not be completely accurate. Understanding this dynamic does not detract from counselors' advocacy role of their clients, but rather supports the counselor's ability to help clients reframe various incidences and experiences in their lives, and to help them gain a healthier and more balanced perspective.

Generalist Practice Assessment Tools

In addition to conducting a clinical inventory, human services professionals often use assessment tools to evaluate their clients' mental health functioning and psychosocial needs. Assessment tools may consist of psychological inventories, such as Beck's Depression Scale or the Rosenberg Self-Esteem Scale, which can be facilitated by any mental health professional, or may involve the use of psychological testing, such as an IQ test, or the Minnesota Multiphasic Personality Inventory (MMPI), which must be facilitated by a licensed psychologist or psychiatrist.

Another type of assessment tool includes those based on a particular theory, such as a **family genogram**, developed by Dr. Murray Bowen and based on a theory he developed in 1978, called family systems theory (Bowen, 1978). Bowen's family systems theory postulates that individuals can best be understood within the context of their familial environments. A family system is composed of individuals operating as interdependent components that impact the other components. Patterns of behaving and functioning, including relational patterns with self and others, not only impact other members of the system but are also transmitted from one generation to the next.

Examples of intergenerational relational patterns include how feelings are managed (are anger and grief expressed openly?), how communication is handled (is open communication embraced or is it threatening to the family system?), how discipline is meted out to children (is it authoritarian? authoritative? permissive?), even whether families are generally open or closed systems (are outsiders, such as new partners, accepted with open arms, or are they treated with wariness and caution?). Relational styles also tend to be passed down from generation to generation, such as the types of behaviors that are most likely to result in alliances (and **enmeshment**) or estrangement from the family.

Having a client develop a *family genogram* is a very effective way of better understanding the big picture of the client's life. A genogram provides a visual picture of these intergenerational patterns, helping the human services provider (and the client) study this intergenerational transmission as it relates to issues such as communication style, emotional regulation, and various other functioning styles and patterns. What has the client taken for granted as normative functioning that was actually passed down from generation to generation? What are the intergenerational transmissions of communication styles, emotional regulation, and relational styles? Some examples of relational styles include how conflict is managed, whether feelings are expressed directly or indirectly, how shame is used and handled, how crises and loss have reverberated through the generations, whether families are open systems or closed, whether family members' independence is encouraged or discouraged, and very important, how culture and religion impact all of these processes.

Bowen believes that for people to achieve positive well-being they must be able to have a healthy personal autonomy and individuation while maintaining appropriate closeness with one's family system. Those who are so close to their family system that they cannot make decisions without family approval (or risk being considered betrayers of the family) may be *enmeshed* with certain family members. Those who find it necessary to emotionally distance themselves to the point of estrangement to achieve independence are considered *cut off* from their family systems. The goal for achieving positive well-being, personally and within one's family system, is to find the balance between achieving personal autonomy and individuation while maintaining appropriate closeness with one's family system.

A family genogram can assist a client in developing a level of objectivity about their family systems, which can ultimately help them to see that they are not victims, but viable participants in choices about future behaviors. Thus, rather than fearing shame and disapproval from a parent, the client can recognize that shaming in response to increased autonomy is a relational style that has been passed down from generation to generation, perhaps in response to some trauma related to a loss experienced several generations back. And perhaps the seemingly negligent parent isn't being purposely distant and unloving but is reacting to his own parent's harsh and authoritarian parenting style.

Creating a family genogram takes considerable time and effort. Most people have some information about their parents, limited information about their grandparents, and oftentimes no information about their great-grandparents. They may have grown up hearing one-sided (and unquestioned) versions of family feuds or odd distant relatives. To gain accurate and valuable information about one's family system, information seeking must be intentional. This can be uncomfortable and may even ruffle the feathers of certain family members, because it is often the family members who have been cut off, or are considered the black sheep, who hold the family secrets that will unlock the hidden underlying dynamics of a family system. Poking around the skeleton closet may threaten family members, particularly in closed family systems.

Genograms use a variety of symbols designed to indicate gender, the type of relationship (married, divorced, etc.), *and* the nature of the relationships (cut off or enmeshed). Traumatic events, such as deaths, divorces, and miscarriages, are noted, as are the family's responses to these events (e.g., losses are openly talked about, never discussed, or denied). Typically, shameful events are also relevant, such as out-of-wedlock births (particularly relevant in earlier generations), abortions, extramarital affairs, domestic violence, alcohol abuse, sexual abuse and assault, and job losses. Traumatic events are often kept secret but can affect family members for generations to come. The shame of an extramarital affair and an out-of-wedlock birth that was hushed up several generations back can have a profound effect on how emotions are handled and how feelings are communicated.

One's culture, religion, and the region where one grew up also have a profound impact on how relational patterns are passed down from generation to generation, without any knowledge of their origin. I once worked with a woman who struggled to understand why her mother never seemed to accept or approve of her. She was raised in a conservative rural community and had spent years in counseling attempting to understand her mother's intense perfectionism and refusal to accept even the smallest of mistakes. My client was convinced that her mother was ashamed of her, and this belief affected every area of her functioning. A genogram revealed that her grandmother was raped as a young woman, and my client's mother was the product of that rape. Both the grandmother and my client's mother lived their lives in constant shame, and their high

Emotional relationships legend

Indifferent/Apathetic	Harmony	Hostile	Violence	Abuse	Manipulative
Distant/Poor	Friendship/Close	Distant-Hostile	Distant-violence	Physical abuse	Controlling
Cutoff / Estranged	Best Friends / Very Close	Close-Hostile	Close-Violence	Emotional abuse	Focused on
Discord / conflict	Love	Fused-Hostile	Fused-Violence	Sexual Abuse	Fan / Admirer
Hate	In Love	Distrust	Fused	Neglect (abuse)	Limerence

©MELCORNEY / WIKIMEDIA FOUNDATION

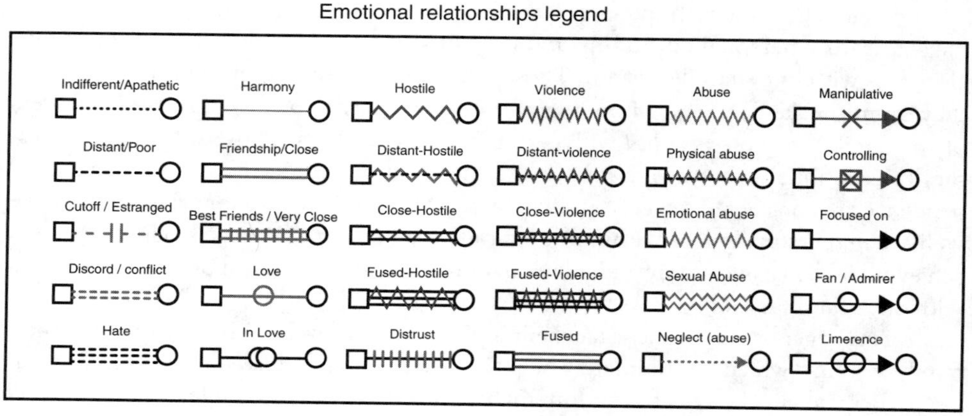

Figure 3.2
Genogram emotional relationships legend.

expectations of my client were really a reflection of their desire to protect her from the shame they endured due to cultural restraints common in that era. What my client perceived as her mother's rejection of her was not a statement of her disapproval, but rather actually an expression of love and protection. It was through the development of a family genogram that my client was able to take a few steps back emotionally and see herself and her family system with more clarity and objectivity.

A family genogram provides a structured way of obtaining a comprehensive family history so that the practitioner and client can develop a more complete understanding of the broader family dynamics that are affecting the client in ways perhaps never before recognized or acknowledged. A family genogram also provides a nonshaming way to gain a level of objective understanding, including an objective understanding of the nature of conflict-filled family relationships (Prest & Protinsky, 1993). A family genogram is an effective assessment tool, as well as a very effective intervention tool that can be used to address long-standing psychosocial issues that have potentially kept clients in emotional bondage for years.

The Nature of Clinical Diagnosing

Many human services practitioners working as paraprofessionals will not be formally diagnosing clients, but it is important that they understand the nature of mental health diagnosing since their clients may have one or more clinical diagnoses. Additionally, licensed human services professionals will likely be required to diagnose clients as a part of the assessment process depending on the nature of their work and the practice setting in which they are working.

There are many components of conducting a clinical diagnosis, including a comprehensive awareness of mental and emotional disorders. Mental health providers in the United States use the *Diagnostic and Statistical Manual of Mental Disorders*, fifth edition (*DSM-5*) to diagnose the mental and emotional disorders of their clients. The *DSM-5* is a classification system developed by the American Psychiatric Association (APA, 2013) that includes criteria for mental and emotional disorders, such as schizophrenia, depressive disorders, and anxiety disorders, and personality disorders such as narcissistic personality disorder and antisocial personality disorder (sociopathy).

In 2013 the *DSM-5* shifted away from a multiaxial system toward a more dimensional approach. Disorders that used to be diagnosed on three different axes—Axis I (clinical disorders), Axis II (personality disorders and mental retardation), and Axis III (general medical conditions)—are now recorded on one axis. Psychosocial and environmental stressors used to be recorded on Axis IV but are now reflected in clinical descriptions. Axis V used to reflect the client's Global Assessment of Functioning (GAF), but, due to the overwhelming consensus among mental health experts that an individual's level of functioning cannot be sufficiently captured with a single number, clinicians are now encouraged to evaluate a client's mental and psychosocial functioning within a separate assessment of the client's severity and disability.

Another important consideration when evaluating someone's level of functioning and mental-health status is to recognize that virtually all behaviors occur on a continuum. It is only when a particular behavior occurs frequently enough, and at an intensity level high enough to interfere with normal daily functioning for a significant amount of time, that it becomes the subject of clinical attention. All of us feel sad at times, but if we are so intensely sad that we stop eating and want to stay in bed all day, then we may be suffering from clinical depression. Similarly, many of us become concerned from time to time that our friends might be gossiping about us or that one of our coworkers is trying to get us fired, but if we're convinced that everyone is out to get us, even people we've never met, then we may be suffering from some form of clinical paranoia.

The *DSM-5*

The *DSM-5* accounts for the continuum of mental health experiences by including criteria relating to the frequency and intensity of psychological experiences in the diagnosis process. For instance, meeting the criteria for major depressive disorder requires that an individual not just be depressed, but also have a depressed mood nearly every day for at least a 2-week period. An individual who meets the criteria for generalized anxiety disorder isn't someone who worries from time to time, but someone who worries excessively, more days than not, for at least 6 months.

Although the diagnostic criteria of the *DSM-5* rely significantly on professional peer consensus and review, and are backed by a large body of research, many professionals in the human services field have some concerns because of the DSM's reliance on the medical model. The human services discipline uses the strengths-based approach, and the DSM's tendency to pathologize certain thoughts and behavior can be problematic if certain behaviors are rooted in different cultures or unique (but not maladaptive) personality styles. For instance, it wasn't too long ago that the DSM considered those with same-sex attractions mentally ill. In many respects, the DSM reflects cultural values. There are numerous examples of feminists during suffragette being diagnosed with a mental illness. Similarly, slaves and indentured servants who ran away from highly abusive situations were also considered mentally ill! Both of these examples predate the DSM, but they highlight how society's perspective of what behaviors are aberrant changes significantly over time.

Pathologizing normative behavior tends to create a stigma for those who behave in ways that are not necessarily maladaptive but lie outside of cultural norms, or those who are responding in an adaptive way to a traumatic experience. Consider those who have recently been victims of violent crime. If they experience mental flashbacks of the traumatic event, are they exhibiting behaviors that are adaptive and expected, perhaps even healthy? Or, in the alternative, are they suffering from posttraumatic stress disorder? Are angry adolescents whose parents just experienced a divorce exhibiting a normal grief response to this loss? Or do they have oppositional defiant disorder? Even if human services professionals do not inherently view human behavior from a disease perspective, using the *DSM-5* can influence practitioners to view their clients from a pathological perspective (Duffy et al., 2002).

Yet, even if one believes that the medical or disease model is appropriate to use when evaluating psychological disorders, an important distinction between the diagnostic system used to diagnose medical conditions and the system used to diagnose mental disorders is that the *DSM-5* uses criteria based on symptoms, whereas medical conditions are diagnosed based on the etiology (cause or origin) of the disorder. Thus, rather than diagnosing a patient with a stomachache, which could potentially have many causes, the medical diagnosis could be a virus, an ulcer, or cancer. Yet, when considering mental disorders, one is not diagnosed with a neurotransmitter disorder, negative thinking, or an abusive childhood, but with major depressive disorder based on the symptoms the client is experiencing, and not on the etiology of their distress.

Despite these concerns, the *DSM-5*, if used in conjunction with other assessment tools, can be an effective way of evaluating clients' emotional and psychological struggles. As referenced at the beginning of this section, the *DSM-5* is based on professional consensus and years of clinical research, and thus can help clinicians make sense of a compilation of complex feelings and behaviors. Human services practitioners trained to use the *DSM-5* will likely find it an effective tool in diagnosing clients as long as it is balanced with a range of other diagnostic tools drawn from empowerment and strengths-based approaches.

INTERVENTION ACTIVITIES AND STRATEGIES FOR GENERALIST PRACTICE

Once the initial assessment is complete, a treatment plan is developed to address the client's identified issues. I will explore *direct practice* and counseling techniques appropriate for clients served in particular practice settings in more detail in subsequent chapters. However, there are basic techniques involved in generalist practice that apply in a broad way to most counseling situations that will be explored in this section.

Effective intervention strategies are based on counselors' ability to build a positive alliance and mutual trust with their clients. We may use the most successful, theoretically based strategies available, but if our clients don't trust us (and if we don't trust ourselves), or if our clients don't feel safe to share what they're thinking, then our work with them, regardless of the strategies we use, will not be successful.

Many individuals seeking services at a human services agency will need assistance with developing better coping skills. Regardless of whether the problems experienced by the client are pervasive or more limited, most clients can benefit from learning to better manage high levels of stress, prioritize the various problems in their lives, and manage the current crisis in a way that diminishes the possibility of a "domino effect" of crises. A crisis with one's child requiring a significant amount of time and attention can quickly result in a job loss, which can in turn result in housing insecurity.

Most mental health experts recognize that one of the best opportunities for personal growth is a crisis because it can disrupt long-standing and entrenched maladaptive behavior patterns (Park & Fenster, 2004; Shigemoto et al., 2016). Thus, learning how to deal with a crisis more effectively can have a positive impact on one's life, including increased self-esteem, the development of new and more effective coping skills and strategies, the gaining of wisdom, the development of new social skills, and the development of a better overall support system. Consider the impact of the 2020 coronavirus pandemic. Virtually every country in the world shut down for months hoping to "flatten the curve" (a phrase used in reference to slowing the transmission of the virus, thus lessening the impact on hospitals and fatality rates). While the nature and length of stay-athome orders varied from state to state in the United States, most states implemented some sort of lockdown, requiring people to work from home or be furloughed from their jobs. Schools were closed across the country, requiring students to engage in online learning or parents to homeschool their children. People were told not to leave their homes except for essential tasks, to wear masks, and to socially distance from others (defined as remaining at least 6 feet apart, with no touching, except for those living in the same home). To discourage congregating, many states and local communities closed hiking trails, parks, and beaches.

The economic stress, the social isolation, and the fear of contracting the COVID-19 (the diseased caused by the novel coronavirus) created a crisis for many people in the United States, and while at this time there is not a body of empirical evidence to show the various ways that people responded to the pandemic, anecdotally, I'm sure all of us know people who ultimately experienced the coronavirus crisis as a wake-up call, promising themselves that they would value their friendships more and never take their freedom for granted again. For me personally, the anxiety and sadness I felt in response to not being able to see my colleagues and students, not being able to go to the beach or hike, not being able to see my son (who lived in another state) was profound. But by the second month, I became determined to use the difficult experience for something good, or at least to be more productive. I surveyed my life and wrote down everything I could think of that I'd ever said I would do "if I just had the time," and I made a commitment to be more purposeful and proactive in creating a life of greater meaning—more meditation, more creativity, less time on social media, and in general, feeling more gratitude for everything and everyone in my life. Was I successful? Not entirely, but I was far more productive than I would have been, had I not been proactive in my approach to being socially and physically isolated.

It's important to note that not everyone had the luxury to respond to the pandemic in the way I did. Many people were suddenly without a job and had no means of support. Many people lost their health insurance, experienced food insecurity, or lost loved ones without being able to say goodbye. Many people were already struggling with debilitating depression and anxiety (or other mental health challenges), and the pandemic created an even more urgent crisis for them. And we now know that people of color, particularly members of the Black community, Latina/os, and Native Americans, were disproportionately impacted by COVID-19. But for those who weren't already marginalized or experiencing a significant crisis, the crisis had the potential to manifest personal growth.

There is some older research to back up these anecdotal experiences I've referenced. Park and Fenster (2004) studied stress-related growth in a group of college students who experienced a stressful life event. The study showed that such struggles ultimately produced personal growth, but only for those who expended the necessary energy to work through their struggles in a positive way. Those in the study who remained negative and avoided dealing with the problems resulting from the crisis did not take advantage of the growth-producing opportunities and thus did not experience any significant personal growth. Recognizing the potential for personal growth from a crisis provides the counselor with a framework for assisting clients in developing more effective coping skills that can better assist them in the management of concrete problems. Of course, it is important that the counselor not jump too quickly to pointing out the positive aspects of a stressful situation, since that may feel trivializing to the client. But once a client feels heard, and senses the counselor's authentic empathy, then the counselor can slowly transition to reframing the stressful situation as a growth opportunity, when the client is ready.

Case Management

Case management is likely one of the most common activities of human services practitioners, often consuming more than 50% of their time (Whitaker et al., 2006). Case management is defined as the coordination of services and advocacy for clients and involves human services professionals working with other professionals to coordinate an array of services for the client that diminishes fragmentation and service gaps (Barker, 2003).

The Center for Credentialing & Education (CCE) (2011) provides the following description of case management duties in the Human Services-Board Certified Practitioner Examination handbook:

- Collaborate with professionals from other disciplines,
- Identify community resources,
- Utilize a social services directory,
- Coordinate delivery of services,
- Participate as a member of a multidisciplinary team,
- Determine local access to services,
- Maintain a social services directory,
- Participate in case conferences,
- Serve as a liaison to other agencies,
- Coordinate service plan with other service providers (p. 5).

There are numerous differences between case management and direct counseling services, and while both encompass a broad range of activities, they are distinctly different. Direct practice with clients is focused more on an individual's psychological growth and the development of emotional insight and personal growth, whereas case management involves coordinating services with other systems impacting the life of the client.

A case manager might coordinate services with a client's school social worker, the housing authority, the local rape crisis center, or even a court liaison, all in an attempt to meet the needs of the client who is interacting in some manner with each of these systems. The goal of the case manager is to assist the client in plugging into necessary and supportive social services within the community and to learn how to improve the reciprocal relationships or transactions with each of these social systems. These efforts have many purposes and goals, but chief among them is the caseworker's proactive attempt to strengthen and broaden the client's social support network.

The Task-Centered Approach

Most of us can relate to feeling completely overwhelmed when facing a life crisis. We know there are things we need to do to manage the crisis, but all we see is a gigantic mountain looming before us. For some, this has a motivating effect, and they attack the mountain until every issue is resolved. But for some, particularly those with a history of crises, those with poor coping skills, or those suffering from emotional or psychological problems with diminished personal management skills, the mountain can seem insurmountable, and their response is to shrink away with a feeling of despair and defeat.

A counseling technique called the *Task-Centered Approach,* an intervention strategy developed by the School of Social Services at the University of Chicago (Reid, 1975), works well with clients who feel paralyzed in response to the challenges of various psychosocial problems and crises. Treatment is typically short, lasting anywhere between 2 and 4 months, and sessions focus on problem solving. The client and counselor or caseworker define the problems together and develop mutually agreed-upon goals. Each problem is broken down into smaller and more easily manageable tasks.

Goals can be as tangible as finding a new job or as intangible as learning how to more effectively manage frustration and anger. Rather than having one broad goal of obtaining a job, a client might have a Week 1 goal of doing nothing more than looking at job ads on a major online job board and a Week 2 goal of submitting a resume to one job posting. Dividing large goals into smaller stepping-stone goals diminishes the possibility that clients will allow their anxiety to overwhelm them. By focusing on specific problems and breaking them into bite-sized manageable pieces, clients not only learn effective problem-solving skills, but also gain insight into the nature of their problems, develop increased self-esteem as they experience successes rather than failures in response to meeting goal expectations, and learn to manage their emotions, such as anxiety and depression, without allowing such states to overtake and overwhelm them.

The counselor or caseworker assists clients in meeting goal expectations through a variety of intervention strategies specific to the actual problem, but can include planning for obstacles, role-playing (where the client can actually act out difficult situations in the safety of the counselor's office as a way of practicing communication), and mental rehearsal—similar to role-playing but involving the client thinking or fantasizing about some specific situation, such as an upcoming job interview or a difficult confrontation (Reid, 1975). Revisiting original goals and evaluating client progress are also powerful tools in helping clients experience a sense of personal mastery and empowerment as they are helped to recognize and acknowledge their progress. Consider Case Study 3.2 and then reflect on how you might use the Task-Centered Approach with a similar client.

Case Study 3.2   The Case of Using the Task-Centered Approach

Kara is the 34-year-old single parent of a 5-year-old boy. She has been living with her mother since her divorce 3 years ago. This is a negative situation because her mother is verbally abusive to Kara and her son, abuses alcohol, and smokes inside the home. In addition, their living space is small, and Kara and her son share a bedroom. Kara's original goal was to live with her mother for only 6 months, but whenever she considers moving out she becomes overwhelmed with the prospect of not only finding a nice apartment, but finding childcare as well, because despite her mother's abusive behavior, Kara has been relying on her mother for before- and after-school childcare while she works. Kara feels trapped but completely powerless to do anything about her situation.

During Kara's intake interview she described her prior counseling experiences, sharing that she quit counseling because whenever she was faced with the prospect of finding an apartment, her fears would snowball into so many fears that she simply couldn't bring herself to make the first phone call in search of housing. She ended up feeling embarrassed, as if she were letting the counselor down, and decided she could not deal with any more failures, so she stopped going to counseling. Kara explained that throughout the past several years her mother has consistently reminded her that she would never make it on her own, that she would surely fail, and that she would end up destroying her life and the life of her son. Her mother also told Kara that if she moved out and ran out of money, she would not bail Kara out again and would instead force Kara and her son to go to a shelter. Going online to look for rentals resulted in a flood of worries and concerns for Kara—some specific and some she could not put into words. She worried about everything from whether she would know what to say when calling an apartment manager to whether she would be able to support herself and her son. What if she was laid off from her job and could no longer afford her apartment and had to live in a shelter? What if she couldn't find a babysitter she could afford? What if she found an apartment and got a babysitter, but the babysitter ended up abusing her son more than her mother did? She heard about such things all the time on the news, she reasoned. Or what if she found an apartment, but she had a financial emergency, such as her car breaking down, and she started falling behind in her rent and was evicted? She couldn't fathom the thought of moving out and then having to move back in with her mother again, or worse what if her mother made good on her threat and refused to allow them to move back in with her? Once confronted with this slippery slope of catastrophizing, she would resist even taking the first step toward independence and could not bring herself to even look at online rental listings. Kara's mood became increasingly melancholy over the years, and after years of verbal abuse from her mother when she was younger, and then her ex-husband, and now her mother again, she had no confidence in her ability to financially support herself or her son.

Kara's caseworker reassured her that there was absolutely no rush in finding an apartment. In fact, she reminded Kara that she was in charge of her own life and could make the choices she thought were best for her and her son. During the first two sessions, Kara and her caseworker developed realistic goals for her, including securing an apartment when Kara had the funds to ensure financial security. Kara

and her caseworker developed a detailed budget and determined that she would need 3 months' salary put away in a savings account to ensure against any realistic financial emergencies. By identifying possible obstacles to Kara achieving independence, decisions were made based on facts and realistic risks, not on undefined and generalized fear and anxiety. Once goals were developed and obstacles identified, Kara and her caseworker agreed on tasks to be accomplished by the following week. Kara's task for the first week was to look through the newspaper and circle rental listings within her price range. She was not to call any of them, though, even if she found one that seemed ideal. Kara came in the second week with rental listings saved on her phone. Kara and her caseworker spent the first portion of the session discussing how Kara felt while tagging these rentals. Kara explained that her initial excitement was quickly followed by intense anxiety, but when she realized she could not call about the apartments even if she had wanted to, she calmed down almost immediately. The next portion of the session was spent on determining tasks for the following week. The first task included calling about two apartments but for informational purposes only. Because she had a significant amount of anxiety about calling and talking to a stranger, Kara and her caseworker wrote a script and rehearsed it by doing a role-play with the caseworker playing the part of the potential landlord. Kara's additional task for the week was to talk to her boss to seek reassurance that her employment was secure.

Kara returned the following week excited. She called on two apartments and followed the script on the first one, but the second call went so well she did not even need the script. Her discussion with her boss also went well, and he assured her that her job was secure. Kara shared excitedly that her boss was pleased that Kara showed assertiveness in approaching him and offered her an opportunity to attend some training courses so that she could be promoted. For the next 3 months, Kara's counseling proceeded in a similar fashion with weekly tasks that inched her along slowly enough that she did not become overwhelmed by unmanageable fears, but quickly enough that she gained confidence and courage with each successive step. Kara rented an apartment during her fourth month of counseling with 3 months' income safely tucked away in a savings account, a promotion with a raise, and reputable and affordable day care.

Perceptual Reframing, Emotional Regulation, Networking, and Advocacy

Another generalist intervention strategy involves perceptual reframing—reframing a client's perception of a situation, emphasizing the importance of viewing various events, relationships, and experiences from a variety of possible perspectives. For some reason it seems easier to assume the negative in many situations, imagining the worst possible outcome. Whether considering the intentions of a partner or the prospects of getting a better job, or even whether good things can happen to good people, many people tend to gravitate toward negative assumptions, particularly during times of crisis.

Many people in the midst of a physical or emotional crisis of any proportion will often resort to taking a somewhat polarized negative stance on an issue and would benefit from some assistance in viewing situations and relationships from a different perspective. A client's perception that life is unfair and nothing good ever happens to her can be encouraged to see life's struggles as normative and even positive because they promote personal growth, including the development of resilience and better coping skills. Clients who feel shame because they were recently fired from a job (one they didn't really like in the first place) can be encouraged to see this incident as an opportunity to find a career for which they are far better suited.

Additional generalist intervention goals include assisting clients with *emotional regulation,* teaching them how to effectively manage their emotions, particularly intense emotions, rather than acting on them in an unhealthy way. For instance, clients can be taught how to sit with their emotions, despite the discomfort this may involve, rather than getting angry and behaving in an impulsive manner. Developing a better social support network is another example of a generalist intervention goal. Healthy social support systems assist clients in becoming emotionally independent and self-reliant.

Cultural Competence and Diversity

Because human services professionals work with such a wide range of people across various cultures, socioeconomic levels, and backgrounds, it is vital that human services education and training be presented in a context of **cultural competence** and cultural sensitivity. *Cultural competence* is reflective of a counselor's ability to work effectively with people of color and ethnic minority populations by being sensitive to their needs and recognizing their unique experiences, both historic and current. Cultural competence is a required component of working in the human services field. For instance, the NOHS ethical standards specify the requirements and competencies human services professionals are required to maintain. Specifically, Standards 17 through 21 deal with issues related to cultural competence, focusing in particular on anti-discrimination, cultural awareness, self-awareness relating to personal cultural bias, and requirements for ongoing training in the field of cultural competence.

The human services field is not the only discipline to require cross-cultural training. Most professional organizations require that their mental health professionals obtain cultural competence training based on a foundation of respect for and sensitivity to cultural differences and diversity (Conner & Grote, 2008). Yet, cultural competence extends beyond that of racial and ethnic differences. For instance, counselors who undergo cultural competence training will learn the importance of remaining sensitive to populations from different income levels, religions, physical and mental capacities, genders, age cohorts, ability levels, and sexual orientations. Therefore, they will learn the importance of avoiding what is commonly referred to as ethnocentrism—the tendency to perceive one's own background and associated values as being superior or more normative than others. In recent years, the issue of cultural or multicultural competence has become so important that training protocols have been developed with recommendations that all those who work in the helping fields engage in some form of cultural competence training.

Cultural competence is somewhat of a general term, though, and is often used synonymously with other terms such as cultural sensitivity. Despite the relatively universal belief among human services and mental health experts that cultural competence is a vital aspect of practice, very little consensus exists as to what constitutes cultural competence on a practice level (Fortier & Shaw-Taylor, 2000). Although broad themes of respect and sensitivity tend to be universally accepted as foundational to culturally competent practice, the concept of cultural competence has tended to remain a general philosophy that has not yet been operationalized in a concrete way.

For instance, Cunningham et al. (2002) surveyed counselors who considered themselves culturally competent and found a vast difference in terms of which counseling methods they believed were most effective with culturally diverse clients. This lack of consensus among experts on which specific counseling approaches and counselor responses constituted cultural competence makes it difficult, if not impossible, to determine what methods will have the greatest likelihood of having a positive outcome in counseling a particular ethnically diverse client group. Although recent research has attempted to develop what is called *evidence-based practice* with regard to cultural competence, to date there remains very little research on what constitutes culturally competent practice.

EFFECTING CHANGE AT THE MACRO LEVEL

Learning Outcome 3.5   **Explore the role of macro practice in affecting change on a broad level**

When students consider entering the field of human services, they often do so because they want to help people meet their basic needs by counseling them by helping them deal with past trauma and current crises and obtain much-needed services. In other words, most students think of direct practice with individuals and families when considering a career in the human services profession. But many times, the challenges clients encounter are caused by some external force—an injustice that is structural or systematic. Some of these external forces might be a school system that offers no bus service and therefore inadvertently contributes to low-income students' truancy rates, a government social welfare policy that inadvertently punishes single mothers who work part-time by cutting their benefits, or a **"three strikes"** law that sends a young man to jail for 25 years for a third, yet relatively minor, offense. How do human services professionals combat harmful policies that punish when they should reward or unfair legislation that hurts certain segments of the population, while benefiting others?

Cesar Chavez 1976, Los Angeles, USA.

© REED SAXON / AP / SHUTTERSTOCK

The human services profession is grounded in the notion that people are a part of larger systems and that to fully understand the individual one must understand the broader systems within which the individual is operating. As such, there is a reciprocal dynamic involving both the individual and the system, where each has an impact on the other. Hence, an individual can be very motivated and respond well to direct intervention, but until structural deficiencies are addressed within society, they will likely continue to experience difficulty in some manner.

It is important, then, for human services professionals to recognize that people can be helped best by approaching problems on various levels. Consider that as a human services provider you are committed to eradicating violence within society. You might choose to work with survivors of domestic violence, focusing on their personal empowerment. This approach would involve micro practice—practice with individuals. You might also decide to facilitate treatment groups for batterers, believing that the greatest likelihood of change can be accomplished by addressing the perpetrators of violence in a group setting where each group member can learn from others and hold each other accountable. This approach would involve mezzo practice—practice with groups. But if you decided to address the problem of violence by working on a community, national or perhaps even a global level—leading a human services agency, conducting a public awareness campaign within a community, developing a national public service advocacy campaign, or lobbying for the passage of antiviolence legislation—then you would be engaging in macro practice.

Macro practice includes three practice areas:

1. Administration and management (focusing on the organizational environment),
2. Community practice (focusing on the community environment defined by geography, identity, or issue)
3. Policy practice (focusing on the public policy environment).

Macro practice is a multidisciplinary field shared by those in the human services, social sciences, political sciences, public policy, and urban planning disciplines. Macro practice involves addressing social issues—those that can act as barriers to getting one's basic needs met—on a community and societal level by creating structural change through social action of some type. The most basic themes involved in macro practice include advocating for social and economic justice and human rights for all members of society to end human oppression and exploitation (Reisch, 2016). There are several ways **social change** is accomplished through macro practice, including community development, community organizing, and policy practice. Thus, although direct practice is important, working with entire systems to promote positive structural change on all fronts is equally important.

Some human services professionals work solely in macro practice in administrative positions, working with a community development organization or engaging **policy advocacy**, conducting no direct practice whatsoever. But many human services professionals involved in micro practice are also involved in macro practice at least to some extent (Austin et al., 2016). For instance, when I was the director of victim-witness assistance at a county state attorney's office, I provided generalist counseling to victims of violent crime, but I also served on community policy action committees and engaged in legislative action with community coalitions, making recommendations to the state legislature on behalf of victims' advocacy groups.

Human services professionals might ask themselves why they should be concerned about what is happening to people in an entire community, in a different part of the country, or in a completely different part of the world. The rationale for engaging in broad-based activities lies in the human services profession's commitment to social justice and human rights achieved through social action and social change. This foundational commitment to social justice is so integral to the human services profession that the professional obligation to social action is reflected in the ethical principles of the discipline (Knight & Gitterman, 2018; Reisch, 2016). For instance, the NOHS (2015) ethical standards reference the human services professional's responsibility to society, which includes remaining aware of social issues that impact communities and initiating social action when necessary by advocating for social change.

As human services professionals we must be aware of the history of social injustices and human rights abuses against certain populations so that we may better understand the context within which they currently struggle. These insights will also help us to gain an awareness of what groups are most likely to be targets of discrimination and oppression in the future. At all times we must be vigilant in avoiding being influenced by the stigma surrounding many challenges experienced by historically marginalized and oppressed populations. Examples include ethnic minority populations that experience disparities within the criminal justice system or populations that are underserved in the areas of mental and physical health (Calkin, 2000).

In some respects, the human services profession has shifted away from its original call to community action, turning instead to a model of individualized care (McBeath, 2016; Rothman & Mizrahi, 2014). This is likely due to the increased popularity of direct (micro) practice within all the mental health professions in the 20th century. This doesn't mean that macro practice or social advocacy has ceased. Rather, as those in the human services fields have moved away from community work, other disciplines have moved in to fill the gap, such as urban and public planners and those in the political sciences. This shift in priorities has resulted in the human services profession often being out of the loop of community building and organizing efforts (Johnson, 2004).

Concerns have also been expressed regarding the neglect of macro and community practice in human services and social work educational programs, which has compounded the tendency for human services professionals to avoid macro practice in their careers as they feel ill equipped and unprepared (Polack, 2004). The movement away from macro practice is apparently an international trend as well. For instance, Weiss (2003) cited examples of how many human services professionals in Israel do not feel competent addressing social issues on a community or global level because the majority of their training focused on practice with individual clients. Weiss encourages those in the human services professions both in Israel and abroad to reengage in policy-related activities and social advocacy on a macro level.

McBeath (2016) provides 10 recommendations for those working in the human services to reaffirm the commitment to macro practice, including developing advocacy networks and partnerships, strengthening interprofessional partnerships, using technology for networking and advocacy purposes, strengthening the connections between micro and macro practice, and using a human rights framework. The reality is that structural issues contributing to poverty, racism, violence, labor abuses, and other forms of human exploitation must be addressed through advocacy efforts for social change on a macro level as well as a micro level to create much-needed changes within society.

Working with At-Risk and Marginalized Populations

Before beginning any discussion on social advocacy efforts on a macro level it is important to identify populations that are often the target of marginalization, social injustice, oppression, and human rights violations. In essence, an at-risk population can include any group of individuals who are vulnerable to exploitation due to lifestyle or the lack of political power, financial resources, and societal advocacy and support, and, generally, the lack of a powerful voice in society. Some of the current at-risk and oppressed populations include ethnic minorities, immigrants, and refugees (particularly those who do not speak English), indigenous people, older adults, women (particularly women of color), children in foster care, prisoners, the poor, the homeless, single parents, LGBTQ$_+$ populations, members of religious minorities, and the physically and intellectually disabled. At-risk populations often share unique characteristics not shared by others within a particular culture, and it is often this uniqueness that can increase the risk of oppression, discrimination, injustice, and exploitation. At-risk populations are thus at greater risk of experiencing a variety of social problems compared to other populations within the mainstream of society (Brownridge, 2009).

An individual or population's risk of marginalization, oppression, and exploitation increases with the interconnectedness or **intersectionality** of multiple vulnerabilities (Cho et al., 2013; Nash, 2008). The more types of discrimination, prejudice, and oppression individuals face—racism, sexism, **xenophobia**, homophobia, ageism, ableism, classism— the more they are at risk for a range of social injustices, including increased risk of disadvantage, stigmatization, and oppression (Cho et al., 2013). The concept of intersectionality was originally applied to race and gender, although the concept is now applied to a variety of marginalizing categories such as level of disability, sexuality and gender expression, social class and socioeconomic status, immigration status, nationality, and family status (Knudsen, 2005; Samuels & Ross-Sheriff, 2008). An example of intersectionality of vulnerabilities would be an older, transgendered Black woman who is economically disadvantaged, physically disabled, and struggling with homelessness. This profile reveals a woman who likely experiences multiple forms of vulnerability to injustice on a variety of levels, likely needing various types of advocacy (Martin, 2014). Within the human services field there is growing recognition that at-risk populations often need advocacy because so many of the challenges they experience are rooted in policies, laws, and attitudes that create an "uneven playing field," where some groups have had greater access to benefits within society (currently and historically) unavailable to other groups.

A Just Society.

Before human services professionals can effectively engage in work on a macro level, they must first become aware of what a just society looks like, so they have a conceptual ideal to strive for. At the root of any discussion of an ideal society is the assumption that all human beings have inalienable rights simply because they are human. History is replete with examples of egregious human rights violations against certain populations, often waged in the belief that such actions are justified on some level. Slavery, a **caste system** that deems one group of people more worthy than another, a patriarchal system that subjugates females within society, the genocide or **ethnic cleansing** of a particular cultural or religious group, and the sale and exploitation of women and children for sexual purposes are all examples of the gross mistreatment of individuals, often because there is some defining characteristic that makes them different from groups possessing political and social power. Such differences are often used to justify mistreatment, where members of a more powerful group place themselves above members of less powerful groups.

Members of a just society recognize that one group should not have oppressive power over another because all human beings have basic rights that must be protected. There are many ways human services professionals can work on a macro level to give at-risk populations a voice, including community development, community organizing, and policy practice. Gaining at least a cursory understanding of the different types of macro practice and the associated activities can aid in understanding how human services professionals' work transitions from identifying social problems within society to finding ways of effectively addressing them, all the while working within a human rights framework.

Types of Macro Practice

Within the general field of macro practice, models and approaches have been developed to frame the various ways of approaching social concerns on a broad level. The Internet has in many ways changed the way that macro practice occurs. Whether engaging in macro-related activities solely online or using the Internet as a vehicle for facilitating offline activities, the Internet, particularly social media, has dramatically increased the reach and power of social activists in ways not dreamed of in pre-Internet eras. Although there are many models and approaches to macro practice, most have at their core the basic goal of social transformation where a community on any level (local, national, or global) incorporates values that reflect the human dignity and worth of *all* its members.

Community Development.

Community development dates back to the settlement house movement when Jane Addams and her colleagues worked with politicians, various community organizations, political activists, and community members to create a better community for all members. Addams was concerned about many civic issues and social ills, including immigrant rights, civil rights, child labor, compulsory education, the extrajudicial lynching of Black men, and **women's suffrage**. By engaging residents, community leaders, local politicians, and other community organizations, Addams was able to develop a sense of community cohesion in urban Chicago, which resulted in collective social action and several laws being passed that benefited the members of her community, including those who resided in the settlement houses.

Community development in Addams's day is similar in many respects to civic and political activism today, where effective community building depends on the participation of community organizations and community members working together to address issues that are of concern to the entire community (Austin, 2005; Clarke, 2018). The issues involved could include civic or political issues, such as addressing crime in the community; educational concerns, such as low state test scores and development of an after-school program to combat juvenile delinquency; bringing new businesses to the community to create jobs for community members; or rallying community leaders to develop more open spaces, such as parks, in densely populated neighborhoods.

Empowerment strategies are used in most macro practice approaches focusing on civic issues, such as social and economic development that involves creating liaisons between community organizations and community members. Partnering with those within the community who are most impacted by the identified problems is vitally important since an empowerment approach presumes that community members are experts at solving their own problems and just need guidance, resources, and political power. A community development approach can tackle problems in ways not possible through individual efforts. A particularly empowering aspect of community development is how the collaboration process can create a sense of collective self-sufficiency that often leads to civic pride for community members. In fact, effective community development is based on the conviction that any community is capable of mobilizing necessary resources to support families (Austin, 2005).

The various aspects of macro practice will vary depending on the area of concern and the at-risk population most affected. However, virtually all models of macro practice include a focus on community development, which can refer to the development of a geographic community, such as a neighborhood or city, or a community of individuals, such as women, immigrants, or children (Netting et al., 2017). There are several necessary components of effective community development, including diversity among group members, a sense of shared values among members, positive and collaborative teamwork, good communication, equal participation of all team members, and a good network of connections outside the community (Gardener, 1994). Good community development also depends on the ability to secure enough funding to support group members' efforts and activities. Good networking skills are also essential as are good technology skills because so much of networking in contemporary society is accomplished through e-mail and other technological means (Austin, 2005; Clarke, 2018; Weil, 1996).

Community Organizing.

Community development depends on community organizing efforts, which in turn depend on the efforts of community organizers. The first step in community organizing is to create a consensus on what the community needs, in particular what challenges the community is facing or areas of needed improvement. Once community members agree on the problems to be addressed, community organizers set about to recruit members to join in the effort to effect change. It is important to once again note that the term *community* does not necessarily refer to a geographic community, but might also refer to a community of people, such as women, survivors of domestic violence, prisoners, or foster care children.

Community organizers can be professional policy makers or licensed practitioners, or they can be everyday individuals with a particular passion and calling for social action. A schoolteacher who gets a group of his students together to remove graffiti from public buildings is a community organizer. The single mother of three who organizes a voluntary after-school tutoring program for the kids in her neighborhood is a community organizer. The father of a child victim of sexual abuse who organizes a campaign to increase prison time for sexual offenders is a community organizer. The human services provider whose agency is hired to canvas a neighborhood in an antidrug educational campaign is a community organizer. There are many famous community organizers, for example, Jane Addams, who organized community action around immigrant rights; Rev. Martin Luther King Jr., who organized community action around civil rights; and Cesar Chavez, who organized community action around farmworkers' rights.

Community organizing efforts usually begin with the *identification of a problem* that is of concern to many people in a community. Once a problem has been identified, community organizers must *conduct research* to define the issues so they can better understand how the problems developed and what, if any, forces exist that are keeping the problems in place. For instance, the community activist who is organizing efforts to increase the labor rights of undocumented immigrants may encounter opposition from factory owners who benefit by paying untaxed low wages to undocumented workers. Thoroughly researching this issue will enable community organizers to identify constituents in the community who will support their cause as well as those who may oppose it. Research will also enable community organizers to identify additional harm done by unfair labor practices not initially identified that might increase the strength of any collating forces.

Once the problem has been identified and research has been conducted, *a plan of action* must be determined based on the research conducted. Community organizers might decide to picket factories where they believe abuse of undocumented workers is occurring. They might decide to distribute press releases and have a press conference to gain media involvement, organize a work walkout, or conduct a letter-writing campaign to local political leaders. Effective community organizers also organize fundraising efforts to support their social activism. Fundraising can include a number of strategies, including direct requests for donations, auctions, fundraising dinners, membership fees, or government grants.

Policy Practice.

Policy practice is a narrower form of macro practice in which the human services professional works within the political system to influence government policy and legislation on a local, state, federal, or even global level. The form that policy practice takes depends in large part on the issues at hand, but certain activities in policy practice are consistent despite the issues involved. This is a relatively new field within human services, with few researchers focusing on policy practice prior to the 1980s. Policy practice has been a somewhat neglected area of macro practice, both within human services and social work education and within human services practice settings. One possible reason for this is that policy practice requires in-depth understanding of complex laws and policies, which often falls outside of what is taught in many human services educational programs. But human services and social work professionals are ideal policy-level advocates due to their training in human and society systems at various levels, as well as the professions' commitment to macro social justice (Weiss Gal, 2016).

Policy practice activities center on either reforming current social policy or initiating the development of new policies that address the needs of the underserved and marginalized members of society, with the primary goal of achieving social justice through social action and policy reform. Policy practice is based on the belief that many problems in society, such as poverty, are structural in nature and can best be addressed by making structural changes within society, including the passage of fair and equitable legislation (Weiss, 2003; Weiss Gal, 2016).

Policy practice may be a singular activity or a part of community development and community organizing. Consider the group of human services professionals who are working with a coalition of agencies and concerned citizens on building a park in town where kids can play rather than loitering in the streets. Then consider that a few months after organizing efforts have begun, the coalition learns of an old law that permits the building of a park only in areas zoned for commercial use, and that the land donated to the coalition is zoned for residential use only. Members of the coalition would need to engage in policy practice to change the zoning laws, alongside community development and community organizing efforts. In other words, while there may be times where those engaging in macro practice will only be involved in one macro approach, most often numerous approaches are used in order to best address the issues so that macro goals can be achieved.

Cyberactivism.

Community organizers and social justice activists are increasingly using the Internet, and particularly social media, to draw attention to social issues, as well as for civic engagement and political advocacy (Castells, 2007; Chalmers & Shotton, 2016; Vissers et al., 2008). Individuals and organizations around the globe now use the Internet to create awareness, increase social mobilization, and effect change on local, national, and global levels. According to Pew Research Center, in 2018 about 63% of people in the United States use some form of social media, with Facebook being the most popular platform (Perrin & Anderson, 2019). Further, about 53% of Americans have used a social media platform, such as Facebook or Twitter, for civil engagement and political purposes (Anderson et al., 2018). Political activity on social media may include liking, posting, and reposting content about civic, social, and political issues on their social media account; encouraging others to take action on an issue; joining a politically related group on a social media site; and following an elected official or political candidate on a social media site (Rainie et al., 2012).

Online advocacy is referred to by many different names, but one of the more popular terms is **cyberactivism** (Morris & Langman, 2002). Macro-level practitioners use the Internet in a variety of ways to engage in cyberactivism. For instance, they can use social media to increase awareness about a particular issue, mobilize supporters, create alliances, and encourage action, whether in the form of writing letters or attending protests. One form of online social justice advocacy that is growing in popularity is called hashtag activism, or *hashtivism*—the development and use of a hashtag that goes viral, thus dramatically increasing the reach and power of a social cause (Ibahrine, 2017; Stache, 2015). Examples of successful hashtivism include the #MeToo movement, which highlighted the significant problem of sexual harassment in the U.S. workforce, and #BlackLivesMatter, which is a social justice campaign started by Patrisse Cullors, Alicia Garza, and Opal Tometi to highlight the fight against systemic racism and violence toward Black people. Both of these online campaigns were largely facilitated by the use of a hashtag, which allows social media posts to be searchable.

Many social media sites also allow users to engage in cyberactivism, both individually and collectively. For instance, Facebook allows individuals and organizations to create campaigns for a nominal fee. Users create the content of their campaign, which may include information, a petition, and/or a link to a website. Users can target their campaigns broadly (Facebook users in the United States), or they can target a particular demographic (women between the ages of 25 and 45, with elementary school-aged kids) using Facebook targeting algorithms. The campaign will then appear on the newsfeeds of Facebook users who meet the campaign's specified criteria. Users receive regular updates on their campaigns, including how many people clicked on the campaign post or took some other action such as liking or commenting on the post.

One of the many challenges traditional activists face is targeting groups most likely to be interested in their cause (Taylor & Van Dyke, 2003). Cyberactivism is more successful than traditional forms of activism because it's less expensive, faster, allows for far broader dissemination of information, and increases the ease of engagement. First, social media "herds" like-minded people together through hashtags and other search methods. Additionally, cyberactivists can more easily develop a sense of solidarity among like-minded users, leading to greater engagement and action. Consider how a petition was circulated in the pre-Internet era: Organizations used professional printers to mass-produce informational leaflets, which were then passed out via the U.S. postal service, through door-to-door in-person canvassing, and perhaps even placed on the windshields of cars in parking lots. Activists stood in shopping malls or busy streets for hours disseminating information in an attempt to increase concern and empathy. They asked for signatures on petitions and for volunteers to make phone calls or attend demonstrations, and if they were fortunate perhaps one person in 25 was effectively engaged. The process was slow, expensive, and cumbersome, and results were often minimal compared to other mobilizing efforts. Now consider civic and political campaigns facilitated through cyberactivism. People can click a link, type their name, and then click the share button.

There are several online advocacy platforms used by many cyberactivists as a tool for engaging in macro-level activities online. Two of the most popular are MoveOn.org and Change.org, both of which boast millions of followers on their social media sites, and more than 100 million users on their civic and political action websites. MoveOn.org describes itself as a service for busy but concerned citizens who want to assert their collective power. Its motto is "Democracy in Action," and its mission is to elevate the voices and power of real people in the political process. Change.org describes itself as the world's largest online platform allowing everyday people to transform their worlds on a local, national, and global level. Its motto is "The World's Platform for Change," and its mission is to use technology to empower users to create the change they want to see.

Community organizers and social justice activists have been flocking to online platforms such as MoveOn.org and Change.org in the last few years because such platforms allow for the immediate and broad dissemination of information, as well as these platforms' ability to facilitate agency cooperation, which increases reach and effectiveness. For instance, recently Greenpeace, the League of Conservation Voters, and Environment America teamed up in support of clean air protections. By using Change.org to facilitate their campaign, they were able to collect 1.4 million digital signatures and 2.1 million comments in less than 10 weeks, successfully countering the very powerful anti-EPA (Environmental Protection Agency) lobbyists. Change.org asserts that the Clean Air Protection campaign resulted in the most signatures and largest number of comments ever submitted to a federal agency (Change.org, n.d.). MoveOn.org has also been used successfully by a number of cyberactivists, ranging from restoring funding to a popular music program at a local high school to stopping the passage of anti-gay legislation (MoveOn.org, n.d.).

Unfortunately, social media has also opened the door for the dissemination of propaganda and disinformation campaigns, and other forms of interference and manipulation of social media users. And while individuals certainly facilitate the dissemination of propaganda on social media, the majority of online disinformation campaigns are presumed to be facilitated by *amplifier accounts* run by governments, political parties, and political candidates (amplifier accounts are defined as social media accounts that post disinformation 50 or more times per day). Since most amplifier accounts operate under pseudonyms, though, it is very difficult to identify the owner of the originating accounts (Bradshaw et al., 2020). But methods are being developed by researchers to better identify whether the source of "fake news" posted on social media are individual users or organized entities (often called "troll farms") attached to a government or other political entity.

Some examples of how researchers are identifying troll farms include examining posting patterns, such as the synchronized posting of identical false material on numerous "bot" (automated) sites, synchronized retweets, and content duplication disseminated by automated accounts such as those associated with Russia's targeted disinformation campaigns (Dawson & Innes, 2019; Pacheco et al., 2020). Also, a recent study found that social media disinformation campaigns organized by governments and political parties increased by 150% between 2017 and 2019, from 28 countries participating in such activities in 2017, to 48 countries in 2018 and to 70 countries in 2019. The primary goals of these online disinformation campaigns were to limit the human rights of some groups of people (such as immigrants), discredit political opponents, and disparage opposing political candidates and political movements (Bradshaw & Howard, 2019).

This study also found that groups affiliated with authoritarian regimes engaged in highly sophisticated social media campaigns in order to influence foreign attitudes using human accounts, bots accounts, cyborg accounts (humans using bot technology), and hacked accounts. The countries most commonly associated with organized social media propaganda disinformation campaigns to interfere with foreign elections and influence foreign audiences are China, India, Iran, Pakistan, Russia, Saudi Arabia, and Venezuela. Bradshaw and Howard (2019) found that the most popular social media platforms used by governments and political parties to influence global audiences were Facebook and Twitter. An example of a propaganda tactic is to create hashtags to either promote or counter popular social justice movements or political candidates deemed threatening to a governmental regime.

In summary, social media has changed the way that social justice advocacy is done on a macro level, both in the United States and globally, offering human services professionals and other advocates increased reach and influence when engaging in a range of macro activities. Advocacy may be solely online, as is the case with the #MeToo movement, or it may involve online to offline activities, as is the case with using social media to get the word out about social protests. In the era of #fakenews, advocates must be unrelenting in their efforts to assess the veracity of social media posts, so that we do not inadvertently disseminate false information.

CONCLUSION

This chapter began with an exploration of the ethical nature of human services practice, including a discussion of the importance of engaging in ethical practice in accordance with NOHS ethical standards. Ethical dilemmas, which are unavoidable, are best managed when human services practitioners have insight into their own value system, and plan ahead for possible ethical challenges. This chapter also explored the nature of generalist practice, including the generalist practice model and generalist intervention strategies most commonly used with diverse clients, experiencing a range of psychosocial challenges. This chapter concluded with a discussion of macro practice approaches and how social media has changed the way community organizing, policy practice, and social justice advocacy is conducted.

SUMMARY

- Ethics and morality within a professional context are defined and discussed within a broader framework of what constitutes moral thinking and action, as well as how people know what is and is not moral or ethical behavior.
- The nature of ethical and professional standards in the human services is explored with a particular focus on the nature of ethical and moral behavior, including how moral reasoning ability develops in association with cognitive development.

- The ways that professional ethical standards and codes of conduct can assist professionals in resolving ethical dilemmas are described. The purpose and nature of professional ethical standards, with a focus on the human services profession, are explored.
- Ethical standards in the human services are explored, including their parameters and purpose. The ways that cultural diversity affects ethical perceptions and decision making within the context of the human services profession are analyzed. The importance of human services practitioners being culturally sensitive when evaluating ethical behaviors is explored, with a particular focus on how culture plays a significant role in ethical decision making.
- The primary tenets of generalist practice are explored including the importance of informed consent and the limits of confidentiality. The generalist practice model is explained, including common skills and competencies of human services providers, including the role of basic helping skills such as empathy and active listening.
- Common assessment tools are described and explored, such as psychosocial assessments and other diagnostic evaluations. Common intervention strategies used in generalist practice are also explored.
- Practice on a macro level is explored, including community development, community organizing, policy practice, and cyberactivism. The importance of advocating for marginalized and at-risk populations is also explored.

END-OF-CHAPTER QUESTIONS

1. Identify at least three ways that the NOHS Ethical Standards help human services providers navigate ethical dilemmas.
2. What do *Tarasoff I* and *Tarasoff II* require of mental health providers in order to protect clients and the public?
3. How can using the task-centered approach and perceptual reframing help clients who are feeling overwhelmed?
4. Describe how a client's intersectionality increases their vulnerability to oppression, discrimination, and marginalization within society.
5. Provide an example of how a population experiencing human rights violations was effectively advocated for online. Cite some positive impacts and describe any online disinformation campaigns facilitated in response.

References

American Counseling Association. (2014). *Code of ethics*. Author. https://www.counseling.org/resources/aca-code-of-ethics.pdf

American Psychiatric Association. (2013). *Diagnostic and statistical manual of mental disorders* (5th ed.). Author.

American Psychological Association. (2016). *Ethical principles of psychologists and code of conduct*. Author. http://www.apa.org/ethics/code/

Anderson, M., Toor, S. Raine, L., & Smith, A. (2018). *Activism in the social media age: Public attitudes toward political engagement on social media*. Pew Research Center. https://www.pewresearch.org/internet/2018/07/11/public-attitudes-toward-political-engagement-on-social-media/

Austin, M. J., Anthony, E. K., Knee, R. T., & Mathias, J. (2016). Revisiting the relationship between micro and macro social work practice. *Families in Society, 97*(4), 270–277.

Austin, S. (2005). Community-building principles: Implications for professional development. *Child Welfare, 84*(2), 105–122.

Barker, R. L. (2003). *The social work dictionary* (5th ed.). NASW Press.

Barsky, A. (2018). *Ethics alive! Cultural competence, awareness, sensitivity, humility, and responsiveness: What's the difference?* The New Social Worker. https://www.socialworker.com/feature-articles/ethics-articles/ethics-alive-cultural-competence-awareness-sensitivity-humility-responsiveness/.

Bowen, M. (1978). *Family therapy in clinical practice.* Jason Aronson.

Bradshaw, S., & Howard, P. (2019). *The global disinformation order: 2019 global inventory of organized social media manipulation.* Computational Propaganda Research Project, Oxford Internet Institute. https://comprop.oii.ox.ac.uk/wp-content/uploads/sites/93/2019/09/CyberTroop-Report19.pdf

Bradshaw, S., Howard, P. N., Kollanyi, B., & Neudert, L. M. (2020). Sourcing and automation of political news and information over social media in the United States, 2016-2018. *Political Communication, 37*(2), 173–193.

Brownridge, D. (2009). *Violence against women: Vulnerable populations.* Routledge.

Calkin, C. (2000, June). Welfare reform. *Peace and Social Justice: A Newsletter of the NASW Committee for Peace and Social Justice, 1*(1). http://www.naswdc.org/practice/peace/psj0101.pdf

Castells, M. (2007). Communication, power and counter-power in the network society. *International Journal of Communication, 1,* 238–266.

Center for Credentialing & Education. (2011). *Human services-board certified practitioner exam candidate handbook.* Author.

Chalmers, A. W., & Shotton, P. A. (2016). Changing the face of advocacy? Explaining interest organizations' use of social media strategies. *Political Communication, 33*(3), 374–391.

Change.org. (n.d.). *Victories.* https://www.change.org/victories.

Child Welfare Information Gateway. (2016). *Mandatory reporters of child abuse and neglect.* U.S. Department of Health and Human Services, Children's Bureau.

Cho, S., Crenshaw, K. W., & McCall, L. (2013). Toward a field of intersectionality studies: Theory, applications, and praxis. *Signs: Journal of Women in Culture and Society, 38*(4), 785–810.

Clarke, S. (2018). *Social work as community development: A management model for social change.* Routledge.

Clinton, C. (2004). *Harriet Tubman: The road to freedom.* Little Brown & Company.

Cloud, H. C., & Townsend, J. (1992). *Boundaries.* Zondervan.

Conner, K., & Grote, N. (2008, October). Enhancing the cultural relevance of empirically-supported mental health interventions. *Families in Society, 89*(4), 587–595.

Cunningham, P., Foster, S., & Henggeler, S. (2002, July). The elusive concept of cultural competence. *Children's Services: Social Policy, Research & Practice, 5*(3), 231–243.

Dawson, A., & Innes, M. (2019). How Russia's Internet research agency built its disinformation campaign. *The Political Quarterly, 90*(2), 245–256.

Drollinger, T., Comer, L. B., & Warrington, P. T. (2006). Development and validation of the active empathetic listening scale. *Psychology and Marketing, 23,* 161–180.

Duffy, M., Gillig, S. E., Tureen, R. M., & Ybarra, M. A. (2002). A critical look at the DSM-IV-TR. *The Journal of Individual Psychology, 58*(4), 362–373.

Escalas, J. E., & Stern, B. B. (2003). Sympathy and empathy: Emotional responses to advertising dramas. *Journal of Consumer Research, 29,* 566–578.

Fitzgerald, P., & Leudar, I. (2010). On active listening in person-centred, solution-focused psychotherapy. *Journal of Pragmatics, 42*(12), 3188–3198.

Fortier, J. P., & Shaw-Taylor, Y. (2000). *Assuring cultural competence in healthcare: Recommendations for national standards and an outcomes-focused research agenda.* Resources for Cross-Cultural HealthCare and the Center for the Advancement of Health. U.S. Department of Health and Human Services, Office of Minority Health.

Fulero, S. M. (1988). Tarasoff: 10 years later. *Professional Psychology: Research and Practice, 19,* 184–190.

Garcia, J. G., Cartwright, B., Winston, S. M., & Borzuchowska, B. (2003). A transcultural integrative model for ethical decision making in counseling. *Journal of Counseling & Development, 81*(3), 268–277.

Gardener, J. W. (1994). *Building community for leadership training programs.* Independent Sector.

Gibbs, J. (2003). *Moral development and reality: Beyond the theories of Kohlberg and Hoffman.* Sage Publications Ltd.

Greenberg, L. S., Elliot, R., Watson, J. C., & Bohart, A. C. (2001). Empathy. *Psychotherapy: Theory, Research, Practice, Training, 38*(4), 380–384.

Greenberg, M. T., & Mitra, J. L. (2015). From mindfulness to right mindfulness: The intersection of awareness and ethics. *Mindfulness, 6*(1), 74–78.

Gustafson, K. E., & McNamara, J. R. (1987). Confidentiality with minor clients: Issues and guidelines for therapists. *Professional Psychology: Research and Practice, 18*(5), 503.

Handy, F., & Russell, A. R. (2018). A road map for ethical decision-making. In *Ethics for Social Impact* (pp. 89–118). Palgrave Macmillan, Cham.

Hepworth, D. H., Rooney, R. H., Rooney, G. D., & Strom-Gottfried, K. (2016). *Empowerment series: Direct social work practice: Theory and skills*. Nelson Education.

Houser, R., Wilczenski, F. L., & Ham, M. (2006). *Culturally relevant ethical decision-making in counseling*. Sage.

Ibahrine, M. (2017). Women hashtactivism: Civic engagement in Saudi Arabia. *International Journal of Information and Communication Engineering, 11*(3), 79.

Johnson, A. (2004). Social work is standing on the legacy of Jane Addams: But are we sitting on the sidelines? *Social Work, 49*(2), 319–322.

Kabat-Zinn, J. (2014). Meditation is not for the faint-hearted. *Mindfulness, 5*(3), 341–344. doi:10.1007/s12671-014-0307-1

Kenny, M. C., Abreu, R. L., Helpingstine, C., Lopez, A., & Mathews, B. (2018). Counselors' mandated responsibility to report child maltreatment: A review of US laws. *Journal of Counseling & Development, 96*(4), 372–387.

Kirst-Ashman, K., & Hull, G. (2015). *Brooks/Cole empowerment series: Understanding generalist practice*. Cengage Learning.

Kitchener, K. S. (1984). Intuition, critical evaluation, and ethical principles: The foundation for ethical decisions in counseling psychology. *The Counseling Psychologist, 12*, 43–55.

Knight, C., & Gitterman, A. (2018). Merging micro and macro intervention: Social work practice with groups in the community. *Journal of Social Work Education, 54*(1), 3–17.

Knudsen, S. (2005, October 26–29). *Intersectionality: A theoretical inspiration in the analysis of minority cultures and identities in textbooks* [Conference presentation]. Eighth International Conference on Learning and Educational Media: Caught in the Web or Lost in the Textbook? IUFM DE CAEN (France). http://www.caen.iufm.fr/colloque_iartem/pdf/knudsen.pdf

Koocher, G. P., & Keith-Spiegel, P. (2018). *Necessary secrets: Ethical dilemmas involving confidentiality*. Continuing Education Courses.

Lamont-Mills, A., Christensen, S., & Moses, L. (2018). *Confidentiality and informed consent in counselling and psychotherapy: a systematic review*. Psychotherapy & Counseling Federation of Australia.

Lloyd-Hazlett, J., Moyer, M. S., & Sullivan, J. R. (2018). Adolescent risk-taking behaviors: When do student counselors break confidentiality? *Journal of Child and Adolescent Counseling, 4*(2), 178–193.

Martin, M. E. (2014). *Advocacy for social justice: A global perspective*. Pearson Publishing.

McBeath, B. (2016). Re-envisioning macro social work practice. *Families in Society, 97*(1), 5–14.

Morris, D., & Langman, L. (2002). Networks of dissent: A typology of social movements in a global age. In M. Gurstein & S. Finquelievich (Eds.), *Proceedings of the 1st International Workshop on Community Informatics*. Montreal, Canada, October 8, 2002.

MoveOn.org. (n.d.). *Success stories*. Retrieved from http://petitions.moveon.org/victories.html.

Nash, J. C. (2008). Re-thinking intersectionality. *Feminist review, 89*(1), 1–15.

National Association of Social Workers [NASW]. (2017). *Code of ethics of the National Association of Social Workers*. Author. https://www.socialworkers.org/About/Ethics/Code-of-Ethics

National Organization for Human Services. (2015). *Ethical standards of human service professionals*. Author. https://www.nationalhumanservices.org/ethical-standards-for-hs-professionals.

Netting, E., Kettner, P., & McMurtry, S. (2017). *Social work macro practice*. Pearson Publishing.

Pacheco, D., Flammini, A., & Menczer, F. (2020, April). Unveiling coordinated groups behind white helmets disinformation. In *Companion Proceedings of the Web Conference 2020* (pp. 611–616).

Park, C. L., & Fenster, J. R. (2004). Stress-related growth: Predictors of occurrence and correlates with psychological adjustment. *Journal of Social and Clinical Psychology, 23*(2), 195–215.

Perrin, A., & Anderson, M. (2019). *Share of U.S. adults using social media, including Facebook, is mostly unchanged since 2018*. Pew Research Center. https://www.pewresearch.org/fact-tank/2019/04/10/share-of-u-s-adults-using-social-media-including-facebook-is-mostly-unchanged-since-2018/

Polack, R. (2004). Social justice and the global economy: New challenges for social work in the 21st century. *Social Work, 49*(2), 281–290.

Pollard, J. W., Disabato, D. J., Polychronis, P. D., & Scalora, M. J. (2019). Counseling center clinicians experience providing assessments of risk to self versus risk to others. *Journal of College Student Psychotherapy, 34*(2): 125–137.

Prest, L. A., & Protinsky, H. (1993). Family systems theory: A unifying framework for codependency. *American Journal of Family Therapy, 21*(4), 352–360.

Rainie, L., Smith, A., Schlozman, K., Brady, H., & Verba, S. (2012). *Social media and political engagement.* Pew Research Center's Internet & American Life Project/Pew Research Center. http://pewInternet.org/~/media/Files/Reports/2012/PIP_SocialMediaAndPolitical Engagement_PDF.pdf

Reid, W. J. (1975). A test of a task-centered approach. *Social Work, 20*(1), 3–9.

Reisch, M. (2016). Why macro practice matters. *Journal of Social Work Education, 52*(3), 258–268.

Rothman, J., & Mizrahi, T. (2014). Balancing micro and macro practice: A challenge for social work. *Social Work, 59*(1), 91–93.

Saleebey, D. (2005). *The strengths perspective in social work practice* (4th ed.). Allyn & Bacon.

Samuels, G. M., & Ross–Sheriff, F. (2008). Identity, oppression, and power: Feminisms and intersectionality theory. *Affilia, 23*, 5–9.

Schatz, M. S., Jenkins, L. E., & Sheafor, B. W. (1990). Milford redefined: A model of initial and advanced generalist social work. *Journal of Social Work Education, 26*(3), 217–231.

Shigemoto, Y., Ashton, M. W., & Robitschek, C. (2016). Predictors of growth in the aftermath of traumatic events: The role of personal growth initiative. *Journal of Loss and Trauma, 21*(5), 399–409.

Stache, L. C. (2015). Advocacy and political potential at the convergence of hashtag activism and commerce. *Feminist Media Studies, 15*(1), 162–164.

Swerdlow, B. A. (2018). Tracing the evolution of the Tarasoff duty in California. *Journal of Sociology & Social Welfare, 45*, 25.

Tarasoff v. Regents of the University of California, 118 Cal. Rptr. 129, 529 P.2d.533 (Cal. 1974).

Tarasoff v. Regents of the University of California, 113 Cal. Rptr. 14, 551 P.2d.334 (Cal. 1976).

Taylor, V., & Van Dyke, N. (2003). Get up, stand up: Tactical repertoires of social movements. In D. Snow, S. Soule & H. Kriesi (Eds.), *The Blackwell companion to social movements reader* (pp. 262–293). Blackwell.

Visser Soule, Hooghe, M. (eds.), V., & Stolle, D. (2008). The potential of political moilization: An experiment on Internet and face-to-face mobilization: *Conference Papers—American Political Science Association,* 1–43.

Weger, H., Jr., Castle Bell, G., Minei, E. M., & Robinson, M. C. (2014). The relative effectiveness of active listening in initial interactions. *International Journal of Listening, 28*(1), 13–31.

Weil, M. O. (1996). Community building: Building community practice. *Social Work, 41*(5), 481–499.

Weiss, I. (2003). Social work students and social change: On the link between views on poverty, social work goals and policy practice. *International Journal of Social Welfare, 12*, 132–141.

Weiss Gal, I. (2016). Policy practice in social work education: A literature review. *International Journal of Social Welfare, 25*(3), 290–303.

Whitaker, T., Weismiller, T., & Clark, E. (2006). *Assuring the sufficiency of a frontline workforce: A national study of licensed social workers—Executive summary.* http://workforce.socialworkers.org/studies/nasw_06_execsummary.pdf

Child and Youth Services

© RAWPIXEL.COM / SHUTTERSTOCK

Vanessa is a a 16-year-old girl who is currently in foster care, but in the process of transitioning to an independent living program where she will learn daily living skills designed to prepare her for self-sufficiency in adulthood. Some of the goals of the independent living program include money management, healthy nutrition, goal planning, education and career development, and self-care skills, including hygiene, birth control, and safe sex. Vanessa has been in and out of foster care since she was about 8 years old. She lived with her biological mother off and on before that, but her grandmother was really her primary caregiver, although her grandmother had an alcohol problem as well and fought with Vanessa's mom on a regular basis. When her grandmother died when Vanessa was 7, her life seemed to spin out of control. Her biological mother struggled with untreated bipolar disorder and alcohol abuse and would often leave Vanessa alone for days at a time when she was in a mania and drinking. Vanessa's neighbors tried to help out, but they were unable to provide the level of care Vanessa needed. Vanessa's mother worked hard to get Vanessa back, but was unable to secure consistent treatment without health insurance, and since they lived in a rural community, there were very few providers in her area that accepted Medicare. In fact, the closest Medicare provider was about 100 miles away, so she began a tragic pattern of becoming stabilized only to psychologically decompose again and then relapse when she ran out of her medication. During one of several sessions with Vanessa's county caseworker, Vanessa's mom disclosed that she was a survivor of sexual abuse and was neglected by her mother, who was an alcoholic and experienced depression.

Vanessa had been an excellent student prior to entering the foster care system. She loved going to school, riding horses, and playing outside. Her placement several miles away was in an adjacent rural community, so she was able to continue many of her rural-related activities, such as spending time with horses, but the placement was far enough away from her mother that challenges with transportation meant she had more limited visitation. Vanessa responded by becoming angry and feeling increasingly isolated and lonely. Also, even though Vanessa was supposed to be in counseling, a lack of access due to her geographical isolation meant that very few counselors were available in her area. Vanessa didn't like her first counselor, and although her foster care caseworker placed her on a waiting list with another counseling center, years went by with no action. When a counselor was available, Vanessa refused to go. Last year Vanessa disclosed to one of her foster parents that she had been sexually abused by one of the neighbors who offered to help out during her mother's longer absences. She did not disclose the abuse earlier because she was afraid it would get her mother in trouble. Her foster parents were sensitive to her past trauma, but when Vanessa began acting out, including spending time with boys without permission, staying out past her curfew, and missing school, the foster parents asked that she be removed from their home. At 15, the chances of Vanessa being adopted were slim, especially because of her acting-out behavior, so Vanessa's county caseworker decided that the best option for her was to be placed in a therapeutic group home, with a focus on transitioning to adulthood. Unfortunately, the group home was in the city, about 100 miles away from her home community, which meant she had very limited access to her mother. It also meant that she was now living in a city, away from the life she knew in the country, and thus felt very out of place. The staff at the group home have caught Vanessa sneaking out to meet boys several times late at night, and they are highly concerned about the possibility of her becoming sexually active and getting pregnant. In response to their concerns, they enrolled her in a sex education course that explores sexuality and safe sex practices from an empowerment perspective. Vanessa's county caseworker has worked closely with the caseworkers in the group home to develop a program for Vanessa that includes trauma-informed treatment, including group and individual counseling, in addition to the other programs focused on self-sufficiency. Vanessa had been very resistant to all forms of treatment, but recently both of her caseworkers developed a plan that allowed her to visit her mother on some weekends, as long as she is safe and checks in periodically. They also arranged for her to receive horseback riding lessons in exchange for volunteering 1 day a week at a local horse stable. These efforts seemed to decrease Vanessa's oppositional behavior, leading to her agreeing to attend group counseling twice a month and see a counselor on a weekly basis.

INTRODUCTION TO WORKING WITH CHILDREN, YOUTH, AND FAMILIES

The field of child, youth, and family services is a broad practice setting that focuses on strengthening families, primarily through the care and protection of children and youth. Child welfare is a more focused area involving the protection of children who cannot for whatever reason be appropriately cared for by their biological parents. Child welfare services also include providing assistance to those who need support in the care and provision of their children through counseling and case management services.

Child, youth, and family agencies offer a range of services, from providing for children in foster care placement to facilitating family preservation programs and adoption services. with the ultimate goal of ensuring the protection and care of children, and the strengthening of families. Human services practitioners may engage in a number of different activities within this broad practice setting, including child abuse investigations; child abuse assessments; case management and counseling of children, youth, foster families, and biological parents; case management and counseling of families in crisis; outreach for runaway and homeless youth; and case management and counseling of potential adoptive parents, adult adoptees, and birth parents.

Some of the more common psychosocial issues human services practitioners working with children and youth experience include feelings of abandonment and loss, post-traumatic stress disorder (PTSD), child development dynamics, parenting issues, substance abuse, **anger management**, and child development issues. Human services professionals working in child, youth, and family agencies also work with clients who are experiencing a broad range of life stressors (often with maladaptive responses) that can ultimately lead to breakdowns within the family if effective intervention strategies are delayed. Consider the opening vignette and how Vanessa experienced many of these psychosocial dynamics. She was abandoned by her depressed and alcoholic mother, and her feelings of abandonment extended well into her adolescence. She likely struggled with PTSD in response to her history of sexual abuse, which then influenced all of her adolescent relationships. This vignette demonstrates the complexity involved in many child welfare cases.

Human services practitioners working in practice settings serving families must be culturally competent, which in this context means being aware of and sensitive to the ways systemic poverty, racism, and disenfranchisement (including government-sponsored abuse) have impacted family systems within certain populations. This chapter will explore many examples of systemic abuse of families of color, such as the forced separation of Native American families and the disparate treatment of Black families within schools and the U.S. criminal justice system. Understanding the history of mistreatment of ethnic and racial minority children, youth, and families within various social and political systems in the United States will help those working with these populations to have increased empathy and understanding of the enduring consequences such families experience.

One of the largest practice settings that focuses on child welfare services is **child protective services (CPS)**, because child protection is mandated by federal legislation. Human services practitioners may also work for not-for-profit agencies (some of which are contracted by the state to provide mandated services to children in substitute care) and some of which provide voluntary services to families seeking assistance. Within these agencies a human services practitioner may be involved in a number of activities, including counseling, case management, administrative functions, interprofessional collaboration, policy work, advocacy, and perhaps even grant writing.

Many working in the field of child, youth, and family services do so on a volunteer basis, and although these individuals are not paid professionals, the work they do is so vital that their role in the welfare of children and families must be mentioned. An example is the **Court Appointed Special Advocate (CASA)** program, which trains volunteers to work in juvenile courts as advocates for children and youth in the foster care system. CASA volunteers are sworn in by dependency judges, allowing them to access confidential information about the children on their caseload. Although CASA volunteers are not paid professionals and do not need a degree, they serve a vitally important role as the voice of the children assigned to them.

THE HISTORY OF CHILD WELFARE IN THE UNITED STATES

The child welfare system in the United States has undergone significant changes in the last few hundred years due to numerous factors such as urbanization, industrialization, immigration, mass life-threatening illness, changes within the family system, changing social mores (including the reduction of shame associated with divorce, out-of-wedlock births, and single parenting by choice), and the eventual availability of government financial assistance for those in need. Thus, to fully understand the current child welfare system, it is vital to understand its past.

Child Labor in Colonial America: Indentured Servitude and Apprenticeships

Learning Outcome 4.1   Examine how children from marginalized populations were historically treated in the United States

There are many ways in which children were mistreated in early America, but in this section, I will be exploring primarily two areas of mistreatment of children in Great Britain and **Colonial America**. First, the use of children in the labor market, otherwise known as child labor, will be explored, and second, the treatment of children who were, for whatever reason, without parents, including **orphans** and street children. By exploring primarily child labor and the treatment of orphans and street children, it should not be presumed that other forms of maltreatment did not occur in America's early history. The rationale for exploring these two areas of historic maltreatment is that they represent a significant departure in how children are treated today. Another rationale is that these areas of maltreatment highlight key areas within child welfare, with regard to early child welfare advocacy and the development of laws, policies, and programs intended to protect children.

The historical treatment of children in England and Colonial America has in many respects served as a precursor for child welfare laws in the United States, including child labor laws and other child protective legislation. There was no official government child welfare system during Colonial America, but there was considerable mistreatment of children. If the government did get involved in child welfare issues, it was either because a child was orphaned or, for whatever reason, living on the streets. Government involvement was not particularly compassionate and the solutions were often punitive in nature.

During Colonial America, poor and orphaned children were expected to work, often within their own households and farms alongside their families. The hope of most parents during this era was that their children would be able to afford to buy farms of their own when they grew to adulthood. But children from poor and immigrant families were often expected to work in adult-like capacities, with children under 12 working alongside their parents in factories or other industrial-like settings, and children 12 and older working in apprenticed positions outside of their homes and away from their families.

During the many waves of early immigration, people seeking a better life in America often paid for their passage to the United States through a process called indentured

© GLASSHOUSE IMAGES / SHUTTERSTOCK

Young Boys Working as Doffers at Cotton Mill, Cherryville, North Carolina, USA, circa 1908.

service, which required that servants work off the cost of their travel by working for a master in some capacity once they arrived in America. If a family immigrated to the United States in this manner, their children, regardless of age, were required to work as well. The economic system of **indentured servitude** was extremely exploitative. Ship owners would often recruit unsuspecting and desperate individuals from other countries with stories of abundant life in America (Greene, 1995). Many individuals and families accepted the call, believing they could make a better life for themselves in Colonial America where opportunities for economic self-sufficiency were believed to be abundant. Indentured servants were often told that the terms of their service would last for about 3 years, and then they would be free—free to buy land and to make a life for themselves that was not possible in many European countries (Alderman, 1975). In reality, the cost of their passage would be paid off in only about a year, and the remaining years of service were essentially free work. Masters often treated their bonded labor quite poorly. Servants received no cash wages, but were supposed to be provided with basic necessities, which, depending on the nature and means of the master, might range from sufficient sustenance to meager sustenance and substandard shelter. Thus, while indentured servants were not considered slaves per se, the treatment of them was quite similar (Martin, 2014).

Although most indentured servants were in their early 20s, Greene (1995) notes that children who immigrated with their families on bonded contracts were expected to work as well and were often treated no differently than their parents. Children were not allowed to enter into bonded labor contracts without the permission of their parents. However, very poor and orphaned children, particularly in London, were often kidnapped and sold to ship captains, who then brought them to America and sold them as indentured servants, most often to masters who used them as house servants. Also, local governments that were responsible for the poor would **bind out** poor and orphaned children in early America as a form of poor relief (Katz, 1996). Most local laws favored masters, as virtually all judges were in fact masters themselves, stipulating that **child bonded servants** could be kept until the age of 24. Laws also dictated that if a bonded servant ran away prior to the ending of their contract, they could legally face a range of punitive consequences, including having the time remaining on their contract doubled (Greene, 1995).

Indentured servitude eventually waned in favor of slavery, but the binding out of children who were poor and orphaned continued well into the 19th century. During the 400 years of the Atlantic slave trade, over 15 million Africans were brought to the United States through the West Indies or directly from Africa. Among these Africans were many children who were either forced or born into slavery along with their parents. In time, masters realized that slaves who had once experienced freedom were far more difficult to control than those born into captivity; thus, a market developed for captive slave children because they tended to be more submissive servants.

Children under the age of about 7 were more often sold with their mothers, but once the children reached the age of about 10, they were often sold off and separated from their families, particularly to fill this growing need for young African slave children born into captivity. Slavery was outlawed in 1865 with the passage of the Thirteenth Amendment to the U.S. Constitution, but the plight of Black children did not improve significantly, since the mistreatment of Black people in the United States became codified into law (Klarman, 2006). In fact, the legacy of slavery has created significant challenges for Black children to this day, including persistent high infant mortality rates, among other social problems (Matoba & Collins, 2017; Moras et al., 2018).

Another form of work that children engaged in during the early years of America was **apprenticeship**, which involved the training of children in some type of craft or artisan work such as making shoes or woodworking. Essentially, apprenticeship involved an artisan taking on an apprentice in early adolescence and teaching him a trade. Some children went to live with the artisan who trained them, while others did not (Schultz, 1985). Often the apprentices who left their families and lived with the artisan served as unpaid assistants. In fact, parents often had to pay to have their children apprenticed because they knew this was likely the only way their children would learn a trade. While most apprenticeships did not involve overt exploitation, the practice did reflect the focus on working children, rather than on education and play. Apprenticeships eventually became less popular when industrialization began in the late 18th century, as machines were developed, replacing the need for many craftsmen.

Child Labor During the Industrial Era: Children and Factories

By the mid-19th century, virtually all apprenticeships and indentured contracts had disappeared, and families were moving into the cities to work in factories (Bender, 1975). Children were the bulk of the workforce in many factories throughout the 19th century, with some children working 6 days a week, 14 hours a day. **Child labor** scholars estimate that hundreds of thousands of children—some as young as 6—were employed in factories in the mid-19th century, with the bulk working in the textile industry such as cotton mills.

Excerpts of autobiographies written by individuals who worked in factories throughout their childhoods reference dismal conditions, with poor sanitation and air quality, repetitive work on machinery that left small hands bleeding, and very long days on their feet, which in many cases significantly shortened the life spans of these child workers.

Garment industry sweatshops began to spring up throughout New York and other large cities in the mid- to late 19th century. Although sweatshops eventually occurred in factory-like settings, their origin involved what was called "outwork," where workers sewed garments and other textiles in their homes. Women and children were primarily hired for these tasks since they could be paid a lower wage. Because they were paid by the piece, they often worked 14 or more hours per day, 7 days a week. Children worked alongside their mothers, because their small fingers enabled them to engage in detail work, such as sewing on buttons—work that was challenging for adults.

Jane Addams and her friend Ellen Gates Starr founded the Hull-House of Chicago, the first U.S. **settlement house** that provided advocacy and what we now call **wraparound services** to marginalized populations working in sweatshop conditions in Chicago. Addams was appalled by the conditions of those living in poverty in urban communities, particularly the plight of recently arrived immigrants, who were forced to live in substandard tenement housing and work long hours in factories, often in very dangerous working conditions. Hull-House offered several services for children and their widowed mothers, including after-school care for those children whose mothers worked long hours in factories.

Providing comprehensive services to those in need and living among them in their own community were some of the ways in which Addams became aware of the plight of children forced to work in the factories. In her autobiography *Twenty Years at Hull-House,* Addams wrote of her first encounter with child labor, including how during their first Christmas party at Hull-House, when Addams knew nothing of child labor, she noticed several young girls who refused to eat the candy at the party. When asked why, the girls stated that because they worked in a candy factory, they could no longer stand the sight of candy. Addams noted how girls as young as 7 would work at the candy factory from early in the morning until late at night.

Because of unsafe conditions many of the children were injured, and a few of the child workers were even killed. Addams described the indifference on the part of factory owners and the lack of recourse of parents, who signed away all of their rights when they "allowed" their children to work (Addams, 1912). Addams and her colleagues began an advocacy campaign against sweatshop conditions in Chicago factories early in the Hull-House's existence, advocating in particular for the women and children who were most likely to work in these factories. Their activism seemed to pay off quickly when the Illinois state legislature passed a law limiting the workday to just 8 hours (from the previous 12- to 14-hour day). Their excitement was soon tempered though when the new law was quickly overturned by the Illinois Supreme Court as being unconstitutional.

Addams and the Hull-House networked quite extensively, joining efforts with trade unions and even the Democratic Party, which in 1892 adopted into its platform union recommendations prohibiting children under the age of 15 years old from working in factories. In her autobiography, Addams discussed how the greatest opposition to child labor laws came from the business sector, which considered such legislation as radicalism. Business leaders, such as those who worked in the Chicago area candy factories and glass manufacturing companies, argued that their companies would not be able to survive without the labor of children (Addams, 1912; Martin, 2014).

Addams and her Hull-House colleagues advocated on a federal level as well, with their support for the *Sulzer Bill*, which when passed allowed for the creation of the Department of Labor. In 1904 the National Child Labor Committee was formed, and Addams served as chairman for one term. In 1912, Julia Lathrop, Addams's Hull-House colleague, was appointed chief of a new federal agency by President William Taft, focusing on child welfare, including child labor. As chief of the Children's Bureau, Lathrop was responsible for investigating and reporting all relevant issues pertaining to the welfare of children from all classes and spent a considerable amount of time researching the dangers of child labor (Martin, 2014).

After several failed attempts, federal legislation barring child labor was finally passed in 1938 and signed into law by President Franklin D. Roosevelt, 3 years after Addams' death. The Fair Labor Standards Act is a comprehensive bill regulating various aspects of labor in the United States, including child labor. The act outlawed what was deemed *oppressive child labor* and set minimum ages of employment and a maximum number of hours children were allowed to work. This act is still in existence today and has been amended several times to address such issues as equal pay (Equal Pay Act of 1963), age discrimination (Age Discrimination in Employment Act of 1967), and low wages (federal minimum wage increases).

The U.S. Orphan Problem

Throughout early America, one of the most vulnerable groups of children was orphans, both in terms of how they were treated as well as how they were exploited in the labor force. During the 1700s and 1800s in particular, attitudes toward children were harsh, and many orphaned or uncared for children roamed the streets, particularly in growing urban areas such as New York and Chicago. Street children were often treated harshly and punitively. If children were on the streets because their parents were destitute, they were sent to almshouses to work alongside their homeless parents. Older orphaned children were sold into indentured servitude or forced into apprenticeships, which provided cheap labor during an era that saw many economic depressions and a shortage of available workers (Katz, 1996).

The plight of the orphan did not appear to tug at the heartstrings of the average American during that era, not only because of the vast number of abandoned and orphaned children, but also because during the 17th through the early 19th century, children were not perceived to be in need of special nurturing because childhood was not considered a distinct stage of development. The influence of Puritanical religious beliefs as well as the general **social mores** of the times led to the common belief that children needed to be treated with harsh discipline and compelled to work or they would fall victim to sinful behaviors such as laziness and vice (Trattner, 2007).

A significant shift in child welfare policy occurred in the mid-19th century (1861 to 1865), when the Civil War left thousands of children orphaned, making tragedy a visitor in some respect to virtually every family in America. Coinciding with an increased concern for the plight of orphaned and disadvantaged children was a dramatic transition in the way childhood was viewed. The development of psychology as an academic discipline and a profession led to the emerging belief that children were essentially good by nature and needed to be treated with kindness, love, and nurturing to enhance their development and ultimate potential as adults (Trattner, 2007). As a result, settlement house workers, **Charity Organization Societies** (COS), and government officials were eager to address the problem of orphaned and abused children in the latter part of the 19th century. The most commonly suggested solution was the creation of institutions designed solely for the care of orphaned and needy children, which at the time seemed a quite compassionate alternative to living in almshouses or on the streets (Addams, 1990; Trattner, 2007).

Although some orphanages existed in the 1700s, they did not become the primary method of caring for orphaned and needy children until the middle to late 1800s. By the 1890s there were more than 600 orphanages in the United States (Trattner, 2007). Orphanages, or orphan asylums as they were often called, housed both parentless children and also half-orphans. And in fact, toward the early 1900s, the majority of children placed in orphan asylums were half-orphans placed into care primarily for economic reasons (Hacsi, 2017). Parents who were unable to financially support their children could leave them in the temporary care of an orphanage for a small monthly fee, but if they missed some payments the children could become wards of the state and the parents could lose all legal rights to them (Hacsi, 2017; Trattner, 2007).

Poor safety conditions in factories resulted in a relatively high prevalence of work-related injuries and death among the poorest members of society, leaving many children orphaned or half-orphaned. Additionally, a significant influx of poor immigrants in the late 1800s and early 1900s resulted in a vulnerable segment of society that often did not have an extended family on which to rely in cases of parental death or disability (Gratton & Moen, 2004). In addition, although infectious disease was nothing new to early America, several infectious disease epidemics spread through urban areas between the mid-1800s and the early part of the 1900s, including smallpox, influenza, yellow fever, cholera, typhoid, and scarlet fever, leaving many children orphaned (Condran & Cheney, 1982).

Orphan asylums were racially segregated until the 1960s, with many Black children being completely excluded from state-supported orphanages (Morton, 2000). By the latter part of the 1800s there were 353 orphanages, most of which were public (or government supported). Just over 78% of these institutions completely excluded Black children, while 19% accepted only a handful of Black children (Morton, 2000). There were only nine Black orphanages in the United States, which led to a movement among Black Christian women to raise funds for the creation of Black orphanages. An example is the efforts of Black church women, led by Mrs. E. Belle Mitchell Jackson in Lexington, Kentucky, who raised funds for the Lexington Colored Orphan Industrial Home (Byars, 1991).

Although the orphanage system was originally perceived as a significant improvement over placing children in almshouses or forcing them into indentured servitude, these institutions were not without their share of trouble, and in time reports of harsh treatment and abuses became commonplace. Although some orphanages were government run, most were privately run with governmental funding, but with little if any oversight or accountability. Because the government paid on a per-child basis, there was a financial incentive to run large operations, with some orphanages housing as many as 2,000 children under one roof. Obedience was highly valued in these institutions out of sheer necessity, whereas individuality, play, and creativity were discouraged through strict rules and harsh discipline.

The Orphan Train Movement

The next wave of child welfare reform involved the gradual shift from institutionalized care to substitute family care—the placing-out of children into private homes. This transition was prompted by a few different social trends, including increased complaints about institutionalized care, the development of compulsory public education (which meant that the education of an orphan was no longer linked with the provision of housing), and a growing problem of street children in big cities. In fact, have you ever wondered where the expression "farming kids out" came from? The origin of this term is rooted in the Orphan Train Movement, a program developed by The New York Children's Aid Society that sent kids living on the streets to farms out west. Rev. Charles Loring Brace founded the orphan train program in the mid-19th century. Brace estimated that as many as 5,000 children were homeless and forced to roam the streets in search of money, food, and shelter. Brace was shocked at the cruel indifference of most New Yorkers, who called these children "street Arabs" with "bad blood." He was also appalled at reports of children as young as 5 years old who were arrested for **vagrancy** (Bellingham, 1984; Brace, 1967).

Many factors contributed to the serious orphan problem in New York. Historians estimate that approximately 1,000 immigrants flooded New York on a daily basis in the mid-1800s (Von Hartz, 1978). Additionally, mass urbanization was occurring with poor rural families flocking to the cities looking for factory work. Industry safety standards were essentially nonexistent, and thus factory-related deaths were at an all-time high. An outbreak of typhoid fever also left many children orphaned or half-orphaned, their widowed mothers having no way to support them because there was no federal social welfare safety net. Harsh social conditions, coupled with the absence of any organized governmental subsidy, left many children to fend for themselves on the streets of New York, resorting to any means available for survival.

Brace feared that the temptations of street life would preclude any possibility that orphaned children would grow up to be God-fearing, responsible adults. He reasoned that children who had no parents, or whose parents could no longer care for them, would be far better off living in the clean open spaces of farming communities out west, where fresh air and the need for children and workers were plentiful. Because the rail lines were rapidly opening up the West, Brace developed an innovative program where children would be loaded onto trains and taken west to good Christian farming families who were open to caring for more children. Notices were sent in advance of train arrivals, and communities along the train line would come out and meet the train so that families who had expressed an interest in taking one or more children could examine the children and take them right then, if they desired.

Many survivors of the **orphan trains** have described their experiences of being paraded across a stage like cattle, with interested foster parents checking their teeth and feeling their muscles before deciding which child they would take. Few parents would take more than one child, and thus siblings were most often split up, sometimes without even a passing comment made by the childcare agents or the new parents (Patrick et al., 1990). It was almost as if the breaking of lifelong family bonds was considered trivial compared to the gift these children were receiving by being rescued from their hopeless existence on the streets.

Most children on the orphan train were not legally adopted but were placed with a family under an indentured contract, which served two purposes. First, this type of contract allowed the placement agency to take the children back if something went wrong with the placement. Second, children placed under an indentured contract could not

Pearson eText

Video Example 4.1

In this video a survivor of the orphan trains tells his story of being relocated to a farming family out west. Evaluating the historical context of this movement, what are some of the negative consequences of the orphan trains?

https://www.youtube.com/watch?v=9Z3djWoTGFU

inherit property; thus, farming families could take in boys to work on the farm or girls to assist with the housework but didn't have to worry about them inheriting family assets (Trattner, 2007; Warren, 1995).

The orphan trains ran from 1853 to 1929, delivering approximately 150,000 children to new homes across the West, from the Midwestern states to Texas, and even as far west as California. Whether this social experiment was a glowing success or a miserable failure (or somewhere in between) depends on whom one asks. Some children placed in good homes and eventually legally adopted by wonderful and loving parents, and they grew up to be happy and responsible adults. But others have shared stories of heartache and abuse, describing their new lives as no better than that of slaves, where they were taken in by families for no reason other than to provide hard labor for the cost of bed and board. Some orphan train survivors describe stories of having siblings torn from their sides as families chose one child (typically a younger child), leaving brothers and sisters on the train. And still others tell stories of failed placements, where farming families exercised their 1-year right-of-return option, sending the children back to the orphanage or allowing the children to drift from farm to farm to earn their keep (Holt, 1992).

Eventually new child welfare practices caught up with new child development theories, leading to a shift in focus from one of work and virtue to one of valuing childhood play. By the early 20th century the practice of farming out children received increasing criticism, and the last trainload of children was delivered to its many destinations in 1929. Despite the controversy surrounding the Orphan Train Movement and similar outplacement programs across the country, even its harshest critics agree that it was a far better alternative than allowing children to fend for themselves on the streets of New York and other large urban cities. The Orphan Train Movement is also considered the forerunner of the current foster care system in the United States, representing a shift away from institutionalized care and toward a system where children are placed in private homes with substitute families.

OVERVIEW OF THE CURRENT U.S. CHILD WELFARE SYSTEM

Learning Outcome 4.2   Explore the nature and purpose of the U.S. child welfare system

The U.S. child welfare system exists to provide a safety net for children and families in crisis, with the primary objective of keeping families together or reuniting children with their biological parents if they have to be removed from the home (Sanchirico & Jablonka, 2000). Federal and state laws have established three basic goals for children in the child welfare system:

- To ensure *safety* from abuse and neglect
- To ensure *permanency* in a stable, loving home (preferably with the biological parents)
- To ensure *well-being* of children with regard to their physical health, mental health, and developmental and educational needs.

Children living in contemporary Western societies face very different challenges than children living 100 or so years ago. Child protection has slowly transitioned from institutionalized care to primarily substitute family care or foster care over the past 100 years. By 1980, virtually no children remained in institutionalized care in the United States, excluding group homes, treatment centers, and homes for developmentally disabled children (Shughart & Chappell, 1999). Government public assistance programs, which developed in the 1960s, reduced the necessity for the removal of children from their homes due to poverty, because single mothers now had some place to go for financial help in raising their children (Trattner, 2007). Further, child labor laws now prohibit child exploitation in the workforce, and companies that violate these laws often face harsh fines.

The Mexican fast food chain Chipotle was recently fined $1.4 million for violating child labor laws in Massachusetts, including allowing adolescent employees to work in excess of 9 hours per day, and over 48 hours per week, sometimes late into the evening on school nights. The Massachusetts Attorney General estimated that Chipotle violated child labor laws 13,253 times in all 50 states! And Chipotle wasn't the only restaurant chain to receive a hefty fine for violating child labor laws. Other offenders include fast-food chains, Burger King, McDonalds, and Wendy's (Yaffe-Bellany & Zaveri, 2020).

Additionally, federal and state social welfare programs now exist that help alleviate poverty and also help protect families from the impact of various catastrophes such as natural disasters and health pandemics. For instance, the 2020 novel coronavirus pandemic prompted the rapid passage of federal emergency relief packages targeting lower-income individuals and families, as well as small businesses. Vulnerable groups of children are also far better protected from disparity in treatment through the passage of such federal legislation as the Civil Rights Act of 1964 and the Americans with Disabilities Act.

Despite these advances, there remain serious issues with how some children are treated within U.S. society. For instance, there remains significant disparity in treatment of children from certain ethnic groups, such as Black, Latina/o, and Native American children (Davidson et al., 2019; Lovato-Hermann et al., 2017; White, 2017). This disparity exists both with regard to the overrepresentation of children of color in foster care, as well as in other areas of child welfare, particularly Black and Native American children (Child Welfare Information Gateway, 2016b; U.S. Department of Health and Human Services [DHHS], 2018).

There are also serious problems with how older children are treated within U.S. society, particularly children of color and sexual minorities. For instance, very few effective systems are in place to assist runaway and homeless youth. Thus, many adolescents who experience physical and sexual abuse in their homes choose to live on the streets rather than trust the "system" to provide for their safety and care (Cochran et al., 2002). This is particularly true for children of color who face an increased risk of living on the streets (Morton et al., 2018). Another area of disparity involves the vast number of children charged as adults for crimes they committed as children, and most of these are children of color—primarily Black boys (Mallett, 2016). Black girls also experience disparity in treatment by organizations charged with the responsibility for their protection. For example, there is a growing recognition that Black and Native American female youth are far more likely to be victims of **domestic sex trafficking** and if they are apprehended, they are far more likely to be charged as prostitutes and sent back to the streets, rather than treated as victims (Hume & Sidun, 2017).

Demographics of Children in Substitute Care

The demographic makeup of children currently in the foster care system has changed considerably as well since the 1800s. Gone are the days where the majority of children placed into substitute care were orphaned due to industrial accidents, war, or illness. Instead, the majority of children currently in child protective custody have been removed from their homes due to serious maltreatment. Also, unlike earlier eras when orphanage placements were most often permanent, just over half of all children currently in foster care will be reunified with their biological parents (DHHS, 2018).

As of September 30, 2017 (the most recent statistics available), there were approximately 442,995 children in the U.S. foster care system. This represents about a 1.5% increase from 2016, but almost a 10% increase from 2013 (DHHS, 2018). Although the increase in children in care is modest, it still represents a steady upward trend, which is concerning. Also concerning is the disparity that exists with regard to which ethnic minority groups are more likely to have children in out-of-home placements. For instance, according to the latest statistics, approximately 44% of all children in foster care are White followed by 23% Black, and 21% Latina/o (DHHS, 2018). These demographics indicate an overrepresentation of Black children in the foster care system because Black people constitute only 13.4% of the general population and Latinos/as constitute 18.1%, whereas White people constitute 60.7% of the general population (U.S. Census Bureau, 2018).

Most children who enter the foster care system are less than 1 year old, with the average age of children in care being between 7 and 8 years old. Most children enter the system because of neglect (62%) followed by parental drug abuse (32%), a parent's inability to cope (14%), physical abuse (12%), and housing (10%). Interestingly, while the primary reason children were placed in orphanages a century or so ago was parental death, this now accounts for only 1% of all children entering the foster care system. The majority of children removed from their homes are placed in licensed nonrelative foster care homes (about 45%), followed by about one-third who are placed with relatives (32%). A smaller percentage are placed in pre-adoptive homes, group homes, and supervised independent living facilities (DHHS, 2018).

The average (mean) length of stay in foster care is about 20 months, but it appears that if children aren't returned home or placed in a permanent home situation in the first 20 months of out-of-home care, chances increase that they will remain in placement between 2 and 4 years, with a small percentage remaining in substitute care for longer than 5 years (Child Trends, 2018). The greatest number of children who left the child welfare system in 2010 were infants and toddlers under 3 years of age, as well as those exiting the system at 17 years old and above (UDHHS, 2018). A significant problem that will be explored later in this chapter relates to children who are aging out of the foster care system. Despite an increase in services targeting this older adolescent population, kids who have spent most of their formative years in foster care face considerable challenges later on in their lives (Bender et al., 2015).

IMPORTANT CHILD WELFARE LEGISLATION

The U.S. Constitution guarantees certain liberties to parents by giving them the right to parent their child in the manner they see fit. But such liberties have limits, and as such are balanced by the parents' duty to protect their child's safety and ensure their well-being. If parents cannot or will not protect their children from *significant* harm, the state has the legal obligation to intervene (Goldman & Salus, 2003).

The U.S. Congress has passed several pieces of legislation that support the state's obligation to protect children, including the *Child Abuse Prevention and Treatment Act* (CAPTA) of 1974, which was established to ensure that child maltreatment is reported to the appropriate authorities. This act also provides minimum standards for definitions of the different types of child maltreatment. Among the many provisions in the legislation, CAPTA provides federal funding to states to support prevention efforts, as well as for the investigation and prosecution of child abuse, and also provides grants to public agencies (including Native American tribes) for treatment efforts and activities. CAPTA has been reauthorized and amended several times, most recently on January 7, 2019, as a part of the Victims of Child Abuse Act Reauthorization Act. The 2015 authorization expanded the definition of "child abuse and neglect" and "sexual abuse" to include child sex trafficking. The 2019 amendment provided increased civil protection for those who report suspected child abuse in good faith (Child Welfare Information Gateway, 2019).

The Adoption Assistance and Child Welfare Act of 1980 (Pub. L. No. 96–272), focuses on family preservation, with the goal of keeping families together by requiring that states develop supportive programs and procedures enabling maltreated children to remain in their own homes. This act also provides for the assistance of **family reunification** following out-of-home placements, and provides funding for adoption assistance, particularly for children with special needs. Other legislation is aimed at (1) improving court efficiency so that child abuse cases will not languish in the court system for years, (2) providing assistance to foster care children approaching their 18th birthday, and (3) bolstering family preservation programs designed as early intervention measures to circumvent out-of-home placement (Goldman & Salus, 2003; Whittaker, 2017).

In 1997 President Bill Clinton signed into law the *Adoption and Safe Families Act* (ASFA) (Pub. L. No. 105–89), which amended *The Adoption Assistance and Child Welfare Act of 1980*. The primary goal of the ASFA of 1997 was to amend problems in the foster care system presumably caused by the previous legislation, including placing family reunification as a priority over a child's health and well-being. Although this was not necessarily the intention of legislators when passing *The Adoption Assistance and Child Welfare Act of 1980*, many caseworkers interpreted this legislation as requiring that biological families remain intact regardless of circumstances, which resulted in children remaining in foster care for much of their childhoods due to a hesitancy to terminate parental rights.

The ASFA of 1997 was passed as a way of addressing this ambiguity in the former legislation, making the best interest of the child a clear priority. Among the various amendments of the act are a shortened timeframe for a child's permanency hearing, financial incentives to states for increasing the number of adoptions of children in the foster care system, new requirements for states to petition for termination of parental rights, and the reauthorization of the Family Preservation and Support Program, which was renamed the Safe and Stable Families Program.

There have been both positive and negative consequences of the ASFA. Certainly no one wants abused and neglected children to languish in temporary placement, but expediting finding permanent homes should not be at the expense of biological parents' rights to have an appropriate amount of time to meet the state's criteria for regaining the custody of their children. Balancing the rights of the biological parents with the best interest of their child is challenging, particularly in light of the complexity involved in many foster care cases, but most human services professionals believe that striving for this balance must remain a priority.

In 2006, the *Safe and Timely Interstate Placement of Foster Children Act* (Pub. L. No. 109-239) was passed, which made it easier to place children in another state, if necessary. This legislation holds states accountable for the orderly, safe, and timely placement of children across state lines by requiring that home studies be completed in less than 60 days and that the children be accepted within 14 days of completion. The legislation also provides grants for interstate placement and requires caseworkers to make interstate visits when necessary.

Quite likely, the most significant federal legislation passed recently is the *Fostering Connections to Success and Increasing Adoptions Act of 2008* (Pub. L. No. 110-351), which former president George W. Bush signed into law in October 2008. This law amends Title IV-E of the Social Security Act by enhancing incentives, particularly in regard to kinship care, including providing the kinship guardian financial assistance as well as providing family connection grants designed to facilitate and support kinship care. This legislation also includes provisions related to education and health care, particularly for children in kinship care, many of whom were not eligible for special assistance programs unless they were in nonrelative care. In fact, the *Fostering Connections to Success and Increasing Adoptions Act of 2008* was the first child welfare law that mandated educational stability for foster care youth. And finally, in 2011, the *Child and Family Services Improvement and Innovation Act* was passed, reauthorizing Title IV-B of the Social Security Act (Pub. L. No. 112-34) and extending funding authorization for the Stephanie Tubbs Jones Child Welfare Services Program and the Promoting Safe and Stable Families Program.

An earlier act that bears mention is the *Indian Child Welfare Act of 1978* (ICWA), which is a federal law that seeks to keep Native American children with Native American families. The ICWA was passed in response to a long history of forced child removal from Indian reservations, including forced removal of children into Indian boarding schools from about the 1880s through the early part of the 1900s, and then the subsequent removal of Native children by state child protection service agencies for maltreatment and placement into White homes. The intention of Congress was to protect the best interest of Native American children and promote the stability and security of Native tribes and families.

The ICWA serves as a policy framework for how to handle the placement of children who are eligible for membership in a federally recognized tribe, with the goal of promoting the role of tribal governments and preserving tribal families (on and off the reservation). The ICWA requires training for social workers about the law (including the historical injustices and reasons for this legislation) and its implementation, the development of tribal-based family programs, the development of intergovernmental agreements, funding for tribes to develop family supportive programs, and case consultation to tribal family members, agencies, human services practitioners, attorneys, and the court system. Essentially, the ICWA requires that prior to a Native American child being placed with a non-Native family, the identified tribe must first be contacted with the goal of keeping the child within the tribal community. Although there has been some erosion of the ICWA with recent court decisions that critics claim violated the ICWA in contested adoption proceedings, the overall goals of the ICWA remain intact with the goal of promoting Native families and righting the wrongs of past injustices against the Native American population (National Indian Child Welfare Association, n.d.).

CHILD ABUSE INVESTIGATIONS

There are several ways that a child abuse investigation may be initiated, but all have their origin in a concern that a child is being mistreated in some manner. **Mandated reporters** are required by law to file a report with their state's child abuse hotline immediately if they suspect that a child is being abused or neglected. Mandated reporters typically fall into several categories and include professionals who work with children as a part of their normal work duties, such as mental health professionals (social workers, counselors, and psychologists), teachers (and other school personnel), medical personnel (such as physicians and nurses), and law enforcement personnel.

Child welfare laws are designed to protect children from maltreatment such as physical abuse.

Most states have strict laws that define the parameters of child abuse reporting, including delineating what constitutes a reportable concern, the timeframe in which a mandated reporter must report the suspected abuse, and the consequences of failing to report, including professional sanction such as probation or the temporary suspension of one's professional license. In fact, in most states, the failure to comply with mandated reporting requirements is a crime (a misdemeanor or even a felony for repeated failures).

The most common reasons for not reporting a case of suspected child abuse include not being properly trained on the signs of potential abuse, not wanting to get a client in trouble, and failing to recognize that a mandated reporter is not an investigator, and thus does not need conclusive evidence of abuse prior to making a report. The majority of calls made to the child abuse hotline are from mandated reporters, but this does not preclude private citizens from calling the child abuse hotline if they suspect a child is being abused or neglected by a parent or caregiver. Thus, it is not uncommon for neighbors, friends, or even relatives to report suspected child abuse. Those who are not mandated reporters are allowed to call anonymously.

Due to the intrusive nature of an abuse investigation, federal and state laws exist to protect the privacy of family life. Thus, child abuse hotline workers must adhere to strict guidelines regarding what reports can and cannot be accepted, and which reports rise to the level of warranting an investigation. If the report of alleged abuse meets the stated criteria, then the report will be accepted and investigated in a reasonable timeframe. In fact, federal funding of state CPS agencies is tied to compliance with federal mandates that all child abuse reports be screened immediately and investigated in a timely manner (CAPTA, 2010). Although federal law does not specify a particular timeframe for conducting an investigation, most states have compliance laws stipulating specific guidelines mandating that reports of abuse be investigated anywhere from immediately for cases involving imminent risk to 10 days for cases involving moderate to minimal risk to the child (Kopel et al., 2003).

Once a child abuse report is accepted, the case is sent to the appropriate regional agency and assigned to an abuse investigator, who is a licensed social worker or other licensed human services professional. The actual investigation will vary depending on the specific circumstances of the allegations, but most investigations will involve interviewing the child, the nonoffending parent(s), and the alleged perpetrator. Although the sequence of the interviews might change depending on the specific circumstances of the case, often investigators prefer to interview the child before the parents or caregivers to avoid the potential for the alleged abusive parent(s) influencing or intimidating the child (Cronch et al., 2006).

Types of Child Maltreatment

Child maltreatment is a crime regardless of who the perpetrator is and should always be reported to legal authorities, but CPS becomes involved only when the abuse is perpetrated by someone in a caregiving role to the child. This includes a parent, a relative, a parent's boyfriend or girlfriend, a teacher, a childcare provider, or even a babysitter. The federal government has developed a definition of what constitutes the minimum standard for child abuse and neglect, establishing four general categories of child maltreatment: neglect, physical abuse, sexual abuse, and emotional abuse (Child Welfare Information Gateway, 2016a). Each state and U.S. territory has the responsibility of defining child abuse and neglect according to state statute, in accordance with federal definitions. The following is the U.S. Health and Human Services' definition of each type of abuse and maltreatment. However, again it is important to remember that each state, although bound to this minimum standard, will likely have additional criteria and scenarios that qualify as abuse (National Clearinghouse on Child Abuse and Neglect, 2005).

Neglect of a child involves the failure to provide for a child's basic needs. Neglect may be

- physical (e.g., failure to provide necessary food or shelter or lack of appropriate supervision)
- medical (e.g., failure to provide necessary medical or mental health treatment)
- educational (e.g., failure to educate a child or attend to the child's special education needs)
- emotional (e.g., inattention to a child's emotional needs, failure to provide psychological care, or permitting the child to use alcohol or other drugs) (CAPTA, 2018).

The existence of some of these indicators does not necessarily indicate child neglect, particularly because cultural values, standards of care in the community, and poverty may be contributing factors in caregiving challenges in meeting a child's physical, medical, and educational needs. Rather, the manifestation of certain problems within a family system, such as not sending a child to school, may be an indicator of an overwhelmed family's need for information and general assistance. Yet, if a family fails to utilize the information, assistance, and resources provided for them, and the child's health and/or safety is determined to be at risk, then a CPS intervention may be warranted.

According to CAPTA (2018), physical abuse of a child includes intentional or unintentional physical injury ranging from burning, minor bruises, severe fractures, or even death, as a result of punching, beating, kicking, biting, shaking, throwing, stabbing, choking, or hitting with a hand, stick, strap, or other object. Sexual abuse includes activities by a parent or caretaker that include fondling a child's genitals, penetration, incest, rape, sodomy, indecent exposure, and exploitation through prostitution or the production of pornographic materials. Emotional abuse of a child involves a pattern of behavior that impairs a child's emotional development or sense of self-worth. This may include constant criticism, threats, or rejection, as well as withholding love, support, or guidance. Emotional abuse is often difficult to prove, and therefore most CPS agencies may not be able to intervene without evidence of significant harm to the child or an indication of another form of abuse (which almost always occurs alongside emotional abuse).

It's important to understand the nature of child abuse, particularly how it can be transmitted from one generation to the next (Bentovim, 2002, 2004; Ehrensaft et al., 2003; Newcomb et al., 2001; Pears & Capaldi, 2001), and although the majority of parents who have been abused in childhood do not go on to abuse their own children, those who commit child abuse likely were abused in their own childhoods. Homes marked by violence, drug abuse, neglect, and sexual abuse contribute to the development of maladaptive patterns that can be passed down to the next generation. Although it might not make intuitive sense that someone who endured the pain of abuse would inflict this same abuse on their own child, the complex nature of child abuse oftentimes renders abuse patterns beyond the control of the abuser without some form of intervention. For instance, consider the opening vignette about Vanessa and then ask yourself how this information would impact your work as a child abuse investigator or child welfare caseworker.

Vanessa illustrates some of the dynamics at play with the intergenerational transmission of abuse and why it is so important for caseworkers to understand how trauma and behavioral patterns are often transmitted from one generation to the next. Individuals who have suffered significant childhood abuse and neglect often suffer from problems with emotional regulation, difficulty attaching to others, and an unstable self-identity (Bentovim, 2002, 2004). Issues such as poor parental modeling, lack of understanding about normal child development, and an individual's level of residual anger and frustration tolerance affect a person's ability to positively parent their children. This does not mean that all parents who come from abusive homes are destined to repeat the mistakes of their parents; far from it, in fact. Rather, what it does mean is that child abuse and neglect does not exist in a vacuum, and the more child welfare professionals understand the systemic nature of child abuse and maltreatment, the better they will be able to serve the families on their caseloads.

The Forensic Interview

Prosecutions of child abuse, particularly child sexual abuse, have steadily increased since 2000 (Connolly et al., 2017). Reasons for this include increased public awareness, mandatory reporting requirements, a significant change in attitudes regarding what constitutes child abuse, as well as the belief that abuse is no longer a private family matter. Yet, as the pendulum swung, the 1970s witnessed a sort of frenzy in child sexual abuse reporting, fueled in part by a popular contention among mental health experts that children were incapable of making false allegations (Bussey & Grimbeek, 1995). This belief fostered overzealousness among some therapists, who used misleading interviewing techniques to encourage disclosures, many of which were false. Examples of the types of questions most likely to lead to false confessions include leading questions, such as: "Did he touch you on your privates?", forced choice questions, such as: "Did he touch you under your clothing or over your clothing?", option posing questions such as: "I heard that your uncle has been bothering you", or suggestive questions, such as: "Many kids at your school have said that your teacher has touched them. Did he touch you, too?"

The use of these types of leading questions used by well-meaning therapists was eventually met with harsh criticism, particularly among members of the legal community who represented those individuals falsely accused of sexually abusing children in their charge. By the 1990s considerable research existed that showed how asking children leading questions during abuse investigations significantly increased the likelihood of false and erroneous disclosures, particularly with preschool-aged children (Hewitt, 1999; Peterson & Biggs, 1997; Poole & Lindsay, 1998). In response to criticism and new research, CPS agencies across the country developed pilot programs that combined the resources of several investigative agencies, including CPS, police departments, and prosecutors' offices. This coordinated approach not only prevents the trauma of duplicative interviews by separate enforcement agencies, but also allows for the highly specialized training of investigators on **forensic interviewing techniques** that avoid any type of suggestive or leading questions (Cross et al., 2007).

Although there is a general understanding among investigators of what constitutes a forensic interview, there was still concern that many interviewers used questions that were somewhat leading in nature, including an interviewer's inadvertent reaction to a child's response that either encouraged or discouraged an honest disclosure. For instance, an investigator who strongly believes that a child has been abused may inadvertently respond with frustration if a child denies the abuse, which may influence a child who wants to please the investigator to give a false disclosure of abuse. Even an expression of sympathy on the part of the interviewer in response to disclosures of abuse can inadvertently encourage a child to embellish somewhat to receive more of the interviewer's compassion.

The National Institute of Child Health and Human Development (NICHD) developed a forensic interviewing protocol that teaches interviewers how to ask open-ended questions, using retrieval cues that rely on free recall. "Can you tell me everything you can remember?" is an example of an open-ended question. "Tell me more about the room you were in" is an example of a retrieval cue (Bourg et al., 1999; Sternberg et al., 2001). The idea behind the NICHD investigative protocol is that questions probing free recall will result in more accurate information than questions relying on other types of memory (Benia et al., 2015; Orbach et al., 2000). New research is being conducted all the time, examining a range of issues related to interviewing children when suspected abuse is involved. Examples include exploring appropriate interview settings, how to build rapport with the child, how to pace the interview, the use of body maps, and best practices for interviewing special populations such as immigrant children (Fontes, 2010; Morgan et al., 2013).

Risk Assessment and Decision-Making Models

Child abuse investigators are responsible for assessing the safety of children who are at risk of maltreatment, deciding what types and levels of services may be immediately needed to keep children safe, and determining under what conditions children are placed in out-of-home care for their protection (DePanfilis & Scannapieco, 1994). Many variables influence the outcome of an investigation, including the criteria a CPS agency uses to determine whether abuse is occurring and, if so, whether it rises to the level of warranting an intervention.

The process of investigating an incident of potential child abuse and maltreatment is complex and fraught with the possibility for bias. For instance, how does an investigator evaluate parental cooperation versus resistance? What about forthrightness versus deception? Such decisions require good clinical skills, the ability to read people, to determine whether someone is being truthful or hiding something significant. In other words, the process of investigating a suspected case of child abuse is wrought with the potential of personal bias influencing the investigative process, which could lead to some cases of abuse being unfounded, as well as cases where the family is meeting the federal minimum parenting standard being founded.

The importance of relying on a bias-free and fact-based decision-making model in making intervention decisions has been discussed among child welfare experts for decades (DePanfilis & Scannapieco, 1994), and according to the Child Welfare League of America (CWLA), there are several approaches now available to making risk assessments of child maltreatment in child protection cases. Safety assessments using structured decision-making tools are either statistically based (also called actuarial models) or consensus based (relying on the opinions of experts in the field, and existing research in child maltreatment).

Actuarial models of risk assessment assess families based on factors and characteristics that are statistically associated with the recurrence of maltreatment, whereas consensus-based models of risk assessment rely on the professional opinions of child maltreatment experts. Because the actuarial models of risk assessments are based on a statistical calculation, the validity of the inventories may be considered higher than the consensus-based model risk assessments. An example of an actuarial model for risk assessment and decision-making is the CRC Actuarial Models for Risk Assessment, which uses two subscales—one that assesses the risk for neglect, and one that assesses the risk for physical and sexual abuse. The subscales then provide a risk level based on the existence of variables statistically associated with child maltreatment, foster care placement, and recidivism within a 2-year period (Austin et al., 2005).

Many within the child welfare fields have expressed concern that actuarial models do not rely enough on clinical judgment, advocating for a dual approach to child abuse assessment. For instance, Shlonsky and Wagner (2005) encourage using both an actuarial risk assessment model and a clinical assessment that includes a comprehensive needs assessment and a strengths-based clinical evaluation that considers contextual factors such as poverty, mental illness, domestic violence, and other social and personal dynamics that highlight the causes of maltreatment. So, while actuarial risk assessment instruments are vitally important because they are effective at predicting the likelihood of future abuse, the caseworker's clinical judgement is also vitally important because it highlights what the parenting plan should focus on and what services and intervention strategies will be most helpful in addressing the identified needs and contextual factors impacting the family system.

Another type of decision-making model are consensus-based approaches, which include theoretically and empirically guided approaches that rank a series of factors that have empirical support for their association with child maltreatment (CWLA, 2005). Some examples of consensus-based models for risk assessment and decision making include the Washington Risk Assessment Matrix, the California Family Assessment and Factor Analysis (also called the "Fresno Model"), the Child Emergency Response Assessment Protocol (Austin et al., 2005), and the Child at Risk Field System (CARF). The CARF provides the following guidelines for abuse investigators making a determination about abuse:

Where children were determined to be maltreated and unsafe, the offending parents

1. were out of control
2. were frequently violent

3. showed no remorse

4. may actually request placement

5. did not respond to previous attempts to intervene

6. location was unknown.

And the caseworker believed that

1. the parents were a flight risk

2. the child had special needs the parents could not meet

3. the conditions in the home are life-threatening

4. the nonoffending parent could not protect the children.

Where children were determined to be maltreated and safe, the parents

1. possessed a sufficient amount of impulse control

2. accepted responsibility for the situation in their home

3. had appropriate understanding of the child, showed concern for the child and remorse for the maltreatment

4. had a history of accessing help and services

5. exhibited knowledge of good parenting skills.

Structured decision-making models, such as the British Framework for the Assessment of Children in Need and their Families (FACNF), tend to be more child-centered and holistic in their approach to decision making because they consider both a child's developmental needs and also environmental (contextual) influences on a parent's ability to meet those needs. In other words, structured models take the child's family situation into account. Research has shown that when investigators used the FACNF instrument, they made better decisions, particularly in complex cases (Bartelink et al., 2015). Another promising risk assessment model involves shared decision making, where children are included in the decision-making process (Vis et al., 2011).

Family group decision-making models, such as the Family Group Conferencing (FGC) model, includes the involvement of the family system in child protection decision-making and problem-solving processes (Merkel-Holguin, 1996, 2004). The FGC model was developed in New Zealand in response to the large number of indigenous Maori children placed in out-of-home care. While research on the effectiveness of FGC in reducing future out-of-home placements has been mixed (Dijkstra et al., 2016), the model is valued by many in child welfare because the model acknowledges the impact of historic systemic factors involved in family problems, especially those experienced by **indigenous populations**.

GENERALIST PRACTICE IN CHILD WELFARE

Learning Outcome 4.3   **Examine role and function of child welfare professionals working with children in placement and their families**

When a child abuse investigator determines a child must be placed into protective custody, the child may be removed from the home and placed in one of many environments, including relative foster care, nonrelative foster care, or an emergency shelter pending more permanent placement. The case is then transferred to a family caseworker who evaluates all the relevant dynamics of the case (i.e., reason for placement, nature of abuse, attitude of the parents). The family caseworker also assesses the strengths and deficits of the biological parent(s) as well as the family structure. A permanency goal for the child is then determined and can include the following:

1. Reunification with the biological parents
2. Living with relatives (kinship care)
3. Guardianship with close friends
4. Short-term or long-term nonrelative foster care
5. Emancipation (with older adolescents)
6. Adoption with termination of parental rights.

Although reunification with the biological parents remains the most common permanency plan, recent changes in many state and federal laws have shifted the focus from protecting the biological family unit to considering the best interest of the child. The reason for this shift can be traced to several high-profile cases in the mid-1990s where children were either seriously abused or killed after being reunified with their biological parents. In response, well-meaning child advocates launched campaigns in Washington, D.C., appealing to Congress to do something about the horrible plight of children who were returned to their biological families only to face further abuse and sometimes their deaths in a failed effort to keep biological families together. There was a perception that the government was failing vulnerable children, and while this was certainly the case in some situations, broadly speaking, there was little evidence of a systemic failure (Roberts, 2002).

Thus, while there was no documented increase of child maltreatment during this time period, newspaper and magazine articles highlighting tragic (albeit rare) cases of continued abuse or deaths when children were reunited with their biological parent(s) were passed around Congress. Articles such as "The Little Boy Who Didn't Have to Die" were utilized in an effort to make an emotional appeal to legislators to shift priorities from family reunification to parental termination and subsequent adoption (Spake, 1994). The result of this campaign was the passage of the ASFA of 1997, which marked a clear departure away from family preservation and toward more rapid termination of biological parents' rights, clearing the way for adoption of children in foster care placement.

The **best interest of the child doctrine** may sound great on the surface. Who wouldn't want the best interest of the child to be the standard when considering the future of an abused child's future? The problem noted with this standard among child welfare experts is that the doctrine does not specify who makes the determination of what is actually in the best interest of the child. In other words, the best interest of the child according to whom? According to the foster parents? The courts? The caseworker? Congress? Society in general? It doesn't take much analysis to recognize how easily this standard could be abused. For instance, what if the caseworker determines that it is in the best interest of the child to be adopted by a family with two parents who are financially secure rather than be returned to the child's poor single mother who, regardless of how diligently she tries to regain custody, works late nights and has no supportive family? The potential to make permanency plans that discriminate against biological parents who are marginalized members of society—such as parents who are poor, single, an ethnic minority, undocumented immigrants, gay or lesbian; who work too many jobs; who are too young or too old (and the list goes on)—is significant.

Dorothy Roberts, author of *Shattered Bonds: The Color of Child Welfare* (2002), cautioned that the AFSA of 1997 and the ensuing best interest of the child doctrine created many problems, including ethical dilemmas when caseworkers are required to pursue two permanency plans at the same time to comply with the new permanency plan timeframes—reunification with the biological family and adoption. What many caseworkers have done to accomplish this task is to place foster children in *preadoptive* homes, while at the same time planning for reunification with the biological parent(s). This creates a situation where the biological parents' rights are often in conflict with the children's rights, and where foster care families, who are by definition charged with the responsibility of fostering a relationship between the children and their biological parent(s), are now competing with the biological parent(s) for the children.

Another possible conflict according to Roberts includes the act's adoption incentive program, where states are given financial incentives of $4,000 for each child placed for adoption (above a baseline), $4,000 for foster care youth identified as special needs, and $8,000 for youth between the ages of 9 and 18. The potential for agency conflict of interest, and in some cases abuse, is evident as states scramble to replace lost revenue due to cutbacks to social service programs. Roberts warns that this new legislation was not directed at effecting faster termination of parental rights in cases with severe abuse because these cases were already relatively "open and shut." Rather, it was the cases involving poverty-related maltreatment, most often in Black and Native American homes, that have been most affected by this new federal law. Roberts feared the new priorities have led to increases in social injustice in many CPS agencies, particularly against the poor, people of color, immigrants, and indigenous populations.

Despite these concerns, a review of the U.S. Department of Health and Human Services Adoption and Foster Care Analysis and Reporting System (AFCARS) annual reports shows that placements in pre-adoptive homes have remained relatively steady at about 4%, whereas relative placements (also called kinship care), have increased from 24% in 2001 (DHHS, 2006) to 32% in 2017 (DHHS, 2018). This increase may indicate that rather than placing children in the pre-adoptive homes of nonrelatives, most states opted to place children with relatives, an option made easier by the passage of the Fostering Connections to Success and Increasing Adoptions Act of 2008 (referenced earlier in this chapter). In fact, AFCARS reports indicate that relative care placements didn't begin to increase until 2010, just after the implementation of the Fostering Connections act, which placed kinship care as a priority (DHHS, 2011).

Pearson eText

Video Example 4.2

This video highlights the complexity involved in many child welfare cases. What skills did the provider use to manage the mother's defensiveness?

Working with Biological Parents of Children in Substitute Care

A caseworker works with the biological parents most closely when it is determined that the most appropriate permanency plan is parent reunification. Once a child has been placed into foster care, the caseworker must prepare a detailed service plan, typically within 30 days, outlining goals that the biological parent(s) must accomplish before regaining custody of their child. The specific goals must be related to the identified parenting deficits. It is then the responsibility of the caseworker to facilitate the biological parents' achieving these goals. This might involve giving referrals to the parents or securing services for them, as well as monitoring their ongoing progress.

In fact, a part of any good case plan will involve a visitation schedule that supports and encourages the child's relationship with the biological parents and provides them with opportunities to apply new parenting techniques that they've learned in **parenting classes** and counseling (Sanchirico & Jablonka, 2000). An effective caseworker will give consistent feedback to the biological parents about their progress toward meeting service plan goals, will balance constructive feedback with encouragement, and will protect the parent–child relationship. The effective caseworker will do whatever possible to remove barriers to complying with service plans, such as finding alternate mental health providers when waiting lists would cause unreasonable delays or resolving conflicts between goals, such as not scheduling visitation during the parents' working hours when maintaining stable employment is a service plan goal.

It is also important for caseworkers to be aware that biological parents who have had their children removed are likely enduring emotional trauma in response to this loss, which may result in them behaving in ways that could be uncharacteristic for them. The strain of having to be accountable to external forces exerting control over their lives may render many biological parents vulnerable to feeling overwhelming shame, which may manifest in defensiveness that could be misinterpreted as indifference or a lack of remorse. An effective caseworker will understand this possible dynamic and will create an environment where biological parents will be able to overcome the barrier of defensiveness and shame and work on the issues identified in their service plan.

For instance, parents who are members of historically disenfranchised groups, such as Native Americans, may respond to child protection investigations with aggression or passivity, with some even opting to abandon their children rather than work with government and tribal agencies to regain custody. Child protection workers who are trained in the U.S. government's historic abuses of Native American populations, including the forced removal of almost all Native children from their reservations in the late 1800s and again in the 1950s and 1960s, will likely have increased understanding and empathy for Native American parents who respond to investigations with resistance (Horejsi et al., 1992).

Pearson eText

Video Example 4.3

This video highlights the importance of providing comprehensive information to the biological parent(s) when a report of potential maltreatment is being investigated. Why is providing all relevant information to parents so important?

Working with Children in Substitute Care

The clinical issues that a child welfare caseworker may experience when working with children in foster care will vary depending on variables such as the age of the child, the length of time in placement, the reasons for placement (and the nature of the abuse and maltreatment), and the **permanency plan** (i.e., adoption or family reunification). Younger children are typically easier to place and may display fewer oppositional behaviors than adolescents, who are often placed in residential group homes, but behavioral problems exhibited by children removed from their homes are both expected and understandable, as such a disruption involves a significant amount of **grief** and psychological adjustment.

Children involved in the child welfare system are contending with either issues related to separation from their biological family members or the threat of separation (Riebschleger et al., 2015). The seminal work by Siu and Hogan (1989) on child welfare dynamics provides recommendations for caseworkers, including the importance of being familiar with the psychological dynamics involved in such separations as they relate to each developmental stage. It is important for caseworkers to acknowledge that these children are not just being separated from their biological parents, but are experiencing multiple separations, such as separation from their extended family, perhaps their siblings and their familiar surroundings, including their bedroom, house, neighborhood, and even their family pets. Caseworkers need to confront these separation issues head-on with the children on their caseload, resisting the temptation to avoid them in response to their own separation anxiety.

Caseworkers can respond to children dealing with separation issues by being honest with them (in an age-appropriate manner) regarding what is happening with their families, and by helping to prepare them for upcoming changes in order to reduce the anxiety associated with anticipating the unknown. Younger children are far more likely to be operating in the "here and now." Thus, it is important for the caseworker to reassure the child that the separation is only temporary (if the goal is family reunification) and that the feelings of sadness and discomfort experienced after being separated will not last forever.

Children who have been removed from their homes also need to be reassured that they are not the cause of the family disruption. It is quite common for foster care children to feel responsible for their parents "getting into trouble," and they may even be tempted to recant their disclosures of abuse in the hope that they can return home. Such children often reason that enduring the abuse is better than having their family torn apart and their parents being in trouble. In fact, some abusive parents tell their children that if they disclose the abuse the parents will go to jail and the children will be taken away. Thus, it is important that caseworkers anticipate the possibility of such prior conversations between children and parents and address this by reassuring the children that the current course of action will ultimately benefit and strengthen the entire family system.

Coming alongside children who have experienced a loss and permitting them to grieve involves having a high tolerance for a wide range of emotions. Lee and Whiting (2007) discuss the concept of ambiguous loss with regard to children in foster care. Ambiguous loss is defined as loss that is unclear, undefined, and, in many instances, unresolvable. Ambiguous loss in foster care situations can involve losses that are confusing for the child, such as the loss of an abusive parent. Children who are removed from an abusive home and placed in a foster home with caring, nonabusive parents may feel conflicted about the loss of the biological parent and entry into the child welfare system. Feelings may include confusion, ambivalence, and guilt.

Earlier research studies have found that people who endure ambivalent loss tend to experience similar reactions and feelings, including the following:

- "Frozen" grief, including outrage and an inability to move on
- Confusion, distress, and ambivalence
- Uncertainty leading to immobilization
- Blocked coping processes
- Feelings of helplessness, depression, and anxiety, and relationship conflicts
- Denial of changes or losses, including a denial of the facts
- Anger at the lost person being excluded
- Confusion in boundaries and roles (e.g., who the parental figures are)
- Guilt, if hope has been given up
- Refusal to talk about the individuals and the situation (Boss, 2004 as cited in Lee & Whiting, 2007).

With these reactions and feelings in mind, Lee and Whiting (2007) interviewed 182 foster children, aged 2 through 10. Children were asked about each of the reactions and feelings identified in Boss' study as typical responses to ambiguous loss. The study showed that virtually all of the children interviewed exhibited these typical feelings, particularly feelings associated with confusion, ambiguity, and outrage about their situation. Several children noted confusion about their future—not knowing when they would see their parent(s) again, or how long they would be in foster care. The children also expressed feelings of uncertainty, guilt, and immobility.

Lee and Whiting (2007) recommend using the model of ambiguous loss when working with children in foster care, cautioning against pathologizing children's feelings (and the consequential behaviors). In describing the application of this model of loss, Lee and Whiting urged child welfare professionals, including therapists, case managers, court personnel, and foster family members, not to see these feelings and their associated behaviors as pathological, but as coping strategies that were understandable considering their circumstances. Lee and Whiting discouraged child welfare professionals from encouraging children in substitute care to suppress their feelings and behaviors just because it might be easier for the foster parents. In fact, they theorize that the behaviors that often cause a disruption in foster care placements are the very behaviors that need to be expected and understood since they are manifestations of fears of interdependency and self-fulfilling prophesies that they are unlovable. If child welfare professionals adopt a strengths-based approach they will no longer perceive grief-based behaviors as deficits, but rather as strengths.

Siu and Hogan (1989) also cite the importance of caseworkers understanding the nature of grieving and thereby assisting foster care children to grieve the loss of their families. It is vital for caseworkers to be familiar with the range of possible expressions of depression among grieving children, which often manifest as irritability and can easily be mistaken for oppositional behavior. It is also quite common for children to express heartfelt grief for parents who have abused them. Even children who have been sexually abused may express that they miss an abusive parent. Effective caseworkers can express understanding and empathy for children as they express their grief and **mourn** their losses, without necessarily minimizing the reasons why the children are in placement.

A child's identity is based on many external factors, including playing sports and having a special pet.

Another trauma children in foster care experience is the disruption of their identity development. Removing children from their biological homes (and potentially their neighborhood and school) can be highly traumatic, resulting in a range of psychological and behavioral problems (Frederico et al., 2017). A considerable amount of children's identities resides outside of themselves; thus, many children are dependent on external validation and encouragement. Consider the case of Vanessa in the opening vignette. Her identity was at least partly rooted in living in a rural community and being a lover of horses. She struggled when she was placed in a group home in the city, where she had limited access to outdoor space and no access to horses. An effective caseworker will understand the various dynamics of identity development, including understanding how removing children from their homes, even abusive homes, can undermine their identity development. Any **acting out behavior** on the part of the child should be viewed through this lens of identity disruption. Caseworkers can respond by providing comfort and encouragement to the child during the transition to a new environment, as well as by coming up with unique remedies to challenging situations in an attempt to address these identity dynamics, such as when Vanessa's caseworkers made arrangements for her to take horseback riding lessons and volunteer at a local stable and visit her mom more regularly.

Continuity of Family Ties and the Need for Post-placement Counseling.

Picture yourself in a boat moored to a dock on the shore of a large lake. Being anchored to the dock provides you with a connection to the mainland and a sense of security, without fearing that you'll become adrift at sea. But what if you need to get to the other side of the lake? You would have to pull up your anchor and drift across the water, and it wouldn't be until you reached the other side and safely anchored yourself against that shore that you would feel secure and stable again. Many significant life transitions are like this—adrift at sea, caught between two shores, where continuity and stability are temporarily lost. Children who have been removed from their biological homes will undoubtedly lose their sense of continuity with their biological families and will feel adrift at sea during the time period when they have not yet established new bonds with their foster family. This is a temporary phenomenon and will pass in time, thus continuity and stability can be reestablished once again.

A 2016 study found that children in foster care remain strongly attached to their biological parents, even when their parents were highly abusive (Baker et al., 2016). In fact, Baker (et al.) found that all of the children in the study "yearned" for their parents, even the abusive parent. They further found that the majority of the children were afraid of being removed from their abusive homes, and blamed themselves for the removal, while at the same time feeling relieved and grateful for being placed in foster care. The results of this and similar studies highlight the importance of caseworkers recognizing the confusing and conflictual feelings most children experience when they're removed from their home, in addition to the strong attachments they maintain with their biological parents, even when a parent is abusive and rejecting.

Siu and Hogan (1989) strongly recommend that caseworkers consider the importance of **family continuity** and stability when considering where to place a child. Ready access to the biological family and even close friends should be a priority in placement decisions. Although this can become challenging, particularly in areas where there is a limited number of available foster families, consideration should still be given to a placement that will facilitate ongoing parental involvement and the possibility of continuing ties with family members and friends. For instance, at times siblings must be placed in separate foster homes, and consideration to continuity issues needs to be extended in this situation. Often siblings in foster families do not visit each other regularly because of the geographic constraints placed on foster families, who are often responsible for providing transportation.

Far too often the foster care system, with all its complications, is ill-equipped to effectively *foster* a relationship between children in placement and their biological families. This is because if children do not have ready access to their biological families, they will most likely search for continuity and connectedness with their foster families, which, although necessary and important, can pose a risk to the continuing bond with their biological parents. Research has clearly shown that children who visit their biological parents more frequently have a stronger bond with them and have fewer behavioral problems, are less apt to take psychiatric medication such as antidepressant medication, and are less likely to be developmentally delayed. This underscores the importance of strengthening the attachment between foster children and their biological parents through regular and consistent visitation (McWey & Mullis, 2004). Restricting visitation for any reason other than the safety of the child will have a negative effect on this attachment and might even be subsequently used against the biological parents when the time comes to make reunification plans.

Removing children from their biological homes and placing them into foster care constitutes a psychosocial crisis. Siu and Hogan (1989) referred to this crisis as a critical transition, which throws an already fragile family into complete disequilibrium. In fact, most child welfare experts put foster care placement in the category of a *catastrophic crisis*, warranting a clinical intervention that involves trauma counseling (often referred to as trauma-informed therapy). Surprisingly, despite the vast amount of research on the trauma foster children experience—in relation to both their maltreatment and their out-of-home placement, only about half of children in placement receive the counseling that they need. One national survey found that the children who were the most likely to receive mental health services were younger children who had been sexually abused. Black children were the least likely to receive mental health services, as were children who remained living in their biological homes (Burns et al., 2004). Research on the needs of foster children is clear: All children in out-of-home placement need trauma-informed therapy to heal from their past and become fully functioning and healthy adults (Riebschleger et al., 2015).

Working with Foster Parents

Foster care can involve many different types of placement settings, including kinship care, a foster care emergency shelter, a child residential treatment center, a group home, or even an independent living program for older adolescents, but most frequently foster care involves placing a child with a licensed foster family (two-parent or single-parent family). Every state has certain guidelines and standards that prospective foster parents must meet (Barth, 2001). Licensure typically requires that families participate in up to 10 training sessions focusing on topics such as the developmental needs of at-risk children, issues related to child sexual abuse, appropriate disciplining techniques for at-risk children, ways that foster parents can support the relationship between the foster children and their biological parents, and ways to manage the stress of adding new members to their family. In addition, individuals who will be foster parenting children of a different ethnicity will undergo training focusing on transcultural parenting issues.

Pearson eText

Video Example 4.4

In this video the human services provider provides clear information to a mother whose son is in protective care on what steps she needs to take to regain custody. What skills did the provider use to address the mother's concerns?

Foster parents provide an invaluable service by accepting abused and maltreated children into their homes and providing love, nurturing, and security, even though they know the children may be in their homes for only a short time. In addition to good training, foster parents benefit from caseworkers who are consistently supportive and available to them, particularly during high stress times when foster children are acting out. Foster placement will be far less likely to fail if the foster parents feel sufficiently well prepared and supported by their caseworker, which includes receiving sufficient training (Miller et al., 2019).

The success of a reunification plan depends largely on the cooperation of the foster parents. A foster parent who eagerly facilitates visitation and the sharing of vital information with the biological parents will help protect and maintain the continuity between the foster children and their biological parents. The caseworker plays a pivotal role in providing support and assistance to foster parents. A foster parent who feels unsupported by the caseworker will be far more likely to either purposely or inadvertently undermine the relationship between the foster child and the biological parents. Much of the time this action comes in the form of advocacy for the child, but unfortunately, this advocacy, as well meaning as it may be, has the potential of disrupting the necessary process of reunification. Thus, although it is certainly understandable that the process of emotional bonding with the foster child may make foster parents vulnerable to advocating for their perception of the best interest of their foster children, foster parents who take it upon themselves to protect their foster child by discouraging the relationship with the biological parents in any way are violating their designated roles, and their effectiveness as foster parents will likely be seriously compromised (Randle et al., 2017).

FAMILY REUNIFICATION: KNOWING WHEN IT'S TIME TO RETURN HOME

Decisions about reunifying children in foster care placement with their biological parents are based on many factors, including the biological parents' success in meeting their service plan goals. Even if these goals are sufficiently met, the timing of reunification will depend on factors related to minimizing disruptions in the child's life, such as not switching schools during breaks if possible. If reunification is the plan from the beginning of placement, then the caseworker should be planning for this event from the initial stages of the case.

Problems arise when issues such as court postponements, additional service plan goals, changes in caseworker assignments, and other factors lead to delays in reunification. A judge may deem it perfectly reasonable to postpone a reunification hearing so that a child can complete the final 4 months of school without disruption. Such a decision can be devastating for the biological parents who have worked diligently to reach all service plan goals and go to court expecting to leave with their biological child, only to be told they must wait an additional 4 months to avoid their child changing schools in the middle of the school year. The potential for a biological parent to give up attempting to regain custody and to relapse into unhealthy behaviors out of discouragement and frustration is great, and caseworkers must be sensitive to the possibility of such frustrations leading to despair or relapse.

Therefore, even though reunification with biological parents is associated with several changes in the child's life, many of which may be negative in nature (Lau et al., 2003), an effective caseworker will begin preparing the child for these transitions from the beginning of placement in foster care. Simply verbalizing what is going to happen, telling the child what to expect in the future, and giving children a voice in expressing their fears and frustrations, even if they do not have decision-making power, will go a long way in minimizing the negative effect of reunification, particularly for children who have been in placement for a significant amount of time.

Reunification is not just stressful for the child, it is stressful for the biological parents as well, and many biological parents are the most vulnerable to stress-related relapse in the weeks leading up to and following reunification (Lau et al., 2003; Mowbray et al., 2017). The combination of increased stress and the acting out of the child due to yet another transition can create a potentially volatile situation where negative behavior patterns resurface and unhealthy coping mechanisms are resumed. Any good reunification plan involves ongoing monitoring and provision of in-home services to prevent such problems during the reunification process. These services can be provided by the county child welfare office directly or by a contracted agency-based practice that specializes in providing services such as in-home case management and support. With good support services, many reunifications go quite smoothly, and in time the children and parents settle into a regular routine where healthier communication patterns and positive parenting styles will eventually lead to a positive response from the children.

FAMILY PRESERVATION PROGRAMS

Family preservation programs are comprised of a variety of short-term, intensive services designed to immediately reduce stress and teach important skills designed to reduce the need for out-of-home placement by intervening in a family crisis process before the dynamics deteriorate to the point of requiring the removal of the children. Services can include family counseling, parenting training, child development education, child behavior management, life-skills training, assistance with household budgeting, stress management, respite care for caregivers, and, in some cases, cash assistance (Nelson, 2017).

Research has found that family preservation programs are generally quite successful, with most remaining intact in the years following the suspension of services (Bezeczky et al., 2020). Higher-need families with complex problems have higher rates of repeat mistreatment, but even these families have relatively good success with intensive family preservation services (Schweitzer et al., 2015).

Despite the success of family preservation programs, including for high-risk families, certain populations, such as Blacks, are not consistently selected for family preservation programs. Reasons for this include caseworker bias based on the belief that the needs of the Black community may be too great to be appropriately handled by this program. And yet, when caseworkers underwent cultural sensitivity training, they increased their referrals for Black families who, as a whole, did quite well in the program (Denby & Curtis, 2003).

There are many types of family preservation programs, including different goals, program elements, services provided, and theoretical orientations. Most states will typically adopt a particular program and then implement it within the state's county CPS agencies. Most family preservation programs typically offer 24-hour referral and response; in-home services offered on a 24-hour, 7-day-a-week availability; small caseloads; and emergency services. An example of a family preservation programs is the Homebuilders® program from the Institute for Family Development, which provides a range of in-home services for identified at-risk families involved in the child welfare system, including crisis intervention, parenting training, life-skills education, and counseling. Currently, more than half of all states in the United States use the Homebuilders® program.

Project Connect is another family preservation program that provides a wide array of services to identified at-risk families in the child welfare system, with a particular focus on parental substance abuse. Project Connect also provides 18 weeks of in-home skills training to parents focusing on child behavior management, child health care skills, and home safety training. Another family preservation program, Functional Family Therapy, provides in-home services to identified at-risk parents with adolescents.

ETHNIC MINORITY POPULATIONS AND MULTICULTURAL CONSIDERATIONS

Learning Outcome 4.4   **Analyze the relationship between historic mistreatment of ethnic minority populations and their current involvement in the U.S. child welfare system**

Black Children and the U.S. Child Welfare System

Children of color are overrepresented in the foster care system, comprising nearly 54% of all placements in the year 2018 (DHHS, 2018). Black children are especially overrepresented in the foster care system, consisting of 23% of all children in substitute care in 2018, while constituting only 14% of the U.S. population. Black children also tend to be treated differently in the foster care system, including being less likely to receive in-home care and being more likely to be removed from the home than White children, despite experiencing similar level of maltreatment. While it is difficult to isolate specific reasons for disparities in treatment, experts suggest that racial bias and cultural misunderstanding are key components in case worker decision making (Child Welfare Information Gateway, 2016b).

Black families are more likely to be referred to child protective services, Black children tend to remain in foster care far longer and are reunited with their families less often (Curtis & Denby, 2011). It's somewhat ironic that Black children were initially excluded from government child protection programs and now they are the most overrepresented among all other racial and ethnic groups (DHHS, 2018). Some reasons for this overrepresentation relate to complex social issues such as the impact of institutionalized racism and intergenerational poverty, but as referenced earlier, other causes include cultural misunderstanding and racial bias on the part of case workers, including **implicit bias** (personal biases that an individual is not necessarily aware of) (Bruster et al., 2019).

A 2003 study found some very interesting trends with regard to the types of racial bias that existed in many child welfare agencies when comparing how Black and White children were treated in foster care, including how decisions were made, and while this study is several decades old, the findings appear to be quite relevant today. For instance, Surbeck (2003) found that most caseworkers exhibited racial partiality in how they assessed parent–child attachment, which led to delays in returning children to their biological parents. Although this finding was reciprocal (meaning that Black caseworkers showed partiality toward Black families and White caseworkers show partiality toward

White families), the effect of this pattern has particular relevance to the Black community because the majority of caseworkers are White and Black children are disproportionately represented in foster care placements. Surbeck theorized that the White caseworkers' lack of cultural understanding may have led them to misunderstand the nature of the parental bond between Black mothers and their children. A more recent study's findings that Black families involved in the foster care system were far less likely to be referred for a range of services due to racial bias appear to support these earlier findings (Lovato-Hermann et al., 2017).

Native Americans and the U.S. Child Welfare System

Native Americans have a unique history with the U.S. government with regard to child welfare and protection policies that warrants special attention. The British colonization of North America involved an organized and methodical campaign to decimate the Native American population through invasion, trickery (such as trading land for alcohol), and ultimately the forced relocation of all Native Americans onto government-designated reservations, where the assimilation into the majority culture became a primary goal of the British and then U.S. governments (Brown, 2001). The few Native Americans who survived this genocide were broken physically, emotionally, and spiritually, suffering from alcoholism, rampant unemployment, and debilitating depression.

In the early part of the 19th century the U.S. government assumed full responsibility for educating Native American children. It is estimated that from the early 1800s through the early part of the 20th century, virtually all Native American children were forcibly removed from their homes on the reservations and placed in Indian boarding schools, where they were not allowed to speak in their native tongues, practice their cultural religion, or wear their traditional dress. During school breaks, many of these children were placed as servants in White homes rather than being allowed to return home for visits. The result of this forced assimilation amounted to cultural genocide where an entire generation of Native Americans was institutionalized, deprived of a relationship with their biological families, and robbed of their cultural heritage.

Native Americans posing on the steps of Carlisle Indian School, c. 1890.

The ongoing campaign to assimilate the Native Americans into European American culture became even more aggressive between 1950 and 1970, when social workers with governmental backing removed thousands of Native American children from their homes on the reservations for alleged maltreatment, placing them in adoptive White homes. In reality, many of the problems on the reservations were the product of years of governmental oppression resulting in extreme poverty and other commonly associated social ills, and the U.S. government's response to this was to tear Native American families apart rather than intervene with mental health services.

Pearson eText

Video Example 4.5

This video highlights the importance of the Indian Child Welfare Act. Why is this federal legislation as important today as when it passed in 1978?
https://www.youtube.com/watch?v=JyW42Rk7lvw

Between 1941 and 1978, approximately 70% of all Native American children were removed from their homes and placed either in orphanages or with White families, many of whom later adopted them (Marr, 2002). In truth, few of these children were removed from their homes because of maltreatment as it is currently defined. Rather, approximately 99% of these children were removed because social workers believed that the children were victims of social deprivation due to the extreme poverty common on most Indian reservations (U.S. Senate, 1974). The result of this government action has been nothing short of devastating. Native Americans have one of the highest suicide rates in the nation, with Native American youth, particularly those who have spent time in U.S. boarding schools, having on average 5 to 6 times the rate of suicide compared to the non-Native population. When these children graduated from high school, they were adults without a culture—no longer feeling comfortable on the reservation after years of being negatively indoctrinated against their cultural heritage, yet not being accepted by the White population either. The response of many of these individuals was to turn to alcohol in an attempt to drown out the pain.

As explored earlier in this chapter, in 1978, the Indian Child Welfare Act (Pub. L. No. 95-608) was passed, which prevented the unjustified removal of Native American children from their homes. The act specifies that if removal is necessary, then the children must be placed in a home that reflects their culture and preserves tribal tradition. Tribal approval must be obtained prior to placement, even when the placement is a result of a voluntary adoption proceeding (Kreisher, 2002). This act has for the most part successfully stemmed the tide of mass removal of Native American children from their homes on the reservations, but unfortunately many caseworkers still do not understand the reason why such a bill was passed in the first place, or why it is necessary, and they mistakenly believe that this act hampers placing at-risk children in loving homes.

Overall Native American families experience disproportionately high rates of poverty, alcohol and substance abuse, and health problems. Native American children experience neglect and physical abuse at higher than average rates, and Native American children on reservations experience excessively high rates of sexual abuse and assault, with lower than average rates of criminal justice intervention. Child welfare professionals are faced with complex challenges, including broken family systems, tribal corruption, remote and isolated communities, chronic and intergenerational substance abuse, domestic violence, and poverty-related stressors. Culturally appropriate intervention strategies can address these complexities in a way that honors and reflects cultural traditions and values.

Latina/o Children and the U.S. Child Welfare System

Latina/o children—including **native-born** children to native-born or immigrant parents (64%) and foreign-born (36%), primarily from Mexico, Cuba, the Dominican Republic, and Central and South America—have historically been slightly underrepresented in the child welfare system on a national level. But this trend has shifted in the past two decades, with Latina/o children now being slightly overrepresented in the child welfare population. For instance, in 2000 Latina/o children represented about 14% of the child welfare population while they represented just over 15% of the U.S. population, but by 2007 Latina/o children represented just over 20% of the child welfare population (Dettlaff & Earner, 2012; Dettlaff et al., 2009). On a state-by-state basis Latina/o children are significantly overrepresented in at least six states, particularly border states with a higher Latina/o population.

There is very little research on intergroup differences within the broader Latina/o population, but this should not be interpreted as there being complete homogeneity between the various country-of-origin subpopulations, or between native- and foreign-born children. The research that does exist reveals differences in the demographic characteristics and nature of maltreatment between native-born and immigrant children. For instance, native children were more likely to be emotionally and physically abused, as well as have neglectful supervision, while immigrant children were more likely to be emotionally and sexually abused, as well as experience far higher rates of family stress. Additionally, immigrant children were far more likely to be living in a two-parent home with at least one grandparent also residing in the home (Dettlaff & Earner, 2012). A new demographic trend includes Latina/o immigrant children who come across the border alone. These unaccompanied migrant youth represent a rather small percentage of the total Latina/o child welfare population, but they are a group worth noting because their numbers are increasing, they tend to be highly traumatized with complex needs, and they have little to no in-country social support (Frydman et al., 2014).

Risk factors for abuse in native Latina/o families involved in the child welfare system include alcohol abuse, drug abuse, poor parenting skills, domestic violence, excessive discipline, a history of child maltreatment, a recent arrest, low social support, high family stress, and difficulty meeting children's basic needs. Risk factors in immigrant families include alcohol abuse, poor parenting skills, domestic violence, excessive discipline, a history of child maltreatment, low social support, high family stress (often related to their immigration experience), and difficulty meeting children's basic needs. With regard to community risk factors, native-born families are far more likely to live in unsafe neighborhoods with high crime rates and with large numbers of unsupervised teens compared to immigrant families (Dettlaff & Earner, 2012).

Latinas/os in general have a number of cultural strengths that child welfare professionals can tap into when working with Latina/o families involved in the child welfare system. For instance, culturally, Latina/o families tend to have very close attachments to their children, have strong connections to their community, and have strong intergenerational ties and family-centered traditions. Additionally, although the stereotype of the macro Latina/o culture is that it is patriarchal in nature, the reality is that many subcultures within the larger Latina/o culture, such as Puerto Ricans, have a long history of feminism (CASCW, 2014).

Child welfare professionals using a strengths-based approach and who are appropriately trained can draw on these cultural values and traditions when working with Latina/o families, providing culturally congruent services. Another important factor relates to the history of trauma many Latina/o families and children experience, primarily as a part of their immigration experience. Thus, it's highly beneficial for child welfare workers working with Latina/o families to be trauma-informed so that they can both recognize and appropriately respond to acute and chronic trauma within their caseloads of migrant populations (Igelman et al., 2007).

Native Hawaiians and Other Pacific Islanders

Native Hawaiians and other Pacific Islanders (NHPIs) consist of a group of diverse people indigenous to the State of Hawai'i and the U.S. territories of American Samoa and Guam, with Polynesian, Micronesian, and Melanesian backgrounds. There are approximately 1.2 million NHPIs living in the United States, constituting 0.05% of the U.S. population. While the majority of NHPIs reside in Hawai'i, other states with high NHPI populations include California, Washington, and Florida. NHPIs are the fastest growing and most diverse racial groups in the United States.

NHPIs generally experience poorer health than other cultural groups in the United States, with higher than average rates of alcohol consumption, smoking, obesity, and diabetes. They also have the highest rates of cancer than any other U.S. cultural group and have the second highest rates of HIV infection and have the second shortest survival rate (White House, n.d.). NHPIs also experience higher-than-average poverty rates and higher-than-average levels of family stress related to social conditions and histories of mistreatment and bias. They also experience disproportionate rates of poverty, barriers to educational opportunities, and quality health care (Communities, E. P. I., 2014).

All of these factors impact family systems and increase vulnerability to becoming involved in the child welfare system. While the overall numbers of NHPI children involved in the child welfare system is small, they are overrepresented in all aspects of the child welfare system, including the juvenile justice system, particularly in Hawai'i (Fong et al., 2014; Office of Hawaiian Affairs, 2010; Okamoto, 2011). Additionally, NHPIs experience disproportionate rates of incarceration, which also has implications for children and the child welfare system (OHA, 2010). These issues are actively being addressed with the human services and broader advocacy communities. However, the complex nature of the dynamics involved, the overt and covert racial bias and discrimination, and the highly diverse nature of the NHPI population creates a challenging situation for child welfare professionals that can be addressed only through extensive culturally based training and a multipronged approach that pairs case management, counseling, and advocacy on the micro and macro levels.

Alaska Natives

Alaska Natives consist of 13 federally recognized tribes of people indigenous to the State of Alaska. Although many Alaska Natives are genetically similar to Native Americans in mainland United States and South America, their histories of migration, cultures, and treatment by Russian and European settlers and the U.S. government are somewhat different. Similar to other indigenous populations, Alaska Natives have a long history of oppression, marginalization, exploitation, and annihilation, dating back to the 1700s, including being treated as servants and slaves and losing their land to Russian and later American ruling powers. Also similar to mainland Native Americans, Alaska Natives were historically not allowed to practice their native traditions or speak their native languages.

Many Alaska Natives fought against such treatment and attempts to rob them of their culture. While many of the remaining tribes remain strongly attached to their cultural traditions, the impact of centuries of mistreatment has resulted in a range of problems within their social structure and family systems, resulting in, among other dynamics, an overrepresentation in the child welfare system. In fact, children from Alaska are twice as likely to be placed in foster care than children from other states, with Alaska Native children being 7 times more likely to be in foster care than non-Native children (Vadapalli et al., 2014). Native Alaskan children are physically and sexually abused at significantly higher rates than the rest of the population. Girls are particularly vulnerable to rape and other forms of violence and abuse, exacerbated by excessively high rates of alcohol abuse, long dark winters, and a culture of secrecy.

A unique challenge facing child welfare professionals in Alaska is the remote location of many of the tribes, which makes regular visits and the offer of support difficult. But research clearly shows that, historically, child welfare caseworkers showed a lack of cultural integrity toward Alaska Natives by removing children from tribal lands despite members of the community being willing to care for them (Rieger & Kandel, 1999). More recent macro interventions focus on social justice issues and cultural rights of Alaska Natives as autonomous people who continue to suffer the consequences of mistreatment by the majority White culture. As with other indigenous people, child welfare professionals working with these populations must be appropriately trained so they can provide culturally congruent services that allow Native children to remain within their communities whenever possible.

WORKING WITH ADOLESCENT YOUTH

Learning Outcome 4.5   Explore the role and function of human services professionals within practice settings serving adolescent populations

Adolescents from troubled families face many unique challenges, particularly in out-of-home placement. About 35% of all children in foster care are youth between the ages of 11 and 20 (Kids Count, 2019). And of the 232,374 children who exited the foster care system in 2018, 43,103 of them were 14 years of age and older (just over 18%) (DHHS, 2018). Among this youth population, about 25,000 were 16 years of age or over, with many likely heading into very uncertain futures. While some adolescents are placed in kinship and nonrelative care, most are placed in group homes (also called **therapeutic foster homes**), particularly if they struggle with behavioral health challenges (behavior disorders or mental illness) and are not safe or compliant in a family home setting.

Group homes can be small and informal, or larger and more structured. Adolescents in the former typically attend a local public school, whereas teens who are placed in more structured environments often attend high schools located within the facility where they are housed. **Treatment modalities** in these facilities often include a combination of behavior modification where desirable behaviors are rewarded and undesirable behaviors are punished, individual therapy, group therapy, and family therapy.

Teens aging out of the foster care system are placed in specialized programs for transitioning youth, called supervised independent living programs. Despite specialized services, including life skills training and educational support, many foster alumni experience multiple challenges and considerable difficulty emerging into adulthood. For instance, one study found that between 31% and 46% of foster care alumni had experienced homelessness by the time they reached 26, over 40% of former foster youth drop out of high school, and fewer than half were unemployed as young adults (Dworsky et al., 2013). Another study found that aging-out foster youth faced increased risk for homelessness and housing instability in their early adulthood, but this trend was mediated for those youth who maintained a relationship with their foster parents (Fowler et al., 2017). An even more distressing finding is that many foster care alumni have been arrested at least once by the time they are 18 and close to half of all girls formerly in foster care had been pregnant one or more times by the time they were 21 years of age (Combs et al., 2018; Ryan et al., 2016). All of these dynamics increase the risk of aging-out foster youth to experience a lifetime of instability related to a range of social problems, including becoming involved in the child welfare system as parents.

Foster care alumni have reported that what they needed more than anything was stable and caring relationships with adults, preferably their family (Geenen & Powers, 2007). One potential solution developed to address these challenges is the Extended Foster Care Beyond 18 program, which allows youth to remain in foster care until their 21st birthday, or in some states even longer. Currently there are 25 states that offer this program (at the state's expense). The Fostering Connections to Success Act of 2008 provides for some Title IV-E funding for states providing extended foster care under certain circumstances, such as if the youth is in school and working part-time (Child Welfare Information Gateway, 2017).

Runaway and Homeless Youth

Unaccompanied youth who are homeless because they are kicked out of their home or they have run away face a number of challenges and are a focus of advocacy and federal policy responses. It's difficult to determine the exact number of runaway and homeless youth because of varying ways this population is defined and various ways counts are conducted. For instance, the 2017 federal point-in-time count estimated that there were up to 41,000 runaway and homeless youth between the ages of 13 and 21, but an advocacy organization relying on phone surveys yielded an estimation of 70,000 (Fernandes-Alcantara, 2018), and an empirical study conducted in 2013 estimated there were up to 2 million runaway and homeless youth, aged 16 to 22, in the United States (Fernandes-Alcantara, 2013). The authors of the latter study found that many of these youth had run away from a foster care placement or had aged out of the foster care system and are living on the streets.

Runaway and homeless youth (sometimes called "throwaway youth") are far more likely to be living on the streets than in a shelter. They are also far more likely to participate in dangerous behaviors such as drug abuse (including needle sharing), panhandling, theft, and survival sex (sex for food, money, and shelter). These risky behaviors put homeless adolescents and youth at risk for HIV, hepatitis B, hepatitis C, and a range of other sexually transmitted diseases (Beech et al., 2002). Runaway and homeless youth are also at high risk for physical and sexual victimization, particularly those youth who are sexual minorities (McCauley et al., 2018; Xu et al., 2016).

Most youth who live on the streets left home because of physical and sexual abuse. In one seminal study of over 600 runaway and homeless youth, sexual abuse was cited as the chief reason they chose to live on the streets rather than remaining in their homes (Yoder et al., 2001). The fact that many of these teens will continue to experience sexual exploitation while living on the streets, whether through sexual attacks, trading sex for basic needs, or sex trafficking, highlights the tragic and cyclical nature of life for these kids.

Most runaway and homeless youth living in urban communities operate as a somewhat cohesive group on the streets, protecting each other and helping one another survive (Auerswald & Eyre, 2002). In fact, it appears that the more seasoned adolescents often take new homeless teens under their wings, teaching them survival tactics and welcoming them into the "fold." Newer homeless youth who were interviewed talked about what a relief it was to have someone essentially mentor them into the ways of surviving street life. But without glamorizing this life, most teens, both boys and girls, talked of the horrors of being victims of domestic sex trafficking rings. In fact, runaway and homeless youth living on the streets identified the many ways in which they felt exploited, both by older teens and by adults who forced them into drug dealing and prostitution (Auerswald & Eyre, 2002).

Interestingly, many runaway and homeless youth have reported a strong belief in God, who they believe watches out for them and keeps them alive. In Auerswald and Eyre's 2002 study, one teen stated that when they were not really in need, they would often get no offer of food and little money while panhandling. Yet when they were really in need, having gone without food for a few days, then whatever they needed would just come to them. One teen attributed this phenomenon to God knowing what he needed and providing for him when he needed it the most. In another study researchers found that over half of all runaway and homeless youth interviewed cited a faith in God as the primary motivation for survival (Lindsey et al., 2000).

Yet even with this surprisingly high percentage of faith-seeking runaway and homeless youth, an estimated 40% attempt suicide (Auerswald & Eyre, 2002). They are also at high risk for **posttraumatic stress disorder (PTSD)**, anxiety disorders, depression, substance abuse, and delinquency (Thrane et al., 2008). Many runway and homeless youth report losing all contact with people in their former lives, even siblings, extended family, and those who had been supportive of them in the past. Many also talked of feeling extremely lonely and distrustful but in desperate need of love and affection. Because the majority of runaway and homeless youth have run away from abusive homes, it seems likely that many were suffering from some form of emotional disturbance even prior to entering street life (Kidd, 2003).

Unfortunately, many of the runaway and homeless youth who were interviewed reported being highly suspicious of all adults, including outreach workers with social service agencies providing assistance to the homeless adolescent population. The overall perception among runaway and homeless youth of outreach agencies is quite negative, and adolescents who accepted assistance from these agencies were considered "sellouts" and foolish. The prevailing belief was that social workers and other outreach workers would force the teens to return to an abusive home environment, or they'd be turned over to the police or child protective services. Knowing these attitudes can aid social service agencies in developing outreach efforts and other services designed to overcome these negative perceptions (Kidd, 2003).

The Runaway and Homeless Youth Act (RHYA) is federal legislation that provides programmatic funding for unaccompanied homeless youth, particularly the most vulnerable of these youth, such as racial and ethnic minorities and sexual minorities (lesbian, gay, bisexual, transgender, and queer/questioning youth). Originally passed in 1974, this act has been reauthorized several times, most recently in 2016. The RHYA provides funding for three types of services: (1) Street outreach services, (2) short-term shelter, and (3) transitional living services, consisting of longer-term housing. All three service domains include counseling and other supportive services. The Runaway and Homeless Youth Act is currently up for reauthorization as the Runaway and Homeless Youth and Trafficking Prevention Act, to address the significant risk of domestic trafficking among youth living on the streets.

Adolescents Who Join Gangs

Gangs consist of groups of individuals who actively participate in criminal activities on an organized or coordinated basis. Gang activity has become an increasingly severe problem in recent years, not only with regard to the number of gangs in operation within the

United States (estimated to be somewhere between 700,000 and 800,000 nationwide), but also with regard to the type of violent activities in which many gang members participate. Gang activity remains primarily a big-city phenomenon, with some of the larger cities having more than 30 gangs operating at one time (National Youth Gang Center, 2005). Smaller towns and rural communities also experience gang problems, but these tend to be relatively sporadic with gangs that are loosely organized.

Gang members commit crimes such as theft, drug trafficking, assault, and intimidation. When gang members engage in turf wars where one gang is in conflict with another, gang fights often ensue, involving both serious assaults and homicides. In some urban communities, such as Chicago and Baltimore, drive-by shootings are a way of life, and parents respond by keeping their young children off the streets and away from windows. And even that doesn't keep some children safe, as evidenced by the alarming number of children who are shot inadvertently by bullets that crash through living room windows.

Most gang members are between the ages of 13 and 25, but some studies found gangs that have members as young as 10. Most gang members come from backgrounds of poverty and racial oppression, live in high-crime urban communities, and live in neighborhoods with high gang activity (Vigil, 2003). Although there has been a recent increase in female gang activity most gangs are still primarily comprised of males (Chesney-Lind, 1999).

Every year the FBI releases a report on gang activity in the United States called the National Gang Report (NGR), which provides an assessment of gang activity across the country. The report is based on surveys of law enforcement agencies throughout the United States. The report categorizes gang activity into four categories: (1) street gang activity (neighborhood gangs and national gangs), (2) prison gang activity, (3) **outlaw motorcycle gang (OMG)** activity, and (4) cross-border gang activity (gang activity between the U.S./Mexico border). This year's report shows an increase in the size of all gangs in the past 2 years, as well as increases in gang-related crime (National Gang Intelligence Center, 2015).

Neighborhood gangs pose a threat to residents, industry, and law enforcement. Prison gangs pose a threat to prison efficiency and the safety of both staff and other prisoners, as well as to the community in general since there remains a strong connection between prison gangs and street gangs. Gangs in general are increasing their criminal activities as well as the seriousness of the crimes they are committing. For instance, gangs consistently engage in drug trafficking crimes (e.g., manufacturing, trafficking, distribution), intimidation (e.g., threats, assaults, murder), and financial crimes (e.g., identity theft, credit card theft, money laundering). More recently street gangs have been increasingly involved in sex trafficking (international and domestic) and prostitution and have formed alliances with other gangs across the country and international sex trafficking rings to increase sex trafficking across the country. Activity between U.S. gangs and gangs and cartels in Mexico, referred to as Mexican Transnational Criminal Organizations (MTCO), has also increased significantly in the last 2 years, with prison gangs often facilitating the connection between the two. Threats against law enforcement, while remaining stable in numbers, have increased in boldness and level of violence (National Gang Intelligence Center, 2015).

According to the FBI, gangs have two primary goals: to make money and increase their power. They accomplish both goals through criminal activity, the former through trafficking and robbery, and the latter through intimidation and violence. The NGR

(2015) also reports that street gangs and OMGs have increased their power and reach by seeking employment in law enforcement agencies, the military, and other government institutions, as well as coordinating with other criminal organizations, such as international sex trafficking rings and MTCOs.

Another interesting trend is the dramatic increase in gangs using social media for recruiting new members, communicating between gang members and other gangs, targeting rivals, facilitating criminal activity, and circumventing law enforcement. Social media has also been used to make threats to law enforcement. The most popular social media sites used by gang members are Facebook, YouTube, Instagram, and Twitter. Additionally, prison gangs use smuggled cell phones to communicate with street gangs and new recruits via social media sites such as Facebook. In 2014 alone, the California Department of Corrections confiscated close to 15,000 cell phones from prisoners, many of which were smuggled in by corrupt prison staff in exchange for cash and sex (National Gang Intelligence Center, 2015). In response to the dramatic rise of gangs using social media, law enforcement agencies are now actively monitoring social media as a part of their surveillance of gang activity.

There are several theories regarding why people (primarily men) join gangs. Most sociological and anthropological theories focus on the sense of solidarity and feelings of belonging that gangs can provide members, particularly disenfranchised youth. Identifying risk factors is important so that effective intervention strategies can be developed and implemented. A comprehensive study facilitated by the U.S. Department of Justice evaluated the gang membership and backgrounds of over 800 gang members from 1985 to 2001 in an attempt to identify some of the reasons why adolescents join gangs. This study, referred to as the Seattle Social Development Project, confirmed that the majority of gang members were men (90%) and that gang members came from diverse ethnic backgrounds including White (European American), Asian, Latino, Native American, and Black, with Blacks having the highest rates of gang membership. Interestingly, the study found that the majority of gang members joined for only a short time, with 70% of youth belonging to a gang for less than a year (Hawkins et al., 2003).

The study identified multiple risk factors for gang membership, including living in high-crime neighborhoods, coming from a single-parent household, poverty, parents who approved of violence, poor academic performance, learning disabilities, little or no commitment to school, early drug and alcohol abuse, and associations with friends who commit delinquent acts. The study's authors recommended early prevention efforts that target youth with multiple risk factors. Programs need to focus on all aspects of the adolescent's life, including family dynamics, school involvement, peer group, and behavioral issues such as drug and alcohol abuse, as well as any antisocial and delinquent behaviors.

What this study seems to underscore is that for youth with multiple risk factors gang membership may be less an option and more a way of life. Adolescents who are fortunate enough to have cohesive families, where high-functioning parents work hard to maintain structure, provide accountability, and keep teens engaged in positive activities, can often avoid the temptation to join a gang. This is particularly true for Black youth living in large urban areas (Walker-Barnes & Mason, 2001).

Adolescents without the benefit of such positive influences, including those who have neglectful and uninvolved parents, often face a reciprocal pull into gang life where they are targeted by existing gang members who recognize the existence of these risk factors. Many adolescents are drawn to gang life because of the benefits gangs appear to provide such as a sense of belonging, a life of excitement, and the feeling of empowerment. The NGR (National Gang Intelligence Center, 2015) referenced aggressive attempts on the part of many gangs to recruit adolescents as young as 11. One example of recruitment tactics using social media include gang members posting rap music on YouTube in an attempt to engage interested youth and convince them to join their gang. Another example included a gang member who contacted a middle school student using an online chat platform and not only told him to join the gang but also demanded that he provide names of other middle school students.

Human services providers who work with youth gang populations may do so on school campuses, in agencies that target at-risk youth, in faith-based outreach agencies, at police departments, or within the juvenile justice system. Most outreach programs target adolescents who live in large urban communities where gang activity is prolific and violent behavior a fact of life, especially those who come from single-parent homes, have poor academic histories, and have shown early signs of delinquent behaviors. Human services providers also target social conditions on a macro level, such as poverty, racism, and the lack of opportunities in urban communities, because these factors contribute to the development of gang activity.

Many human services programs that target at-risk adolescents operate after-school programs or evening community programs that give adolescents a place to go to socialize other than the streets. This is particularly important for youth who are in search of a sense of cohesion, security, and social belongingness, elements that might be missing from their home life. In light of the research indicating that most gang members have relatively loose, short-term affiliations with gangs, these types of programs have the potential of being successful in steering even active gang members away from gang life. Finally, human services programs committed to reducing the gang problem must be willing to engage in active and aggressive outreach efforts, maintain a highly visible presence in the community, coordinate services with other gang intervention programs, and be willing to engage at-risk adolescents and their family on multiple levels.

CONCLUSION

Human services practitioners who work with troubled families have the opportunity to effect change that positively affects not only the present families but all future generations within that family system as well. While the area of child, youth, and family services is broad, what agencies have in common is a focus on strengthening and supporting families in need. One of the largest practice settings within the broader area of child, youth, and family services is child welfare. Child welfare agencies are charged with the responsibility of protecting children from neglect and abuse.

The challenges families in the child welfare system experience are often of a very complex nature, and can include mental health illness, substance abuse, poor anger management, and low coping skills on the part of the parents, and behavior problems, trauma, school problems, and identity issues on the part of the children. Child welfare workers are most effective when they develop expertise in the area of child development, as well as become acutely familiar with the history of government-sanctioned racism targeting certain ethnic minority populations such as Black and Native American and Alaska Native populations.

An increased focus on family preservation programs and other early intervention programs offers the best opportunity for reducing out-of-home placements, but these programs must be offered to all potentially appropriate families without bias. This can occur through sufficient federal and state funding of child welfare programs and the effective recruitment and training of social workers willing to work with a variety of families, from various cultures dealing with a wide range of life challenges.

Adolescents present a complicated and challenging case for social workers, particularly those exiting the foster care system with little to no support. Youth transitioning out of foster care face tremendous difficulty in adulthood and poor outcomes across a range of life domains. Youth opting to live on the streets rather than in abusive homes, foster care, or group homes, face even more hardship such as risks of HIV and STIs, physical and sexual violence, and sex and labor trafficking. Child welfare experts, including social workers, have been instrumental in developing innovative programs to address these challenges, such as extending foster care beyond a child's 18th birthday. Federal legislation can assist by driving expectations and providing funding.

SUMMARY

- The ways in which children were treated historically in the United States, with a particular focus on children from marginalized populations, are examined. The treatment of children since Colonial times, including how poor, migrant, and children of color were abused and exploited within the labor market, as well as how orphaned children and children without parental care were managed and cared for, are also explored.
- The role and function of the human services professional in the current U.S. child welfare system are analyzed. The structure and purpose of the U.S. child welfare system, with a particular focus on the role and function of human services professionals working within each phase of the child welfare system process, are explored.
- The various ways that child abuse investigations are initiated and managed are assessed. The child abuse investigation process within the U.S. child welfare system within the context of the various types of child maltreatment and abuse is explored.
- The role and function of child welfare professionals working with children in placement and their families are explored. The impact on children of being involved in the child welfare system is explored, with a particular focus on removal, as well as how human services professionals can effectively respond to children in placement.
- The relationship between historic mistreatment of ethnic minority populations and their current involvement in the U.S. child welfare system is analyzed. The **disproportionality** of children of color in the child welfare system is explored, including the role of racial bias in decision making and the nature of historic mistreatment of many ethnic minority populations, including Black, Latina/o, Asian, Native American, Native Hawaiian and other Pacific Islander, and Alaska Native populations.
- Important factors related to working with the adolescent population are explored with a particular focus on key challenges many adolescents face. Challenges related to substance abuse and runaway and homeless youth are explored, as is the role of human services providers working with this at-risk population.

END-OF-CHAPTER QUESTIONS

1. Describe how ethnic minority children were historically abused and exploited, and provide an example of its lasting effects.
2. What is the purpose of family preservation programs?
3. Provide an example of ways that removing children from their homes and placing them in foster care can impact their identity development.
4. What are some reasons for the overrepresentation of certain ethnic minority populations in the child welfare system?
5. Why are runaway and homeless youth so resistant to treatment, and what are some ways that the Runaway and Homeless Youth Act assists human services providers working with this population?

References

Addams, J. (1912). *Twenty Years at Hull House*; with autobiographical notes. Kindle Edition.

Addams, J. (1990). *Twenty years at Hull-House*. University of Illinois Press.

Alderman, C. L. (1975). *Colonists for sale: The story of indentured servants in America*. Macmillan.

Auerswald, C. L., & Eyre, S. L. (2002). Youth homelessness in San Francisco: A life cycle approach. *Social Science & Medicine, 54*(10), 1497–1512.

Austin, M. J., D'Andrade, A., Lemon, K., Benton, A., Chow, B., & Reyes, C. (2005). *Risk and safety assessment in child welfare: Instrument comparisons*. University of California, Berkeley, School of Social Welfare (BASSC), 2, 1–16.

Baker, A. J., Creegan, A., Quinones, A., & Rozelle, L. (2016). Foster children's views of their birth parents: A review of the literature. *Children and Youth Services Review, 67*, 177–183.

Bartelink, C., van Yperen, T. A., & Ingrid, J. (2015). Deciding on child maltreatment: A literature review on methods that improve decision-making. *Child Abuse & Neglect, 49*, 142–153.

Barth, R. P. (2001). Policy implications of foster family characteristics. *Family Relations, 50*(1), 16–19.

Beech, M., Meyers, L., & Beech, D. J. (2002). Hepatitis B and C infections among homeless adolescents. *Family Community Health, 25*(2), 28–36.

Bellingham, B. (1984). *Little wanderers: A socio-historical study of the nineteenth century origins of child fostering and adoption reform, based on early records of the New York Children's Aid Society* [Unpublished doctoral dissertation]. University of Pennsylvania. (Available from University Microfilm Incorporated (UMI), Ann Arbor, MI.)

Bender, K., Yang, J., Ferguson, K., & Thompson, S. (2015). Experiences and needs of homeless youth with a history of foster care. *Children and Youth Services Review, 55,* 222–231.

Bender, T. (1975). *Toward an urban vision: Ideas and institutions in nineteenth century America*. The John Hopkins University Press.

Benia, L. R., Hauck-Filho, N., Dillenburg, M., & Stein, L. M. (2015). The NICHD investigative interview protocol: A meta-analytic review. *Journal of Child Sexual Abuse, 24*(3), 259–279.

Bentovim, A. (2002). Preventing sexually abused young people from becoming batterers, and treating the victimization experiences of young people who offend sexually. *Child Abuse & Neglect, 26*(6–7), 661–678.

Bentovim, A. (2004). Working with abusing families: General issues and a systemic perspective. *Journal of Family Psychotherapy, 15*(1–2), 119–135.

Bezeczky, Z., El-Banna, A., Petrou, S., Kemp, A., Scourfield, J., Forrester, D., & Nurmatov, U. B. (2020). Intensive family preservation services to prevent out-of-home placement of children: a systematic review and meta-analysis. *Child Abuse & Neglect, 102*, 104394.

Bourg, W., Broderick, R., & Flagor, R. (1999). *A child interviewer's guidebook*. Sage Publications.

Brace, C. L. (1967). *The dangerous classes of New York and twenty years work among them*. Patterson Smith.

Brown, D. (2001). *Bury my heart at Wounded Knee: An Indian history of the American West*. Henry Holt and Company.

Bruster, B. E., Lane, T. Y., & Smith, B. D. (2019). Challenging implicit bias: preparing students to practice with African American families. *Social Work Education*, 38(5), 654–665.

Burns, B. J., Phillips, S. D., Wagner, H. R., Barth, R. P., Kolko, D. J., Campbell, Y., & Landsverk, J. (2004). Mental health need and access to mental health services by youth involved with child welfare: A national survey. *Journal of the American Academy of Child & Adolescent Psychiatry*, 43(8), 960–970.

Bussey, K., & Grimbeek, E. J. (1995). Disclosure processes: Issues for child sexual abuse victims. In K. J. Rotenberg (Ed.), *Cambridge studies in social and emotional development. Disclosure processes in children and adolescents* (pp. 166–203). Cambridge University Press.

Byars, L. F. (1991). Lexington's Colored Orphan Industrial Home, 1892–1913. *The Register of the Kentucky Historical Society*, 89(2), 147–178.

CAPTA Reauthorization Act of 2010 (P.L. 111–320). Retrieved September 9, 2012, from http://www.govtrack.us/congress/bills/111/s3817/text

CAPTA Reauthorization Act of 2018 (P.L. 111–320). http://www.govtrack.us/congress/bills/111/s3817/text

Center for the Advanced Studies in Child Welfare [CASCW]. (2014). *Latina/o cultural guide building capacity to strengthen the well-being of immigrant families and their children: A prevention strategy.* http://cascw.umn.edu/wp-content/uploads/2014/02/CulturalGuide-Latino.pdf

Chesney-Lind, M. (1999). Challenging girls' invisibility in juvenile court. *Annals of the American Academy of Political and Social Science*, 564, 185–202.

Child Trends. (2018). *Foster care.* https://www.childtrends.org/indicators/foster-care

Child Welfare Information Gateway. (2016a). *Definitions of child abuse and neglect.* U.S. Department of Health and Human Services, Children's Bureau. https://www.childwelfare.gov/topics/systemwide/laws-policies/statutes/define/

Child Welfare Information Gateway. (2016b). *Racial disproportionality and disparity in child welfare.* https://www.childwelfare.gov/pubs/issue-briefs/racial-disproportionality/

Child Welfare Information Gateway. (2017). Extension of foster care beyond age 18. U.S. Department of Health and Human Services, Children's Bureau.

Child Welfare Information Gateway. (2019). About CAPTA: A legislative history. U.S. Department of Health and Human Services, Children's Bureau.

Child Welfare League of America [CWLA]. (2005). *A comparison of approaches to risk assessment in child protection and brief summary of issues identified from research on assessment in related fields.* http://www.childwelfare.gov/responding/iia/safety_risk/

Cochran, B. N., Stewart, A. J., Ginzler, J. A., & Cauce, A. M. (2002). Challenges faced by homeless sexual minorities: Comparison of gay, lesbian, bisexual, and transgender homeless adolescents with their heterosexual counterparts. *American Journal of Public Health*, 92(5), 773–777.

Combs, K. M., Begun, S., Rinehart, D. J., & Taussig, H. (2018). Pregnancy and childbearing among young adults who experienced foster care. *Child maltreatment*, 23(2), 166–174.

Communities, E. P. I. (2014). Native Hawaiians and Pacific Islanders in the United States: A community of contrasts. Empowering Pacific Islander Communities. https://www.empoweredpi.org/research.html

Condran, G. A., & Cheney, R. A. (1982). Mortality trends in Philadelphia: Age and cause-specific death rates 1870–1930. *Demography*, 19(1), 97–123.

Connolly, D. A., Coburn, P. I., & Chong, K. (2017). Twenty-six years prosecuting historic child sexual abuse cases: Has anything changed? *Psychology, Public Policy, and Law*, 23(2), 166.

Cronch, L. E., Viljoen, J. L., & Hansen, D. J. (2006). Forensic interviewing in child sexual abuse cases: Current techniques and future directions. *Aggression and Violent Behavior*, 11(3), 195–207.

Cross, T. P., Jones, L. M., Walsh, W. A., Simone, M., & Kolko, D. (2007). Child forensic interviewing in Children's Advocacy Centers: Empirical data on a practice model. *Child Abuse & Neglect*, 31(10), 1031–1052.

Curtis, C. M., & Denby, R. W. (2011). African American children in the child welfare system: Requiem or reform. *Journal of Public Child Welfare*, 5(1), 111–137.

Davidson, R. D., Morrissey, M. W., & Beck, C. J. (2019). The Hispanic experience of the child welfare system. *Family Court Review*, 57(2), 201–216.

Denby, R. W., & Curtis, C. M. (2003). Why special populations are not the target of family preservation services: A case for program reform. *Journal of Sociology & Social Welfare*, 30(2), 149–173.

DePanfilis, D., & Scannapieco, M. (1994). Assessing the safety of children at risk of maltreatment: Decision-making models. *Child Welfare*, *73*(3), 229–246.

Dettlaff, A. J., & Earner, I. (2012). Children of immigrants in the child welfare system: Characteristics, risk, and maltreatment. *Families in Society: The Journal of Contemporary Social Services*, *93*, 295–303.

Dettlaff, A. J., Earner, I., & Phillips, S. D. (2009). Latino children of immigrants in the child welfare system: Prevalence, characteristics, and risk. *Children and Youth Services Review*, *31*(7), 775–783.

Dijkstra, S., Creemers, H. E., Asscher, J. J., Deković, M., & Stams, G. J. J. (2016). The effectiveness of family group conferencing in youth care: A meta-analysis. *Child Abuse & Neglect*, *62*, 100–110.

Dworsky, A., Napolitano, L., & Courtney, M. (2013). Homelessness during the transition from foster care to adulthood. *American Journal of Public Health*, *103*(S2), S318–S323.

Ehrensaft, M. K., Cohen, P., & Brown, J. (2003). Intergenerational transmission of partner violence: A 20-year prospective study. *Journal of Consulting & Clinical Psychology*, *71*(4), 741–753.

Fernandes-Alcantara, A. L. (2013). *Runaway and homeless youth: Demographics and programs* (CRS Report No. RL33785).

Fernandes-Alcantara, A. L. (2018). *Runaway and homeless youth: Demographics and programs*. Congressional Research Service, The Library of Congress.

Fong, R., Dettlaff, A., James, J., & Rodriguez, C. (Eds.). (2014). *Addressing racial disproportionality and disparities in human services: Multisystemic approaches*. Columbia University Press.

Fontes, L. A. (2010). Interviewing immigrant children for suspected child maltreatment. *Journal of Psychiatry & Law*, *38*(3), 283–305.

Fowler, P. J., Marcal, K. E., Zhang, J., Day, O., & Landsverk, J. (2017). Homelessness and aging out of foster care: A national comparison of child welfare-involved adolescents. *Children and Youth Services Review*, *77*, 27–33.

Frederico, M., Long, M., McNamara, P., McPherson, L., & Rose, R. (2017). Improving outcomes for children in out of home care: the role of therapeutic foster care. *Child & Family Social Work*, *22*(2), 1064–1074.

Frydman, L., Dallam, E., & Bookey, B. (2014*). A treacherous journey: Child migrants navigating the US immigration system*. Center for Gender & Refugee Studies. University of California Hastings College of the Law. http://www.uchastings.edu/centers/cgrsdocs/treacherous_journey_cgrs_kind_report.pdf

Geenen, S., & Powers, L. E. (2007). Tomorrow is another problem: The experiences of youth in foster care during their transition into adulthood. *Children and Youth Services Review*, *29*, 1085–1101.

Goldman, J., & Salus, M. (2003). *A coordinated response to child abuse and neglect: The foundation for practice*. U.S. Department of Health and Human Services, National Center on Child Abuse and Neglect.

Gratton, B., & Moen, J. (2004). Immigration, culture, and child labor in the United States, 1880–1920. *Journal of Interdisciplinary History*, *34*(3), 355–391.

Greene, J. W. (1995). *From forge to fast food: A history of child labor in New York State. Volume I: Colonial times through the Civil War*. New York Labor Legacy Project, Council for Citizenship Education, Russell Sage College.

Hacsi, T. (2017). From indenture to family foster care: A brief history of child placing. In *A history of child welfare* (pp. 155–173). Routledge.

Hawkins, J. D., Smith, B. H., Hill, K. G., Kosterman, R., Catalano, R. F., & Abbott, R. D. (2003). Understanding and preventing crime and violence: Findings from the Seattle Social Development Project. In T. P. Thornberry & M. D. Krohn (Eds.), *Taking stock of delinquency: An overview of findings from contemporary longitudinal studies* (pp. 255–312). Plenum.

Hewitt, S. K. (1999). *Assessing allegations of sexual abuse in preschool children: Understanding small voices*. Sage Publications.

Holt, M. (1992). *The orphan trains: Placing out in America*. University of Nebraska Press.

Horejsi, C., Craig, B. H. R., & Pablo, J. (1992). *Reactions by Native American parents to child protection agencies: Cultural and community factors*. Child Welfare League of America.

Hume, D. L., & Sidun, N. M. (2017). Human trafficking of women and girls: Characteristics, commonalities, and complexities. *Women & Therapy*, *40*(1–2), 7–11.

Igelman, R., Conradi, L., & Ryan, B. (2007). Creating a trauma-informed child welfare system [Electronic version]. *Focal Point*, *21*(1), 23–26.

Katz, M. B. (1996). *In the shadow of the poorhouse: A social history of welfare in America*. Basic Books.

Kidd, S. A. (2003). Street youth: Coping and interventions. *Child and Adolescent Social Work Journal*, *20*(4), 235–261.

Kids Count. (2019). *Children in foster care by age group in the United States.* Kids Count Data Center. https://datacen-ter.kidscount.org/data/tables/6244-children-in-foster-care-by-age-group?loc=1&loct=1#detailed/1/any/false/37,871, 870, 573,869,36,868,867,133,38/1889,2616, 2617,2618,2619,122/12988,12989

Klarman, M. J. (2006). *From Jim Crow to civil rights: The Supreme Court and the struggle for racial equality.* Oxford University Press.

Kopel, S., Charlton, T., & Well, S. J. (2003). Investigation laws and practices in child protective services. *Child Welfare, 82*(6), 661–684.

Kreisher, K. (2002). Coming home: The lingering effects of the Indian Adoption Project. *Children's Voice, 11*(2). 9–11.

Lau, A. S., Litrownik, A. J., Newton, R. R., & Landsverk, J. (2003). Going home: The complex effects of reunification on internalizing problems among children in foster care. *Journal of Abnormal Child Psychology, 31*(4), 345–358.

Lee, R. E., & Whiting, J. B. (2007). Foster children's expressions of ambiguous loss. *American Journal of Family Therapy, 35,* 417–428.

Lindsey, E. W., Kurtz, D. P., Jarvis, S., Williams, N. R., & Nackerud, L. (2000). How runaway and homeless youth navigate troubled waters: Personal strengths and resources. *Child and Adolescent Social Work Journal, 17*(2), 115–140.

Lovato-Hermann, K., Dellor, E., Tam, C. C., Curry, S., & Freisthler, B. (2017). Racial disparities in service referrals for families in the child welfare system. *Journal of Public Child Welfare, 11*(2), 133–149.

Mallett, C. A. (2016). The school-to-prison pipeline: A critical review of the punitive paradigm shift. *Child and Adolescent Social Work Journal, 33*(1), 15–24.

Marr, C. (2002). *Assimilation through education: Indian boarding schools in the Pacific Northwest.* University of Washington Libraries Digital Collections. http://content.lib.washington.edu/aipnw/marr/marr.html

Martin, M. (2014). *Advocacy for social justice: Local and global implications.* Pearson Publishing.

Matoba, N., & Collins, J. W. Jr. (2017, October). Racial disparity in infant mortality. In *Seminars in perinatology* (Vol. 41, No. 6, pp. 354–359). WB Saunders.

McCauley, H. L., Coulter, R. W., Bogen, K. W., & Rothman, E. F. (2018). Sexual assault risk and prevention among sexual and gender minority populations. In Orchowski, L., Gidycz, C. (Eds.), *Sexual assault risk reduction and resistance: Theory, research, and practice* (pp. 333–352). Elsevier.

McWey, L., & Mullis, A. K. (2004). Improving the lives of children in foster care: The impact of supervised visitation. *Family Relations: Interdisciplinary Journal of Applied Family Studies, 53*(3), 293–300.

Merkel-Holguin, L. (1996). Putting families back into the child protection partnership: Family group decision making. *Protecting Children, 12*(3), 4–7.

Merkel-Holguin, L. (2004). Sharing power with the people: Family group conferencing as a democratic experiment. *Journal of Sociology & Social Welfare, 31,* 155.

Miller, A. E., Green, T. D., & Lambros, K. M. (2019). Foster parent self-care: A conceptual model. *Children and Youth Services Review, 99,* 107–114.

Moras, A., Shehan, C., & Berardo, F. M. (2018). African American families: Historical and contemporary forces shaping family life and studies. In *Handbook of the sociology of racial and ethnic relations* (pp. 91–107). Springer, Cham.

Morgan, K., Dorgan, K., & Hayne, H. (2013). Body maps do not facilitate older children's report of touch. *Scandinavian Journal of Psychology, 54*(1), 51–55.

Morton, M. H., Dworsky, A., Matjasko, J. L., Curry, S. R., Schlueter, D., Chávez, R., & Farrell, A. F. (2018). Prevalence and correlates of youth homelessness in the United States. *Journal of Adolescent Health, 62*(1), 14–21.

Morton, M. J. (2000). Institutionalizing inequalities: Black children and child welfare in Cleveland, 1859–1998. *Journal of Social History, 34*(1), 141–162.

Mowbray, O., Victor, B. G., Ryan, J. P., Moore, A., & Perron, B. E. (2017). Parental substance use and foster care reentry. *Journal of Social Work Practice in the Addictions, 17*(4), 352–373.

National Clearinghouse on Child Abuse and Neglect. (2005). *Definition of child abuse and neglect state statutes.* Series 2005. U.S. Department of Health and Human Services, Administration for Children & Families. http://www.childwelfare.gov/systemwide/laws_policies/statutes/define.cfm

National Gang Intelligence Center. (2015). *National Gang Report 2015.* Federal Bureau of Investigation. https://www.fbi.gov/file-repository/stats-services-publications-national-gang-report-2015.pdf/view

National Indian Child Welfare Association (NICWA). (n.d.). *Indian Child Welfare Act of 1978.* http://www.nicwa.org/Indian_Child_Welfare_Act/

National Youth Gang Center. (2005). *Highlights of the 2002–2003 national youth gang surveys*. U.S. Department of Justice, Office of Justice Programs, Office of Juvenile Justice and Delinquency Prevention. https://www.ncjrs.gov/pdffiles1/ojjdp/fs200501.pdf

Nelson, D. (2017). Recognizing and realizing the potential of "family preservation." In J. K. Whittaker, J. Kinney, E. M. Tracy, & C. Booth (Eds.), *Reaching high-risk families* (pp. 13–30). Routledge.

Newcomb, M., Locke, D., & Thomas, F. (2001). Intergenerational cycle of maltreatment: A popular concept obscured by methodological limitations. *Child Abuse & Neglect, 25*(9), 1219–1240.

Office of Hawaiian Affairs [OHA]. (2010). *The disparate treatment of Native Hawaiians in the criminal justice system*. http://www.justicepolicy.org/uploads/justicepolicy/documents/10-09_exs_disparatetreatmentofnativehawaiians_rd-ac.pdf

Okamoto, S. K. (2011). Current and future directions in social work research with Native Hawaiians and other Pacific Islanders. *Journal of Ethnic & Cultural Diversity in Social Work, 20*(2), 93–97.

Orbach, Y., Hershkowitz, I., Lamb, M. E., Sternberg, K. J., Esplin, P. W., & Horowitz, D. (2000). Assessing the value of structured protocols for forensic interviews of alleged child abuse victims. *Child Abuse & Neglect, 24*(6), 733–752.

Patrick, M., Sheets, E., & Trickel, E. (1990). *We are a part of history: The orphan trains*. The Donning Co.

Pears, K. C., & Capaldi, D. M. (2001). Intergenerational transmission of abuse: A two-generational prospective study of an at-risk sample. *Child Abuse & Neglect, 25*(11), 1439–1461.

Peterson, C., & Biggs, M. (1997). Interviewing children about trauma: Problems with "specific" questions. *Journal of Traumatic Stress, 10*(2), 279–290.

Poole, D. A., & Lindsay, D. S. (1998). Assessing the accuracy of young children's reports: Lessons from the investigation of child sexual abuse. *Applied & Preventive Psychology, 7*(1), 1–26.

Randle, M., Ernst, D., Leisch, F., & Dolnicar, S. (2017). What makes foster carers think about quitting? Recommendations for improved retention of foster carers. *Child and Family Social Work, 22*(3), 1175–1186.

Riebschleger, J., Day, A., & Damashek, A. (2015). Foster care youth share stories of trauma before, during, and after placement: Youth voices for building trauma-informed systems of care. *Journal of Aggression, Maltreatment & Trauma, 24*(4), 339–360.

Rieger, L., & Kandel, R. (1999). *Child welfare and Alaska Native tribal governance: A pilot project in Kake, Alaska—Report of findings*. University of Alaska Anchorage Justice Center.

Roberts, D. (2002). *Shattered bonds: The color of child welfare*. Basic Civitas Books.

Ryan, J. P., Perron, B. E., & Huang, H. (2016). Child welfare and the transition to adulthood: Investigating placement status and subsequent arrests. *Journal of Youth and Adolescence, 45*(1), 172–182.

Sanchirico, A., & Jablonka, K. (2000). Keeping foster children connected to their biological parents: The impact of foster parent training and support. *Child and Adolescent Social Work Journal, 17*(3), 185–203.

Schultz, C. B. (1985). Children and childhood in eighteenth century. In J. M. Hawes and N. R. Hiner (Eds.), *American childhood: A research guide and historical handbook* (Vol. 70, pp. 79–80). Greenwood Press.

Schweitzer, D. D., Pecora, P. J., Nelson, K., Walters, B., & Blythe, B. J. (2015). Building the evidence base for intensive family preservation services. *Journal of Public Child Welfare, 9*(5), 423–443.

Shlonsky, A., & Wagner, D. (2005). The next step: Integrating actuarial risk assessment and clinical judgment into an evidence-based practice framework in CPS case management. *Children and Youth Services Review, 27*(4), 409–427.

Shughart, W. F., & Chappell, W. F. (1999). Fostering the demand for adoptions: An empirical analysis of the impact of orphanages and foster care on adoptions in the U.S. In R. D. McKenzie (Ed.), *Rethinking orphanages for the 21st century* (pp. 151–171). Sage Publishers.

Siu, S., & Hogan, P. T. (1989). Common clinical themes in child welfare. *Social Work, 34*(4), 229–345.

Spake, A. (1994, November). The little boy who didn't have to die. *McCall's*, 142.

Sternberg, K. J., Lamb, M. E., & Orbach, Y. (2001). Use of a structured investigative protocol enhances young children's responses to free-recall prompts in the course of forensic interviews. *Journal of Applied Psychology, 86*(5), 997–1005.

Surbeck, B. C. (2003). An investigation of racial partiality in child welfare assessments of attachment. *American Journal of Orthopsychiatry, 73*(1), 13–23.

The White House. (n.d.). *White House initiative on Asian Americans & Pacific Islanders (WHIAAPI) fact sheet: What you should know about Native Hawaiians and Pacific Islanders (NHPI's)*. https://www2.ed.gov/about/inits/list/asian-americans-initiative/what-you-should-know.pdf

Thrane, L., Chen, X., Johnson, K., & Whitbeck, L. B. (2008). Predictors of police contact among Midwestern homeless and runaway youth. *Youth Violence and Youth Justice, 6*(3), 227–239.

Trattner, W. I. (2007). *From poor law to welfare state: A history of social welfare in America* (6th ed.). Simon and Schuster.

U.S. Census Bureau. (2018). *Quickfacts data*. https://www.census.gov/quickfacts/fact/table/US/PST045218

U.S. Department of Health and Human Services. (2006). *The AFCARS report: Final estimates for FY 1998 through FY 2002*. U.S. Dept. of Health and Human Services, Administration for Children and Families, Administration on Children, Youth and Families, Children's Bureau. https://www.acf.hhs.gov/sites/default/files/cb/afcarsreport12.pdf

U.S. Department of Health and Human Services [DHHS]. (2011). *The AFCARS report 18*. U.S. Dept. of Health and Human Services, Administration for Children and Families, Administration on Children, Youth and Families, Children's Bureau. https://www.acf.hhs.gov/cb/resource/afcars-report-18

U.S. Department of Health and Human Services [DHHS]. (2018). *The AFCARS report 25*. U.S. Dept. of Health and Human Services, Administration for Children and Families, Administration on Children, Youth and Families, Children's Bureau. https://www.acf.hhs.gov/cb/resource/afcars-report-25

U.S. Senate. (1974). Hearings before the Subcommittee on Indian Affairs of the Committee on Interior and Insular Affairs, 99th Cong., 2nd Session (testimony of William Byler). U.S. Government Printing Office.

Vadapalli, D., Hanna, V., & Passini, J. (2014). Trends in age, gender, and ethnicity among children in foster care in Alaska. http://www.iser.uaa.alaska.edu/Publications/2014_12-TrendsInAge-GenderAndEthnicity-AmongFosterChildrenInAlaska.pdf

Vigil, J. M. (2003). Urban violence and street gangs. *Annual Review Anthropology, 32*, 225–242.

Vis, S. A., Strandbu, A., Holtan, A., & Thomas, N. (2011). Participation and health: A research review of child participation in planning and decision-making. *Child and Family Social Work, 16*, 325–335.

Von Hartz, J. (1978). *New York street kids*. New Dover.

Walker-Barnes, C. J., & Mason, C. A. (2001). Ethnic differences in the effect of parenting upon gang involvement and gang delinquency: A longitudinal, HLM perspective. *Child Development, 72*, 1814–1831.

Warren, A. (1995). *Orphan train rider: One boy's true story*. Houghton Mifflin Co.

White, V. (2017). *Disproportionality of American Indian children in foster care*. Retrieved from Sophia, the St. Catherine University repository website: https://sophia.stkate.edu/msw_papers/812

Whittaker, J. K. (2017). *The child welfare challenge: Policy, practice, and research*. Routledge.

Xu, L., Carpenter-Aeby, T., Aeby, V. G., Lu, W., Fisher, L., Hardee, M., & Rowson, N. (2016). A systematic review of the literature: Exploring correlates of sexual assault and homelessness. *Tropical Medicine & Surgery, 4*(2), 212–223.

Yaffe-Bellany, D., & Zaveri, M. (2020). Chipotle is fined $1.4 Million in vast child labor case. *The New York Times*. https://www.nytimes.com/2020/01/28/business/chipotle-child-labor-laws-massachusetts.html

Yoder, K. A., Whitbeck, L. B., & Hoyt, D. R. (2001). Event history analysis of antecedents to running away from home and being on the street. *American Behavioral Scientist, 45*(1), 51–65.

5

Human Services with Older Adults

© SHUTTERSTOCK

Glenn was shocked as he walked down La Salle Avenue, in the heart of the business district in Chicago. He was used to seeing homeless people, either standing or sitting along the side of the road with signs asking for money, but he had never seen an older couple begging for money before. What was unique about this couple was that they looked as though they could be his own mother and father. He began to walk by them, avoiding their stare as he usually did when people begged for money, but this time was different, and he could not resist approaching this couple. "Hi, my name is Glenn, and I'd love to give you some money." The couple looked at him sheepishly, and he noticed the shame in their eyes. "Thank you," the woman said quietly, averting her glance downward. Glenn handed them $10 and started to walk away, but curiosity got the better of him. He turned around and asked them if he could talk to them about their situation. The husband and wife looked at each other, and Glenn did not know if it was with suspicion or simple caution, but they eventually agreed. Over their meals of hot soup and sandwiches, Rosemary and Donald shared about their "all-American" lives. They raised two children in a suburb of Chicago, owned a home, and even had a family dog. They were like anyone else in the neighborhood, until that is, Donald was laid off 2 years before his scheduled retirement when his company was sold and then downsized. Donald had worked for this company for 40 years. Donald was unable to find a job because of his age, and eventually they had to let their health insurance lapse because they could no longer afford the high monthly premiums. Unfortunately, Rosemary became ill the following month with a bout of influenza that ultimately developed into pneumonia. The hospital bill for her 2-week stay was over $40,000. With no retirement and only Social Security benefits to count on, and with their two adult children serving overseas in the military, Donald and Rosemary began a downhill financial descent that didn't stop until they depleted their life savings and ultimately lost their home in foreclosure. Although many couples like Donald and Rosemary spend their "golden years" playing golf in Florida, Donald and Rosemary spend their days sitting outside the train station, begging for money.

Clara was sitting in a classroom filled with people half her age and wondered if she'd made the right choice. It's not that she regretted her choice to stay home and raise her children, but since her divorce last year, she realized she wanted more out of life than wondering what could have been. What if she had not married at 18 and started a family by 20? What if she had pursued her dream of graduating from college? What if she'd had the courage and support to pursue her career goals, in addition to being married and raising a family? When her therapist, a very nice woman with an LCSW, first suggested she return to school, she thought that was a ridiculous idea. She was 60 years old, certainly too old to start her life over again. But her therapist pointed out a few things Clara had not considered. First, people are living longer. If Clara lived even slightly longer than her parents, she could easily have another 20 years or more on this earth. She was healthy and active, so living until she was 85 or 90 was a definite possibility. And second, with the increased availability of technology, there were more opportunities than ever for people willing to take a risk. Clara realized that while others may have held her back when she was younger, the only person holding her back now was herself. So, she told herself that 60 wasn't too old to grow and change, and she applied for and was accepted to a college program for mature students. She wasn't sure what to expect, but in a way, that was a part of the excitement.

THE GRAYING OF AMERICA

Learning Outcome 5.1 **Examine the impact of changing demographics associated with the current and projected growth of the older adult population**

The opening vignettes illustrate the range of experiences of those considered "old" in the United States. Today's older adults experience a broader range of lifestyles than ever before, but they also experience a broad range of challenges. There are several dynamics that have led to increased opportunities and lifestyle choices for older adults. An increase in the human lifespan, changes in the perception of old age in general, and changes in the economy have all opened increased opportunities for a range of life trajectories for older adults that didn't exist a few decades ago, particularly for women. For some older

Pearson eText

Video Example 5.1

This video explores the challenges facing many older adults and a unique alternative to longterm care. Is the Village Network an approach that would work through the country? Why or why not? https://www.youtube.com/watch?v=oLKTThGrAxw

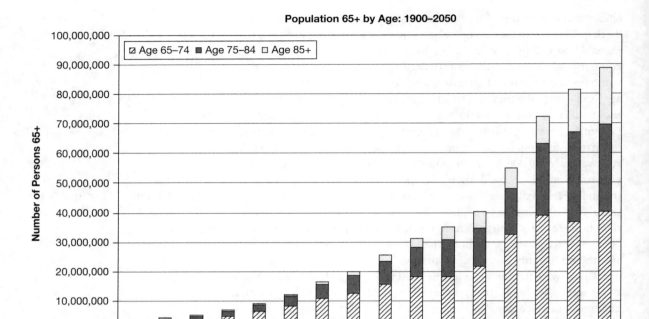

Figure 5.1
Increase in U.S. Population by Age, 1900 to 2050, Showing Increase in Population Age 65+
Compiled by the U.S. Administration on Aging using data from Table 5. Population by Age and Sex for the United States: 1900 to 2000, Part A. Number, Hobbs, Frank and Nicole Stoops, U.S. Census Bureau, Census 2000 Special Reports, Series CENSR-4, Demographic Trends in the 20th Century.

adults, these societal shifts have led to positive outcomes, but for others, life has become more complicated and difficult to navigate. Take the lengthening lifespan, for instance. For many, living longer means increased opportunities to remain in the workforce longer and maybe even switch careers. But for others, living longer doesn't necessarily equate to living better due to a range of challenges such as economic challenges and chronic illness.

The United States is getting grayer, meaning the number of older people in the United States is growing. The term "the graying of America" refers to an increase in the older adult population in the United States. The U.S. Census (2018) predicts that by the year 2035, there will be more older adults than children, and that by 2060, 25% of the U.S. population will be over the age of 65 (compared to about 14% currently) (Vespa et al., 2018). The current population increase coupled with a projected increase in the U.S. older adult population between now and 2050 is directly related to the aging of a cohort of individuals referred to as the baby boomers. The **baby boomers** are popularly defined as those having been born between 1946 and 1964. The name refers to the boom of births after World War II, which caused an unusual population spike in the United States.

Approximately 76 million individuals (roughly 29% of the U.S. population) fall into the baby boomer cohort; thus, it is obvious why this cohort has been the focus of interest to social scientists, the media, politicians, and others (Colby & Ortman, 2014). One reason for the intense interest in this phenomenon is that despite the somewhat broad range of ages within this cohort, similarities between members are numerous, including their socioeconomic status, which tends to be higher than earlier cohorts, consumer habits, and political concerns. As the boomers age, there has been much discussion and some concern regarding the consequences of this large cohort heading into their retirement years, including their increased lobbying power. The **graying of America**, then, refers to the projected increase in the older adult population because of the aging boomers.

The aging of the baby boomers is not the only variable leading to the increase in the older adult population. Other factors include the 50% increase in the human life expectancy in the United States during the 20th century. In 1900 the average human lifespan in the United States was about 47 years, but by 1999 life expectancy had increased to about 77 years, and topped out at 78.9 years in 2014 for all races (life expectancy for Whites was 78.9, and 75.3 for Blacks and 81.8 for Hispanics) (Murphy et al., 2015). Despite earlier projections of a continued upward trend in U.S. life expectancy (particularly among high-income earners) (Arias, 2004), new projections have yielded lower estimates by 2040 (Foreman et al., 2018).

These new projections are based on mortality data from 2014 to 2017, which showed a surprising decrease in lifespans in the United States for adults between the ages of 25 and 64, in large part due to the opioid crisis and rising obesity rates (Murphy et al., 2017; Woolf & Schoomaker, 2019). But even with these lowered lifespan projections the U.S. Census estimates that by the year 2060, there will be almost 95 million people in the United States over the age of 65 (Vespa et al., 2018). That's almost double the number in 2014!

According to the 2017 U.S. Census data, there were an estimated 48,164,303 people living in the United States who were 65 years of age or older, which means that older adults comprise just over 15% of the population (U.S. Census Bureau, 2018). If the 2060 projections are accurate, older adults will comprise about 23% of the population. Additionally, the U.S. Census Bureau projects that the number of people 85 years of age and older will double by 2035 (6.4 million) and triple by 2060 (19 million)! The U.S. population will continue to become more diverse as well, which is why some have referred to the shifting demographic phenomenon as the "graying and browning of America."

So far this all sounds pretty good—we're living longer, and in the next 10 or 20 years a third of the population will be classified as older adults, which no doubt will increase attention paid to social and political issues important to those in their later years of life. However, the landscape for older adults in the United States is not without concern; quite the opposite, in fact. Some older adults will enjoy their longer lifespan, but for many, their additional years on this earth may be spent in a long-term care facility with chronic health problems and increased financial strain.

As rates of opioid use and chronic diseases, such as diabetes, **dementia**, and hypertensive chronic heart problems, continue to rise globally and in the United States, concerns among researchers and policy makers has risen as well (Silberner, 2018). A driving force in the rise of chronic disease is obesity, a reversible condition but one that requires both personal and political will. The academic journal, *The Lancet*, publishes a detailed report on a range of global health indicators every 10 years called the Global Burden of Disease Study, and accompanying the November 2018 reports was an editorial that issued a dire warning to the world: We may be living longer, but we're not living better. Our physical and mental health is compromised due to lifestyle and dangerous social conditions (conflict, terrorism), and we don't have enough health care workers to meet this growing need (Lancet, 2018).

Table 5.1   Older Population by Age Group: 1900 to 2050 with Chart of the 65+ Population

Census Year	Age 60–64	Age 65–74	Age 75–84	Age 85+	Age 60 and older	Age 65 and older	Total, all ages
1900	1,791,363	2,186,767	771,369	122,362	4,871,861	3,080,498	75,994,575
1910	2,267,150	2,793,231	989,056	167,237	6,216,674	3,949,524	91,972,266
1920	2,982,548	3,463,511	1,259,339	210,365	7,915,763	4,933,215	105,710,620
1930	3,751,221	4,720,609	1,641,066	272,130	10,385,026	6,633,805	122,775,046
1940	4,728,340	6,376,189	2,278,373	364,752	13,747,654	9,019,314	131,669,275
1950	6,059,475	8,414,885	3,277,751	576,901	18,329,012	12,269,537	150,697,361
1960	7,142,452	10,996,842	4,633,486	929,252	23,702,032	16,559,580	179,323,175
1970	8,616,784	12,435,456	6,119,145	1,510,901	28,682,286	20,065,502	203,211,926
1980	10,087,621	15,580,605	7,728,755	2,240,067	35,637,048	25,549,427	226,545,805
1990	10,616,167	18,106,558	10,055,108	3,080,165	41,857,998	31,241,831	248,709,873
2000	10,805,447	18,390,986	12,361,180	4,239,587	45,797,200	34,991,753	281,421,906
2010	16,757,689	21,462,599	13,014,814	5,751,299	56,986,401	40,228,712	310,232,863
2020	21,008,851	32,312,186	15,895,265	6,597,019	75,813,321	54,804,470	341,386,665
2030	20,079,650	38,784,325	24,562,604	8,744,986	92,171,565	72,091,915	373,503,674
2040	20,512,884	36,895,223	30,145,467	14,197,701	101,751,275	81,238,391	405,655,295
2050	23,490,423	40,112,637	29,393,295	19,041,041	112,037,396	88,546,973	439,010,253

Source: From "Administration on Aging (AoA). Projected Future Growth of the Older Population." Published by Administration for Community Living © 2000.

The United States has experienced several economic and social shifts that have impacted the older adult population in the last few decades. The **Great Recession of 2007** caused, among other things, forced retirement and unanticipated layoffs of many older adults within the workforce. In addition, changes in the U.S. and global economic landscape resulted in many individuals approaching retirement in economically vulnerable positions as companies shifted away from offering lifelong and secure pensions and toward self-funded and less secure retirement strategies. Sharp increases in the cost of medical care, increased housing costs, and other complexities of life are also putting some older adults at risk of financial insecurity. Thus, the growth of the older adult population is having a significant impact on their economic, housing, medical, mental health, and even transportation needs; their families; and the communities in which they reside.

Additionally, changes in the U.S. family structure, such as the significant increase in divorce rates, have put some older adults, particularly women, in economically fragile positions. Other older adults are in the position of having to provide day care for their grandchildren and, in some cases, even are parenting their grandchildren. Thus, although some older adults will be able to take advantage of the many medical advances, healthier lifestyles, and increased opportunities for enjoying life, many others may not.

This chapter will explore the wide range of issues and challenges many in the older adult population experience in the United States, as well as explore some issues projected to be relevant in the future. The role of the human services professional will be explored as well, with a special focus on how the field of gerontology has changed in recent years, expanding the role of the human services professional in various practice settings.

DEVELOPMENTAL PERSPECTIVES OF OLDER ADULTHOOD

Learning Outcome 5.2   **Explore the stage of older adulthood within a developmental context**

Working with the older adult population warrants knowledge of older adult developmental theory. Adults do not go through systematic and uniform developmental stages in the same way that children do; thus, many developmental theories typically stop at early adulthood or lump all adult development into one category stretching from post-adolescence and beyond. One reason for this approach is that if development is conceptualized as involving the combined impact of physical, cognitive, and emotional development, then development must involve progression, such as children who push themselves from a crawl to a walk in their quest to explore their social worlds. Yet, once one has reached physical and cognitive maturity, this interplay between physical ability and emotional desire (where one dynamic serves as the incentive for the other) subsides, and the motivation to pursue a particular life course becomes based more on personal choice and internal motivation, making adult maturity anything but systematic or universal.

Most of us have heard about the infamous **midlife crisis** marking the entry into middle age, or **empty nesting**, the life transitions some women experience in response to their adult children leaving home. Regardless of the validity of the universality of such life events, it does seem reasonable to assume that individuals within a particular society will respond and adapt in similar ways to both internal and external demands and expectations placed on them by cultural mores and norms. For example, cultural expectations in the United States, such as marriage, parenting, employment, and home ownership, certainly have an impact on those in early and middle adulthood, just as retirement, increased physical problems, and widowhood will have an impact on those in later adulthood. Yet, because the options and choices available to adults are so broad, any developmental theory must be considered in more general and descriptive terms compared to the narrower and more prescriptive terms often used to evaluate and consider child developmental theories.

Erikson's Stages of Psychosocial Development

Erik Erikson (1959, 1966), a psychodynamic theorist who studied under Sigmund Freud (the father of psychoanalysis), developed a theory of psychosocial development, beginning with birth and ending with death. According to Erikson, each stage of development presented a unique challenge or crisis brought on by the combining forces of both physiological changes and psychosocial needs. Successfully resolving each developmental crisis resulted in being better prepared for the next stage of development. The eighth stage of Erikson's model is *integrity versus despair* and spans from the age of 65 to death. Although Erikson's theory is no longer considered universal in the sense that we cannot assume that all individuals progress through these stages in a uniform manner, his theory is useful as a lens to better understand the psychosocial experiences of the older adult population.

Erikson believed that adults over the age of 65 reflected on their lives, taking stock of their choices and the value of their various achievements. If this reflection results in a sense of contentment with their choices and life experiences, older adults will be more likely to accept death with a sense of integrity. But if they do not like the choices they made, the relationships they developed, and the wisdom they gained throughout their lives, they risk facing death with a sense of despair.

Because the successful navigation of each stage is dependent on the successful navigation of the preceding stages, Erikson believed that individuals who did not develop a sense of basic trust in others or in the world (Stage 1) struggled with developing a sense of personal autonomy (Stage 2), had difficulty developing any personal initiative (Stage 3) or a sense of accomplishment (Stage 4), and faced challenges in adolescence when attempting to discover a personal identity (Stage 5). This made it difficult to develop truly intimate relationships with others (Stage 6), leaving them incapable of offering true guidance and generativity to the younger generations (Stage 7), which meant they would be less likely to reflect back on their lives with a sense of contentment and satisfaction, and would likely face impending death with a deep sense of despair.

A ninth stage was added posthumously by Erikson's wife, Joan Erikson. That ninth stage was based on discussions she and her husband had prior to his death in recognition of the lengthening lifespan, as well as his notes from interviews (Erikson & Erikson, 1998). The ninth stage, *very old age* (despair and disgust versus integrity) pertains to those in their 80s and 90s, who are dealing with the reality of death in a way not experienced in previous generations. Joan Erikson cites the increasing isolation of the *old-old adult* as they deal with loss in numerous realms. She cites cultural implications common in many Western countries, noting that older adults are often marginalized and dismissed and no longer perceived as sources of life wisdom, but instead as burdens (Erikson & Erikson, 1998). This is an extremely challenging time, according to Joan Erikson, where the old-old adult must in some respects rework or confront earlier stages of development, with the negative outcome at times becoming more dominant. She argues that many cultural determinants are destructive forces, negating the "grand-generative" contributions adults in their 80s and 90s (and older) can make.

Tornstam's Theory of Gerotranscendence

Similar to Joan Erikson's conceptualization of grand-generativity is Tornstam's theory of **gerotranscendence**, which posits that the old-old transcend above their everyday realities toward a more cosmic connection with the universe. Tornstam (1994) describes the changes individuals experience from middle to older adulthood on emotional, cognitive, and physical levels as gerotranscendence (Tornstam, 1994). Tornstam's theory explores how an individual moves from a strong connection to the material world to transcending above material aspects of the world into a more existential approach to living. Tornstam describes how individuals progressing from midlife onward transition from an externalizing perspective, where they are focusing outward toward the world, to a more internally focused approach in life.

According to Tornstam (2003) there are three dimensions of transcendence. The first is the cosmic dimension, in which individuals change their notions of time and space, such as reorienting themselves to how they view life and death, ultimately accepting death with a sense of peace. The second dimension relates to "the self" where individuals increasingly move away from self-centeredness, transcending above a focus on the physical and move toward more altruism. The third dimension involves social and individual relationships, where relationships are viewed in a new light with new meaning, including developing new insights into the differences between "the self" (who they really are) and the roles they play in life (mother/father, son/daughter, friend, etc.), and the ability to rise above black-and-white thinking and embrace the gray in life (Degges-White, 2005).

There are key issues involved in the process of personal transcendence across the three dimensions (cosmic, self, and relationships with others). For instance, Degges-White cites the importance of counselors becoming personally comfortable with the concept of death within, so they can help their aging clients accept the inevitability of death without overwhelming fear and anxiety. With regard to transcendence in the "self" dimension, Degges-White describes how counselors can help their older clients conduct a "life review" where they seek to better understand and accept their life choices, thus finding a level of peace and self-acceptance about their choices and experiences, particularly the challenging and painful ones. The ultimate goal of counseling older adults using a gerotranscendence model is to assist older adults move toward increased self- and other-acceptance and wisdom in various dimensions and domains in life—in a sense, giving them permission to draw intrinsically inward as they let go of the more transitory dimensions of life and move toward a more existential existence.

Daniel Levinson's Theory of Middle Adulthood

Daniel Levinson (1978, 1996) is probably one of the most well-known adult developmental theorists, having developed a lifespan theory extending from birth through death. Levinson wrote two books explaining his theory, *The Seasons of a Man's Life* (1978) and *The Seasons of a Woman's Life* (1996), where he focused on middle adulthood. What is rather revolutionary about his theory is his argument that adults do continue to grow and develop on an age-related timetable. Levinson noticed that adults in the latter half of their lives are more reflective, and as they approach a point in their lives where they have more time behind them than ahead of them, this reflection intensifies. Levinson also believes that individuals progress through periods of stability followed by shorter stages of transition (and instability). The themes in his theory most relevant to human services professionals include the notion of life reflection—the taking stock of one's life choices and accomplishments, the need to be able to give back to society, which encompasses an acknowledgment that at some point the goal in life is not solely to focus on one's own driving needs, but to give back to others and to one's community through the sharing of gained wisdom and mentoring.

Finally, Levinson's belief that as people age they need to become more intrinsically focused rather than externally based, is equally relevant. Consider the man who in his 30s gains self-esteem and a sense of identity through working 80 hours per week and running marathons. How will this same man define himself when he is 70 years old and no longer has the physical stamina or agility to perform these activities? Levinson believes that a developmental task for aging adults is to become more internally anchored, more intrinsic in their self-identity, lest they develop a sense of despair and depression later in life when they are no longer able to live up to their previous youthful expectations.

SUCCESSFUL AND ACTIVE AGING

Learning Outcome 5.3   **Identify key aspects of successful and active aging**

In light of the growing concern about the declining physical and mental health of older adults, the concept of **successful aging** is more important than ever. The concept of successful aging has been around since the early 1960s (Havighurst, 1961), but was developed as

Pearson eText

Video Example 5.2

In this video researchers discuss factors relating successful aging. How can the results of this study influence human services agencies serving the older adult population? https://www.youtube.com/watch?v=UgaPdSWEIlQ

© RAWPIXEL.COM / SHUTTERSTOCK

Older adults who are physically active age more successfully.

a model by researchers Rowe and Kahn in 1987 and further developed in the late 1990s (Rowe & Kahn, 1997). According to Rowe and Kahn's earlier model of successful aging (called the MacArthur Model), successful aging encompasses three components: (1) having low levels of disease and related disability, (2) having high levels of mental and physical functioning and (3) having high levels of social engagement. While Rowe and Kahn's earlier model has been criticized for not including more variables (such as spirituality and more medical literature) (Crowther et al., 2002), they remain notable for being some of the first researchers to suggest that aging poorly was not inevitable.

A lot of the research on successful aging examines individuals who age better than others to determine what differences might account for their success, as well as identifying variables at play in helping individuals live healthier lives longer. Some of the variables identified in research studies that have a positive impact on the aging process include maintaining a moderately high physical activity level; remaining socially engaged, including keeping active with hobbies, social events, and regular exercise (Gopinath et al., 2018; Hsu, 2007; Warr et al., 2004); and having a positive sense of spirituality (Crowther et al., 2002).

Research clearly shows that most adults prefer to remain in their home as they age (a concept called "aging in place"), and yet this is difficult for many older adults because of physical limitations that contribute to social disengagement (Johnson & Appold, 2017). For example, few older adults play on intramural softball teams due to physical limitations, and even something like poor night vision can keep an older adult from being able to hop in the car and visit family. Employment provides most people with the greatest opportunities for social interaction, and when individuals retire, a significant portion of their social life is lost along with their career. Thus, many older people naturally begin withdrawing from the world, both physically and socially, in response to diminished capability and opportunity. And with such disengagement comes an increase in physical and emotional problems such as depression and loneliness (Singh & Misra, 2009).

A recent study seems to indicate that good psychological health is one of the most important factors in ensuring good quality of life in later years (Bowling & Iliffe, 2011). For instance, the ability of older adults to rely on their psychological resources, such as good **self-efficacy** and **resilience**, was more strongly linked to successful and **active aging** than were biological and social factors. This does not mean that good physical health and an active social life aren't important, but as Tornstam (2005) and Degges-White (2005) suggest, older adults who can mentally and emotionally transcend the physical and social limitations inherent in the aging process seem to have a better quality of life compared to older adults who lack these psychological resources.

Consider an individual's level of psychological resilience, which encompasses one's coping strategies that can be relied upon during challenging times. Many older adults must not only face increased health problems and physical limitations but also deal with multiple losses as they begin to lose friends, siblings, and even their spouses to death. Many older adults may also need to move from their longtime home into residential care or the home of a family member, and the loss of independence can have a devastating effect on their ability to optimize opportunities for active engagement. Those with better coping mechanisms, psychological resilience, and optimism will be able to manage these multiple losses in a healthier manner, even perhaps finding some existential meaning in facing these losses with a sense of wisdom and acceptance despite the deep pain and sense of powerlessness many older adults may feel. Those who have a lifetime of poor coping mechanisms, who are not particularly resilient and who tend toward pessimism, will likely fare much worse.

As the older adult population has increased in numbers, the government has shifted its priorities and developed programs aimed at long-term health care needs, with a particular focus on vulnerable populations such as women, ethnic minorities, and older adults living in rural communities. It is difficult to define who is particularly vulnerable within the older adult population because in many senses, *all* older adults could conceivably be considered vulnerable to social, economic, physical, and psychological harm or exploitation simply by virtue of their advancing age and corresponding dependency needs. But many gerontologists classify various subpopulations as more vulnerable for various reasons, thus warranting increased attention. For instance, successful aging has been linked to good economic status, good health care, relatively low stress levels, and high levels of social connections. A 2004 study also showed a link between good health and financial stability, finding that Whites tend to have greater economic wealth and better health than members of the Black and Latina/o populations (Lum, 2004).

Other research has shown how institutionalized racism can lead to feelings of being invisible, stress, depression, and ultimately despair as the person experiences a sense of futility in combating a lifetime of discrimination and White privilege (Franklin, 2019; Franklin et al., 2006; Graham et al., 2016). These are all issues that social workers address when working with the older adult population, warranting an awareness of the various ways that aging impacts different racial and ethnic minority groups.

Another group warranting increased attention are lesbian, gay, bisexual, transgender, queer/questioning (LGBTQ) older adults. These populations are not counted in the U.S. Census, so social scientists must rely on community-based studies. LGBTQ older adults experience higher rates of mental illness and psychosocial challenges such as loneliness due to social isolation. This is particularly true for lesbians, who are more likely to be single and childless than their cisgender counterparts (Perone et al., 2020). Another issue to consider is how many members of the LBGTQ community are dealing with effects of cumulative discrimination, rooted in an era when the majority of Americans (and the U.S. government) conflated same-sex attractions and sexual minorities with pedophilia or worse. Consider "Boys Beware," the 1955 public service announcement cosponsored by the police department and Unified School District of Inglewood, California, that warns the public against the dangers of homosexuality. The video featured a "homosexual" man who cruises adolescent boys playing basketball and on the beach, and finally coaxes one into his car. The narrator explains that this mistake cost the boy

Pearson eText

Video Example 5.3

In this video human services providers meet with a State Representative to advocate for LGBTQ older adults. What are some of the reasons why human services professionals are effective at advocating on a policy level?

his life, intimating that the man assaulted and then murdered the teen. Many older adults lived through this era and internalized these negative stereotypes of sexual minorities.

In light of the overt attack on sexual minorities, the "coming out" experiences of older adults are vastly different than many sexual minorities today. This is particularly true of those older adults born between 1926 and 1945, often referred to as the "Silent Generation." Many of these adults may keep their sexual orientation or gender identity hidden from health care providers and assisted living personnel, which can have a detrimental effect on their physical and mental health (Yarns et al., 2016). Coming out to primary care physicians and providers involved in end-of-life care can be challenging for members of the LGBTQ community, and when social workers are aware of these common dynamics they can better serve this population and serve as their advocates in a range of situations and life domains (Law et al., 2015).

COMMON PSYCHOSOCIAL CHALLENGES IN OLDER ADULTHOOD

Learning Outcome 5.4   Examine major challenges facing many older adults

There are many challenges facing the older adult population in the United States, many of which have a direct impact on the aging process. Some examples include age-related discrimination (ageism), economic disadvantage impacting housing stability (and quality of housing), challenges associated with retirement, depression, dementia, and elder abuse. Of particular concern to human services professionals and others working in the field of gerontology are the populations that are disproportionally impacted by these challenges, such as some ethnic minority populations, women, and veterans, particularly those experiencing a lifetime of economic disadvantage.

Ageism

Ask some typical young Americans what they think it's like to be a man in his seventies, and they may well tell you that an average 75-year-old man is in poor health, drifts off to sleep at a moment's notice, talks of nothing but the distant past, and unproductively sits in a rocking chair, rocking back and forth all day long. They might even throw in a comment or two about his general grouchy disposition. Ask if older adults still have the desire for sexual intimacy, and you might get a good hearty laugh in response. However, this description of older adults is a myth based on deeply entrenched negative stereotypes of older adults and can serve as a foundation of a form of prejudice and discrimination of older adults called ageism.

The term *ageism* was first coined by Robert Butler (1989), chairman of a congressional committee on aging in 1968. He described ageism in a similar vein as racism and sexism, where older adults are negatively stereotyped on a systematic basis and are then discriminated against on that basis. Butler theorized that at the root of this negative stereotyping was perhaps a fear of growing old. Ageism typically involves any attitude or behavior that negatively categorizes older adults based either on partial truth (often taken out of context) or on outright myths of the aging process. Such myths often describe old age as inherently involving poor health, senility, depression, irritability, a sexless life, a lack of vitality, an inability to learn new things, and a loss of productivity (Thornton, 2002).

Gerontologists caution that the promotion of such negative stereotypes of old age not only trivializes older adults but also risks displacing the older adult population as communities undervalue them based on the perception that older adults are a drain on society. A further risk of ageism is that older adults may internalize negative stereotypes held by the majority population, creating a **self-fulfilling prophecy** of sorts, in much the same way that some marginalized ethnic minority groups internalize historic negative perceptions held by the majority population (Snyder, 2001; Thornton, 2002).

Old age hasn't always been viewed negatively in the United States. In fact, earlier in the 20th century, societal attitudes reflected a relatively positive view of older adults and the aging experience. Older adults were respected for their wisdom and valued for their experience; thus, they were not perceived as a drain on society. Yet, sometime around the mid-1900s, as life expectancy began to grow in response to safer lifestyles and medical advances, professionals such as physicians, psychologists, and gerontologists began discussing older adults in terms of their burden rather than their contributions (Hirshbein, 2001).

Many social psychologists and gerontologists cite the media as contributing to the creation of negative stereotypes of older adults and the aging process, noting the consistent negative portrayal of older adults in television shows and commercials as dimwitted individuals who live in the past. And yet, the results of a study conducted in 2004 did not support these concerns. The study's authors reviewed television commercials from the 1950s through the 1990s and found that media depictions of older adults have been generally positive during this time period and actually improved in the latter two decades (Miller et al., 2004). This study is not only good news, but also highlights the power of the media and how it can be used to confront existing negative stereotypes as older adults are cast in active and vibrant roles.

NBC's hidden camera show *Off Their Rockers*, starring Betty White, is an excellent example of a television show that confronts negative stereotypes of older adulthood. The premise of the show was similar to other popular shows about pranks being played on unsuspecting people in front of a hidden camera. The twist with this show was that the pranks involved scenarios designed not just to confront stereotypes, but to shatter them with humor. Each episode began with a "warning" screen informing viewers that the show involved senior citizens who played pranks on real unsuspecting young people. The theme song was "We're Not Going to Take It." Betty White then welcomed viewers, describing the show as one where seniors prefer to age disgracefully.

Most pranks involved stark contradictions, each beginning with an expected stereotype of an older adult, and concluding with something that was unexpected—a nun cruising down the street in an electric wheelchair (expected), swearing at people to get out of her way (unexpected); an older woman asking a younger woman on the street for help with her smartphone (expected), and then asking her to help decipher sexts from her senior citizen boyfriend (unexpected); an old blind man with a red-tipped cane asking a younger man for assistance walking across a path (expected), and then getting into his convertible and driving off at a fast speed (unexpected); and finally, Betty White in several skits talking about the importance of remaining active in later years (expected), and then walking away with a shirtless younger man (unexpected). What was so effective about this show is that it used humor to confront negative stereotypes about older adults (and confront them it does!).

It's very important that human services professionals explore their own misconceptions and negative stereotypes of older adults and the aging process, such as assuming that older adults are incapable of learning something new, gaining new insights, resolving old conflicts, and growing emotionally. Since research shows that internalized negative stereotypes about aging can increase feelings of loneliness and dependency, practitioners are wise to address any misconceptions they personally have prior to working with the older adult population (Coudin & Alexopoulos, 2010). Practices such as talking down to older adult clients and not directly addressing difficult issues based on a belief that the older client lacks the capacity to understand will undoubtedly affect the level of investment the client makes in the counseling relationship. This type of behavior on the part of the practitioner can also encourage a self-fulfilling prophecy within older adult clients, where they begin to act the part of the incompetent, unproductive, and cognitively dull individual. Making positive assumptions about older adult clients will increase the possibility of bringing out the most authentic and dynamic aspects of older adult clients.

Older Adult Housing

Residents of an assisted living facility tend their gardens in wheelchair accessible containers.

The majority of older adults in the United States remain in their homes, often alone, throughout their senior years, which is a trend that is relatively unique to the United States. In most countries around the world, older adults live with family members who provide continuity and care (Ausubel, 2020). An increasing number of older adults in the United States, though, need to move out of their homes when they reach a certain level of physical and/or cognitive decline because, while medical technology may be allowing people to live longer, that doesn't always equate with living long and healthy lives. Older adults who need additional care may move into the home of a family member or they may move into a retirement community that offers independence and facility-offered services to meet their needs, such as shuttle services and handicapped-accessible facilities.

Private residential communities for the older adult population are typically quite costly, though, with the price increasing substantially in relation to the services provided. As a consequence, many older adults find themselves in situations where they cannot afford the exorbitant cost of many private communities. Government-subsidized senior housing, such as the Section 202 Supportive Housing for the Elderly program, Section 8 Housing for the general population (choice vouchers and project-based), and Section 515 for rural communities, can make housing costs more affordable for low-income older adult populations by providing a subsidy directly to older adults in the form of tax credits, loans, or rental vouchers to housing communities, which then pass on this discount to residents. There are several problems with government subsidy programs, though, including a lack of available units and the inappropriateness of many units for older adults due to location and condition.

A 2003 longitudinal study that followed 1,200 older adults in their transition from independent living to age-restricted housing found that older adults who transitioned to more-expensive communities fared the best with regard to physical health and overall life satisfaction, while those who transitioned to government-subsidized housing programs fared the worst. Although the study investigators acknowledged that levels of life satisfaction might be related to a cumulative effect of a lifetime of poverty, they concluded that, overall, the quality of housing had a direct relationship to life satisfaction (Krout, 2003).

Housing Insecurity among Older Adults

The story of Rosemary and Donald in the opening vignette highlights the issue of homelessness in the older adult population. Older adults are at a lower risk for homelessness than other age groups, but homelessness in the older adult population is a growing concern because the percentage is expected to grow as the baby boomer generation ages (Gonyea et al., 2010). Additionally, for years the problem of homelessness among the older population has been for the most part ignored by policy makers and legislators, rendering this population somewhat invisible (Gonyea et al., 2010).

The common causes of homelessness in the older adult population include many of the same underlying factors as in the general population, such as a lack of affordable housing, a lack of employment opportunities, mental illness, substance abuse, a history of adverse life experiences, bad childhoods, a history of incarceration, low educational attainment and underemployment, and a reduction in social services support (Fernald, 2014; Glynn & Fox, 2019; U.S. Conference of Mayors, 2016). Research shows that about half of the older adult homeless population experienced their first bout of homelessness after the age of 50, having lived relatively conventional lives up until that point.

This group presents with a different picture—most homeless adults over age 50 had been spending more than 50% of their income on housing, which increased their risk of homelessness. Most also experienced chronic illnesses that when combined with a job loss or other adverse life experience placed them in a financially vulnerable position (Brown et al., 2016). Ethnic and racial minorities were also at higher risk of homelessness later in life due to historic disadvantage and the loss of affordable housing (Fernald, 2014). One marked difference between younger homeless cohorts and older adults who did not experience homelessness until after 50 is that in the latter group substance abuse does not appear to be a risk factor for homelessness. What this means from a social service perspective is that less-intensive intervention strategies would likely be effective with this population (Brown et al., 2016).

Gaining more insights into the differences between younger homeless and older homeless populations becomes important when considering programs designed to assist the older adult homeless population. And yet, while some research has been conducted that indicates several differences, including older adult populations having significantly lower incidences of substance abuse and domestic violence, more research is needed to better understand the patterns of older adult homelessness, including frequency and duration of homeless episodes, the nature of their needs, and their patterns of service utilization. Any human services programs designed to assist the older adult subgroups with housing issues need to focus on issues related specifically to the older adult population, such as insufficient income, health concerns, low-income housing needs, and supportive services designed for an older adult population.

Retirement

Another issue impacting the older adult population is the notion of retirement—the practice of leaving one's employment to permanently enter a phase of chosen nonemployment. The concept of retirement is so common to the 21st century that it rarely needs explanation. The most common conceptualization of retirement involves an employee permanently surrendering his or her position at approximately 65 years of age and drawing on a pension or retirement account that has likely been accruing for decades.

Of course, there are numerous variations on this theme—some people never fully retire, choosing instead to dabble in part-time work, and some people work in fields that have mandatory retirement ages, such as the airline industry, which requires all pilots retire at the age of 65. For others, retirement is simply not an option due to financial constraints. The traditional notion of retirement is an experience that only those with higher incomes can afford; thus, it would be inappropriate to assume that everyone in the workforce has accrued a pension sizeable enough to permit them to live on for years. But despite the range of retirement experiences, certain generalizations can be made about the retirement experience for the majority of those living in the United States during the 21st century.

Robert Atchley (1976) was one of the first researchers who attempted to describe the retirement experience for men and women. He identified five distinct yet overlapping stages that most retirees progress through when they formally retire:

1.   The honeymoon phase: Retirees embrace retirement and all their newfound freedom in an optimistic but often unrealistic manner.

2.   Disenchantment: Retirees become disillusioned with what they thought retirement was going to be like and get discouraged with what often feels like too much time on their hands.

3.   Reorientation: Retirees develop a more realistic view of retirement with regard to both increased opportunities and increased constraints.

4.   Stability: Retirees adjust to retirement.

5.   Termination: Retirees eventually lose independence due to physical and cognitive decline.

There has been some controversy about whether retirees actually progress through such distinct stages or whether there is just too much of a range of experiences among retirees in the United States to categorize experiences in a **linear stage theory**. A study by

Reitzes and Mutran (2004) appears to support Atchley's stage theory, finding that retirees experience a temporary lift right after retiring (for about 6 months), but then develop an increasingly negative attitude after about the 12-month mark, with some retirees starting to experience increased optimism after about 2 years. The study also found that an individual's level of self-esteem preretirement seemed to have an effect on their overall mental health after retirement, with those who had higher levels of self-esteem faring better.

A more recent study on postretirement dynamics seems to support some of Atchley, and Reitzes and Mutran's findings, while refuting others. The study, which was funded by the National Institute on Aging, found that men and women who continued to work for a period of time after retirement, on a part-time or temporary basis (called bridge employment), had much better physical and psychological quality of life during their later years. This would seem to indicate that sudden and complete retirement without any transition period may have negative consequences for an older adult's physical and mental health. Interestingly, the positive effects gained from **bridge employment** existed regardless of the retiree's preretirement mental and physical health status (Zhan et al., 2009).

Because nearly 50% of the U.S. population is now over the age of 50, the implications of retirement preparation and adjustment to retirement for the human services field cannot be ignored. Human services professionals will likely come into contact with retired or retiring adults in many different settings. Thus, it is important to realize that impending retirement can become an issue for someone even in middle adulthood.

Finally, **race** and gender have a significant effect on retirement experiences. Research has shown that women and many ethnic minority groups often have different attitudes and experiences surrounding retirement issues due to disparity in income and education levels (McNamara & Williamson, 2004). Thus, the human services professional must understand that most factors affecting a client's retirement experience are going to be influenced by the client's gender and racial status. In fact, in many senses, the notion that one voluntarily leaves employment for an older adulthood filled with golf and travel is a very White male conceptualization. This conceptualization of retirement also is based on the notion that retirement is necessary to allow room for younger generations to enter the workforce. Contemporary realities are shifting notions of retirement, even for White male workers, driven by changes in the pension industry, shifts in employment trends, and the impact of technology on retirement (Czaja, 2020).

Grandparents Parenting

The practice of grandparents raising grandchildren (known as grandfamilies) is not new, but it has increased dramatically over the past several years, signaling many challenges in U.S. society that have emerged since the 1970s. In response to an increase in grandparents becoming primary caregivers to their grandchildren, beginning in 2000 the U.S. Census includes questions regarding grandparents residing with grandchildren, including whether they had primary responsibility for them and what length of time they had acted in a parental role (i.e., revealing whether the situation is temporary or permanent).

As of 2017 (the most recent data available) the U.S. Census estimated that approximately 7.2 million U.S. households (about 20% of the population) had grandparents co-residing with grandchildren under the age of 18 (called intergenerational co-residents). Among these households, about 2.7 million grandparents had primary caregiving responsibilities for about 2.6 million children (Lent & Otto, 2018; U.S. Bureau of the Census, 2014; Wiltz, 2016).

There are three primary issues of concern in relation to grandparents parenting their grandchildren: (1) these households face increased risk of disadvantage (Glaser et al., 2018; Pilkauskas & Dunifon, 2016), (2) grandchildren raised by their grandparents face increased risk of behavioral and emotional problems (Ellis & Simmons, 2014; Ge & Adesman, 2017; Smith & Palmieri, 2007), and (3) the number of grandparents parenting their grandchildren is steadily increasing among all racial groups, although ethnic minority populations experience increased levels of poverty (Cohn & Passel, 2018; Dunifon et al., 2014; Ellis & Simmons, 2014).

Parenting one or more children is challenging even for the most financially, mentally, and physically fit couple, but research shows that most grandparents raising their grandchildren are not only battling normal everyday age-related fatigue, but a range of other challenges as well. The majority of grandparents with primary parenting responsibilities for their grandchildren are female-headed households with low incomes (U.S. Bureau of the Census, 2017). Also, about 25% have an age-related disability (Lent & Otto, 2018), just over one third have not graduated from high school, and about half of parenting grandmothers and one third of parenting grandfathers are unemployed, which adds significant economic stress to an already stressful situation (Glaser et al., 2018; Pilkauskas & Dunifon, 2016).

There are many reasons for the increase in grandparents taking on the primary role of parenting their grandchildren, including an increase in divorce rates, child abuse and parental incarceration (Smith & Palmieri, 2007), and mental illness (Generations United, 2016), but a chief reason for recent increases in this trend relates to substance abuse, most notably the opioid crisis (Generations United, 2018; Lent & Otto, 2018). The opioid crisis has impacted thousands of families across the country, with the rate of people in their childbearing years who overdose increasing sharply between 2015 and 2016 (Hedegaard et al., 2017). One result of this increase is an equally sharp increase in the number of children entering the foster care system and being placed with relatives, most frequently their grandparents under kinship care arrangements. In fact, a 2019 U.S. Census report found an increase in grandparents parenting their grandchildren in the five states with the highest opioid prescription rates, indicating that when parents become incapacitated by an opioid addiction, grandparents are stepping in to help (Anderson, 2019).

Grandparent caregivers tend to be younger, belong to ethnic minorities, be poor with low education levels, and suffer from depression. Additionally, grandparent caregivers in the Southeast and in urban areas have the highest levels of poverty and the lowest levels of education (Simmons & Dye, 2003; Whitley & Kelley, 2007). Even though older Black grandmothers are disproportionately represented in custodial grandparent arrangements, a recent research study indicates that older grandparents may experience less emotional strain related to their primary parenting role than do younger grandparents, likely related to their increased ability to manage stressful life situations (Conway et al., 2011).

Ethnic minority children are far more likely to be raised by a grandparent than White children, with Black children in the Southeastern states having a significantly higher rate of living with custodial grandparents than children in other regions in the United States. Black grandparents are far likelier to experience poverty (despite being in the workforce). They are also far likelier to be underinsured and experience greater physical and emotional stressors (Whitley & Kelley, 2007). There are several reasons why grandparents become surrogate parents, but the chief reasons include the following:

1. Substance abuse
2. Maltreatment
3. Poverty
4. Incarceration
5. Mental and physical illness
6. Abandonment
7. Divorce
8. Military deployment (Davey et al., 2016).

The issues facing grandparents raising grandchildren are complex, involving emotional as well as financial, legal, and physical challenges. Many grandparent caregivers are forced to live in limbo, not knowing how long they will remain responsible for their grandchildren, particularly when the biological parents are either in jail or suffering from drug addiction that prevents them from resuming their primary parenting role. The choice to act as a surrogate parent is in many instances made in a time of crisis. Thus, older adults who may have been planning their retirement for years often find themselves in a position to either take on this parenting role in the face of the situation that rendered the biological parents unable to continue parenting or allow their grandchildren to enter the foster care system. Parenting younger children has its unique challenges, but often comes with some level of social support, at least within the primary school system, but this is often not the case with older children, particularly adolescents.

Parenting adolescents often presents significant challenges for grandparents, particularly when the grandparent caregivers are advanced in years. Parenting adolescents can be an exhausting endeavor for the young or middle-aged parent, but imagine the demands placed on someone who is an older adult, who has limited physical capacity and even more limited financial means. Adolescents who have endured significant loss through death or abandonment, have been raised in abusive homes, or have been raised by parents who abuse drugs or are serving time in prison may act out emotionally and even physically, putting even greater stress on an already fragile family system.

Human services professionals may enter a grandparent-led family system in numerous ways—they could be the school social worker or counselor working with the children, they might be the child welfare caseworker assigned to assist the grandparent who is serving as a kinship foster care parent, or they might work for a human services agency offering outreach services to grandparent caregivers. The generalist skills human services professionals must have are relatively expansive due to the nature of the work they will likely be doing within the family system. These include knowledge of adolescent development, cultural competence, knowledge of a range of psychosocial issues ranging from effective parenting styles to knowledge of grief and loss processes, and excellent case management skills.

Dementia

Dementia is a progressive degenerative illness experienced during old age that impairs brain function and cognitive ability. Dementia is an umbrella term encompassing numerous disorders, but the two most common forms of dementia are **Alzheimer's disease** and **multi-infarct dementia** (small strokes in the brain). Dementia involves the comprehensive shutting down of all bodily systems. In general, the symptoms include progressive memory loss, increased difficulty concentrating, a steady decrease in problem-solving skills and judgment capability, confusion, hallucinations and delusions, altered sensations or perceptions, impaired recognition of everyday objects and familiar people, altered sleep patterns, motor system impairment, inability to maintain ADL (such as dressing oneself), agitation, anxiety, and depression. Ultimately, the dementia sufferer enters a complete vegetative state prior to death.

According to a Pew Research Internet Report (2018), about 37% of adults over the age of 65 use at least one social media platform, such as Facebook, compared with only 2% in 2005. This increase has been driven in large part by an increase in older adults using tablets (compared to laptops or desktop computers). Another study suggests that retired older adults who use the Internet are about one-third less likely to experience depression (Cotten et al., 2014). And finally, a 2013 study found that adults between the ages of 65 and 91 years of age improved their cognitive functioning by about 25% if they used Facebook on a daily basis in an interactive manner by creating online social connections (compared with older adults who used Facebook in a noninteractive manner and those who did not engage in any online activity). The results of the study suggest a possible link between online social interaction and cognitive functioning (Myhre, 2013). The power of social media, when used in a healthy manner, can have the strongest implications for those older adults who are socially isolated due to geography or physical limitations.

Human services professionals may work directly with clients diagnosed with dementia or with the caregiver (typically a spouse or adult child) if they work in a practice setting that serves the older adult population. However, dealing with dementia as a clinical issue can occur in any practice setting because any client may have a relative suffering from dementia and may therefore need counseling and perhaps even case management. Consider the practitioner who assists clients in managing an ailing parent. The practitioner may need to help the client with questions about whether the parent is suffering from cognitive impairment, with grieving the slow loss of the parent they love, and with support in making difficult decisions such as determining when their parent can no longer live alone. Or, consider the school social worker who is counseling a student whose grandfather has recently been diagnosed with Alzheimer's disease. The pressure on the entire family system will affect the student in numerous ways—academically, emotionally, perhaps even physically—and may even magnify any existing issues with which the student is currently struggling.

Elder Abuse

The National Center on Elder Abuse (2018) defines elder abuse as any "knowing, intentional, or negligent act by a caregiver or any other person that causes harm or a serious risk of harm to a vulnerable adult." The specific definition of elder abuse varies from state to state, but in general elder abuse can include physical, emotional, or sexual abuse; neglect and abandonment; or financial exploitation. Older adults are at an increased risk of abuse due to factors such as their physical frailty, dependence, social isolation, and any existence of cognitive impairment.

Elder abuse was not legally defined until 1987, when it was directly addressed in an amendment of the **Older Americans Act**. While it's difficult to determine with any level of accuracy how many older adults are being abused and/or neglected, reports of elder abuse have increased significantly over the last several years. For instance, in 1986 there were 117,000 reports of elder abuse nationwide, and by 1996 the number had more than doubled, reaching 293,000 reported cases (Tatara, 1997). By the year 2000 the number of elder abuse reports had risen to an alarming 47,281 (Acierno et al., 2010) and by 2004 that number had increased to 565,747 (Teaster, 2006). Currently, about one in four older adults are at risk of being abused (Nagaratnam & Nagaratnam, 2019).

Homes leveled by the Camp Fire line the Ridgewood Mobile Home Park retirement community in Paradise, Calif. Northern California authorities arrested a woman they say scammed $63,100 from a 75-year-old who lost a home in the wildfire in 2018. The Butte County Sheriff's Office announced Tuesday, Nov. 5, 2019, the arrest of 29-year-old Brenda Rose Asbury for elder abuse, embezzlement and grand theft.

© NOAH BERGER / AP / SHUTTERSTOCK

One reason for the rise in abuse reports is that the newest figures include not only abuse in domestic settings, but also abuse in institutional settings. Despite the more comprehensive data collection methods, there is no escaping the fact that elder abuse is increasing within the United States (Teaster, 2006). Elder abuse is expected to continue to rise in the coming years due to the increased lifespan and the resultant increase in chronic illnesses, changing family patterns, and the complexity involved with contemporary caregiving.

Sixty percent of all reported abuse victims are women, and 65% of all abuse victims are White, more than 60% of abuse incidences occurred in domestic settings, and about 8% of abuse incidences occurred in institutionalized settings. Family members were the most commonly cited perpetrators, including both spouses and adult children (Teaster, 2000). A recent study found that elder abuse and neglect were associated with being single (separated or divorced), being poor, being in poor health, and having a disability. The study also found that Hispanics were less likely to be abused and/or neglected (Burnes et al., 2015).

In March 2010, the Elder Justice Act of 2009 was passed and signed into law by President Obama as part of the Patient Protection and Affordable Care Act (ACA). The act sets forth numerous provisions for addressing the abuse, neglect, and exploitation of older adults, with both preventative and responsive measures. For instance, the legislation provides grants for a number of training programs focusing on prevention of abuse and exploitation of older adults; provides measures for expanding long-term care services, including a long-term care ombudsman program; establishes mandatory reporting requirements for abuse against older adults occurring in long-term care facilities; and includes provisions for creating national advisory councils (National Health Forum Policy, 2010).

Every state is required to have an **adult protective services agency**. There is significant variation among states with regard to how abuse is to be reported and investigated. Some states have separate agencies handling elder abuse, and some combine the protection of older adults with the protection of disabled adults of all ages. Despite increases in reporting requirements, elder abuse is still considered to be underreported not only due to the range of reporting requirements, but also due to the hidden nature of elder abuse (Rosenthal Gelman et al., 2018). It is for this reason that it's essential that those working in the human services field be aware of the elder abuse reporting laws and requirements in their state in addition to the early signs of abuse and neglect, including financial abuse.

Caregiver burnout is one of the primary risk factors of elder abuse. The most common scenario involves a loving family member who becomes intensely frustrated by the seemingly impossible task of caring for a spouse or parent with a chronic illness such as dementia. Providing continuous care of someone with Alzheimer's disease, for example, can be frustrating, provoking an abusive response from someone with no history of abusive behavior. One of the most effective intervention strategies can be a caregiver support group. These groups are typically facilitated by a social worker or other human services provider and focus on providing caregivers, many of whom are older adults themselves, a safe place to express their frustrations, sadness, and other feelings related to caring for their dependent older adult loved one.

LEGISLATION AFFECTING OLDER ADULTS

In anticipation of the increase in the older adult population as well as an increase in the needs and complex nature of the issues facing many older adults, the *Older Americans Act* was signed into federal law in 1965. This act led to the creation of the **Administration on Aging**, which funds grants to states for various community and social service programs for age-related research and the development of social service agencies called **Area Agencies on Aging (AAA)** operating at the local level. The Administration on Aging also acts as a clearinghouse, disseminating information about a number of issues affecting the older adult population in the United States.

Several additional federal laws have been passed in recent years that have or likely will have a significant impact on the older adult population. The American Tax Relief Act of 2012 (Pub. L. No. 112-240), signed by President Obama on January 2, 2013, mandated the creation of a 15-member commission to examine the issue of long-term care on a national level. The goal of the commission was to develop a plan for the implementation and funding of a high-quality and coordinated national long-term care system serving older adults and people with disabilities. The Commission on Long-Term Care submitted a report to Congress in September 2013 that included a projection that the number of adults needing long-term care in the United States would increase from 12 million in 2012 to 27 million n 2050. The report outlined a number of challenges in meeting this need but made a case for the urgency in doing so, which the authors asserted warranted immediate action (U.S. Senate, 2013). To date, it's unclear what steps have been taken to address the projected shortage of long-term care facilities, including nursing homes and skilled nursing units serving older adults, although a 2019 report cited a severe workforce shortage in long-term care facilities, noting that this issue remains one in need of an aggressive federal response (Bradford, 2019).

The *Patient Protection and Affordable Care Act* (Pub. L. No. 111-148) was signed into law on March 23, 2010. This broad-based legislation is the first federal law designed to overhaul the U.S. health care system. The legislation was phased in beginning in 2010, with full implementation in 2014. Benefits for seniors include automatic discounts of up to 50% on prescription drugs covered by Medicare Part D, an end to insurance carrier-imposed limits on lifetime care, access to no-cost prevention and wellness services, protection of

Medicare benefits prohibiting future cuts, better coordination between different Medicare programs, and legislative efforts to prohibit Medicare fraud and waste. The law also provides for grants to educational institutions providing training for direct care workers through the *Direct Care Training Grants Program*, as well as grant programs providing incentives for entering the field of geriatrics, including those in the human services fields (Lewis-Burke Associates, 2011).

The ACA has undergone some changes under the Trump administration to weaken the legislation, such as the decision to halt the government's

NEW YORK - 11 NOV 2016: The belongings of a homeless US Army veteran on a park bench outside the opening ceremony in Madison Square Park before the annual Americas Parade on Veterans Day in Manhattan.

payment of subsidies for those with low incomes. The ACA in its original form used a standard of affordability, which specified that the cost of health care should not exceed 8.16% of an individual's adjusted gross income, which means that those who earned up to 400% of the federal poverty level could receive a subsidy.

The ending of government subsidies won't affect those with incomes under the federal poverty level or those who qualify for Medicare, but Trump's decision significantly impacted those who earn incomes above the poverty level. In fact, those between the ages 50 and 65 who are low income, but not considered to be statistically poor (according to federal guidelines), have been affected the most (Jones et al., 2018). A recent report indicates that adults near 60 who do not yet qualify for Medicare, must earn an additional $46,658 to be able to afford health insurance (eHealth, 2017).

PRACTICE SETTINGS SERVING OLDER ADULTS

Learning Outcome 5.5   **Explore the roles and functions of human services professionals working in practice settings serving the older adult population**

Working with older adults is gaining in popularity within the human services field, driven in part by an increased focus on gerontology in human services educational programs. For human services professionals wishing to provide direct services to the older adult population, a wide array of choices in practice settings awaits them. AAAs, discussed earlier in this chapter, often serve as human services agencies offering direct service to the older adult community on a local level. Generally, these agencies offer a multitude of services for older adults, such as nutrition programs, services for homebound older adults, programs for low-income minority older adults, and other programs focusing on the needs of older adults within the local community. Many AAAs also act as a referral source for other services in the area. For instance, the Mid-Florida AAAs offer programs for those suffering from Alzheimer's disease (including caregiver respite), a toll-free elder hotline that links older adults in the area with resources, an emergency home energy

Pearson eText

Video Example 5.4

In this video a human services supervisor and a colleague discuss some upcoming funding cuts to the agency's adult day care program. Since most agencies are reliant at least in part on government funding, what are some skills that human services professionals can develop to adapt to changes in program funding?

Pearson eText

Video Example 5.5

In this video the human services provider explains to a client the potential impact of funding cuts on the adult day care program that the client's elderly parent attends. What skills does the provider illustrate during their discussion?

assistance program, paralegal services, home care for older adults, Medicaid waivers, and practitioners who work with older adults in helping them make informed decisions.

Most AAAs offer both in-house services, many of which are facilitated by human services professionals, and off-site programs. Human services professionals working at an AAA-funded center might facilitate **caregiver respite** programs, or they might provide case management for an agency that provides employment services for clients over 60 years old. Even at centers where services are primarily medical in nature, human services professionals often provide counseling and case management as a support service.

Other practice settings include adult day cares, geriatric assessment units, nursing home facilities, veterans' services, elder abuse programs, adult protective services, bereavement services, senior centers, and hospices. A human services professional working in one of these practice settings may engage in direct services, consultations, and educational services focused on assisting older clients maintain or improve their quality of life, independence, and level of self-determination. Tasks are typically performed using a multidisciplinary team approach and can include conducting psychosocial assessments, providing case management, developing treatment plans, providing referrals for appropriate services, and providing counseling to older adult clients and their families. Services are also provided to family caregivers offering support and respite care.

MULTICULTURAL CONSIDERATIONS

As the frail older adult population has increased in numbers, the government has shifted its priorities to long-term health care needs, with a particular focus on at-risk populations such as women, ethnic minorities, nursing home residents, and older adults living in rural communities who are socially isolated. It's difficult to define who among the adult population is at particular risk of a range of psychosocial problems because in many senses all older adults are at risk in that they are vulnerable to social, economic, physical, and psychological harm or exploitation simply by virtue of their advanced age and corresponding dependency needs. But many gerontologists classify various subpopulations as more vulnerable than others for various reasons. For instance, successful aging has been linked to good economic status, good health care, relatively low stress levels, and high levels of social connections. A 2004 study also showed a link between good health and financial stability, finding that Whites tend to have greater economic wealth and better health than Black and Latina/o populations (Lum, 2004). A more recent study found that predictors of successful aging are rooted in early childhood, with those who had positive childhood experiences, including a higher socioeconomic status, having a greater likelihood of aging more successfully (Brandt et al., 2012).

Women are often considered a special population because as a group they are more prone to depression and typically have a worse response to antidepressant medication (Kessler, 2003). Women also experience greater financial vulnerability, particularly if divorced or widowed, and are often in lower-wage jobs, undereducated, and underinsured. Widowhood is a common occurrence for women because they live an average of 7 years longer than men, and although the majority of women in the United States marry, 75% of women are unmarried by the age of 65. Widowhood puts women at increased risk for lower morale and other mental health problems, even though these symptoms abate with time and intervention (Bennett, 1997). Other research indicates that in some settings, women tend to fare better, at least in assisted living facilities (Kozar-Westman et al., 2013). This may be due to the tendency for women to engage in social activities in such settings at a higher level compared to men.

Another at-risk population is older veterans, and while most older veterans rate themselves as aging successfully (Pietrzak et al., 2014), other studies show that exposure to trauma, pre- and post-service socioeconomic status, and health status impact successful aging in this population. For instance, veterans who experienced combat had a history of financial insecurity and mental health problems, including depression and posttraumatic stress disorder (PTSD), and experienced more challenges in their advanced years (Daniels et al., 2015). In fact, it appears as though exposure to combat-related trauma in early adulthood may decrease veterans' ability to effectively manage stressors later in life. Sachs-Ericsson et al. (2016) found that veterans who had been exposed to combat-related trauma earlier in life actually developed PTSD symptoms in older adulthood, becoming more reactive to stressors in older adulthood than non-veterans.

Research has also shown a link between stress and racism that often affects quality of life, exacerbated in later years for certain populations. A study conducted in 2002 found that racism, and particularly institutionalized racism (such as government-sanctioned racism through discrimination in housing, education, employment, and health care), had a detrimental effect on older members of the Black community, particularly men, who experienced greater stress throughout lives and lower life satisfaction during older adulthood (Utsey et al., 2002). In fact, institutionalized racism has been linked to feelings of invisibility, stress, depression, and ultimately despair as affected individuals experience a sense of futility in combating a lifetime of discrimination and disparity in treatment related to White privilege (Franklin et al., 2006).

Identifying special populations within the older adult population will allow the human services professional to explore issues that can potentially place older adult clients at increased risk of a lower quality of life during old age. A human services professional who is well versed in common risk factors for older adults in the United States, as well as the increased risk factors facing special populations, will be far more effective in protecting and advocating for their older adult clients.

CONCLUSION

The older adult population is increasing at a dramatic rate in the United States (as well as globally), rendering this one of the fastest growing target populations of human services agencies. As the baby boomer cohort continues to age and as life continues to become increasingly complex, many within the older adult population will rely on human services professionals to meet many of their psychosocial needs. Many human services educational programs are adding the field of older adult care, or social gerontology, as an area of specialization in response to the growing need for practitioners committed to working with this population.

Future considerations include continued efforts to identify at-risk populations, as well as addressing ongoing concerns such as the shortage of available affordable housing, the availability of long-term care and health care services directed at the older adult population, and the increased role of parenting responsibilities placed on the older adult population. Human services professionals can make a positive impact on the lives of older adults and their family members by addressing both ongoing and anticipated needs of this population.

SUMMARY

- The impact of changing demographics associated with the current and projected growth of the older adult population is examined. Changing population demographics involving the dramatic growth of the older adult population, also referred to as the graying of America, is explored. Dynamics include the impact of the extended lifespan on older adults, their family systems, and society in general.
- Older adulthood from a developmental perspective is discussed, including discussion of Erikson's theory of psychosocial development, Tornstam's theory of gerotranscendence, and Daniel Levinson's theory on middle age framed as seasons of life, each providing insights into how the aging process evolves holistically.
- Key aspects of successful and active aging are identified. The concepts of successful aging and active aging are discussed within the context of what factors are related to aging well, such as remaining physically active and engaged on a social level.
- Major challenges facing many older adults are examined. Challenges facing many older adults are discussed, including ageism, housing and homelessness, retirement, grandparents parenting, depression, dementia, and elder abuse. Populations that are at increased risk of experiencing these challenges are also explored, as are underlying factors such as economic disadvantage and ethnic minority status.
- The roles and functions of human services professionals working with the older adult population in a range of practice settings are explored. Practice settings serving the older adult population are explored within the context of the roles and functions of human services professionals. Practice settings such as AAAs, adult day cares, geriatric assessment units, nursing home facilities, veterans' services, elder abuse programs, adult protective services, bereavement services, senior centers, and hospices are also explored as are multicultural considerations.

END-OF-CHAPTER QUESTIONS

1. What are some ways that the "Graying of America" may impact older adult human services in the next few decades?
2. Identify one aspect each of Tornstam's theory of gerotranscendence and Daniel Levinson's theory of middle adulthood that you believe is the most impactful in understanding transitions experienced by many older adults.
3. What are some ways that human services providers help older adults facing challenges identified in this chapter?
4. What are some reasons for the increase in grandparents raising their grandchildren?
5. In what ways is aging more difficult for ethnic minority populations with histories of disadvantage?

References

Acierno, R., Hernandez, M. A., Amstadter, A. B., Resnick, H. S., Steve, K., Muzzy, W., & Kilpatrick, D. G. (2010). Prevalence and correlates of emotional, physical, sexual, and financial abuse and potential neglect in the United States: The National Elder Mistreatment Study. *American Journal of Public Health*, 100(2), 292–297.

Anderson, L. (2019). *The opioid prescribing rate and grandparents raising grandchildren: State and county level analysis*. U.S. Census Bureau. https://www.census. gov/library/stories/2019/04/opioid-crisis-grandparents-raising-grandchildren.html

Arias, B. (2004). United States life tables, 2002. *National Vital Statistics Reports, 53*(6). National Center for Health Statistics.

Atchley, R. C. (1976). *The sociology of retirement*. John Wiley.

Ausubel, J. (2020). *Older people are more likely to live alone in the U.S. than elsewhere in the world*. Pew Research Center. https://www.pewresearch.org/fact-tank/2020/03/10/older-people-are-more-likely-to-live-alone-in-the-u-s-than-elsewhere-in-the-world/

Bennett, K. M. (1997). Widowhood in elderly women: The medium- and long-term effects on mental and physical health. *Mortality, 2,* 137–148.

Bowling, A., & Iliffe, S. (2011). Psychological approach to successful ageing predicts future quality of life in older adults. *Health and Quality of Life Outcomes, 9*(1), 13–22.

Bradford, K. (2019). Shoring up the long-term care workforce. *NCSL, 27*(28), 1–2. https://www.ncsl.org/Portals/1/Documents/legisbriefs/2019/AugustLBs/Long-Term-Care-Workforce_28_V02.pdf

Brandt, M., Deindl, C., & Hank, K. (2012). Tracing the origins of successful aging: The role of childhood conditions and social inequality in explaining later life health. *Social Science and Medicine, 74*(9), 1418–1425.

Brown, R. T., Goodman, L., Guzman, D., Tieu, L., Ponath, C., & Kushel, M. B. (2016). Pathways to homelessness among older homeless adults: Results from the HOPE HOME Study. *PloS one, 11*(5).

Burnes, D., Pillemer, K., Caccamise, P. L., Mason, A., Henderson, C. R., Berman, J., & Salamone, A. (2015). Prevalence of and risk factors for elder abuse and neglect in the community: A population-based study. *Journal of the American Geriatrics Society, 63*(9), 1906–1912.

Butler, R. N. (1989). Dispelling ageism: The cross-cutting intervention. *Annals of the American Academy of Political and Social Science* 503: 138–147.

Cohn, D., & Passel, J. (2018). *A record 64 million Americans live in multigenerational households*. Pew Research Center. https://www.pewresearch.org/fact-tank/2018/04/05/a-record-64-million-americans-live-in-multigenerational-households/

Colby, S. L., & Ortman, J. M. (2014). *The baby boom cohort in the United States: 2012 to 2060*. U.S. Census Bureau. https://www.census.gov/prod/2014pubs/p25-1141.pdf

Conway, F., Jones, S., & Speakes-Lewis, A. (2011). Emotional strain in caregiving among African American grandmothers raising their grandchildren. *Journal of Women and Aging, 23*(2), 113–128.

Cotten, S. R., Ford, G., Ford, S., & Hale, T. M. (2014). Internet use and depression among retired older adults in the United States: A longitudinal analysis. *Journals of Gerontology Series B: Psychological Sciences and Social Sciences, 69*(5), 763–771.

Coudin, G., & Alexopoulos, T. (2010). "Help me! I'm old!" How negative aging stereotypes create dependency among older adults. *Aging and Mental Health, 14*(5), 516–523.

Crowther, M. R., Parker, M. W., Achenbaum, W. A., Larimore, W. L., & Koenig, H. G. (2002). Rowe and Kahn's model of successful aging revisited: Positive spirituality—The forgotten factor. *The Gerontologist, 42*(5), 613–620.

Czaja, S. J. (2020). Setting the Stage: Workplace and Demographic Trends. In *Current and emerging trends in aging and work* (pp. 3–11). Springer, Cham.

Daniels, L. R., Boehnlein, J., & McCallion, P. (2015). Aging, depression, and wisdom: A pilot study of life-review intervention and PTSD treatment with two groups of Vietnam veterans. *Journal of Gerontological Social Work, 58*(4), 420–436.

Davey, M., Kissil, K., & Lynch, L. (2016). Helping Children and Families Cope with Parental Illness: A Clinician's Guide. Routledge.

Degges-White, S. (2005). Understanding gerotranscendence in older adults: A new perspective for counselors. *Adultspan: Theory Research and Practice, 4*(1), 36–48.

Dunifon, R. E., Ziol-Guest, K. M., & Kopko, K. (2014). Grandparent coresidence and family well-being: Implications for research and policy. *The ANNALS of the American Academy of Political and Social Science, 654*(1), 110–126.

eHealth. (2017, October). *Obamacare affordability analysis for individual coverage: Major metro areas 2018 projections*. https://news.ehealthinsurance.com/_ir/68/20179/2018%20Projected%20Obamacare%20Affordability%20Analysis%20for%20Individuals%20in%2025%20Cities.pdf

Ellis, R. R., & Simmons, T. (2014). *Coresident grandparents and their grandchildren: 2012. Current population reports,* P20-576, U.S. Census Bureau.

Erikson, E. H. (1959). Identity and the life cycle. *Psychological Issues, 1,* 1–171.

Erikson, E. H. (1966). Eight ages of man. *International Journal of Psychiatry, 2*, 281–300.

Erikson, E. H., & Erikson, J. M. (1998). *The life cycle completed* (extended version). W. W. Norton & Company.

Fernald, M., ed. (2014). Housing America's older adults: Meeting the needs of an aging population. Joint Center for Housing Studies of Harvard University. 2014. http://www.jchs.harvard.edu/sites/jchs.harvard.edu/files/jchs-housing_americas_older_adults_2014.pdf

Foreman, K. J., Marquez, N., Dolgert, A., Fukutaki, K., Fullman, N., McGaughey, M., Pletcher, M. A., Smith, A. E., Tang, K., Yuan, C.-W., Brown, J. C., Friedman, J., He, J., Heuton, K. R., Holmberg, M., Patel, D. J., Reidy, P., Carter, A., Cercy, K., ... Murray, C. J. L. (2018). Forecasting life expectancy, years of life lost, and all-cause and cause-specific mortality for 250 causes of death: Reference and alternative scenarios for 2016–40 for 195 countries and territories. *The Lancet, 392*(10159), 2052–2090.

Franklin, A., Boyd-Franklin, N., & Kelly, S. (2006). Racism and invisibility: Race-related stress, emotional abuse and psychological trauma for people of color. *Journal of Emotional Abuse, 6*(2/3), 9–30. doi:10.1300/J135v06n02-02

Franklin, J. D. (2019). Coping with racial battle fatigue: Differences and similarities for African American and Mexican American college students. *Race Ethnicity and Education, 22*(5), 589–609.

Ge, W., & Adesman, A. (2017). Grandparents raising grandchildren: A primer for pediatricians. *Current Opinion in Pediatrics, 29*(3), 379–384.

Generations United. (2016). *Children thrive in grandfamilies.* Author.

Glaser, K., Stuchbury, R., Price, D., Di Gessa, G., Ribe, E., & Tinker, A. (2018). Trends in the prevalence of grandparents living with grandchild(ren) in selected European countries and the United States. *European Journal of Ageing, 15*(3), 237–250.

Glynn, C., & Fox, E. B. (2019). Dynamics of homelessness in urban America. *The Annals of Applied Statistics, 13*(1), 573–605.

Gonyea, J. G., Mills-Dick, K., & Bachman, S. S. (2010). The complexities of elder homelessness, a shifting political landscape and emerging community responses. *Journal of Gerontological Social Work, 53*(7), 575–590.

Gopinath, B., Kifley, A., Flood, V. M., & Mitchell, P. (2018). Physical activity as a determinant of successful aging over ten years. *Scientific Reports, 8*(1), 10522.

Graham, J. R., West, L. M., Martinez, J., & Roemer, L. (2016). The mediating role of internalized racism in the relationship between racist experiences and anxiety symptoms in a Black American sample. *Cultural Diversity and Ethnic Minority Psychology, 22*(3), 369.

Havighurst, R. J. (1961). Successful aging. *Gerontologist, 1*(1), 8–13.

Hedegaard, H., Warner, M., & Miniño, A. M. (2017, December). Drug overdose deaths in the United States, 1999–2016. NCHS Data Brief, no 294. National Center for Health Statistics. https://www.cdc.gov/nchs/data/databriefs/db294.pdf

Hirshbein, L. D. (2001). Popular views of old age in America, 1900–1950. *Journal of American Geriatrics Society, 49*, 1555–1560.

Hsu, H. (2007, November). Does social participation by the elderly reduce mortality and cognitive impairment? *Aging and Mental Health, 11*(6), 699–707. doi:10.1080/13607860701366335

Johnson, J. H. Jr., & Appold, S. J. (2017). *US older adults: Demographics, living arrangements, and barriers to aging in place.* Kenan Institute.

Jones, D. K., Gusmano, M. K., Nadash, P., & Miller, E. A. (2018). Undermining the ACA through the executive branch and federalism: What the Trump administration's approach to health reform means for older Americans. *Journal of Aging & Social Policy, 30*(3–4), 282–299.

Kessler, R. C. (2003). Epidemiology of women and depression. *Journal of Affective Disorders, 74*(1), 5–13.

Kozar-Westman, M., Troutman-Jordan, M., & Nies, M. A. (2013). Successful aging among assisted living community older adults. *Journal of Nursing Scholarship, 45*(3), 238–246.

Krout, J. A. (2003). *Residential choices and experiences of older adults: Pathways for life quality.* Spring Publishing Company.

Lancet. (2018). GBD 2017: A fragile world. *Lancet (London, England), 392*(10159), 1683.

Law, M., Mathai, A., Veinot, P., Webster, F., & Mylopoulos, M. (2015). Exploring lesbian, gay, bisexual, and queer (LGBQ) people's experiences with disclosure of sexual identity to primary care physicians: A qualitative study. *BMC family practice, 16*(1), 175.

Lent, J. P., & Otto, A. (2018). Grandparents, grandchildren, and caregiving: The Impacts of America's substance use crisis. *Generations, 42*(3), 15–22.

Levinson, D. (1978). *The seasons of a man's life.* Knopf.

Levinson, D. (1996). *The seasons of a woman's life.* Knopf.

Lewis-Burke Associates. (2011). *CSWE Patient Protection and Affordable Care Act of 2010: A resource guide for social workers.* http://www.cswe.org/File.aspx?id=48334

Lum, Y. (2004). Health-wealth association among older Americans: Racial and ethnic differences. *Social Work Research, 28*(2), 106–116.

McNamara, T. K., & Williamson, J. B. (2004). Race, gender, and the retirement decisions of people ages 60 to 80: Prospects for age integration in employment. *International Journal of Aging and Human Development, 59*(3), 255–286.

Miller, D., Leyell, T., & Mazacheck, J. (2004). Stereotypes of the elderly in U.S. television commercials from the 1950s to the 1990s. *International Journal of Aging and Human Development, 58*(4), 315–340.

Murphy, S. L., Kochanek, K. D., Xu, J. Q., & Arias, E. (2015). Mortality in the United States 2014, NCHS data brief, no 229. National Center for Health Statistics.

Murphy, S. L., Kochanek, K. D., Xu, J.Q., & Arias, E. (2017). Mortality in the United States, 2017 (NCHS Data Brief, no 328). National Center for Health Statistics.

Myhre, J. W. (2013). *Effects of online social networking on the cognitive, social, and emotional health of older adults* [Doctoral dissertation]. University of Arizona.

Nagaratnam, K., & Nagaratnam, N. (2019). Elderly abuse and neglect. In *Advanced age geriatric care* (pp. 19–24). Springer, Cham.

National Center on Elder Abuse. (2018). What is elder abuse? https://ncea.acl.gov/FAQ-(2).aspx

National Health Forum Policy. (2010, November). *The Elder Abuse Act: Addressing elder abuse, neglect, and exploitation.* The George Washington University. https://hsrc.himmelfarb.gwu.edu/cgi/viewcontent.cgi?article=1243&context=sphhs_centers_nhpf

Perone, A. K., Ingersoll-Dayton, B., & Watkins-Dukhie, K. (2020). Social isolation loneliness among LGBT older adults: Lessons learned from a pilot friendly caller program. *Clinical Social Work Journal, 48*(1), 126–139.

Pew Research Center. (2018). Social Media Fact Sheet. https://www.pewinternet.org/fact-sheet/social-media/

Pietrzak, R. H., Tsai, J., Kirwin, P. D., & Southwick, S. M. (2014). Successful aging among older veterans in the United States. *The American Journal of Geriatric Psychiatry, 22*(6), 551–563.

Pilkauskas, N. V., & Dunifon, R. E. (2016). Understanding grandfamilies: Characteristics of grandparents, nonresident parents, and children. *Journal of Marriage and Family, 78*(3), 623–633.

Reitzes, D. C., & Mutran, E. J. (2004). The transition to retirement: Stages and factors that influence retirement adjustment. *International Journal of Aging and Human Development, 59*(1), 63–84.

Rosenthal Gelman, C., Ghesquiere, A., Rogers, G., Williams, L., & Notto, A. (2018). Elder abuse, mistreatment, and interventions. *Innovation in Aging, 2*(Suppl 1), 524–525.

Rowe, J. W., & Kahn, R. L. (1997). Successful aging. *The Gerontologist, 37*(4), 433–440.

Sachs-Ericsson, N., Joiner, T. E., Cougle, J. R., Stanley, I. H., & Sheffler, J. L. (2016). Combat exposure in early adulthood interacts with recent stressors to predict PTSD in aging male veterans. *The Gerontologist, 56,* 83–91.

Silberner, J. (2018). We're living longer, but a medical journal sees many causes for alarm. NPR. https://www.npr.org/sections/goatsandsoda/2018/11/27/668233128/were-living-longer-but-a-medical-journal-sees-many-causes-for-alarm

Simmons, T., & Dye, J. L. (2003, October). *Grandparents living with grandchildren: 2000.* U.S. Bureau of the Census.

Singh, A., & Misra, N. (2009). Loneliness, depression and sociability in old age. *Industrial Psychiatry Journal, 18*(1), 51.

Smith, G. C., & Palmieri, P. A. (2007). Risk of psychological difficulties among children raised by custodial grandparents. *Psychiatric Services, 58*(10), 1303–1310.

Snyder, M. (2001). *Self and society.* Blackwell Publishers.

Tatara, T. (1997). *Summaries of the statistical data on elder abuse in domestic settings.* National Center on Elder Abuse.

Teaster, P. B. (2000). *A response to the abuse of vulnerable adults: A 2000 survey of state adult protective services.* National Center on Elder Abuse.

Teaster, P. B. (2006). *A response to abuse of vulnerable adults: The 2000 survey of state adult protective service.* http://www.ncea.aoa.gov/NCEAroot/main_site/pdf/research/apsreport030703.pdf.

Thornton, J. E. (2002). Myths of aging or ageist stereotypes. *Educational Gerontology, 28,* 301–312.

Tornstam, L. (1994). Gerotranscendence—A theoretical and empirical exploration. In L. E. Thomas & S. A. Eisenhandler (Eds.), *Aging and the religious dimension.* Greenwood Publishing Group.

Tornstam, L. (2003). *Gerotranscendence from young old age to old age.* www.soc.uu.se/Download.aspx?id=SpeY85Xb-P%2Bg%3DShare

Tornstam, L. (2005). *Gerotranscendence: A developmental theory of positive aging.* Springer Publishing.

U.S. Bureau of the Census, Population Estimates Program (PEP). (2014). Updated annually. http://www.census.gov/popest/

U.S. Bureau of the Census, Population Estimates Program (PEP). (2017). Updated annually. http://www.census.gov/popest/

U.S. Census Bureau. (2018). U.S. Census Bureau, 2018 American Community Survey 1-Year Estimates. Author.

U.S. Conference of Mayors' Report on Hunger and Homelessness. (2016). *A status report on hunger and homelessness in U.S. cities.* Author.

U.S. Senate, Commission on Long-Term Care. (2013). *Report to the Congress.* https://www.govinfo.gov/content/pkg/GPO-LTCCOMMISSION/pdf/GPO-LTCCOMMISSION.pdf

Utsey, S. O., Payne, Y. A., Jackson, E. S., & Jones, A. M. (2002). Race-related stress, quality of life indicators, and life satisfaction among elderly African Americans. *Cultural Diversity and Ethnic Minority Psychology, 48*(3), 224–233.

Vespa, J., Armstrong, D., & Medina, L. (2018). *Demographic turning points for the United States: Population projections for 2020 to 2060. Current Population Reports,* P25-1144, U.S. Census Bureau.

Warr, P., Butcher, V., & Robertson, I. (2004). Activity and psychological well-being in older people. *Aging and Mental Health, 8*(2), 172–183.

Whitley, D. M., & Kelley, S. J. (2007, January). Grandparents raising grandchildren: A call to action (Prepared for the Administration for Children and Families, Region IV). http://www.acf.hhs.gov/opa/doc/grandparents.pdf

Wiltz, T. (2016). *Why more grandparents are raising children.* Pew Trust. https://www.pewtrusts.org/en/research-and-analysis/blogs/stateline/2016/11/02/why-more-grandparents-are-raising-children

Woolf, S. H., & Schoomaker, H. (2019). Life expectancy and mortality rates in the United States, 1959-2017. *JAMA, 322*(20), 1996–2016.

Yarns, B. C., Abrams, J. M., Meeks, T. W., & Sewell, D. D. (2016). The mental health of older LGBT adults. *Current Psychiatry Reports, 18*(6), 60.

Zhan, Y., Wang, M., Liu, S., & Shultz, K. S. (2009). Bridge employment and retirees' health: A longitudinal investigation. *Journal of Occupational Health Psychology, 14,* 374–389.

6

Behavioral Health Services

© TINXI / SHUTTERSTOCK

Sara is a 45-year-old recently separated mother of two school-aged children. She has recently sought the services of a local human services agency at the request of her divorce attorney who believes her periodic bouts with depression and anxiety—conditions she has struggled with for years—may impact her custody case. Sara described in her first session how she has struggled with bouts of depression and anxiety since she was a teenager. Sara shared that her depression manifested as melancholy, with low energy, intense sadness, loss of appetite, negative thinking, and a general feeling of malaise. During these periods, Sara disclosed that she had tremendous difficulty completing tasks, such as keeping her home clean, cooking dinner for her kids, and, at times, even mustering the motivation to shower regularly. She also tends to drink more alcohol when she's depressed and anxious, but loses her appetite when she's feeling down, and just wants to sleep all the time. Sara described her anxiety as a sense of foreboding, where she feels like something bad is going to happen to her. Part of her knows these fears are likely irrational, but she also wonders if some mysterious force is warning her about an impending threat. Because she isn't always sure what's causing her fears, she often withdraws and doesn't want to leave her home, sometimes for weeks at a time.

Sara has struggled with substance abuse through the years, including an opioid addiction in her early adulthood for which she underwent residential rehabilitation. Sara shared how her depression and anxiety got worse after her husband filed for divorce. She explained that the divorce proceedings have been very contentious and rather traumatic, largely due to a protracted custody battle and having to find a job after being home with her kids for years. In subsequent sessions, Sara shared that her depression and anxiety began when she was about 14 years old, shortly after her childhood home caught fire during the night when she and her family were sleeping. Everyone got out, but her younger brother later died from smoke inhalation. Sara talked about how this traumatic event seemed to get lumped onto earlier traumatic events related to her father's alcoholism and her mother's depression, a considerable amount of neglect, and the subsequent divorce of Sara's parents. Sara shared how she couldn't sleep for months after the fire because she kept replaying the various events that night in her head again and again—waking up to the smoke alarm, seeing flames, having to escape through an upstairs window, and watching her younger brother taken away in an ambulance. Sara described how she has beaten herself up for years because she saved herself but didn't stay behind and look for her brother, who hid in his smoke-filled closet until firefighters found him. She shared that there are times even now where she can think about almost nothing else, and she worries all the time about her own home burning down, especially if her kids are home with a babysitter and she's not there to make sure everyone is safe.

Sara admitted that her depression and anxiety, particularly her reluctance to leave the kids alone, was a huge focus of the conflict between her and her estranged husband, who consistently expressed frustration that they never took a vacation away from their kids, let alone have a nice dinner out. If they did go out, invariably Sara would become so anxious that they would need to cut the evening short and go home to check on the kids. Sara also disclosed that she has never had counseling for her earlier trauma and loss, which was also frustrating for her husband, who asked her on multiple occasions to see a counselor. Sara shared that she was reluctant because talking about her problems only seemed to make them worse. She's only seeking counseling now because her mental health has become a focus of the custody case.

BEHAVIORAL HEALTH IN THE UNITED STATES

Mental illness is a serious social problem in the United States. Depression and anxiety seem to have skyrocketed in the last decade or so, and there has been an equally large surge of self-help books offering anecdotal advice on how to live a calmer, more stress-free life. According to a Gallup Health and Wellbeing Index poll, well-being also appears to be at an all-time low, particularly for middle-aged women (Davis & Francis, 2011). Violence, especially mass gun violence, seems to be at an all-time high, and the coronavirus pandemic exacerbated people's existing diagnoses at the same time that they were cut off from seeing providers for face-to-face counseling sessions.

According to the Substance Abuse and Mental Health Services Administration (SAMHSA, 2019), 47.6 million adults 18 years of age and older had a diagnosable mental illness in 2018 (defined as having any mental, behavioral, or emotional disorder in the past year that met *DSM-5* criteria). That equals about 15% of the adult population in the United States. Within this population, about 12.6 million adults 18 years of age and older struggled specifically with a major depressive disorder, which is equal to about 4% of the U.S. adult population. While the rate of any mental illness has remained stable in the last few years, overall there has been an increase since 2009, especially in young adults (18 to 25 years of age) (SAMHSA, 2019).

As one of the largest groups of behavioral health providers in the United States, human services providers play a vital role in the care of those struggling with mental illness and behavioral health challenges (Council on Social Work Education, 2014). Because of the unique nature of the human services profession, with its focus on social problems and underserved populations, human services providers are more likely than other helping professions to serve in liaison roles coordinating services of several disciplines such as psychiatry and psychology. Thus, they are often frontline workers in the area of behavioral health care.

This chapter explores the nature of behavioral health in the United States, providing a summary overview of how behavioral health and mental illness have been viewed and treated throughout the years, the types of psychological disorders human services providers are most likely to encounter in their client populations, different service delivery models (and their levels of effectiveness), and how mental illness impacts various groups, such as member of the Black population, Latina/o populations, Native Americans and Alaska Natives, LGBTQ populations, military personnel, homeless populations, and prisoners.

Before jumping in, though, I want to share a word about words. Traditionally, *mental health* was used as a catchall term used to describe one's emotional and psychological functioning. More recently, though, the mental health field has increasingly preferred to use the term *behavioral health*, based on the contention that the term is broader, encompassing the multidimensional nature of mental wellness. Behavioral health includes the reciprocal nature of behavior and mental well-being, both positive and negative. The terms "mental health" and "behavioral health" are still used interchangeably in the literature, but it's important to note that the term "mental health" refers primarily to the biological aspects of mental illness and well-being, while the term "behavioral health" is more inclusive. Within this chapter I have selected the term I believe best reflects the intention of its use and whichever term was used by the authors I am drawing from. When I am referring to both the biological nature of mental wellness and the behavior/well-being connection—I have used the term "behavioral health."

THE HISTORY OF MENTAL ILLNESS: PERCEPTIONS AND TREATMENT

Learning Outcome 6.1   **Examine how people with mental illness have historically been perceived and treated**

Early in human history, mental illness, called madness, lunacy, insanity, or feeble-mindedness, was commonly believed to be caused by demon possession. Archeologists have found skulls dating back to at least 5000 BCE with small holes drilled in them, presumably to allow the indwelling demons to escape. This practice, called trepanning, was practiced through the **Middle Ages**. Demonic possession, including witchcraft, was still thought to be the cause of most mental illnesses throughout the Middle Ages, driven primarily by early Western Christianity (Covey, 2005). A common "cure" involved tying up those suspected of being witches or demon-possessed with a rope and lowering them into freezing cold water. If they floated, they were believed to be witches and were then killed. If they sunk, they were not considered witches, and the cold water was believed to be a cure for whatever ailed them (Porter, 2002).

Mental Illness during America's Colonial Era

How mental illness was perceived and treated during Colonial times is difficult to ascertain because information is rather sparse and contested (Eldridge, 1996). But what is known is that mental illness was considered a private family matter to be handled at the local level by family and perhaps the church. But as populations in the cities grew, those suffering from some form of mental illness increasingly became a problem for the entire community. Almshouses, typically used as poorhouses or workhouses, were often used to house the mentally ill. By the mid-1700s, many towns in **Colonial America** were following the trend in Europe of building separate almshouses and even specialized hospitals for the insane (Torrey & Miller, 2002). The first hospital with space reserved exclusively for the mentally ill was opened in 1752 by the Quakers at Pennsylvania Hospital. But mistreatment was common, evidenced by the fact that the space for mentally ill patients was located in a damp basement and contained shackles in each room. Several Black slaves were admitted by their owners for "insane" behavior (typically manifested by running away), and by 1762, bars were erected securing each room. To help defray costs and meet the public's growing curiosity about the "insane," the hospital allowed the public to view patients for a modest admission fee (Grob, 1973; Torrey & Miller, 2002).

The Moral Movement and Aftercare Movement

By the early 18th century, mental health reform had begun with the **moral treatment movement**, led in part by Dr. Philippe Pinel, a French physician, who rejected the prevailing belief that insanity was caused by demonic possession. Pinel became interested in mental illness when a friend developed symptoms, which Pinel referred to as a "nervous mania" that eventually evolved into a full mania. Pinel was ultimately forced to admit his friend into an asylum where his treatment was mismanaged. Pinel's friend left the asylum to return home with his parents, where his condition continued to deteriorate, leading to his untimely death when he wandered into the forest and was found dead several weeks later. This experience prompted Pinel to seek employment in 1792 at La Bicêtre hospital, which had an asylum for the incurably insane. Pinel served as chief physician at La Bicêtre for five years (Goldstein, 2002).

The conditions Pinel found at the hospital shocked him—patients chained to walls, some for decades, regular beatings, and some patients being put on public display for money. Although Dr. Pinel receives most of the credit for stopping this inhumane treatment at the hospital by unchaining thousands of patients, it was actually Jean-Baptiste Pussin, the superintendent of the mental ward, who in 1784, along with his wife and colleague, Marguerite, who advocated for a more humane treatment of patients.

In 1793 Pinel, the new chief physician of the hospital, visited Pussin in the ward to learn more about his approach to patient care. In 1797 Pinel officially banned the use of all chains and shackles as well as other forms of abuse at the hospital. Pinel and Pussin worked together again at another hospital where Pinel was chief and Pussin was his assistant. Together they instituted what is now referred to as moral treatment of the mentally ill, described in detail in Pinel's book *Treatise on Insanity*, published in 1800. Unfortunately, Pinel and Pussin's work did not end the abuse of the mentally ill, and in time, the cruel treatment of those considered insane and incurable became prolific throughout both Europe in the United States.

The human services professional involvement in the practice of caring for the mentally ill began during the *aftercare movement* of the late 1800s and early 1900s. Aftercare, a social reform issue of the time, involved the short-term care of the formerly "insane" and "lunatics" (Vourlekis et al., 1998). Aftercare was typically managed by private charitable societies that offered temporary assistance and housing for those coming out of the state asylum system. Human services professionals, particularly social workers, were on the forefront of this helping model, which was really before its time because this type of "continuum of care" was not a part of the psychological mainstream during that era. It wasn't long before aftercare programs were considered the sole domain of social workers who were paid by the state, and ultimately by public or private hospitals. This program served as the foundation for the contemporary role of those in the human services field who provide both advocacy and direct service to those who suffer from mental illness.

Dorothea Dix was a leader in advocating for more compassionate treatment of the mentally ill in insane asylums in the United States. Her plea to the Massachusetts state legislature in 1843 poignantly described the deplorable conditions those with mental illness were forced to endure, including being held in cages by chains, often naked, enduring beatings with rods, and being whipped to ensure obedience. Dix pleaded for the legislators to intercede on behalf of society's most vulnerable members. Dix's efforts resulted in an improvement in the conditions in both hospitals and asylums (Torrey & Miller, 2002), but these improvements were rather short-lived.

By the beginning of the 20th century most of the almshouses and insane asylums had closed, and state mental institutions became the primary facilities housing the mentally ill. While institutionalized care was considered revolutionary, compassionate, and far better than almshouses and asylums, rampant abuses involving cruel treatment, neglect, and physical and emotional abuse were increasingly reported throughout the early and middle 1900s. In fact, Dix's description of mid-century insane asylums could easily have described the early 20th-century state system, which ultimately led to what is now referred to as deinstitutionalization.

The Deinstitutionalization of the Mentally Ill

Although horrible abuses in state and private mental hospitals were well documented through the mid-1900s, institutionalized care remained the primary method of treating the seriously mentally ill for another 50 years (Deutsch, 2013). The U.S. government's first legislative involvement in the care of the mentally ill occurred in 1946, when President Harry Truman signed the National Mental Health Act into law. The signing of this act allowed for the creation of National Institute of Mental Health (NIMH) in 1949, one of the first of four institutes under the National Institutes of Health (Mannekote et al., 2019).

In 1955 the Mental Health Study Act was passed, which directed the convening of the Joint Commission on Mental Health and Illness under the auspices of the NIMH. The Joint Commission was charged with the responsibility of analyzing and assessing the needs of the country's mentally ill, as well as making recommendations for a more effective and comprehensive national approach to the treatment of those with mental disorders and disabilities (Grob & Goldman, 2006). The committee was comprised of professionals in the mental health field such as psychiatrists, psychologists, therapists, educators, and representatives from various professional agencies, including the American Academy of Neurology, the American Academy of Pediatrics, the American Psychological Association, the National Association of Social Workers (NASW), and the National Association for Mental Health.

Generally, in addition to making recommendations for increasing funding for both research and training of professionals, the committee recommended transitioning from an institutionalized treatment model to an outpatient community mental health model, where patients were treated in the **least restricted environment** within the community. This report led to the creation of the Community Mental Health Centers (CMHC) Act of 1963, which was passed under the Kennedy administration. The CMHC enabled the funding of a new national mental health care system focusing on prevention and community-based care rather than on institutionalized custodial care (Feldman, 2003). The passage of the CMHC Act set the **deinstitutionalization movement** into motion, prompted by dissatisfaction with public mental hospitals, as well as the development of psychotropic medications and a new focus on the brain–behavior connection (Mowbray & Holter, 2002).

Several decades after President Kennedy described the CMHC program as a bold new approach to dealing with mental illness, many in the behavioral health field cited frustration and discouragement with what was perceived as numerous failures of the deinstitutionalization process and the new national system. A part of the challenge of implementing a community-based program was related to overoptimism about new treatments and an underestimation of the complexity of mental illness.

Early proponents of deinstitutionalization had hoped that through early detection, increased research, psychotropic medication, and better intervention strategies, mental illness could be greatly reduced and perhaps even eliminated. Yet mental illness remained pervasive regardless of significant efforts to curb its devastating impact on individuals, families, and society. The most serious criticisms of the deinstitutionalization movement are leveled at the federal government, which many claim fell short of funding commitments, resulting in far fewer community mental health centers being opened across the United States.

Among those centers that did open, most were poorly staffed and generally unprepared to deal with the rapid transition from institutionalized to community care.

With insufficient funding and an inability of government services to keep pace with need, the burden of care for the country's mentally ill shifted from the public mental hospital system to nursing homes, the prison system, and even the streets (Dear & Wolch, 2014; Kim, 2016; Raphael & Stoll, 2013). Patients seeking treatment with community mental health centers appear to have been a previously undertreated population that were experiencing life challenges, such as substance abuse and child welfare issues, not chronic and severe mental illness (Grob, 2014).

CURRENT LEGISLATION AFFECTING ACCESS TO SERVICES AND MENTAL HEALTH PARITY

Learning Outcome 6.2   Describe common legislation impacting mental health provision in the United States

Some mental illnesses take a lifetime to develop. Others seem to hit out of nowhere, such as schizophrenia. Mental illness cuts across all socioeconomic, racial, and gender lines; in fact, one could say that mental illness is an "equal opportunity" affliction. I have worked with both the lower-income and undereducated population and the upper-income and highly educated population, and my only observation about the difference regarding these two groups is that oftentimes those on the upper end of the income/education continuums do a better job of hiding their mental illnesses and emotional disorders, at least for a time. For this reason, as well as the increasing evidence of the biological basis of many mental illnesses formerly believed to be solely psychological in nature, most behavioral health advocates argued the importance of requiring health insurance companies to cover mental health conditions in the same manner as they cover general medical conditions. Yet in the 1980s, when managed care became the norm in health insurance coverage, many advocates complained that managing costs became synonymous with limiting much-needed benefits, particularly in the area of mental health coverage.

Through bipartisan efforts, the *Mental Health Parity Act* was passed in 1996, which bars employee-sponsored group health insurance plans from limiting coverage for mental health benefits on a greater basis than for general medical or surgical benefits. This initial bill removed annual and lifetime dollar limits commonly used by insurance companies to limit mental health benefits. Unfortunately, the majority of health insurance companies found loopholes, allowing them to avoid complying with this legislation. *The Mental Health Parity and Addiction Equity Act of 2008* (sponsored by President Obama when he was a senator), which was attached to the 2008 federal bailout legislation, promised significant reform of mental health parity in the United States. The act went into effect January 1, 2010 and required group health plans (covering 50 or more employees) that already provided medical and mental health coverage to provide mental health and substance abuse benefits at the same level as medical benefits are provided (i.e., it does not require employers to provide mental health and substance abuse coverage). Thus, if an employer-sponsored insurance plan offered mental health benefits, the benefits must be consistent with what is offered in the medical plan with regard to deductibles, copays, number of visits allowable per year, and so on. Although some exemptions existed in this act, it went a long way in securing parity of mental health and substance abuse benefit coverage.

Perhaps one of the most significant federal laws to be passed in years is the Affordable Care Act (ACA), a comprehensive health care reform bill signed into law by President

Obama in March 2010. The ACA took effect incrementally between 2010 and 2014 and, as referenced earlier, has and will continue to have an impact on behavioral and mental health care coverage. Overall, this legislation is designed to make it easier for individuals and families to obtain quality health insurance, despite pre-existing conditions, and will make it more difficult for health insurance companies to deny coverage. The ACA also incorporates mental health parity legislation, and expands Medicare in a variety of ways, including bolstering community- and home-based services, as well as providing incentives for preventive, holistic, and wellness care.

According to the Centers for Disease Control and Prevention, public health experts are increasingly recognizing the significant impact of mental illness on society, including its economic impact (Reeves et al., 2011). The cost of mental health treatment (which may require frequent hospitalizations and long-term residential care) is often quite high, and because of the debilitating nature of most mental illnesses, which often impacts an individual's ability to maintain consistent employment, a disproportionate number of the mentally ill do not have private health care insurance or are underinsured, and thus are dependent on the often-inadequate U.S. public health care system. The ACA addresses some of these issues by significantly reducing uninsured rates and expanding Medicaid coverage for low-income adults, and requires compliance with mental health parity (as of January 2014).

With respect to behavioral health care, the ACA provides increased incentives for coordinated care; school-based care, including behavioral health care; and substance abuse treatment. Additionally, it includes provisions that require the inclusion of mental health care, including substance abuse coverage, in benefits packages; this includes prescription drug coverage and wellness and prevention services, incorporating earlier mental health parity legislation.

LAWRENCE, MA, USA – JULY 20, 2017: Demonstrators protest US Representative Paul Ryan's visit to the New Balance factory due to Ryan's opposition to government subsidized healthcare.

The expansion of Medicaid and private insurance coverage through the passage of the ACA meant that millions of previously uninsured Americans now had mental health coverage and coverage for substance abuse. The Trump administration's efforts to repeal and replace the ACA placed those struggling with mental illness and substance abuse at risk and threatened mental health parity (Wishner, 2017). When the efforts of the Trump administration and the Republican Congress to repeal the ACA were unsuccessful, Trump responded by taking executive action to dismantle the ACA (Jost, 2018). On October 12, 2017, Trump signed an executive order removing the mandate penalty that all individuals must have health insurance, as well as removing some of the regulatory requirements for insurance companies (The White House, 2017). Trump also announced that he was halting federal cost-sharing payments, essentially ending government subsidies for low-income policy holders.

The concern among ACA advocates is that these actions are designed to entice healthy people away from the ACA, which will ultimately increase premium costs for those who need the

© HEIDI BESEN / SHUTTERSTOCK

insurance the most and are less likely to be able to afford comprehensive plans. The NASW expressed particular concern about the U.S. Department of Health and Human Services plan to require recipients of Medicare to work if they are childless, since there is no consideration of recipients' mental health and ability to work (NASW, 2019). A recent analysis of the actual and potential impact of Trump's efforts to dismantle the ACA has found that insurance companies raised their rates up to 16% (average of about 8%). The analysis projected additional future increases for those lower-income individuals who had previously received a government subsidy (Kamal et al., 2018). Regardless of the Trump administration's actual intent, the actions of the administration have had a negative impact on those struggling with mental illness and substance abuse, particularly those who relied on federal subsidies to supplement their policies (Friedmann et al., 2017; Wishner, 2017).

Mental Health Courts

A significant social problem in U.S. society is the *criminalization of the mentally ill*. This term refers to the trend of chronically mentally ill people being arrested for behaviors directly related to their mental illness, such as loitering, trespassing, and resisting arrest. The development of **Mental Health Courts** (**MHC**) in the early 2000s is a significant step forward in addressing this issue on a national and local level. MHCs are specialized courts that divert mentally ill defendants into court-mandated community-based treatment programs, with the ultimate goal of addressing public safety and providing compassionate and effective care for people struggling with chronic and **serious mental illness** who come into contact with the criminal justice system.

The MHC program was developed pursuant to the America's Law Enforcement and Mental Health Project (Pub. L. No. 106-515, passed in November 2000), reauthorized under the Mentally Ill Offender Treatment and Crime Reduction Act (MIOTCRA), and was reauthorized again more recently under the 21st Century Cures Act of 2016. The MHC is administered under the Bureau of Justice Assistance (BJA), a component of the U.S. Department of Justice, in cooperation with SAMHSA.

Currently, the Justice and Mental Health Collaboration Program (authorized under the MIOTCRA) funds MHC programs, as well as mental health and substance-use treatment for individuals in the criminal justice system, community reentry service programs, and training for local law enforcement on how to deal with the mentally ill population and their families. As of 2019, the MIOTCRA has funded 186 mental health courts, provided funds for training in about 146 local police departments, and provided almost 500 grants across the country (Council of State Governments Justice Center, 2019).

The goal of the BJA is to encourage, lead, and fund the development of comprehensive programs run by criminal justice systems across the country that offer alternatives to incarceration as well as help to avoid future court involvement. MHC program goals include the following:

- Increase public safety for communities—by reducing criminal activity and lowering the high recidivism rates for people with mental illnesses who become involved in the criminal justice system
- Increase treatment engagement by participants—by brokering comprehensive services and supports, rewarding adherence to treatment plans, and sanctioning nonadherence

- Improve quality of life for participants—by ensuring that program participants are connected to needed community-based treatments, housing, and other services that encourage recovery
- More effectively use resources for sponsoring jurisdictions—by reducing repeated contacts between people with mental illnesses and the criminal justice system and by providing treatment in the community when appropriate, where it is more effective and less costly than in correctional institutions.

Research indicates that the MHCP has been successful at diverting the mentally ill from jail to programs offering much needed services. One study researching one of the first mental health courts (located in Broward County, Florida) found that participants spent 75% less time in jail, received needed mental health services on a more frequent basis, and were less likely to commit a new crime, compared with mentally ill defendants who proceeded through the traditional court process (Christy et al., 2005).

As successful as mental health courts have been, particularly at helping states save unnecessary costs and providing services for the mentally ill involved in the criminal justice system, the Board of Directors of the advocacy organization Mental Health America (2019) expressed several concerns in a recently released policy statement. The organization's concerns include an opposition to the expansion of mental health courts to serve as a substitute for the development of a comprehensive community-based national mental health care system. Mental Health America also expressed concerns about the possibility that the MHCP would bring more people into the criminal justice system, rather than divert them to community resources as quickly as possible.

COMMON MENTAL DISORDERS AND PSYCHOSOCIAL ISSUES

Learning Outcome 6.3   **Explore serious mental illnesses and common mental disorders within the context of diagnostic approaches used in the human services field**

Human services professionals may encounter mental illness directly when clients seek therapy for previously diagnosed disorders or they may encounter mental illness indirectly when clients seek services from a human services agency for reasons unrelated to their own behavioral health and then symptoms of mental illness begin to surface in the midst of the counseling relationship. Whether clients present with prior diagnoses or have no previously identified mental health issues, mental health providers must be able to recognize the common signs and symptoms of mental illness in their clients.

The *DSM-5* categorizes mental disorders based on common symptomology, and certain criteria must be met to diagnose someone with a mental, emotional, or behavioral disorder. There is some controversy surrounding the possibility that the *DSM-5* contributes to pathologizing people rather than focusing on their strengths, but it is to date the most effective evidence-based tool available for assessing individuals in a systematic and organized manner (APA, 2013).

The *DSM-5* is organized into three sections—Section I includes introductory information, Section II includes diagnostic criteria and diagnostic codes, and Section III includes information on emerging measures and models (e.g., alternative models,

Pearson eText

Video Example 6.1

In this video a human services provider assesses the nature of a client's challenges and selects an appropriate intervention strategy. What were some factors that likely influenced the provider's perspective?

conditions for further study). One of the most significant changes from the *DSM-IV* is that the *DSM-5* no longer uses a multiaxial system to categorize mental disorders. Disorders formerly diagnosed on Axis I (clinical disorders), Axis II (personality disorders and intellectual disabilities), and Axis III (general medical conditions) are now all included in Section II. Axis IV, which clinicians used to note psychosocial and contextual functioning that affected the client's functioning, has now been omitted (although counselors are encouraged to holistically note psychosocial and environmental in their primary diagnosis). Axis V, formerly the Global Assessment of Functioning (GAF)—a hypothetical continuum of behavioral health and functioning ranging from 0 to 100— was discontinued due to a perception that a singular score of functioning was unreliable and not particularly useful.

It's important for human services providers to also use a **strengths-based approach** with clients because it encourages the practitioner to recognize and promote a client's strengths rather than solely focus on deficits. A strengths perspective also presumes a client's ability to contribute to addressing their own problems through the development of self-sufficiency and self-determination. Saleebey (1996) developed several principles for practitioners to follow that can help clients struggling with mental illness and emotional disorders experience a sense of empowerment in their lives. Saleebey encourages practitioners to recognize that all clients

1. have resources available to them, both within themselves and their communities;
2. are members of the community and as such are entitled to respect and dignity;
3. are resilient by nature and have the potential to grow and heal in the face of crisis and adversity;
4. need to be in relationships with others in order to self-actualize; and
5. have the right to their own perception of their problems, even if this perception isn't held by the practitioner.

Sullivan (1992) was one of the first theorists to apply the strengths perspective to the area of chronic mental illness where clients suffering from mental illness are encouraged to recognize and develop their own personal strengths and abilities. Sullivan compared this approach to one often used when working with the physically challenged, where focusing on physical disabilities is replaced with focusing on the development of physical abilities. Sullivan claimed that by redefining the problem (rather than continuing to search for new solutions), by fully integrating the mentally ill into society, and by focusing on strengths and abilities rather than solely on deficits, an environment can then be created that is more consistent with the early goals of mental health reformers who sought to remove barriers to treatment and promote respectful, compassionate, and

Suicide Prevention Walk, Cincinnati, USA - 15 Oct 2017.

© AP / SHUTTERSTOCK

Pearson eText

Video Example 6.2

In this video a human services provider facilitates a group for clients struggling with depression and anxiety. What is the value of using an ecological systems approach with this type of support group?

comprehensive care of the mentally ill. Operating from a strengths perspective is important regardless of what the clinical issues are or what intervention strategies are used.

Every society has members who struggle with some form of mental illness—those people whose behavior is considered outside what is considered normal and appropriate. Each society has also developed ways in which to handle or manage such individuals so that healthy societal functioning is not disrupted. But because the criteria for what is considered normative behavior changes from era to era, as well as from culture to culture, it is important to keep cultural mores and generational issues in mind when characterizing someone's behavior as maladaptive or unhealthy.

The following section includes some of the more serious mental illnesses that human services professionals may encounter when working with clients who have been (or could be) diagnosed with a mental, behavioral, or emotional disorder that significantly interferes with multiple life domains, warranting extensive case management and counseling services. Clients experiencing a serious mental illness may come into contact with a human services professional in a range of agencies such as an outpatient community mental health center, an inpatient psychiatric facility, the court system (mental health court or a probation department), a prison, or a homeless shelter. It is important, then, that generalist human services professionals be familiar with some of the more common disorders so their clients' cases can be managed as effectively as possible.

Psychotic Disorders

Psychotic disorders are among the most serious of all mental illnesses because they impact an individual's sense of reality, often resulting in the marked impairment in most, if not all, life domains. Common symptoms of a psychotic disorder include hallucinations, delusions, and generally bizarre and eccentric behavior. The most common psychotic disorder is **schizophrenia**, an umbrella term for a number of brain disorders with similar symptoms, manifesting most often in the late teens and early adulthood. The symptoms of schizophrenia affect how people think, perceive, feel, and act. While there is no known cause of schizophrenia, researchers believe there are genetic components involved and likely numerous causes (Skene et al., 2018).

According to the *DSM-5*, symptoms of schizophrenia are divided into four domains: **positive symptoms**, including psychotic symptoms such as hallucinations; **negative symptoms**, including an absence of appropriate emotion and/or loss of speech; **cognitive symptoms**, including neurocognitive deficits such as issues with memory, attention, and social skills; and **mood symptoms**, including alterations in mood manifesting in either excessive happiness or sadness (APA, 2013).

According to the *DSM-5*, an individual may be diagnosed with schizophrenia if they experience two of the following five symptoms for at least one month.

1. **Delusions**: Strongly held false beliefs or misperceptions that are not consistent with the person's culture, many of which could not possibly be true. Examples include believing that the government is monitoring one's activities through the television set or that one has special powers such as speaking to others through mental telepathy.

2. **Hallucinations**: Sensations that are experienced as real, but are not, such as hearing voices, seeing things that are not there, smelling smells that do not exist, or feeling sensations when nothing is present.

3. **Disorganized speech**: Speech often reflects thinking that makes no sense, with frequent trailing off into incoherent talk often referred to as "**word salad**."

4. Disorganized or **catatonic behavior**: Inability to dress oneself, poor self-care, or catatonic behavior such as holding a rigid pose for hours.

5. Negative symptoms: Affective flattening, alogia (a complete lack of any speech), and extreme apathy or disinterest.

Schizophrenia used to be diagnosed based on subtype (paranoid, disorganized, catatonic, undifferentiated, and residual types), but because patients often experience overlapping symptoms, the APA omitted subtypes in its most recent edition of the *DSM* (APA, 2013).

There is no cure for schizophrenia, and thus treatment consists primarily of custodial care and medication to minimize symptoms, particularly destructive ones. Antipsychotic medication has been available since the mid-1950s, but negative side effects of these medications, such as sexual impotence, tardive dyskinesia (involuntary jerking spasms of the muscles), and tranquilizing effects, often result in many patients refusing to take their medication consistently. New **atypical antipsychotic drugs**, such as Vraylar (approved by the FDA in September 2015), Seroquel, and Risperdal, have shown promise in reducing symptoms of schizophrenia such as hallucinations and delusion without nearly the number of side effects (Agarwal et al., 2016).

Bipolar Disorder

Bipolar disorder is a disorder of the brain that causes dramatic shifts in mood, called mood episodes, where affected individuals swing from periods of mania to periods of depression. Manic episodes can include inflated self-esteem, insomnia, rapid speech, a rush of ideas, and impulsive or dangerous behavior in response to elation and overexcitement, as well as irritability, particularly in response to someone attempting to stop their activities. People with bipolar disorder often feel isolated and misunderstood. During a manic episode, an individual may believe they have special powers or a unique contribution to make to the world that does not match the reality of their situations. They may go days without sleep, appear extremely restless, talk rapidly, act in a grandiose manner, behave impulsively, and experience a mental rush in response to rapidly firing ideas and extreme creativity. They may go on unrestrained spending sprees, have unprotected sex with strangers, or engage in other high-risk behaviors (APA, 2013).

Depressive episodes are more frequent than manic episodes and involve deep depression or complete despondency. During a depressive episode, individuals with bipolar disorder may experience profound guilt and feelings of worthlessness, difficulty thinking and making decisions, may have no appetite, may want to do nothing but sleep, and may think about or plan their suicide. If someone experiences both manic and depressive symptoms, they are experiencing what is called a mixed episode. When bipolar disorder first manifests, patients often experience what is called rapid cycling—a more extreme form of bipolar involving four or more mood episodes within a 12-month period (APA, 2013).

While the exact cause of bipolar disorder is unknown, earlier studies show a genetic link, and recent stem cell research found that people with bipolar disorder had significant differences in their brains compared to those without bipolar disorder. Specifically, researchers found that people diagnosed with bipolar disorder experienced genetic vulnerabilities in their early brain development, including differences in how calcium signals

Pearson eText

Video Example 6.3

In this video a human services provider illustrates
how to work with a client
from a different culture.
What are three ways that
the provider connected to
the client's culture in order
to learn more?

were sent and received (Chen et al., 2014). The most common treatment of bipolar disorder involves a combination of drug therapy, including mood stabilizers, lithium (a salt),
and psychotropic medications, along with case management and counseling.

Depressive Disorders

People who have a depressive disorder often feel sad, anxious, empty, hopeless, irritable,
guilty, worthless, helpless, and lethargic. While there are several types of depressive disorders, one of the most common is major depressive disorder. Everyone feels depressed
sometimes. We experience heartbreak when our partner breaks up with us or a dear
friend or family member dies, and we are likely going to have difficulty sleeping, eating,
and concentrating as a result. We may even experience a stomachache or headache and
other somatic symptoms. But major depressive disorder is far more than a temporary
down mood in response to a difficult time in life. The vignette at the beginning of this
chapter meets several *DSM-5* criteria for major depressive disorder.

According to the *DSM-5*, in order for a diagnosis of major depressive disorder to
be given, an individual must experience two episodes of five or more of the following
symptoms for at least a two-week period:

1. Depressed mood most of the day
2. Lack of interest or pleasure in all or almost all activities
3. Significant unintentional weight loss or weight gain
4. Insomnia or sleeping too much
5. Agitation or cognitive slowness that is noticed by others
6. Fatigue or loss of energy
7. Feelings of worthlessness or excessive or toxic guilt
8. Difficulty concentrating or making decisions
9. Recurrent thoughts of suicide,

Additionally, the symptoms must cause significant impairment in the individual's
important areas of life, such as work, their social life, and interpersonal relationships
(APA, 2013).

Depression is quickly becoming one of the most significant disorders of our time,
with an estimated 350 million people experiencing major depression throughout the
world (World Health Organization, 2015). The impact of depression is broad and deep,
particularly for women, who experience depression in greater numbers than men.
Depression doesn't just rob people of joy and happiness; it also has a negative impact on
society in the form of lost productivity and the residual impact on family members who
are caring for a loved one suffering from chronic depression.

Depression is not a new disorder even though it seems to be increasing in prevalence. References to depression date back to the beginning of recorded time. Hippo-
crates wrote about melancholy in the 4th century, believing such sadness was caused
by an imbalance in the body's "humors" or liquids (blood, bile, phlegm, and black bile).
Depression is considered productive if it motivates people to change themselves and
their circumstances, when complacency might otherwise keep someone in an unhealthy
situation. But debilitating depression is rarely productive and can leave people feeling ashamed, particularly in a productive-oriented society such as the United States.

Such shame and guilt only serve to add an increased burden to the depressed person, exacerbating depressive symptoms, which can lead to a downward emotional spiral.

There are several theories regarding the cause of major depression, and most experts agree there are likely numerous causes of depression, involving a combination of psychological and biological systems. One popular theory of depression is drawn from cognitive-behavioral theory—a somewhat hybrid model incorporating aspects of Aaron Beck's cognitive theory of depression and behaviorism theory. Cognitive-behavioral theory hypothesizes that depression is often the result of negative and irrational thinking. Thoughts such as "I'm a horrible person," "Nothing good will ever happen to me," or "I will always fail," if thought consistently enough, can ultimately lead to feelings of sadness, despair, and hopelessness (Beck, 1964; Beck, 2006).

Another popular theory, particularly with human services professionals and human services providers, draws from social-contextual theory. In this theory, negative life events within one's social world, such as racial discrimination, gender bias, and poverty, are believed to contribute to depression, particularly if the depressed individual does not have adequate coping skills to deal with these negative experiences in a productive manner (Swindle et al., 1989).

In the last several decades, a biological model of depression has emerged positing genetic vulnerabilities and neurohormonal irregularities such as problems with neurotransmitter functioning. Most human services professionals tend to embrace a **biopsychosocial model** of depression that recognizes the biological basis of many depressions, as well as other influences such as those in the psychological and social realms. Because depression often co-occurs with other disorders such as anxiety, eating disorders, and substance abuse disorders, it is essential that all human services professionals involved in direct service be able to screen for depression, even if a client is not seeking services for this purpose.

Human services professionals utilize many tools and interventions when working with clients struggling with depression. Some of these intervention strategies include insight counseling, where clients develop self-awareness skills intended to help them cope more effectively with their behavioral health–related challenges. A popular and effective intervention strategy often used to treat depression is cognitive behavioral therapy (CBT), based on Beck's (1964) theory of depression. CBT is an intervention strategy used with a range of client populations, including those struggling with depression and anxiety disorders. CBT is a hybrid theory drawing from **cognitive theory** and **behaviorism**.

Essentially, CBT is based on the premise that people will function more effectively if they change their negative and maladaptive thinking and behavioral patterns. Examples of negative thinking include self-statements such as "Nobody will ever love me" or "I can't do anything right." CBT theorists believe that such statements not only influence our beliefs, but also our behaviors. People create meaning around their experiences, and the meaning they create is based on their belief system, which is built up over years of conditioning. CBT challenges clients' negative beliefs about themselves, others, and the world in an attempt to undo previous negative conditioning and replace limiting negativity with more hopeful and optimistic beliefs and behaviors (Beck, 2006).

CBT was originally developed as an intervention with depression, but it has since been used with a range of disorders, including anxiety, eating disorders, and obsessive-compulsive disorder (OCD) (Fava et al., 1998; McKay et al., 2015; Norton & Price, 2007). In addition to individual counseling, group counseling can be effective in assisting clients gain strength and support from others in similar situations—some a few steps ahead of them and some a few steps behind. Psychotropic medications are often used in collaboration with individual and group counseling, and they offer many clients hope of controlling the often-debilitating symptoms common to many serious mental illnesses.

Trauma-Informed Care.

Many people who have a major depressive disorder are also struggling with posttraumatic stress disorder (PTSD), which is characterized by exposure to some type of significant trauma such as a death (or threatened death), serious injury, or sexual assault (or threatened sexual assault). People with PTSD often re-experience the trauma through flashbacks, nightmares, or unwanted and intrusive memories, which they attempt to avoid by avoiding anything that may trigger their trauma. They also experience negative thoughts or feelings about their trauma, which can leave them feeling depressed, anxious, and socially isolated. Depending on the nature of the trauma, they may blame themselves for not acting in a certain way (just as Sara did, as described in the opening vignette). They may also feel chronic irritability or even aggression, experience sleep problems, have difficulty concentrating, and have an exaggerated startle reflex in response to relatively normative stimuli, such as a veteran who was exposed to combat becoming startled in response to a car backfiring (APA, 2013).

The majority of people exposed to trauma may experience some negative symptoms but do not go on to develop PTSD (Frissa et al., 2013); however, research is increasingly showing that some people are more at risk than others to develop PTSD after experiencing a trauma (McLaughlin et al., 2017). For instance, Dorrington et al. (2019) found that people who experience child adversity, such as abuse and neglect, were more vulnerable to developing PTSD in response to a later trauma. There is also an established relationship between cumulative trauma exposure and the development of PTSD, meaning that the more trauma an individual is exposed to, the more they will be vulnerable to PTSD (Dorrington et al., 2014).

It appears that vulnerability to PTSD is greatest when one has experienced interpersonal violence such as domestic violence (Dorrington et al., 2014). There are many possible reasons for these risk factors, including changes that occur in the brain in response to child abuse and neglect that may influence decision making later in life. Another reason may be related to association between childhood trauma and the engagement in risky behaviors later in life, which can then lead to additional traumas (Felitti et al., 1998). For instance, there is a strong link between childhood trauma and later substance abuse (Elwyn & Smith, 2013; Levenson & Grady, 2016).

Individuals who have experienced significant childhood trauma, including emotional, physical, and sexual abuse, and/or have been exposed to domestic violence in the home are best served with a trauma-informed approach. Trauma-informed therapy integrates certain principles that acknowledge the complex nature of trauma and its impact on the brain, body, emotions, and psychological well-being, as well as the impact trauma has on society in general (van der Kolk, 2014). Trauma-informed therapy isn't as much a specific modality as it is a philosophical approach to working with trauma survivors. The National Center for Trauma-Informed Care has published a set of guiding principles for trauma-informed care, asserting that counseling of trauma survivors should be conducted in a way that (1) is safe; (2) is transparent and trustworthy; (3) involves peer support; (4) is collaborative and mutual; (5) focuses on empowerment, voice, and choice; and (6) acknowledges cultural, historic, and gender issues (SAMHSA, 2014).

Consider the case of Sara in the opening vignette. Sara experienced significant childhood trauma, including her father's alcoholism and her mother's depression, both of which appeared to result in Sara and her younger brother being neglected. She then experienced the highly traumatic event of a house fire, which led to her brother's death, and ultimately her parents' divorce. The cumulative traumas Sara experienced throughout her life led to interpersonal problems in her marriage and parenting, as well as substance abuse. There are many therapeutic interventions Sara might benefit from, including CBT, to address her negative thinking and her feelings of powerlessness, but whatever modality the counselor selects must be informed by a trauma-informed approach and by a counselor who is well aware of the impact cumulative trauma likely had on Sara's brain as well as her emotions. Using a trauma-informed approach would help Sara recognize that her fears about leaving her children were a very natural response to losing her brother in the fire. Among the many benefits of a trauma-informed approach is the ability to de-shame a client's thoughts and behaviors, which can then lead to the creation of a safer, more transparent, and empowering counseling experience.

Anxiety Disorders

Other disorders that are frequently experienced by clients seeking treatment in human services agencies include anxiety disorders, such as generalized anxiety disorder (GAD), which involves excessively worrying (that cannot be easily controlled) about a number of different things more days than not for at least six months. Symptoms of GAD include restlessness, being easily fatigued, difficulty concentrating, irritability, muscle tension, and disturbances in sleep, although a client only needs to experience three of these symptoms in order to be diagnosed with GAD, and the symptoms cannot be associated with a substance, medication condition, or PTSD (APA, 2013).

Obsessive-compulsive disorder (OCD) is also quite common and includes compulsive behaviors such as intrusive thoughts and impulses that the individual realizes are coming from inside, not being imposed from the outside (to distinguish OCD from psychotic disorders). In addition, OCD includes compulsions, or ritual behaviors, such as repetitive handwashing, used to manage the obsessive thoughts. For example, an individual who has intrusive thoughts about family members dying might flip his blinds seven times every hour based on the irrational belief that this activity will keep his family safe (while knowing that the behavior is irrational). Another OCD-type disorder includes body dysmorphic disorder (now included in the *DSM-5*), a body image disorder where people are preoccupied with imagined or exaggerated flaws in their appearance (Phillips & Castle, 2015).

Because human services professionals work in practice settings that serve high-crisis clients, they often come into contact with individuals who have experienced a significant amount of trauma. Some of these clients will then likely be experiencing trauma-and-stressor-related disorders, such as PTSD; PTSD is a particular clinical focus when working with survivors of domestic violence and veterans. PTSD involves a history of exposure to a traumatic event, referred to as the stressor, which results in symptoms that fall into four clusters:

- *Intrusive recollections* involving, for instance, mental images or intrusive thoughts about the original traumatic event repeatedly playing through the person's mind

- *Avoidance behaviors* that serve as strategies to avoid psychological triggers related to the trauma, such as avoiding people, places, or things that remind the person of the original traumatic event
- *Negative cognitions*, such as blaming oneself for the traumatic event or believing that the world is a bad place
- *Moods*, such as ongoing depression and rage; alternations in arousal or reactivity, such as generalized anxiety; or hypervigilance, such as a heightened startle reflex (APA, 2013).

Personality Disorders

People with personality disorders view themselves and others in a way that significantly and negatively impacts their lives and ability to function across many areas of their lives. Personality disorders used to be diagnosed on Axis II of the *DSM-IV*, but the *DSM-5* now includes personality disorders and clinical disorders in the same section based on the contention that distinguishing between clinical disorders and personality disorders is somewhat arbitrary (APA, 2013).

Students and newer clinicians often express confusion about how to tell the difference between clinical disorders and personality disorders because some of the symptomology is overlapping, but more seasoned counselors can pretty easily make a distinction. In fact, when I was in graduate school I had a professor who told us that the easiest way a clinician could tell the difference between someone with a clinical disorder and a personality disorder is that clients with clinical disorders express fears that there is something terribly wrong with them, whereas clients with personality disorders express outrage that there is something wrong with everyone else. Of course, my professor was exaggerating to make a point, and while there is certainly no validity to such universal catchall phrases, anyone who has known someone with a diagnosable personality disorder would understand my professor's point.

Generally speaking, a key difference between clinical disorders and personality disorders is that those with clinical disorders for the most part have insight and awareness into the maladaptive nature of their feelings and behaviors, whereas those with personality disorders often do not. For instance, clients with OCD for the most part know their intrusive thinking and obsessive need to engage in rituals is irrational and they will often come into counseling expressing fears that they are "crazy," while clients with obsessive-compulsive personality disorder believe their way is the right way, and they may come into counseling complaining that the entire world is out of step except them (IOCDF, 2014).

Individuals with personality disorders often experience rigid and inflexible patterns of feelings and behavior, including unhealthy and maladaptive patterns of perceiving things, difficulty controlling or regulating emotions, and difficulty controlling emotional impulses. People with personality disorders will often perceive things differently than others, including misperceiving another's behavior and intentions. Close to 8% of the world population is estimated to have a personality disorder, but in high-income countries, such as the United States, the estimate is closer to 11% (Winsper et al., 2020). Before you begin diagnosing your family and friends (or your exes!), it's important to know that just because someone has personality traits that are irritating or somewhat eccentric, it does not mean they have a personality disorder. One of my best friends can be defensive if someone criticizes her children. She often misperceives innocent comments as slights or criticism of her parenting. But does this mean she has a personality disorder? Not necessarily. But what if her defensiveness was so intense that she started arguments constantly with friends and family members? What if she could not enjoy going out socially because all she could think about was protecting her children? What if she perceived insults everywhere and could not get along with anyone, including her children's teachers? This behavior might then push her in the direction of a personality disorder—a collection of maladaptive and rigid personality traits that are exhibited across different life domains and that interfere with one's ability to function effectively in life, including interfering with one's ability to enjoy reasonably healthy relationships with others.

For instance, it might be perfectly normal for a woman to feel emotionally attacked whenever she gets into an argument with her husband if he has an aggressive way of expressing his needs and frustrations. But it is not necessarily healthy or normative

Table 6.1   Personality Disorders Organized by Clusters

Cluster	Cluster Description	Personality Disorders	Personality Disorder Characterization
A	Odd and eccentric	Paranoid	A pattern of suspicion and mistrust of others that is irrational and not based in reality
		Schizoid	A lack of interest and detachment from social relationships, feelings of apathy toward others, and a restricted range of emotions
		Schizotypal	A pattern of extreme discomfort in social interaction with distorted thinking and perceptions
B	Dramatic, emotional, or erratic	Antisocial	A pervasive pattern of disregard for others with a violation of others' rights, a lack of empathy, bloated self-image, manipulative and impulsive behavior
		Borderline	A pervasive pattern of instability in relationships, self-image, identity, and behavior. Emotions often lead to self-harm, intense anger in response to perceived abandonment, and impulsivity
		Histrionic	A pervasive pattern of attention-seeking behaviors and excessive emotionality
		Narcissistic	A pervasive pattern of grandiosity, a constant need for admiration, and a general lack of empathy toward others
C	Anxious and fearful	Avoidant	Pervasive feelings of social inhibition and feelings of inadequacy, extreme sensitivity to negative evaluation
		Dependent	A pervasive psychological need to be cared for by others, highly dependent on the approval of others, inability to make choices on their own
		Obsessive compulsive	A pervasive and rigid conformity to rules, perfectionism, an excessive need for control

for a woman to feel emotionally attacked whenever she receives constructive feedback that she perceives as criticism from her husband, friends, family, coworkers, supervisor, teachers, and children. It also might be perfectly healthy for a man to consistently focus on himself in certain situations where perhaps he feels somewhat insecure, such as in large social environments. But it might not be considered normative and healthy if this person excessively focuses on himself in virtually all areas of his life—at home, at work, with family, in social situations large and small, often at the expense of others.

Far more people exhibit features of personality disorders (meaning they have some traits, but do not meet the criteria for a personality disorder); thus, human services providers must be careful not to overdiagnose clients based on irritating or eccentric tendencies. The relative health or adaptive nature of one's personality traits is always assessed on a continuum, like so many other mental and emotional conditions. If someone is a bit on the rigid side with certain issues, it wouldn't necessarily be appropriate to diagnose this person with a personality disorder. Yet, if someone gets far enough out on the continuum with regard to rigidity, for example, so that it interferes with an ability to function at work, with family, or in social situations, then this person might have what is considered a disordered personality.

According to the *DSM-5*, the key difference between someone who has a normally structured personality and one who has a personality disorder is that the structure of a disordered personality must cause distress and impairment of functioning in several important areas of functioning (APA, 2013). The *DSM-5* categorizes the 10 personality disorders into three groups, or clusters, based on similar features and symptoms. Cluster A includes odd and eccentric behaviors (paranoid, schizoid, and schizotypal personality disorders), Cluster B includes dramatic, emotional, and erratic behaviors (antisocial, borderline, histrionic, and narcissistic personality disorders), and Cluster C includes anxious and fearful behaviors (avoidant, dependent, and obsessive-compulsive personality disorders). Although there are distinct diagnostic differences between the different personality disorders, most have some features in common, such as rigid thinking, problems perceiving experiences accurately, and significant interpersonal problems.

Counseling individuals with personality disorders can be frustrating for practitioners because progress is slow and clients are often resistant to change due to the inherent nature of personality disorders. Yet, many new counseling techniques are being developed, some with a fair amount of success. One reason for the slower progress is because authentic change requires that clients with personality disorders change the entire way they perceive the world and themselves within it. They must also learn how to "sit with their emotions" and control their impulses rather than act on them, which can be particularly challenging when the personality disorder involves impulsivity and high emotionality.

Antidepressant and antianxiety medications are often used in combination with individual and group counseling, where even clients who struggle with insight can focus on skill building, such as developing anger management skills, delaying gratification, and increasing social skills. A counseling approach that has shown some promise is dialectical behavior therapy (DBT), pioneered by Marsha Linehan. DBT uses a combination of cognitive behavioral therapy with group work and skills training. A relatively recent study showed that DBT was effective in treating suicidal clients with borderline personality disorder, which is particularly promising in light of the difficulty of working with this population (Linehan et al., 2015).

COMMON BEHAVIORAL HEALTH
PRACTICE SETTINGS

Learning Outcome 6.4   Describe the roles and functions of human services professionals within common mental health practice settings serving mainstream and special populations

Human services professionals working with the mentally ill population do so in a variety of practice settings, including outpatient mental health clinics, community mental health centers, not-for-profit agencies, outreach programs, job training agencies, housing assistance programs, prisoner assistance programs, government agencies such as departments of mental health and human services, and probation programs. Generalist human services practitioners might be case managers responsible for conducting needs assessments and coordinating the mental health care of clients, they might be providing counseling services on an individual and/or group basis, or they may provide more concrete services such as job training. In truth, a human services practitioner will likely encounter clients with serious mental illnesses in just about any practice setting, but in this section, I will focus on those settings where the seriously and chronically mentally ill are the target population.

Community mental health centers provide direct services to the seriously and chronically mentally ill population. These centers are typically licensed by the state and designated to serve a certain catchment area within the community. Services offered often include outpatient services for adults and children, 24-hour crisis intervention, case management services, community support, psychiatric services, alcohol and drug treatment, psychological evaluations, and various educational workshops. They might also offer partial hospitalization and day treatment programs. Although most community mental health centers operate on a sliding scale, most centers are funded through federal grants, so they typically will not turn clients away who have no ability to pay; thus, they are highly reliant on public funding.

The seriously mentally ill are often served by full-service not-for-profit human services agencies, which typically offer an array of services aimed at various target populations, including the seriously mentally ill. Human services agencies can range broadly in terms of the level of services they provide, and what client populations they target, but generally most agencies provide general counseling and case management services, group counseling, family intervention services, and a range of special programs specific to the agency's mission, such as vocational programs, housing assistance, parenting training, childcare, crisis intervention, and substance abuse counseling.

A human services practitioner might work in a number of capacities within a human services agency, depending in large part on what types of programs the agency offers. For instance, a human services practitioner might offer general case management services, coordinating all the care the client is receiving and acting as the point person for the psychologist, psychiatrist, and any other service providers involved in a client's case. They might provide direct counseling services or run support groups focusing on a number of psychosocial and daily life issues. If the agency provides outreach services, the human services practitioner might be out in the community providing emergency crisis intervention services for the local police department or other emergency personnel. The list of program services that a human services agency may offer is almost endless, particularly because a part of the role of the human services agency is to identify needs within a community and address those needs whenever possible.

An alternative to inpatient hospitalization is partial hospitalization or day treatment programs. These programs, often operated within a hospital setting, are intensive and offer services for individuals who are having difficulty coping in their daily lives but are not at a point where inpatient hospitalization is a necessity. Clients typically attend the program 5 days a week, for approximately 7 hours a day, and work with a multidisciplinary team of professionals, including a psychiatrist, psychologist, and human services provider. Family involvement is highly encouraged. Certain partial hospitalization programs focus on specific issues, such as eating disorders, self-abuse, or substance abuse, whereas others focus on a wider range of clinical issues, such as severe depression, anger management, and past abuse issues. The nature of the program will also vary depending on whether the target population consists of adults, adolescents, or children. These structured programs can either serve as an alternative intervention to inpatient hospitalization or be utilized when a patient is transitioned out of inpatient hospitalization back into the community.

Although the deinstitutionalization movement has resulted in a dramatic reduction in long-term hospitalization of persons with severe mental illness, some individuals who are acutely disturbed or suicidal are hospitalized on a short-term basis for diagnostic assessment and stabilization in inpatient or acute psychiatric hospitals. Psychiatric units are typically locked for the safety of the patients, who are often actively psychotic and may be a danger to themselves or others. Again, services are focused on assessment and stabilization, with a particular emphasis on discharge planning. Human services practitioners often provide case management and discharge planning in inpatient settings. Licensed mental health care providers engage in more intensive counseling services such as facilitating individual and group counseling, as well as behavior management if the program is focused on children and adolescents.

An interesting approach increasingly adopted by practitioners and agencies working with substance abusing populations and clients with dual diagnoses is the *harm reduction model*. The basic premise behind the harm reduction model is that clients are helped the most when they are accepted as they are (Vakharia & Little, 2017). Providing clean needles to drug users to ensure a reduction of HIV infections, or not requiring complete sobriety in homeless shelters, since the majority of mentally ill homeless individuals have a dual diagnosis and need the assistance the most, are examples of programs using a harm reduction model.

The harm reduction model, and harm reduction therapy (HRT), is based on the principle of client autonomy and self-determination, which is congruent with the human services profession. According to Vakharia and Little (2017), one of the greatest strengths of using the harm reduction model with clients who abuse substances and have mentally illness is that it helps create a strong therapeutic bond (because the client does not feel judged), and it lowers the threshold of treatment, since many substance abusing clients are resistant to treatment because they are not ready to commit to complete abstinence, particularly if they are using substances as a form of self-medication.

WORKING WITH SPECIAL POPULATIONS

Working with Homeless Populations

One unanticipated consequence of deinstitutionalization was the shifting of literally thousands of mentally ill patients from institutions to the streets due to a shortage of housing for the severely mentally ill (Torry et al., 2015). In fact, a 2005 study found that nearly one in six mentally ill individuals are homeless (Folsom et al., 2005). And since it is so difficult to track intermittent homelessness—where a mentally ill person cycles in and out of homelessness—the actual number is likely far higher.

Many of these individuals previously would have been institutionalized, but with the closing of the majority of public mental hospitals and the transitioning of most psychiatric units to a focus on short-term stays, the severely mentally ill who do not have a network of supportive and able family members are often left with no place to live except on the streets. Even individuals who do have supportive families may live on the streets due to the nature of psychosis, which clouds judgment and impairs the ability to think without distortion, leading some individuals to disappear for years at a time.

The link between homelessness and mental illness is not solely related to deinstitutionalization. Certainly, warehousing the mentally ill kept them off the streets, but the nature of this association is far more complex and likely reciprocal in nature. Severe mental illness leaves many incapable of providing for their basic needs, and the stressful nature of living on the streets—not knowing where one will sleep at night, dealing with exposure to violence and inclement weather, not knowing where one's next meal will come from—would put the healthiest of individuals at risk for developing some mental illness.

Government sources estimate that approximately 26% of the homeless population is severely mentally ill (U.S. Conference of Mayors, 2016; Henry et al., 2020), and if mental illness is broadened to include clinical depression and substance abuse disorders (often used to self-medicate), that percentage jumps to 35 to 50% (North et al., 2004; Shern et al., 2000). The mentally ill homeless population is a diverse group, but single Black men and veterans are most likely to be homeless and suffering from mental illness (Folsom et al., 2005; Koerber, 2005; Shern et al., 2000).

Although deinstitutionalization is credited for being the primary cause of increases of the mentally ill homeless population, the increase escalated in the 1980s due to a shortage in affordable housing and a lack of funding of housing assistance programs targeting at-risk middle-aged men and veterans. Examples of other driving factors in the increase of homelessness are the increase in rental prices (Glynn & Fox, 2019) and an increase in single parenting and violence against women, the fastest growing homeless demographic (Phipps et al., 2019). There is considerable controversy surrounding the relationship between substance abuse and homelessness, particularly whether substance abuse is a risk factor for homelessness, or whether homelessness is a risk factor for substance abuse (i.e., which came first, the "chicken or the egg"). One recent study found that homeless youth were particularly vulnerable to using drugs and alcohol as a way of handling living on the streets (Lightfoot et al., 2018). In other words, it wasn't using drugs that led to youth homelessness, but rather, the mental and emotional stressors of living on the streets.

One of the biggest challenges in getting individuals with mental illness off the streets is engaging them in treatment. One of the rights the mentally ill achieved in post-deinstitutionalization legislation was the right to refuse treatment. A deeper look into this issue reveals that it may not be as simple as individuals in need not wanting help, but may be far more related to the difficulty and complexity of accessing needed services (Shern et al., 2000). Barriers to accessing services often include difficulties in applying for government assistance such as Medicaid and Medicare to pay for both treatment and medication. Another barrier involves the actual service delivery model most popular in counseling and mental health centers, where the client comes to the psychologist, not the other way around. History clearly reveals that this model simply does not work with most seriously mentally ill individuals, particularly those living on the streets. Such individuals are often confused, disoriented, and frequently distrusting of others, particularly if they are suffering from some sort of psychotic disorder. To expect a person who is homeless and suffering from mental illness to remember a weekly appointment and somehow figure out how to navigate transportation to a doctor's office in a business center or other urban location is likely unrealistic.

Another barrier to seeking treatment involves the many stipulations and requirements common in standard treatment models used by many community mental health centers. Most standard behavioral health programs have strict participation requirements, particularly related to behavioral issues, such as maintaining sobriety to remain in a housing assistance program or requiring clients to participate in weekly counseling support groups in order to receive other services. In fact, most standard programs are directive with seriously mentally ill clients, often determining treatment goals and interventions for the client, rather than empowering clients to assist in determining their own treatment goals and interventions (Shern et al., 2000). Programs using a harm reduction model reduce this barrier to treatment.

The problem of homelessness among the mentally ill population will not be resolved until sufficient long-term housing assistance can be provided. Housing assistance programs typically have long waiting lists and often allow only women with children accelerated access to the program. Because Black men and veterans are overrepresented in the mentally ill homeless population, more programs need to be developed that target these populations. Such programs must also be designed to address issues related to alcohol and substance abuse problems as well, because many within the mentally ill homeless population have co-occurring substance abuse problems.

Working With Prisoners

Another unintended by-product of deinstitutionalization is the inadvertent shifting of chronically mentally ill patients from public mental hospitals to jails and prisons. In fact, many behavioral health advocates have argued that prisons are now the primary institutions within the United States warehousing severely mentally ill individuals. About 60% of state and federal prisoners have a diagnosable and often untreated mental illness, and about 15% have a diagnosable severe mental illness (e.g., schizophrenia, bipolar disorder) (Fields & Phillips, 2013; Palermo et al., 1991; Raphael & Stoll, 2013; Torrey, 1995).

There are more mentally ill men than mentally ill women in jails and prison. However, mentally ill women are overrepresented in the prison population, with approximately 31% of women in state prisons suffering from some form of serious mental illness compared to about 14% for men (Torrey et al., 2010). Most mentally

Jailed and Mentally Ill, Chicago, USA.

© AP / SHUTTERSTOCK

ill prisoners are poor and either were undiagnosed prior to their incarceration or were untreated in the months prior to entering the prison system. Female mentally ill inmates were twice as likely to have a history of physical abuse and four times as likely to have been the victim of sexual abuse. In fact, almost 65% of mentally ill female inmates reported having been physically and/or sexually abused prior to going to prison (Ditton, 1999).

But what does this really mean? Could it simply mean that mentally ill individuals break the law more than mentally healthy individuals? Couldn't it be argued that one must certainly be mentally ill to commit serious crimes in the first place? After all, what sane person sexually abuses children, or robs a bank, or drinks alcohol and drives? Depending on how mental illness is defined, it could be argued that those who commit heinous crimes are by definition mentally ill, and that their mental illness does not and should not negate the appropriateness of sending them to prison for their crimes. But even in situations where offenders clearly should be incarcerated, a retrospective look at their behavioral health histories might reveal a history of poor service utilization, including multiple barriers to effective treatment.

While prisons have always held mentally ill prisoners, the number of incarcerated mentally ill persons has increased, in large part because of a decrease in treatment options available for the mentally ill population within the general population. The reasons for this decrease include a reduction in funding of community mental health centers, barriers to access for lower-income and ethnic minority populations, and increasing difficulty in securing involuntary hospitalization of the severely mentally ill. The majority of the mentally ill who are incarcerated have been convicted of nonviolent petty crimes related to their mental illness. In fact, far too often mentally ill prisoners, particularly those in the general prison population, are consistent targets of victimization, particularly sex-related crimes, many of which go unreported (Marley & Buila, 2001).

Many military personnel and veterans are provided with service dogs to help with anxiety, depression, and the symptoms of PTSD.

The incarceration of the mentally ill is not a simple problem, and thus it has no simple answers. Mental health and prison advocates cite barriers to accessing mental health services, problems with early intervention, and the high cost of mental health care as direct causes of seriously mentally ill individuals ending up in the penal system rather than in psychiatric facilities. The **Affordable Care Act (ACA)**, with the inclusion of **mental health parity**, is a promising step forward, but challenges related to service availability, cost, and patient compliance remain significant.

Once again the controversial issue of an individual's right to refuse treatment is relevant in this matter as well, evidenced by the many family members of the mentally ill who consistently complain that the courts have refused to order involuntary treatment, only to have their mentally ill family member commit a violent crime some time later. What is so unfortunate in these incidences is that the majority of mentally ill defendants are amenable to treatment, but many were not receiving any treatment at the time of their incarceration (Marley & Buila, 2001).

Working with Military Personnel and Veterans

A relatively recent phenomenon within the armed services involves a dramatic spike in behavioral health disorders, including suicide, among military personnel—both within service members who have been deployed to combat zones as well as those deployed within the United States. Suicides among military personnel (active duty and post-enlistment) have skyrocketed in recent years, particularly between 2007 and 2009 (during the Iraqi and Afghanistan conflicts). In fact, despite efforts to confront this epidemic, in 2012 the number of military suicides outpaced the number of soldiers killed in combat (Briggs, 2013). The mental health community is scrambling to figure out why and also to find viable and enduring solutions to this mental health crisis.

These wars were far more protracted and violent than past wars and involved unprecedented redeployments and longer-than-average deployment times (Kang et al., 2015). Soldiers returned home with a range of behavioral health, medical, and psychosocial challenges, including traumatic brain injuries, stress-related disorders such as PTSD and "combat stress," intimate partner violence, substance abuse, trauma resulting from sexual abuse and assault, and readjustment issues. Many soldiers returned to face a lack of support, including insufficient (and stigmatized) behavioral health services, financial difficulties, and challenges finding employment. Suicides among soldiers returning from the Afghanistan and Iraq wars have been significantly higher than in the general population, which has been attributed to the unique nature of these conflicts (Kang et al., 2015). Additionally, there have been numerous cases of soldiers behaving in ways that were seemingly uncharacteristic, presumed to be fueled by substance abuse, depression, and trauma. Consider the following case study detailing true events:

Case Study 6.1   The Case of Military Trauma and Violence

On March 11, 2012 Staff Sgt. Robert Bales, a U.S. Army Staff Sergeant, who was serving his fourth combat deployment since enlisting in the Army in November 2001 shortly after the 9/11 terrorist attacks, opened fire on 17 innocent Afghani civilians, primarily women and children. The Kandahar Province massacres were committed in the middle of the night, solely by Sgt. Bales, following a night of drinking with his buddies. The married father of two from Washington State described in court how he brutally attacked victims in two villages by gunning them down and then stacking some like firewood and setting them on fire. This incident is certainly disturbing (to say the least), but what is almost equally disturbing is what Sgt. Bales' defense attorney described as a normal family man turned homicidal maniac due to the horrific stress endured on the battlefield—four combat deployments in high-violence combat zones; two injuries, one including traumatic brain injury (TBI); exposure to high levels of violence and trauma, including numerous roadside bombings and carrying dead bodies, some burned beyond recognition, off the battlefield—coupled with excessive drinking to relieve stress and taking valium and steroids allegedly supplied by his superiors. Fellow soldiers described Sgt. Bales as "competent and positive." His wife described him as a wonderful husband and father. But when he returned from each of his tours, he described how his depression and anger worsened, how his drinking and misuse of sleeping pills increased, and how ineffective counseling caused him to withdraw from family and friends even more. In court Sgt. Bales stated that while he could not explain the murders, he believed he just snapped because he could no longer manage his mounting anger and stress resulting from the trauma he had endured from multiple deployments. Brown, his defense attorney, described Sgt. Bales as "crazed and broken" the night of the attack—"He's broken, and we broke him" (Johnson, 2013). In June 2013, Bales pled guilty to murder to avoid the death penalty and was sentenced in August of 2013 to life in prison without the possibility of parole. In December 2019, a military advocacy group, United American Patriots, filed a civil suit on Bales' behalf accusing the U.S. government of denying Bales his constitutional rights. The lawsuit claimed that Bales experienced a psychotic break due to taking mefloquine, an anti-malaria drug, which can cause behavioral health problems, including hallucinations (South, 2019).

Behavioral health issues, such as PTSD, depression, explosive disorders, and substance abuse, have long been associated with military service and are increasingly prevalent among the veteran population. There has been increased attention on the behavioral health of military personnel recently due to several high-profile cases involving homicide, suicide, and domestic violence. Research on the impact of trauma on military personnel and their families focuses on answering important questions about the causes, nature, and extent of mental illness. For instance, was Sgt. Bales' murderous rampage a result of longstanding homicidal tendencies rooted in childhood or adolescence? Or was it brought on solely by the stress of multiple deployments and untreated PTSD and a TBI? What were the warning signs, if any, that Bales' struggles were beyond his ability to cope? What structures did the Army have in place to deal with Bales' deteriorating mental health status?

In response to the recent spike in mental health disorders and suicides among service members, the Army, in cooperation with the National Institute of Mental Health, has initiated the largest research study of military service members and veterans ever commissioned. The study is called the Army Study to Assess Risk and Resilience in Servicemembers (STARRS). STARRS consists of a series of studies categorized into five study types:

- The Historical Administrative Data Study—The examination of administrative and health records of 1.6 million active-duty soldiers between 2004 and 2009 in search of evidence of psychological risk (e.g., a past history of depression) and protective factors (e.g., evidence of psychological resilience)
- The New Soldier Study—The assessment of the health, personalities, and prior experiences of new soldiers
- The All Army Study—The assessment of soldiers' psychological and physical health during combat and non-combat periods
- The Soldier Health Outcomes Study—Two studies that compare service personnel who have experienced suicidal behavior with those who have not
- Special Studies—The examination of the effects of deployment to a combat zone with the goal of identifying risk factors for suicide and factors relating to psychological resiliency among service members who have faced combat.

According to three STARRS studies published in March 2014, suicide rates more than doubled for soldiers who served in Iraq and Afghanistan between 2004 and 2009, but almost even more alarming was that suicide rates nearly tripled for soldiers who were not deployed but remained in the United States (Schoenbaum et al., 2014). Additionally, most subjects who were diagnosed with post-deployment mental disorders (e.g., PTSD, anxiety, depression, attention-deficit/hyperactivity disorder [ADHD], anger management, substance abuse), as well as those who experienced suicide ideation and suicide attempts, had a history of pre-enlistment mental disorders, most often rooted in childhood and adolescence (Nock et al., 2015; Ursano et al., 2014). These findings are vitally important because not only do they highlight the nature of the problems experienced by many current and former service members (active duty, deployed, and veterans), they also provide insights into ways that the mental health community can better support recruits, soldiers, and veterans through better behavioral health screening and the development of prevention and treatment programs.

Human services practitioners have long been members of multidisciplinary teams serving on military bases as both officers and civilian employees, dating back to at least

World War I. Currently, a range of human services practitioners contribute to the development and facilitation of effective treatment programs to address contemporary issues facing soldiers and their family members. Human services practitioners work within all branches of the armed services throughout the world, the Department of Defense, and the U.S. Department of Veteran's Affairs hospitals. They serve on emergency response teams that are deployed in times of crisis, such as a violent incident occurring on a military base, or during a natural disaster, providing humanitarian and disaster relief.

Working with LGBTQ Populations

Lesbian, gay, bisexual, transgender, and queer/questioning (LGBTQ) adults and youth experience higher rates of behavioral health challenges than the cisgender population (Whaibeh et al., 2019). Transgender and gender non-conforming youth (those who do not identify as either male or female) are at particular risk of behavioral health issues, primarily due to how sexual and gender minorities are treated in society and the ensuing trauma (Becerra-Culqui et al., 2018). Of course, there is great variation, with some sexual and gender minorities who live with accepting families and in accepting communities experiencing minimal trauma, and others who reside in hostile environments and experience considerable distress.

A study based on the 2017 Institute Southern Survey found that members of the LGBTQ community living in the southern regions of the United States, where religiosity is high and acceptance of sexual minorities is low, experienced significantly higher rates of serious mental illness compared to cis men and women. Those who were out had lower rates of mental illness, and a lifetime of discrimination was associated with higher rates of discrimination (Caldwell, 2019). When race intersects with sexual orientation, behavioral health is even more significantly impacted. A 2016 study found that discrimination based on race had a negative impact on an individual's behavioral health, but when discrimination was based on LGBTQ status, not only was the victim's behavioral health impacted, but the LGBTQ-based discrimination also increased thoughts of suicide (Sutter & Perrin, 2016).

LGBTQ youth are at increased risk of mental health problems and suicide, as well as running away (Choi et al., 2015; Rhoades et al., 2018). Runaway and homeless youth were explored in Chapter 4, but understanding the running away experiences of LGBTQ within the context of behavioral health is important, particularly because this is a group with elevated risk and with few advocates. A 2015 study found that running away was often prompted by sexual and gender minority youth coming out to their parents, who then kicked them out of the house. Living on the streets after being kicked out was associated with increased risk of physical and behavioral health problems. Transgender youth were at a particularly high risk of having behavioral health problems, particularly problems with substance abuse (Choi et al., 2015). Research has found that social support clubs run by counselors and human services providers can have a positive impact on LGBTQ youth with mental illness by providing them with a safe and accepting place to hang out, in many cases reducing the need for inpatient hospitalization (Klein, 2017).

In the past, anti-LGBTQ rhetoric would have suggested that the reason sexual and gender minorities struggled with behavioral health issues, including substance abuse and suicidality, was because their "lifestyle" was making them "sick." And yet, the research is clear. When sexual and gender minorities live in an accepting and supportive environment, they experience lower rates of mental illness, and when they live in hostile and unaccepting environments, where they're subject to discrimination and social isolation, they experience higher rates of mental illness.

WORKING WITH RACIAL AND ETHNIC MINORITY POPULATIONS

Pearson eText

Video Example 6.4

In this video the human services provider explores a client's experiences as a recently arrived immigrant. What is the value of asking open-ended questions to explore the client's feelings and sense of belonging?

Learning Outcome 6.5   **Critically analyze the relationship between racial bias and disparity in treatment among ethnic minority populations**

Early studies have shown that ethnic minority populations are often poorly served in mental health centers because of a lack of culturally competent and bilingual counselors, as well as a lack of available services offered in ethnic minority communities (Alegría et al., 2008; Horvitz-Lennon et al., 2015; Sue, 1977). Other studies have shown that while Latina/o, Asian, and Pacific Islander populations were underrepresented in community mental health center settings, those within the Black and Native American populations were overrepresented (Diala et al., 2001; Hernandez et al., 2015; Sue & McKinney, 1975). This pattern may be partly due to cultural acceptance or rejection of psychotherapy within different cultural groups, and it may also be related to the relative complexity of issues facing the populations served, particularly Native Americans, who traditionally have high rates of substance abuse and depression and often reside in remote areas. Regardless of inter-ethnic minority utilization comparisons, the research clearly shows that lower-income ethnic minority populations are poorly served in almost all respects, including a lack of available individual counseling, case management, and front-line psychotropic medications (Hernandez et al., 2015).

Other types of bias can enter the counseling relationship as well. Consider the bias that many in the United States (particularly European Americans) have about time. The U.S. culture tends to highly value time and promptness. When someone is timely, they are often considered to be respectful, responsible, considerate of others, and organized. Conversely, those who are consistently late are often presumed to be disrespectful, irresponsible, inconsiderate of others, disorganized, and perhaps even lazy. Yet, not all cultures value or perceive time in the same manner, and a stereotyped bias is that individuals from cultures that do not perceive time in a similar manner as the majority culture are in some way deficient. Human services professionals who have been enculturated in U.S. values might not even realize they hold this stereotype and might unconsciously attribute negative traits to clients who consistently show up late to their appointments. Thus, although it might be worth exploring whether a pattern of lateness is related to lacking motivation or resistance, a human services professional should consider whether racial bias is resulting from negative assumptions about a client's character based solely on the fact that the client is from a culture that does not value time in the same manner as U.S. culture.

Hence, although rarely is someone eager to admit holding negative stereotypes and biases about certain races, cultures, or lifestyles, it is imperative, particularly when working with the seriously mentally ill population, that these negative stereotypes are explored, challenged, and discarded. Otherwise they will remain powerful forces in how human services professionals subtly or overtly evaluate and assess client actions, motivations, strengths, and deficits, including assessment of accountability and causation for their life circumstances.

Pearson eText

Video Example 6.5

In this video the human services provider uses a strengths-based approach with a client who is adjusting to living in a new country. What strengths does the provider identify and how did this process shift the perspective of the client?

Working with Native Americans and Alaska Natives

One of the first studies to provide national averages for mental illness among Native American and Alaska Native (AI/AN) populations found that 70% of AI/AN men and 63% of AI/AN women had a psychiatric disorder, and over half met the criteria for at least one psychiatric disorder in the past year (Brave Heart et al., 2016). These rates were significantly higher than for non-Hispanic Whites and other ethnic minority populations. The types of mental disorders AI/AN populations were most vulnerable to were substance abuse, depression, and certain personality disorders (obsessive personality disorder, paranoid personality disorder, and antisocial personality disorder).

Many communities of color experience an increased risk of behavioral health problems due to racism, discrimination (Oh et al., 2016; U.S. Commission on Civil Rights, 2003), and physical and health disparities (Bailey et al., 2017; Indian Health Service, 2009). But AI/AN populations face several risk factors unique to indigenous populations, including as historic cultural losses such as land and water loss, a history of family separations (Whitbeck et al., 2004) (also experienced by many in the Black community and certain immigrant groups), and physical and cultural genocide (Brave Heart, & DeBruyn,1998).

Working with the Black Community

The Black population experiences higher rates of mental illness, often due to the stress associated with historic trauma, economic disadvantage, overt racism, and microaggressions (Durham, 2018; Pachter et al., 2018). Recent research has also shown a correlation between mental illness and food insecurity among the Black population (Allen, Becerra & Becerra, 2018). Blacks also face a disproportionate number of barriers to treatment such as stigma and lack of access (Flores & Tomany-Korman, 2008; Thornicroft, 2008; Williams & Wyatt, 2015). These barriers are particularly prevalent among Black families living in rural communities (Douthit et al., 2015).

There have been several recent high-profile cases involving alleged police brutality against unarmed Black people that have highlighted the disparate treatment of Blacks living in the United States. These cases, while too many to include in this section, reflect the impact of racial bias within many law enforcement agencies, both with regard to assumptions made about the potential threat posed by Blacks, particularly Black men, as well as their treatment in the criminal justice system. Three of the more high-profile cases of police killing unarmed Blacks, leading to widespread outrage and sustained national and global protests in 2020, include the killings of 25-year-old Ahmaud Arbery in Georgia, 26-year-old Breonna Taylor in Kentucky, and 46-year-old George Floyd in Minnesota.

On March 13, 2020, Louisville, Kentucky, police used a battering ram in the middle of the night to forcibly enter the home of Breonna Taylor, a health care worker. Police had obtained a "no knock" warrant to enter the residence based on the belief that Taylor may have been involved in a drug deal, despite already apprehending the primary target, who lived a considerable distance away from Taylor. When the police rammed into the residence during the middle of the night, Breanna's boyfriend, Kenneth Walker, a licensed gun owner, fired a shot, believing someone was breaking into their home. In response, police showered the residence in bullets, hitting Taylor eight times. Although Walker was initially charged with attempted murder of a police officer, the charges were later dropped, in what some have suggested was a response to inconsistencies contained in the police incident report. Taylor's family and Walker denied any connection to drug dealing, and believe the police identified the wrong residence. Law enforcement experts have asserted that using a battering ram in the middle of the night based on a belief that Taylor's home might have been used to receive a package of drugs, was completely unnecessary and led to the justifiable response of Walker, and the needless death of Taylor (Oppel & Taylor, 2020).

George Floyd was killed on May 25, 2020, during an arrest for allegedly using a counterfeit $20 bill to purchase cigarettes. Video evidence showed that four Minneapolis police officers engaged in a series of activities in violation of Minneapolis Police Department regulations, including kneeling on Floyd's neck for 8 minutes and 46 seconds, which resulted in Floyd's death. Prior to his death, several witnesses were heard on video screaming at officer Derek Chauvin, who is White, to remove his knee from Floyd's neck, as Floyd was clearly in distress. Not only did Chauvin refuse to remove his knee, he kept it there more than a minute after Floyd became unresponsive. All four officers involved in Floyd's death have since been terminated and criminally charged. Chauvin was charged with second-degree murder, and the other three officers were charged with aiding and abetting a murder (Hill et al., 2020).

On Sunday, February 23, 2020 at about 1 p.m., Ahmaud Arbery, was jogging through a south Georgia neighborhood near his home when he was chased down and killed by two White men in their truck—Gregory McMichael, a former police officer and former investigator with the local district attorney's office, and his son, 34-year-old son Travis. The McMichaels stated that they saw Arbery jogging by their home and believed he looked like someone suspected of series of residential burglaries. They grabbed a shotgun and a .357 magnum pistol and took chase in their truck with the intention of making a citizen's arrest. The district attorney declined to charge the McMichaels, asserting that the McMichaels had a right to make a citizen's arrest and were acting in self-defense. A graphic video emerged online more than 2 months after the killing, which appeared to show quite a different story than originally reported. The graphic video showed the McMichaels chasing down Arbery in their truck, maneuvering the truck to block Arbery's path on several occasions. A second car joined in the chase, and the pair finally successfully blocked him, exited the truck with weapons in hand, and after a brief scuffle, Arbery was shot three times and killed. The district attorney released a statement that Arbery had burglarized a construction site, but it was later determined by the owners that Arbery was merely checking out the construction progress and did not steal anything (Fausset, 2020). The video caused outrage across the country, particularly since by the time of its release, it was clear that a decision had been made not to charge the McMichaels with Arbery's death. On May 5, 2020, the Georgia Bureau of Investigations took over the case, and by May 7, 2020, the McMichaels and the third man who videotaped (and later posted) the video were charged with murder (Rojas, 2020). It's also worth noting that there had not been any reported residential burglaries in the area for months, raising questions about the McMichaels' claim that they were concerned about a series of recent burglaries (Andone & Barajas, 2020). A witness later reported that Travis McMichael used a racial slur, including the "n-word" after shooting Arbery three times. The same witness stated that Travis McMichael had also used the "n-word" on numerous occasions in social media (Booker, 2020).

In response to these and similar racially fueled incidents targeting Black Americans, protests broke out across the country, many of them organized by Black Lives

Matter (BLM), an organization advocating for increased awareness about police brutality against Black people. These protests led to other racial justice movements as well, including banning Confederate symbols such as statues of Confederate soldiers and the Confederate flag—symbols many perceive as being racially divisive (Ortiz & Diaz, 2020; Philimon et al., 2020). As advocates for social change, human services professionals are involved in advocating for racial justice on both a micro and macro level, including advocating for their Black clients and engaging in grassroots advocacy on a macro level.

It is vitally important that before human services professionals engage in this work, they become aware of the history of racial bias in the United States, particularly since racial bias can influence many factors associated with the lives of many Black people in the United States, whether on a macro or micro level. On a clinical level, studies have shown that Blacks are far more likely to be diagnosed with disruptive behavioral disorders in counseling compared with Whites, who were far more likely to be diagnosed with less serious clinical disorders such as adjustment disorder (Feisthamel & Schwartz, 2009). Racially disproportionate clinical diagnoses may be due to personal racial biases on the part of human services practitioners, but may also be due to counselors not taking into consideration the disproportionate challenges facing many ethnic minorities, such as increased levels of poverty, racial oppression, and higher rates of unemployment compared with Whites in America (Feisthamel & Schwartz, 2009).

Working with Latina/o Populations

Mental health providers and social justice advocates have increasingly expressed concerns about the impact of anti-immigration policies on the Latina/o community, particularly with regard to the additional stress such as legislation and the associated *xenophobia* (an irrational fear of immigrants or those presumed to be foreigners) that can affect the immigrant community (Ayon et al., 2010). A study of Latina/o youth and their families in the Southwest, which has higher levels of anti-immigrant policies and attitudes, showed that the majority of the Latina/o youth and parents surveyed had experienced significant discrimination related to their ethnic backgrounds and perceived immigrant status, even if they were born in the United States. Yet, their strong ties to family (immediate and extended) and their communities (referred to as *familismo*) seemed to counter some of the effects of discrimination (Ayon et al., 2010). Mental health providers, including human services practitioners who embrace Euro-American values of individualism, could potentially view the cultural tradition of *familismo* as something negative, such as maladaptive family enmeshment, rather than as a cultural strength that can serve as protection from the negative effects of discrimination and xenophobia.

According to the Southern Poverty Law Center, xenophobia-related hate crimes have soared since 2016 (Beirich, 2019). White nationalist groups increased 50% between 2017 and 2018. Hate groups spiked when Barack Obama was first elected president in 2008 in response to his race, but then dropped 23% (Beirich, 2019). Beirich noted how President Trump's rhetoric about the Central American migrants seemed to fuel the anti-immigrant sentiments of many White nationalists. Much of what is stoking this rage is fear that the Latina/o population will overtake Whites in numbers and in opportunity.

After his election in 2016, Trump signed the "zero tolerance" executive order that significantly increased the criminalization of immigrants and political asylum seekers crossing the border without legal authorization; he canceled several humanitarian and community-based programs helping immigrants and refugees and instead initiated a policy of forced family separations and extended detention of noncriminal undocumented immigrants and asylum-seekers in for-profit prisons; he revoked the Obama-era Deferred Action for Childhood Arrivals (DACA) that allowed youth who arrived in the country as children to legally remain in the country pending the passage of permanent legislation (although this decision was reversed in a June 18, 2020, Supreme Court decision); and he dramatically lowered the refugee admissions ceiling and instituted a travel ban on primarily Muslim majority countries.

Trump is known for his anti-immigrant rhetoric, and particularly for targeting migrants crossing the U.S. southern border. For instance, on January 12, 2018, he tweeted about the high number of crimes new immigrants commit, and a few days later during a speech, Trump strongly intimated that Central American political-asylum seekers coming through the southern border were primarily criminals, including murderers: "You'll have killings, you'll have murders, you'll have this, you'll have that, and you'll have crime" (The White House, 2018a).

So, what do government reports, empirical research, and policy analyses show about the criminality of undocumented immigrants? Well, if immigration-related charges are omitted, the statistics do not support these claims. Research and government statistics have consistently shown that undocumented immigrants have significantly lower crime rates, particularly violent crimes, compared to documented immigrants and native-born Americans, including murder, manslaughter, sexual abuse, rape assault, drug trafficking, and firearms violations (Bondarenko & Gould, 2017; Stowell et al., 2009; United States Sentencing Commission, 2015; U.S. Sentencing Project, 2015; Ye Hee Lee, 2015).

Additionally, Trump and members of his administration have on numerous occasions asserted that the majority of political asylum seekers, particularly those from Central America, do not show up to their immigration court proceedings and instead disappear into the country, never to be found again (National Immigrant Justice Center, 2019; White House, 2018b). However, U.S. Justice Department records show that 89% to 94% of asylum seekers appeared at their immigration hearings in fiscal years 2014 through 2018, as did 99% of political asylum seekers participating in an Obama-era pilot program involving community monitoring (U.S. Department of Homeland Security, 2016).

Stoking fears that our southern border was being overrun by immigrants, intimating most immigrants are criminals in speeches and on Twitter, and claiming that few showed up for their immigration hearings left many Americans afraid of losing their country, and White nationalists fearing "White genocide" (Beirich, 2019). Anti-immigrant rhetoric and political action has increased disparities in the behavioral health of undocumented and documented immigrants, who internalize anti-immigrant stigma (Morey, 2018). In fact, research clearly shows that undocumented students, including those with DACA status, experience an increase in fear, anxiety, and depression during times of political upheaval (Andrade, 2019). Andrade also found that DACA students in particular were experiencing significant stress since Trump's election, but many were supported by school faculty and administration, which helped mediate the negative impacts. Although the June 18, 2020, Supreme Court decision provided some breathing room for DACA recipients, the program remains temporary pending the passage of federal legislation such as the Dream Act (*U.S. Department of Homeland Security et al. v. Regents of University of California et al.*, 2020; Dream and Promise Act, 2019).

It is important that human services providers be aware of their own potential negative biases when working with immigrant populations. Anti-immigrant rhetoric often relies on simplistic arguments in justification for harsh policies, such as "they're flooding our border," "illegals are victimizing innocent Americans," and "they should just follow the law and enter the right way" (Quinonez, 2018). Such stances can influence even socially aware and caring people to support anti-immigrant policies. And yet, such statements negate the complexity of U.S. immigration and asylum-seeking law, which permits immigrants to cross the border without documentation (or overstay an immigration visa) if they request asylum within 1 year of arrival. Such stances also negate the actions of many U.S. companies in the agricultural and meat processing sectors that have actively recruited undocumented labor from south of the border for decades.

Some human services providers may deny having negative or stereotypical biases against cultures different from their own. No one wants to be characterized as racist, xenophobic, or elitist. But the reality is that all of us possess some biases, and if human services providers do not confront their biases through increased personal awareness and clinical consultation, even subtle biases will undoubtedly unfold within the counseling relationship.

CONCLUSION

The field of behavioral health is a dynamic practice area for the human services professional for many reasons. Human services professionals have the ability to truly make an impact while working with some of society's most vulnerable members. Because mental illness is such a broad term, encompassing a wide array of psychological, emotional, and behavioral issues, the human services professional works as a true generalist, whether in a direct service capacity or providing advocacy within the community. The United States has experienced dramatic shifts in its behavioral health delivery system during the past 60 years and will no doubt continue to experience changes, some intended and some unintended. Human services professionals are on the front lines of many intended changes, lobbying for increased funding, changes in legislation, and new programs to meet the complex needs of the seriously mentally ill population.

SUMMARY

- The ways in which people with mental illness have historically been perceived and treated are examined. The history of mental health treatment dating back to 18th-century France and through deinstitutionalization in the United States in the 1960s is discussed. The ways in which advocacy efforts impacted the treatment of the seriously mentally ill are also examined.
- The history of deinstitutionalization of the mentally ill is explored, including the impact of transitioning to a community-based model. Challenges and advantages are explored, identifying key aspects of the deinstitutionalization process that continue to influence behavioral health care today.

- Serious mental illnesses and common mental disorders within the context of diagnostic approaches used in the human services field are explored. A range of mental disorders experienced by client populations commonly encountered by human services professionals is discussed, including psychotic disorders, depressive disorders, anxiety disorders, and personality disorders. *DSM-5* criteria are explored and compared to using a strengths perspective in evaluating clients.
- The roles and functions of human services professionals within common mental health practice settings serving mainstream and special populations are described. Practice settings serving client populations experiencing serious mental illnesses within the context of the roles and functions of human services professionals are examined. An exploration of special populations, including the homeless mentally ill and mentally ill prisoners, is also included.
- The nature of working with special populations, including working with the homeless population and those struggling with housing insecurity, is explored. Working with prisoners, including the importance of understanding disparities within the criminal justice system, is described. Working with military personnel, their families, and veterans is also explored, with a particular focus on current challenges and stressors impacting those who have served in combat. Additionally, working with LGBTQ people is explored with a particular focus on the impacts of challenges facing these communities.
- The relationship between racial bias and disparity in treatment among ethnic minority populations is critically examined. Multicultural considerations with a particular focus on people of color are examined, including the nature of barriers to and disparities in treatment for ethnic minority populations. The importance of cultural competence is stressed, particularly when working with historically marginalized populations.

END-OF-CHAPTER QUESTIONS

1. Identify at least two ways that advocacy improved the lives of the mentally ill during the late Middle Ages and early Colonial period.
2. Describe some of the social forces that led up to the deinstitutionalization of the mentally ill and what barriers prevented the full implementation of Kennedy's plan for community-based care.
3. What is the difference between clinical disorders and personality disorders?
4. What is the role of human services providers working with the homeless populations?
5. Describe at least three reasons why younger veterans have become a population in need of special attention.
6. What is the relationship between racial bias and disparity in sentencing laws, and how can human services providers advocate for ethnic minority populations impacted by unfair policies and practices within the criminal justice system?

References

Agarwal, P., Sarris, C. E., Herschman, Y., Agarwal, N., & Mammis, A. (2016). Schizophrenia and neurosurgery: A dark past with hope of a brighter future. *Journal of Clinical Neuroscience, 34*, 53–58

Alegría, M., Chatterji, P., Wells, K., Cao, Z., Chen, C. N., Takeuchi, D., & Meng, X. L. (2008). Disparity in depression treatment among racial and ethnic minority populations in the United States. *Psychiatric Services, 59*(11), 1264–1272.

Allen, N. L., Becerra, B. J., & Becerra, M. B. (2018). Associations between food insecurity and the severity of psychological distress among African-Americans. *Ethnicity & Health, 23*(5), 511–520.

American Psychiatric Association [APA]. (2013). *Diagnostic and statistical manual of mental disorders* (5th ed.). Author.

Andone, D., & Barajas, A. (2020). Crime stats call into question Georgia men's 'burglary' claims. *Mercury News*. https://www.mercurynews.com/2020/05/08/crime-stats-call-into-question-georgia-mens-burglary-claims/

Andrade, L. M. (2019). "The war still continues," Part II: The importance of positive validation for undocumented students one year after Trump's presidential victory. *Journal of Hispanic Higher Education* [Advance online publication]. http://doi.org/10.1177/1538192718823186

Ayón, C., Marsiglia, F. F., & Bermudez-Parsai, M. (2010). Latino family mental health: Exploring the role of discrimination and familismo. *Journal of Community Psychology, 38*(6), 742–756.

Bailey, Z. D., Krieger, N., Agénor, M., Graves, J., Linos, N., & Bassett, M. T. (2017). Structural racism and health inequities in the USA: Evidence and interventions. *The Lancet, 389*(10077), 1453–1463.

Becerra-Culqui, T. A., Liu, Y., Nash, R., Cromwell, L., Flanders, W. D., Getahun, D., Giammattei, S. V., Hunkeler, E. M., Lash, T. L., Millman, A., Quinn, V. P., Robinson, B., Roblin, D., Sandberg, D. E., Silverberg, M. J., Tangpricha, V., & Quinn, V. P. (2018). Mental health of transgender and gender nonconforming youth compared with their peers. *Pediatrics, 141*(5), e20173845.

Beck, A. T. (1964). Thinking and depression: 2. Theory and therapy. *Archives of General Psychiatric, 10*, 561–571.

Beck, J. S. (2006). Cognitive-behavioral therapy. *Primary Psychiatry,13*(4), 31–34.

Beirich, H. (2019). White supremacy flourishes amid fears of immigration and nation's shifting demographics. *Intelligent Report, Southern Poverty Law Center*. Spring Issue.

Bondarenko, V., & Gould, S. (2017). Despite Trump's speech, immigrants commit far fewer crimes than native-born Americans. Business Insider. http://www.businessinsider.com/immigrants-commit-less-crime-than-native-born-americans-trump-speech-2017-3/#native-born-americans-commit-a-lot-more-crime-than-immigrants-2

Booker, B. (2020). White defendant allegedly used racial slur after killing Ahmaud Arbery. NPR. https://www.npr.org/2020/06/04/869938461/white-defendant-allegedly-used-racial-slur-after-killing-ahmaud-arbery.

Brave Heart, M. Y. H., & DeBruyn, L. M. (1998) The American Indian holocaust: Healing historical unresolved grief. *American Indian and Alaska Native Mental Health Research 8*(2), 56–78.

Brave Heart, M. Y. H., Lewis-Fernández, R., Beals, J., Hasin, D. S., Sugaya, L., Wang, S., Grant, B. F., & Blanco, C. (2016). Psychiatric disorders and mental health treatment in American Indians and Alaska Natives: Results of the National Epidemiologic Survey on Alcohol and Related Conditions. *Social Psychiatry and Psychiatric Epidemiology, 51*(7), 1033–1046.

Briggs, B. (2013). Why modern soldiers are more susceptible to suicide. Military Suicide Research Consortium. https://msrc.fsu.edu/news/msrcs-david-rudd-consulted-why-modern-soldiers-are-more-susceptible-suicide

Caldwell, J. A. (2019). Outness, discrimination, and serious mental illness among LGBTQ Southerners [Thesis]. Georgia State University. https://scholarworks.gsu.edu/iph_theses/638

Chen, H. M., DeLong, C. J., Bame, M., Rajapakse, I., Herron, T. J., McInnis, M. G., & O'Shea, K. S. (2014). Transcripts involved in calcium signaling and telencephalic neuronal fate are altered in induced pluripotent stem cells from bipolar disorder patients. *Translational Psychiatry, 4*(3), e375.

Choi, S. K., Wilson, B. D., Shelton, J., & Gates, G. J. (2015). *Serving our youth 2015: The needs and experiences of lesbian, gay, bisexual, transgender, and questioning youth experiencing homelessness.* The Williams Institute with True Colors Fund.

Christy, A., Poythress, N. G., Boothroyd, R. A., Petrila, J., & Mehra, S. (2005). Evaluating the efficiency and community safety goals of the Broward County mental health court. *Behavioral Sciences and the Law, 23,* 227–243.

Council of State Governments Justice Center Staff. (2019). *U.S. House members express support for key justice programs.* Justice Center: The Council on State Governments. https://csgjusticecenter.org/jc/u-s-house-members-express-support-for-key-justice-programs-3/

Council on Social Work Education. (2014). *The role of social work in mental and behavioral health care Principles for public policy.* CSWE. https://www.cswe.org/getattachment/Advocacy-Policy/RoleofSWinMentalandBehavorialHealthCare-January2015-FINAL.pdf.aspx

Covey, H. C. (2005). Western Christianity's two historical treatments of people with disabilities or mental illness. *The Social Science Journal, 42*(1), 107–114.

Davis, L., & Francis, E. (2011). 'Most stressed out' in U.S.? Middle-aged women have lowest well-being, study finds. ABC News. https://abcnews.go.com/Health/MindMoodNews/stressed-us-middle-age-women-lowest-study-finds/story?id=14174138

Dear, M. J., & Wolch, J. R. (2014). *Landscapes of despair: From deinstitutionalization to homelessness.* Princeton University Press.

Deutsch, A. (2013). *The mentally ill in America-A History of their care and treatment from colonial times.* Read Books Ltd.

Diala, C. C., Muntaner, C., Walrath, C., Nickerson, K., LaVeist, T., & Leaf, P. (2001). Racial/ethnic differences in attitudes toward seeking professional mental health services. *American Journal of Public Health, 91*(5), 805–807.

Ditton, P. M. (1999). *Mental health and treatment of inmates and probationers* (Special report NCJ 174463). Washington, DC: U.S. Department of Justice, Office of Justice Programs, Bureau of Justice Statistics.

Dorrington, S., Zavos, H., Ball, H., McGuffin, P., Rijsdijk, F., Siribaddana, S., Sumithapala, A., & Hotopf, M. (2014). Trauma, post-traumatic stress disorder and psychiatric disorders in a middle-income setting: Prevalence and comorbidity. *The British Journal of Psychiatry, 205*(5), 383–389.

Dorrington, S., Zavos, H., Ball, H., McGuffin, P., Sumathipala, A., Siribaddana, S., Rijsdijk, F., Hatch, S. L., & Hotopf, M. (2019). Family functioning, trauma exposure and PTSD: A cross sectional study. *Journal of affective disorders, 245,* 645–652.

Douthit, N., Kiv, S., Dwolatzky, T., & Biswas, S. (2015). Exposing some important barriers to health care access in the rural USA. *Public Health, 129*(6), 611–620.

Dream and Promise Act. (2019). H.R. 2820.

Durham, J. I. (2018). Perceptions of microaggressions: Implications for the mental health and treatment of African American youth. *Journal of Infant, Child, and Adolescent Psychotherapy, 17*(1), 52–61.

Eldridge, L. D. (1996). "Crazy Brained": Mental Illness in Colonial America. *Bulletin of the History of Medicine, 70*(3), 361–386.

Elwyn, L., & Smith, C. (2013). Child maltreatment and adult substance abuse: The role of memory. *Journal of Social Work Practice in the Addictions, 13*(3), 269–294.

Fausset, R. (2020). What we know about the shooting death of Ahmaud Arbery. *The New York Times.* https://www.nytimes.com/article/ahmaud-arbery-shooting-georgia.html.

Fava, G. A., Rafanelli, C., Grandi, S., Conti, S., & Belluardo, P. (1998). Prevention of recurrent depression with cognitive behavioral therapy: Preliminary findings. *Archives of General Psychiatry, 55*(9), 816–820.

Feisthamel, K. P., & Schwartz, R. C. (2009). Differences in mental health counselors' diagnoses based on client race: An investigation of adjustment, childhood, and substance-related disorders. *Journal of Mental Health Counseling, 31*(1), 47–59.

Feldman, S. (2003). Reflections on the 40th anniversary of the U.S. Community Mental Health Centers Act. *Australian and New Zealand Journal of Psychiatry, 3,* 662–667.

Felitti, V. J., Anda, R. F., Nordenberg, D., Williamson, D. F., Spitz, A. M., Edwards, V., & Marks, J. S. (1998). Relationship of childhood abuse and household dysfunction to many of the leading causes of death in adults: The Adverse Childhood Experiences (ACE) Study. *American Journal of Preventive Medicine, 14*(4), 245–258.

Fields, G., & Phillips, E. E. (2013). The new asylums: Jails swell with mentally ill. *Wall Street Journal, 25.*

Flores, G., & Tomany-Korman, S. C. (2008). Racial and ethnic disparities in medical and dental health, access to care, and use of services in US children. *Pediatrics, 121*(2), e286–e298.

Folsom, D. P., Hawthorne, W., & Lindamer, L. (2005). Prevalence and risk factors for homelessness and utilization of mental health services among 10,340 patients with serious mental illness in a large public mental health system. *American Journal of Psychiatry, 162*(2), 370–376.

Friedmann, P. D., Andrews, C. M., & Humphreys, K. (2017). How ACA repeal would worsen the opioid epidemic. *New England Journal of Medicine, 376*(10), e16.

Frissa, S., Hatch, S. L., Gazard, B., Fear, N. T., Hotopf, M., & SELCoH Study Team. (2013). Trauma and current symptoms of PTSD in a South East London community. *Social psychiatry and psychiatric epidemiology, 48*(8), 1199–1209.

Glynn, C., & Fox, E. B. (2019). Dynamics of homelessness in urban America. *The Annals of Applied Statistics, 13*(1), 573–605.

Goldstein, J. E. (2002). *Console and classify: The French psychiatric profession in the nineteenth century.* University of Chicago Press.

Grob, G. N. (1973). *Mental institutions in America.* Transaction Publishers.

Grob, G. N. (2014). *From asylum to community: Mental health policy in modern America.* Princeton University Press.

Grob, G. N., & Goldman, H. H. (2006). *The dilemma of federal mental health policy: Radical reform or incremental change?* Rutgers University Press.

Henry, M., Watt, R., Mahathey, A., Ouellette, J. & Aubrey Sitler, Abt Associates. (2020). U.S. Department of Housing and Urban Development Office of Community Planning and Development. In *The 2018 annual homeless assessment report (AHAR) to Congress.* https://files.hudexchange.info/resources/documents/2019-AHAR-Part-1.pdf

Hernandez, M., Nesman, T., Mowery, D., Acevedo-Polakovich, I. D., & Callejas, L. M. (2015). Cultural competence: A literature review and conceptual model for mental health services. *Psychiatric Services, 60*(8), 1046–1050.

Hill, E., Tiefenthäler, A., Triebert, C., Jordan, D., Willis, H. & Stein, R. (2020). How George Floyd died in police custody. *The New York Times.* https://www.nytimes.com/2020/05/31/us/george-floyd-investigation.html

Horvitz-Lennon, M., Frank, R. G., Thompson, W., Seo Hyon Baik, M. S., Alegría, M., Rosenheck, R. A., & Normand, S. L. T. (2015). Investigation of racial and ethnic disparities in service utilization among homeless adults with severe mental illnesses. *Psychiatric Services 60*(8), 1032–1038.

Indian Health Service. (2009). Trends in Indian health 2002–2003. U.S. Department of Health and Human Services.

International OCD Foundation [IOCDF]. (2014). Obsessive compulsive personality disorder [Factsheet]. https://iocdf.org/wp-content/uploads/2014/10/OCPD-Fact-Sheet.pdf

Johnson, G. (2013). U.S. soldier to admit to massacre in Afghanistan. *The Mercury.* https://www.pottsmerc.com/u-s-soldier-to-admit-to-massacre-in-afghanistan/article_2d03a87c-4099-5e32-ae66-1c1ba9908356.html

Jost, T. (2018). The Affordable Care Act under the Trump administration. *The Commonwealth Fund.* https://www.commonwealthfund.org/blog/2018/affordable-care-act-under-trump-administration

Kamal, R., Cox, C., Fehr, R., Ramirez, M., Horstman, K., & Levitt, L. (2018). *How repeal of the individual mandate and expansion of loosely regulated plans are affecting 2019 premiums.* The Henry J. Kaiser Family Foundation.

Kang, H. K., Bullman, T. A., Smolenski, D. J., Skopp, N. A., Gahm, G. A., & Reger, M. A. (2015). Suicide risk among 1.3 million veterans who were on active duty during the Iraq and Afghanistan wars. *Annals of Epidemiology, 25*(2), 96–100.

Kim, D. Y. (2016). Psychiatric deinstitutionalization and prison population growth: A critical literature review and its implications. *Criminal Justice Policy Review, 27*(1), 3–21.

Klein, E. (2017). Using social support for LGBTQ clients with mental illness to be out of the closet, in treatment, and in the community. *Journal of Gay & Lesbian Social Services, 29*(3), 221–232.

Koerber, G. (2005). *Veterans: One-third of all homeless people.* National Alliance on Mental Illness, Issue Spotlight. http://www.nami.org/Template.cfm?Section=Issue_Spotlights&template=/ContentManagement/ContentDisplay.cfm&ContentID=26958

Levenson, J., & Grady M. (2016). Substance abuse, violence, and childhood adversity: Implications for trauma-informed social work practice. *Journal of Social Practice in the Addictions, 16*(1), 2445. https://doi.org/10.1080/1533256X.2016.1150853

Lightfoot, M., Wu, N., Hughes, S., Desmond, K., Tevendale, H., & Stevens, R. (2018). Risk factors for substance use among youth experiencing homelessness.

Journal of Child & Adolescent Substance Abuse, 27(5–6), 288–296.

Linehan, M. M., Korslund, K. E., Harned, M. S., Gallop, R. J., Lungu, A., Neacsiu, A. D., ... & Murray-Gregory, A. M. (2015). Dialectical behavior therapy for high suicide risk in individuals with borderline personality disorder: A randomized clinical trial and component analysis. *JAMA Psychiatry, 72*(5), 475–482.

Mannekote, S., Pillai, A., & Harbishettar, V. (2019). Civil commitment of persons with mental illness: Comparison of the Mental Healthcare Act 2017 with corresponding legislations of the USA. *Indian Journal of Psychiatry, 61*(Suppl 4), S821.

Marley, J. A., & Buila, S. (2001). Crimes against people with mental illness: Types, perpetrators, and influencing factors. *Social Work, 46*(2), 115–124.

McKay, D., Sookman, D., Neziroglu, F., Wilhelm, S., Stein, D. J., Kyrios, M., Matthews, K., & Veale, D. (2015). Efficacy of cognitive-behavioral therapy for obsessive–compulsive disorder. *Psychiatry Research, 225*(3), 236–246.

McLaughlin, K. A., Koenen, K. C., Bromet, E. J., Karam, E. G., Liu, H., Petukhova, M., Ruscio, A. M., Sampson, N. A., Stein, D. J., Aguilar-Gaxiola, S., Alonso, J., Borges, G., Demyttenaere, K., Dinolova, R. V., Ferry, F., Florescu, S., de Girolamo, G., Gureje, O., Kawakami, N., ... & Kessler, R. C. (2017). Childhood adversities and post-traumatic stress disorder: Evidence for stress sensitisation in the World Mental Health Surveys. *The British Journal of Psychiatry, 211*(5), 280–288.

Mental Health America Board of Directors. (2019). *Policy statement 53 Mental health courts.* Mental Health America. https://www.mentalhealthamerica.net/positions/mental-health-courts

Morey, B. N. (2018). Mechanisms by which anti-immigrant stigma exacerbates racial/ethnic health disparities. *American Journal of Public Health, 108*(4), 460–463.

Mowbray, C. T., & Holter, M. C. (2002). Mental health & mental illness: Out of the closet? *Social Service Review, 76*(1), 135–179.

National Association of Social Workers [NASW]. (2019). *NASW will continue to monitor efforts to sabotage Affordable Care Act* [Press Release]. Retrieved online from https://www.socialworkers.org/News/News-Releases/ID/1953/NASW-will-continue-to-monitor-efforts-to-sabotage-Affordable-Care-Act.

National Immigrant Justice Center. (2019). *The Trump administration's manipulation of data to perpetuate anti-immigrant policies* [Policy brief]. https://immigrantjustice.org/research-items/policy-brief-trump-administrations-manipulation-data-perpetuate-anti-immigrant

Nock, M. K., Ursano, R. J., Heeringa, S. G., Stein, M. B., Jain, S., Raman, R., Sun, X., Chiu, W. T., Colpe, L. J., Fullerton, C. S., Gilman, S. E., Hwang, I., Naifeh, J. A., Rosellini, A. J., Sampson, N. A., Schoenbaum, M., Zaslavsky, A. M., Kessler, R. C., on behalf of the Army STARRS collaborators. (2015). Mental disorders, comorbidity, and pre-enlistment suicidal behavior among new soldiers in the US Army: Results from the Army Study to Assess Risk and Resilience in Service members (Army STARRS). *Suicide and Life-Threatening Behavior, 45*(5), 588–599.

North, C. S., Eyrich, K. M., Pollio, D. E., & Spitznagel, E. L. (2004). Are rates of psychiatric disorders in the homeless population changing? *American Journal of Public Health, 94*(1), 103–108.

Norton, P. J., & Price, E. C. (2007). A meta-analytic review of adult cognitive-behavioral treatment outcome across the anxiety disorders. *The Journal of Nervous and Mental Disease, 195*(6), 521–531.

Oh, H., Cogburn, C. D., Anglin, D., Lukens, E., & DeVylder, J. (2016). Major discriminatory events and risk for psychotic experiences among Black Americans. *American Journal of Orthopsychiatry, 86*(3), 277.

Oppel, R. A., & Taylor, D. B. (2020). Here's what you need to know about Breonna Taylor's death. *The New York Times.* https://www.nytimes.com/article/breonna-taylor-police.html

Ortiz, A., & Diaz, J. (2020). George Floyd protests reignite debate over Confederate statues. *The New York Times.* https://www.nytimes.com/2020/06/03/us/confederate-statues-george-floyd.html

Pachter, L. M., Caldwell, C. H., Jackson, J. S., & Bernstein, B. A. (2018). Discrimination and mental health in a representative sample of African-American and Afro-Caribbean youth. *Journal of Racial and Ethnic Health Disparities, 5*(4), 831–837.

Palermo, G. B., Smith, M. B., & Liska, F. J. (1991). Jails versus mental hospitals: A social dilemma. *International Journal of Offender Therapy and Comparative Criminology, 35*(2), 97–106.

Philimon, W., Hughes, T., & della Cava, M. (2020). Will the Black Lives Matter movement finally put an end to Confederate flags and statues? *USA Today*. https://www.usatoday.com/story/news/nation/2020/06/12/confederate-statues-flags-banned-black-lives-matter-movement-grows/5346701002/

Phillips, K. A., & Castle, D. J. (2015). Body dysmorphic disorder. *Widiger, TA.; Frances, AJ.; Pincus, HA.*

Phipps, M., Dalton, L., Maxwell, H., & Cleary, M. (2019). Women and homelessness, a complex multidimensional issue: Findings from a scoping review. *Journal of Social Distress and the Homeless, 28*(1), 1–13.

Porter, R. (2002). *Madness: A brief history*. Oxford University Press.

Quinonez, E. S. (2018). (Un)welcome to America: A critical discourse analysis of anti-immigrant rhetoric in Trump's speeches and conservative mainstream media [Thesis]. California State University, San Bernardino.

Raphael, S., & Stoll, M. A. (2013). Assessing the contribution of the deinstitutionalization of the mentally ill to growth in the US incarceration rate. *The Journal of Legal Studies, 42*(1), 187–222.

Reeves, W. C., Strine, T. W., Pratt, L. A., Thompson, W., Ahluwalia, I., Dhingra, S. S., McKnight-Eily, L. R., Harrison, L., D'Angelo, D. V., Williams, L., Morrow, B., Gould, D., & Safran, M. A. Centers for Disease Control and Prevention (CDC), 2011. Mental Illness Surveillance among Adults in the United States. *Morbidity and Mortality Weekly Report. Surveillance Summaries/CDC, 60,* 1–29.

Rhoades, H., Rusow, J. A., Bond, D., Lanteigne, A., Fulginiti, A., & Goldbach, J. T. (2018). Homelessness, mental health and suicidality among LGBTQ youth accessing crisis services. *Child Psychiatry & Human Development, 49*(4), 643–651.

Rojas, R. (2020). Investigators say one man shot Ahmaud Arbery. Why are three charged with murder? *The New York Times*. https://www.nytimes.com/2020/05/23/us/ahmaud-arbery-william-bryan-travis-mcmichael-gregory-mcmichael.html

Saleebey, D. (1996). The strengths perspective in social work practice: Extensions and cautions. *Social Work, 41*(3), 296–305.

Schoenbaum, M., Kessler, R. C., Gilman, S. E., Colpe, L. J., Heeringa, S. G., Stein, M. B., Ursano, R. J., Cox, K. L., & Army STARRS Collaborators. (2014). Predictors of suicide and accident death in the Army Study to Assess Risk and Resilience in Service members (Army STARRS): Results from the Army Study to Assess Risk and Resilience in Service members (Army STARRS). *JAMA Psychiatry,71*(5), 493–503.

Shern, D. L., Tsemberis, S., Anthony, W., Lovell, A. M., Richmond, L., Felton, C. J., Winarski, J., & Cohen, M. (2000). Serving street-dwelling individuals with psychiatric disabilities: Outcome of a psychiatric rehabilitation clinical trial. *American Journal of Public Health, 90*(12), 1873–1878.

Skene, N. G., Bryois, J., Bakken, T. E., Breen, G., Crowley, J. J., Gaspar, H. A., Giusti-Rodriguez, P., Hodge, R. D., Miller, J. A., Muñoz-Manchado, A. B., O'Donovan, M. C., Owen, M. J., Pardiñas, A. F., Ryge, J., Walters, J. T. R., Linnarsson, S., Lein, E. S., Major Depressive Disorder Working Group of the Psychiatric Genomics Consortium, Sullivan, P. F., & Hjerling-Leffler, J. (2018). Genetic identification of brain cell types underlying schizophrenia. *Nature Genetics, 50*(6), 825.

South, T. (2019, December). Advocacy group takes on latest case – Army staff sergeant convicted in Afghan massacre. *Army Times*. https://www.armytimes.com/news/your-army/2019/12/12/advocacy-group-takes-on-latest-case-army-staff-sergeant-convicted-in-afghan-massacre/.

Stowell, J. I., Messner, S. F., McGeever, K. F., & Raffalovich, L. E. (2009). Immigration and the recent violent crime drop in the United States: A pooled, cross sectional time series analysis of metropolitan areas. *Criminology, 47*(3), 889–928.

Substance Abuse and Mental Health Services Administration. (2014). *SAMHSA's concept of trauma and guidance for a trauma-informed approach*. HHS Publication No. (SMA) 14–4884. Author.

Substance Abuse and Mental Health Services Administration. (2019). *Key substance use and mental health indicators in the United States: Results from the 2018 National Survey on Drug Use and Health* (HHS Publication No. PEP19-5068, NSDUH Series H-54). Center for Behavioral Health Statistics and Quality, Substance Abuse and Mental Health Services Administration. https://www.samhsa.gov/data/

Sue, S. (1977). Community mental health services to minority groups: Some optimism, some pessimism. *American Psychologist, 32*, 616–624.

Sue, S., & McKinney, H. (1975). Asian Americans in the community mental health system. *American Journal, 45*, 111–118.

Sullivan, W. P. (1992). Reclaiming the community: The strengths perspective and deinstitutionalization. *Social Work, 37*(3), 204–209.

Sutter, M., & Perrin, P. B. (2016). Discrimination, mental health, and suicidal ideation among LGBTQ people of color. *Journal of Counseling Psychology, 63*(1), 98.

Swindle, R. W., Cronkite, R. C., & Moos, R. H. (1989). Life stressors, social resources, coping, and the 4-year course of unipolar depression. *Journal of Abnormal Psychology, 98*(4), 468–477.

The White House. (2017). Presidential executive order promoting healthcare choice and competition across the United States. https://www.whitehouse.gov/presidential-actions/presidential-executive-order-promoting-healthcare-choice-competition-across-united-states/.

The White House. (2018a). Remarks by President Trump at the National Federation of Independent Businesses 75th anniversary celebration. https://www.whitehouse.gov/briefings-statements/remarks-president-trump-national-federation-independent-businesses-75th-anniversary-celebration/

The White House. (2018b). Remarks by President Trump on the illegal immigration crisis and border security. https://www.whitehouse.gov/briefings-statements/remarks-president-trump-illegal-immigration-crisis-border-security/

Thornicroft, G. (2008). Stigma and discrimination limit access to mental health care. *Epidemiology and Psychiatric Sciences, 17*(1), 14–19.

Torrey, E. F. (1995). *Surviving schizophrenia*, 3rd ed. Harper-Perennial.

Torrey, E. F., & Miller, J. (2002). *The invisible plague: The rise of mental illness from 1750 to present*. Rutgers University Press.

Torrey, E. F., Entsminger, K., Geller, J., Stanley, J., & Jaffe, D. J. (2015). The shortage of public hospital beds for mentally ill persons. *Montana,303*(20.9), 6–9.

Torrey, E. F., Kennard, A, D., Eslinger, D., Lamb, R., & Pavle, J. (2010). More mentally ill persons are in jails and prisons than hospitals: A survey of the states. Report for the National Sheriff's Association and the Treatment Advocacy Center.

U.S. Commission on Civil Rights. (2003). *Not in my backyard: Executive Order 12,898 and Title VI as tools for achieving environmental justice*. US Commission on Civil Rights.

U.S. Conference of Mayors. (2016). *Hunger and homelessness survey: A status report on hunger and homelessness in America's cities*. Author. https://endhomelessness.atavist.com/mayorsreport2016

U.S. Department of Homeland Security et al. v. Regents of University of California et al., No. 18–587 (2020). https://www.supremecourt.gov/opinions/19pdf/18-587_5if1.pdf

U.S. Department of Homeland Security. (2016). U.S. Immigration and Customs Enforcement's Award of the Family Case Management Program Contract (Redacted). Office of Inspector General, OIG–18–22.

U.S. Sentencing Commission. (2015). Citizenship of offenders in each primary offense category 1. https://drive.google.com/file/d/0B0kkOiAWUCUGMXgwcEcwbkN5Ylk/view

U.S. Sentencing Project. (2015). Interactive sourcebook. Commission's fiscal year 2015 Datafile, USSCFY2015. https://drive.google.com/file/d/0B0kkOiAWUCUGMXgwcEcwbkN5Ylk/view

Ursano, R. J., Colpe, L. J., Heeringa, S. G., Kessler, R. C., Schoenbaum, M., Stein, M. B., & Army STARRS Collaborators. (2014). The Army Study to Assess Risk and Resilience in Servicemembers (Army STARRS). *Psychiatry: Interpersonal and Biological Processes, 77*(2), 107–119.

Vakharia, S. P., & Little, J. (2017). Starting where the client is: Harm reduction guidelines for clinical social work practice. *Clinical Social Work Journal, 45*(1), 65–76.

Van der Kolk, B. (2014). *The body keeps the score: Mind, brain and body in the transformation of trauma*. Penguin Books.

Vourlekis, B. S., Edinburg, G., & Knee, R. (1998). The rise of social work in public mental health through aftercare of people with serious mental illness. *Social Work, 43*, 567–575.

Whaibeh, E., Mahmoud, H., & Vogt, E. L. (2019). Reducing the treatment gap for LGBT mental health needs: The potential of telepsychiatry. *The Journal of Behavioral Health Services & Research, 47*, 424–431.

Whitbeck, L. B., Adams, G. W., Hoyt, D. R., & Chen, X. (2004). Conceptualizing and measuring historical trauma among American Indian people. *American Journal of Community Psychology, 33*(3–4), 119–130.

Williams, D. R., & Wyatt, R. (2015). Racial bias in health care and health: Challenges and opportunities. *JAMA, 314*(6), 555–556.

Winsper, C., Bilgin, A., Thompson, A., Marwaha, S., Chanen, A. M., Singh, S. P., Wang, A., & Furtado, V. (2020). The prevalence of personality disorders in the community: A global systematic review and meta-analysis. *The British Journal of Psychiatry, 216*(2), 69–78.

Wishner, J. B. (2017). *How repealing and replacing the ACA could reduce access to mental health and substance use disorder treatment and parity protections*. Urban Institute.

World Health Organization. (2015, October). Depression: Fact Sheet No 369. http://www.who.int/mediacentre/factsheets/fs369/en/

Ye Hee Lee, M. (2015). Donald Trump's false comments connecting Mexican immigrants and crime. *Washington Post*. https://www.washingtonpost.com/news/fact-checker/wp/2015/07/08/donald-trumps-false-comments-connecting-mexican-immigrants-and-crime/

7

Housing and Homelessness

© EMA WOO/SHUTTERSTOCK

Ana is currently homeless and looking for permanent housing, while attempting to put the pieces of her life back together. Ana was raised in an unstable and abusive home environment where she had been told repeatedly throughout her childhood that she was worthless and that she would amount to nothing in her life. Her every move was criticized and served as proof that she was no good. Ana had the natural need and desire to be loved and accepted, and by the time she was 17 this need peaked to a point that she could not resist the affections of an older man who promised her the world. Although she initially resisted his attempts to become sexually active with her, he eventually convinced her by telling her that the only way he would know she loved him was if they had sex, and that if she refused, he would leave her. Ana's insecurities and her deep need to be cared for made her vulnerable to his manipulative threats, so she relented and agreed to have sex with him, believing that she had finally found someone who truly loved and accepted her. Yet when she got pregnant, he became abusive and used many of the same abusive statements she had

225

confided that her father had used to manipulate and control her. She wondered if her father must have been right all along, because how else could she explain yet another man seeing such ugliness in her? Ultimately, this man abandoned her and her unborn child, and when her father learned of her pregnancy, he kicked her out of the house and refused to allow her to return.

For the next 4 years Ana was intermittently homeless, finding temporary stability through various transitional housing programs that helped her secure employment and an apartment. However, any crisis put her on the streets again, such as the time her son got the chicken pox, resulting in her needing to stay home with him for 2 weeks. Ana was fired even though she had medical verification of her son's illness. This led to yet another financial downward spiral and another episode of homelessness. By the time her son was 5 years old, he was acting out, considerably adding to her sense of frustration and burden. So when she met a new man who showered her with attention and compliments, all she could think of was that she had finally met the man of her dreams. He said all the right things, offered to let her and her son move in with him, and offered to manage every part of her life. He even told her that she would not have to work and could stay home with her son, so she gladly quit her job and embraced being a stay-at-home mom at last—something she had wanted to do for years.

Ana wanted desperately to believe this was real and accepted this man's seemingly generous offers because she believed that to do otherwise would mean robbing her son of his only opportunity for a real home and family. When her new boyfriend told her that she was the first woman he'd ever wanted to have a baby with, she was so flattered she immediately agreed to get pregnant. She believed with all her heart that she finally had it all, and that all the years of suffering were behind her. Ana became pregnant quickly and dreamed of her new life with her new boyfriend. Although she wanted to get married, he claimed not to be ready yet and she didn't want to rock the boat, so she did not push the subject. She talked endlessly to her son about their good fortune in finding this man who was going to take care of them forever. When her new boyfriend hit her for the first time, she convinced herself that it was a one-time incident caused by the stress of having a new family. When she noticed that he drank too much alcohol and seemed impatient with her son, she convinced herself that he needed time to adjust to having an instant family. Then one day he did not come home from work, and when a few days had gone by and he still had not returned with her car, she contacted an agency that helped single mothers experiencing a financial crisis, because she had no money to pay for the rent due in a few days.

A caseworker helped Ana evaluate her situation, identifying her strengths and needs. Her caseworker was with her when she went to the police department to report her car having been stolen. When she gave the police officer the name of her now ex-boyfriend, they told her that he had a record of domestic violence and financial fraud. This was not the first time he had encouraged a single mom to depend on him only to flee when the good feelings ended, leaving the woman with debt. The police told her that unfortunately she had no recourse against him, even for taking her car, because to make insurance matters easier, she had agreed to put his name on the title—a decision that seemed foolish in hindsight but at the time seemed the least that she could do in light of all that he was offering her and her son. Now she had no money, no job, no car, a devastated and angry child, and a baby on the way. She would also be homeless again within the month.

Adding to her burden was the intense sense of humiliation she felt when she realized that she had once again been taken advantage of. She firmly believed that she deserved this treatment and argued that there must be something terribly defective about her because these things kept happening to her. She was devastated that she was so completely abandoned in the wake of breathing her first sigh of relief in years. She was extremely depressed, which increased her risk for either inadvertently abusing her child or neglecting him in some way, particularly when he expressed anger at her for driving his "new daddy" away. Her additional loss of self-esteem left her in no shape to solve problems by gaining employment, finding low-cost housing, and searching out assistance programs, most of which would require her to disclose her reasons for becoming homeless. She simply did not have it in her to repeatedly tell her story of blind trust and exploitation. Although her caseworker suggested she go to the hospital for a suicide evaluation due to her severe depression, she refused because she feared that hospitalization would mean placing her son in temporary foster care.

Ana was evicted from her apartment and began "couch surfing"—**doubling up** with friends for a few weeks at a time while she tried to save enough money to stay in a motel. She continued working with the agency periodically, primarily when she experienced another crisis. During her most recent visit, she admitted that she got paid for having sex, just so she could avoid sleeping on the streets. She also shared that her depression had gotten so bad, that she started taking Vicodin—an opioid—to keep going. Ana's caseworker asked her if she had a prescription, and Ana admitted that she did not. She had a friend who got them on the black market and shared some with her. The problem was that she was now taking several Vicodin daily because that was the only way she could function.

Ana's case plan included entering a residential drug treatment center for 30 days, attending parenting classes, joining a weekly support group for victims of domestic violence, entering a vocational training program so she could obtain a job, and applying for **Temporary Assistance to Needy Families** (**TANF**), including childcare assistance for when she began working.

Ana did not believe she could complete the case plan and refused substance abuse treatment because she didn't believe she needed it and refused to allow her children to be placed in temporary substitute care. Although she had no solid plan for permanent housing, Ana shared that she did have an acquaintance who was living in an illegal tented community just outside of town, who invited them to stay with him for a while. Her caseworker asked about his expectations and expressed concerns about the safety of this plan, particularly for her children. Ana said she couldn't think about that, nor could she think about getting a real job or doing any of the other things on the case plan. Her sole focus was figuring out how to find food and shelter for the night.

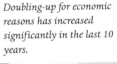

Doubling-up for economic reasons has increased significantly in the last 10 years.

© MJTH / SHUTTERSTOCK

THE CURRENT STATE OF HOMELESSNESS IN THE UNITED STATES

Homelessness is a very complex social problem, as reflected in the opening vignette, often encompassing issues related to physical and mental health, domestic violence, child welfare, and chronic financial insecurity. The rate of homelessness began to increase between 1970 and 1980 due to a decrease in **affordable housing** and an increase in poverty. The 2007 recession exacerbated this trend of financial vulnerability, as reflected in the finding that in 2014 two thirds of cities in the United States reported increases in requests for food and emergency shelter (U.S. Conference of Mayors, 2014). Among those cities reporting an increase in emergency service requests, 56% were families, 38% were employed, and just over 20% were older adults. Not all of those requesting emergency food assistance were homeless, but the two dynamics are certainly related. City officials identified the lack of affordable housing as one of the primary causes of homelessness among families with children, but unemployment, poverty, and low-paying jobs were referenced as well. For single individuals, unemployment, poverty, untreated mental illness, and untreated substance abuse were all correlated with housing insecurity and homelessness (U.S. Conference of Mayors, 2014).

How Homelessness Is Defined

Learning Outcome 7.1   **Evaluate the different ways that homelessness is defined, and the impact definitions have on policy responses**

Determining an accurate scope of homelessness in the United States is challenging because currently there is no universally agreed-upon definition of homelessness. The federal definition of homelessness includes only those individuals or families who do not have a fixed, regular, or adequate nighttime residence, and who spend the night in a shelter or in an area not intended as a regular sleeping accommodation for humans, such as a car, abandoned building, a train station, or an airport. But homeless advocates have long criticized this definition for being far too narrow, thus failing to capture the entire scope of the homeless problem. Those in the human services fields, including homeless advocates, define homelessness far more broadly to include the 'hidden homeless,' such as those who couch surf (staying on various friends' or family members' couches for a few nights before moving on to someone else's couch), double up (moving in with a friend or family member temporarily), or live in motels.

In response to criticism that the federal definition of homelessness was too narrow, it was broadened somewhat when the *McKinney-Vento Act* —comprehensive federal legislation that provides funding for a range of shelter services—was reauthorized and amended as the *Homeless Emergency Assistance and Rapid Transition to Housing (HEARTH) Act* in 2009. The definition now includes those who are in imminent danger of losing their housing, whether it is a home they own, rent, live in without paying rent, or share with others. Also included in the definition of homelessness are those who have been evicted from their homes and have no home to move into because they lack the resources to obtain permanent housing. Much of the impetus for the expanded definition of homelessness was the 2007 recession that resulted in over 7 million home foreclosures, affecting not only homeowners, but renters as well. The *HEARTH Act* also expanded the definition of homelessness to include unaccompanied youth and families with chronic housing instability due to health problems such as physical disabilities and illnesses, mental health conditions, substance abuse, and domestic violence and child abuse (42 U.S.C. § 11302, et seq., 2009).

Homeless Counts

Learning Outcome 7.2   Identify past and current demographic trends within the homeless population

The federal government counts homelessness in two ways—estimates of the total number of sheltered and unsheltered people who experience homelessness within a year and point-in-time counts, which provide an estimated number of people who are sheltered and unsheltered on any given night in the last week of January of a particular year (thus, a "snapshot"). The federal government began requiring **Continuums of Care (CoC)** Homeless Assistance Programs (local community agencies) to submit annual point-in-time counts to Congress in 2005. The estimates are then released in an annual report by The U.S. Department of Housing and Urban Development (HUD), called the **Annual Homeless Assessment Report (AHAR)**. The report is also published on the **U.S. Housing and Urban Development (HUD)** Exchange website.

Although the federal definition of homelessness was broadened, many homeless advocates believe that the amendments in homeless legislation, while a step in the right direction, don't go far enough because point-in-time counts still only include sheltered and unsheltered persons, and not the hidden homeless. This impacts service provision eligibility and funding, since the federal government significantly undercounts the homeless population and those experiencing housing insecurity. For instance, according to the 2019 federal point-in-time count included in the 2019 AHAR to Congress, there were 567,715 people on any given night in January 2019 who were homeless (Henry et al., 2020), but when definitions are broadened to include the hidden homeless, estimates of homelessness jump to between 2.5 and 3.5 million people, with an additional 7.4 million people who were doubling up with friends or family (National Law Center on Homelessness and Poverty, 2018).

According to the 2019 point-in-time count, just under two thirds of homeless individuals were in some type of shelter and just over one third were unsheltered, such as living on the streets or in tent encampments. About 69% of the 567,715 homeless individuals were adults without children, about 30% were families with children, and about 1% were unaccompanied children. Sixty percent were male, 38.7% were female, 0.57% were transgender, and 0.24% were gender nonconforming. When measured by race, 40% of the homeless population in 2019 were Black, which reflects their overrepresentation in the homeless population, as they are only 13% of the national population. Whites constitute 77% of the national population

Pearson eText

Video Example 7.1

This video explores the escalating homeless problem in California. What role can human services professionals play in providing assistance to the chronically homeless population?

https://www.youtube.com/watch?v=xydPnMW3zjg

The stereotypical homeless person is an unkempt alcoholic man.

© PHOTOGRAPHEE.EU/SHUTTERSTOCK

and are almost half (48%) of the homeless population. Just over 3% of the homeless population were Native American or Alaska Natives and 6.5% identified as multiple races. When measured by ethnicity, 22% of the homeless population were Hispanic/Latina/o (Henry et al., 2020).

The 2019 point-in-time count reflects only a slight increase (2.7%) from 2018, but there are several trends reflected in the point-in-time count report that are a cause for concern. For instance, there was a 9% increase in unsheltered homeless, most of whom reside in larger urban communities in West Coast states. Additionally, there was a significant increase (16%) in homelessness in California between 2018 and 2019, most of which was in the unsheltered population. In fact, 26.6% (151,278) of all homeless individuals in the 2019 count reside in California, with Los Angeles experiencing the greatest 1-year increase in homelessness. For instance, California experienced a 21% increase in unsheltered homeless, many of whom reside in Los Angeles in various tented communities strewn throughout the city. Additionally, the number of people nationwide who are **chronically homeless** increased 9% from 2018, after several years of declines (Henry et al., 2020).

There were some positive trends as well, including a 5% decrease in homeless families with children from 2018. This decrease is a part of a longer-term trend beginning in 2007, primarily among unsheltered families. In fact, the number of homeless families has decreased 27% from 2007, likely due to ambitious housing assistance programs targeting homeless children. Veteran homelessness decreased slightly (2%) from 2018, and the number of unaccompanied youth decreased by 4% (Henry et al., 2020).

Homelessness remains primarily an urban/suburban concern, with about 75% of all homeless individuals living in large cities or suburban communities. In fact, almost a quarter of all homeless people in the United States in 2019 lived in either New York City or Los Angeles. Unsheltered homeless are highly concentrated in urban communities, such as Oakland, California, and Los Angeles, California. Even though rural communities only account for 18% of homelessness in the United States, they tend to be concentrated in just five areas: Texas, Oregon, Washington, Georgia, and Indiana, while the homeless problem in California is primarily in urban areas (Henry et al., 2020).

Pearson eText

Video Example 7.2

In this video Timothy B. Watt discusses his mission to visit every county in Indiana as a homeless man, to fight the stigma of homelessness and advocate for the housing insecure. What are some ways that Watt's willingness to put a face to the plight of the homeless directly impacts stigma?

https://www.
youtube.com/
watch?v=E2lXakPydlo

PERCEPTIONS OF THE POOR

Learning Outcome 7.3   **Examine how negative perceptions of the poor and homeless impact funding and service provision**

Homelessness, particularly among certain subpopulations, tends to be highly stigmatized, which can lead to a lack of sympathy toward the homeless. For instance, research shows that many people in the United States believe that unsheltered homeless in particular are dangerous drug addicts. This is particularly true if they are Black unsheltered males (Markowitz & Syverson, 2019). Perceptions do not match reality, though, as homeless individuals are far more likely to be victims of crime than perpetrators (Ellsworth, 2019). Schanzer et al. (2007) point out that it is often the condition of many unsheltered homeless individuals, such as being malnourished, unshowered, mentally ill, and disabled, that contributes to their stigmatization.

The negative view many people have of homeless people, particularly those living in tent encampments or openly on the streets, can also negatively affect funding for homeless services as well as service provision. Research shows that most people tend to support homeless services in general, but not having programs or homeless individuals living in their neighborhoods. This negative attitude toward community-based housing programs is often referred to as the "not in my backyard" phenomenon, or NIMBY, and is based primarily on the fear that such programs will cause increased crime and decreased property values. And yet, research does not support these negative perceptions. A 2019 study on the impact of affordable housing programs in Los Angeles (a city that has experienced a 40% increase in homelessness in the last 5 years) found that affordable housing programs actually had a positive impact on the neighborhoods in which they were located, including leading to a significant decline in crime and tent encampments and an increase in property values (Cohen et al., 2019).

It's not just homeless people who are stigmatized in the United States though—it's poverty overall. The negative attitude about those who are poor and homeless is reflected in several studies and national public opinion surveys. Generally, it appears as though most people blame the poor for their bad lot in life. For instance, a seminal national survey conducted in 1975 found that the majority of those in the United States attributed chronic poverty to personal failures such as having a poor work ethic, poor money management skills, a lack of any special talent that might translate into a positive contribution to society, and low personal moral values. Those questioned ranked social causes, such as economic disadvantage, racism, poor schools, and the lack of sufficient employment, the lowest of all possible causes (Feagin, 1975).

Surveys conducted in the mid-1990s revealed a growing trend to blame the poor for their poverty (Weaver, Shapiro, & Jacobs, 1995), even though a considerable body of research points to social and structural dynamics, such as income inequality, as the primary causes of poverty (Shelton et al., 2009; Wilkinson & Pickett, 2017). A 2007 study comparing attitudes toward homelessness among respondents in five countries—the United States, the United Kingdom, Belgium, Germany, and Italy—found that respondents in the United States and the United Kingdom, the only two English-speaking countries, reported higher rates of lifetime homelessness and fewer social programs, yet had lower levels of compassion for the homeless population (Toro et al., 2007).

Compassion for poverty in general and poverty-related homelessness tends to be greater during difficult economic times and lower during economic booms, and general compassion for families tends to be greater as well, particularly if the family members do not match the negative stereotype of homeless people living on the streets. Several studies have examined the dehumanization of the poor, noting that much of the resentment of the poor comes from misunderstanding of what causes poverty. These misunderstanding then makes it easier for people to believe the stereotype that poverty is caused by laziness and other forms of poor moral character (Tagler & Cozzarelli, 2013). Haslam and Loughnan (2014) point out how a major component of the dehumanization of those in poverty involves seeing them as animals—socially and intellectually inferior and lacking human qualities, including self-control.

The dehumanization of people struggling with poverty, particularly those who are homeless, is what often influences public discourse about the causes of extreme poverty and also justifies social and economic inequality (Sainz et al., 2019). It's far easier to support harsh and punitive social policies toward the poor and homeless, when people are convinced that the homeless caused their own problems because they are somehow inferior members of the human race.

The negative attitudes toward those struggling with poverty are not a one-way street though. It appears that people in lower socioeconomic strata also feel negatively toward the economically wealthy. A 2012 study examining attitudes related to **class conflict** during and after the 2007 economic crisis found that about half of lower-income respondents felt resentment toward the wealthy, believing they earned their wealth not through hard work, but through inheritance and social connections (Taylor et al., 2012).

Despite intermittent increases in compassion toward the poor and homeless, the general public does not appear to understand the underlying causes of poverty and homelessness, which may make it easier for them to jump to incorrect conclusions based on negative stereotypes. Negative perceptions of homeless people do not seem to be consistent across the board, as some subgroups are more stigmatized than others, such as being perceived as more dangerous. For instance, research shows that homeless Black males are perceived as being more dangerous than Whites (Markowitz & Syverson, 2019; Weisz & Quinn, 2018).

A concept that may help explain why certain groups are more stigmatized than others is the fundamental attribution error (FAE), a tendency for people to attribute causality of events and circumstances incorrectly due to bias (Ross, 1977). In typical circumstances when people attempt to explain why they failed, or someone they know well or can relate to failed, they have a tendency to blame situational factors outside of the person's control. They give them the benefit of the doubt. But if they are attempting to explain why a complete stranger failed, particularly someone they cannot relate to, or someone they know but do not like, they will have a tendency to blame personal factors (personality traits or choices), such as personal moral failing or being a bad person, and disregard situational factors.

Assuming that FAE is at play when people are trying to figure out why someone is homeless, people who have never experienced housing insecurity or known anyone who has may have a tendency to assume that most homeless individuals are without housing due to their own personal shortcomings such as an inability to manage money well, a history of poor choices, a poor work ethic, and substance abuse. Yet, if they or someone they knew well became homeless, they would be more likely to attribute the homelessness to situational factors such as a bad economy, being unfairly laid off from work, or abruptly leaving an abusive relationship.

Human services professionals will be more effective if they understand the stigmas associated with homelessness as well as why they occur so they can acknowledge and challenge them. Human services professionals who internalize macro negative stereotypes and biases about certain subpopulations, including those experiencing homelessness, risk harming their clients in a range of ways, including contributing to their existing sense of invisibility and lost sense of self.

POPULATIONS AT RISK FOR BECOMING HOMELESS

Learning Outcome 7.4   **Analyze common risk factors that increase housing insecurity among vulnerable populations**

There are many risk factors associated with homelessness. For instance, chronic homelessness is correlated with mental illness and substance abuse (U.S. Department of Housing and Human Development [HUD], 2020). Additionally, individuals who have adverse childhood experiences, such as child maltreatment, a parent with mental illness or substance abuse, and violence (witnessed or experienced), are at far higher risk of homelessness (Montgomery, 2013; Montgomery et al., 2013; Shelton et al., 2009). Domestic violence and chronic economic insecurity also increase the risk of homelessness, particularly among single mothers and their children (Staggs et al., 2007). And finally, single middle-aged men, many of whom are veterans, are also at increased risk of homelessness for a variety of reasons that include post-war social isolation and untreated mental health issues such as posttraumatic stress disorder, depression, and substance abuse (Creech et al., 2015; Rosenbeck & Fontana, 1994).

Homeless Single-Parent Families

For years, families have been one of the fastest-growing subgroups among the homeless population. Currently, about one third of the homeless population are families, with the majority of those being female head-of-households (Kim & Garcia, 2019). Although family homelessness has declined in recent years, single mothers and their children remain a highly vulnerable group. The increase of homeless single mothers began several decades ago in large part due to a lack of affordable housing. Affordable housing programs began to decrease in the mid-1970s in response to a decline in federal funding. For instance, federal support for housing assistance declined by 50% between 1976 and the early 2000s (Covert, 2014). The combination of an increase in divorces and single parenting and the dramatic decrease in affordable housing resulted in many single mothers not being able to find safe and appropriate housing. Welfare reform in the mid-1990s added to this negative dynamic by significantly limiting cash assistance and housing subsidies.

Pearson eText

Video Example 7.3

In this video, two colleagues explore the challenges many homeless single moms face in traditional shelters. What types of questions could be asked in a national survey on the needs of homeless single mothers?

Women of color are overrepresented in the single-parent homeless population, with Black women comprising the majority of female head-of-household homeless families, relative to their proportion in the general U.S. population (Henry et al., 2020). Black female-headed households also tend to remain homeless longer than other racial groups (Meanwell, 2012). Most homeless single mothers have never been married, and although more than half are high school graduates, most have never established a solid work history for many reasons. Many single mothers cite either never having had stability in their housing situations (some dating back to their childhoods) or having experienced unstable housing for several years prior to becoming homeless. Most have experienced homelessness chronically on a cyclical basis, securing housing for a short time only to experience a financial crisis, such as a job loss, that resulted in a domino effect of negative life events and ultimately another episode of homelessness (U.S. Conference of Mayors, 2016).

Causes and Correlates of Single Mother Homelessness.

There's a stereotype that's been floating around for decades about lower income single moms on public assistance (particularly single moms of color). The stereotype goes something like this: Poor single moms on public assistance are lazy and commit welfare fraud to make money, including having additional children for extra assistance. As discussed in Chapter 2, the colloquial term for this stereotype is a "welfare queen"—a term made popular by former President Ronald Reagan's story about a woman on the south side of Chicago who had several children from multiple fathers, and used 80 names, 30 different addresses, and 15 phone numbers to fraudulently collect welfare and veteran benefits totaling $150,000 per year (Levin, 2019; Zucchino, 1997).

It's assumed that Reagan's story was based on Linda Taylor, a mentally ill woman born in 1926 to a White woman and a Black man in Alabama, during a time when interracial relationships were a illegal. Taylor, whose real name was Martha Louise White, endured extreme racism and poverty throughout her life, including being expelled from public school in the second grade due to her biracial status. Taylor had her first child at 14, and had four more during her lifetime, with each relationship involving exploitation and abandonment. She was charged earlier in her life for being a "promiscuous woman," rendering it impossible for her to secure any type of legitimate employment (her male suitors were never charged). She used at least one false name and claimed to have children she did not have in order to receive public assistance, and in 1974 she was indicted for welfare fraud for illegally receiving payments of $7608.02. She did not use 80 names, and she did not use 30 addresses, or 15 phone numbers, and she certainly was not receiving $150,000 per year (Covert, 2019; Levin, 2019).

When Reagan used Taylor's story to drive down support for public assistance and increase support for slashing social welfare benefits, he never once referenced the harsh realities Taylor experienced throughout her life, including being the victim of an extremely racist system. He did not mention that she was forced to quit school in the second grade because her father was Black, and he did not point out that Taylor, like many Black and biracial women (particularly those from the South), were victims of sexual exploitation and had no educational or employment opportunities available to them due to a system of White privilege and power. Rather, he exaggerated her "crime" in such a way that he significantly contributed to the racialization and genderization of poverty (Gilman, 2013; Levin, 2019). Further, although single mothers receiving public assistance were already stigmatized in U.S. society, Reagan's actions turned a stereotype into American folklore, and attempts to later challenge this dangerous myth with factual information seemed to fall on deaf ears (Zucchino, 1997). Rather, politicians who do not support social welfare programs have continued to promote the myth that people of color are lazy and promiscuous and cheat (White) taxpayers out of their hard-earned money (Daniels, 2016; Gilman, 2013).

So, what's the truth about most single moms struggling with poverty in the United States? Are they a lazy lot with multiple children from multiple fathers who keep having children, so they don't have to work? Well, according to the U.S. Census Bureau (2019) there are about 11 million single parent households in the United States with no spouse present, and 87% of these families are headed by women. About 75% of all single mothers worked full or part time in 2019, but most work in low-wage jobs such as those in the service industry. These jobs are notoriously unstable and insecure. Most pay minimum wage and have unstable hours, some are seasonal, and most do not provide benefits. Because of the tendency for single mothers to work in primarily low-wage jobs, 34% are considered poor, with about 25% of all single mothers living in poverty (30% of Black and Hispanic single mothers) (U.S. Census Bureau, 2019). By comparison, the poverty rate for the general population is 11.8% and for married couples it's 4.7%.

Among single mothers who work full time in minimum-wage jobs, 80% paid more than 30% of their income toward the cost of housing in 2018 and nearly one third paid over 50%, a trend being driven by stagnant wages and increasing rents (U.S. Conference of Mayors, 2016). The high cost of childcare remains one of the most significant barriers to meaningful employment among the single-parent population. The annual cost of full-time, center-based childcare for one infant in 2019 ranged from $5436 (Mississippi) to $24,434 (Washington, DC). When calculated on a monthly basis, the national average for childcare is about $1,230 per month and family-based care averages about $800 a month (Economic Policy Institute, 2019). Additionally, most service-sector jobs, in which the bulk of low-income single mothers are employed, offer employment with nontraditional hours, such as evenings and weekends, which makes it even more difficult and cost-prohibitive to secure appropriate and accessible childcare services.

Additionally, federal childcare subsidies are difficult to obtain, and most states have either long waiting lists or enrollment freezes (U.S. Department of Health and Human Services, 2017). Other studies have shown that a very small percentage of eligible children actually receive the subsidy. For instance, one of the largest federally supported grants is the Child Care and Development Block Grant (CCDBG), and a 2019 analysis showed that only 8% of the 17.4 million children eligible for this grant received a subsidy. Some reasons for the lack of access to this and other subsidy programs relate to stagnant or decreased funding; difficult qualifying processes including qualifying work and educational requirements; and provider eligibility limitations.

The analysis also revealed that children of color, primarily Black and Hispanic children, had the lowest levels of access, despite having the highest rates of need. For instance, 79% of eligible Black children did not receive a childcare subsidy (Ullrich et al., 2019). No one is suggesting quality childcare workers shouldn't be paid well, but the governments in most other Western countries have universal childcare, which means that childcare is either free or highly subsidized for all children. This scheme reduces stigma, increases quality, and benefits all of society in a number of ways (Chzhen et al., 2019).

For the average single mother with two children (the national average for single mothers receiving federal aid), the cost of housing is about 50% of her monthly income, and the cost of childcare without any subsidies is also about 50% of her income (Martin-West, 2019). Such a situation is clearly untenable, and, unfortunately, safety nets in the form of public assistance programs have significantly shrunk since the passage of federal welfare reform legislation in 1996. Welfare reform effectively ended the Aid to Families with Dependent Children program and initiated the **Temporary Assistance for Needy Families (TANF)** program, which provides assistance at about one third of the federal poverty level (Nickelson, 2004). A driving force behind the change in approaches to poverty alleviation was the belief that poverty was more effectively addressed through increased personal accountability, a focus on employment (and less reliance on government), and a policy strategy that decreased out-of-wedlock births and increased incentives for single mothers to marry.

As discussed in Chapter 2, the United States, for the most part, still uses a male breadwinner model in relation to family policies, which creates structural challenges for single mothers to rise up out of poverty. Essentially, the change in policy priorities and approaches after welfare reform shifted the rhetoric from focusing on macro-level poverty dynamics to characterizing single-parent homelessness as one of poor women of color having sex outside of marriage and getting pregnant. Such a characterization negates the complexity of poverty and also contributes to a perception that single-parent poverty and homelessness is not a social problem but a personal one that needs to be managed through increased stigmatization and punishment.

Research on single-parent homelessness reveals a quite different picture of the one painted by proponents of welfare reform—one of incredible complexity where the "problem" of single-parent homelessness is deeply rooted in numerous other social issues related to race, gender, violence, and mental illness. For instance, over 90% of homeless single mothers report unstable childhoods filled with physical

In many emergency shelters teenage boys are required to stay on the men's side of the shelter rather than remain with their mothers and sisters.

and sexual abuse (Nunez & Fox, 1999; Shelton et al., 2009). About 85% of homeless single mothers surveyed experienced domestic violence as adults, with most reporting that they became homeless after leaving an abusive relationship. Other issues include high rates of behavioral health problems, including co-occurring substance abuse disorders at about 4 times that of the nonhomeless population (Shelton et al., 2009). These types of social problems are exacerbated by longstanding societal disparities such as the overrepresentation of children of color in the child welfare system (Bradley-King et al., 2013) and increased barriers to mental health treatment experienced by many ethnic minority populations (Alegría et al., 2015).

Single-Parent Families and Shelter Living.

The increase in single-mother homelessness has resulted in the need for significant changes in social welfare policy regarding how homelessness is managed at local, state, and federal levels. When the homeless population was more homogeneous, consisting primarily of single men living in single residency occupancies or in tented encampments, the community response was less complex, focusing on low-cost housing and substance abuse counseling. But the current homeless demographic presents more challenging problems requiring a more multifaceted approach. For instance, emergency shelters are not equipped to serve families, which poses a considerable number of challenges for single mothers and their children, which in turn can exacerbate existing problems.

Single parents and their children often proceed through a series of unstable housing situations, such as doubling up with family and friends prior to living in a shelter. When a single-parent family does become homeless, the parent often attempts to avoid traditional shelter settings, but that is not always possible. There are a lot of studies showing just how difficult living in a homeless shelter is for families, particularly children, but probably one of the most compelling studies involved interviewing single mothers who were living in shelters with their children (Lindsey, 1998). In this older but seminal study, single homeless mothers discussed the vast number of outdated rules, such as not allowing their sons to sleep in the same area as them (some boys as young as eight years old were required to sleep alone on the men's side of the shelter). If the mothers refused, for fear of their sons' safety, the only choice they had available to them was to allow their sons to enter the county foster care system.

Several single mothers in the study also shared how shelters applied the same rules to families as they did to singles, forcing single mothers and their children to leave the shelter between 7:00 a.m. and 5:00 or 6:00 p.m., even if they had infants or preschool-aged children. This policy was enforced regardless of weather conditions or the lack of safety of the community where the shelter was located. Many single mothers also complained that there was no way to look for a job when they had to stay out of the shelter with their kids for most of the day. Other complaints included staff who seemed insensitive to their children's needs, for instance enforcing rules barring children from running around and playing, creating a difficult situation for parents who were required to keep their children quiet at all times even though the children lacked distractions such as television or toys. If the mothers didn't or couldn't comply, they risked being asked to leave the shelter.

By far the most difficult aspect of shelter living according to the single mothers surveyed involved staff who would override their parenting decisions. For example, staff might correct a mother in front of her child and other shelter residents for how she was disciplining her child. Such actions on the part of shelter staff made the mothers feel as though their authority was diminished in the eyes of their children. Other shelter rules that made parenting difficult included not being able to have food at any time other than during designated mealtimes, including not allowing mothers to give snacks to their young children.

Lindsey (1998) concluded that most rules and policies in traditional shelters were not created with families in mind and had a potentially devastating effect on the parent–child relationship. Most mothers she interviewed felt as though they were no longer the head of household with the power to make parenting decisions in the best interest of their children—even basic decisions such as when to bathe and feed their children were taken away from them, leaving many of them feeling just as powerless as they felt when living with an abusive partner. Lindsey also noted that the disintegration of the mother–child relationship was often not a temporary disruption, but rather one that continued on long after the family left the shelter, degrading and disempowering parents who were already feeling shamed and powerless by their homeless status.

It's important to also discuss the strengths that many homeless single mothers exhibit, particularly because human services professionals will need to work with the single-parent client to identify and build on existing strengths. Another older but seminal study found that single mothers living in shelters had a surprising level of determination, a sense of personal pride, and an ability to confront their problems directly. Many of the single mothers interviewed exhibited a strong commitment to the welfare of their children (such as choosing homelessness over remaining in an abusive relationship) and had strong moral values that acted as a guide in decision making. Many homeless single mothers also had deep religious convictions that provided them with a sense of purpose and meaning. Many overcame what seemed to be insurmountable odds to keep their children with them rather than have them placed in foster care, despite harsh living conditions (Montgomery, 1994).

A more recent study evaluating the resiliency of single mothers in general (not solely homeless families) found that single mothers were very resilient, despite all of the challenges they faced. Most shared that they disagreed with the negative stereotypes of single mothers as inadequate and immoral, and believed they had personally grown through the challenges they faced in raising their children alone. Many also shared that they found the experience of single parenting transformative and confidence building (Levine, 2009). Human services professionals can tap into these strengths when working with single parents in order to help them gain self-sufficiency in the face of multiple challenges.

Homeless Children and School Attendance.

Children are the fastest growing segment of the homeless population. According to the Department of Education (which uses the broader definition of homelessness) there were over 1.5 million students who were homeless during the 2017–2018 school year, which represents a 15% increase over the prior year (National Center for Homeless Education, 2020). Most of these children were living with at least one parent and were doubling up with family and friends, but the report also found that there were 129,370 unaccompanied youth enrolled in schools who were living alone on the streets and in shelters, which represents a 15% increase from 2015.

The staggering increase in the number of homeless students creates challenges for human services agencies and public schools. Homeless children are at increased risk of a range of social problems and challenges, including physical illnesses such as asthma, mental disorders such as depression and anxiety, behavioral problems, and low self-esteem (Masten et al., 2015; Needle, 2014). Homeless children also fare worse academically, with significantly poorer school readiness and high rates of absenteeism, particularly those already struggling with other social problems (such as violence and food insecurity) (Canfield et al., 2016; Manfra, 2019). Developing effective programs designed to address the wide array of risk factors associated with child homelessness, as well as keeping homeless children in school and succeeding academically, is essential; otherwise, they will be at increased risk of homelessness in their adulthood, in addition to experiencing a host of other social problems related to chronic poverty.

Enrolling in school and maintaining a consistent pattern of attendance is a significant challenge for homeless children due to the transient nature of homelessness, as well as other problems that result from homelessness. For instance, homeless students are far more likely to transfer schools several times during a school year, and experience significantly higher rates of absenteeism (National Center for Homeless Education, 2018). Even though the McKinney-Vento act (reauthorized as the HEARTH Act) requires that schools allow homeless children to remain at their original school if they move out of the district, regardless of residency requirements, it is often just not feasible to remain due to difficulties in transportation and other complications. In addition to family mobility, other barriers to school enrollment and attendance include delays in the transfer of school records, poor health and hygiene, a lack of clothing, and an inability to obtain required school supplies (National Center for Homeless Education, 2019; National Coalition for the Homeless, 2007).

I recall when I was working as a school social worker in Los Angeles having several school-aged homeless children on my caseload. The children would get settled and acclimated to their classroom and start the long process of building a trusting relationship with their teachers and me, and then suddenly, one day, they would disappear. I would typically learn at some point that the family was forced to move to a different shelter, and even if remaining at the school of origin was a legal possibility, it was not a realistic one because there was no guarantee that the next shelter would be anywhere close to our school. Although the McKinney-Vento Act requires that the original school provide transportation for homeless students, the commute was often several hours each way, which was simply not sustainable.

Homeless Individuals

The largest portion of the homeless population consists of homeless single adults—primarily middle-aged men who are often a member of a racial or ethnic minority. Veterans used to be a relatively large percentage of the individual homeless population, but the number of veterans living alone in shelters or on the streets has been cut in half since 2009, from 73,000 to 37,000 in 2019. What has driven the percentage of homelessness up in the United States for the most part is the number of sole individuals experiencing unsheltered homelessness, particularly in major cities such as Los Angeles and New York City (Henry et al., 2020).

The risk factors associated with single adult homelessness are similar to those noted earlier in the section on single-parent family homelessness—experiencing abuse and instability in childhood, growing up in the foster care system, having little or no family or social support, being undereducated and stuck in minimum wage jobs, having physical illness and disabilities, and having mental illness and co-occurring substance abuse disorders (Caton et al., 2005; Koegel et al., 1995; Tsai & Rosenheck, 2018). Social causes of homelessness among middle-aged and older Black men include institutionalized racism and oppression, lack of opportunity and chronic disadvantage, lack of access to mental health services, and increased stigmatization that impacts service provision (Markowitz & Syverson, 2019; Timmer et al., 2019). Research also shows that being older and having a criminal record (even for nonviolent offenses) are correlated with longer episodes of homelessness for single adults (Caton at al., 2005). But having said all of that, the most significant driver of homelessness among all subpopulations is the lack of affordable housing (Cohen et al., 2019; Henry et al., 2020).

Tent Encampments.

Many urban communities, such Los Angeles, Denver, and Seattle, have experienced a significant spike in tent encampments strewn throughout the city. Such encampments are important to understand because they create considerable conflict between tent dwellers and residents and business owners (Lopez, 2019), and present challenges for resource management and service provision. There are several reasons for the increase in tent encampments, but two key reasons include a severe shortage of affordable housing, particularly in urban communities, and limitations of traditional shelters, with most being out of date with regard to the current state of homelessness. For instance, most shelters have a severe shortage of available beds and don't have enough funding to increase capacity. Many also lack supportive services such as transitional (bridge) housing and/or supportive housing for those needing additional services. Also, most traditional shelters have policies that mandate the separation of men and women. This means that couples are separated, and boys as young as 8 to 12 may be forced to stay on the "men's side" rather than remain with their mothers. Most shelters do not permit pets, and most have rigid entry and exit policies, which create challenges for residents' who work or have other responsibilities that require coming and going during the

Tent encampments are increasing in many urban communities, particularly in the western part of the United States.

day. Many shelters also have security issues that can result in stolen personal belongings. And finally, many shelters have strict policies about substance abuse but offer little to no case management or other human services (Cohen et al., 2019).

Some tent encampments are highly organized and structured, with rules and policies, security, and cooperative practices, such as food and resource sharing, but at the same time offer flexibility, a perception of greater autonomy, a sense of community, and increased security (Lutz, 2015). Others are more loosely organized without any real formal structure or sense of community (Sparks, 2017). There do not appear to be any

© BILLY F BLUME JR/SHUTTERSTOCK

meaningful patterns in terms of racial composition, except that research does show that many encampments are organized along racial and ethnic lines. Some tent encampments are organized around drug use, particularly the use of opioids, but encampments comprised primarily of families often prohibit substance use and have other rules to ensure safety and cohesion (Cohen et al., 2019).

Many encampments have the support of cities and local human services agencies that provide services and resources, while others are subject to consistent sweeps and dismantling. How a city responds to tent encampments is often influenced by the size and location of the encampment. If encampments are interfering with local businesses and residents, or if there are concerns about public health safety, they will be more likely to be subject to a sweep by law enforcement. For instance, in early 2018 city officials closed down a historic tented encampment with over 700 residents spread along the Santa Ana riverbed in Orange County, California. The county was sued by homeless advocates and was compelled by a federal judge to temporarily halt the sweep until residents could be placed in motels and shelters, assessed by mental health experts, and then referred for social services. Many residents of tent encampments have highly complex problems and can be difficult to serve, creating challenges for city officials and human services providers (Cohen et al., 2019).

Research on tent encampments is limited, and many government agencies and researchers are in the beginning stages of researching the factors involved in their development and their impact on both their residents and the local community. Encampments may be small, sprinkled along a major road, or under a freeway underpass, while others may be far larger, taking up considerable space in open fields or parking lots. People's motivations for residing in encampments vary, which requires a varied response by local officials and human services professionals.

THE HOUSING FIRST MODEL

As referenced earlier, a key barrier to getting individuals off the streets and into shelters are rigid policies, including the requirement that residents maintain sobriety while in the shelter or risk being asked to leave. A more contemporary approach to **permanent housing programs** is called the *Housing First* model, an evidence-based approach that prioritizes permanent housing over everything else. This approach is based on the belief that people will be more able and willing to seek behavioral health services, including substance abuse treatment, once their most basic needs for food and shelter are met. Additionally, Housing First models prioritize client choice, which means that potential residents have a say in the trajectory of their lives (National Alliance to End Homelessness, 2016).

Pearson eText

Video Example 7.4

In this video, the Housing First Model is compared to more traditional housing programs. What are some key differences noted in the video?

Housing First programs serve both families and individuals, are flexible and responsive to clients' unique situations and circumstances. One type of Housing First program is *permanent supportive housing* (PSH), which works with chronically homeless individuals and families who are struggling with chronic illnesses, including disabilities, behavioral health issues, and substance use disorders. PSH programs provide support with long-term rental assistance, case management, and other supportive services. Another type of Housing First program is called *rapid rehousing*, which provides short-term rental assistance and supportive services. The goal of rapid rehousing programs is to help people obtain housing quickly.

Research shows that Housing First programs are far more successful at helping people remain housed. A 2019 study of chronically homeless people in Indiana who received housing along with a range of holistic services (counseling, substance use treatment, job coaching, etc.) found that 6 months after housing was secured, 63% were still housed (Macy et al., 2019). A 2016 study explored the effectiveness of the Housing First approach with chronically mentally ill ethnic minority populations compared to a traditional housing program. The selected Housing First program employed anti-racism and anti-oppression policies and practices; did not require participants to achieve sobriety prior to placement; and offered a range of supportive services, including substance abuse treatment and behavioral health counseling, after housing was secured. The study found that 24 months after placement, 75% of those placed in the Housing First program remained successfully housed, compared to 34% of those in the traditional housing program (Stergiopoulos et al., 2016).

Housing First programs are now being used globally, with several subpopulations, including those that are notoriously challenging to serve. The Housing First approach is complementary to the values of human services, particularly the right of clients to determine their own life course (self-determination), and prioritizes cultural competence. Housing First programs exist in most urban communities throughout the country, providing human services providers opportunities to work with a wide range of clients experiencing chronic housing insecurity and homelessness, including survivors of domestic violence, single mothers with children, and individuals who have experienced chronic homelessness.

COMMON PRACTICE SETTINGS SERVING HOMELESS POPULATIONS

Learning Outcome 7.5   **Identify the nature of service provision at agencies serving homeless populations**

There are many agencies that offer services for people who are experiencing housing insecurity and homelessness. Agencies that provide direct services to the homeless population are likely the recipient of grants provided in response to federal legislation, such as the McKinney-Vento Act. Under the McKinney-Vento Act (prior to reauthorization), government funding for homeless programs was facilitated through a number of competitive grant programs within the federal Homeless Assistance program. These included the Shelter Plus Care Program, the Supportive Housing Program, and the Section 8 Moderate Rehabilitation **Single Room Occupancy** Program. Under the HEARTH Act, grants were consolidated into a single program called the Emergency Solutions Grants program, which funds community-based programs through the Continuum of Care (CoC) program. The CoC program provides competitive grants for not-for-profit agencies as well as state and local governments. Programs focus on **rapid rehousing** to minimize the trauma of homelessness, as well as on funding permanent housing programs, transitional housing programs, supportive services, and programs that focus on homelessness prevention.

Permanent housing programs, also called supportive housing, include any housing program that doesn't have a limit on the amount of time a client can stay. Permanent supportive housing provides services to individuals with disabilities, and rapid rehousing

Pearson eText

Video Example 7.5

In this video, a human services provider explores a client's feelings about the stigmatization of being homeless. How do professional ethics drive their responses to clients' challenges?

involves services that assist homeless individuals and families with obtaining permanent housing as quickly as possible. Other examples of permanent housing that are not necessarily funded through the CoC program include subsidized housing programs facilitated through HUD. An early type of government-subsidized housing consisted of clusters or communities of apartments, often in high rises. **Housing projects**, as such communities were often called, did not effectively resolve homelessness, in large part due to the inadvertent creation of segregated communities of poverty and crime.

A more current form of permanent low-cost housing includes HUD's housing voucher program, which is based on the scattered model: **Section 8 housing** for the general population (although women with children have priority) and **Section 811 housing** for individuals with disabilities (including mental illness). HUD's housing voucher programs involve recipients finding their own rental that accepts a government voucher for rental payment. Theoretically the voucher can be used with any approved rental property, but either through bias or because of a competitive rental market, many landlords in more upscale communities will not accept rental vouchers. Thus, even though one intention of the voucher program was to avoid segregation, the result in some communities is still much the same because the landlords most likely to accept vouchers are owners of large apartment complexes in low-income, higher-crime areas. Unfortunately, the need for low-cost housing has outpaced availability.

Emergency and **transitional housing programs** offer temporary housing on an emergency or longer basis, with comprehensive programs sometimes offering housing for up to 24 months. Housing is usually only one part of the program package, and residents are often required to participate in a wide range of adjunct social services such as job training, budgeting classes, adult literacy, substance abuse treatment, and parenting training. Other support services may include childcare, job placement, medical care, and counseling. Most transitional housing programs focus on a specific target population, such as survivors of domestic violence, single-mother families, single men struggling with a substance abuse disorder, runaway and homeless youth, or the older adult population.

Emergency shelters and daytime drop-in centers offer crisis services for individuals who have no other housing options available. While emergency shelters are definitely needed, particularly when dealing with a population that might experience a crisis resulting in sudden homelessness, many emergency shelters are criticized for their often unsafe and inflexible environments where residents must leave after only a short stay. Transitional housing programs that offer housing for a year or two tend to be more successful, particularly if they provide a wide range of intensive services aimed at addressing the root causes of chronic poverty and homelessness. Transitional housing programs are also challenging to facilitate due to the complexity of the issues being addressed and the cost associated with administering programs offering comprehensive services. Other permanent housing programs focus on subpopulations such as veterans. There has been a push in recent years to address veterans' homelessness. In addition, many new programs have been developed to provide comprehensive services, as well as permanent housing in the form of rental apartments that are subsidized through government grants and grassroots organizations.

Domestic violence shelters offer transitional housing to women and children who are fleeing violent partners. Domestic violence shelters operate on a 24-hour emergency basis, providing safe houses whose locations remain confidential. Many domestic violence shelters have various homes and apartments spread throughout the community, each shared by a few women and children. Shelter stays range from 1 month to several months, and residents and their children participate in a broad range of services, including age-appropriate support groups. Human services professionals provide counseling, case management, and advocacy services, including assisting clients in obtaining orders of protection through the court system and advocating for them during any criminal or civil court hearings. Support groups focus on empowerment issues, including educating the women on the nature of intimate partner violence, supporting parenting from a perspective of strength, developing self-sufficiency skills, and understanding healthy relationship boundaries. Services may also include job training skills and job networking, childcare services, referral for substance abuse treatment (if necessary), and assistance in locating permanent housing. In general, human services professionals provide as many services as are needed by the client.

Supportive services provided in any practice setting that focus on homeless populations can include anything from outreach to sheltered and unsheltered homeless persons and families, to linking clients with housing or other necessary services. Programs may include mental health counseling and case management for homeless individuals, budgeting assistance, and substance abuse counseling—really any service that focuses on an associated risk factor or correlate to homelessness. The one thing that all homeless programs have in common is a focus on housing. Homeless prevention programs can include any community-based services that focus on stabilization in order to prevent homelessness.

Pearson eText

Video Example 7.6

In this video the human services professional provides concrete assistance to a homeless client seeking housing assistance. What are the advantages and disadvantages of providing hands-on services to clients in this manner?

CONCLUSION

Homelessness is a complex social problem with multifaceted causes and risk factors, including domestic violence, substance abuse, mental illness, and physical disabilities. Social causes include institutionalized racism and oppression and structural causes related to a changing U.S. economy. Structural issues include high income inequality, salaries that have not kept pace with the cost of living, and escalating housing prices, which when combined create an abundance of low-income renters competing for fewer affordable housing units. The development of affordable housing, although a good idea in theory, is challenging due to the high cost of land and appropriate housing in safer areas. Regardless of how rental subsidies are structured, focusing on affordable subsidized housing as the primary resolution to the homeless problem negates the complex nature of homelessness (Wright, 2000).

Housing First programs that prioritize securing housing over other issues, such as sobriety, and offer a wide array of supportive services are the most effective at achieving enduring housing solutions. Human services agencies are on the front lines of developing such programs designed to promote self-sufficiency, optimal functioning, and housing permanence.

SUMMARY

- Past and current demographic trends within the homeless population are identified, with a particular focus on how the definitions of homelessness impact funding and service provision. Homelessness demographics are explored, with an examination of overrepresented populations.

- The ways in which negative perceptions of the poor and homeless impact funding and service provision are examined. Stigmatization of homelessness is examined, with a focus on the origin of negative stereotypes of poverty and homelessness, particularly of certain subgroups, and the impact stigmatization has had on funding and service provision.
- The nature of homelessness within a range of subpopulations at risk of housing insecurity is explored. The nature of homelessness within a range of subpopulations that are at risk of housing insecurity, including single mothers and children, individuals, and runaway and homeless youth, is explored.
- The Housing First Model is explored as a more holistic approach to addressing the chronically homeless population.
- The nature of service provision at agencies serving homeless populations is identified, including various types of housing programs serving at-risk populations.

END-OF-CHAPTER QUESTIONS

1. Describe some of the challenges associated with accurately estimating the homeless population.
2. What is the connection between perceptions of the poor and the development of homeless policy?
3. What are some of the risk factors for homelessness, and how do human services professionals advocate for these populations?
4. What is the Housing First model, and how does this model differ from the traditional housing assistance model?

References

Alegría, M., Chatterji, P., Wells, K., Cao, Z., Chen, C. N., Takeuchi, D., & Meng, X. L. (2015). Disparity in depression treatment among racial and ethnic minority populations in the United States. *Psychiatric Services*, 59(11), 1264–1272.

Bradley-King, C., Perry, M. A., & Donohue, C. (2013). Race, racial disparity, and culture in child welfare. In H. Cahalane (Ed.), *Contemporary social work practice: Contemporary issues in child welfare practice* (pp. 159–181). Springer New York.

Canfield, J. P., Nolan, J., Harley, D., Hardy, A., & Elliott, W. (2016). Using a person-centered approach to examine the impact of homelessness on school absences. *Child and Adolescent Social Work Journal*, 33(3), 199–205.

Caton, C. L., Dominguez, B., Schanzer, B., Hasin, D. S., Shrout, P. E., Felix, A., McQuistion, H., Opler, L. A., & Hsu, E. (2005). Risk factors for long-term homelessness: Findings from a longitudinal study of first-time homeless single adults. *American Journal of Public Health*, 95(10), 1753–1759.

Chzhen, Y., Gromada, A., & Rees, G. (2019). *Are the world's richest countries family friendly?. Policy in the OECD and EU*. UNICEF Office of Research, Florence.

Cohen, R., Yetvin, W., Khadduri, J., & Abt Associates. (2019). *Understanding encampments of people experiencing homelessness and community responses: Emerging evidence as of late 2018*. Office of Policy Development and Research.

Covert, B. (2014). *The racist housing policies that helped fuel the anger in Ferguson*. Think Progress.

Covert, B. (2019). The myth of the welfare queen: The right turned Linda Taylor into a bogeyman but her real life was much more complicated. *The New Republic*. https://newrepublic.com/article/154404/myth-welfare-queen.

Creech, S. K., Johnson, E., Borgia, M., Bourgault, C., Redihan, S., & O'Toole, T. P. (2015). Identifying mental and physical health correlates of homelessness among first-time and chronically homeless veterans. *Journal of Community Psychology*, 43(5), 619–627.

Daniels, J. (2016). *White lies: Race, class, gender and sexuality in White supremacist discourse*. Routledge.

Economic Policy Institute. (2019). Family budget fact sheets. https://www.epi.org/resources/budget/budget-factsheets/

Ellsworth, J. T. (2019). Street crime victimization among homeless adults: A review of the literature. *Victims & Offenders, 14*(1), 96–118.

Feagin, J. R. (1975). *Subordinating the poor*. Prentice Hall.

Gilman, M. E. (2013). The return of the welfare queen. *American University Journal of Gender, Social Policy & the Law, 22*, 247.

Haslam, N., & Loughnan, S. (2014). Dehumanization and infrahumanization. *Annual Review of Psychology, 65*, 399–423. https://doi.org/10.1146/annurev-psych-010213-115045

Henry, M., Watt, R., Mahathey, A., Ouellette, J., Aubrey Sitler, & Abt Associates. (2020). U.S. Department of Housing and Urban Development Office of Community Planning and Development. In *The 2018 annual homeless assessment report (AHAR) to Congress*. https://files.hudexchange.info/resources/documents/2019-AHAR-Part-1.pdf

Kim, K., & Garcia, I. (2019). Why do homeless families exit and return the homeless shelter? Factors affecting the risk of family homelessness in Salt Lake County (Utah, United States) as a case study. *International Journal of Environmental Research and Public Health, 16*(22), 4328.

Koegel, P., Melamid, E., & Burnam, M. A. (1995). Childhood risk factors for homelessness among homeless adults. *American Journal of Public Health, 85*(12), 1642–1649.

Levin, J. (2019). *The queen: The forgotten life behind an American myth*. Little, Brown and Company.

Levine, K. A. (2009). Against all odds: Resilience in single mothers of children with disabilities. *Social Work Health Care, 48*(4), 402–419.

Lindsey, E. W. (1998). The impact of homelessness on family relationships. *Family Relations, 47*(3), 243–252.

Lopez, S. (2019). When an L.A. homeless camp rises outside your window: 'You have no idea the hell I was living.' *Los Angeles Times*. https://www.latimes.com/california/story/2019-11-17/column-steve-lopez-hollywood-homelessness-three-perspectives.

Lutz, M. 2015. "Uncommon claims to the commons: Homeless tent cities in the US." In M. Dellenbaugh, M.

Kip, M. Bieniok, A. Müller, & M. Schwegmann (Eds.), *Urban commons: Moving beyond state and market* (pp. 101–116). Birkhäuser:.https://www.academia.edu/26014671/Uncommon_Claims_to_the_Commons_Homeless_Tent_Cities_in_the_US_2015_book_chapter_in_Dellenbaugh_Mary_et_al._Urban_commons_Moving_beyond_state_and_market. Bauwelt_Fundamente_Vol._15_Birkh%C3%A4user_101–117.

Macy, J. T., Hanauer, M., Watterson, K., Ragatz, M., Suisman, S., & Sinclair, E. (2019, November 2–6). Predictors of successful housing in a Housing First program [Paper presentation]. American Public Health Association Annual Meeting and Expo, Philadelphia, PA, United States.

Manfra, L. (2019). Impact of homelessness on school readiness skills and early academic achievement: A systematic review of the literature. *Early Childhood Education Journal, 47*(2), 239–249.

Markowitz, F. E., & Syverson, J. (2019). Race, gender, and homelessness stigma: Effects of perceived blameworthiness and dangerousness. *Deviant Behavior*, 1–12.

Martin-West, S. (2019). The role of social support as a moderator of housing instability in single mother and two-parent households. *Social Work Research, 43*(1), 31–42.

Masten, A. S., Fiat, A. E., Labella, M. H., & Strack, R. A. (2015). Educating homeless and highly mobile students: Implications of research on risk and resilience. *School Psychology Review, 44*(3), 315.

Meanwell, E. (2012). Experiencing homelessness: A review of recent literature. *Sociology Compass, 6*(1), 72–85.

Montgomery, A. E. (2013, November 2–6). Relationship between adverse childhood experiences and adult homelessness: A secondary analysis of behavioral risk factor surveillance system data [Paper presentation]. American Public Health Association Annual Meeting and Expo, Philadelphia, PA, United States.

Montgomery, A. E., Cutuli, J. J., Evans-Chase, M., Treglia, D., & Culhane, D. P. (2013). Relationship among adverse childhood experiences, history of active military service, and adult outcomes: Homelessness, mental health, and physical health. *American Journal of Public Health, 103*(S2), S262–S268.

Montgomery, C. (1994). Swimming upstream: The strength of women who survive homelessness. *Advances in Nursing, 16*(3), 34–45.

National Alliance to End Homelessness. (2016). *Housing First*. https://endhomelessness.org/resource/housing-first/

National Center for Homeless Education. (2018). *In school every day: Addressing chronic absenteeism among students experiencing homelessness* [Best practices in homeless education brief series]. https://nche.ed.gov/wp-content/uploads/2018/10/chron-absent.pdf

National Center for Homeless Education. (2019). *Transporting children and youth experiencing homelessness* [McKinney-Vento law into practice brief series]. https://nche.ed.gov/wp-content/uploads/2019/01/transportation.pdf

National Center for Homeless Education. (2020). *Federal data summary school years 2015–16 through 2017–18: Education for homeless children and youth*. https://nche.ed.gov/wp-content/uploads/2020/01/Federal-Data-Summary-SY-15.16-to-17.18-Published-1.30.2020.pdf

National Coalition for the Homeless. (2007). *Education for homeless children and youth*. http://www.nationalhomeless.org/publications/facts/education.pdf

National Law Center on Homelessness and Poverty. (2018). Homelessness in America: Overview of data and causes. https://nlchp.org/wp-content/uploads/2018/10/Homeless_Stats_Fact_Sheet.pdf

Needle, C. M. (2014). *Another piece of baggage: A literature review and data analysis on the needs of young homeless children in emergency shelter programs* [Doctoral dissertation]. University of Pittsburgh.

Nickelson, I. (2004). *The district should use its upcoming TANF bonus to increase cash assistance and remove barriers to work*. DC Fiscal Policy Institute. http://dcfpi.org/?p=69

Nunez, R., & Fox, C. (1999). A snapshot of family homelessness across America. *Political Science Quarterly, 114*(2), 289–307.

Rosenbeck, R., & Fontana, A. (1994). A model of homelessness among male veterans of the Vietnam War generation. *American Journal of Psychiatry, 151*, 421–421.

Ross, L. (1977). The intuitive psychologist and his shortcomings: Distortions in the attribution process. In *Advances in Experimental Social Psychology* (Vol. 10, pp. 173–220). Academic Press.

Sainz, M., Martínez, R., Sutton, R. M., Rodríguez-Bailón, R., & Moya, M. (2019). *Less human, more to blame: Animalizing poor people increases blame and decreases support for wealth redistribution*. Group Processes & Intergroup Relations, 1368430219841135.

Schanzer, B., Dominguez, B., Shrout, P. E., & Caton, C. L. (2007). Homelessness, health status, and health care use. *American Journal of Public Health, 97*(3), 464–469.

Shelton, K. H., Taylor, P. J., Bonner, A., & van den Bree, M. (2009). Risk factors for homelessness: Evidence from a population-based study. *Psychiatric Services, 60*(4), 465–472.

Sparks, T. (2017). Citizens without property: Informality and political agency in a Seattle, Washington homeless encampment. *Environment and Planning, 49*(1): 86–103. https://doi.org/10.1177/0308518X16665360

Staggs, S. L., Long, S. M., Mason, G. E., Krishnan, S., & Riger, S. (2007). Intimate partner violence, social support, and employment in the post-welfare reform era. *Journal of Interpersonal Violence, 22*(3), 345–367.

Stergiopoulos, V., Gozdzik, A., Misir, V., Skosireva, A., Sarang, A., Connelly, J., Whisler, A., & McKenzie, K. (2016). The effectiveness of a Housing First adaptation for ethnic minority groups: Findings of a pragmatic randomized controlled trial. *BMC Public Health, 16*(1), 1110.

Tagler, M. J., & Cozzarelli, C. (2013). Feelings toward the poor and beliefs about the causes of poverty: The role of affective–cognitive consistency in help-giving. *The Journal of Psychology: Interdisciplinary and Applied, 147*, 517–539.

Taylor, P., Parker, K., Morin, R., & Motel, S. (2012). *Rising share of Americans see conflict between rich and poor*. Pew Research Center, Social and Demographic Trends. http://www.pewsocialtrends.org/files/2012/01/Rich-vs-Poor.pdf

Timmer, D. A., Eitzen, D. S., Talley, K. D., & Eitzen, D. S. (2019). *Paths to homelessness: Extreme poverty and the urban housing crisis*. Routledge.

Toro, P. A., Tompsett, C. J., Lombardo, S., Philippot, P., Nachtergael, H., Galand, B., Schlienz, N., Stammel, N., Yabar, Y., Blume, M., MacKay, L., & Harvey, K. (2007). Homelessness in Europe and the United States: A comparison of prevalence and public opinion. *Journal of Social Issues, 63*(3), 505–542.

Tsai, J., & Rosenheck, R. A. (2018). Risk factors, service delivery, and prevention of veteran homelessness. In *Military and Veteran Mental Health* (pp. 183–195). Springer.

U.S. Census Bureau. (2019). *America's families and living arrangements: 2019 family groups*. Table FG10. https://www.census.gov/data/tables/2019/demo/families/cps-2019.html

U.S. Conference of Mayors. (2014, December). *Hunger and homelessness survey* https://endhomelessness.atavist.com/mayorsreport2016

U.S. Conference of Mayors. (2016, December). *Hunger and homelessness survey.* https://www.usmayors.org/category/task-forces/hunger-and-homelessness/

U.S. Department of Health and Human Services. (2017). *Wait list vs. enrollment freeze.* National Center on Subsidy Innovation and Accountability, https://childcareta.acf.hhs.gov/sites/default/files/public/wait_list_vs_enrollment_freeze.pdf

U.S. Department of Housing and Urban Development [HUD]. (2020). The 2019 annual homeless assessment report (AHAR) to Congress. https://files.hudexchange.info/resources/documents/2019-AHAR-Part-1.pdf

Ullrich, R., Schmit, S., & Cosse, R. (2019). *Inequitable access to child care subsidies.* Center for Law and Social Policy (CLASP).

Weaver, R. K., Shapiro, R. Y., & Jacobs, L. (1995). Trends: Welfare. *Public Opinion Quarterly, 59*(4), 606–627.

Weisz, C., & Quinn, D. M. (2018). Stigmatized identities, psychological distress, and physical health: Intersections of homelessness and race. *Stigma and Health, 3*(3), 229.

Wilkinson, R. G., & Pickett, K. E. (2017). The enemy between us: The psychological and social costs of inequality. *European Journal of Social Psychology, 47*, 11–24. https://doi.org/10.1002/ejsp.2275

Wright, T. (2000). Resisting homelessness: Global, national and local solutions. *Contemporary Sociology, 29*(1), 27–43.

Zucchino, D. (1997). *Myth of the welfare queen: A Pulitzer Prize-winning journalist's portrait of women on the line.* Scribner Book Company.

Medical, Health Care, and Hospice

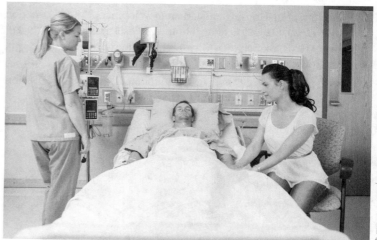

© TYLER OLSON / SHUTTERSTOCK

At 9 a.m. Glenn is called to the labor and delivery department of a large hospital where he tries to talk with a teenage girl who just had a baby. The young girl holds her new infant as Glenn initiates a conversation with her. He explains that he is visiting her because it is hospital policy for a human services provider to visit with all adolescents who have just had babies. He asks the young mother a few basic questions such as whether she has a place to live once she and her infant leave the hospital, whether her parents knew about her pregnancy, whether the father of the baby is involved, and whether she has a plan for raising her child. The young mother admits that her parents knew nothing of her pregnancy, as she managed to hide it by wearing large clothing and spending a lot of time in her room. She admits she is frightened that if she shares the news with them, they will force her to leave their home. And she admits that the father is no longer in her life and that she has no ability, nor any real desire, to raise a child.

    Glenn understands that this mother's ambivalence about raising her child is far more related to her age than her character. After some further discussion, Glenn asks her if she'd be interested in talking with a counselor who can assist her in sorting through all of the options available to her. After learning that her parents were generally supportive and loving people, he offers to call them for her so that they can help her decide how to best manage this unplanned pregnancy. The young mother appears relieved and admits that she considered just leaving the hospital without her baby because she was so desperately frightened and didn't know what else to do. When Glenn returns to his office, he makes the call to the parents; after a 20-minute emotional phone call, he makes plans to meet them in 30 minutes in their daughter's hospital room. After meeting with the entire family, he supplies them with several names of counseling agencies that can assist the young mom in either parenting or placing her infant for adoption.

While walking out of the hospital room Glenn is paged to the emergency room. When he arrives, he finds the entire unit in chaos. Three cars collided and many people were injured. After talking to the emergency room nurses and physicians, Glenn learns that one of the cars had several children in it, many of whom were seriously injured. Glenn gets to work right away collecting identifying information, making sure that each child's parent is accounted for, and obtaining phone numbers of parents who need to be notified of the accident and their child's condition. After obtaining all necessary information, Glenn makes himself available to the parents who had children in surgery—parents who were not in the accident, whom he recently called to the hospital—and the children who are not seriously injured but had parents who were. He offers to contact friends and family for support. After contacting spouses and two family pastors, Glenn sits with one family who had two seriously injured children and provides crisis counseling so that they can be calm enough to understand all that is going on with their children. Glenn also offers to be the conduit between the waiting families and the medical team, so for over an hour he goes back and forth between the medical personnel working on the injured and delivering any new information to the family members. Two hours later, all parties are out of crisis and have support systems by their sides, and Glenn is cleared to return to his office.

Next, Glenn begins working on several discharge planning cases for various patients who are scheduled to be released from the hospital within the next 2 days. One is an older patient who is not healthy enough to return home, and it is Glenn's responsibility to assist the family in finding either appropriate alternate housing or in-house services that will enable the patient to remain in his home. Another case involves a survivor of a serious car accident who needs continued therapy but can no longer remain in the hospital. Glenn's job is to locate a rehabilitation center close to family that will be covered under his insurance plan.

As Glenn's day is coming to a close, he is paged again to the emergency room, where he learns there is a potential victim of sexual assault. Glenn asks the victim whether she is comfortable talking to him, but she states that she is not—she prefers a female counselor. Glenn then calls the local county rape crisis center and asks for a volunteer to come to the hospital immediately to counsel and support a sexual assault victim.

On his way out of the emergency room he is asked to consult on a potential child abuse case. Glenn interviews the parents of a 6-year-old boy who suffered a spiral fracture of the arm. Glenn becomes concerned when he interviews each parent separately and their stories differ significantly. Because of this and the child's inability to describe in detail how he injured his arm, Glenn feels the case warrants a call to child protective services (CPS). He explains to the parents that he will be making an abuse allegation report and that the child will not be released until a CPS caseworker comes to the hospital and interviews everyone in the family.

Prior to Glenn leaving for the day, he is asked to visit with a patient and her adult son who just learned of her terminal diagnosis. Glenn provides both with some crisis counseling and makes a referral to a local hospice agency. He offers to meet with them again tomorrow and to meet with them and the hospice team if they wish. Glenn's last case for the day is to provide counseling to a 60-year-old man who recently underwent a liver transplant and is about to be released from the hospital. Research indicates that transplant patients often experience depression after being released from the hospital. Therefore, Glenn's focus is to help this patient adjust to the realities of being a transplant patient, as well as preparing him for experiencing some depression in the coming weeks. He makes sure this patient leaves armed with names of counselors who have experience working with transplant patients.

Pearson eText

Video Example 8.1

In this video a patient experiencing persistent pain expresses resistence to seeing a medical social worker. Why is it important for human services providers working in medical settings to not react personally to clients who are resistant?

HUMAN SERVICES IN MEDICAL AND OTHER HEALTH CARE SETTINGS

Learning Outcome 8.1   Explore the role and functions of human services providers in medical and other health care settings

Glenn's day depicted in the opening vignette reflects a typical day of a human services provider working in a medical or health care setting—essentially a day with very little predictability. In other words, there is no such thing as a "typical day" in the life of a human services provider working in a medical or health care setting! In fact, someone interested in a career in the human services field and looking for structure and predictability would probably not fare well in a health care setting, whereas human services providers who embrace change and unpredictability will likely thrive in a typical health care setting.

Human services providers have traditionally worked in hospital settings in a variety of capacities. Yet as the health care field branched out to other arenas, including community-based health care centers, primary care full-service clinics, and specialized health centers serving particular populations (such as veterans, children, intensive care patients with infectious diseases, women, cancer patients, and older adults), human services providers can now be found in a variety of health care-related practice settings.

Health care is one field in which most professionals working in human services are required to be licensed human services providers in some capacity—licensed social workers, therapists, or psychologists. There is some variation from state to state, but health care settings in particular are highly regulated fields and as such mental health providers working in these environments are typically required to have both advanced degrees and state licenses. For instance, most human services providers working in a hospital setting are required to have a master's in social work (MSW) and be registered as a **licensed clinical social worker (LCSW)**. Psychologists working in health care settings must typically have a doctorate in philosophy or psychology and also be licensed by the appropriate professional and state agency.

Human services providers working in medical settings are true generalists. They must be flexible and able to deal with a variety of issues, in a setting that is often wrought with crisis and trauma. But despite their broad generalist functions, the scope of human services functions in medical and health care settings, such as hospitals, can be quite specific. Most medical positions require an MSW or LCSW, but paraprofessionals may be hired for other roles as well, such as bereavement counselor and case manager, positions that may only require a bachelor's degree. Assuming someone is working on a master's level, the functions and responsibilities may include the following:

Pearson eText

Video Example 8.2

In this video a medical social worker working on an interdisciplinary medical team demonstrates the importance of communicating clearly with a patient experiencing chronic pain. Why do you think the patient is responding defensively, and what are some ways that a human services provider can respond to ensure the patient feels heard?

- Conducting initial screenings and evaluations of patient and families
- Preparing comprehensive psychosocial assessments of patients and families
- Providing education to patients and families regarding the nature of treatments and their consequences
- Providing support during hospital admissions and stays
- Educating patients on the roles of each member of the health care team and acting as a liaison for communication
- Assisting patients and families understand the different levels of care, available community resources, and the creation of advance directives
- Helping patients and families make difficult decisions about the course of treatment
- Providing crisis intervention
- Making referrals for individual, family, and group psychotherapy and other services, as needed
- Providing information to hospital staff on psychosocial issues patients and families may be experiencing
- Facilitating communication and collaboration among members of the health care team
- Helping patients during the discharge process
- Coordinating continuity of care planning (National Association of Social Workers, 2011).

Crisis and Trauma Counseling

A large part of a human services provider's role in a medical or health care setting is comprised of providing crisis and trauma counseling to patients who are experiencing a medical crisis, as well as their family members. In fact, when a hospital has notified a family of a patient's injury or illness, it is often someone from the human services or social work department who meets the family at the emergency room doors.

A good model for how to approach an individual or family in crisis is one based on a theory developed by Abraham Maslow. Maslow (1954) created a model focusing on needs motivation that helps us to better understand how people are motivated to get their needs met, and how we as mental health providers can help them meet their needs. As the illustration shows, Maslow believed that people are motivated to get their most basic physiological needs met first (i.e., the need for food and oxygen) before they meet higher-level needs, such as their need for safety (i.e., the security we find in the stability of our relationships with family and friends), or their need to develop self-esteem (i.e., to gain respect from others and have confidence in who they are). According to Maslow, most people would find it difficult to focus on developing a more positive

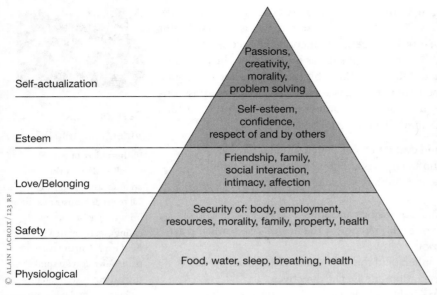

© ALAIN LACROIX / 123 RF

Figure 8.1
Maslow's Hierarchy of Needs.

self-esteem when they are hungry and homeless. In other words, thoughts about how to gain more self-confidence will quickly take a back seat as worries about mere survival take hold.

Hospital social workers and other mental health providers working in a medical setting understand that when individuals are facing a significant crisis, they often feel compelled to get their most basic needs met before anything else. In situations where family members or close friends have been called to a hospital in response to a loved one having been in a serious accident or suffering from a life-threatening illness, their first priority is often to obtain information about the medical status of the patient. Therefore, it is very important for the human services provider to provide as much information as possible without escalating in panic or anxiety along with the family. In fact, it is vital that professionalism be maintained in the midst of the crisis so the human services provider can serve as a calming influence that the family can rely on as they attempt to navigate the crisis and regain emotional stability.

Each family handles a crisis differently and an effective human services provider will recognize the family's particular coping style quickly. Some families will focus on seemingly mundane details, such as inquiring about meals or clothing, while others will focus more directly on crisis-related issues. Some families may ask the same questions repeatedly, or ask questions that have no answers, such as repeatedly asking whether the patient will survive the surgery, even though there might be no way to answer such a question at that time.

Regardless of people's individual coping styles, the human services provider must be able to read between the lines, recognizing that a family confronted with the shocking news of a loved one having a life-threatening condition often leaves them feeling disoriented and powerless. Many of the questions family members have, or actions they take, may be attempts to regain some sense of control over the situation. By understanding this dynamic, the human services provider can take concrete steps to assist the family in gaining as much control as possible in a chaotic situation with numerous unknowns. For instance, the human services provider can act as the conduit between the medical staff and the family; can assist the family in developing an immediate plan of action, such as finding childcare for younger children or having someone go to the patient's house to care for pets; and can help notify friends and employers on behalf of the patient. By addressing clients' more basic needs, the human services provider meets clients where they are.

Human services providers' role may be limited to the immediate crisis. Though they may meet with patients and family members for only a few hours, they also may continue working with the family as the situation progresses, perhaps for days or even weeks, depending on the nature of the health care crisis. In the latter instance, providers may assist the patient and family in adjusting to any limitations posed by the patient's condition or injury, as well as assist the family and patient in securing necessary resources as a part of discharge planning when the patient is well enough to leave the hospital. The human services provider may even follow up with the patient and family after discharge to check on their progress and ensure that they've been able to successfully connect with services within their community.

For many patients and their family members, the trauma associated with a serious illness or injury will continue for years. In fact, in the last few decades considerable research has shown that trauma can have a profound effect on an individual's life, at times evolving into **posttraumatic stress disorder** (**PTSD**). Those who meet the criteria for having features of PTSD exhibit physical and emotional symptoms that are pervasive and interfere with daily functioning. When individuals experience a significant trauma, their brains react accordingly, going into a "survival mode," which often doesn't go away when their lives return to normal. People with PTSD continue to react in many respects as if they are still in danger. They may have an exaggerated startle reflex, they often replay various aspects of the trauma again and again in their minds, and they may experience heightened anxiety and a fear response to new experiences, particularly those experiences that remind a person of the original trauma (called triggers).

Human services providers can respond with trauma-informed counseling, a healing approach to trauma that was developed in recognition of the powerful and profound impact trauma has on people physically, psychologically, emotionally, and even spiritually. According to the Substance Abuse and Mental Health Services Administration's (SAMHSA) National Center for Trauma-Informed Care, a trauma-informed approach acknowledges the significant impact of trauma on people's lives and integrates the knowledge of the nature of trauma and its comprehensive impact on individuals, family systems, and society into policies, procedures, and practices, with the dual goal of helping people heal and avoiding retraumatization (SAMHSA, 2015). The six key principles of a trauma-informed approach focus on the following:

1. Creating an environment that emphasizes the importance of *safety*,
2. Developing relationships with clients based on *trustworthiness* and *transparency*,
3. The importance of *peer support*,
4. *Collaboration* and *mutuality* between client and counselor,
5. Providing clients with a sense of *empowerment, voice, and choice*, and
6. Respecting and honoring *cultural, historical, and gender issues*.

Using a trauma-informed approach in a hospital setting requires that human services providers become aware of the nature of trauma, including how it impacts people across the lifespan, how it affects the human brain, and common ways that individuals who have and are experiencing trauma may react at various stages of the trauma experience. An example of a trauma-informed approach to policies in a hospital setting would be to have more flexible visitation policies, including providing family members with the option of spending the night. A trauma-informed policy may also require an expansion of the definition of "family" to include close friends and partners with no legal status, but who are integral parts of a patient's life. A trauma-informed approach to case management involves recognizing the importance of ensuring patients and their family members are provided trauma-focused resources within their community.

Pearson eText

Video Example 8.3

In this video a medical social worker demontrates how to act as an intermediary for a patient with the medical team. What skills and theoretical approaches did the provider utilize in her interaction with the patient?

Single Visits and Rapid Assessment

Because lengths of stays in hospitals are decreasing, the reality for most human services providers is that they will have very brief access to the majority of their patients in a hospital setting. In fact, it may be that a human services provider working in a hospital setting will see patients only one or two times. Because of the abbreviated nature of client work in medically related settings, there is a growing body of literature on single-session encounters with clients, addressing how human services providers can develop a set of skills that allow for rapidly assessing the patient and his or her situation, as well as how to assist clients most effectively in a short period of time.

Gibbons and Plath (2009) explored the area of rapid assessment by interviewing several patients and asking what they found helpful in these single sessions, including what skills and qualities were helpful and which were not. They isolated seven basic skill sets that medical social workers need in order to engage successfully with patients during a single session. These include the ability to

1. quickly put the patient at ease
2. establish a rapport and a sense of trust quickly
3. exhibit a sense of competence
4. engage in active listening and exhibit empathy
5. be nonjudgmental
6. provide needed information quickly
7. organize support services.

Since many hospitals hire human services providers with certificates and bachelor's degrees to conduct discharge planning, case management, and patient advocacy, as well as other functions related to patient care, the skill set discussed by Gibbons and Plath can be applied to a broader range of roles within the human services profession.

WORKING WITH PATIENTS WITH INFECTIOUS DISEASES

Learning Outcome 8.2   **Identify ways human services providers can serve those impacted by pandemics on a micro and macro level**

Human services providers working in a medical setting, particularly in public health, commonly work with various health-related crises and epidemics. In the last few decades, the United States has confronted several health crises such as COVID-19, influenzas (H1N1, SARS, Influenzas A and B), the Ebola virus, **HIV/AIDS**, and other infectious diseases. In this section I will explore a few infectious diseases that impacted a large proportion of the population because they were infected, knew someone who was infected, or their lives were impacted in some way because of an infectious disease epidemic or pandemic. Because human services providers work with clients across a range of practice settings, particularly vulnerable populations experiencing a crisis, they are well situated to provide services to those most impacted by the outbreak of an epidemic or pandemic (Dice et al., 2020).

The 2020 Global Pandemic: The Novel Coronavirus

On January 8, 2020, the New York Times published an article about a new virus identified by Chinese researchers that had infected "dozens of people across Asia" (Wee & McNeil, 2020, para 1). The article described the virus as "pneumonia-like," but optimistically stated that the virus did not appear to be readily spread by humans. At the time of publication, what was later determined to be a novel coronavirus that causes COVID-19 had infected only 59 people in Wuhan, China (the presumed epicenter of the virus). By January 20, 2020, several Asian countries had reported confirmed cases, and by January 21, 2020, the United States confirmed its first COVID-19 case in Washington State. The initial cases involved people who had traveled to Wuhan or had been in the proximity of those who had, but in a relatively short period of time there were several cases of community spread—infections among people who had no contact with those who had traveled to COVID-19 "hotspots."

The human-to-human spread of the novel coronavirus was so rapid that on January 30, 2020, the World Health Organization (WHO) declared a global health emergency. By January 31, 2020, the Trump administration implemented travel restrictions from China, but it was likely too late since the virus was far more contagious than most experts originally believed, and the virus had already spread to Europe, and it was the European strain that spread to the United States. By late February news outlets were reporting that Italy and Iran were being overwhelmed with COVID-19 cases (Taylor, 2020).

While there was considerable political wrangling about an appropriate U.S. response, few people, other than perhaps statisticians and virologists with expertise in pandemics, suspected that in just a few months, the United States would be leading the globe in infections and deaths, in numbers and per capita. On February 15, 2020, the United States had 15 reported cases of coronavirus, and by May 4, 2020, that number skyrocketed to 1,209,702, although estimates were presumed far higher because of a significant shortage of tests plaguing the country. By October 26, 2020, the United States was heading into a third wave, with a reported 8,962,783 cases, and by November 17, 2020 the number of COVID-19 cases spiked to 11,136,253 as the United States experienced another surge (CDC, 2020).

Pearson eText

Video Example 8.4

This video explores how the novel coronavirus impacted communities of color, particularly African Americans, at a far highr rate than Caucasians. What are some of the intersects explored in the video and how can human services providers address the range of social problems experienced by communities of color impacted by public health crises?

https://www.
youtube.com/
watch?v=tgyZXMCJYDY

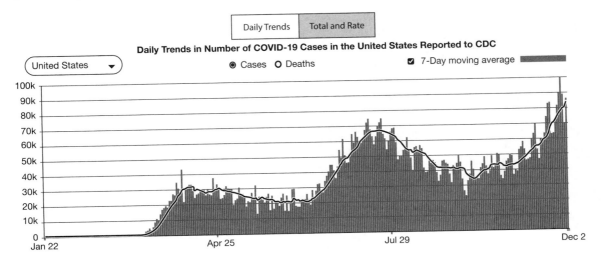

Graph 8.1 Graph of COVID-19 Infections.

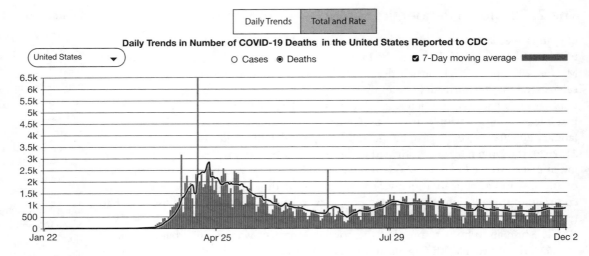

| Daily Trends | Total and Rate |

Daily Trends in Number of COVID-19 Deaths in the United States Reported to CDC

United States ▼   ○ Cases ● Deaths   ☑ 7-Day moving average

Graph 8.2 Graph of COVID-19-Related Deaths.

The United States reported its first suspected death due to COVID-19 on February 29, 2020, and by May 4, 2020, the number of deaths soared to 69,476. By October 26, 2020, 231,045 people had died due to COVID-19 (CDC, 2020).

The global pandemic led to unprecedented global shutdowns in March 2020, including the United States, in an attempt to "flatten the curve," a term adopted to indicate the dramatic upswing in infection rates, which on a graph looks like a backwards "L." The United States experienced a dramatic economic downturn in response to strict lockdown orders that required most businesses to close, except for businesses considered "essential." Initial jobless claims (the number of people applying for unemployment benefits) were 211,000 on February 1, 2020. By the week of March 28, that number jumped to 6.86 million (CDC, 2020). Jobless claims peaked at over 11 million in October 2020 and appeared to be declining toward the end of the year (Department of Labor, 2020).

Freeway signs around the country warning people to wear a mask.

© F. ARMSTRONG PHOTOGRAPHY / SHUTTERSTOCK

The coronavirus pandemic of 2020 led to numerous challenges in the areas of public health and mental health care, while also exacerbating many other social problems, such as economic, housing, and food insecurity due to COVID-related job losses, increased depression and anxiety, increased substance abuse, increased bias-based bullying against Asians, and service delivery barriers for vulnerable populations, particularly those at increased risk for becoming extremely ill (or even dying) from COVID-19. Human services providers were on the front lines helping to prevent the spread of the coronavirus, as well as providing services to those experiencing the range of impacts from this novel virus.

One specific challenge for providers and community leaders was the impact of coronavirus on the U.S. health care system. Many hospitals across the country reported being at or over capacity with patients infected by COVID-19. Because the virus caused a pneumonia-like condition in the lungs, impacting patients' ability to breathe, many were placed on ventilators in a hospital's intensive care units—departments for seriously ill patients that often have limited capacities. New York City was particularly hard hit because it's an international hub with high population density. The country's stockpile of personal protective equipment (PPE; medical gloves, gowns, and N95 respirators) was quickly depleted, leaving many first responders with little protection from the virus other than inefficient surgical masks or homemade masks donated by the general public (Miroff, 2020). Many human services providers, including psychologists and social workers, were considered "essential workers" but also lacked proper PPE, placing them at risk for infection.

Human services providers were integral to providing frontline assistance to those most impacted by the pandemic, including those populations most at risk for contracting the novel coronavirus, such as those living in close proximity to others (e.g., older adults in nursing homes, teens in residential settings, residents of substance abuse treatment centers). Human services providers also worked with those experiencing housing insecurity, such as people living in homeless shelters and those doubling up or couch surfing, who often are unable to socially distance from others, which put them at significantly higher risk for infection. Other people who were significantly impacted by the national shutdowns and shelter-in-place orders and were in need of human services intervention included victims of domestic violence living in social isolation with their abusers. On a macro level, during the height of the pandemic human services professionals led community efforts to disseminate factual information relating to the virus, including medical and safety protocols, as well as how to access a range of community-based resources, including services focusing on those living in unsafe conditions (Dice et al., 2020).

When most state shutdowns occurred in mid-March 2020, just about everyone's lives changed immediately and profoundly. Because nursing homes became early hotspots for the spread of the coronavirus, most residential facilities serving older adults barred visitors, leaving families to wonder and worry about their loved ones. For those who contracted COVID-19, hospital stays were lonely places, as visitation also was barred. Clients who relied on the support of human services providers were suddenly in the position of having to rely on telehealth services—the use of technology to provide counseling and other confidential services typically provided in person.

Telehealth services have been practiced for some time now, and there has been considerable interest in using telehealth services in rural communities, many of which lack access to services available in urban and suburban communities (Fairchild et al., 2020; Hilty et al., 2020; Myers, 2019). Telehealth services typically involve using some technological interface, such as FaceTime or Skype, that provides real-time video chat capabilities using a device such as a laptop, tablet, or smart phone. Telehealth services provided by human services providers can include counseling and case management, and within health care settings may include medical consultations with a team that includes human services professionals.

When the coronavirus pandemic hit the United States, the Centers for Medicare and Medicaid Services (CMS) issued guidelines for the use of telehealth during the public health crisis, and also temporarily relaxed HIPAA restrictions, although certain unsecure applications such as Facebook Live and Google Hangouts were still not permitted. The CMS also determined that telehealth services could be used by clinicians in their home or office with clients in their homes or a health care setting, and that licensed providers would be reimbursed at the same rate as if the services were provided in person. One application that became very popular during the pandemic, for business, educational purposes, and telehealth is Zoom, an application that provides one-on-one video chatting as well as group engagement.

Although telehealth technologies enabled many services to continue uninterrupted, including those in medical settings, they also raised concerns about access. Consider clients who have limited access to the internet because they have plans with limited data allowances, or they live in rural communities with limited broadband access. Clients who live in homes with multiple family members or are doubling up may lack the space to have a private 1-hour session with a provider. Other clients may not have a smartphone or other device that has the capacity for quality interactive wireless video chats. Thus, although the majority of Americans have some type of internet access, many do not have the level of access needed for an hour-long interactive, real-time video chat that requires a clear picture and excellent sound quality.

The AIDS Pandemic

HIV and AIDS were first discussed in the medical literature in 1981 (Gottlieb et al., 1981). Medical treatment during these early years typically occurred in a crisis setting with patients presenting in the emergency room with advanced or end-stage AIDS infections, such as **Pneumocystis carinii pneumonia (PCP)** or **Kaposi's sarcoma**, both opportunistic infections common in end-stage AIDS patients. In August 1981, the Centers for Disease Control and Prevention (CDC) reported 108 AIDS cases were reported in the United States, and by 1988 the CDC estimated that approximately 1.5 million people were living with the HIV infection. The dramatic increase in the HIV infection rate indicates just how quickly HIV/AIDS spread throughout the United States (CDC, 1988).

The WHO (2013) estimates that 78 million people in the world have been infected with the HIV virus and 39 million people have died from AIDS since 1981. When HIV/AIDS first emerged in the United States, there were no medical treatments available to address the actual disease process; thus, treatment was focused on symptomatic relief only. By the 1990s significant medical advances were gained, in large part through grassroots efforts that led to significant fund-raising efforts for medical research. Currently, HIV/AIDS is considered a chronic rather than terminal disease for those individuals fortunate enough to have access to expensive antiviral therapy. Despite medical advances, however, the treatment of HIV/AIDS remains a serious public health concern, particularly for those individuals who have no access to advanced medical treatment or who do not respond positively to the most aggressive antiviral therapy, commonly referred to as the **AIDS cocktail**.

Human services providers, such as social workers, psychologists, counselors, and behavioral health care providers, work not only with those diagnosed with HIV/AIDS, but also with their family members; thus, there is a wide spectrum of psychosocial issues involved. Examples of commonly associated psychosocial issues include grief and loss, learning to manage the stigma associated with an **HIV-positive status**, adjustment issues related to learning to live with a chronic disease that requires a daily medical regime, and co-occurring mental illnesses such as substance abuse issues and disorders.

During the early years of the AIDS crisis, the role of human services providers focused almost exclusively on the crisis of receiving a terminal diagnosis and included conducting emergency discharge planning, death preparation, arranging for acute care, and initiating hospice services. By the 1990s, education efforts led to earlier diagnoses and better medical treatment for those who could afford it, and clinical intervention focused more on the psychosocial issues involved with having a chronic, debilitating, and sometimes terminal disease that was highly stigmatized. These psychosocial issues typically included a fear of discrimination, concerns about receiving quality medical care, job accommodations and finding other income sources when they could no longer work, and housing accommodations when a client's physical health began to decline (Kaplan et al., 2004). More current treatment protocols for working with HIV/AIDS-affected clients include evaluating a spectrum of biopsychosocial issues impacting the entire family system.

The most recent statistics available from the CDC (2020) indicate that at the end of 2013, about 1.2 million people in the United States were living with a diagnosed case of HIV/AIDS, which includes 37,968 new cases diagnosed in 2018. The CDC estimates that there are approximately 50,000 people newly diagnosed with HIV each year in the United States. According to the CDC, the populations at greatest risk of infection are **men who have sex with men (MSM)** and people of color. For instance, in 2018 almost twice as many in the Black community were diagnosed with HIV as Whites (CDC, 2020). Despite aggressive public awareness campaigns in both the general public and the professional community designed to increase general awareness and remove stigma, many individuals with HIV/AIDS endure numerous barriers to getting their basic needs met—some of which are related to the stigma associated with HIV/AIDS, some related to institutionalized racial discrimination, and some related to a combination of both (Algarin et al., 2019; Kaplan et al., 2004).

An example of disparities in treatment is the lack of quality medical care available on most Native American reservations. Native American advocates have argued that the reason for these deficits relates to racial disparity and historic mistreatment and oppression of indigenous people. When reservations were first confronted with rapidly increasing rates of HIV/AIDS in the 1980s and 1990s, the U.S. government did very little to address the issue, and Native American elders complained that the medical neglect experienced on most reservations was yet another form of racial discrimination and **marginalization** (Weaver, 1999).

Human services providers working within the medical field must be aware of the various ways that racial **prejudice** and **discrimination** play out within ethnic minority and other displaced communities, whether such prejudice and discrimination is direct and overt or institutionalized (such as the allocation of federal funding). This awareness can then translate into advocacy and outreach as well as increased sensitivity as practitioners challenge their own perception of the HIV/AIDS crisis, including their attitudes about those populations that are currently most affected by this virus.

When confronting the HIV/AIDS crisis, human services providers engage in a three-pronged approach to psychosocial care, including prevention and educational awareness (such as the practice of safe sex), client advocacy, and case management/counseling. Human services providers are actively involved in both practice and policy aspects of the HIV/AIDS pandemic. This includes focusing on meeting the psychosocial needs of those diagnosed with HIV/AIDS; being on the front lines of prevention efforts, and engaging in community and patient educational and awareness campaigns, advocating for increased funding of intervention and treatment programs; and participating in lobbying efforts and advocating for the passage of laws designed to protect the privacy and legal rights of HIV-positive populations.

Other tasks involve helping HIV-positive clients obtain necessary medical services, including advocating for the necessary funding for treatment and providing counseling for HIV-positive clients and their families and caregivers. The nature of the counseling will change depending on the progression of the virus and the personal dynamics associated with each client. Newly diagnosed clients will likely need counseling focusing on acceptance of a potentially terminal disease, whereas other clients will need counseling focusing more on living with a chronic illness, accepting a life of potential disability, accepting a life that includes multiple medications taken on a daily basis, and learning to live with the consequences of a stigmatized disease.

When human services providers and allied health workers engage with populations that are at higher risk for HIV infection and the AIDS virus and have lower levels of health care engagement, such as the Latino MSM population, cultural competence and sensitivity are vitally important, as is creativity in accessing this difficult-to-reach population. The intersectionality of characteristics that increase a population's level of vulnerability is considerable among the ethnic minority populations who are in same-sex relationships or are bisexual and are HIV-positive. When evaluating clients within the context of stigmatizing characteristics and issues, it is understandable why HIV-positive Latino MSM can be a challenging population to engage in counseling and active health care management.

Several studies have found that many people with HIV are not actively engaged in their own health care, which is of great concern since research clearly shows a strong relationship between personal health care engagement and positive health outcomes (CDC, 2012; Colasanti et al., 2017). Research has also shown that individuals who are not actively engaged in their medical care are more likely to be diagnosed later in the disease progression and begin taking antiviral drugs late or not at all (Mugavero et al., 2013). This makes sense, of course—if patients aren't proactive about their health care, including accessing medical care on a regular basis and accessing accurate information about HIV/AIDS (transmission, treatment, etc.), they will be less likely to advocate for themselves in receiving the best possible medical care. This is particularly important information for human services providers working with ethnically diverse HIV-positive clients who are known to have lower levels of health care engagement.

Telehealth and the Internet (for informational purposes) are used for outreach and as educational tools for HIV-positive clients, particularly those who tend to be resistant to treatment. In fact, research on Internet usage for health purposes and the effectiveness of online engagement with the HIV-positive population reveals just how powerful this medium is in breaking through a number of barriers. For instance, there is a positive connection between using the Internet for health-related purposes (e.g., engaging with medical personnel via e-mail or video-chat, using a smartphone calendar for appointment reminders, asking health-related questions on social media and blogs, watching educational health-related online videos, reading health-related articles posted on social media and blogs) and better psychosocial and health outcomes (Colasanti et al., 2017; Mbuagbaw et al., 2013).

But research also shows that HIV-positive members of the Black and Latinas/o communities, particularly those with lower education levels and lower incomes, tend not to use the internet nearly as often as Whites or those with higher education levels and higher incomes (Saberi & Johnson, 2015). Thus, one way of promoting better psychosocial and health-related outcomes among ethnically diverse HIV-positive clients is to encourage their use of social media and telehealth for health care purposes. Human services providers can make suggestions that their HIV-positive clients e-mail their doctors or use online calendars and smartphone reminders for appointments, and they can provide them with valid and relevant online sources for information about HIV/AIDS, such as social media sites, informational websites, online articles, and blogs. HIV-positive clients who are hesitant to reach out to the medical community because they are embarrassed or afraid may be far more likely to take initial steps in the direction of more active health care engagement if they can do so from the privacy of their own homes.

THE U.S. HEALTH CARE CRISIS: A LEGISLATIVE RESPONSE

Learning Outcome 8.3   **Examine how the Affordable Care Act changed the U.S. health care system**

In 2007, Michael Moore, American film director, writer, and social justice advocate, released his documentary called *Sicko*, highlighting a range of problems with the U.S. health care system. Throughout the film, Moore featured everyday Americans who faced insurmountable challenges in attempting to receive quality health care at a reasonable cost. In some cases, patients did not have sufficient health care insurance either because it was unaffordable or because they were unable to obtain health care insurance due to a range of insurance industry policies designed to avoid providing coverage—policies that Moore alleged were designed to benefit the for-profit insurance industry, not the consumer. The crux of Moore's film was that the United States was the only industrialized country where an individual could face financial ruin and in some cases death because of increasingly unaffordable health care and unsavory practices by a for-profit insurance industry that, according to Moore, was more concerned about its financial bottom line than the health care of its consumers.

After a contentious partisan battle over the role of government in ensuring that all Americans have access to quality and affordable health care, the Patient Protection and Affordable Care Act (ACA) was signed into law by President Obama on March 23, 2010. Proponents of the ACA (also referred to as "Obamacare" and the PPACA) framed the health care crisis in the United States as a human rights issue, often relying on arguments that all individuals deserve affordable health care, and that to deny people quality medical care because they couldn't afford it was a violation of their human rights. Advocates of the ACA cited the recent trend of employer-provided health care benefits to employees being drastically reduced, either by increasing employee contributions or by restricting benefits to only a small pool of employees. This trend was making it impossible for many lower- and middle-class individuals to obtain affordable health care insurance despite being employed full-time.

Linking compulsory health care insurance coverage to employment dates back to the early 1900s, when Congress passed legislation limiting wage increases, and employers

responded by offering employees "fringe benefits" to increase the rank of quality workers (Scofea, 1994). Employment-provided insurance benefits were also thought to guarantee a full-time work force, since people would be required to work in order to receive
much-needed benefits. Yet many of the incentives to provide employees with health care
benefits (such as government tax breaks) did not keep pace with the cost of health care;
thus, many employers have found it necessary to reduce their benefit packages. In other
words, a system that worked for decades—employers offering employees health care
benefits to secure a strong full-time workforce—no longer appears to be feasible because
of changes in the U.S. health care and economic structure.

The concept of a single-payer government-sponsored health care program is not
new. In fact, President Truman attempted to introduce such a program for all Americans
and had considerable public support, but any reference to a universal health care program was vehemently opposed by the American Medical Association (Corning, 1969). In
response to strong opposition to a government-sponsored single payer system, no such
program was implemented in the United States (despite several attempts), until, that is,
when the ACA was voted into law in 2010. The ACA isn't a true universal health care
program; rather, it is a complex network of legislative policies and requirements that
place limitations on third-party payers (e.g., private insurance companies) and employers
with regard to the nature of the benefits they provide and how such benefits are to be
facilitated. Implementation of the ACA was incremental, with various components of
the legislation being rolled out between 2010 and 2014.

The goal of the ACA is to reform health care insurance in the United States by
expanding coverage, making health care more affordable, and increasing consumer protections. The ACA includes an emphasis on prevention and wellness, while attempting to
limit rising health care costs. The following list includes key provisions of the legislation:

- Employers must provide health insurance for their employees (citizens and legal
  residents), or pay penalties, with exceptions for small employers.
- Tax credits are provided for certain small businesses that reimburse certain costs
  of health insurance for their employees (began in 2010).
- Citizens and legal residents were required to sign up for health insurance by April
  1, 2014, with some exceptions such as financial hardship or religious belief.
- Policies must provide what is called "Essential Health Benefits" at varying rates
  of coverage, starting at the bronze level (covers 60% of health care costs) or the
  platinum level (covers 90% of health care costs) (Note: The minimum benefit
  level is referred to as "Essential Health Benefits").
- State-based insurance exchanges were created to help individuals and small
  businesses purchase insurance. Federal subsidies are provided for individuals
  and families to 2% of income for those with incomes at 133% of federal poverty
  guidelines and 9.5% of income for those who earn between 300% and 400% of
  the poverty guidelines.
- Medicaid was expanded to cover people with incomes below 138% of federal poverty guidelines.
- Temporary high-risk pools were created for those who could not purchase insurance on the private market due to preexisting health conditions (began in 2010).
- Young adults are covered under parents' policies until age 26 (began in 2010).
- A national, voluntary long-term care insurance program for "community living
  assistance services and supports" (CLASS) was established (in 2012).

- A range of consumer protections were established so consumers can retain their insurance coverage (began in 2010), such as allowing no lifetime monetary caps or exclusions for preexisting conditions, prohibiting insurance plans from rescinding coverage if consumers become ill (unless fraud is involved), and limiting insurance premium increases due to illness and/or gender, etc.

Experts estimated that the ACA has extended health insurance coverage to at least 32 million people (Gorin, 2010). Human services providers have played a key role in the debate about health care by being advocates for individuals' rights to quality and affordable health care. Human services providers also serve an important role in providing assistance to clients as they navigate their way through what can be a confusing process of obtaining health insurance through the government **Health Insurance Marketplace** and can also help clients better understand the nature of their benefits.

The ACA is not without its critics, though, from both sides of the political fence. Some common criticisms include the government's ability to compel millions of uninsured (or underinsured) individuals to purchase health care insurance or else face financial penalties. Some critics were concerned about the high cost of implementing the ACA, particularly in the first several years. There also were concerns about the ACA's impact on small businesses, as well as on the medical community, particularly in terms of whether physicians accept policies generated through the marketplace, or whether insurance providers will pull out of certain markets (this latter trend is occurring in some states).

A significant concern relates to the fact that consumers must reapply for insurance on an annual basis, providing insurers with an opportunity to raise rates. The ACA mandates that insurance providers disclose if they will be raising their rates more than 10%. Several insurance companies did just that in 2015, highlighting the need for these protections. On June 1, 2015, several health care insurance companies filed a notice that they intended to increase their rates for 2016 on an average of 5 to 40%. For example, Blue Cross Blue Shield increased the cost of health plans offered through the government Health Insurance Marketplace an average of 13.5% in 2015 and an additional 25.7% in 2016 (Tajlili, 2015). Despite consistent gains in profits each year, the company cited an increase in costs as justification for the almost 40% rate hikes in the last 2 years, and yet many of the losses involved moving funds into reserves for anticipated losses and did not constitute actual declines in profits (Wang, 2014).

President Trump was sworn into office on Jan. 20, 2017. On that same day he signed Executive Order 13765 (2017), "Minimizing the Economic Burden of the Patient Protection and Affordable Care Act Pending Repeal," paving the way to repeal and replace the ACA with a Republican-sponsored health care legislation (p. 8351). The executive order not only clearly stated that it was the intention of the Trump administration to promptly repeal the ACA, but it also granted all relevant agencies the authority to "waive, defer, grant exemptions from, or delay the implementation of any provision or requirement of the Act" if they perceived that the cost of its continued implementation was a financial burden to any party, including individuals, families, health care providers, health insurers, patients, recipients of health care services, purchasers of health insurance, or makers of medical devices, products, or medications" (p. 8351). The Republican Party's plan to repeal and replace the ACA with the "American Health Care Act" failed when the late Sen. John McCain (R-AZ) voted against the legislation.

What occurred next was an orchestrated attempt by the Trump administration to dismantle the ACA piece by piece, with a promise to give Americans better health care legislation. Aspects of the ACA legislation that were effectively dismantled include the *Individual Mandate*, which required that all U.S. residents have at least a minimum-level policy or pay a penalty. The 2017 Republican-backed tax overhaul reduced the penalty to $0, essentially nullifying the mandate. The purpose of the individual mandate was to increase the pool of healthy policy owners, thereby lowering premiums on market-place policies. After Congress reduced the incentive to purchase a marketplace policy, premiums increased between 17 and 32% in 2018, depending on the plan level (Seman-skee et al., 2018).

Another change implemented by the Trump administration was halting the payment of Federal subsidies for low-income individuals and families. These subsidies were paid to insurance companies to offset the cost of offering lower-cost plans to qualified buyers. Finally, the Trump administration significantly cut funding to advertise open enrollment periods and assist people in applying for marketplace policies. There have been many impacts as a result of these actions, but the most significant is that more people are uninsured in the United States, than were previous to these changes. In 2010, prior to the ACA, 46.5 million Americans did not have health insurance. That number dropped to 26.7 million, the lowest rate ever in 2016. After the Trump administration's attempts to dismantle the health care legislation, by 2018 the number of people who were uninsured increased to 27.9 million, with most people citing the cost of coverage as the primarily prohibitive factor in remaining insured (Tolbert et al., 2019). Those most affected by premium increases have been those with lower and moderate incomes living in states that offer minimal subsidy assistance (Aron-Dine & Broaddus, 2019).

A key issue in the 2020 Democratic presidential campaigns was health care reform. Bernie Sanders (I–VT) and Elizabeth Warren (D–MA), both progressive Democratic 2020 presidential candidates, expressed strong support for the implementation of a single-payer universal health plan in the United States labeled "Medicare for All." In 2019, Senator Bernie Sanders and House Rep. Pramila Jayapal both introduced *Medicare for All* legislation, S. 1129 in the Senate, and H.R. 1384 in the House of Representatives. Both proposed pieces of federal legislation introduce a universal single-payer plan, similar to the National Health System in the United Kingdom. The proposed Acts would cover all U.S. residents, regardless of income and cover medically necessary services, preventative care, mental health care, reproductive care, prescription drugs, and vision and dental care. Both proposed Acts also cover long-term services at home and within the community. Patients would have the freedom to choose their physicians, and there would be no cost for services except a nominal annual copay of about $200.00.

Sanders notes on his Senate website that the United States pays far more per capita in health care costs than other industrialized countries, noting that a universal health care plan would significantly reduce costs (Sanders, 2019). A 2020 analysis of Sanders' plan found the proposed legislation would save the United States approximately $450 billion per year, and save approximately 68,000 lives (Galvani et al., 2020). This independent analysis also placed the number of underinsured in the United States at 37 million and estimated the number of people who are underinsured and have poor access to medical care at 41 million. Both the Senate and the House versions of the *Medicare for All Act* are currently in committee but are not expected to pass due to strong Republican opposition.

THE HOSPICE MOVEMENT

Learning Outcome 8.4   Explore the role and function of the human services professional working with patients in a hospice care setting

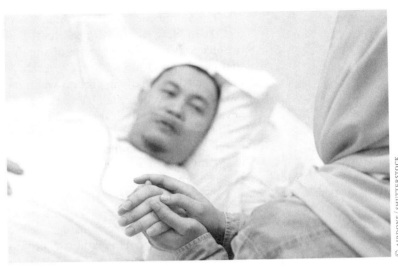

Hospice workers often provide comfort to their dying patients.

© AIRDONE / SHUTTERSTOCK

Hospice care is a service provided to the terminally ill that focuses on comprehensive care addressing the physical, emotional, social, and spiritual needs of the dying and their family members. Although hospices have existed since about the 4th century, the biblical and Roman concepts of hospice involved providing refuge for the poor, sick, travelers, and soldiers returning from war. Hospice as a refuge or service for the terminally ill was not developed until the mid-1960s.

The modern hospice movement emerged from the general dissatisfaction with how dying individuals were being treated by the established medical community. Western medicine is curative by design, with a focus on restoring individuals back to a state of healthy functioning. This model left the majority of the traditional medical community at a loss as to how to treat those who were beyond the hope of recovery. Dying patients often felt neglected and isolated in depersonalized hospital settings where they were typically subjected to needless and futile medical interventions. The hospice movement challenged the treatment provided by the traditional medical community that often failed to address pain management effectively and often neglected the psychosocial and spiritual needs of the dying patient.

Dame Cicely Saunders, the founder of the modern hospice movement, recognized this lapse of appropriate care for the dying and set about to make significant changes that would affect how the world viewed the dying process. Originally trained as a nurse, Saunders eventually earned her degree in medicine and quickly challenged what she saw as the medical community's failure to address the comprehensive needs of terminally ill patients. Saunders was passionate about the care of the terminally ill and in 1958 wrote her first paper, entitled "Dying of Cancer," which addressed the need to approach dying as a natural stage of life. Through her work with the terminally ill, Saunders recognized that dying patients required a far different approach to treatment than the traditional one that tended to see death as a personal and medical failure.

In Saunders's personal letters, she describes in detail her discussions with terminally ill patients in the hospice where she worked, as well as her dedication to the prospects of developing a system of care committed to a dying process without pain while enabling terminally diagnosed patients to maintain their sense of dignity throughout the dying process (Clark, 2002). Saunders founded St. Christopher's Hospice of London in 1967. Her model of care used a multifaceted approach, where dying patients were treated with compassion so that their final days were spent in peace rather than undergoing invasive and futile medical treatments and where they were free to attend to the business of dying, such as saying goodbye to their loved ones.

The Connecticut Hospice, Inc., was the first hospice opened in the United States in 1974 in New Haven, Connecticut, funded by the National Cancer Institute. The hospice was created for many of the same reasons noted by Saunders—the belief that good end-of-life care was severely lacking within the U.S. hospital system and the belief that the dying process was a meaningful one worthy of honor and respect (Stein, 2004). When the HIV/AIDS crisis first began in the 1980s, and prior to the development of antiviral treatment, hospices took on a significant role in the end-of-life care of those dying of the AIDS virus. Although there are some freestanding hospices, hospice is not a "place," but rather it is a concept of care and can be provided anywhere a patient resides (Paradis & Cummings, 1986).

The hospice movement has grown immensely in a relatively short period of time, and what began as a grassroots effort of trained volunteers supported by philanthropic agencies, such as the United Way, has become a highly regulated and profitable industry staffed by a team of professional service providers. Although the core goals and philosophy of hospice remain the same, the professionalization and governmental regulation of this field has influenced its service delivery model. For instance, although hospice care was originally developed as an alternative to hospital care, many hospices in the United States are now in some way affiliated with a hospital or other health care organization, most are accredited, and almost all are Medicare certified (Paradis & Cummings, 1986).

The Hospice Philosophy

The hospice philosophy employed today is similar to the one envisioned by Saunders. Dying is seen not as a failure, but as a natural part of life in which every human being has the right to die with dignity. Hospice care involves a team approach to the care and support of the terminally ill and their family members. A core value of the hospice philosophy is that each person has the right to die without pain and that the dying process should be a meaningful experience. Because Western culture often perceives accepting death as synonymous with giving up, individuals battling illness are often inadvertently encouraged to fight for their survival to the "bitter end"; thus, the hospice philosophy is counterintuitive to Western cultural wisdom.

Hospice treatment involves **palliative care** rather than curative care. The hospice movement is highly supportive of patients remaining in their homes, but when that is not possible, hospice service is provided in hospitals, nursing homes, and long-term care facilities and can be an adjunct to other medical services provided. The only stipulation of most hospice agencies is that the patient has stopped pursuing **curative treatment** and that the patient received a terminal diagnosis of 6 months or less.

The hospice team is interdisciplinary by design, and although there is considerable overlap in many of the roles of the various service providers, the hospice human services provider serves a unique purpose on the team, emanating from the distinct values underlying the human services discipline (MacDonald, 1991). The hospice team typically consists of a hospice physician who makes periodic visits and monitors each case through weekly reports from other team members; a nurse who visits patients wherever they reside at least three times per week; and a human services provider, most often a social worker, who provides case management services and counseling to the patient and family. The social work professional might help the patient say goodbye to friends and family, help resolve any past conflicts, and assist with end-of-life issues, including preparation of legal documents such as wills and advance directives (which will be explored in the next section). The hospice team might also include a chaplain who provides spiritual support; a home health aide who provides daily care such as personal hygiene; a trained volunteer who provides companionship, including reading to patients or taking them for strolls in a wheelchair; and a bereavement counselor, a human services provider (licensed, paraprofessional, or volunteer) who provides counseling and support to surviving family members after the death of the patient. One might question whether the interdisciplinary team model works when so many varied professions are involved, but research indicates that the hospice interdisciplinary team model is effective as long as there is good communication, trust, and mutual respect among team members as well as administrative support (Oliver & Peck, 2006).

The Hospice Team and the Role of the Hospice Human Services Provider

The hospice team is interdisciplinary by design, and although there is considerable overlap in many of the roles of the various service providers, the human services provider serves a unique purpose on the team, emanating from the distinct values underlying the human services discipline (MacDonald, 1991).

The hospice social worker provides numerous services to hospice patients and their families, including providing advocacy for patients, particularly in regard to obtaining services and financial assistance, crisis intervention when emergencies arise, case management and coordination of services for the comprehensive care of patients and their family members, and case consultation services among hospice and other health care staff. The hospice social worker assists the patient and family in planning for the patient's eventual death, provides bereavement counseling to assist patients in accepting their terminal illness and in saying goodbye to loved ones, and counsels surviving family members after the patient's death. Bereavement counselors also provide counseling and support to surviving family members after the death of the patient, including regular outreach, telephone support, home visits, support group and educational workshop facilitation, and even condolence cards sent on the anniversary of the death.

Prior to engaging in any intervention strategy with hospice patients, human services providers working in the capacity of counselor and case manager will complete a thorough psychosocial assessment to evaluate the strengths and deficits of the patient and family members. How are the client and family accepting the reality of the terminal illness? What are the family's emotional, social, and financial resources? Is there a history of mental illness in the family and/or the client? Can the family realistically provide for the current and future needs of the patient? Family members who are still reeling from the news of their loved one's terminal diagnosis are often unrealistic in their expectations of the rigors involved with caring for a terminally ill person and may need help to recognize their limitations and need for outside assistance.

Conducting a thorough psychosocial assessment is the first step in making these clinical determinations and ascertaining what services are needed. Although there are basic criteria of a psychosocial assessment, the information sought and the focus of the assessment change depending on the issues at hand. Thus, a psychosocial assessment of a hospice patient living at home will focus more on the patient's current living conditions, including whether they are appropriate in relation to the patient's declining health, as well as on end-of-life issues. Other dynamics explored may include the state of the patient's current relationships and whether there are any unresolved issues that need

Pearson eText

Video Example 8.5

In this video a hospice worker shares her experiences providing comfort and counseling dying patients. What aspects of the hospice philosophy are noted in this video?

https://www.youtube.com/watch?v=yX3U5XM-Fk6Y&t=35s

to be resolved before the patient's death. Once a thorough psychosocial assessment has been conducted, the human services provider will determine the nature and level of intervention necessary to meet the needs of the patient and family members. In fact, the psychosocial assessment in many respects acts as a blueprint for the human services provider, determining the course of case management and counseling intervention strategies for the patient and involved family members.

One of the most common roles for human services providers working in hospice includes providing case management and bereavement counseling services to patients and their family members that address the issues noted in the psychosocial assessment. For instance, issues related to how the patient and family are dealing with the terminal illness, the patient's loss of control because of increasing debilitation, and the impending death are all explored, and counseling is provided as necessary. Because each family is different, the counseling will vary pretty significantly from patient to patient. For instance, if the patient is a 5-year-old child dying of cancer, the counselor will need to assess the needs of the parents and siblings involved. Yet, if the patient is 85 years old with an ailing spouse and adult children in their 60s, the clinical issues will be different, and although it would be incorrect to automatically assume that the level of grief is lessened simply because this death is expected in the natural course of life, the needs of the different parties involved are obviously going to vary significantly. Thus, the actual nature of the illness or condition, the age of the patient, and the specific demographics and characteristics of the family members, including their cultural and religious background, all combine to determine the nature of the counseling.

I recall working with one client who was dying of amyotrophic lateral sclerosis (ALS), also known as Lou Gehrig's disease. She was suffering from almost complete paralysis and was unable to communicate once hospice was hired, so I worked primarily with her husband. This couple was in their early 80s and had been married for over 50 years. The surviving spouse was heartbroken at the prospect of losing his wife, who was also his best friend. Our counseling relationship lasted for months and consisted primarily of him talking about his wife, their relationship, and how agonizing it was for him to watch his once-capable, articulate wife, who was a leader both in the community and within their family, become slowly imprisoned and paralyzed by ALS.

My role was not to reframe this tragedy in some more positive light, as might be appropriate in another type of counseling in another practice setting. Rather, my role was to remain comfortable when in the presence of his emotional expressions of grief and sadness, which in some sense gave him permission to have these necessary feelings. I did my best to provide comfort and a forum for his sadness, but I never gave him the impression that his feelings were in any way wrong or that he should work harder to see the positive side of the situation. Rather I accompanied him on his grief journey as best I could, making sure he knew I was emotionally available and comfortable with his emotions.

Well-meaning but misguided counselors are often uncomfortable when confronted with a client's intense emotions of sadness and anger and, in an attempt to alleviate their client's pain and their own discomfort, try to make the client feel better by pointing out the positive side of a crisis or encouraging the client to avoid dwelling on feelings of sadness and anger. This approach often leaves grieving clients feeling as though their emotions are somehow unacceptable, or at the least burdensome, which in turn results in them potentially withdrawing and struggling in isolation. Hence, one of the greatest challenges facing hospice workers lies in their ability to increase their comfort level with painful and unpleasant emotions. Many people who are grieving can intuitively sense the comfort levels of those around them, and many hospice clients report that hospice counselors are the only people with whom they feel safe and comfortable sharing their deepest and most painful feelings of loss, grief, sadness, and anger. We don't need to offer magic words to make it better to be effective counselors, we just need to be present, open, and accepting.

There are several common issues that human services providers may encounter when working with terminally ill patients and their family members. Ways in which patients and family members manage the impending death on an emotional and practical level often determine the nature of the intervention strategies used in the counseling process. For instance, do the patient and family accept the diagnosis and grieve openly and collectively? Or do they perceive such acceptance as a sign of lost hope and giving up? Are they prepared to deal with the more practical aspects of dying, such as getting the affairs of the patient in order? What coping mechanisms do they use to help them through difficult life experiences?

Most likely human services providers will encounter a broad range of attitudes, approaches, and coping strategies used by their clients, with some families presenting a unified approach and others presenting a complex system of contradictory perspectives and approaches to death—many of which are rooted in intergenerational, cultural, and/or religious traditions. An effective human services provider helps terminally ill patients and their families navigate this difficult path, using a range of client-centered and culturally sensitive strategies.

Accepting the Reality of the Death

Hospice patients and their family members often struggle with the realities associated with a terminal diagnosis. As mentioned earlier, embracing death often feels all too much like letting go of life, and North American culture encourages embracing life and even fighting for it. Many people are fearful that if they accept the reality of the terminal diagnosis, they are essentially letting go of their loved one, which they fear not only sends the wrong message, but also feels like they're giving up. This culturally based attitude has helped create a sort of taboo surrounding death where many people don't want to think about their own deaths, let alone the impending death of a loved one.

In some families, if accepting the reality of the terminal diagnosis is synonymous with losing hope, then resisting the acceptance of a terminal diagnosis can feel like fighting for life, and a human services provider might be seen as someone who is trying to rob the patient and family of their hope. Thus, many times families make the decision to either reject social services when first signing up for hospice care or prohibit the human services provider (the social worker or bereavement counselor) from talking about the terminal diagnosis in front of the patient. Yet, because many of the issues addressed by hospice workers are anticipatory, meaning that they are designed to also deal with problems that may confront surviving family members at some point in the future, it is important that the human services provider address the family's denial and assist them in understanding that to accept the impending death of their loved one is not synonymous with hastening the death or with losing hope. Rather, it is more about seeing death as a natural part of life, as a transition.

Counseling can be particularly challenging when the patient is asking for information and the family does not want the information about the terminal diagnosis to be shared. In this situation, the human services provider must be sensitive to the family's feelings, but remain clear that the patient is the identified client, and what is in the best interest of the patient will also eventually be in the best interest of the family, even if they do not initially recognize this. A human services provider will assist the family with the tasks of accepting the terminal illness, facing this approaching loss, and addressing each emotional complication that arises with as much sensitivity and compassion as possible.

Human services providers working in hospice must be comfortable confronting the realities of death within themselves before they will be comfortable dealing with this often-taboo or at least uncomfortable subject with patients and families. Knowing how to respond effectively and compassionately when a family accepts social services, but prohibits any discussion of the terminal illness, requires clinical skills based not only on good training and education, but also on the human services provider's self-awareness and own comfort level in dealing with these difficult issues.

Planning for the Death

Human services providers working in hospice settings also assist the patient and family with the practical aspects of planning for increased disability and eventual death. Such practical planning may include something as specific as assisting the patient and family prepare **advance directives** or as broad as helping the patient and family sort through their feelings of sadness and even anger in response to the impending death. Generally, advance directives include the spelling out of one's end-of-life wishes. Legal documents such as **do-not-resuscitate** orders, **living wills**, and a **medical power of attorney** are designed to clearly define a patient's wishes regarding the nature of their medical care if and when they reach a point where they are no longer able to make decisions for themselves. Preparing advance directives is an emotional process. Imagine sitting with a patient who recently learned he is terminally ill and will likely die in less than 6 months and discussing whether or not the patient and his family want extraordinary measures taken to save his life when a point is reached in his disease process where he is unresponsive and stops breathing. The clients may respond with shock and confusion—why are you asking us these questions when we already know he's going to die? The process may seem unnecessary, but it is not, because these are legal documents required by medical settings providing care in end-of-life situations.

Making a decision that essentially will mean allowing a family member to die without intervention, either through the removal of a feeding tube or not using cardiopulmonary resuscitation (CPR) to revive their loved one, often generates feelings of immense guilt at the prospect of abandoning their family member and allowing him to die. Such emotional turmoil has the potential to create significant conflict and rifts within a family system that may already be buckling under the emotional strain of their impending loss. A human services provider's role, then, is not simply to assist the patient and family with the practical matters involved with preparing advance directives, but also to help the family navigate this emotionally rocky path.

Another role of the human services provider is to assist the patient with the preparation of funeral arrangements. The thought of planning one's own funeral might seem rather morbid to some, but it can actually be rather therapeutic for someone who is facing a terminal illness or other life-limiting condition. Consider experiencing a life event that stripped you of all control—you can no longer plan for your future because you have only 6 months to live, you can no longer bound out the door for a morning jog or even run errands whenever the mood strikes. A terminal illness robs people of their hopes for the future, but it also robs them of their control in their present, and patients—even aging patients—often struggle with the reality of their increasing dependence on others. Planning their funeral, such as selecting scriptures, music to be played, whether it will be a celebration of life or a more traditional and formal funeral, a graveside service, or a memorial service, gives patients a sense of control in the midst of their increasing powerlessness.

The hospice human services provider can utilize what might initially appear to be a practical matter (making funeral arrangements) to facilitate discussions with clients and elicit feelings about their increasing debilitation, confinement, and dependence. I recall working with a hospice patient who at the age of 93 shared heartfelt grief at the thought that he could no longer take his dog for a walk or run to catch up with a friend. In his confinement to a bed, he recalled how he had taken his physical freedom for granted and felt powerless and hopeless in response to the realization that his body could no longer cooperate with what his mind wanted it to do. Planning his funeral was the one thing he felt he still had control over in the midst of the powerlessness he felt in every other aspect of his life.

The Spiritual Component of Dying

Hospice care has its roots in the caring for the dying by religious orders, because religious leaders recognized the spiritual component of facing one's mortality and eventual death. Even though religious issues and spiritual concerns may technically fall under the purview of the hospice chaplain, every professional on the hospice team will likely be asked by a patient or family member to pray with them, and human services providers, including bereavement counselors, are more effective if they are comfortable in doing so, even if they do not happen to share the same faith as the patient. Facing one's mortality can be a frightening experience for many, and relying on or reconnecting to the faith of one's youth is a common experience for those dying of a terminal illness.

Counseling commonly takes on a spiritual tone as hospice patients attempt to make sense out of their terminal diagnosis. Patients might experience anger, confusion, and a loss of hope, and may seek answers from God yet pose these questions to the human services provider. Although no one expects someone in human services to be an expert in theology, it is important that the human services provider feel comfortable enough to help the patient sort through these questions, and even if questions cannot be answered, the human services provider can then direct a pastor or other religious leader to the patient to provide answers and comfort.

Death and Dying: Effective Bereavement Counseling

Several research surveys have noted that about 60% of human services and social work programs at both the bachelor's and master's levels offered courses related to death and dying. These courses were primarily offered as electives, and only about 25% of students actually took them. Related studies found that over 60% of new human services providers felt as though their educational program did not adequately prepare them for counseling clients dealing with end-of-life issues (Kramer, et al. 2003). This is unfortunate because many human services providers work directly or indirectly with death and dying issues, including issues related to grief and loss. In light of this, it is essential that those in the human services field obtain the necessary education and training so they feel competent in providing services to clients dealing with death and dying.

Several theoretical models are available for dealing with grief and loss related to death and dying. Traditional grief models often include Elisabeth Kübler-Ross's (1969) model of grief, which depicts grieving as a process involving overlapping stages, where a mourner meets a loss initially with a sense of denial and disbelief, then moves on to the anger stage, where the mourner feels a sense of injustice and rage in response to the loss. The object of the anger varies depending on the circumstances surrounding the loss and the values of the mourner, but might include being angry with God, the loved one who died, at themselves for not doing more, or at the world in general. The next stage is marked by the mourner bargaining to avoid the loss. Individuals whose loss is due to a death may bargain with God—perhaps promising a sinless life if their loved one can be returned to them, or they wish they were the ones to die, rather than their loved one. The stage of depression is marked by sadness, where mourners experience deep melancholy, hopelessness, and despair. The final stage of grieving involves the mourner's acceptance of the loss, which allows the mourner to move on in life. Although Kübler-Ross's stage theory has dominated the field of grief and loss for many years, there has been a recent turn away from perceiving the mourning process as one where mourners progress through distinct emotional stages, culminating in acceptance.

A more contemporary approach focuses on task theories, which suggest that mourners are confronted with tasks or needs to address as they navigate their grief journey. Alan Wolfelt (1996), a **thanatologist**, developed a task-based practice theory for grief and loss that involves seven reconciliation needs that both adults and children need to address to find healing. It is interesting to note that Wolfelt does not discuss healing in terms of acceptance, which he believes puts too much pressure on the bereaved, particularly those mourning a significant loss such as the death of a child.

Wolfelt's seven reconciliation needs include (1) acknowledging the reality of the death, (2) embracing the pain of the loss, (3) remembering the person who died through memories, (4) developing a new self-identity in the absence of the loved one, (5) searching for some meaning in the loss, (6) receiving ongoing support from others, and (7) reconciling the grief, which is different than acceptance. Bereavement counseling can be facilitated by human services providers from various disciplines, including a human services generalist with a bachelor's or master's degree, a licensed therapist or social worker, or even hospice volunteers. In fact, it is often a volunteer bereavement counselor who follows up with family members after the death of the patient to explore how the surviving family members are faring, as well as to determine the need for ongoing bereavement counseling.

Human services providers who conduct bereavement counseling may do so on an individual basis but also may facilitate support groups focusing on a particular loss. Support groups for children surviving the loss of a parent or groups for widows or widowers are examples of grief-specific support groups. Most hospices offer free bereavement counseling for up to 1 year after the death of the patient as a part of the full continuum of care. Bereavement counseling is an important component of hospice care, particularly because knowing their loved ones will be cared for after their death can provide a sense of comfort for dying hospice patients.

Multicultural Considerations in Hospice Care

Learning Outcome 8.5   Examine multicultural factors and diversity issues involved in health care access, provision, and affordability

Individuals from many ethnic minority and migrant groups tend to underutilize hospice care. The reasons for this underutilization are related to numerous factors, including a general lack of awareness of hospice care; Medicare regulations, which create barriers for immigrants, low-income populations, and certain minority groups from accessing hospice; a lack of diversity within the hospice staff leading to a general mistrust and discomfort with hospice services; and a lack of knowledge of hospice care among many physicians who serve ethnic minority populations.

Many ethnic groups perceive the acceptance of death negatively, values that are inconsistent with hospice values. For instance, one study that examined barriers to hospice service for people of color found that many in the Black community held religious beliefs that conflicted with the hospice philosophy. Subjects stated that they did not feel it was appropriate to talk about, plan for, or accept their impending death. In addition, a majority of the subjects interviewed stated they felt more comfortable turning to those within their own community, particularly their church, for support during times of crisis, rather than turning to strangers within the health care system (Reese et al., 1999).

It's important not to push hospice services on anyone if they are culturally and morally opposed to the hospice philosophy. However, if the reason why hospice care is rejected lies more in the lack of knowledge about the services provided, then it is appropriate for hospice workers to advocate for increased access to underutilizing populations. Thus, rather than accepting differences in philosophy on their surface, hospice agencies can adapt their services to meet the needs of the Black community and other ethnically diverse groups (Greiner et al., 2003; Reese et al., 1999).

Little research has been conducted on usage patterns or barriers to service for Asian Americans, Latina/o Americans, or Native Americans, but similar issues may emerge within these communities as well. By remaining flexible in their policies and practices, hospice agencies can meet the needs of a range of culturally diverse groups and avoid either directly or inadvertently discriminating against ethnic minority groups. Although there may be multiple barriers facing some populations in receiving hospice care services—some financial and some cultural—one of the foundational values of the hospice philosophy is that hospice care will be available to every dying individual.

Certainly, hospice administrators are responsible for developing admittance policies that do not directly or inadvertently discriminate against low-income patients while protecting the financial status of the hospice. But human services providers who are professionally committed to advocating for economically disadvantaged and underserved populations are in the unique position of securing financial assistance in the form of private and government assistance.

Another ethical dilemma facing hospice staff involves the issue of **euthanasia** and physician-assisted suicide. Dr. Jack Kevorkian made national headlines in the 1990s for assisting numerous terminally ill patients in the ending of their lives and was then sent to prison for his actions. Currently, euthanasia remains illegal in most states, but **physician aid-in-dying (PAD)** is legal in California, Oregon, Washington, Vermont, and some parts of New Mexico. The difference between euthanasia and PAD is that in the former, a physician administers the lethal dose of medication, whereas with PAD, the patient does. Requests for PAD or physician-assisted suicide present a particularly challenging ethical dilemma for conservative faith-based hospice agencies that believe that issues related to death and dying fall under the sole dominion of God (Burdette et al., 2005).

Those who believe that PAD should be legalized typically cite an argument based on the inalienable human right to choose death when pain and suffering robs a person of a meaningful life. Although a counterargument could be based on the meaningful nature of suffering, a better argument might be based on the hospice philosophy that dying persons have a right to die without physical, emotional, and spiritual pain—the heart of palliative care. In fact, several studies examining similarities among terminally ill patients expressing a desire to hasten their deaths found that the chief reasons cited included (1) depression and a sense of hopelessness, (2) poor symptom management, (3) poor social support, (4) fear of becoming a burden on family members, and (5) a poor physician–patient relationship (Kelly et al., 2002; Leman, 2005). If these issues could be addressed effectively, would these same patients still seek physician-assisted suicide? That is a difficult question to answer and likely would vary from person to person.

Although the hospice philosophy advocates for neither hastening nor postponing death, hospice agencies have more in common with supporters of physician-assisted suicide than one might initially think. In fact, the leading reasons among terminally ill patients for requesting a quicker end to their lives include the very issues hospice care is designed to manage. Hospice workers can respond to this ethical dilemma by advocating for the meaningful nature of the dying process from spiritual, psychological, and social perspectives, made possible when patients are helped to confront feelings of sadness and hopelessness, when symptoms are well managed, when social support is bolstered, when families are assisted with the care of the patient, and when the hospice physician maintains a close relationship with patients based on a palliative care model. In fact, one human services provider working in hospice explained that if a choice is made to cut the dying process short, then many opportunities for growth and even last-minute revelations may be lost, as it is often the last weeks, days, hours, or even minutes of a person's life that many lifelong problems are resolved. Hospice advocates cite the value of every life experience and remind us how these types of end-of-life realizations and resolutions also benefit surviving family members and friends (Mesler & Miller, 2000).

CONCLUSION

Hospital social workers and other human services providers provide crisis counseling, case management, discharge planning, and a range of other generalist services focused on the care of clients receiving services in relation to a medical issue. Some examples include providing counseling and case management services to patients and their family members experiencing a medical emergency and providing psychosocial support to those struggling with HIV/AIDS. Hospital social workers and other human services providers commonly work on interdisciplinary teams and possess an array of skills that equip them to manage a wide range of issues within a client population seeking medical services.

The passage of the ACA health care delivery, management, and reimbursement models have changed the health care model dramatically in the United States, impacting both patients receiving medical care and those who care for them.

Hospice care grew out of a general discontent with western curative treatment models, which often involve subjecting the terminally ill to unnecessary, futile, and often painful treatment, as well as a loss of dignity in their final months of life. The hospice philosophy is based on a palliative model, which involves a patient- and family-centered approach that allows patients to die with dignity with the least amount of pain possible. Although hospice care has been around for over four decades, many patients and their families are resistant to accepting hospice services because they believe that doing so is tantamount to accepting defeat and losing hope. Human services providers play a key role in helping families perceive hospice care in a different light, where embracing the dying process is recognized as an important and meaningful part of living.

SUMMARY

- The roles and functions of human services providers in medical and other health care settings are explored, with a particular focus on access, provision, and affordability.
- Recent pandemics were explored, examining the impact on vulnerable and at-risk individuals and communities, including exploring the role of human services providers assisting at the individual and community levels.
- Legislation, such as the Affordable Care Act, was analyzed with a particular focus on recent changes that threaten access and affordability for low- and moderate-income populations.
- The role and function of the human services professional working with patients in a hospice care setting is explored, including the hospice approach, multicultural and diversity factors impacting access and care, and spiritual and cultural approaches to dying.

END-OF-CHAPTER QUESTIONS

1. In what ways does applying Maslow's Hierarchy of Needs assist human services providers in better understanding the impact of crises on individuals experiencing a health care trauma?
2. Apply the six characteristics of the trauma-informed approach to a health care-related crisis such as families who have recently had a member hospitalized with COVID-19.
3. Identify at least three dynamics that increased an individual's physical and psychosocial vulnerability to the 2020 coronavirus pandemic.
4. Why are low- and middle-income individuals and families the most impacted by recent changes in the implementation of the ACA?
5. Compare and contrast Kubler-Ross's stage theory of grief and Alan Wolfelt's task- or needs-based approach.

References

Algarin, A. B., Zhou, Z., Cook, C. L., Cook, R. L., & Ibañez, G. E. (2019). Age, sex, race, ethnicity, sexual orientation: Intersectionality of marginalized-group identities and enacted HIV-related stigma among people living with HIV in Florida. *AIDS and Behavior*, 23(11), 2992–3001.

Aron-Dine, A., & Broaddus, M. (2019*). Improving ACA subsidies for low-and moderate-income consumers is key to increasing coverage.* Center on Budget and Policy Priorities. https://www.cbpp.org/sites/default/files/atoms/files/3-21-19health2.pdf

Burdette, A. M., Hill, T. D., & Moulton, D. E. (2005). Religion and attitudes toward physician-assisted suicide and terminal palliative care. *Journal for the Scientific Study of Religion*, 44(1), 79–93.

Centers for Disease Control and Prevention [CDC]. (1988). Quarterly report to the domestic policy council on the prevalence and rate of spread of HIV and AIDS—United States. *Morbidity and Mortality Weekly Report*, 37(36), 551–554.

Centers for Disease Control and Prevention [CDC]. (2012). *HIV in the United States: The stages of care.* Author.

Centers for Disease Control and Prevention [CDC]. (2020). Coronavirus disease (COVID-19): Cases in the U.S. https://www.cdc.gov/coronavirus/2019-ncov/cases-updates/cases-in-us.html

Centers for Disease Control and Prevention [CDC]. (2020). *Statistics overview. HIV surveillance report.* Division of HIV/AIDS Prevention, National Center for HIV/AIDS, Viral Hepatitis, STD, and TB Prevention, Centers for Disease Control and Prevention. https://www.cdc.gov/hiv/statistics/overview/index.html

Clark, D. (2002). *Cicely Saunders: Founder of the hospice movement: Selected letters 1959–1999.* Clarendon Press.

Colasanti, J., Stahl, N., Farber, E. W., del Rio, C., & Armstrong, W. S. (2017). An exploratory study to assess individual and structural level barriers associated with poor retention and re-engagement in care among persons living with HIV/AIDS. *Journal of Acquired Immune Deficiency Syndromes,* 74(Suppl 2), S113.

Corning, P. A. (1969). *The evolution of Medicare: From idea to law* (No. 29). U.S. Social Security Administration, Office of Research and Statistics.

Dice, T., Simmons, J., & Wolfenden, O. (2020). Responding to epidemics and pandemics: The role of human services professionals. *Human Services Today*, 1(1), 12.

Executive Order No. 13765, 82 F.R. 8351 (2017). https://www.federalregister.gov/documents/2017/01/24/2017-01799/minimizing-the-economic-burden-of-the-patient-protection-and-affordable-care-act-pending-repeal

Fairchild, R. M., Ferng-Kuo, S. F., Rahmouni, H., & Hardesty, D. (2020). Telehealth increases access to care for children dealing with suicidality, depression, and anxiety in rural emergency departments. *Telemedicine and e-Health.* Advance online publication. https://doi.org/10.1089/tmj.2019.0253

Galvani, A. P., Parpia, A. S., Foster, E. M., Singer, B. H., & Fitzpatrick, M. C. (2020). Improving the prognosis of health care in the USA. *The Lancet*, 395(10223), 524–533.

Gibbons, J., & Plath, D. (2009). Single contacts with hospital social workers: The clients' experiences. *Social Work in Health Care*, 48(8), 721–735.

Gorin, S. H. (2010). The Patient Protection and Affordable Care Act, cost control, and the battle for health care reform. *Health & Social Work*, 35(3), 163–166.

Gottlieb, M. S., Schroff, R., Schanker, H. M., Weisman, J. D., Fan, P. T., Wolf, R. A., & Saxon, A. (1981). *Pneumocystis carnii* pneumonia and mucosal candidiasis in previously homosexual men: Evidence of a new acquired cellular immunodeficiency. *New England Journal of Medicine*, 305(24), 1425–1431.

Greiner, K. A., Perera, S., & Ahluwalia, J. S. (2003). Hospice usage by minorities in the last year of life: Results from the National Mortality Follow Back Survey. *Journal of the American Geriatrics Society*, 51, 970–978.

Hilty, D. M., Gentry, M. T., McKean, A. J., Cowan, K. E., Lim, R. F., & Lu, F. G. (2020). Telehealth for rural diverse populations: Telebehavioral and cultural competencies, clinical outcomes and administrative approaches. *Mental Health*, 6, 1–9.

Kaplan, L. E., Tomaszewski, E. S., & Gorin, S. (2004). Current trends and the future of HIV/AIDS services: A social work perspective. *Health & Social Work*, 29(2), 153–159.

Kelly, B., Burnett, P., Pelusi, D., Badger, S., Varghese, F., & Robertson, M. (2002). Terminally ill cancer patients' wish to hasten death. *Palliative Medicine, 16*, 335–339.

Kramer, B. J., Hovland-Scafe, C., & Pacourek, L. (2003). Analysis of end-of-life content in social work textbooks. *Journal of Social Work Education, 39*(2), 299–320.

Kübler-Ross, E. (1969). *Living with death and dying.* Macmillan Publishing Co.

Leman, R. (2005). *Seventh annual report on Oregon's death with dignity act.* State of Oregon, Department of Human services, Office of Disease Prevention and Epidemiology. http://oregon.gov/DHS/ph/pas/docs/year7.pdf

MacDonald, D. (1991). Hospice social work: A search for identity. *Health and Social Work, 16*(4), 274–280.

Maslow, A. (1954). *Motivation and personality.* Harper.

Mbuagbaw, L., Van Der Kop, M. L., Lester, R. T., Thirumurthy, H., Pop-Eleches, C., Smieja, M., & Thabane, L. (2013). Mobile phone text messages for improving adherence to antiretroviral therapy (ART): A protocol for an individual patient data meta-analysis of randomised trials. *BMJ Open, 3*(5), e002954.

Mesler, M. A., & Miller, P. J. (2000). Hospice and assisted suicide: The structure and process of an inherent dilemma. *Death Studies, 24*, 135–155.

Miroff, N. (2020, April). Protective gear in national stockpile is nearly depleted, DHS officials say. *Washington Post.* https://www.washingtonpost.com/national/coronavirus-protective-gear-stockpile-depleted/2020/04/01/44d6592a-741f-11ea-ae50-7148009252e3_story.html

Mugavero, M. J., Amico, K. R., Horn, T., & Thompson, M. A. (2013). The state of engagement in HIV care in the United States: From cascade to continuum to control. *Clinical Infectious Diseases, 57*(8), 1164–1171.

Myers, C. R. (2019). Using telehealth to remediate rural mental health and healthcare disparities. *Issues in Mental Health Nursing, 40*(3), 233–239.

National Association of Social Workers [NASW]. (2011). *Social workers in hospitals & medical centers: Occupational profile.* https://www.socialworkers.org/LinkClick.aspx?fileticket=o7o0IXW1R2w%3D&portalid=0

Oliver, D., & Peck, M. (2006, September). Inside the interdisciplinary team experiences of hospice social workers. *Journal of Social Work in End-of-Life and Palliative Care, 2*(3), 7–21.

Paradis, L., & Cummings, S. (1986). The evolution of hospice in America toward organizational homogeneity. *Journal of Health and Social Behavior, 27*(4), 370–386.

Reese, D. J., Ahern, R. E., Nair, S., O'Faire, J. D., & Warren, C. (1999). Hospice access and use by African Americans: Addressing cultural and institutional barriers through participatory action research. *Social Work, 44*(6), 449–559.

Saberi, P., & Johnson, M. O. (2015). Correlation of internet use for health care engagement purposes and HIV clinical outcomes among HIV-positive individuals using online social media. *Journal of Health Communication, 20*(9), 1026–1032.

Sanders, B. (2019). *Medicare for All Act of 2019.* Bernie Sanders Senate website. https://www.sanders.senate.gov/download/medicare-for-all-2019-summary?id=FA52728F-B57E-4E0D-96C2-F0C5D346A6E1&download=1&inline=file

Scofea, L. A. (1994). The development and growth of employer-provided health insurance. *Monthly Labor Review, 117*(3), 3–10.

Semanskee, A., Claxton, G., & Levi, L. (2018). *How premiums are changing in 2018.* Kaiser Family Foundation. https://www.kff.org/health-costs/issue-brief/how-premiums-are-changing-in-2018/

Stein, G. (2004). Improving our care at life's end: Making a difference. *Health and Social Work, 29*(1), 77–79.

Substance Abuse and Mental Health Services Administration [SAMHSA]. (2015). *About NCTIC.* National Center for Trauma-Informed Care & Alternatives to Seclusion and Restraint. http://www.samhsa.gov/nctic.

Tajlili, B. (2015). *Yes, you'll probably pay more for your health insurance in 2016, and here's why* [Blog]. Blue Cross Blue Shield. from http://blog.bcbsnc.com/2015/06/yes-youll-probably-pay-more-for-your-health-insurance-in-2016-and-heres-why/

Taylor, D. B. (2020, April). How the coronavirus pandemic unfolded: A timeline. *New York Times.* https://www.nytimes.com/article/coronavirus-timeline.html

Tolbert, J., Orgera, K., Singer, N., & Damico, A. (2019). *Key facts about the uninsured population* [Issue brief]. Kaiser

Family Foundation. http://files.kff.org/attachment/Issue-Brief-Key-Facts-about-the-Uninsured-Population

Wang, A. (2014, March 5). *Blue Cross parent expecting losses in 2014 due to Obamacare*. Crain's Chicago Business. http://www.chicagobusiness.com/article/20140305/NEWS03/140309917/-blue-cross-parent-expecting-losses-in-2014-due-to-obamacare

Weaver, H. N. (1999). Through indigenous eyes: Native Americans and the HIV epidemic. *Health and Social Work, 24*(1), 27–34.

Wee, S. L., & McNeil Jr, D. G. (2020). China identifies new virus causing pneumonialike illness. *New York Times*.

Wolfelt, A. (1996). *Healing the bereaved child: Grief gardening, growth through grief, and other touchstones for caregivers*. Companion Press.

World Health Organization. (2013). *Global health observatory data: HIV/AIDS*. http://www.who.int/gho/hiv/en/

9

Human Services in the Public School System

© SHUTTERSTOCK

Mario is a junior at a public high school in a large urban school in a state bordering Mexico. He does not have a behavior problem and does relatively well in his academic studies, but he has come to the attention of school social workers due to excessive absences. His teachers also report that he seems particularly "stressed out" lately and is not himself. There is concern that he may be withdrawing emotionally and socially due to an increase in anti-immigrant sentiments expressed among some students and even some school personnel. A psychosocial evaluation revealed that Mario is the oldest of four children. Mario's parents are undocumented immigrants from Mexico who have been living in the United States for approximately 15 years, having been recruited to work in the United States by a large agricultural company.

Mario's parents do not speak English, and Mario disclosed that he often misses school so that he can translate for his parents or advocate for them when they are too frightened to seek out services themselves, in light of an increase in anti-immigration sentiments in their community. Mario also disclosed that he has been the target of anti-immigrant bullying at school and in public places, including derogatory statements made toward him. For instance, on several occasions while walking down the halls in school he has heard random students shout out to him asking for proof of his legal status or telling him to go back to Mexico. He has also experienced negative statements directed toward all Latina/o students, including a few teachers and some office assistants who have made statements appearing to scapegoat this population for everything from escalating violence to high regional unemployment rates.

The school social worker, Rosa, who is bilingual, recently reached out to Mario's parents to see how she and the school could help. Rosa met with Mario and his parents to gain a greater understanding of their challenges and to offer support, including school and community-based services. During the meeting Mario shared that he just learned that he does not in fact have legal status. Mario grew up believing that he was born in the United States, but after applying for financial aid for college next year, Mario was informed that his Social Security number was not valid. His parents then told him that they were given paperwork by the U.S. agricultural company that recruited them, and they learned years later that the paperwork was fraudulent. Mario was 6 months old when they emigrated from Mexico, and he has no memory of living in Mexico. Since he only returned a few times much earlier in his childhood, he has no real connections there. Mario shared with Rosa that he became extremely distraught when he learned about his immigration status, including feeling discouragement and fear that he would not be able to attend college, despite having lived in the United States since infancy. He also shared feeling frightened and distraught at the prospect of being deported to Mexico, since his entire family lives in the United States, and his younger two siblings, who were born in the United States, have legal status. Mario shared that he always worked so hard in school, but when he learned he did not have legal status, he just gave up.

Rosa did her best to offer Mario hope, but she knew his situation required coordination with advocacy and legal services outside of the school, so she was careful not to make promises she could not keep. Shortly after the meeting, Rosa reached out to a community immigration advocacy organization and set up a joint meeting with the agency, herself, Mario, and his parents. Before their next meeting Rosa did some research on immigration-related issues, particularly surrounding situations like Mario's. She read about the history and current status of Deferred Action for Childhood Arrivals (DACA), a program created through an Executive Order signed by former President Barack Obama, as well as other federal and state legislation that could protect Mario from forced deportation. She also read several scholarly articles about the impact of living in limbo on youth like Mario so she could be better prepared to offer him psychosocial support and encouragement. Gaining awareness of both the micro and macro issues affecting the Latina/o students at Rosa's school is a vital part of providing culturally competent human services in a school setting.

THE HISTORY AND FUNCTIONS OF HUMAN SERVICES IN U.S. PUBLIC SCHOOLS

Human services providers have been associated with the U.S. public school system since the passage of compulsory attendance laws in the early 1900s. Although the titles of these positions have changed throughout the years, human services providers in the public school system can be categorized into three basic professional groups: school social workers, who focus primarily on psychosocial issues that create barriers to students' academic performance; school counselors, who focus primarily on academic guidance; and school psychologists, who focus primarily on academic testing and placement. Each of these disciplines has a unique professional identity, as well as unique academic and licensing requirements, and each discipline has its own professional organization that provides ethical standards, guidance, and leadership. But in reality, since school social workers, school counselors, and school psychologists working in the public school system are all concerned with student health, well-being, and success, there is considerable overlap in their functions and duties.

Human services professionals are an integral part of the public school system, providing academic support, psychosocial counseling, and career guidance to millions of students every year, as well as programmatic leadership and support within the public school system. School social workers, school counselors, and school psychologists comprise what is often called the **student services team**—a multidisciplinary team where each support professional works within their respective specialties to meet students' psychosocial and academic needs, increasing student success in a range of important domains.

School social workers, school counselors, and school psychologists all provide psychosocial services, but they use somewhat different approaches to counseling and student support provision, having different standards of practice and even different service and treatment goals. Social workers tend to focus more on the psychosocial aspects of students' lives, providing counseling and case management that focus on traditional social work concerns such as the students' overall mental health, diversity and cultural competence, and social problems within the community that can impact students' lives in a way that creates barriers to learning (e.g., violence, homelessness, poverty). School counselors have a similar focus as school social workers but tend to focus more on academic counseling and career guidance, while also focusing on emotional or psychological issues that pertain to student achievement. School psychologists focus more on testing, particularly in response to numerous federal and state mandates that require the academic testing of students to place them in the proper educational setting, but school psychologists may also provide counseling for students who are experiencing emotional difficulties affecting their academic achievement.

In general, the goals of each member of a student services team focuses on (1) supporting academic achievement, (2) fostering emotional and mental health, (3) encouraging prosocial behavior, (4) supporting diverse learners and students from diverse backgrounds, (5) creating safe school environments, and (6) building strong connections between school, home, and community. Thus, while there is some overlap in the duties and functions of school social workers, school counselors, and school psychologists, each professional serving on a student services team accomplishes these goals in ways

Pearson eText

Video Example 9.1

In this video a team of human services professionals discuss concerns regarding a student's behavior. What are the advantages of the interprofessional collaboration?

that reflect the evidence-based and data-driven practices and foundational values unique to their respective professional disciplines.

SCHOOL SOCIAL WORK

Learning Outcome 9.1   Explore the nature of school social work in the public school system, including the duties and functions of a school social worker

School social workers serve as important liaisons between students and their families, the school system, and the community. Most states require that school social workers have an MSW with a specialization in school social work; accrue 1200 hours in an internship, which includes 720 hours in a public school setting; and pass a state content-area test. School social workers serve the vital role of providing students with psychosocial support in a range of contexts—in the classroom, at home, in the community—addressing dynamic challenges that present barriers to academic success.

The Historical Roots of Social Work in Schools

Social workers have served an important role in supporting a wide range of at-risk and marginalized students and their families for over 100 years, ensuring that students were attending school regularly, that children's adjustment needs were met, and that children with disabilities received the services they needed (Allen-Meares, 2006; McCullagh, 1993). Early school social workers were called visiting teachers and were a part of the **Visiting Teacher Movement**, which began in 1906 and ended in 1940.

Visiting teachers were primarily social workers from **settlement houses**—community-based organizations that provided services primarily to low-income immigrant populations in large urban areas. Thus, most of the children who were the original focus of early school social work services were the children of immigrants, many from non-English-speaking countries. The communities where settlement houses were located were frequently overcrowded, both within the neighborhoods as well as within the classroom, where some schools had as many as 50 students per classroom (McCullagh, 1993, 1998).

The role of visiting teachers expanded quickly to focus not only on immigrant children but also on maladjusted children (including those with conduct problems) and children with intellectual disabilities (often referred to as **feeble-minded** or unintelligent in the early education literature). Among the many goals of visiting teachers was to save the unadjusted child—those children who were not faring well amidst all of the dramatic social and economic changes occurring during that era that were impacting children and their families, and thus the educational system as a whole.

In addition to mass immigration, another social force driving the need for increased psychosocial support in the public school system was the passage of **compulsory education laws** from the mid-1800s through about 1920. Mandatory school attendance laws meant that thousands of children who had previously been omitted from the educational system—poor children, orphans, immigrant children, and children who were cognitively disabled—were now compelled to attend school or face sanctions, which in some states involved the termination of parental rights. **Mass urbanization** was another socioeconomic force involving scores of people moving away from their farms and into the cities for factory jobs. With them came children, many of whom struggled in their adjustment to city life, particularly when it involved living in cramped quarters with parents who worked long hours. The maladjustment of these children created challenges within the school systems in large cities, such as New York, Philadelphia, and Chicago, in the form of conduct problems and truancy.

By the 1920s the number of visiting teachers placed in schools had increased significantly, with boards of education and teachers in low-income, high-need, urban neighborhoods looking to visiting teachers for advice and assistance with several psychosocial issues related to their students. In fact, many larger school districts were lobbying to have school social workers become paid members of the school district and board of education, rather than being contracted volunteers of the settlement houses supported by philanthropic organizations (McCullagh, 1993, 1998; Terry, 1925).

One of the first professional organizations representing visiting teachers was the National Committee of Visiting Teachers and Home and School Visitors, established in 1919. In 1929 the name of the organization was changed to the American Association of Visiting Teachers, and in 1942 the name was changed again to the American Association of School Social Workers. Just a few years later, the name was changed yet again to the National Association of School Social Workers to reflect the growing professionalization of school social workers as a distinct field.

In 1955 the American Association of Social Workers (AASW), American Association of Medical Social Workers, American Association of Psychiatric Social Workers, American Association of Group Workers, Association for the Study of Community Organization, Social Work Research Group, and the National Association of School Social Workers (NASSW) merged to form the National Association of Social Workers (NASW). The NASSW still exists but it is now under the auspices of the NASW.

The role of the school social worker continued to grow and expand through the 1960s and 1970s, fueled in part by the social turbulence that marked these decades, as well as the 1975 passage of the Individuals with Disabilities Education Act [IDEA] (Pub. L. No. 94–142), which required that public schools provide "free and appropriate" public education to all school-aged children between 3 and 21 years of age, regardless of their disability. The passage of IDEA meant that schools were now legally required to serve a far broader student population, many with complex needs. Social workers contributed to compliance efforts, along with other members of the student services team. Today, school social work remains a growing field that offers excellent practice opportunities for those wanting to work with school-aged children. Issues such as international academic competition, concerns about increasing violence in schools, and continued reliance on social work services for the regular as well as special education students have continued to propel school social work forward into the 21st century.

Duties and Functions of School Social Workers

The traditional model of school social work involves the social worker providing school-based social work services as an employee of the school district and as a part of a multidisciplinary team (Costin, 1975). Although some districts utilize school-based social workers employed by outside agencies (primarily as a cost-saving measure), most school districts in the United States still use the traditional school social work model. School social workers' roles and functions are typically generalist in nature but have become increasingly specialized as challenges experienced by students have become more complex (Gherardi, 2017; Teasley & Richard, 2017).

Pearson eText

Video Example 9.2

In this video a school social worker evaluates a student for the risk of suicide. What elements of the student's disclosures are a cause for alarm and why?

School social workers perform a variety of duties, serve numerous functions, and operate within several different roles depending on the demographics of the school population, the age of children served, and the capacity in which the social worker is functioning. In general, school social workers serve as an important liaison between schools, parents, and the community (Sherman, 2016). Within school settings, they serve as counselors, advocates, mediators, and community liaisons. They assist children in managing psychosocial issues that are creating a barrier to learning and academic achievement, including physical barriers to learning in the form of a physical disability, cognitive barriers such as intellectual or learning disabilities, and behavioral barriers such as students who are depressed, anxious, or acting out. School social workers also work to develop, enhance, and maintain a close working relationship between student families and the school, advocating for students and their family members in a variety of situations (Villarreal Sosa et al., 2017).

According to the NASW (2012), school social workers should be competent in providing individual, group, and family counseling, be well versed in theories of human behavior and development, and have knowledge of and be sensitive to the demographic makeup of the school population in which they work, including students' socioeconomic status, gender, race, sexual orientation, and any community stressors that might affect a student's ability to perform (such as a high crime rate or community gang infiltration). School social workers must also have competencies in the areas of psychosocial assessment, be familiar with local referring agencies, and be committed to the values and ethics of the social work profession, including those relating to social justice, equity, and diversity.

Pearson eText

Video Example 9.3

In this video the school social worker summarizes the session with her supervisor. What rationale is the foundation for the social worker's plan of action?

School social workers may work with the general school population or may work solely within the special education department, with physically, cognitively, or behaviorally disordered students. Direct practice often includes individual and group counseling, as well as family counseling if necessary. In many school settings, social work services are designated as a required part of a student's **Individualized Education Plan**, which serves as a sort of contract between the school and family for students identified with special education needs. But school social workers are often called upon to work with the general population of students, as needed (SSWAA, n.d.).

The intervention tools a school social worker uses depends on the ages of the students and the issues they are experiencing, School social workers often facilitate support groups focusing on social–emotional skill development such as healthy conflict resolution (Haymovitz et al., 2018). Other examples of skills such support groups may focus on include effective anger management, positive peer relations, and management of grief and loss related to death and divorce. Many schools also offer "newcomer clubs" for new students who are struggling to make friends. There are ample resources in the marketplace to help school social workers facilitate such groups, such as anger management and social skills curriculum, and therapy games such as the *Ungame*.

Case management is also provided by school social workers and can include the organization and coordination of numerous services received by a student. For instance, a student's case might involve an outside therapist who is providing psychological counseling, a psychiatrist who supervises psychotropic medication such as antidepressants, a truancy officer, the police department, a child welfare agency, the family, all the student's teachers, and the school principal. Thus, depending on the issues the student is experiencing, the social worker will likely be involved in the coordination of services and the appropriate dissemination of information to a number of involved parties (assuming confidentiality has been waived) (Richard et al., 2019).

Crisis intervention is also an important function of a school social worker (Teasley & Richard, 2017). Crises may include a natural disaster, such as a tornado or earthquake; a student suicide; or on-campus violence, such as student-on-student assaults (Powell & Holleran-Steiker, 2017). School social workers, in coordination with other members of the student services team, provide crisis counseling to the entire student population, families, and school staff as needed. Crisis counseling includes helping students face the initial shock of a tragedy and also includes ongoing counseling as a part of a safety and prevention plan. For instance, the suicide of a student often elicits emotional distress among a student population and can lead to the increased risk of other students committing suicide (Mirick et al., 2018). A school social worker will be involved in creating awareness (through classroom presentations or staff meetings), maintaining a visible presence on campus, and conducting outreach services to vulnerable students

School social workers also work as a part of a multidisciplinary team when a natural disaster, such as a tornado, hurricane, flood, wildfire, or earthquake, occurs within a school community (Bauwens & Naturale, 2017). Natural disasters create a series of traumas, beginning with the acute reaction to a life-threatening experience, followed by subsequent traumas related to loss, called secondary effects (Daniell et al., 2017). For instance, once students recover from the shock of living through a tornado, they will likely experience additional traumas, perhaps related to losing their home, losing friends or family, witnessing others' traumas (vicarious trauma), as well as secondary effects related to economic losses experienced by their family, friends, and even the community. Many people are forced to abandon their pets because of limitations imposed by emergency shelters, which can produce significant psychological trauma, particularly if the pets are harmed or run away during the disaster (Chadwin, 2017). School social workers provide crisis counseling in response to natural disasters, but also provide important follow-up services once the initial crisis has calmed and students (and their families) are continuing to deal with the crisis.

Ethical Dilemmas Facing School Social Workers

School social workers face ethical dilemmas on a daily basis that require knowledge of the NASW ethical standards, as well as an awareness of common ethical dilemmas experienced in a school setting. Some ethical dilemmas are pretty straightforward, such as maintaining confidentiality of student counseling and related records and reporting child abuse in accordance with mandatory child abuse reporting laws. But there are other areas of ethical concern that are not so clear cut, requiring school social workers to rely on a systematic method for managing difficult situations.

For instance, consider the White school social worker who, without awareness, seems to automatically show bias toward White students and against students of color because he relates better to students he better understands and relates to (Kaliades, 2017). It's important to consider at what point a personal affinity becomes bias toward one subpopulation and over another. Or, consider the female school social worker who is passionate about advocating for female students because of what she endured as a child in school related to her gender. Her motivation to advocate for girls is good, but if she doesn't thoroughly evaluate the circumstances surrounding situations involving similar dynamics, she might be biased toward girls and potentially against boys. There are certain ethnic and racial minorities who are in need of targeted advocacy, and an important role for school social workers is to advocate

JOPLIN, MO - MAY 22: The ruins of an elementary school in Joplin, Missouri stand testament to the power of the tornado that cut a path of destruction 7 miles long and a half mile wide on May 22, 2011.

for human rights issues on behalf of these special populations. For instance, a recent call to action for school social workers is to increase targeted advocacy for Latinas/os who have been impacted by the separation of immigrant families at the U.S. southwest border (Villarreal Sosa, 2019). It may be school social workers of the same **ethnicity** or race who are most likely to identify human rights violations involved within this population. There is no inherent ethical dilemma here, except that the social worker's advocacy must be balanced and not compromise their other student-centered responsibilities.

School social workers deal with very complex situations on a daily basis and must make decisions about how to best handle these situations based on their professional training as well as their clinical judgment and personal experiences. Having personal experiences that allow us to empathize with certain situations that clients are experiencing is absolutely fine. In fact, it is often those very experiences that draw people to the social work career to begin with. But it is important for school social workers (and social workers in general) to be aware of how an emotional desire to help can easily evolve into ethical breaches, as passionate advocacy blinds well-meaning social workers to important ethical boundaries. School social workers are bound by the NASW Code of Ethics and can benefit from additional training in ethical management from a variety of sources. School social workers can also seek additional guidance from the specialty practice section of the NASW website that focuses on school social work, where, for example, articles on issues related to confidentiality and boundary setting are posted.

SCHOOL COUNSELING

Learning Outcome 9.2   Explore the nature of school counseling in the public school system, including the duties and functions of a school counselor

School counselors serve a vital role in maximizing student success (Dahir & Stone, 2006; Lapan et al., 2007; Mau et al., 2016). They are licensed professionals with a minimum of a master's degree in school counseling, typically offered within the education department at universities offering this degree. School social workers provide leadership, advocacy, and collaboration, with the goal of promoting equity in access to the best educational experience possible for all students. School counselors work on student services teams to promote safe and effective learning environments for all students by delivering culturally relevant services as a part of a comprehensive school counseling program (Hines et al., 2020; Lee, 2005).

The Historical Roots of School Counseling

School counseling also has a history dating back to the late 1880s and early 1900s, with roots in the vocational guidance counseling movement (Schmidt & Ciechalski, 2001). In fact, early school counselors focused primarily on matching male high school graduates in an appropriate vocational or job placement. In the 1920s, theories of intelligence and cognitive development became popular, influencing the work of school guidance counselors who, with the advent of intelligence and aptitude testing, now had new tools with which to do their jobs.

The 1930s saw advancements in the areas of personality development and motivation, which directly influenced the field of school counseling, enabling counselors to further assist students in identifying areas of aptitude, as well as developing motivational techniques to increase academic performance and all-around personality development. Social trends and political movements were chief among various influences that led to a gradual shift from a primary focus on guidance and the vocational needs of students to a more comprehensive focus where school counselors proactively meet various developmental and psychosocial needs of students (Schmidt & Ciechalski, 2001). As with school social work, the passage of IDEA—which required, among other things, that children with special needs receive all support services necessary for their academic success—led to school counselors becoming involved in special education departments. Government committee reports, such as *A Nation at Risk* (National Commission on Excellence in Education, 1983), and additional federal legislation, such as the *No Child Left Behind Act* (NCLB) of 2001, and the more recent *Every Student Succeeds Act* (ESSA) of 2015 have meant an increase in funding for many schools, some of which has been directed to school counseling programs.

Duties and Functions of School Counselors

School counselors perform vitally important services in public schools, providing a range of direct and indirect services to students, parents, the school, and the community. The American School Counselor Association (ASCA) developed a national framework for school counseling programs with the goal of promoting student achievement by addressing students' personal, social, educational, and career needs. The framework ensures the development of skills, knowledge, and attitudes necessary for students to achieve success in school, and their lives in general, so they can become well-adjusted and successful adults (ASCA, 2019a).

A national model for school counseling programs was developed by the ASCA to ensure that school counseling across the nation has a unified vision based on four themes: (1) leadership, (2) advocacy, (3) collaboration, and (4) systemic change. The model has four components:

1. *Foundation:* Includes components such as a vision and mission statement that articulates the program's focus; a plan for goal setting for student achievement; the development of student competencies that focus on academic, career, and personal development; and professional competencies for school counselors based on the ASCA Ethical Standards for School Counselors.

2. *Delivery:* Includes all activities necessary to deliver the school counseling program, including guidance curriculum, which is integrated into the broader K–12 curriculum; individual student planning; services that respond to students'

Pearson eText

Video Example 9.4

In this video a school counselor facilitates a group exploring the ideal college fit. What ASCA school counselor professional standards and competencies did this counselor demontrate?

needs, such as individual counseling focusing on psychosocial issues and academic needs; and systems support that facilitates the administration of the school counseling program.

3. *Management:* Includes the development and ongoing management of organizational processes involved in the school counseling program, such as ways in which school counselors manage the delivery of services, including the overall facilitation of the program to ensure that program goals are met.

4. *Accountability:* Includes information on the collection and evaluation of data to illustrate how the program is meeting the needs of students and its organizational and program goals (ASCA, 2019a).

School counselors generally focus on three basic areas: academic counseling, career development, and personal–social development (Dahir et al., 2010). Their role began to shift in about the late 2000s to include more advocacy (Education Trust, 2009). The focus and role of school counseling depends in large part on whether the school counselor is working at an elementary school, middle school, or high school. Other factors that influence the focus and role of school counselors include the size of the student population, whether the school is in an urban or rural area, the nature of the surrounding community, and the demographic makeup of the school. For instance, a school counselor who works at an overcrowded high school in the city of Chicago will perform different duties and functions than a school counselor working in a high-income suburban or rural elementary school. Despite the variation in duties and functions, all school counseling activities are drawn from the ASCA school counselor professional standards and competencies (ASCA, 2019b).

School counselors work as an important part of the multidisciplinary student services team, collaborating with school social workers, school psychologists, teachers, and school administrators on student matters related to student academic performance and behavior. In general, school counselors provide individual student guidance, such as helping students develop good study skills, develop effective coping strategies, and foster good peer relationships through the development of prosocial skill, such as exhibiting empathy, showing kindness to others, and managing anger appropriately. School counselors also develop and facilitate programs on substance abuse awareness and multicultural awareness, including perhaps running a diversity support group. They assist students with goal setting, academic planning, and planning for college. They facilitate crisis intervention with individual students, the student body, families, and the school as a whole as a part of the student services team.

School counselors collaborate with parents, teachers, and school administrators and provide community referrals as necessary. They may also facilitate programs focusing on making the transition to the next level of schooling or to a working environment. School counselors identify and then work with at-risk students, managing behavioral and mental health issues such as substance abuse, suicide threats, classroom disruptions, student–teacher conflicts, and other issues as they arise. Finally, they are leaders in educational reform and the ability to effectively communicate with and collaborate with other educational professionals (ASCA, 2019b; Lee, 2005).

Common Ethical Dilemmas Facing School Counselors

As with many other human services-related disciplines, school counselors face ethical dilemmas on a daily basis that require them to be aware of not only the ethical standards

A school counselor runs a group on diversity and multicultural awareness.

of the school counseling profession, but also the common dynamics they may face that could result in unintentionally transitioning from genuine caring about students to the violation of ethical boundaries. Some of these challenges are pretty straightforward, such as maintaining confidentiality of student counseling and related records or reporting child abuse in accordance with mandatory child abuse laws. But there are other areas of ethical concern that are not so clear-cut (Bodenhorn, 2006).

Several articles posted on the ASCA website focus on common ethical dilemmas encountered by school counselors with the goal of assisting school counselors recognize the ethical and unethical nature of various approaches to student problems and situations. For instance, one article entitled *Boundary Crossing: The Slippery Slope* features a vignette of a student from a particularly chaotic and neglectful home who develops a strong attachment to the school counselor, popping into her office spontaneously whenever he needs some additional support. The student then invites the school counselor to a wrestling match a considerable distance from the school on a Saturday evening. The school counselor attends the match, and then drives the student home, stopping for dinner on the way as a gesture of congratulations for a job well done. Readers are asked whether any aspect of this scenario violated ethical boundaries and why. Most respondents were somewhat mixed on whether the fluidity of the office visits and traveling a long distance to attend a student's school-related event were ethical, but all respondents perceived the school counselor driving the student home from the match and stopping for dinner as clearly representing an ethical boundary violation, or at least a potential one (Stone, 2011).

Stone (2011) explains each type of boundary violation and the associated risks, including the violation of boundaries regarding *roles* (confusing the role of school counselor with a caregiver), the violation of boundaries regarding *time* (allowing the student to so frequently make impromptu office visits, an arrangement that cannot be maintained for all students), and the violation of boundaries regarding *place* (attending an event outside of school hours and such a long distance away, driving the student home, and stopping for dinner). Such boundary violations, while coming from a place of good intentions on the part of the school counselor, can lead to confusion on the part of the student who may develop unrealistic expectations of the school counselor, and then face disappointment when the school counselor is unable to maintain that level of attention. The behavior of the school counselor may also reflect bias toward one particular student, when many students have similar backgrounds and needs.

Stone believes that many ethical boundary violations among school social counselors, even more significant ones, most often come from good intentions, and not from bad character or an overt attempt to behave unethically. Ethical breaches often begin with a desire on the part of the school counselor to be helpful and supportive, but at some point, either because of **counter-transference** or some other dynamic, ethical boundary lines are crossed, and originally gray situations become much clearer (particularly in retrospect).

A new ethical concern for the school counseling profession (and other helping professions as well) relates to an increase in school counseling occurring online, either as an additional service provided to brick-and-mortar schools, or counseling services in support of virtual schools. Online school counselors deal with many of the same issues as face-to-face counselors, but they must also deal with ethical concerns around online communication, keeping records online, and the parameters around using social media (King-White et al., 2019). This issue became particularly salient during the 2020 coronavirus pandemic when most public schools in the United States rapidly transitioned to virtual instruction. The 2016 version of the ASCA ethical standards included some guidance on virtual school counseling, related both to expectations and limitations, such as difficulties in reading tone and subtle gestures. For instance, virtual school counselors have noted that they had more difficulty assessing suicide risks with at-risk students compared to school counselors who spent face-to-face time with students (Poh Li et al., 2013).

A 2019 survey of school counselors found that most believed that virtual counseling was relatively similar with regard to ethical dilemmas compared to face-to-face counseling, but several did note that counseling students online presents challenges relating to maintaining confidentiality, referring students to outside services, managing crises, and engaging child protective services (King-White et al., 2019). Interestingly, the authors of this study never defined "virtual counseling," and primarily referenced concerns about e-mails. Newer technological platforms, such as Zoom and Google Hangouts that offer face-to-face video interaction, may mediate some of these concerns, but more empirical research needs to be conducted to evaluate the nature of virtual counseling when using platforms with increased levels of functionality.

SCHOOL PSYCHOLOGISTS

Learning Outcome 9.3   **Explore the nature of school psychology in the public school system, including the duties and functions of a school psychologist**

School psychologists provide services that focus on the academic, social, and emotional success of students, with the goal of creating healthy and safe learning environments. They also focus on developing strong connections between the school and students' home.

While the goals of school psychologists are similar in nature to school social workers and school counselors, their duties and functions are quite different in that school psychologists focus on student learning, which also includes supporting teachers in their efforts to teach all learning styles. School psychologists have either a master's degree in educational psychology or a doctoral degree. They complete a 1200-hour internship in a school setting and complete a licensing exam, which enables them to obtain a special credential designating them as a school psychologist (National Association of School Psychologists, 2017).

Duties and Functions of School Psychologists

School psychologists work directly with students, teachers, administrators, families, and other members of the student services team with the goal of helping students achieve their optimal level of academic performance. Some of their specific duties include conducting psychological and academic testing, developing programs that increase student motivation and engagement, and creating individualized education programs that include instructional programs and interventions tailored to a student's specific needs. School psychologists also monitor student progress through observation, testing, and evaluation.

School psychologists focus on the promotion of positive mental health, which includes assessing students' emotional and behavioral needs and providing direct services to students to foster better life skills, including communication skills, social skills, coping skills, and problem-solving skills. School psychologists develop these skills through individual and group counseling, as well as through coordination with other members of the multidisciplinary student services team and through collaborative efforts with community agencies.

Similar to the mission of the school social work and school counseling professions, school psychologists are committed to supporting diverse learners. Diversity can include a student's ethnic minority status, immigration status, gender identity, sexual orientation, ability level, or learning style. Some of the ways school psychologists perform this function are conducting testing to assess diverse learning needs and providing culturally appropriate services to students with diverse backgrounds. They may also modify curricula and instruction methods as needed and as appropriate. School psychologists communicate regularly with students' parents and guardians, fostering the connection between home and school.

School psychologists also work with other members of the student services team to create and foster a positive and safe learning environment. Their activities in this regard may include developing programs focused on the development and support of prosocial skills, such as character building and ethical behavior. They also develop and facilitate programs addressing online and offline bullying, conflict resolution, violence prevention, and crisis intervention. These can include prevention programs, positive discipline programs that address negative behaviors, and restorative justice programs that help foster an environment of healing and positive growth.

Common Ethical Dilemmas Facing School Psychologists

The National Association of School Psychologists (NASP) Professional Standards (2020) are based on four broad themes: (1) respect for the dignity and rights of all persons, (2) professional competence and responsibility, (3) honesty and integrity in professional relationships, and (4) responsibility to schools, families, communities, the profession, and society. Similar to the other student services team professions, school psychologists often face ethical dilemmas when they are attempting to help students. Ethical dilemmas can also occur when ethical principles conflict, such as when a school psychologist attempts to balance a student's right to privacy with the parents' rights to know what's going on with their child (Iyer & Baxter-MacGregor, 2010). Other ethical dilemmas relate to complying with federal legislation, such as IDEA (2006) and ESSA (2015) (the successor to the **No Child Left Behind Act**), in a way that respects the rights of students with disabilities, while at the same time not compromising the learning of mainstream students or a safe school environment.

Achieving this balance can be challenging when students with significant disabilities have psychiatric or behavioral disorders that can disrupt learning environments or pose a danger to other students (Koppelman, 2004). For instance, students with serious behavioral problems may require restraint and seclusion, practices that are highly controversial among education and child development experts who question their effectiveness (Ryan & Peterson, 2004; Scheuermann et al., 2015). Experts also cite the history of abuse and trauma to children when such tactics are used inappropriately (Frueh et al., 2005; Prince & Gothberg, 2019). There are times, though, when students behave in ways that require restraint to ensure their safety or the safety of others. School psychologists are often responsible for developing programs that assess the appropriateness of **restraint** and **seclusion**, including under what circumstances they are used and how restrain is to be carried out.

But what if parents refuse to agree to the program of restraint or seclusion, even if their child's behavior warrants it? In a situation such as this, a school psychologist faces an ethical dilemma because NASP Ethical Standard I.1.5 stipulates that school psychologists respect the wishes of parents who object to school psychology services. But consider the example posed by Yankouski et al. (2012) of a significantly disabled child with a history of self-injurious behavior, including banging her head against a wall so hard she has caused damage to her head and potentially to her vision. Her parents refuse to allow her to be restrained under any circumstance because they believe that restraining their child in the past did not help her or discourage her self-injurious behavior. Thus, the ethical dilemma—the school psychologist cannot keep the child safe and respect the parents' wishes at the same time.

In cases where ethical and legal standards conflict, the use of an ethical and legal decision-making model that provides school psychologists with evidence-based options for dealing with difficult situations is recommended. Using an ethical and legal decision-making model in the case of the head-banging child whose parents object to her being restrained would likely recommend that the school psychologist contact the parents when the child is banging her head and require that they pick her up immediately. In the event that the student has already injured herself, then the appropriate course of action would be to contact emergency services (Yankouski et al., 2012).

MENTAL HEALTH AND OTHER PSYCHOSOCIAL CONCERNS

Learning Outcome 9.4   **Examine responses of school-based human services providers to mental health challenges, such as behavioral health disorders and other psychosocial issues**

In 2018 approximately 3.5 million children between the ages of 12 and 17 experienced at least one episode of major depression, with female youth experiencing almost double the rate of depression for male youth (SAMHSA, 2019). Depression among the adolescent population is on the rise, having increased an estimated 25% since 2014 (Center for Behavioral Health Statistics and Quality, 2015). Additionally, about 70% of these youth were severely impaired during the depressive episode and experienced significant problems in functioning in one or more areas of their lives, including severe problems with school (SAMHSA, 2019). Symptoms of depression in children and adolescents are similar to those of adults, except that oftentimes children exhibit symptoms of irritability rather than melancholy (Abrams et al., 2005; Shapero & Mazzone, 2019). Depression in adolescences is also associated with substance abuse and suicide; thus, it's very important for student services personnel to be familiar with the early signs of this disorder.

Using an **ecological model**, where the student is evaluated holistically, as a lens for evaluating students struggling with major depression has been shown to be highly effective (Abrams et al., 2005; Brigman et al., 2017), particularly interventions that are targeted to specific student situations (Werner-Seidler et al., 2017). For instance, in assessing and evaluating a potentially depressed student, the human services provider would evaluate the student's specific situation, including the relationship the student has with peers, family members, even teachers, and then consider whether the student is experiencing conflict with one or both parents, and whether the student recently experienced fights with peers or teachers. Other considerations include understanding the nature of the relationship between the student and the broader community, such as whether the student has been involved with the legal system or with a truancy officer.

In general, school-based human services providers evaluate anything that might be a contributing factor to the student's current mental health status, as well as the strengths and support within the student's world (Brigman et al., 2017). Does the student belong to a faith community that offers or has the potential of offering support? Does the student have any extended family members who might come forward and offer support to the student during a difficult time? Students experiencing depression because a military parent has been deployed, for instance, might have an untapped support system such as a support group for children facilitated by the U.S. Armed Services. By using an ecological model, members of the student services team can assist the student in expanding his or her existing support system, thus helping to not only address existing depression, but also potentially stemming the tide of future psychosocial problems that might evolve if core issues are left unaddressed.

The value of the ecological model is that it is complementary with the overall model of human services, which relies on a **person-in-environment approach** in the evaluation of nearly all psychosocial issues. The ecological model also enables human services providers to provide more effective case management once contributing factors and support systems are identified. This model also encourages inter-professional collaboration on a variety of levels.

Parental involvement is a key factor in the treatment of students experiencing major depression, and members of the student services team should evaluate any barriers that might prevent parents from being involved in the school-based counseling of their child. Barriers might be cultural in nature, such as a less-than-welcoming environment for non-English-speaking parents (Alvarez, 2019), or they may be geographical, such as barriers rural parents face in relation to limited services and difficulty with transportation (van Vulpen et al., 2018). Barriers can also be more concrete, such as a parent's work schedule that makes meeting with school personnel during prescribed times impossible. Flexibility on the part of schools, particularly school services teams, is important, and may include a willingness to conduct home visits, after school hours, if necessary.

Substance Abuse in the Schools

Substance abuse, both on and off campus, continues to be a growing problem across the United States, primarily in high schools but also in some middle schools. School services teams must be able to identify the signs of substance abuse and be prepared to intervene when substance abuse is suspected. Although many graduate programs in the mental health-related fields are addressing this issue by including more courses on substance abuse, the majority of programs still only offer substance abuse courses as electives, leaving many within the human services fields feeling unprepared to deal with substance abuse (Minnick, 2019).

Alcohol and drug use among adolescents have either remained stable or declined since 2009, which is great news, but despite these declines, substance use and abuse remain one of the most significant issues confronting school personnel. This is primarily due to the significant problems that alcohol and substance abuse cause in the lives of teens at home and school. In terms of current use, according to the Substance Abuse and Mental Health Services Administration (SAMHSA), in 2018 about 2.2 million adolescents admitted to drinking alcohol in the past month (about 10% of the adolescent population), about 4.2 million adolescents admitted to using illegal drugs, including opioids (close to 17% of the adolescent population), and about 3 million adolescents admitted to using marijuana (about 12% of the adolescent population) (SAMHSA, 2019). Other studies have found significantly higher rates of alcohol and marijuana use among teens—up to 32% for alcohol and 22% for marijuana (Gray & Squeglia, 2018).

An area of growing concern for parents and mental health providers is the increase in synthetic drugs, which are increasingly available in U.S. high schools. Estimates of how many adolescents use synthetic drugs is difficult to ascertain because often teens may not be aware that the drugs they're consuming are synthetic. A 2018 study estimated that about 4% of U.S. teens have knowingly used synthetic drugs and believed they were easy to obtain. A disturbing finding in the study was that most teens surveyed stated that they did not perceive synthetic drugs to be particularly dangerous, despite evidence to the contrary (Debnam et al., 2018). Another area of concern is teen use of e-cigarettes. While cigarette smoking has dramatically declined in the last few decades, e-cigarette use is on the rise, and in this area, too, teens tend to underestimate its dangers (Bunnell et al., 2015).

Human services providers need to be able to identify adolescent substance abuse and respond with an effective intervention strategy, which includes school engagement as well as the involvement of outside referral sources that will engage the entire family system. The model most often used to describe the nature of adolescent substance abuse is similar to an adult model but often does not take into consideration factors related to adolescent development. Adolescents tend to be developmentally egocentric in the sense that they often act in more self-focused ways than adults. They also tend to display behaviors that are impulsive, not always considering the consequences of their use of alcohol and drug use and abuse. This seeming sense of omnipotence, coupled with normative developmental egocentrism, often complicates the application of traditional models of substance abuse to the adolescent population.

Using a **systems perspective** in evaluating substance abuse in the adolescent population, rather than viewing substance abuse as an individual problem, substance abuse may be a sign of some type of dysfunction going on within the family system, such as when a child is scapegoated for family problems such as domestic violence or general marital problems (Calix et al., 2018). Often, families that are resistant to admitting to underlying problems are forced to deal with their dysfunction when one or more of the children begin acting out in ways that require outside attention and intervention—particularly the abuse of drugs and alcohol.

Another issue to consider when using a systems perspective is whether the adolescent's substance abuse is mirroring a parent's substance abuse. A parent's abuse of alcohol or drugs has been shown to influence an adolescent's decision to begin drinking early (Lambie & Sias, 2005; Solis et al., 2012). Families that have serious systemic problems such as parental substance abuse and other forms of **maladaptive behavior** are often closed-family systems and may lack the ability or capacity to handle the increased stressors associated with children entering the adolescent years. Adolescents demanding changes to longstanding rules, pushing for more privileges, developing a far wider circle of peers, and questioning family rules, including unspoken rules to keep family dysfunction a secret, can often leave a family that is wary of outsiders with few effective coping skills to adapt to these changes. In addition, problems that have their roots in early childhood often manifest during adolescence.

Human services providers working with substance-abusing adolescents must first be able to identify the common signs of abuse, including erratic behavior, mood swings, red eyes, and slurred speech. They must then be able to provide support to the student and the family, acting as a liaison between student, family, school, and community-based treatment programs. On a broader level, student services teams can help institute prevention programs in the school, such as the Drug Abuse Resistance Education program that involves police and other community agencies coming into the schools and creatively (through plays, dance, and songs), and in an age-appropriate manner, educate students about the dangers of drug abuse and provide students with avoidance strategies and avenues for assistance, if needed. Another program that has been very successful at the high school level is the *Every 15 Minutes* program, where four times an hour a student is taken from a classroom, made to look dead (with makeup), and then returned "dead" by the police. A letter is then read by the student's parents, often framed as an obituary, and a mock funeral often follows during a school assembly designed to make the consequences of teen drinking and driving very real to the students. The *Every 15 Minutes* program is a collaborative effort that involves school, home, community, and student engagement.

Napa, CA, U.S. - Valley Oak High School students watch a simulated traffic accident during an Every 15 Minutes event at the school. The purpose of the event is to teach students about the consequences of drinking and driving.

Teenage Pregnancy

Teenage pregnancy in girls between the ages of 15 and 19 has declined 72% since an all-time high in 1991 (Hamilton et al., 2019). For instance, in 1950 there were 86.6 live births per 1000 for teens between the ages of 15 and 17, and in 2018 that number had dropped to 7.9 live births per 1000. Declines have been relatively stable each year, but some years had pretty significant declines—9% from 2013 to 2014 (Hamilton et al., 2015), and another 7.4% from 2017 to 2018 (Martin et al., 2019). While this trend is wonderful news, the

© NAPA VALLEY REGISTER / ZUMA WIRE / ZUMA PRESS / ALAMY STOCK PHOTO

© JEFF CHIU / AP / SHUTTERSTOCK

Justin Pace reads along with classmates during a ninth-grade Teen Talk class at Carlmont High School in Belmont, Calif. Sex education in some American high schools is evolving beyond pregnancy and disease prevention to include lessons aimed at curbing sexual assaults.

United States still has one of the highest rates of teen pregnancy compared to other industrialized nations (Golman et al., 2019).

No one really knows the exact reason for the decrease, but there is speculation that adolescent girls are not as sexually active as in earlier years, and when they are, they are more likely to use birth control due to a decrease in stigmatization of female sexuality. And yet, teen pregnancy remains a serious concern in high school because about 40% of high school students aged 15 to 19 report being sexually active (this percentage jumps to 53% for students aged 17 to 19) (Martinez & Abma, 2020), and because of the serious toll teen pregnancy takes on the psychosocial develop-ment of the teen parents and their child, as well as on their educational advancement and future economic security (Gorry, 2019).

Various research studies have identified many factors that might influence teen pregnancy rates, but the dynamics involved are complex and vary based on race and ethnicity, socioeconomic status, and geographical region (CDC, 2018; Martin et al., 2019; Summers et al., 2017). For instance, in 2018, there were 179,871 live births by teens between the ages of 15 and 19. Birth rates declined for all racial and ethnic groups, but birth rates among socioeconomically disadvantaged Black, Latina, Native American, Alaska Native, and Hawaiian and Pacific Islander youth were still higher than for White and Asian youth (Martin et al., 2019; Summers et al., 2017). Another study that evaluated broad influencing factors found that girls who are not doing well in school, have experienced chronic depression, and have a history of abortions are at higher risk of repeated pregnancies in their teens (Maravilla et al., 2017). Yet another study focusing solely on economically dis-advantaged Black teens found five influencing factors that increased the risk of teen pregnancy: parental influence, influences by peers, substance use, broader social influences, and the desire to become pregnant (Summers et al., 2017). These are all factors that can help human services professionals working in school environments better understand how to address teen pregnancy on a micro and macro level.

Sex and pregnancy prevention programs have been included in school curricula for several decades with mixed reviews. Sex prevention programs in the 1970s and 1980s focused primarily on sexual health and birth control, but in the 1990s *abstinence-only* programs became popular. Proponents of abstinence-only sex education cite research showing a decrease in adolescent sexual activity after participating in an **abstinence-only program**—evidence that they are successful (Toups & Holmes, 2002). Yet others have questioned whether these programs are as successful as some of these studies indicate, citing poor study designs and a wide range of abstinence programs, with some defin-ing abstinence as postponing sex until early adulthood and some more religiously based programs sending the message that premarital sex should always be avoided. With-out a clear definition of "abstinence," it may be impossible to determine the success of these programs (Kirby, 2002; Marseille et al., 2018). A large federally funded study published in 2007 may have provided the definitive word on this issue, when the results clearly showed that youth who had completed abstinence-only programs were no more likely to delay becoming sexually active, have fewer sexual partners, or abstain from sex altogether (Trenholm et al., 2007). A more recent study that examined state-mandated abstinence-only programs found similar results—that state-mandated abstinence-only programs had no effect on teen birth rates or abortion rates, but they may have had a positive impact on the rates of sexually transmitted diseases in some states (Carr & Packham, 2017).

Reasons for the lack of success of abstinence-only programs may be related to the lack of immediate consequences for adolescents who engage in sexual activity. A teen pregnancy prevention program popular in the early 2000s and still used today in many school districts is the *Baby Think It Over* (BTIO) program. The BTIO program provides teens with a computerized doll programmed to cry and fuss intermittently throughout the day and night. The BTIO program is designed to educate teenagers on the realities of having a baby by providing immediate feedback, thus making child raising a reality. The BTIO program is generally believed to be effective, although research has been somewhat mixed. A 2019 study found that program participants found the program helpful (Hussain et al., 2019), while another study found no impact (Barnett, 2006), and yet another study found that the program was actually harmful (Brinkman et al., 2016). A subsequent analysis of the Brinkman et al. study though found it was methodologically flawed due to recruitment bias (Thornton et al., 2020).

Other programs target at-risk groups that have higher pregnancy rates than the general teen populations, such as homeless teens. Wahine Talk is a holistic program that targets homeless female teens using a trauma-informed approach. This program provides resources to program participants focusing on basic needs, peer mentoring, sexual health education support groups, and comprehensive sexual education and health care. The researchers found that the use of birth control among program participants tripled 6 months after program participation, with a little more than a third option for long-acting reversal birth control such as Depo-Prevera (Aparicio et al., 2019).

Identifying the reasons why populations of adolescents engage in unsafe sex practices may provide more information on why some prevention programs work and others don't. For instance, developing culturally sensitive empowerment support groups has shown some success in increasing awareness among a demographic of adolescent girls who often report feeling powerless in making decisions about their sexuality (Vidourek & King, 2019). Examples include the *My Journey* curriculum for sixth- to eighth-grade Native American girls, which taps into traditional indigenous values and culture (Kenyon et al., 2019), and the *Blueprint: A Sexual Risk Avoidance and Wellness* program for Black girls, which taps into hip-hop and Black culture. Both programs offer culturally anchoring curricula steeped in female empowerment. All-girl empowerment groups can provide at-risk girls a safe place to talk about their feelings about sex and support each other in their right to say no to sex (or no to sexual activity without using a condom). They can also provide girls with educational information and tools for boundary setting that reflects their actual desires, increasing an overall sense of personal empowerment, which is likely to result in a reduction of unplanned pregnancies.

Programs grounded in an empowerment approach involve a shift from sex and pregnancy prevention to personal empowerment and healthy sexual choices. One of the first states to transition from a risk-focused paradigm to a youth development model that perceives sexual activity as a normal part of adolescent development is Oregon. A youth development model engages adolescents as partners in the issue, focusing on sexual health and positive choices, destigmatizing sexual activity, and instead focusing on personal empowerment (Nystrom et al., 2013).

MULTICULTURALISM AND DIVERSITY IN THE PUBLIC SCHOOL SYSTEM

Learning Outcome 9.5   Explore how school-based human services providers become culturally competent in working with and advocating on behalf of diverse student populations

In virtually every school, some students fit into the mainstream and others do not. It is often the students who do not fit in who are most likely to be vulnerable to scapegoating, bullying, violence, and other psychosocial problems. Students who do not feel safe in school, who are subject to bullying, and who are made to feel like outcasts because of their gender, race, sexual orientation, religion, body type, family constellation, or any other factor that seems to set them apart from the mainstream, are at increased risk for academic failure or at least academic difficulty. Although the responsibility for keeping students safe rests with all adults associated with the student—teachers, all school personnel, and even parents—school social workers, school counselors, and school psychologists are in a unique position to identify potential problems related to diversity and difference and intervene by advocating for diverse students.

Working with Racial and Ethnic Minority Populations

Racial and ethnic diversity can be a wonderful asset to any school environment, leading to a richness in experiences for students and teachers alike. But in some school environments, racial prejudice and discrimination can lead to violence and conflict among many within the student population. Students who comprise a part of a racial minority either within the school or within broader society are at risk for academic failure for many reasons, including social, economic, and political conditions such as poverty, racial intolerance, and higher rates of violence often associated with the urban school environment. For example, a school environment that is hostile to racial and ethnic minorities contributes to the creation of an unsafe school environment where students feel uneasy, unsafe, and unprotected.

School social workers, school counselors, and school psychologists can assist teachers and school administrators in recognizing and addressing racial and ethnic discrimination and prejudice on campus. They can also assist in the development of cultural diversity training focusing on racial and ethnic sensitivity and respect for diversity. Equally important is the cultural competence of the student services team professionals themselves. It is vital that school-based human services providers participate in racial and diversity training, focusing on the nature of counseling from a multicultural perspective (Cook et al., 2019; Holcomb-McCoy, 2004).

Consider the case of Mario in the opening vignette. While Mario is capable of academic success, he is experiencing extreme stressors on various levels—his parents are undocumented and rely on him extensively, the political climate in the United States has changed considerably since the Obama era, and with the DACA program in jeopardy, Mario is quite likely experiencing considerable stress and fear related to his uncertain status. To most effectively support Mario, Rosa and the other members of the student services team would need to be aware of micro dynamics, such as Mario's depression and anxiety; mezzo dynamics, such as the nature of **bias-based bullying**; and macro dynamics, such as immigration law and the status of the DACA program. Operating as an interprofessional team, Rosa and the team could work collaboratively with the teachers and staff to implement racial diversity training on bias-based bullying. And while keeping Mario's legal status confidential, they could also work together to provide as much support and guidance as possible.

This type of training is particularly important since research shows that traditional counseling theories and interventions are often biased against racial and ethnic minorities, particularly Blacks. For instance, many traditional Euro-American theories tend to pathologize racial minorities rather than recognize the **social oppression** that contributes to violence, gang activity, and juvenile delinquency (Alegria et al., 2010; Fusick & Charkow, 2004). Any theory (or theorist) that disregards the power of long-standing racism and the effect that intergenerational oppression has on a population would be hard pressed to explain why these groups experience significantly higher rates of poverty and violence than other groups that haven't experienced intergenerational racism and oppression. Are the former merely more innately violent? Are they just lazy? Less moral as a whole? Of course, the answer is no, which means that credence must be given to the possibility that behavior deemed maladaptive is not solely a result of individual psychopathology but the result of social causes and clinical interpretation as well.

Decolonization is a term most commonly used to critique and then amend theories and systems influenced by the superiority and privilege associated with White Western ideologies— prioritizing individualism over collectivism, financial wealth over contentment, White male domination over multiculturalism and gender equity, and Christianity over indigenous religions, are just a few examples. Briskman (2008) was one of the first scholars to apply the concept of "decolonization" to practice with the indigenous people in Australia. The concept was then later more fully developed in Coates and Hetherington's (2016) book, *Decolonizing Social Work*, originally published in 2013. As Coates and Hetherington describe, decolonizing practice is rooted in concerns about the effects of Western colonization on indigenous people, particularly how the helping fields approach problems experienced in indigenous communities.

Coates and Hetherington's book is focused primarily on social work practice, but the application of the concept and principles of decolonization is now more broadly applied to include all helping fields, including grassroots work with at-risk populations, when the professionals are primarily White and the populations being served are primarily indigenous, and more recently with all people of color. When a theory or system is decolonized, colonial ideologies are deconstructed to make the implicit, obvious. Perspectives presumed to be common sense or practices taken for granted as "the norm" are challenged during this process. The reconceptualization of theories and practices occurs by keeping diversity and cultural context at the forefront, and by challenging the status quo.

The colonial influences of Western theories and practices are very apparent across a range of disciplines and systems, including the field of education and practices involved in the public school system (Pratt et al., 2018). Child development theories are often steeped in colonial influence (Soto & Swadener, 2002). Consider child development theories that promote independence over inter-dependence as important milestones (e.g., children sleeping alone, attending all-day preschool) and prioritize academics over family or cultural obligations (e.g., attending school rather than family or cultural celebrations). The ideals embedded in developmental theories are often based on colonial narratives of what is "right/wrong" and "healthy/unhealthy," and students and families who resist these Westernized norms are often stigmatized in some manner, with noncomplying students often subjected to disciplinary action.

The process of decolonizing theories and systems often refers to social justice movements in relation to indigenous populations, but the process can be applied to almost any facet of social life that has been impacted by Western ideological superiority. For instance, the decolonization of education begins with an acknowledgement that many of the psychosocial assessment tools, teaching methods, and disciplinary actions used in the public school system are often biased against racial and ethnic minority populations. This is because many of these tools and methods have been developed for the assessment and evaluation of the majority culture based on White middle-class values (Chatmon & Watson, 2018; Fusick & Charkow, 2004). Cultural competency and racial equity training can aid school services personnel in assessing the appropriateness of using standard assessment tools, teaching methods, and disciplinary actions and, if necessary, reconceptualizing them for racial and ethnic populations. This practice will contribute to alleviating the broad-based problem of overidentifying racial and ethnic minority students for behavioral services and disciplinary processes based on culturally rooted behaviors (Sintos, 2020).

Bias-Based Bullying and Cyberbullying

Bullying within the public school system is gaining increasing attention among the general U.S. population, as well as among school administrators and policy makers on a local and national level. The increased attention is due at least in part to what appears to be a vast increase in bullying incidents, including **bias-based bullying**—bullying based on a federally protected characteristic, such as race/ethnicity, religion, nationality, gender identity/expression, gender, sexual orientation, or disability—and **cyberbullying**—bullying and harassment using an electronic medium, such as texting, instant messaging, or social media. One reason for the increase in attention to bias-based bullying in particular is recent studies that have identified the significant harm this type of bullying does to victims (Mulvey et al., 2018).

One out of every five students report having been bullied, and the most common reason for being bullied is related to their physical appearance, race or ethnic identity, gender, religion, disability, or sexual orientation (National Center for Education Statistics, 2019). Students who are particularly at risk for being bullied are those who have a number of these characteristics, such as a disabled, gay Latino, or an obese girl who has a physical disability (Biggs et al., 2009). Whether bullying incidents are actually increasing, or whether reporting rates have increased, remains unclear, but this is an important issue that directly affects the human services profession, particularly those working in schools, because about 75% of students surveyed have reported they do not know how to report bullying incidents (Asian American Legal Defense and Education Fund, 2009).

Bullying can include name-calling and insults, being the object of rumors, threats of harm, physical assaults (shoving, hitting, tripping, spitting), being purposely excluded from activities, and property destruction. Cyberbullying can include posting hurtful, harassing, and threatening information on the internet, as well as unwanted contact via e-mail, text, online gaming sites, or other online communities such as Facebook. Cyber-bullying can also include the purposeful exclusion from an online community such as a Facebook group (DeVoe & Murphy, 2011; Mulvey et al., 2018).

Bullying in schools, particularly bias-based bullying, is an important issue for many reasons, but chief among them is evidence that victims being bullied experience both short- and long-term consequences, including poor school performance, depression, and increased health problems (Mulvey et al., 2018; Rigby, 2003). And while research is not conclusive in this area, there is growing evidence that extreme bullying may contribute to types of retaliation with devastating consequences. For instance, the U.S. govern-ment's bullying website notes that in 12 out of 15 student-initiated campus shootings in the 1990s, the shooters disclosed histories of being bullied, some severely. Research also suggests that many incidents of bullying go unreported to parents and school, which hinders a school's ability to determine the scope of bullying within a school system and effectively address the problem (Petrosino et al., 2010). When bullying is bias-based, the damage to the victim can be even more significant, such as the victim committing sui-cide, since the target of bullying relates to the victim's identity—race, gender, gender identity, or sexual orientation—something that cannot be changed and something that may make the child or adolescent already feel different and socially isolated (Mulvey et al., 2018).

Although to date there is no federal legislation mandating how schools must respond to bullying, there is considerable encouragement from the White House as well as the Department of Education for schools to adopt proactive measures to address bullying on campus, off campus, and online. For instance, in March 2011 former Presi-dent Obama and the first lady reached out to students, parents, educators, and education advocates across the country as well as other concerned parties at the *White House Confer-ence on Bullying Prevention*, acknowledging the very serious nature of school bullying, and announcing several programs designed to assist schools, nonprofit organizations, and other advocates in putting a stop to bullying, both on campus as well as in cyberspace. The Stop Bullying website was launched as a part of this conference, providing informa-tion from numerous government agencies on the nature of bullying, including bullying prevention and intervention strategies. The Trump administration has maintained this website and has provided additional guidance for bullying victims and updated resources for educators, community leaders, and parents (Stop Bullying, 2020).

School-based human services providers are aptly placed to be leaders in the fight against bullying, but far too often they lack the training and resources to effectively address bullying on a macro and micro level. For instance, in a recent study on cyberbul-lying, about half the social workers surveyed reported they felt ambivalent about their role in addressing cyberbullying, despite the majority reporting their recognition of the seriousness of this form of bullying (Slovak & Singer, 2011). Other research indicates that a part of the challenge in effectively addressing school bullying, including cyber-bullying, involves a lack of clear school policies and a general lack of training in man-aging all aspects of the school bullying problem (Mason, 2008). In response to a call for increased training for school personnel, some school districts developed comprehensive training initiatives, including policies and training manuals, which have shown promise in reducing school-based bullying (Williford et al., 2019).

Biggs et al. (2009) recommend that school-based human services providers develop a strategy to address school bullying that involves a multidisciplinary team approach, using a strengths-based perspective. The team approach allows each professional to provide support for the others on the team, and serve as an interdisciplinary consultant sharing resources from a variety of professional perspectives. Most anti-bullying prevention programs are based on a combination of education, awareness, and outreach, such as the Pink Shirt Day anti-bullying campaign, Project Change, use of anti-bullying posters as educational tools, and anti-bullying workshops with speakers. Using trauma-informed approaches is also important because they acknowledge the serious damage bullying can cause, particularly bias-based bullying and cyberbullying (Dombo & Sabatino, 2019).

Bias-Based Bullying of Lesbian, Gay, Bisexual, Transgendered, and Queer/Questioning Students.

Students who are in the sexual minority—such as lesbian, gay, bisexual, transgendered youth; those students who are questioning their sexuality in some way; and other sexual minorities (LGBTQ+)—are often the victims of bias-based bullying, including verbal and physical violence. Many of these children spend a considerable amount of time feeling different and isolated, often believing that no one will understand their feelings and accept them unconditionally. Such individuals have an alarmingly high rate of suicide attempts, with over 30% admitting to having attempted suicide at some point in their lives. Approximately 75% of LGBTQ+ students admit to having been verbally abused at school and over 15% have been physically abused (Pope, 2003).

Most of the youth in Pope's study reported that the violence they experienced was a direct result of their sexual orientation, with boys being abused more often than girls. Pope discussed this type of abuse in terms of the pressure on most high school students to conform to the norms of their peer group. When faced with the overwhelming demands to be just like everyone else, students who stand out because they look or act differently can quickly become outcasts.

In 2016, the advocacy organization Gay, Lesbian and Straight Educational Network (GLSEN) conducted a national survey of LGBTQ+ students about their experiences with the following issues:

- Hearing biased and homophobic remarks in school
- Feeling unsafe in school because of personal characteristics, such as sexual orientation, gender expression, or race/ethnicity
- Missing classes or days of school because of safety reasons
- Experiencing harassment and assault in school.

The results of the study found that overall, bias-based bullying had declined since its previous report in 2005, although many LGBTQ+ students continue to experience verbal and physical harassment on a daily basis in school. For instance, 55% of LGBTQ+ students surveyed heard homophobic terms used in a derogatory manner, such as "gay," "dyke," and "faggot," in school, and most respondents reported feeling distress in response. Over 25% of students heard derogatory remarks about their sexuality from school staff. Almost 74% reported that they had been verbally harassed at school due to their sexual orientation, and almost as many reported that they'd been verbally harassed because of their gender expression (not being feminine or masculine enough). And while reports of physical harassment at school declined significantly since 2005, cyberbullying and harassment through text messaging, e-mails, and social media have increased.

The report details the most frequent consequences of these various types of bullying related to a student's sexual orientation and gender expression, including higher-than-average school absenteeism, lower educational achievement, and a negative impact on their psychological well-being (higher rates of depression, anxiety, and lower levels of self-esteem). GLSEN recommends that schools offer **gay–straight alliance clubs (GSAs)**, an inclusive curriculum (course curriculum that includes positive representations of LGBTQ+ people and events, currently and historically), supportive educators (educators trained in LGBTQ+ awareness and advocacy), and the incorporation of strict bullying and harassment legislation and policies. Schools that incorporate these remedies show marked reductions in LGBTQ+ bias-based bullying (Kosciw et al., 2010).

The recommendations in GLSEN's 2016 report include the following:

- Provide professional development for teachers specifically addressing biased behaviors in relation to LGBTQ+ students issues
- Address issues facing traditionally marginalized students, including LGBTQ+, students of color, students with disabilities, and gender nonconforming students
- Provide up-to-date curricula for teachers, school personnel, and students
- Support Gay-Straight–Alliance (GSA) clubs
- Develop and implement anti-bullying and harassment policies at the district level
- Regularly assess the school climate for bias-based bullying and other forms of harassment (Kosciw et al., 2016).

It is vital that school-based human services providers address the harassment that so many gay and lesbian students experience on a daily basis in the public school system and help to develop programs to combat poor treatment of students in the sexual minority. The first step in this effort is to establish a *zero-tolerance policy*, where teachers, school administrators, and student services team professionals make it clear to the student population through policy and action that harassment will not be tolerated in any respect. Developing a plan for making school safe for all vulnerable students begins with the education of school personnel.

School social workers, school counselors, and school psychologists are the ideal candidates to educate both school staff and students on the importance of accepting diversity. Such a program must begin with the school staff, particularly the teachers, who are most likely to be present when the abuse of LBGTQ+ students occurs. The focus of such programs centers on the belief that regardless of personal opinion, respect for human dignity and everyone's basic right to self-determination cannot be compromised.

A particularly effective program facilitated by schools across the nation is called the Making Schools Safe project (Otto et al., 2002). This program was developed by the American Civil Liberties Union (ACLU) and was designed to combat antigay harassment on school campuses. The ACLU recommends that all teachers and administrators use this curriculum, which focuses on the importance of creating a safe learning environment for all children by challenging the status quo that exists on many school campuses, ranging from overt bullying to more subtle forms of harassment, such as the generalized use of the word "gay" and other terms deemed derogatory and offensive to the LGBTQ+ population.

Bias-Based Bullying of Muslim Students.

In the wake of the September 11, 2001, terrorist attacks in New York and Washington, DC, the media was filled with reports of potential future attacks, many of which have since come to fruition. Many school districts scrambled to develop programs to address students' feelings about the attacks and their concerns about future attacks, particularly

© AP / SHUTTERSTOCK

Chicago high school senior Hira Zeeshan poses for a portrait in the West Ridge neighborhood of Chicago. Zeeshan, a Pakistani Muslim immigrant, said she's been affected personally by the anti immigrant rhetoric that is on the rise in the nation's schools.

for students close to the location of the attacks (Calderoni et al., 2006). Programs were also developed to prevent bias-based bullying and scapegoating of Muslim students (Zempi, 2014).

The events of September 11, 2001, were difficult for adults, but were particularly hard on children, many of whom lacked the ability to effectively communicate their feelings. A 2004 study found that about 65% of students experienced moderate to high levels of distress in the weeks following the attacks (Auger et al., 2004). The most frequently reported symptoms included fear, worry, anxiety, sadness, anger, and aggression. Students who were personally affected by terrorist attacks or who were already suffering from some mental health issues, such as depression, were the most at risk for developing symptoms consistent with PTSD. Auger et al. (2004) also noted that although many schools took appropriate action in responding to students' needs, 12% took no responsive action. In addition, the majority of the schools surveyed took no action to assist school personnel in dealing with their own feelings about increases in terrorism. In fact, over one third of school counselors stated that they did not feel prepared to respond to a serious trauma, suggesting that ongoing training of all school personnel is essential.

Some examples of **Islamophobia** include making constant references to Muslim children as being terrorists and making jokes about Muslim children and their families making bombs (Abdelkader, 2011). Such bias-based bullying should not be tolerated, and school-based human services providers, in coordination with teachers, school administrators, parents, and other students, can counteract Islamophobia through the implementation of educational programs designed to increase awareness of the diversity within mainstream Muslims, both in the United States and abroad.

There is no indication of a reduction in anti-Muslim sentiments, and, in fact, the Southern Poverty Law Center (SPLC) has reported a sharp rise in anti-Muslim hate groups, and an increase in White nationalist hate groups in general, since 2016 (Beirich, 2019). SPLC notes that White nationalist groups rose to an all-time high of 1020 in 2018, which is a 50% increase from 2017. Backlash to the election of former President Barack Obama, the first Black U.S. president, peaked in 2011, with 1018 hate groups. These groups targeted both Blacks and Muslims, as many White nationalists believed Obama was born in Kenya and practiced Islam. The number of hate groups then steadily declined to 784, but sharply increased by 30% after Donald Trump was elected. The SPLC reports that among the 1020 hate groups, at least 100 are solely anti-Muslim.

Social media platforms, such as Facebook and Twitter, are breeding grounds for White nationalist hate groups in the United States. Groups such as Stop Islamization of America, Act! For America, and the Center for Security Policy are nationwide organizations that the SPLC has identified as anti-Muslim hate groups, and each has a strong online presence. These groups (and others like them) spread propaganda designed to influence both people and public policy. While these groups may not be targeting youth specifically, the impact of propaganda disseminated on social media is vast and influences some people's attitudes about the Muslim American population, which includes youth. Human services providers working in a school setting can be most effective in responding to propaganda, including conspiracy theories, spread on social media by being aware of how social media works and its impacts (both positive and negative) and by being prepared with accurate information so they can better advocate for Muslim students.

CONCLUSION

The need for mental health services and psychosocial support in public school settings has never been greater. Teachers are increasingly reporting that children with behavioral problems fare worse in their academic performance and overall school adjustment (Mitchell et al., 2019). Psychosocial issues that can present barriers to academic achievement include mental health problems, teen pregnancy, bias-based and cyberbullying, and a whole host of other dynamics plaguing our school systems.

It is with the complexity of student psychosocial challenges in mind that there has been an increased focus on ways in which school social workers, school counselors, and school psychologists can move beyond mere cooperation toward real collaboration (Kim, 2012). Collaboration within a public school context is defined as a process where professionals within each discipline (school social work, school counselor, and school psychology) provide reciprocal information, informing mutual understanding of the client(s) while acknowledging the expertise and roles played by each respective profession (Axelsson & Axelsson, 2009).

There is the increased need for interprofessional collaboration not only due to shrinking budgets (requiring the pooling of resources) but also because of a national movement toward school-based mental health programs that are dependent on professionals from each helping profession to work together more effectively (Kim, 2012). An example is Expanded School Mental Health (ESMH), a three-tiered framework incorporating prevention, early intervention, and treatment. The ESMH framework expands on existing core mental health services provided in the public school system and emphasizes shared responsibility among all school service professionals, as well as community mental health providers. Recognizing the vital role that each student services team member plays in the public school system in addressing children's mental and psychosocial well-being is important because working together to remove barriers to learning offers students their best opportunity for academic success.

SUMMARY

- The nature of school social work in the public school system, including the duties, roles, and functions of a school social worker, is explored. The history of the visiting teacher movement and the roots of social work in the settlement house movement are explored within the context of how the profession evolved into the career it is today. Ethical dilemmas facing many school social workers are also explored.
- The nature of school counseling in the public school system, including the duties, roles, and functions of a school counselor, is explored. The history of the school counseling profession's roots in academic guidance and its evolution to a broader

focus to include psychosocial counseling and support is discussed. Ethical dilemmas facing many school counselors are also explored.

- The nature of school psychology in the public school system, including the duties, roles, and functions of a school psychologist, is explored. The role of school psychologists on the student services team, including their expanding role beyond academic testing, is discussed.

- Responses of school-based human services providers to mental health challenges, such as depression and substance abuse, are examined. The way in which mental health concerns create barriers to student academic achievement is explored, with a focus on how student services teams collaborate to support students with mental health care concerns and other psychosocial challenges, such as depression, substance abuse, and teen pregnancy.

- The ways in which school-based human services providers become culturally competent in working with and advocating on behalf of diverse student populations are explored. Issues related to diversity in the public school system, with a focus on how school social workers, school counselors, and school psychologists collaborate to create safe and bias-free learning environments, are examined.

- Cultural competence within the context of working with ethnic and racial minority populations is explored, as well as how school-based human services providers respond to a range of challenges in public school settings, such as bias-based bullying, cyberbullying, and disparate treatment of students who are diverse and different.

END-OF-CHAPTER QUESTIONS

1. Compare and contrast the roles and functions of the human services providers who most commonly work with pupil personnel services in a school setting.
2. Describe the nature and importance of interprofessional collaboration.
3. Compare and contrast common ethical dilemmas facing human services providers working in school settings on a face-to-face basis versus virtually.
4. Describe three examples of how theories used in human services within school settings could be decolonized to be more culturally appropriate for indigenous students and other students of color.
5. What are some ways that human services providers working in school settings can address bias-based bullying targeting LGBTQ students, using GLSEN's recommendations?

References

Abdelkader, E. (2011, October 24). Islamophobic bullying in our schools. Huffington Post: Religion.

Abrams, K., Theberge, S. K., & Karan, O. C. (2005). Children and adolescents who are depressed: An ecological approach. *Professional School Counseling, 8*(3), 284–292.

Alegria, M., Atkins, M., Farmer, E., Slaton, E., & Stelk, W. (2010). One size does not fit all: Taking diversity, culture and context seriously. *Administration and Policy in Mental Health and Mental Health Services, 37*(1–2): 48–60. https://doi.org/10.1007/s10488-010-0283-2

Allen-Meares, P. (2006). One hundred years: A historical analysis of social work services in schools. *School Social Work Journal, 30*(3), 24–43.

Alvarez, M. (2019). *Parental involvement for limited or non-English speaking parents/guardians of Hispanic/*

Latino students in public schools [Doctoral dissertation], Southern Connecticut State University.

American School Counselor Association [ASCA]. (2019a). The ASCA National model: A framework for school counseling programs. Author.

American School Counselor Association [ASCA]. (2019b). *ASCA School Counselor Professional Standards & Competencies*. Author.

Aparicio, E. M., Kachingwe, O. N., Phillips, D. R., Fleishman, J., Novick, J., Okimoto, T., Kaleipumehana Cabral, M., Kaʻopua, L. S., Childers, C., Espero, J., & Anderson, K. (2019). Holistic, trauma-informed adolescent pregnancy prevention and sexual health promotion for female youth experiencing homelessness: Initial outcomes of Wahine Talk. *Children and Youth Services Review, 107*, 104509.

Asian American Legal Defense and Education Fund. (2009). *Bias-based harassment in New York City public schools: A report card on the Department of Education's implementation of chancellor's regulation A-832.* http://www.aaldef.org/Bias-based-Harassment-in-NYC-Public-Schools.pdf

Auger, R. W., Seymour, J. W., Roberts, W. B., & Waiter, B. (2004). Responding to terror: The impact of September 11 on K-12 schools and schools' responses. *Professional School Counseling, 7*(4), 222–230.

Axelsson, S. B., & Axelsson, R. (2009). From territoriality to altruism in interprofessional collaboration and leadership. *Journal of Interprofessional Care, 23*(4), 320–330. https://doi.org/10.1080/13561820902921811

Barnett, J. E. (2006). Evaluating "baby think it over" infant simulators: A comparison group study. *Adolescence, 41*(161), 103.

Bauwens, J., & Naturale, A. (2017). The Role of Social Work in the Aftermath of Disasters and Traumatic Events. *Journal of Clinical Social Work, 45*, 99–101. https://doi.org/10.1007/s10615-017-0623-8

Beirich, H. (2019). *The year of hate and extremism: Rage against change. Intelligence report* (pp. 38–61.). Southern Poverty Law Center, https://www.splcenter.org/sites/default/files/intelligence_report_166.pdf

Biggs, M. J. G., Simpson, C. G., & Gaus, M. D. (2009). A case of bullying: Bringing together the disciplines. *Children and Schools, 31*(1), 39.

Bodenhorn, N. (2006). Exploratory study of common and challenging ethical dilemmas experienced by professional school counselors. *Professional School Counseling, 10*(2), 2156759X0601000203.

Brigman, G., Villares, E., & Webb, L. (2017). *Evidence-based school counseling: A student success approach.* Routledge.

Brinkman, S. A., Johnson, S. E., Codde, J. P., Hart, M. B., Straton, J. A., Mittinty, M. N., & Silburn, S. R. (2016). Efficacy of infant simulator programmes to prevent teenage pregnancy: A school-based cluster randomised controlled trial in Western Australia. *The Lancet, 388*(10057), 2264–2271.

Briskman, L. (2008). Decolonizing social work in Australia: Prospect or illusion. In M. M. Gray, J. Coates, & M. Y. Bird (Eds.), *Indigenous social work around the world: Towards culturally relevant education and practice* (pp. 83–93). http://ezproxy.uws.edu.au/login?url=http://ebookcentral.proquest.com/lib/uwsau/reader.action?ppg=112&docID=438278&tm=1494474371045

Bunnell, R. E., Agaku, I. T., Arrazola, R. A., Apelberg, B. J., Caraballo, R. S., Corey, C. G., Coleman, B. N., Dube, S. R., & King, B. A. (2015). Intentions to smoke cigarettes among never-smoking US middle and high school electronic cigarette users: National Youth Tobacco Survey, 2011–2013. *Nicotine & Tobacco Research, 17*(2), 228–235.

Calderoni, M. E., Alderman, E. M., Silver, E. J., & Bauman, L. J. (2006). The mental health impact of 9/11 on inner-city high school students 20 miles north of Ground Zero. *Journal of Adolescent Health, 39*(1), 57–65.

Calix, S. I., Garrett, K. C., & Fine, M. A. (2018). Evidence-based family treatment of adolescent substance-related disorders. In C. G. Leukefeld & T. P. Gullotta (Eds.), *Adolescent Substance Abuse* (pp. 173–190). Springer, Cham.

Carr, J. B., & Packham, A. (2017). The effects of state mandated abstinence based sex education on teen health outcomes. *Health Economics, 26*(4), 403–420.

Center for Behavioral Health Statistics and Quality. (2015). *Behavioral health trends in the United States: Results from the 2014 National Survey on Drug Use and Health* (HHS Publication No. SMA 15–4927, NSDUH Series H–50).

Centers for Disease Control [CDC]. (2018). *Crude birth rates, fertility rates, and birth rates, by age, race, and Hispanic origin of mother: United States, selected years 1950–2017.* https://www.cdc.gov/nchs/data/hus/2018/001.pdf

Chadwin, R. (2017). Evacuation of pets during disasters: a public health intervention to increase resilience. *American Journal of Public Health, 107*(9), 1413–1417.

Chatmon, C. P., & Watson, V. M. (2018). Decolonizing school systems: Racial justice, radical healing, and educational equity inside Oakland Unified School District. *Voices in Urban Education*, 48, 7–12.

Coates, J., & Hetherington, T. (2016). *Decolonizing social work*. Routledge.

Cook, A. L., Brodsky, L., Gracia, R., & Morizio, L. J. (2019). Exploring multicultural and social justice counseling training outcomes on school counselor and youth development. *Counseling Outcome Research and Evaluation*, 10(2), 78–93.

Corcoran, J., Franklin, C., & Bennett, P. (2000). Ecological factors associated with adolescent pregnancy and parenting. *Social Work Research*, 24(1), 29–39.

Costin, L. B. (1975). School social work practice: A new model. *Social Work*, 20(2), 135–139.

Dahir, C. A., Burnham, J. J., Stone, C. B., & Cobb, N. (2010). Principals as partners: Counselors as collaborators. *NASSP Bulletin*, 94(4), 286–305.

Dahir, C. A., & Stone, C. B. (2006). Preparing the next generation: Implementing new paradigms for school counseling preservice and practice. *Vistas: Compelling Perspectives on Counseling*, 43–47.

Daniell, J. E., Schaefer, A. M., & Wenzel, F. (2017). Losses associated with secondary effects in earthquakes. *Frontiers in Built Environment*, 3, 30.

Debnam, K. J., Saha, S., & Bradshaw, C. P. (2018). Synthetic and other drug use among high school students: The role of perceived prevalence, access, and harms. *Substance Use & Misuse*, 53(12), 2069–2076.

DeVoe, J., & Murphy, C. (2011). *Student reports of bullying and cyber-bullying: Results from the 2009 school crime supplement to the National Crime Victimization Survey*. Web Tables. NCES 2011–336. National Center for Education Statistics.

Dombo, E. A., & Sabatino, C. A. (2019). *Creating trauma-informed schools: A guide for school social workers and educators*. Oxford University Press.

Educational Trust. (2009). *The new vision for school counselors: Scope of the work*. https://1k9gl1yevnfp2lpq1dhrqe17-wpengine.netdna-ssl.com/wpcontent/uploads/2014/09/TSC-New-Vision-for-School-Counselors.pdf

Every Student Succeeds Act [ESSA] of 2015. Pub. L, 114–95.

Frueh, B. C., Knapp, R. G., Cusack, K. J., Grubaugh, A. L., Sauvageot, J. A., Cousins, V. C., & Hiers, T. G. (2005). Special section on seclusion and restraint: Patients' reports of traumatic or harmful experiences within the psychiatric setting. *Psychiatric Services*, 56(9), 1123–1133.

Fusick, L., & Charkow, B. (2004). Counseling at-risk Afro-American youth: An examination of contemporary issues and effective school-based strategies. *Professional School Counseling*, 8(2), 102–116.

Gherardi, S. A. (2017). Policy windows in school social work: History, practice implications, and new directions. *School Social Work Journal*, 42(1), 37–54.

Golman, M., Ricks, N., Gallegos, I. D., & Weaver, J. (2019). Utilizing the ocio-ecologic model as a framework for the prevention of teen pregnancy. In D. Akella (Ed.), *Socio-cultural influences on teenage pregnancy and contemporary prevention measures* (pp. 208–233). IGI Global.

Gorry, D. (2019). Heterogeneous consequences of teenage childbearing. *Demography*, 56(6), 2147–2168.

Gray, K. M., & Squeglia, L. M. (2018). Research review: What have we learned about adolescent substance use? *Journal of Child Psychology and Psychiatry*, 59(6), 618–627.

Hamilton, B. E., Martin, J. A., Osterman, M. J. K., et al. (2015). Births: Final data for 2014. *National Vital Statistics Reports*, 64(12). National Center for Health Statistics.

Hamilton, B. E., Martin, J. A., Osterman, M. J. K., & Rossen, L. M. (2019, May). Births: Provisional data for 2018. *Vital Statistics Rapid Release*, 7. National Center for Health Statistics.

Haymovitz, E., Houseal-Allport, P., Lee, R. S., & Svistova, J. (2018). Exploring the perceived benefits and limitations of a school-based social–emotional learning program: a concept map evaluation. *Children & Schools*, 40(1), 45–54.

Hines, E. M., Moore, J. L. III, Mayes, R. D., Harris, P. C., Vega, D., Robinson, D. V., Gray, C. N., & Jackson, C. E. (2020). Making student achievement a priority: The role of school counselors in turnaround schools. *Urban Education*, 55(2), 216–237.

Holcomb-McCoy, C. C. (2004). Assessing the multicultural competence of school counselors: A checklist. *Professional School Counseling*, 7(3), 178–186.

Hussain, H., Jomeen, J., Hayter, M., & Tweheyo, R. (2019). Implications for school nurses using simulator dolls to manage unplanned teen pregnancy. *British Journal of School Nursing*, 14(4), 177–188.

Individuals with Disabilities Education Act [IDEA] (Pub. L. No. 94–142). 89 Stat 775. (1975).

Individuals with Disabilities Education Improvement Act of 2004, Pub. L. 108–446. 118 Stat. 2647. (2006).

Iyer, N. N., & Baxter-MacGregor, J. (2010). Ethical dilemmas for the school counselor: Balancing student confidentiality and parents' right to know. *NERA Conference Proceedings 2010*, 15.

Kaliades, A. (2017). Rethinking disciplinary strategies: Reflections on White privilege in school social work. In M. Jaffe, J. Floersch, J. Longhover, & W. Winograd (Eds.), *The social work and K-12 schools casebook* (pp. 135–153). Routledge.

Kenyon, D. B., McMahon, T. R., Simonson, A., Green-Maximo, C., Schwab, A., Huff, M., & Sieving, R. E. (2019). My journey: Development and practice-based evidence of a culturally attuned teen pregnancy prevention program for Native youth. *International Journal of Environmental Research and Public Health*, 16(3), 470.

Kim, A. J. (2012). *Interdisciplinary collaboration in school social work: Building relationships for ecological change* [Doctoral dissertation]. Smith College.

King-White, D., Kurt, L., & Seck, M. (2019). A qualitative study of online school counselors' ethical practices in K-12 schools. *Journal of Counselor Practice*, 10(1), 40–58.

Kirby, D. (2002). Effective approaches to reducing adolescent unprotected sex, pregnancy and childbearing. *Journal of Sex Research*, 39(1), 51–57.

Koppelman, J. (2004). Children with mental health disorders: Making sense of their needs and the systems that help them. *National Health Policy Forum Issue Brief*, 799, 1–24.

Kosciw, J. G., Greytak, E. A., Diaz, E. M., & Bartkiewicz, M. J. (2010). *The 2009 National School Climate Survey: The experiences of lesbian, gay, bisexual, and transgender youth in our nation's schools*. GLSEN.

Lambie, G. W., & Sias, S. (2005). Children of alcoholics: Implications for professional school counseling. *Professional School Counseling*, 8(3), 266–273.

Lapan, R. T., Gysbers, N. C., & Kayson, K. (2007). *How implementing comprehensive guidance programs improves academic achievement for all Missouri students*. Missouri Department of Elementary and Secondary Education, Division of Career Education.

Lee, C. C. (2005). Urban school counseling: Context, characteristics, and competencies. *Professional School Counseling*, 8(3), 184–188.

Maravilla, J. C., Betts, K. S., Cruz, C. C. E., & Alati, R. (2017). Factors influencing repeated teenage pregnancy: a review and meta-analysis. *American Journal of Obstetrics and Gynecology*, 217(5), 527–545.

Marseille, E., Mirzazadeh, A., Biggs, M. A., Miller, A. P., Horvath, H., Lightfoot, M., Malekinejad, M., & Kahn, J. G. (2018). Effectiveness of school-based teen pregnancy prevention programs in the USA: A systematic review and meta-analysis. *Prevention Science*, 19(4), 468–489.

Martin, J., Hamilton, B., Osterman, M., & Driscoll, A. (2019). Births: Final data for 2018. *National Vital Statistics Reports*, 68(13). National Center for Health Statistics.

Martinez, G. M., & Abma, J. C. (2020). *Sexual activity and contraceptive use among teenagers aged 15–19 in the United States, 2015–2017*. NCHS Data Brief, no 366. National Center for Health Statistics.

Mason, K. L. (2008). Cyberbullying: A preliminary assessment for school personnel. *Psychology in the Schools*, 45(4), 323–348.

Mau, W. C. J., Li, J., & Hoetmer, K. (2016). Transforming high school counseling: Counselors' roles, practices, and expectations for students' success. *Administrative Issues Journal: Connecting Education, Practice, and Research*, 6(2), 83–95.

McCullagh, J. G. (1993). The roots of school social work in New York City. *Iowa Journal of School Social Work*, 6, 49–74.

McCullagh, J. G. (1998). Early school social work leaders: Women forgotten by the profession. *Social Work in Education*, 20(1), 55–64.

Minnick, D. (2019). The state of substance use education in Master of Social Work programs: A content analysis of course listings and faculty profiles. *Substance Abuse*, 40(2), 194–200.

Mirick, R. G., Berkowitz, L., Bridger, J., & McCauley, J. (2018). Lessons learned from ten years of using school-based screenings for suicide postvention. *School Social Work Journal*, 43(1), 20–37.

Mitchell, B. S., Kern, L., & Conroy, M. A. (2019). Supporting students with emotional or behavioral disorders: State of the field. *Behavioral Disorders*, 44(2), 70–84.

Mulvey, K. L., Hoffman, A. J., Gönültaş, S., Hope, E. C., & Cooper, S. M. (2018). Understanding experiences with bullying and bias-based bullying: What matters and for whom? *Psychology of Violence*, 8(6), 702.

National Association of School Psychologists [NASP]. (2017). *Overview of differences among degrees in school psychology*. https://www.nasponline.org/about-school-psychology/who-are-school-psychologists

National Association of School Psychologists [NASP]. (2020). *NASP 2020 professional standards adopted*. https://www.nasponline.org/standards-and-certification/nasp-2020-professional-standards-adopted

National Association of Social Workers [NASW]. (2012). *NASW standards for school social work services*. https://www.socialworkers.org/LinkClick.aspx?fileticket=1Ze4-9-Os7E%3D&portalid=0

National Center for Education Statistics [NCES]. (2019). *Student reports of bullying: Results from the 2017 School Crime Supplement to the National Crime Victimization Survey*. U.S. Department of Education. https://nces.ed.gov/pubs2019/2019054.pdf

National Commission on Excellence in Education. (1983). A nation at risk: The imperative for educational reform. *The Elementary School Journal, 84*(2), 113–130.

No Child Left Behind Act of 2001, Pub. L. 107–110, 115 Stat. 1425 (2002).

Nystrom, R. J., Duke, J. E., & Victor, B. (2013). Shifting the paradigm in Oregon from teen pregnancy prevention to youth sexual health. *Public Health Reports, 128*(Suppl. 1), 89–95.

Otto, N., Middleton, J., & Freker, J. (2002). *Making schools safe: An anti-harassment program from the Lesbian & Gay Rights project of the American Civil Liberties Union*. Lesbian & Gay Rights Project, American Civil Liberties Union. (ERIC Document Reproduction Service No. ED475274).

Petrosino, A., Guckenburg, S., DeVoe, J., & Hanson, T. (2010). What characteristics of bullying, bullying victims, and schools are associated with increased reporting of bullying to school officials? Issues & Answers. REL 2010-No. 092. *Regional Educational Laboratory Northeast & Islands.*

Poh Li, L., Jaladin, R. A. M., & Abdullah, H. S. (2013). Understanding the two sides of online counseling and their ethical and legal ramifications. *Procedia: Social and Behavioral Sciences, 103*, 1243–1251. https://doi.org/10.IO16/j.sbspro.2013.10.453

Pope, M. (2003). *Sexual minority youth in the schools: Issues and desirable counselor responses*. Information Analysis. (ERIC Document Reproduction Service No. ED480481).

Powell, T., & Holleran-Steiker, L. K. (2017). Supporting children after a disaster: A case study of a psychosocial school-based intervention. *Clinical Social Work Journal, 45*(2), 176–188.

Pratt, Y. P., Louie, D. W., Hanson, A. J., & Ottmann, J. (2018). Indigenous education and decolonization. In *Oxford Research Encyclopedia of Education*.

Prince, A. M., & Gothberg, J. (2019). Seclusion and restraint of students with disabilities: A 1-year legal review. *Journal of Disability Policy Studies, 30*(2), 118–124.

Richard, L., Monroe, P. A., & Garand, J. C. (2019). School social work roles, caseload size, and employment settings. *School Social Work Journal, 43*(2), 18–40.

Rigby, K. (2003). Consequences of bullying in schools. *The Canadian Journal of Psychiatry, 48*(9), 583–590.

Ryan, J., & Peterson, R. (2004). Physical restraint in school. *Behavioral Disorders, 29*(2), 154–168.

Scheuermann, B., Peterson, R., Ryan, J. B., & Billingsley, G. (2015). Professional practice and ethical issues related to physical restraint and seclusion in schools. *Journal of Disability Policy Studies*. https://doi.org/1044207315604366.

Schmidt, J. J., & Ciechalski, J. C. (2001). School counseling standards: A summary and comparison with other students services' standards. *Professional School Counseling, 4*(5), 328–333.

School Social Work Association of America [SSWAA]. (n.d.). *Role of school social workers*. https://www.sswaa.org/school-social-work

Shapero, B. G., & Mazzone, E. (2019). Early onset of depression during childhood and adolescence. In B. G. Shapero, D. Mischoulon, & C. Cusin (Eds.), *The Massachusetts general hospital guide to depression* (pp. 59–70). Humana Press, Cham.

Sherman, M. C. (2016). The school social worker: A marginalized commodity within the school ecosystem. *Children & Schools, 38*(3), 147–151.

Sintos, C. R. (2020). Decolonizing urban education. *Educational Studies, 56*(1), 1–17.

Slovak, K., & Singer, J. B. (2011). School social workers' perceptions of cyberbullying. *Children and Schools, 33*(1), 5–16.

Solis, J., Shadur, J., Burns, A., & Hussong, A. (2012). Understanding the diverse needs of children whose parents abuse substances. *Current Drug Abuse Reviews, 5*(2), 135–147.

Soto, L. D., & Swadener, B. B. (2002). Toward liberatory early childhood theory, research and praxis: Decolonizing a field. *Contemporary Issues in Early Childhood, 3*(1), 38–66.

Stone, C. (2011, July). Boundary crossing: The slippery slope. *ACSA School Counselor*. http://www.ascaschoolcounselor.org/article_-content.asp?edition=91&section=140&article=1221

Stop Bullying. (2020). Stop bullying on the spot. https://www.stopbullying.gov/resources/get-help-now

Substance Abuse and Mental Health Services Administration. (2019). *Key substance use and mental health indicators in the United States: Results from the 2018 National Survey on Drug Use and Health* (HHS Publication No. PEP19-5068, NSDUH Series H-54). Center for Behavioral Health Statistics and Quality, Substance Abuse and Mental Health Services Administration. https://www.samhsa.gov/data/

Summers, L., Lee, Y. M., & Lee, H. (2017). Contributing factors of teenage pregnancy among African-American females living in economically disadvantaged communities. *Applied Nursing Research*, 37, 44–49.

Teasley, M., & Richard, L. (2017). Changing the paradigm for school social work roles. In L. Villarreal Sosa, T. Cox, & M. Alvarez (Eds.), *School social work: National perspectives on practice in schools* (pp. 39–54). Oxford University Press.

Terry, P. (1925). Review: The visiting teacher movement, with special reference to administrative relationships by Julius John Oppenheimer. *The Elementary School Journal*, 26(4), 313–315.

Thornton, J., Fadl, H. E., Walker, K. F., & Torgerson, D. (2020). Avoiding biased exclusions in cluster trials. *Acta Obstetricia et Gynecologica Scandinavica*, 99(2), 145.

Toups, M. L., & Holmes, W. R. (2002). Effectiveness of abstinence-based sex education curricula: A review. *Counseling and Values*, 46(3), 237–240.

Trenholm, C., Devaney, B., Fortson, K., Quay, K., Wheeler, J., & Clark, M. (2007). *Impacts of four Title V, Section 510 abstinence education programs. Final report*. Mathematica Policy Research, Inc.

van Vulpen, K. S., Habegar, A., & Simmons, T. (2018). Rural school-based mental health services: Parent perceptions of needs and barriers. *Children & Schools*, 40(2), 104–111.

Vidourek, R. A., & King, K. A. (2019). Preventing teen pregnancy among minority populations: Risk and protective factors. In D. Akella (Ed.), *Socio-cultural influences on teenage pregnancy and contemporary prevention measures* (pp. 189–207). IGI Global.

Villarreal Sosa, L., Cox, T., & Alvarez, M. (2017). *School social work: National perspectives on practice in schools*. Oxford University Press.

Villarreal Sosa, L. (2019). Advocating for Latinx children's rights and supporting their healing from trauma: School social workers as nepantleras. *Children & Schools*, 41(4), 195–201.

Werner-Seidler, A., Perry, Y., Calear, A. L., Newby, J. M., & Christensen, H. (2017). School-based depression and anxiety prevention programs for young people: A systematic review and meta-analysis. *Clinical Psychology Review*, 51, 30–47.

Williford, A., Fite, P. J., DePaolis, K. J., Cooley, J. L., Hawley, P. H., & Isen, D. (2019). A comprehensive training initiative for educators to develop and implement effective anti-bullying policies in K–12 schools. *Journal of Applied School Psychology*, 35(2), 146–175.

Yankouski, B., Masserelli, T., & Lee, S. (2012, December). Ethical issues regarding the use of restraint and seclusion in schools (Practice Forum). Division of School Psychology, American Psychological Association. http://www.apadivisions.org/division-16/publications/newsletters/school-psychologist/2012/12/restraint-in-schools.aspx

Zempi, I. (2014). Responding to the needs of victims of Islamophobia. In N.Chakraborti & J. Garland (Eds.), *Responding to hate crime: The case for connecting policy and research*. Policy Press Scholarship Online.

10

Religion, Spirituality, and Faith-Based Agencies

Yesenia is a case worker at an **interfaith** social service agency serving low-income families experiencing a range of psychosocial challenges. She has a bachelor's degree in human services with an emphasis in community development. Yesenia's caseload consists primarily of single mothers and their children who struggle with poverty, food insecurity, and psychosocial issues such as family conflict, parenting challenges, job training, and other family-related issues. Yesenia is Catholic, but many of her clients are from different Christian denominations, or different faiths altogether, such as Jewish, **Muslim**, Buddhist, or "New Age" (a life philosophy drawn from Eastern philosophies). Sometimes faith and **spirituality** are integral to the nature of the sessions, and sometimes they aren't. Yesenia always makes certain that any discussion of faith is client centered, so she allows her clients to lead, and she responds with reflective questions, perhaps reframing their perspectives, but not in a directive way. Yesenia's agency is also very active in community development projects, and while faith definitely drives their mission, evangelism isn't a motivating factor.

Rather, her agency runs weekly food drives, does outreach within a local refugee community, and offers after-school care for the children of clients. The agency's case management services are offered on a sliding scale, and no one is turned away for a lack of ability to pay. The agency also works with a broad coalition of community-based, faith-based organizations so that clients have access to a range of services, and larger projects, like crisis response, are conducted collectively.

THE ROLE OF RELIGION AND SPIRITUALITY IN HUMAN SERVICES

Learning Outcome 10.1   **Explore how human services providers can integrate religion and spirituality into practice**

The work that Yesenia does with a faith-based agency is common among similar agencies across the country. While some faith-based agencies are explicit about a goal of evangelism, most are not and instead focus on a mission of helping those in need. This type of altruism is integral to many faith traditions. In fact, religious institutions have a long history of caring for the poor and disadvantaged, providing counsel to those in pain, and responding in times of crisis. What people are helped and how the help is provided has been highly influenced by religious teachings, particularly teachings within the **Judeo-Christian** traditions, and then reinforced by church authorities. A policy of charity is not limited to Judeo-Christian faiths; in fact, most religions and faith traditions include charity as a requirement of faithful adherence, not only in the form of financial assistance but also through compassionate service and kindness.

Religion and spirituality have been a part of everyday life for many people in the United States, although the religious landscape has been changing in the last few decades. In the late 1990s to early 2000s, 80 to 90% of people in the United States surveyed identified themselves as being either religious or spiritual, stating that their faith is an important aspect of their daily lives (Gallup & Lindsey, 1999; Grossman, 2002). The predominant religion practiced in the United States is Christianity, but in the last 20 years, rates of religiosity have declined, while levels of general spirituality have increased. For instance, in 2018 and 2019 65% of Americans surveyed identified themselves as Christians, which reflects a decline of 12% compared to the previous decade. Those who identify as atheist, agnostic, or "nothing in particular" rose from 17% in 2009 to 26% in 2019 (Pew Research Center, 2019). But despite these shifting dynamics, the decline in the identification of a specific religious affiliation doesn't necessarily mean that people in the United States are becoming less spiritual. In 2017, just over half (54%) of Americans described themselves as "religious," but an additional 27% considered themselves "spiritual, but not religious," and just fewer than 20% stated that they were neither spiritual nor religious (Lipka & Gecewicz, 2017). Thus, as identification with a particular religious denomination has been steadily declining in the United States, general spirituality has sharply increased.

Religion or religiosity is not the same as spirituality. Religiosity is often defined as a social or cultural experience grounded in a religious tradition, whereas spirituality is often defined as the experience of having an independent relationship with a deity, involving a search for the sacred—a process that involves seeking out that which is considered holy or seeking the divine (Miller & Thoresen, 2003; Pargament & Mahoney, 2009).

Of course, people can be religious *and* spiritual (searching for the divine within the context of a particular religious tradition), religious without being particularly spiritual (a cultural or secular involvement in a religious faith) or spiritual without being grounded in a particular religious tradition (searching for the divine within the context of various spiritual practices such as **New Age spirituality** or **Eastern religious philosophies, but not within a traditional religious doctrine**). When clients use these terms, it's important for human services providers to explore what religion and spirituality mean to them, so that everyone is speaking the same language.

Personal faith is important to many people because it provides them with comfort during difficult times. Faith also binds people together and provides communities with a framework for coming together and depending on one another during good times and bad. And yet, despite the core role that religion, spirituality, and faith play in the lives of so many people, the human services profession as a whole has been rather reluctant to incorporate faith and spirituality into practice (Harris et al., 2017). According to Harris et al., the primary reason cited by practitioners for their reluctance was a concern that they lacked the knowledge of how to effectively integrate faith into the counseling process, particularly if the client had a faith that was different than their own.

Integrating Christianity into human services practice has been of particular concern to some human services professionals, since Christianity is the dominant faith tradition in the United States and often includes directive moral stances that may marginalize certain populations such as the lesbian, gay, bisexual, transgender, and queer/questioning (LGBTQ) communities. Yet, in light of the high percentage of people who cite faith as integral to their identity and a primary source of support during difficult times, many within the human services profession have acknowledged that exploring this area, particularly from a nondirective, client-centered approach, has merit.

Integrating faith and spirituality into practice is a broad topic and often means something different to different people. For instance, there are many faith-based agencies in the United States, but not all faith-based agencies provide services that are religious and/or spiritual in nature, such as the agency referenced in the opening vignette. Similarly, not all mental health counselors who provide spiritual or faith-based counseling work with faith-based agencies. In fact, in many instances it would be difficult to determine any substantive difference between the services provided by a secular agency and those provided by a faith-based agency.

Another reason to consider integrating faith into practice is because of the positive impact spirituality can have on people's lives. Several research studies in the last two decades have focused on the mind–body–soul connection in an attempt to understand the reciprocal relationship of each, with a specific focus on how spirituality affects an individual's overall physical and mental well-being (Chaar et al., 2018; McLaughlin, 2004; Powell et al., 2003). What has been found in most of these studies is that personal spirituality has been linked to a decrease in depression, an increase in greater social support, an increase in cognitive functioning (Koenig et al., 2004), an improvement in the ability to cope with crises (McLaughlin, 2004), and a better ability to cope with substance abuse problems (Fallot & Heckman, 2005). So, it would seem that having a relationship with a faith community and believing in something bigger than ourselves is good for our physical health, our mental health, and our psychosocial well-being.

It is quite likely that as human services providers we will serve our clients more effectively if we can accompany them on *their* faith journey, at least to some extent. Several research studies suggest that counselors should acknowledge and address the religious and spiritual dimensions of mental and emotional disorders within the counseling relationship, particularly if clients identify themselves as being spiritually grounded, at least to some extent (Currier et al., 2018; Kliewer, 2004; Koenig et al., 2017; Miller et al., 2004). And yet, as much as incorporating spirituality into the counseling relationship may be helpful for many clients, there is also the potential for harm, particularly when the religion of a provider is pushed onto a client in a directive manner.

The question pertinent to all human services providers, then, is how to remain client centered while incorporating spirituality into practice. This process will undoubtedly involve engaging in some conceptual or paradigm shifts, from a Western model to a more **holistic** one. Traditionally, the mental health and medical communities in Western societies have had a tendency to divide human beings into biological, intellectual, social, emotional, and spiritual domains, with minimal recognition of how each of these dimensions interacts with the other. But in recent years there has been a growing interest, both within professional circles and within the general public, in moving away from such a compartmentalized view of the human experience and toward regarding humans more holistically, where one is considered as a whole with each part or dimension of the person being inextricably interwoven with the others (Oxhandler & Parrish, 2018).

Essentially, a holistic approach to psychosocial health involves the process of acknowledging, addressing, and evaluating the mind, the body, and the spirit (or soul) when considering issues affecting one's psychosocial functioning. In other words, rather than attempting to determine whether depression is a biological disorder with psychological manifestations or a psychological disorder with biological implications, depression would be considered a condition having a reciprocal impact on the whole person.

Cultural Competency and Religious Literacy

Religious values and ethics are core components of many religious faiths, and it is important to have a basic working understanding of the values of various religions in the event that a human services provider works with clients who practice a different faith. Possessing interfaith competency and religious literacy will enhance the human services provider's ability to provide faith-based or spiritual counseling by enabling them to move beyond their own belief system. It's also important to move beyond the common negative stereotypes of other religions and denominations and see the value of religious diversity. Incorporating spirituality into a counseling relationship requires counseling skills reflecting cultural competence as well as religious literacy, because many religious traditions are rooted in cultural tradition.

A human services provider who does not possess cultural competence risks inflicting harm onto the client, even if the harm is unintentional. For instance, the human services provider may feel unprepared to address the client's spiritual needs, and in response, may simply ignore the client's references to spiritual matters, which may result in the client feeling ashamed or trivialized. Prior to the recent surge of interest in **holistic health**, practitioners in the West were often dismissive of Eastern philosophies, which have acknowledged the mind–body–soul connection for centuries (Wang et al., 2020), rendering many in the human services profession ill-equipped to provide effective services to Asian clients (for instance) from Buddhist or Hindu traditions (Hodge, 2004; Jegathesan & Abdullah, 2019).

A more overt form of lacking cultural competence is when human services providers are inappropriately directive in pushing their religious beliefs onto their clients.

This can be particularly egregious if the human services provider is a member of the dominant culture, practices the dominant religion, and is providing human services to members of a minority religious group. Cultural competence in religion and spirituality requires that human services providers practice religious humility, sensitivity, and receptivity, integrating spirituality into their practice in a way that is client driven and client centered (Hall et al., 2004). One way of accomplishing this task is by developing a sense of community cultural competency so that the broader cultural context is highlighted, rather than solely a personal competency (Garrido et al., 2019). Research has also demonstrated the importance of a foundational framework that is based on openly communicating, having the ability to be sensitive, perceiving counselors as competent, providing sufficient resources to clients, and the fostering of mutual trust. This framework is particularly important in rural communities, as they tend to be more religious demographically and insular; thus, developing a strong and reciprocal relationship based on open communication and trust is key when incorporating faith and spirituality into the counseling relationship (Baldwin & Poje, 2020).

THE NATURE OF FAITH-BASED HUMAN SERVICES DELIVERY

Learning Outcome 10.2   Examine how faith-based human services agencies operate

Human services providers can incorporate matters of spirituality in just about any practice setting in response to their clients' disclosure that faith is an integral part of their lives or something they wish to explore. In addition, there are thousands of faith-based agencies that operate locally and globally, providing valuable services to a range of populations in need. Human services providers who work with these agencies may or may not practice the same faith as the agency, and the populations served may or may not practice the same religion. Some faith-based agencies incorporate spirituality into practice, and some do not. This all leads to the logical question of what, if anything, makes a faith-based organization different—in nature and service delivery—from a secular agency.

It's easy to identify a faith-based agency when it's a synagogue, church, or mosque, filled with religious symbols and a **mission statement** that identifies serving God as a primary function and purpose of the organization. But what about **parachurch organizations** that do not function as churches but more as a human services agency? Or human services agencies that have their roots in a particular religious tradition but don't integrate religion or faith into practice? Would those agencies be considered "faith based"?

The difficulty lies in the fact that many secular agencies provide almost identical services as faith-based agencies, and there is often no distinguishable difference between the two. Policy makers, social scientists, and historians have defined faith-based organizations in various ways in the past, with most criteria relating to an organization's dependence on religious entities or denominations for financial support, whether the mission statement identifies agency goals that reflect core values that are religious in nature, and whether the employees of the organization are religious and adhere to a **statement of faith** (Ebaugh et al., 2003).

In whatever way "faith based" is defined, it is important to remember that a faith-based agency does not necessarily mean Christian, as might be presumed in many

Western countries, such as the United States. In fact, a number of religiously oriented agencies provide faith-based human services grounded in faiths other than Christianity. Thus, although it is true that the majority of faith-based agencies in the United States have Christian roots, many do not. Faith-based agencies may be Jewish, Christian, Muslim, Buddhist, Hindu, or interfaith, each either serving communities broadly or electing to serve only individuals of that particular faith.

Faith-based human services can be facilitated as a ministry of a house of worship, such as a synagogue or church counseling center or food bank, or they can be facilitated as a program within a religious organization that functions as a distinct agency, such as the Salvation Army. Some faith-based agencies have the goal of converting clients to that particular faith (evangelism), believing that conversion is the first step toward wholeness, or they might deliver human services in a manner consistent with the agency's mission—justice, compassion, and kindness, for instance—without integrating religion into practice. It's important for human services providers to be aware of the church or agency's mission because it will have a significant impact on how human services are delivered.

Federal Funding and Regulation of Faith-Based Agencies

Historically, it has been difficult, if not impossible, for a faith-based agency to receive government funding. The Fourth Amendment of the U.S. Constitution, which guarantees freedom of worship, has been interpreted by the courts to mean there must be a separation between government and religion. Thus, unless the agency operated as a secular organization and did not incorporate faith into practice, for the most part it could not receive government funding. The government remains sensitive to those members of society who do not share the same faith as the majority culture and, as such, attempts to protect these individuals with policies and legislation that ensure equity in access and services for those who do not practice a particular faith or are members of a religious minority.

In 2001, then-President George W. Bush signed the Faith-Based Community Initiatives Act, also known as Charitable Choice, or Care Services Act (CSA), which made it easier for faith-based agencies to receive federal funding as long as religious worship, religious instruction, or **proselytizing** was not a part of service provision (at least within the aspect of the agency or program seeking federal funding). Many preceived this as a positive step toward reengaging religious organizations in the care of those in need, though others expressed concern that the CSA would remove the federal government as the primary entity responsible for human services provision.

While acknowledging the important role of faith-based agencies in human services, critics recalled the history of some faith-based organizations enforcing arbitrary conditions on service delivery based on religious or moral grounds. These practices directly or indirectly discriminated against certain groups, such as LGBTQ, single parents, the poor, or individuals who embraced different values than the majority population, such as indigenous populations (National Association of Social Workers [NASW], 2002).

Some might question whether there is anything inherently wrong in making services contingent on the performance of some behavior. Do compliance-based services rob clients of self-determination and personal agency and risk forcing culturally based moral values on those who do not share these same social mores? Take, for example, single women in the 1940s and 1950s who had children out of wedlock. It was not uncommon for these women to have services denied to them unless they agreed to place their babies for adoption—a practice based on the culturally rooted moral belief that premarital sex

Pearson eText

Video Example 10.1

This video describes how faith-based organizations can use government grants to support local human services. What are key factors referenced in this video that ensure equity in funding?

https://www.
youtube.com/
watch?v=eocTF_VVC_w

was wrong and that it would be immoral for a single mother to raise an out-of-wedlock child (Edwards & Williams, 2000). Or what about the common practice of denying services to homeless individuals who are actively engaging in alcohol and drug abuse? Do those without homes and dependent on others for sustenance have the right to consume alcohol, even if it is not in their best interest? The goal of this chapter is not to determine which side of this debate has a stronger argument. Certainly, each side has merit, and a meaningful debate must continue. What is important is understanding the complexities involved in qualifying services based on behavior, particularly when behavioral standards are religiously based.

Most critics of the CSA were not necessarily against faith-based agencies providing services to those in need. Rather, they argued that faith-based agencies should not become the primary human services providers in the United States. For instance, the NASW advocates for the government remaining responsible for providing comprehensive human services to the public, which ensures that everyone has equal and available access to services. The NASW also advocates that utilization remains voluntary, that human services delivery systems remain accountable to the public and the professional community, and that human services providers have appropriate levels of education and are professionally licensed in their field (NASW, 2002).

Balancing rights is never easy, but that is the government's role, particularly with regard to vulnerable populations with a history of marginalization and exclusion from mainstream society. In February 5, 2009, former President Obama signed Executive Order 13199, establishing the White House Office of Faith-Based and Neighborhood Partnerships. After signing the order, President Obama pledged not to favor one faith tradition or denomination over another, changing how decisions on funding practices were made from his predecessor. Among the key priorities of the Office of Faith-Based and Neighborhood Partnerships was a commitment to foster interfaith dialogue with community leaders and scholars (The White House, 2009). The shift in priorities alleviated many of the fears of the NASW and other human services organizations, which recognized the long-term contributions of faith-based agencies but advocated for distribution of agency funding to a wide range of religious agencies, with an equally wide range of views and objectives.

The Obama administration also implemented numerous policies intended to ensure equal access and fair treatment in social service agencies, including barring federally funded religious organizations from discriminating against employees or clients based on religious reasons. Under Obama, federally funded faith-based health and human services agencies were required to provide written notice to clients about the religious nature of the organization and also to provide a list of services they do not provide (based on their religious values), and provide a list of alternate resources where clients could receive those services (The White House Archives, 2012). Specific concerns centered on providing protections for LGBTQ community members as well as those seeking abortion-related services or access to birth control.

The Trump administration began removing Obama-era regulations on faith-based organizations shortly after President Trump took office, citing the need for regulatory reform and increased "religious freedoms" (U.S. Department of Health and Human Services, 2020). Mental health and human services organizations, including the American Psychiatric Association and the NASW, expressed concerns that the effect of these moves was actually lifting regulations designed to bar discrimination based on religious beliefs, most notably discrimination against LGBTQ employees and clients (NASW, 2016), while promoting Christian values (Stern, 2019). Democratic lawmakers also expressed concerns about the "religious freedom" policies, noting that a religious organization, particularly one receiving federal funding, should not be permitted to discriminate against a client or employee based on their sexual orientation, gender identity, pregnancy status, marital status, or other medical conditions, which would represent key violations of the separation of church and state doctrine (Weixel, 2020).

Examples of the Trump administration dismantling protections on behalf of marginalized groups, masked as "religious freedoms," include the attempted dismantling of Obama-era workplace protections for LGBTQ people (reversed in a 2020 Supreme Court decision) (Liptak, 2020). Another example includes Trump's executive order banning Muslim refugees from several predominantly Muslim countries while granting priority status to Christian refugees (Executive Order 13769, 2017; Goodstein, 2017; Shear & Cooper, 2017). A final example is the Department of Justice ruling against Native American tribes seeking to protect their sacred lands from fracking and the installation of oil pipelines on native lands (American Civil Liberties Union, 2019; Lucas, 2018; Thompson, 2017).

Many faith-based agencies make significant contributions to communities and individuals, providing important services from unique perspectives. They should not be arbitrarily prohibited from receiving federal or state funding solely because of their religious roots and/or orientations, but measures must be taken to ensure equal and open access to services, particularly when an agency is performing services within the public domain with federal support. Thus, it is important that the federal government step in to ensure that members of populations that do not align with conservative values, have protections as well. In other words, federally funded faith-based organizations should not be able to discriminate against employees or clients based on religious reasons, because this will then bar certain populations from receiving vitally important federally funded medical and mental health care services.

The Benefits of Faith-Based Services

Since the majority of Americans identify religion and spirituality as an important part of their lives and also identify themselves as being members of a particular faith community, many also rely on their communities and congregations when going through a difficult time. Faith communities provide individuals with a valuable support system during times of crisis, providing both guidance and emotional support. One goal of human services is to connect people to a broad support system, and a faith community can provide this for its active members.

Religious coping and spiritual support have been found to provide more benefits over other coping methods, such as general social support, including mental health counseling (de Rezende-Pinto et al., 2019; Pargament et al., 2001). For instance, one study questioned individuals within a church congregation who had recently experienced a crisis. The subjects were asked to rank various resources they found helpful during the crisis, such as family, friends, religious beliefs, praying, reading scripture, and professional services, including counseling, legal services, and psychological services. The researchers were surprised to learn that most people ranked professional services last in helpfulness and ranked religious beliefs and praying the highest (Stone et al., 2003). A 2017 study found that mindfulness was an effective coping mechanism for older adults with hypertension, and another study found that Muslims' use of religious coping strategies drawn from **Islam** during times of stress was highly effective compared to other coping strategies (Achour et al., 2016).

So, clearly there is a lot of evidence that positive religious and spiritual coping strategies can help people better manage a range of life stressors, but what about major tragedies and catastrophes? Do positive religious coping mechanisms help manage those crises also? A study conducted after the September 11, 2001 terrorist attacks on the World Trade Center and the Pentagon found that of 560 adults questioned in a national telephone survey, 90% sought out positive religion, often in the context of a faith community, as a way of coping with this tragedy. Examples of positive religion include seeing God as a source of strength and support and perceiving God and a faith community as supportive rather than a source of judgment (Meisenhelder & Marcum, 2004). These studies confirm what many people may know anecdotally—that in times of crisis, people tend to draw strength and support from their faith communities, which provide them with a sense of comfort and familiarity while giving them a sense of being a part of a larger whole and reminding them they are not alone.

THE RANGE OF FAITH-BASED HUMAN SERVICES AGENCIES

Learning Outcome 10.3   **Explore service delivery approaches of faith-based agencies from a range of faith traditions**

In this section I will explore examples of faith-based human services agencies operating from **Abrahamic religions** (Jewish, Christian, and Islamic), as they are the major providers of human services, on both a local and global level in the United States. I will also explore the role of the human services provider working in these faith-based agencies, noting any significant differences between their role and those played by human services providers in secular agencies. Most of the agencies featured in this section operate separately from any church or religious entity but are either supported by a particular religious tradition or operate as an extension or branch of a particular religious tradition or denomination. I will also explore ways in which human services providers can incorporate spirituality in practice using spiritually based intervention strategies drawn from Eastern philosophies and religions, such as mindfulness practice, since oftentimes clients are seeking a spiritual connection outside of a traditional mainstream religious framework.

Jewish Human Services Agencies

Pearson eText

Video Example 10.2

In this video, HIAS, a Jewish social service agency, provides humanitarian relief at the border. What types of motivations did volunteers have to help migrants at the border?

https://www.
youtube.com/
watch?v=c8idk7y4Iag

> If one of your countrymen becomes poor and is unable to support himself among you, help him as you would an alien or a temporary resident, so he can continue to live among you. (Leviticus 25:35)

Judaism is an Abrahamic religion that is based on the belief that the Jews are the chosen people of God. Judaism is considered an ancient religion with a history of profound blessings and persecution. The Hebrew Bible, called the **Tanakh** (what Christians call the Old Testament), contains three books, the first of which is called the **Torah**. The Torah contains oral tradition and written law providing Jews with guidance on how to live and treat others.

Tzedakah is the Hebrew word for giving to the disadvantaged. The literal translation of Tzedakah means fairness or justice, as in doing what is fair and just for the poor.

Tzedakah is not really like charity, in that charity is voluntary and based on altruism, while Tzedakah is obligatory. While Jewish law, the **Halakhah**, doesn't necessarily prohibit charitable giving, it does recognize that charity alone isn't sufficient in caring for the poor; thus, Tzedakah is an obligation, somewhat like a public tax, imposed on Jewish followers. Poverty is not considered virtuous in the Jewish religion, as it is in some Christian denominations, and in fact, it is considered pointless and something to be avoided through hard work and good financial stewardship (Eisenberg, 2010). While Jews are required to provide for the poor through mandatory giving, because poverty is not considered a natural state, the most ideal type of giving is providing someone with employment (Lifshitz, 2008).

Volunteer Malka Rodrig unpacks meals at a kosher food drive-thru distribution site, at the Greater Miami Jewish Federation building in Miami.

Jewish human services agencies operate under an umbrella agency that provides coordination and macro services, such as financial support, educational services, and policy support, including political lobbying for social justice causes. For instance, the Jewish Federations of North America (JFNA) serves as an umbrella organization for a network of over 100 Jewish federations and Jewish community centers across North America. The JFNA also provides international funding and coordination for rescue and resettlement of Jews living in high-conflict or unsafe areas worldwide, including regions where anti-Semitism is prolific.

A component of the JFNA is the Human Services and Social Policy Pillar (HSSP), which is responsible for political lobbying action on local and national levels in an attempt to influence policymakers. Whether it's lobbying for increased funding for geriatric services, homeless resources, or refugee programs, the HSSP, or *the pillar* as it is commonly called, relies on human services professionals and volunteers to coordinate services of human services agencies inside and outside the Jewish community.

The Association of Jewish Family and Children's Agencies (AJFCA) serves as an information clearinghouse and support for Jewish Family Services (JFS) agencies located across the country. The AJFCA provides funding, advocates for social justice causes on a policy level, and provides information on education and training opportunities for JFS agencies. Local JFS agencies offer a number of different services, including individual and family counseling, marital counseling, substance abuse counseling, AIDS counseling and educational awareness programs, anger management courses, employment services, parenting workshops, domestic violence services, children's camps, teen programs, and geriatric programs such as Kosher Meals on Wheels and hospice. No one is denied services due to an inability to pay, and payment for services is typically on a sliding scale.

Many JFS agencies also have refugee resettlement programs that assist Jewish and non-Jewish migrants who have fled persecution and need legal and resettlement assistance in the United States. Services typically include short-term housing on arrival, emergency financial support, case management, medical care, assistance with school enrollment, job placement, and language courses. JFC agencies have excellent reputations

© WILFREDO LEE / AP / SHUTTERSTOCK

in assisting refugees gain financial independence, particularly in light of the often tragic circumstances many refugees have faced prior to coming to the United States. Refugee resettlement services may be coordinated with the United Nations and U.S. Department of State, or at times are facilitated without government funding and assistance.

Services focused exclusively on the Jewish community include Holocaust survivor services to Jews who lived under Nazi rule between 1933 and 1945 or were affected by the Holocaust in some manner. In addition to providing counseling services related to posttraumatic stress disorder (PTSD), in-home services related to geriatric care are also provided for Jewish older adults. Other Jewish-related services include counseling and case management services for Jewish armed services personnel, Jewish chaplaincy services, family services, and outreach focusing on assisting families reconnect with their Jewish roots by learning how to incorporate Jewish traditions and values into their family systems. Premarital and marriage services are also offered to Jewish and interfaith couples, focusing on marriage and parenting within the Jewish faith.

The primary difference between the manner in which human services providers deliver services at a JFS agency versus a secular agency is the focus on connecting Jewish clients to the broader Jewish community, both domestically and worldwide, as well as the incorporation of Jewish values throughout the various programs. Counselors and case managers are also primarily Jewish and well connected to the Jewish community, including being familiar with local synagogues and other Jewish services within the local community.

Case Study 10.1 Example of a Client at a Jewish Faith-Based Agency

Raisa, a 77-year-old Jewish widow, began counseling at a local Jewish community center about 1 year ago for depression. Her initial psychosocial assessment revealed a long history of mild depression with mild anxiety that escalated in recent years to a point where intervention was necessary. Raisa shared that her normal sadness increased dramatically when she lost her husband 4 years ago and did not abate even when she found herself feeling more at peace with her husband's death. Raisa and her husband were married for 45 years, both having migrated from Europe shortly after World War II. They were unable to have children of their own and thus adopted one child, a daughter, who resides in a different state about 3 hours away by car. Raisa's daughter is married and has one child, also through adoption.

Sarah, her counselor, presumed that Raisa may have been a Holocaust survivor, and that some of the earlier trauma and grief issues were likely at play in her current depressive state, but Sarah chose not to address this possibility in counseling, choosing to wait until Raisa was ready to share her experience. Despite weekly counseling sessions and several courses of antidepressant medication, Raisa's depression and anxiety continued to worsen. During one session approximately 9 months into their counseling relationship, Raisa was discussing the difficult early years of her marriage when she and her husband first moved to the United States. Raisa became extremely emotional as she shared that they were both orphans because of the war and thus had no family to help or guide them, either in their migration experience or in their marriage.

Sarah recognized the grief Raisa was reexperiencing, and also noted that once Raisa became obviously distressed, she became very uncomfortable, apologizing for her "outburst," and then quickly changing the subject. Sarah did not push Raisa, understanding that Raisa's decision to share her distant but obviously still-powerful memories was just that—Raisa's decision. As the months progressed Raisa began to pensively share more stories of her early marriage, which seemed to be marked by considerable loss and struggle.

She was 18 when the war ended. She met her husband, Reuben, 1 year later, although they had met once or twice several years earlier. They became inseparable almost immediately, likely out of loneliness, Raisa suspected, rather than any type of love at first sight, although in retrospect, Raisa shared, she wasn't sure there was a difference—both were emotions encompassing a significant amount of passion and intensity. Raisa and Reuben spent 2 years searching for family members immediately after the war with the hope of relocating from their home in Amsterdam. Her husband located an aunt and uncle in the United States and Raisa learned that her brother had escaped to Israel at the beginning of the war. They never located any other surviving family members.

After some thought and consideration, they decided to move to the United States in the hope of connecting with her husband's relatives. When they first arrived in New York, they experienced a long-overdue measure of relief, but this was to be short lived when Reuben's aunt and uncle announced plans to move to California. Deciding not to follow, Raisa and Reuben were left to survive on their own in a big city that offered as much risk as opportunity.

Although Raisa spent most of her time focusing on the physical and financial hardships of her early life, she appeared to avoid any discussion of her feelings. In fact, Sarah noted that whenever Raisa risked becoming emotionally upset, such as when Sarah asked any question that required Raisa to reflect on her childhood (even positive aspects of her youth), Raisa became emotionally and physically rigid, as if she were talking herself out of the "nonsense" of her feelings to regain composure.

Sarah became increasingly concerned about Raisa's psychological stability, particularly in light of her very recent increase in anxiety. In fact, there were two occasions where Raisa was so anxious that she did not feel comfortable leaving her home to attend her counseling session. In light of Raisa's worsening condition and a fear that Raisa might be at risk of suicide, Sarah made the decision to have a session with Raisa where she would more assertively address Raisa's Holocaust experience, believing that to be the root of her unresolved grief and the source of complicated mourning related to many of the losses she experienced after the war. Sarah went to Raisa's house for this session so that Raisa could remain in the safety of her surroundings if the session became too difficult. Sarah also implemented a safety plan for Raisa, including collecting a list of emergency numbers and the number of a local geriatric outreach center that Raisa had been involved with intermittently for several years.

Sarah began her session with Raisa by gently expressing her concern about her emotional well-being, as well as sharing her belief that Raisa may be suffering long-term effects from being a Holocaust survivor. Sarah shared her belief that unless Raisa addressed her past grief and losses, her depression and anxiety might not abate and may, in fact, continue to worsen. Raisa was immediately uncomfortable, but Sarah reassured her that although she wanted to push Raisa a bit, she'd made sure she could remain with Raisa for the entire afternoon; thus, Raisa could take her time. Although Sarah had spent considerable time in counseling sessions with Raisa conducting "psychoeducation"—teaching Raisa about the normal stages of grief and the common psychological responses to trauma—Sarah reiterated this information now in the hope that Raisa would begin to accept that her feelings were normal.

During this session Raisa shared that her early childhood was one of constant happiness. Her father was a professor at a local university in Amsterdam. Although they were not very religious, they attended synagogue weekly and observed the Sabbath. Without realizing it at the time, Raisa's family was quite immersed in the Jewish culture, which in her family meant close ties to extended family and friends within the community who had a shared culture, customs, and life perspective. Raisa recalled the emergence of a different feeling in her neighborhood when she was about 11 years old. She is not sure if this marked the slow invasion of the Nazi party into her small town, but she did recall that it was about this time that her parents could no longer protect her brother and her from the fact that their lives were about to change forever.

Raisa shared that her family started closing the front door and drawing the shades more frequently and that various neighbors suddenly began to disappear. She recalls the day, at the age of 13, when almost everyone in her neighborhood was forced to wear yellow stars on their sleeves, and she marked this as the day she realized that some of her favorite neighbors were apparently not Jewish, because they did not have to wear the yellow star.

Raisa shared with great emotion the night she and her brother, 2 years older than she, were awakened in the middle of the night by their parents and told to dress quietly in the dark. They were going on a long trip but had to remain quiet. She shared that she did not recall thinking much about what was happening. Perhaps she was too scared, or maybe she had experienced so much change and shock in the past year, she simply accepted this as one more confusing event in a long line of bewildering experiences.

Months earlier Raisa's father had told her that it was important for her to obey him without asking questions because not obeying him might have serious consequences. She recalled crying when he said this to her because he was so firm, an emotion she rarely saw in her father. He responded by telling her that tears were useless now—they would not help, and that she needed to be strong. She obeyed him now as she folded one change of clothing into a small dark knapsack, confused and afraid, but resolved not to cry. The next thing Raisa remembers is that she and her family were crouching down outside in the dark and running along the hedge line. She recalled that there was no moon, and the night was so dark she was certain she would lose her brother, who was directly in front of her. She kept running, though, trusting that someone would come back for her eventually if she lost her way. They arrived at a stranger's house, and her father knocked on a back door that appeared to lead to a basement. A young woman opened the door and hurried Raisa and her brother through the door.

Raisa had only a quick moment to look back and see her mother and father, who to her horror were not following behind them. Instead, her father and mother were crying, peering into the dark basement with a look of sadness on their faces. Raisa recalled her mother telling her earlier that she loved her very much, yet Raisa could not recall having said it in return. This was something that would haunt Raisa for years. Did she tell her mother that she loved her? She would never be sure that she had. That was the last time that Raisa and her brother saw their parents. Raisa learned after the war that their parents were forced to leave their home shortly after arranging to smuggle their children out of Amsterdam and after a short stay in what became known as a Jewish ghetto, they were sent to a concentration camp. Although she was never able to obtain exact information, Raisa learned that both of her parents had been executed, likely sometime in early 1943.

Raisa and her brother remained in the dark basement with little food or water for about 3 days before being driven, during the middle of the night, to another home.

Raisa recalled crying sometimes but her brother, like her father, told her to stop and to be strong, and she complied. This time period was particularly difficult for both Raisa and her brother, who were tempted to escape and return home to their parents. She is not sure whether it was fear or wisdom that kept them from this course, but she realizes now that had they returned home, their fate would have been the same as their parents'. The next trauma for Raisa occurred when she learned that she would be separated from her brother. Although her parents had arranged for them to remain together, increased risk led her rescuers to conclude that two children suddenly showing up in a home was far riskier than one; thus, in the middle of one night several weeks into their frightening journey, Raisa's brother was hurried into one car, and she into another. This, too, would remain a source of considerable pain for Raisa, as she realized that once again, she was denied a proper good-bye. Her last memory of her brother was his surprised face looking out the car window as he realized that she was being escorted into a different car.

Raisa fled to Italy, where she lived in a converted attic, and although enjoying some measure of freedom, she had to remain relatively hidden until the war was over. Her foster parents were nice, but stern. They were not Jewish, so Raisa was compelled to live a lifestyle very different from the one she had enjoyed in Amsterdam. She dressed differently, attended church rather than synagogue, and ate food very different from what she was used to. It did not occur to Raisa until she was much older that there wasn't any possibility of seeing her family again. Her attitude during the balance of her childhood was one of "waiting it out" until the war was over and she could go home and resume life as she had known it before the war. But of course, that was a dream that would never come true. When the war ended, her host family wished her good fortune, and at 17 years of age Raisa was completely on her own.

Although God had never played much of a role in her life before, Raisa now found herself praying to the God of her childhood that her family was safe and waiting for her at home. She got a job in town so she could earn enough money to return to Amsterdam, and that is where she met Reuben. It was Reuben who told her there was nothing to return to—that his family, and likely hers, were dead, and the only choice Jews had was to go somewhere safe, outside of Europe, perhaps Israel or America. Raisa had been sheltered by her host family and had heard nothing of the concentration camps and the unchecked slaughter of millions of Jews. She had difficulty describing the way she felt once she learned that her entire family was likely dead. She described it as both surreal and numbing. She had no idea where her brother had been taken, and she had fantasized for years about finding him walking down an Italian street or shopping center in town. He was all she could think of now. She had to find him.

She and Reuben made the singular goal of finding whatever family they had left. At some point in their planning, they became a couple and decided to marry. Raisa learned through a charitable organization that her brother was living in Israel. She had shared with Sarah earlier that their decision to immigrate to New York to join Reuben's family was a practical one. She shared now that Reuben was afraid that if they immigrated to Israel, they might find themselves in the same situation as in Amsterdam—in the center of a war—and he could not risk becoming involved in another war ever again. Raisa let go of her hope to return to her brother when Reuben decided it would be wiser for them to move to the United States. Raisa did reconnect with her brother eventually, but they never enjoyed the closeness of their childhood. When she and Reuben visited her brother in Israel many years later, it felt to Raisa as if she were visiting a complete stranger. Her brother had become quite religious, embracing the faith of their youth—a choice antithetical to Raisa's, who chose to distance herself from her Jewish roots. Raisa shared all these stories with emotion, but no tears; she was still being "strong."

Although Sarah decided to hold off on approaching the subject of Raisa and Reuben's infertility, she made a mental note that she would visit this issue in a later session. Sarah knew this too would likely be a very difficult subject for Raisa and a source of great pain—both from a generational perspective (issues related to infertility were typically not discussed in earlier generations) and from a loss perspective. Sarah assumed that Raisa and Reuben looked forward to having their own children not simply as a way of starting a family as so many couples do, but as a way of *replacing* the family that had been taken from them both. Sarah would learn later that Raisa's first child was a stillbirth, that the loss was almost too much for Raisa to bear, and that this was likely when Raisa's melancholy transitioned into a clinical depression. Even when Raisa and Reuben experienced the joy of adopting their daughter, Raisa shared that a sense of sadness remained hidden within her.

After this intense and very long session, Sarah developed a treatment plan for Raisa—one that involved both trauma and grief counseling. Sarah suspected that in addition to depression and anxiety Raisa also suffered from PTSD, so she incorporated aspects of **trauma-informed therapy** designed to help her deal more effectively with being a survivor of trauma and loss. Sarah suspected that Raisa was in many ways still operating with a survivor mentality, which compelled her to obey her father's distant admonition to resist crying and remain strong. Raisa's tendency to equate crying with weakness could be addressed through cognitive behavioral therapy, where Raisa would be encouraged to recognize that such rules about emotion may have been necessary in wartime but were no longer necessary and were actually damaging. The challenge for Raisa would likely lie in a fear that to change her perspective on crying might indicate a betrayal of her father and his wishes.

One of Sarah's ultimate treatment goals for Raisa was to help her develop a more realistic and timely definition of authentic strength that did not dishonor her father's guidance. Another treatment goal involved helping Raisa learn to grieve all her past losses and finally to rebuild the community she lost so many years ago. Although Raisa had a daughter, she had avoided ever getting too involved in the Jewish community, perhaps out of a fear that she might lose again what she had lost as a child—a close-knit community of neighbors who shared a culture and a faith and who operated in many respects as an extended family. Although Sarah suspected that Raisa might have some objections to getting involved in the local Jewish community, Sarah planned to explore the possibility of reconnecting Raisa with the faith and culture of her childhood.

A significant portion of Raisa's healing came from a pilgrimage of sorts that Sarah helped her plan, involving returning to Amsterdam with her daughter and her brother. During this long-overdue visit, Raisa and her brother tearfully revisited their childhood home, as well as other places of nostalgia, and although things had changed significantly since their youth, Raisa and her brother found great healing in their trip "home." The final leg of their trip involved creating a memorial for Raisa and her brother's parents and all her lost family and friends. Raisa's last session with Sarah prior to her trip involved writing a poem they would leave at the site where the Chelmno concentration camp once stood. The trip helped Raisa create meaning around the death of her parents, and it also helped her to reconnect emotionally with her brother and involve her daughter in a part of her life she had previously kept hidden.

In succeeding years Raisa's debilitating depression lifted, and her anxiety receded. She learned how to genuinely grieve her past losses and to recognize how her early trauma and loss impacted virtually every area of her life. She did ultimately become involved in her community, and in the years preceding her death, she even resumed attending synagogue. Sarah's relationship with Raisa involved more than counseling. It involved incorporating aspects of faith and culture into sessions, case management that involved connecting Raisa to a community from which she had been generally estranged. It also involved Sarah drawing on her own Jewish faith, which enabled her to understand much of what Raisa experienced both in her past and in her current life.

Christian Human Services Agencies

> For I was hungry and you gave me something to eat, I was thirsty and you gave me something to drink, I was a stranger and you invited me in, I needed clothes and you clothed me, I was sick and you looked after me, I was in prison, and you came to visit me . . . I tell you the truth, whatever you did for one of the least of these brothers of mine, you did for me. (Matthew 25:35–36, 40)

Christianity is an Abrahamic religion that evolved when a sect of Jews professed their belief that Jesus was the promised Messiah and savior of the world. Christians believe that Jesus is the Son of God and died for their sins. They consider this sacrificial act "the good news" and they consider themselves the adopted children of God. Christians follow both the Old and New Testaments, which contain admonitions to care for the poor, particularly widows, orphans, and the sick. Christians are instructed to provide materially for those in need, as well as tend to their emotional and spiritual needs.

A considerable number of faith-based agencies in the United States are Christian in nature, operating from a wide range of denominations and faith traditions. The Catholic Church and traditional Protestant denominations have a long history of providing for the financial, emotional, spiritual, and social needs of those in need. An earlier Protestant movement called the **social gospel** represented a renewal of commitment to address the social causes of many problems experienced by people in need, particularly poverty and oppression.

Many **conservative Christians**, such as evangelicals, fundamentalists, and Pentecostals, have moved away from the social gospel, focusing instead on individual sin and fallen world as the cause of many problems in society, although this perspective may be changing among younger and more progressive Evangelicals (Gasaway, 2014). Evangelism is seen as the initial priority in helping others, based on the belief that repenting of one's sins and becoming a new creation in Christ will, in most situations, alleviate suffering. Ethical dilemmas can arise when Christian agencies and providers practice evangelism as a component of human services provision, since professional standards in the human services fields, whether human services, social work, counseling, psychology, or psychiatry, prohibit proselytizing to clients, particularly when clients are not driving this process. Critics of evangelical practitioners who evangelize clients as a part of the counseling and case management process suggest that evangelism is more appropriately conducted in the vein of pastoral counseling or ministry efforts, not human services (Belcher et al., 2004).

The Black church, particularly in the rural South, has a long history of providing valuable and important services to the Black community—a typically underserved population (Blank et al., 2002). Many historically Black churches provide for the social and mental health care needs of individuals within the respective churches and communities. Research shows that many in the Black community prefer to seek support, guidance,

Pearson eText

Video Example 10.3

This video describes the role of Catholic Charities in providing relief services in natural disasters. What are some benefits of approaching relief services from a faith-based perspective?

https://www.youtube.com/watch?v=eocTF_VVC_w

Volunteer with Catholic Charities of the Archdiocese of Washington prepares to distribute a grocery box to recipients who have been affected by the coronavirus outbreak and economic downturn, in a parking lot outside Robert F. Kennedy Memorial Stadium in Washington.

and counsel from their pastors, rather than seek assistance from formal human services agencies, which underscores the importance of the Black church and the services they provide. Black churches tend to offer far more human services than predominantly White churches, which may be a reflection of a general sense of distrust of the mainstream mental health community on the part of many Black people, as well as their historic (and current) exclusion from formal services within their communities (Blank et al., 2002; Campbell et al., 2020; Thomas et al., 1994).

Catholic Charities USA is a network of human services agencies linked to the Roman Catholic Church that has a long tradition of caring for those in need, regardless of religious affiliation or ability to pay. Currently, there are about 1600 local Catholic Charities agencies across the United States offering a wide variety of human services designed to serve those in need within the particular community served. According to the Catholic Charities website, services provided at most of its local agencies focus on advocacy and direct services related to reducing poverty, supporting families, and empowering communities. They do this by facilitating programs that focus on child welfare and adoption, housing, counseling, after-school youth programs and youth athletic programs, child care, domestic and international adoptions, domestic violence victim advocacy, employment and job training, health care education, senior services, and homeless services, including providing holiday meals to those in need (Catholic Charities USA, 2010). The majority of funding for Catholic Charities comes from federal and state sources, with only a small percentage coming from the Catholic Church. Catholic Charities has not had significant problems obtaining federal funding because providing services directly linked to religious ministry is not typically an aspect of services the agencies provide. Human services professionals are not required to be Catholic to work at Catholic Charities, and services are not dependent on a client's faith, although service delivery is facilitated in a manner consistent with Catholic teachings.

An example of a Protestant human services agency is Prison Fellowship Ministry (PFM), founded by Chuck Colson, former President Richard Nixon's aide. In 1973 Colson became a Christian, and in 1974 he pleaded guilty to obstruction of justice charges in association with the **Watergate scandal**. Colson served 7 months of a 3-year sentence, and when he was released in 1976 he founded PFM, based on his own religious conversion and his belief that no one is beyond hope. His ministry is now one of the largest prison ministries in the world, serving thousands of prisoners, ex-prisoners, their families, and victims. PFM is also involved in criminal justice reform through a PFM affiliate, Justice Fellowship, which focuses on numerous social justice issues, including prison safety and elimination of prison rape.

Such social advocacy is particularly important for groups of individuals who do not evoke sympathy in the average person, and prisoners certainly fall into this category. Yet, it is essential for people to realize that prisoners are not a uniform group of "evildoers" and "sociopaths" who deserve whatever hardship the prison system can dish out. Most prisoners have had childhoods marked by poverty and abuse, many serve longer sentences because they could not afford adequate legal counsel, and some are innocent, or at least not guilty of the crimes for which they are charged and sentenced. PFM is committed to stopping the intergenerational cycle of crime and poverty by offering prisoners hope for a second chance through the Christian faith.

PFM volunteers facilitate Bible studies and topical seminars, mentor at-risk youth, counsel prisoners and crime victims, serve in youth camps, organize Angel Tree programs, visit prisoners regularly, counsel ex-prisoners and crime victims, and write letters to prisoners in the "pen pal" program. PFM does not receive federal funding because its volunteers focus extensively on the evangelism of prisoners and their family members.

Case Study 10.2 Example of a Client at a Christian Faith-Based Agency

Castle Christian Counseling Center (CCCC) is a not-for-profit, ecumenical counseling center contracted by the county to provide mandated counseling services, including anger management and alcohol counseling for individuals who have been charged with an alcohol offense. Julie was required to attend anger management as a part of her probation for a domestic battery charge. Julie's initial psychosocial assessment recommended that she participate in both group and individual counseling. The group counseling consisted of a 26-week program focusing on anger management and personal accountability.

Julie's individual counseling was designed to help her deal with the underlying reasons for intense anger and inappropriate behavior, such as verbal and physical abuse. Julie was 24 years old when she was charged with domestic battery against her husband of 3 years. When Julie began counseling, she was both emotionally needy and defensive. Her counselor, Dana, suspected that beneath Julie's defensiveness lay a tremendous amount of shame, so she chose not to confront Julie until much later in their counseling relationship.

During the first several months of counseling Julie expressed considerable anger and frustration with her husband, who she perceived as being quite passive. In response to his seeming inability to make decisions or take the lead in any aspect of their life, Julie expressed extreme disappointment and at times rage. It became clear to Dana that Julie's husband was in many respects being set up for failure by Julie. For instance, Julie often expressed to her husband that she wished he would be more proactive in their social life, but if he did forge ahead and make plans without checking with her first, she would become irate that he chose an activity he should have known she would not like. Yet if he checked with her first before making plans, she would become angry that he did not have the confidence to make plans without her input, and she would accuse him of ruining the surprise for her.

The incident that resulted in the charge of domestic battery involved a fight that escalated over their finances. Julie had decided to quit her job and try to get pregnant, even though her husband had expressed concerns that he did not make enough money to be the sole provider. He ultimately supported her decision, and Julie quit her job, but after a few months, when money got tight, and they ultimately did not have enough money to pay bills, Julie lost her temper. During her tirade she accused her husband of not caring about their finances and of sabotaging their plans to start a family. Julie became physically abusive toward her husband when he attempted to stand up to her by telling her that he had not in fact wanted her to quit her job because he feared their current situation would come to fruition. Julie became hysterical, accusing her husband of hating her and of just looking for an excuse to leave her.

Dana recognized Julie's tendency to alter the facts to support whatever theory she was attempting to prove at the moment. She also recognized Julie's all-or-nothing thinking—people either loved her or hated her, were for her or against her. According to secular psychology Julie may have met the criteria for borderline personality disorder, but Dana recognized her behavior as indicative of a contemporary form of idol worship. Julie was expecting her husband to be God, yet there was only one God who could meet all of Julie's needs. Dana knew that over the next several months she would be Julie's representative of God—showing her unconditional love as well as truth. She made a commitment to Julie that she would always be honest with her, and there would be nothing that Julie could do that would lead Dana to end their relationship. She trusted that Julie could handle the truth if it were delivered in love, not shame.

It was only a few days later that Julie seemed to test Dana's commitment. Julie called Dana and left a frantic message, stating that she was very upset and needed to talk immediately. When Dana had not returned her call within the hour, Julie called again but this time was enraged. She accused Dana of being like everyone else—making promises but then abandoning her when she was most in need. Before returning Julie's call, Dana prayed for wisdom and insight. She immediately had an image of truth as light, and for Julie, any truth at all was like a flashlight blaring into her eyes, causing Julie to have to bat the light away to avoid the pain. Dana knew immediately from then on that she would have to be gentle not only in the amount of truth she shared with Julie but also in the way she shared her wisdom.

In the face of Julie's intense and abrasive defensiveness, Dana resisted the natural tendency to force truth on her. Instead she indulged Julie a little, suspecting that Julie's initial feeling when she made a mistake was intense shame, but before she could respond to this emotion she reacted by flipping her shame outward into anger against anyone who represented the source of shame—anyone who made her feel guilty in some way, who exacted accountability, and even who reacted emotionally to one of her rages. Dana's intuition told her that if she could relieve some of Julie's shame—take her off the hook in some manner—this might give Julie the emotional space to explore her feelings of intense shame and guilt. When Dana did call, she suspected that Julie would already be feeling immense shame and guilt, regretting her episode of anger.

Dana also suspected that Julie would not be able to emotionally manage these feelings and thus would have a need to rationalize her behavior by escalating Dana's "sin" to match her own reaction. Dana knew that if she admonished Julie for her tantrum, this would set this process in motion, so she did something different; she took Julie off the hook and rather than admonishing her, she praised her for her ability to communicate her feelings! Julie was so taken off guard that it actually enabled her to experience feeling a small amount of productive guilt. After Dana had finished complimenting Julie on her willingness to communicate, Julie admitted that she should have handled her feelings differently, that she should have been more patient, and that in some respects she believed she was expecting to be let down by Dana, so she didn't even give her a chance to meet her needs. Success! By taking this counterintuitive approach and lifting the burden of shame, Julie was able to actually recognize her internal process without rationalizing her feelings away.

During the course of their counseling Dana addressed Julie's negative feelings about God. Julie shared that she felt very insignificant whenever she thought of God. She then shared new elements of her childhood. She had already disclosed a childhood fraught with abuse and emotional humiliation at the hands of both her father and her mother, but during this particular session, Julie shared that whenever she made a mistake as a child, her father would tell her she was going to hell, that she was a disappointment to God, and that she could not hide from God—He could see her wherever she was and He knew what she was doing and that what she was doing the majority of the time was bad. Julie's father would often physically abuse her, sometimes using a Bible to beat her on the head.

When Dana asked Julie to draw a picture of her relationship with God, Julie drew a picture where she was quite small, crouched down and running, and God, a large presence on the page, was looking down on her with a stern scowl on his face. Dana asked Julie if she ever turned to God when going through a difficult time. Julie looked shocked, expressing her belief that if she were in trouble, God would be the last source she would consider turning toward for support. In fact, Julie shared that she believed that the only time God paid any attention to her was when she had messed up. She imagined God saying, "There you go again—I knew you would blow it eventually!"

Dana told Julie that she would like to spend some time sharing a different type of God with her, not a punishing God, but a loving God who acted as a father to his children—guiding his children when they were walking down the wrong path, like any good father, and applauding when they did well. Dana shared about her own feelings toward her young son. She found herself chuckling even when he got himself into a bit of trouble, like the time he wrote his name in purple crayon all over his closet door, only to deny his culpability when Dana came upon his artwork. Dana was not harsh, nor punishing, but she did want to teach her son that defacing property was not the best choice. She did this in love, extending grace and forgiveness because she understood that at this age her son did not know any better. She also smirked as she admired her son's artwork, knowing that drawing on the wall with crayon was a perfectly normal thing to do. Julie could not fathom a God who was anything but condemning, but she was very interested in learning about the concepts of grace and forgiveness.

Once Dana was confident that Julie trusted her, she began to respond to each of Julie's rage episodes by first empathizing with Julie's emotions—her disappointment, her fear, her anger—followed by gently sharing truth. When Julie asked if Dana thought she was wrong to have such high expectations of her husband, Dana said yes, but that did not mean Julie should have no expectations. Rather, Dana explained that once Julie developed a more solid emotional base within herself, including having a more solid relationship with God, her expectations of her husband would likely be more realistic.

Julie's counseling also consisted of a significant amount of grief counseling, mourning her lost childhood, gaining insight and understanding of the abuse she had endured, and learning her emotional triggers and ways to avoid them. Dana taught Julie to contain her emotions, so that she wouldn't have to react the moment she experienced an intense emotion, such as the intense fear that she was going to be abandoned, which would often turn toward anger. Dana used guided imagery directing Julie to imagine Jesus holding her firmly, but lovingly. Imagery exercises of this type also helped Julie make God more real in her life. Julie began to believe that God had good intentions for her, not evil ones, that He wanted the best for her, not the worst. He would not hide from her, and she did not have to hide from him. Julie continued counseling even after she met her mandated requirement.

In her second year of counseling, Dana shifted focus from Julie's childhood to her current relationships, including the relationship with her husband. Julie's intense fear of abandonment often led her to be so self-focused that she was blinded to the damage she caused other people. As her fear of abandonment subsided and her shame diminished, Dana was able to coach Julie into looking through the eyes of her husband. This process would have been impossible a year ago because the shame would have paralyzed her, but with her increasing internal strength, Julie was able to accept her behavior and the pain it caused. Once she saw herself as deserving of forgiveness, she could address her own abusive behavior.

Within the second year of therapy, Julie's anger receded significantly, and she was able to talk through her feelings rather than act them out. She remained in counseling intermittently for years to maintain her program of faith building, emotional containment, and extension of forgiveness to self and others.

Islamic Human Services Agencies

Pearson eText

Video Example 10.4

This video explores the services provided by a community-based Muslim clinic providing a range of services to those in need. What are some strengths associated with no limiting services to the same faith as the agency?

https://www.youtube.com/watch?v=zlfZhPt_ndQ+7:7

And those in whose wealth is a recognized right; for the needy who asks and those who are deprived. (Qur'an 70:24–25)

Islam is another Abrahamic religion that is based on both the Jewish holy books, as well as the Christian Bible. The word *Islam* means submission, and followers of Islam submit themselves to **Allah**. The Muslim holy book is called the **Qur'an** and is considered by Muslims to be the recited words of God revealed to the Prophet Muhammad in the 7th century. Islam believes the Qur'an to be God's final revelation to humankind.

Islam is a religion that is often misunderstood and mischaracterized by both the general public and the media. This mischaracterization is due in part to the differences between more liberal Western values and the more conservative values held by many in the Islamic community. The terrorist acts of September 11, 2001, and subsequent acts of terrorism have increased cultural misunderstandings and promoted sentiments of **xenophobia** and **Islamophobia**. A negative stereotype of Islam is that the entire Muslim culture endorses violence, extremist dogma, and female oppression. In truth, every culture and every religious faction has its peaceful members and its violent ones, but the extremists do not define the entire population.

There are over 1 billion followers of Islam worldwide, which makes it the second-largest religion in the world. The majority of Muslims live in Southeast Asia, Northern Africa, and the Middle East. There are two primary sects within Islam due to an early dispute over who should have been Muhammad's successor. The Sunnis tend to be more religiously and politically liberal (for instance, they believe that Islamic leaders should always be elected). Approximately 90% of all Muslims are Sunnis. Shiites, on the other hand, tend to be more orthodox in their religious beliefs and political philosophies, having developed a more strictly academic application of the Qur'an. Shiites believe that all successors to Muhammad (**imams**) are infallible and sinless. They appoint their clergy and hold them in high regard.

The majority of Muslims who live in the United States are Sunnis, 75% of whom are foreign born. The Muslim community tends to be college educated and middle class, and Muslims in general tend not tend to rely on government-sponsored human services to meet their basic needs. Much of the focus of Islamic charity is directed toward Muslims in other parts of the world who are suffering, either because of war or some other form of oppression. Local Muslim human services tend to focus on marriage and family services.

Because Muslims come from many different countries there is considerable diversity within the Islamic community, particularly in the United States. Yet despite the variability of cultural beliefs and practices, Islam shares five basic pillars of faith:

- *Shahada:* Faith in one God
- *Salat:* Ritual prayer five times a day while facing Mecca
- *Zakat:* Charitable giving to the poor with the understanding that all wealth belongs to God
- *Sawm:* Fasting from sunrise to sunset during the month of Ramadan
- *Hajj:* Pilgrimage to Mecca.

According to the Qur'an (9:60), there are eight categories of people who qualify to receive zakat. These include the poor, the needy, those who collect zakat, those who are being converted, captives, debtors, those fighting for a cause (that is, those fighting for God), and travelers. The three foundational values within the Islamic community include community, family, and the sovereignty of God. Family is often defined as the joining of two extended families; thus, what might be considered **enmeshment** in North American society is often seen as a sign of respect, as extended families are drawn close and remain an active part of the immediate family's life. Men and women typically adopt traditional roles in families that are close adherents to the Islam faith, with men working outside of the home and women caring for the home and children. This trend is changing, even in more traditional families, just as it is in other cultures within U.S. society. Modesty is seen as an important value necessary for keeping order within society, and women often wear clothing (*hijab*) that covers the greater part of their body (Hodge, 2005).

Areas of obvious conflict between Islamic values and liberal North American values include Western culture's values of individualism, self-expression, and self-determination, compared to Islamic culture values of community, self-control, and consensus (Hodge, 2005). Thus, whether working with an Islamic human services agency, coordinating services with one, or directly serving the Islamic community, Hodge cautions human services workers not to view Islamic values through the eyes of Western culture. For example, it is common for Westerners to view the Islamic tenet of modesty as primitive and oppressive to women, which for some Westerners may seem synonymous to endorsing domestic violence. Yet the Qur'an states that husbands and wives must express respect and compassion toward one another, and domestic violence is not endorsed. To truly understand the values of modesty and traditional roles embraced within the Islamic culture, one must take the time to understand what these values mean to the men and women who embrace them because, as with many other social dynamics, people interpret Islamic gender roles in many different ways. Hence, although human services providers might not share Islamic belief systems, working in

Volunteers with the Islamic Society of Greater Houston, package donations at a mosque that was being used as a shelter. Houston's Muslim community, an estimated 200,000 people, has opened many of its community centers and sent hundreds of volunteers to serve food and deliver donations. Some have rescued neighbors from high water.

© AP / SHUTTERSTOCK

association with Islamic human services agencies can provide them with an opportunity to gain greater cultural competence.

There has been a recent surge of interest in developing human services programs within mosques and Islamic centers across the United States in response to growing concerns about social issues and demonstrated needs within the Muslim community, particularly related to marriage, family, and Islamophobia. The discipline of human services is relatively new to the Islamic community, but charity is not new and has been practiced within Islamic and broader Arab communities for generations. Islamic human services providers may include social workers, counselors, and psychologists, but an imam can also provide human services. Islamic human services agencies provide services to those within Muslim and non-Muslim communities and are increasingly relied on to serve as a liaison for Western aid agencies in Muslim communities experiencing a crisis (De Cordier, 2009).

Islamic charities have suffered since the September 11 terrorist attacks, because many Muslims in the United States are afraid that money they donate in good faith to an Islamic charity may be frozen by the U.S. government and not directed to humanitarian causes as planned. Muslims are also giving less because they are afraid that they might be held in suspicion if a charity to which they donate money is later investigated for diverting funds to terrorist causes. Mosques and Islamic centers across the nation are reaching out to legislators in a campaign called Charity Without Fear, asking them to establish a list of Islamic charities in good standing so that devout Muslims can give to charity without fear of being accused of supporting terrorist organizations (Council of Islamic Organizations, 2005). To date, the federal government has not responded to the request for a "clean" list of Muslim charitable organizations.

There are several Islamic human services agencies operating within the United States, and although not as prolific as Jewish or Christian organizations, Islamic agencies are increasing in numbers and offer important services to the Muslim community. The Islamic Social Services Association (ISSA) acts as an umbrella organization for all Muslim human services agencies in the United States and Canada. The ISSA provides training and educational services, acting as a network linking and equipping Muslim communities. The Inner-City Muslim Action Network (IMAN) focuses on meeting the needs of those in the inner city in Chicago by operating food pantries, health clinics, and prayer services. IMAN, which is located in a storefront on Chicago's South Side, offers a free computer lab with free Internet service, General Educational Development courses, and computer training classes. IMAN is also involved in community activism such as lobbying against the granting of liquor licenses in high-crime areas, community development, and coordination of outreach events with other community agencies both Muslim and non-Muslim.

There is concern within the Islamic faith community that Muslim marriages are being negatively affected by the casual nature of divorce in the United States. Thus, several Muslim human services agencies focus on providing marriage and family services with the goal of strengthening Muslim families. Muslim Family Services (MFS), a division of the Islamic Circle of North America, is a national agency with offices located throughout the United States. They provide marriage and family services for families and couples, teaching them how to have a marriage according to Islamic principles. MFS provides education, such as workshops for married couples and training for imams; premarital, marriage, and parenting counseling; emergency services; foster care; and advocacy in court and with departments of social services. Islamic values are stressed, including the belief that marriage is the foundation of society and the pillar on which family is built. Human services providers working for MFS understand that Muslim couples living in the United States are often caught between two cultures, and many are influenced by the more liberal Western values. This has led to increased divorce rates and also many parenting challenges as adolescents in particular challenge traditional Islamic values such as modesty and embrace more liberal male–female relationships.

Another Muslim human services agency that focuses primarily on women is Niswa (which means "woman in community" in Arabic), located in Southern California. Niswa was founded in 1990 by Dr. Shamim Ibrahim, a psychologist and counselor, who recognized the need for culturally and linguistically competent services for incoming migrant and refugee Muslim women in need of advocacy. The goal of Niswa is to strengthen Muslim families by providing services to South Asian, Afghan, and Middle Eastern immigrant women. Niswa provides counseling, case management, crisis intervention, preventative health education, referrals, and domestic violence services, including a domestic violence shelter called Niswa House. Niswa's primary focus is on women's advocacy and domestic violence but has expanded considerably in the past several decades to keep pace with clients' needs.

In addition to Muslim human services, there are several human services agencies that provide services to the Arabic community, but outside of a religious context. For instance, Arab American Family Services (AAFS) provides services focused on domestic violence prevention and intervention, older adult and disabled services, cultural diversity training, immigration services, community health and education, youth programs, and mental health services. AAFS also provides advocacy services focused on dispelling negative stereotypes about the Arab culture, serving as a bridge between Arab Americans and the mainstream American culture.

The U.S. Muslim community will continue to be confronted with issues related to acculturation and the eroding of traditional values, and problems within Muslim families will likely continue, particularly in light of rising incidences of Islamophobia. Human services agencies can assist Muslim families in feeling less isolated, provide much-needed education and support, and provide a sense of connectedness among Muslims who are feeling unsupported within their communities.

Case Study 10.3 Case Example of a Client at a Muslim Faith-Based Agency

Maya is a 42-year-old Muslim woman who was referred to an Islamic women's center for advocacy and counseling. She has been married to Asad, a 44-year-old physician, for 18 years. Maya is the stay-at-home mother of their three children, aged 10, 12, and 14. Both Maya and Asad are originally from Egypt, having immigrated to the United States shortly after getting married. Maya reports that she and her husband have always been devout Muslims and are very involved in their local mosque. They have had what she considers a traditional Muslim marriage, where her husband is the leader of the home and provides for the family financially, and she takes care of the home and the children.

For the majority of their marriage Maya believed that their marriage has been a good one. She believed that her husband was always very respectful of her and relied on her wisdom and input in making decisions impacting the family, particularly with regard to the children. Because Maya was an accountant prior to getting married, Asad has relied on her to help with financial matters related to his medical practice.

Maya reported that about 5 years ago Asad began to "bring his work home with him," which led to an increase in his general irritability and frustration. In the last 2 years Maya noted that he began to become more controlling of her whereabouts, getting angry with her if he could not reach her at a moment's notice. She did not reach out then because she believed Asad when he said that it was his right to control her in this manner. Although Maya's father did not behave this way, she began to believe that perhaps she needed to endure Asad's behavior in order to be a good Muslim wife.

Maya shared that in the past few months Asad's aggression had escalated to the point of screaming at her, both at home and in public, backing her into corners. His drinking has escalated as well. The incident that prompted Maya to finally reach out for help occurred after she refused to sleep with Asad because he was extremely intoxicated and verbally abusing her. Asad became irate and began beating her, citing his rights according to the Qur'an (4:34–35).

Maya initially went to the imam at her mosque, who supported her completely and also explained that her husband's use of the Qur'an was a misinterpretation. He explained that Islam did not in any way condone abuse. He provided her with a considerable amount of information regarding the "cycle of violence" and services in the community for victims of domestic violence, including support groups for both adults and children. Maya contacted the Muslim women's center that day and saw a counselor later in the week.

During Maya's first counseling center she expressed relief that her community was so supportive of her, but she expressed sadness as well because the information and resources she received seemed so fatalistic and hopeless. Her counselor explained that her husband was acting in a manner inconsistent with the will of Allah and if he was truly committed to following Islam and being a good Muslim husband and father, then perhaps he would be open to receiving counseling as well. Domestic violence, the counselor explained, not only destroyed everyone in the family but also affected the entire community, thus the Muslim community was as concerned about Asad as it was about Maya.

During counseling Maya began to understand the underlying dynamics of her husband's behavior and gained wisdom regarding the difference between a husband who led his family with respect, as described by Muhammad, and the controlling and abusive behavior exhibited by her husband. As Maya gained confidence in herself and her decisions, she felt strongly that Allah was leading her to be strong for the sake of her family. Strength, according to her counselor, meant that she could not tolerate abuse. Asad met with the imam for several weeks and then reluctantly agreed to attend a 1-year anger management program that was led by an imam at the community Islamic center, and Maya agreed not to make any decisions about divorce until after Asad had finished his program. Both the imam and the counselor agreed that family counseling should not occur until after Asad had received enough counseling to recognize the root of the family and marital problems lay mostly within himself and his abusive behavior.

As Maya continued counseling, she began to realize the intergenerational cycle of abuse that existed in her husband's family and how important it was, particularly for the sake of her children, that she become strong enough to break the cycle. The most difficult aspect of this process for Maya was maintaining good boundaries with Asad and realizing that he had the choice not to change, which would force her hand in a sense, compelling her to leave the marriage to avoid repeating the patterns of abuse.

The Mindfulness Movement

Spiritual counseling need not always be facilitated within a traditional religious framework. It can also involve general spirituality, where the social worker provides resources and counseling focusing on a belief that all people are interconnected on some level and are guided by a divine presence. Many clients who wish to seek a deeper connection with a **higher power** but are not comfortable doing so within a particular theological framework can greatly benefit from exposure to general spirituality. Thus, although this chapter focuses more on mainstream traditions, it is important for social workers to be aware of a wide range of spiritual resources, which include traditions rooted in what would be considered Eastern or New Age philosophies, including some yoga traditions and the **mindfulness movement**.

New Age traditions approach the person from a holistic perspective, focusing on making connections between the person and the divine, and often rely on using all of the senses, as well as meditation practices, with the goal of helping individuals gain increased awareness and connectedness. The mindfulness movement (also called **contemplative practice**) rooted in the Buddhist tradition helps individuals develop a sense of awareness and presence in one's daily life.

Mindfulness traditions focus on cultivating an accepting awareness and enhanced attention to present moment experiences, and a belief that with this experience, a sense of interconnectedness to everything else emerges on its own. Practicing living each moment with this awareness promotes resilience in relating to life's obstacles as well as healing, love, and compassion. Those practicing mindfulness believe that if one seeks wisdom and balance in life and a connection with that which is bigger than oneself, then conditions such as depression, anxiety, substance abuse, and unresolved grief can be overcome and ultimately replaced with living mindfully with greater compassion, appreciation, and joy.

Pearson eText

Video Example 10.5

This video explores how yoga and medication can help children on the autism spectrum. How can meditation complement other types of interventions?

https://www.youtube.com/watch?v=n2S-1Se9asTY

Case Study 10.4 Case Study in the Mindfulness Movement

Kim Hunkle, a licensed counselor, owns a drug and alcohol rehabilitation center in Orange County, California, called Dee's House. Kim explains that she named her residential treatment center for women over 30 in honor of a dear friend of hers who died of alcohol-related causes. Dee's House uses mindfulness practices drawing from more New Age philosophies, with an emphasis on holistic treatment and what Kim refers to as "whole-hearted healing." Dee's House serves primarily mature women, and the staff, according to Kim, and reflected on the agency's website, rely on a holistic approach to healing that taps into the mind–body–soul connection. Clients take meditation classes, attend seminars on metaphysical

Gratitude What are you grateful for? rock.

© ISABELLA ROSE 444/SHUTTERSTOCK

healing strategies, and spend a considerable amount of time communing in nature—hiking and taking contemplative walks on the beach. Staff also provide opportunities for clients to engage in mindfulness exercises, including yoga, with a focus on spiritual healing and self-discovery. Kim notes that one of her goals for her clients is to help them learn to value themselves fully, to find their voice, and to experience new ways of looking at the world, while immersed in a community of loving and supportive women.

Dee's House clients often struggle with a range of issues in addition to substance abuse, including depression, anxiety, and PTSD. In fact, most women who come through Dee's House use substances to manage traumatic backgrounds, including domestic violence, sexual assault, child sexual abuse, poverty, and childhood deprivation. Kim recognized early on that almost all her clients experience low self-esteem, have histories of trauma, and are reluctant to speak their truth in life. Referring to her clients as "angels," Kim states, "It's almost like life has beaten them down so much, they've forgotten who they are, or maybe they never knew. And they use alcohol and drugs as a way of forgetting their pain, of blocking out their real feelings, and just to be able to cope with all of life's stressors. But eventually that life catches up to them and they must find new ways of coping, and that's where we come in. We focus on authentic and holistic healing, rooting out all the shame these women are feeling (that often fuels relapses). We give them their voice back." According to the Dee's House website, clients can "finally eliminate the feelings of impending doom and the thoughts of 'I don't want to live anymore, yet I'm too afraid to die.' Kim notes that the Dee's House staff help clients discover the reasons they are here on this earth, uncovering their natural gifts and finding their unique talents. And then "we help her to share those gifts with the world, leaving it a better place than she found it," hopefully knowing she has found her life purpose, her reason for living.

A typical day for a Dee's House residential client includes attending morning and afternoon meditation, doing contemplative exercises, attending a workshop focused on trauma and healing, participating in a spiritual healing book club, and participating in sessions with spiritual counselors, as well as secular case managers and therapists (which involves spiritual modalities, if client-directed). Clients also participate in a 12-step program for women, which includes a weekly "Wing Repair" meeting (a dual reference to the women being angels and having the protection of guardian angels). Clients also go on weekend hikes that often include Dee's House alumni, providing opportunities to commune with nature in a nurturing environment. Kim states "we use everything in nature as life lessons, including how to climb over challenging hills to get to the other side. The activities are nondirective in the sense that the level of integrated spirituality is tailored to each client's desire and comfort level." Kim notes that the rate of relapse is very low, but she keeps her doors open for clients who need to return for what she calls a "spiritual tune up."

CONCLUSION

Far too many of the world's conflicts center on religion, and religious dogma has often been at the heart of marginalization and the justification of oppression of members of the "out-group" population. Yet religion can also be a source of peace, faith, optimism, and hope. Despite the misuse and misapplication of religion by some, religion, particularly personal spirituality, is often key to the self-actualization of many. Thus, human services providers must be comfortable integrating spirituality into practice, if client directed. Further, faith-based agencies from a range of religious traditions have had a long history of providing assistance to underserved and at-risk populations and are often working in partnership with secular and government agencies providing valuable services to clients throughout the country and world.

As the field of human services evolves and matures, the scope with which this discipline is viewed will be broadened and the value of services provided by those not within the mainstream mental health community will be increasingly recognized. Whether these services are delivered informally through church-sponsored programs or through organized faith-based human services agencies, recognizing that human services delivery can occur through a variety of systems acknowledges the reality that different people seek help in different ways.

SUMMARY

- The ways in which human services providers can integrate religion and spirituality into practice are explored, including examining how human services providers develop competency in integrating faith and spirituality into their practice in a manner that is client-centered.
- The ways in which faith-based human services agencies operate are examined. The nature of faith-based institutions, including comparisons with secular agencies, is also examined. The history of government funding of faith-based agencies is explored within the context of federal legislation that determines parameters for which faith-based agencies qualify for federal funding. The benefits of faith-based services are also explored, such as the development of positive religious coping strategies.
- Service delivery approaches of faith-based agencies from a range of faith traditions are explored. The philosophies and human services delivery systems from a range of faith traditions, including Jewish, Christian, and Islamic human services agencies, are discussed. The mindfulness movement, an Eastern faith tradition, is also explored.

END-OF-CHAPTER QUESTIONS

1. Provide an example of a positive religious coping mechanism and a negative religious coping mechanism.
2. Why is it important for human services providers to learn how to integrate spirituality into practice in a way that is client centered?
3. Do you believe it's important that the federal government remains neutral in matters of religion, particularly in relation to the human services profession? Why or why not?
4. What do research studies show regarding the advantages of seeking counseling from a faith-based organization?

References

Achour, M., Bensaid, B., & Nor, M. R. B. M. (2016). An Islamic perspective on coping with life stressors. *Applied Research in Quality of Life, 11*(3), 663–685.

American Civil Liberties Union [ACLU]. (2019). Request for investigation regarding unconstitutional use of State Department resources. https://www.aclu.org/letter/request-investigation-regarding-unconstitutional-use-state-department-resources

Baldwin, I., & Poje, A. B. (2020). Rural faith community leaders and mental health center staff: Identifying opportunities for communication and cooperation. *Journal of Rural Mental Health, 44*(1), 16–25. https://doi.org/10.1037/rmh0000126

Belcher, J. R., Fandetti, D., & Cole, D. (2004). Is Christian religious conservatism compatible with the liberal social welfare state? *Social Work, 49*(2), 269–276.

Blank, M. B., Mahmood, M., Fox, J. C., & Guterbock, T. (2002). Alternative mental health services: The role of the Black church in the South. *American Journal of Public Health, 92*(10), 1668–1672.

Campbell, R. D., & Winchester, M. R. (2020). Let the church say...: One congregation's views on how the Black church can address mental health with Black Americans. *Social Work & Christianity, 47*(2).

Catholic Charities USA. (2010). *Catholic Charities at a glance.* http://www.catholiccharitiesusa.org/document.doc?id=2853

Chaar, E. A., Hallit, S., Hajj, A., Aaraj, R., Kattan, J., Jabbour, H., & Khabbaz, L. R. (2018). Evaluating the impact of spirituality on the quality of life, anxiety, and depression among patients with cancer: an observational transversal study. *Supportive Care in Cancer, 26*(8), 2581–2590.

Council of Islamic Organizations. (2005). *Charity without fear.* http://www.ciogc.org/Go.aspx?link=7654625

Currier, J. M., Pearce, M., Carroll, T. D., & Koenig, H. G. (2018). Military veterans' preferences for incorporating spirituality in psychotherapy or counseling. *Professional Psychology: Research and Practice, 49*(1), 39.

De Cordier, B. (2009). Faith-based aid, globalisation and the humanitarian frontline: An analysis of Western-based Muslim aid organisations. *Disasters, 33*(4), 608–628.

de Rezende-Pinto, A., Schumann, C. S. C., & Moreira-Almeida, A. (2019). Spirituality, religiousness and mental health: Scientific evidence. In *Spirituality, religiousness and health* (pp. 69–86). Springer, Cham.

Ebaugh, H. R., Pipes, P. F., Chafetz, J. S., & Daniels, M. (2003). Where's the religion? Distinguishing faith-based from secular social service agencies. *Journal for the Scientific Study of Religion, 42*(3), 411–426.

Edwards, C. E., & Williams, C. L. (2000). Adopting change: Birth mothers in maternity homes today. *Gender and Society, 14*(1), 160–183.

Eisenberg, R. L. (2010). *What the rabbis said: 250 topics from the Talmud.* ABC-CLIO.

Executive Order No. 13769, 82 Fed. Reg. 8977 (Feb. 1, 2017).

Fallot, R. D., & Heckman, J. D. (2005). Religious/spiritual coping among women trauma survivors with mental health and substance use disorders. *Journal of Behavioral Health Services and Research, 32*(2), 215–226.

Gallup, G., & Lindsey, D. M. (1999). *Surveying the religious landscape: Trends in U.S. beliefs.* Morehouse.

Garrido, R., Garcia-Ramirez, M., & Balcazar, F. E. (2019). Moving towards community cultural competence. *International Journal of Intercultural Relations, 73*, 89–101.

Gasaway, B. W. (2014). *Progressive evangelicals and the pursuit of social justice.* UNC Press Books.

Goodstein, L. (2017). Christian leaders denounce Trump's plan to favor Christian refugees. *The New York Times.* https://www.nytimes.com/2017/01/29/us/christian-leaders-denounce-trumps-plan-to-favor-christian-immigrants.html

Grossman, C. L. (2002, March 7). Charting the unchurched in America. *USA Today*, D1.

Hall, C. R., Dixon, W. A., & Mauzey, E. D. (2004). Spirituality and religion: Implications for counseling. *Journal of Counseling & Development, 82*, 504–507.

Harris, H., Yancey, G., Myers, D., Deimler, J., & Walden, D. (2017). Ethical integration of faith and practice in social work field education: A multi-year exploration in one program. *Religions, 8*(9), 177.

Hodge, D. R. (2004). Working with Hindu clients in a spiritually sensitive manner. *Social Work, 29*(1), 27–38.

Hodge, D. R. (2005). Social work in the house of Islam: Orienting practitioners to the beliefs and values of Muslims in the U.S. *Social Work, 50*(2), 162–173.

Jegathesan, A. J. E., & Abdullah, S. S. E. (2019). *Multicultural counseling applications for improved mental healthcare services*. IGI Global.

Kliewer, S. (2004). Allowing spirituality into the healing process. *Journal of Family Practice, 53*(8), 616–624.

Koenig, H. G., George, L. K., & Titus, P. (2004). Religion, spirituality, and health in medically ill hospitalized elderly patients. *Journal of American Geriatrics Society, 52*(4), 554–562.

Koenig, H. G., Boucher, N. A., Oliver, R. J. P., Youssef, N., Mooney, S. R., Currier, J. M., & Pearce, M. (2017). Rationale for spiritually oriented cognitive processing therapy for moral injury in active duty military and veterans with posttraumatic stress disorder. *The Journal of Nervous and Mental Disease, 205*(2), 147–153.

Lifshitz, J. (2008). Welfare, property and the divine image in Jewish law and thought. In Jonathan B. Imber (Ed.), *Markets, morals and religion* (pp. 117–129). New Transaction Publishers.

Lipka, M. & Gecewicz, C. (2017). *More Americans now say they're spiritual but not religious*. Pew Research Center. https://www.pewresearch.org/fact-tank/2017/09/06/more-americans-now-say-theyre-spiritual-but-not-religious/

Liptak, A. (2020). Civil rights law protects gay and transgender workers, Supreme Court rules. *The New York Times*. https://www.nytimes.com/2020/06/15/us/gay-transgender-workers-supreme-court.html

Lucas, R. (2018). *Deep in the desert, a case pits immigration crackdown against religious freedom*. NPR, All Things Considered. https://www.npr.org/2018/10/18/658255488/deep-in-the-desert-a-case-pits-immigration-crackdown-against-religious-freedom

McLaughlin, D. (2004). Incorporating individual spiritual beliefs in treatment of in-patient mental health consumers. *Perspectives in Psychiatric Care, 40*(3), 114–119.

Meisenhelder, J. B., & Marcum, J. P. (2004). Responses of clergy to 9/11: Post-traumatic stress, coping and religious stress. *Journal for the Scientific Study of Religion, 43*(4), 547–554.

Miller, M. M., Korinek, A., & Ivey, D. C. (2004). Spirituality in MFT training: Development of the spiritual issues in supervision scale. *Contemporary Family Therapy, 26*(1), 71–81.

Miller, W. R., & Thoresen, C. E. (2003). Spirituality, religion, and health: An emerging research field. *American Psychologist, 58*, 24–35.

National Association of Social Workers. (2002, January). *NASW priorities on faith-based human services initiatives.* http://www.naswdc.org/advocacy/positions/faith.asp

National Association of Social Workers [NASW]. (2016, April). *Leading mental health organizations urge an end to harmful 'religious freedom' laws* [Press Release]. http://www.socialworkblog.org/wp-content/uploads/Joint-Statement-on-Religious-Freedom-Laws.pdf

Oxhandler, H. K., & Parrish, D. E. (2018). Integrating clients' religion/spirituality in clinical practice: A comparison among social workers, psychologists, counselors, marriage and family therapists, and nurses. *Journal of clinical psychology, 74*(4), 680–694.

Pargament, K. I., & Mahoney, A. (2009). Spirituality: The search for the sacred. In C. R. Snyder & S. J. Lopez (Eds.), *Oxford handbook of positive psychology* (2nd ed., pp. 611–620). Oxford University Press.

Pargament, K. I., Tarakeshwar, N., Ellison, C. G., & Wulff, K. M. (2001). The relationships between religious coping and well-being in a national sample of Presbyterian clergy, elders, and members. *Journal for the Scientific Study of Religion, 40*(3), 497–513.

Pew Research Center. (2019). *In U.S., decline of Christianity continues at rapid pace*. https://www.pewforum.org/2019/10/17/in-u-s-decline-of-christianity-continues-at-rapid-pace/

Powell, L., Shahabi, L., & Thoresen, C. E. (2003). Religion and spirituality: Linkage to physical health. *American Psychologist, 58*, 36–52.

Shear, M. & Cooper, H. (2017). Trump bars refugees and citizens from 7 Muslim countries. *The New York Times*. https://www.nytimes.com/2017/01/27/us/politics/trump-syrian-refugees.html

Stern, M. (2019). The Trump Justice Department has turned 'religious liberty' into a license to discriminate. *USA Today*. https://www.usatoday.com/story/opinion/2019/06/25/trump-gives-religious-conservatives-license-to-discriminate-column/1540435001/

Stone, H. W., Cross, D. R., Purvis, K. B., & Young, M. J. (2003). A study of the benefit of social and religious support on church members during times of crisis. *Pastoral Psychology, 51*(4), 327–340.

The White House Archives. (2012). *Interagency Working Group on Faith-based and Other Neighborhood Partnerships*.

https://obamawhitehouse.archives.gov/sites/default/files/uploads/finalfaithbasedworkinggroupreport.pdf

The White House, Office of the Press Secretary. (2009, February 5). *Obama announces White House Office of Faith-based and Neighborhood Partnerships* [Press Release]. http://www.whitehouse.gov/the_press_office/ObamaAnnouncesWhiteHouseOfficeofFaith-basedandNeighborhoodPartnerships/

Thomas, S. B., Quinn, S. C., Billingsley, A., & Caldwell, C. (1994). The characteristics of northern Black churches with community health outreach program. *American Journal of Public Health*, 84(4), 575–579.

Thompson, I. (2017). *Discrimination under the guise of 'religious freedom' is still discrimination, Mr. Trump*. American Civil Liberties Union [ACLU]. https://www.aclu.org/blog/lgbt-rights/discrimination-under-guise-religious-freedom-still-discrimination-president-trump?page=3

U.S. Department of Health and Human Services. (2020). *HHS announces proposed rule regarding equal treatment of faith-based organizations in HHS-Supported social service programs* [Press Release]. HHS Press Office. https://www.hhs.gov/about/news/2020/01/16/hhs-announces-proposed-rule-regarding-equal-treatment-faith-based-organizations-hhs-supported-social-service-programs.html

Wang, Y. Y., D'Amato, R. C., Van Damme, C., & Mahmood, S. (2020). Crossing cultural boundaries: Integrating eastern mind–body techniques for diverse Western learners. In C. Maykel & M. A. Bray (Eds.), *Applying psychology in the schools. Promoting mind–body health in schools: Interventions for mental health professionals* (pp. 93–111). American Psychological Association. https://doi.org/10.1037/0000157-007

Weixel, J. (2020). *Democrats demand Trump administration drop religious provider rule*. The Hill. https://thehill.com/policy/healthcare/483679-democrats-demand-trump-administration-withdraw-religious-provider-rule

11

Violence, Victim Advocacy, and Corrections

© DAXIAO PRODUCTIONS / SHUTTERSTOCK

Samuel grew up in a home marked by domestic violence, which oftentimes extended to the children. Samuel's mother was chronically depressed and often resorted to using alcohol to avoid dealing with her feelings. Samuel recalls days and sometimes weeks where his mother refused to get out of bed, and he was responsible for caring for his younger siblings. His father also had an alcohol problem and would fly into nightly rages where he would physically abuse Samuel's mother. When Samuel got older, he attempted to intervene and protect his mother, which only resulted in his father physically abusing him. In addition to physical abuse, Samuel was also the victim of emotional abuse and neglect. Samuel's father would often call him derogatory names and humiliate him by telling him that he would amount to nothing in life and that he was worthless. It seemed as though Samuel could do nothing right, and when he was about 12 years old, he promised himself that he would never allow anyone to hurt or humiliate him again. Samuel married when he was 21 and was hopeful that his life of being victimized was over. He loved his wife Ana very much and was determined to be the best husband

and father he could possibly be. He vowed not to repeat the mistakes of his parents, but deep inside he was plagued with fears that he wasn't good enough for his wife and that she would eventually leave him. He became increasingly jealous and accused his wife constantly of plotting behind his back to leave him, likely with another man. If Samuel's wife tried to convince him otherwise, he accused her of lying. When she became pregnant, he was thrilled, but after the baby was born he became upset because his wife seemed to want to spend all her time with the baby, leaving him to fend for himself.

One day Samuel's boss called him into his office and pointed out a mistake that Samuel made. All Samuel could think of was the promise he had made to himself years ago to never allow anyone to hurt or ridicule him again. Even though his boss's comments would have seemed reasonable to most people, to Samuel they were a recreation of the abuse he endured as a child. He lost control of his temper, slammed his fist into the wall, and quit his job. When he got home, he told Ana and fully expected her to sympathize with him and support his decision to not tolerate such abuse, but instead she complained that his act was selfish, particularly in light of his responsibilities as a father. Samuel completely lost his temper and in a blinding rage accused Ana of betraying him. In the blur that followed, Samuel accused her of cheating on him, of caring about the baby more than him, and even of getting pregnant by another man. In the midst of his angry outburst he shoved Ana against the wall and knocked her down, and then began kicking her in the stomach and head. All he could think of was how this woman, who he thought was his "savior," was really his enemy, and at that moment he hated her for allowing him to lower his guard and trust her. All the pain of his childhood, with all the hurt and humiliation, came rushing back, and he began to choke her. When his baby interrupted his rage, he screamed at his son to shut up. When his baby's crying got louder, he picked him up and shook him violently.

Samuel was arrested on charges of felony domestic violence, unlawful restraint, and child endangerment. After Ana was released from the hospital she listened to her voicemail and heard several frantic and pleading voicemail messages from Samuel crying and profusely apologizing and expressing intense fear about being in jail. The next call was from a social worker at the Victim-Witness Assistance with the local prosecutor's office asking her to return the call so that she could provide her with information about the court case, her order of protection, and resources for counseling. Ana then received a call from the local domestic violence shelter. The social worker asked her several questions about her safety and whether she needed shelter. She also offered Ana court advocacy and resources to help with her baby's medical care. Ana was hesitant to say too much. Mostly she was overwhelmed and felt flood of emotions – fear, sadness, confusion, and guilt. She felt sorry for Samuel. She knew he was a good person and she couldn't stand the thought of him being in jail, alone and scared. The sound of Samuel's voice on the voicemail rang in her ears and she began going over what happened in her mind again and again, questioning her original version of the events that night. Did Samuel mean to knock her down? Did he really shake the baby? Why wasn't she more sympathetic? She really had been neglecting him lately . . . was she a bad wife?

During Ana's first meeting with the prosecutor and court advocate about Samuel's case, she immediately became uncomfortable about the prospect of testifying against her husband. In fact, she couldn't imagine it! She felt sorry for Samuel—he'd had a horrible childhood and she felt like she was the only one he could confide in and that made her feel good. She believed in her heart that good people forgave easily, especially their husbands. Since Samuel was released on bond, and even though he was not allowed to contact her, she had been receiving almost nightly calls from him, begging for her forgiveness. This Samuel was the Samuel she fell in love with—the soft Samuel, the vulnerable Samuel, the sweet Samuel, and the kind Samuel. She reasoned that as awful as this incident had been, maybe it was the wake-up call their family needed to get back on track. When the prosecutor informed Ana that she did not have the power to drop the charges or the order of protection, she became very upset. She neither wanted nor asked for their involvement. She was certain that she could handle this matter on her own, as a family, and she wanted no part of the free advocacy from Victim-Witness or from the local shelter. She found their perception of her as a "battered wife" embarrassing and humiliating.

Despite her numerous attempts to play down what happened, even blaming herself for what happened, denying that it was "that bad," and explaining that Samuel has never kicked her and was actually trying to soothe the baby, not shake him, the prosecutor refused to budge, and in fact warned Ana that if she allowed Samuel back into the house, she too could be facing charges of child maltreatment for putting her baby at risk. Ana left the courthouse upset and confused, feeling misunderstood, scared, embarrassed, and completely alone. She knew none of her friends and family would understand because no one understood Samuel like she did, and they didn't like him. In fact, the only person she believed she could rely on was the one person who was forbidden to see her—her husband Samuel.

VIOLENCE IN AMERICA

According to the FBI Uniform Crime Reporting, in 2018 there were just over 1.2 million violent crimes committed in the United States (a decrease of about 3.3% from 2017). Violent crime includes murder, rape, aggravated assault (including intimate partner violence and hate crimes), and other crimes that cause serious injuries to others. Overall violent crime is down slightly from 2016, including murder, which has decreased 6.2% from 2017. But rape has increased just over 18% since 2014. Violence is one of the most significant social problems in U.S. society. Consider that there were 417 mass shootings in the United States just in 2019 (Gun Violence Archive, 2020). This is a uniquely U.S. problem not experienced in any other Western country. The number of gun-related homicides in the United States are unparalleled as well, with 73% of murders in the U.S. being caused by firearms, compared to only 3% in the United Kingdom (BBC, 2019). The reason for the high gun-related homicide rate in the United States is presumed to be related to the availability of guns in the U.S. as well as the strong gun culture, which has deep historic roots (Igielnik & Brown, 2017).

The impacts of violent crime are many, affecting families, particularly women and children, when violence occurs between intimates; women and girls when violence involves sexual assault and harassment; and people of color when violence involves firearms. And while gun violence is often gang related, a trend that has recently captured the attention of the entire country (actually, the world) is the extent of systemic racism in the U.S. criminal justice system, including law enforcement agencies, that treats people of color more harshly and more violently than White people. The "War on Drugs"—a Nixon-era policy proclaiming drugs as "enemy number one"—was intended by legislators to target king-pin drug dealers, but instead the well-funded policies were used to target primarily Black youth and young adults, who were often charged as adults and sent to prison for decades

(Cooper, 2015). But that's not all. Police brutality toward people of color, particularly Black Americans, is a significant problem that has only recently gained worldwide attention.

In May and June 2020, millions of people protested in the United States, led by the advocacy organization Black Lives Matter and other racial equity advocacy groups, in response to the killing of George Floyd in Minnesota by a White officer who knelt on his neck for almost nine minutes, despite Floyd claiming that he could not breathe. Floyd's killing was not an isolated incident, but rather was one of several such incidents many experts believe reflect a pattern of historically rooted systemic racism in U.S. law enforcement agencies (Owusu-Bempah, 2017). For instance, research shows that Black Americans are 2.5 to three times more likely to die in police custody compared to White people, despite committing similar offenses and even though Black people are 1.3 times less likely to be armed (Edwards et al., 2019). In fact, despite a common narrative that police killings of Black people are correlated to community violence, research shows that there is no correlation between the two, meaning that many of the communities with comparatively lower levels of violent crime have higher rates of police killings of Black people, and in most of these cases the victims were unarmed (Mapping Police Violence, 2019).

FORENSIC HUMAN SERVICES

Human services providers work with victims of violent crime in a variety of capacities and practice settings, providing advocacy and counseling and engaging in advocacy on a micro and macro level. Human services providers also work with perpetrators of violence in correctional facilities, probation departments, and human services agencies contracted to provide mandated services. Practice areas involving work with violence are often referred to as *forensic human services*, which is a multidisciplinary area focusing broadly on the intersects between human services and the legal, judicial, and corrections systems. Human services providers who work in practice settings dealing with violence are often referred to as forensic human services providers.

The role and function of human services providers working in the area of forensics may vary significantly depending on the legal issues involved, but most forensic human services providers require specialized training in areas such as deviant behavior, crime victimization, crisis counseling, trauma responses, and intervention strategies, and develop a thorough understanding of the legal and criminal justice systems. In this chapter, various types of violence will be explored, such as intimate partner violence (IPV); rape and sexual assault; hate crimes against lesbian, gay, bisexual, transgender, queer/ questioning (LGBTQ) people; and general crime victimization. Ways in which violence impacts victims, including how victims become survivors, will also be explored, as well as how society and those within the human services fields intervene to reduce violence.

INTIMATE PARTNER VIOLENCE

Learning Outcome 11.1   Critically analyze the role of the human services provider in working with survivors of intimate partner violence

IPV involves physical violence, sexual violence, stalking, and psychological aggression toward an intimate partner (Breiding et al., 2015). IPV can occur between current or former spouses, cohabitating partners, boyfriends and girlfriends, dates, and sexual partners. Intimate partners can be either heterosexual or same sex. IPV manifests in many different ways and can include physical violence, economic abuse, psychological or emotional abuse, sexual abuse, and stalking, including **cyberstalking**. Most often, perpetrators of abuse start slowly and lure their partners in through honeymooning them, much like Samuel likely did with Ana in the opening vignette. While some abusive relationships may begin with psychological abuse and control, often the physical abuse doesn't manifest until later in the relationship, once the victim becomes immersed in and dependent on the relationship dynamic (Johnson, 2017).

There are various definitions of the types of abuse that rise to the level of IPV drawn from legislation and empirical research, but in general, *physical violence* can include hitting, punching, slapping, pinching, shoving, and throwing objects at or near the victim, or threatening to do so, or using one's body weight and strength to restrain someone, such as backing someone into a corner and not allowing them to leave. *Sexual violence* can include forced penetration of the abuser or someone else; psychological pressure or coercion to engage in unwanted sexual activity; unwanted sexual contact such as being touched or being forced to touch someone else, and non-contact unwanted sexual activity, such as being forced to watch pornography, or being filmed while engaging in some sexual activity. *Stalking* involves a pattern of repeated unwanted contact or harassment that causes fear, such as making phone calls or sending texts, driving by one's house, monitoring someone online (cyberstalking), leaving notes on cars, and showing up where the victim is present. *Psychological aggression* involves the use of verbal or non-verbal communication to cause another person harm, and to exert control over that person, such as name calling, harassment, taunting, put-downs, ridiculing, coercion, monitoring of one's whereabouts, and use of threats and intimidation to tear another person down and control him or her (Breiding et al., 2015).

IPV is a significant public health problem with consequences that extend far beyond the individuals and families involved in the violence. IPV affects the entire community in lost revenue, lost creativity, mental health problems, and uncompensated medical care. According to the most recent statistics available, over 10 million women and men experience physical violence in an intimate relationship each year in the United States (Smith et al., 2018), resulting in over 1.3 million injuries and 2,350 deaths. One in four women (36.4% or 43.6 million) and 1 in 10 men report having experienced IPV during their lifetimes, including physical violence and psychological aggression. In addition, women who have experienced IPV also experience higher rates of psychological trauma and mental illness, including depression, posttraumatic stress disorder (PTSD), anxiety, worry, nightmares, memory problems, and **suicidal ideation** (Karakurt et al., 2014). Women also have significantly higher rates of physical health problems as a consequence of IPV, such as chronic pain, gynecological problems, HIV/AIDS, other sexually transmitted diseases, gastrointestinal problems, unwanted pregnancy, miscarriage, and premature births (Davis et al., 2018; Kapaya et al., 2019; Wall et al., 2019).

Although men are victims of IPV in heterosexual relationships, women are far more likely targets of violence in intimate relationships, with about 75% of IPV victims being females with male perpetrators and about 25% of victims being males with female perpetrators (Karakurt & Cumbie, 2012). The gendered nature of IPV has long been debated, with the question of whether men and women engage in violent behavior equally. Yet research shows that heterosexual relationships with mutual violence tend to involve conflicts that result in either partner "losing their cool," but rarely result in significant injury

(Karakurt & Cumbie, 2012). A 2012 review of several existing studies on the gendered nature of domestic violence revealed that even when women are the perpetrators of violence against their male partners, most incidences occur in self-defense, an attempt to protect their children, or out of fear when violence is being perpetrated against them by a male partner. In relationships with serious violence—often called "intimate terrorism"—men are much more likely to be perpetrators of IPV with female partners being victims (Swan et al., 2008). In other words, when exploring the gendered nature of IPV, context matters (Myhill, 2017).

In a patriarchal culture, such as the United States, IPV is gendered because the violence is often related to societal power structures (Heise, 1998; Jewkes, R., et al., 2015; Ridgeway & Correll, 2004). For instance, in many countries, women are far likelier to be economically dependent on their male abuser, which contributes to societally supported male dominance (Karakurt & Cumbie, 2012; McCarthy et al., 2018). In addition, a woman may be culturally and/or socially expected to remain in the relationship and endure the abuse because passivity and submission are considered "feminine" in a patriarchal social system, including within some more traditional and conservative religions (Knickmeyer et al., 2010; Sultana, 2010).

Children are often silent witnesses to IPV and can be deeply impacted by the violence for their entire lives.

© SHUTTERSTOCK

Children living in homes with IPV are victims as well, even if the violence is not aimed directly toward them. For instance, children who witness **interparental violence** are at increased risk of experiencing a range of problems including being emotionally, physically, and sexually abused, and developing emotional and behavioral problems that often extend well into adulthood (Crawford, 2016). Children exposed to violence in the home often experience a lifetime of challenges and adversities in their lives such as having violent relationships, vocational problems, substance abuse, and housing insecurity (Carneiro, J. B., et al., 2017; Holt et al., 2008). Research also indicates that boys and girls who witness IPV, particularly against their mother, often respond differently, with boys externalizing their feelings by acting like "warriors" and girls internalizing their feelings by acting like "worriers" (Blair et al., 2015). Additionally, boys who witness interparent violence, where their fathers abuse their mothers, can be socialized to become violent and are more likely to perpetrate violence against women as adults, whereas girls in such situations can be socialized to be submissive and compliant and thus are more likely to enter into a domestic violence relationship (Roberts et al., 2010).

The Cycle of Violence

Lenore Walker (1979, 2016) was the first to coin the phrase *cycle of violence* to describe the pattern of interpersonal violence in intimate relationships.

Walker asserted that most abusive relationships begin in a *honeymoon-like state*, with the abusers often telling their new partners that they are the only people in the world they can trust—the only ones who understand them. New partners are usually swept off their feet with compliments and many promises for a wonderful future. Once the abusers feel comfortable in the relationship, a dual process occurs. The abusers begin to feel vulnerable by recognizing their partner's power to hurt them deeply, and, as familiarity in the relationship increases, the abusers often increase their sense of entitlement to have all their needs met.

Abusers, plagued with fears that they will be abandoned, taken advantage of, and humiliated (as many were in their childhoods) exhibit jealousy and possessiveness, and accusations begin. Emotional immaturity often prevents abusers from being able to separate their internal feelings from possible causes (i.e., are their feelings of jealousy caused by their own insecurities or caused by their partner's unfaithfulness?); thus, a common assumption among batterers is that if they feel bad, then their partners must be doing something to cause their pain. In response to these threatening feelings of vulnerability and entitlement, and poised to be hurt once again, batterers often focus their mistrust, fear, and ultimate rage on their partners. Abusers often misinterpret the intentions of their partners, mentally ticking off injustice after injustice. These types of negative misperceptions and misassumptions are prevalent and are rarely checked against fact.

Walker points out that most partners of batterers will sense the increasing tension brought about by the abusers' underlying anger that is bubbling to the surface. Batterers might ask more questions, make sarcastic comments, ask why two cups are out rather than one, or question why the phone wasn't answered more quickly when they called. They will typically have a short fuse, becoming easily frustrated often without provocation. In response, most victims do their best to "walk on eggshells" to avoid an explosion. But no amount of running interference or offered reassurances will help because the process is an internal one, occurring within the mind of the abuser. In fact, most abusers have an actual need to be proven correct in their fear of being hurt and humiliated again because, to a batterer, being too trusting is often synonymous with being an unsuspecting fool.

Eventually the explosion occurs despite all peacemaking efforts. Abusive rages can take on several forms, including frightening bouts of screaming and yelling; intimidation; and physical abuse such as hitting, kicking, scratching, grabbing, slapping, and shoving. Attacks might also include throwing objects at or near the victim, punching walls, and making threats to harm either the person or the personal property of the victim. Once batterers have experienced a violent rage, they are often temporarily relieved of their internal feelings of rage and in many respects take on the persona of a remorseful child, seeking reassurance and approval. Batterers often "honeymoon" their partners and other family members who were victims of the abuse, promising never to repeat the abusive behavior. There is commonly a manipulative aspect to the batterer's professions of regret and apologies, with the extent of authentic remorse being somewhat questionable. One reason for this is that the batterer's apologies are often riddled with a series of "buts": "I'm sorry I hit you, *but* you know how I hate to be awakened early in the morning." "I'm sorry I shoved you, *but* you know I don't like you talking to other men." "I'm sorry I slapped you, *but* you know how stressed I get when work is so busy."

In my own practice I noticed that during the honeymoon phase, rarely was the batterers' focus authentically placed on the pain and trauma caused to the partner or other family members. Rather, the honeymoon phase involves more of a panicked pleading, begging the victim not to leave, to forgive and forget, to move on quickly by minimizing the extent of the abuse. Statements intended to reframe the abuse, such as "You must be crazy. I can't believe you think I shoved you! I clearly remember me reaching out to you and you jerking away and tripping," are common. These types of manipulations are called *gaslighting*, a term used to describe a partner who intentionally and manipulatively tries to make a partner feel "crazy" and doubt their sanity, as a way of gaining increased control in the relationship (Sweet, 2019). Gaslighting may involve intentionally pretending not to understand or remember something, challenging the victim's recall or memories of abusive events, trivializing an abusive event, or pretending to completely forget what happened. What's important to remember about gaslighting is that it's an intentional effort to confuse the victim and make them question themselves, rendering them more easily manipulated in the future (Tracy, 2012).

Gaslighting and honeymooning can be an immensely confusing time for victims, who usually know instinctively that the batterer needs help, though any attempt to point out a pattern of abuse or to hold the batterer accountable (particularly after the batterer gets comfortable once again and stops apologizing) will hasten the tension-building phase, something victims desperately want to avoid. Attempts to demand authentic change in the abuser often result in the batterer accusing the victim of holding a grudge, being unforgiving, and being punishing. Comments such as, "How dare you rub my face in this when I've already apologized! What do you want me to do? I've already said I'm sorry 100 times. Let's move on!" are common.

With the hope that the honeymoon phase might just last forever, victims of IPV often comply with the dangerous demands of the batterer to relinquish their own sense of reality and accept the reality of the batterer instead—that the abuse was not that bad, that it was a one-time event, and that it will never happen again. Again, this is accomplished through the process of gaslighting. Living in the here-and-now allows both the batterer and the victim to avoid seeing the broader pattern of abuse, which in some respects allows them both to avoid their fear of facing the truth and seriousness of the situation. But no matter how many promises the abusive partner makes or how desperately the victim wants to believe the abuse will never occur again, without intervention the cycle is destined to repeat itself.

Many women find leaving an abusive relationship very difficult, particularly because the cycle of violence means that a honeymoon is right around the corner. But there are other forces at play as well. For instance, many women remain in an abusive relationship citing their love and commitment to their abusive partner, despite the abuse (Smith & Randall, 2007). Such women often have a romanticized view of love as a powerful force that can conquer all, a belief system influenced by American culture, particularly the media (Power et al., 2006). Many women in abusive relationships also cite a fear of being alone (and lonely) as a reason for staying, as well as a strong fear of abandonment (Kunst & van Bon-Martens, 2011).

While some dynamics place certain women at higher risk for domestic violence, for the most part women who are in an abusive relationship or have a history of abusive relationships come from all walks of life. And although there are many theories of shared personality factors, most are not supported by research. Walker (1979, 2016) theorized that many battered women shared a common orientation of **learned helplessness**—the tendency to see oneself as powerless in controlling life events. As such, Walker predicted that battered women would have an external locus of control (the tendency to place control of their lives and choices outside of their domain of responsibility), be more passive in relationships, and have poorer problem-solving skills, compared to women who had not experienced IPV. Research has supported aspects of Walker's theory, but not others. Battered women do tend to have significantly poorer problem-solving skills, and they are also more passive in their relationships, but research does not support Walker's theory that battered women have a more external locus of control (Launius & Lindquist, 1988).

The Kunst and van Bon-Martens study cited above found that loneliness or a fear of being alone increased a person's risk for remaining in a domestic violence relationship. Other research found connections between decisions to remain in an abusive relationship and how battered women attribute causality of the abuse. Women who attribute their partner's abuse to personality factors, such as an inability to manage anger, a refusal to take responsibility for his behavior, or a lack of empathy, are more likely to leave the abusive relationship (Pape & Arias, 2000; Truman-Schram et al., 2000), whereas women who attribute their partners' abusive behavior to forces outside his control, such as work stressors or a bad childhood, are more likely to remain in the relationship (Gordon et al., 2004).

Research also found that women who remain in abusive relationships long term (6 or more years) experience far higher rates of self-blame and unreasonable guilt, often citing guilt associated with self-advocacy (such as calling the police) and a belief that they betrayed their partners (Karakurt et al., 2014). It's important to remember that these studies explored correlations, not causation; thus, it is entirely possible that the abuse itself led to many differences in the personalities of battered women, compared to women who were not in abusive relationships.

Pearson eText

Video Example 11.1

This video explores the impact the novel coronavirus had on domestic violence during the nationwide shutdown. What are some of the challenges associated with using technology to support victims in need of assistance?

https://www.youtube.com/watch?v=KpV9aooweqI

Domestic Violence Practice Settings

One of the most common practice settings where human services providers will encounter survivors of IPV is a **women's shelter**, also sometimes called a battered women's shelter, as well as a **transitional shelter** (long-term housing focused on gaining permanent self-sufficiency). Such shelters typically offer numerous services, including the following:

- A 24-hour hotline for immediate access to information and services
- Immediate safety shelters for domestic violence victims and their children
- Individual counseling for all victims
- Survivor support groups
- Court advocacy
- Children's programs
- Teen programs
- Information referral
- Medical advocates who provide onsite support at hospitals
- Immigrant programs (depending on the ethnic makeup of the community).

Most shelters involve communal living, where residents share their living space with other survivors. Residents are often required to participate in group counseling sessions with other residents and assist with the general functioning and maintenance of the shelter. Human services providers are often assigned to each shelter living space and facilitate inhouse programs to maintain smooth functioning within the home, as well as among the residents. Human services providers will also be likely to engage in individual counseling, case management, and court advocacy. The focus of counseling will likely vary depending on the needs of the residents, but most often focus on educational awareness, life skills, self-sufficiency, and learning about healthy relationships, including healthy parenting, and how to be safe.

It is particularly important for human services providers to be familiar with the Internet and social media, since perpetrators can now easily track a survivor's whereabouts online and may even use social media to harass and intimidate the victim (cyberstalking and **digital abuse**). The growing awareness of ways that perpetrators can track the online activity of victims is reflected in domestic violence awareness websites having "quick escape" buttons that pop up when the page loads. Technology can also help in the fight against IPV through online awareness campaigns, such as the *No More* campaign, which includes actors providing public service announcements using YouTube videos. Facebook is also being used to provide an online space for virtual support groups such as the open Facebook group *Domestic Violence Support Group*.

Intervention Strategies with Survivors of IPV

Working with IPV survivors requires specialized training above generalist human services education that focuses on the unique dynamics commonly at play in abusive relationships. Most human services agencies serving the IPV survivor population require that providers and volunteers complete a 40-plus hour domestic violence training and certification program that focuses on topics such as the following:

- The history of domestic violence
- The complexity of domestic violence
- The impact of violence on victims
- The effect of domestic violence on children
- Cultural competency
- Advocacy strategies for victims
- Legal issues such as orders of protection and domestic violence court.

Because IPV involves an abuse of psychological, sexual, economic, and physical power in order to coerce and oppress a partner, most counseling intervention strategies are based on **empowerment theory**, which focuses on increasing the personal relationship and social power of victims (Goodman & Epstein, 2008). Empowerment theory is based on feminist values of social justice, self-determination (personal choice, finding one's voice), and resiliency (overcoming abuse and oppression) (Cattaneo et al., 2014). Using empowerment theory as the foundation of an intervention strategy relies on a strengths-based approach and focuses on helping clients increase their personal empowerment within the context of their intimate relationship.

There are several theoretical models that can be used when working with survivors of IPV that provide structure and guidance to the clinician and client. A relatively new model is the empowerment process model, developed by Cattaneo and Goodman (2015). The model focuses on clients establishing empowerment goals and taking action to achieve these goals. The actions are based on a client's evolving **self-efficacy** (belief in one's abilities), skills (concrete capabilities), knowledge (information the client must learn to achieve empowerment goals), and access to community resources (formal and informal). In this respect, the empowerment process model utilizes a psychosocial approach to self-empowerment, guiding the process of self-evolution while connecting clients to supportive resources within their communities. The model also encompasses a process of reflection, where clients reflect on their progress and make adjustments to their goals, if necessary.

Cattaneo and Goodman stress the importance of their model as encompassing both *process* and *outcome*. Far too often clients in violent relationships are assessed (and assess themselves) based on whether they leave their abusive relationship and become self-sufficient (psychologically, socially, and economically), and yet the process of achieving interim empowerment goals incrementally are highly valuable in and of themselves. Many clients, for instance, gain a personal sense of empowerment by gaining financial literacy, long before they leave an abusive relationship.

Human services providers using the empowerment process model can work with clients in abusive relationships in every step of their empowerment journey. The various "steps" in the empowerment process are interrelated in the sense that each promotes the others. For instance, providing guidance to a client in goal setting provides opportunities to assist clients in increasing their self-efficacy as they assess their strengths and resources. The process of gaining knowledge, such as learning about their legal rights in a divorce process, naturally leads to skills development as clients explore taking concrete steps to protect their rights, such as contacting an attorney and filing an order of protection. The reflection process can increase clients' self-efficacy as they reflect on their progress and all that they've accomplished. Again, it is important to note that "accomplishments" do not necessarily mean leaving an abusive relationship, as there are numerous areas of accomplishment leading up to that point that providers can acknowledge, thus increasing a client's sense of personal empowerment.

What is so powerful about the empowerment process model is that the authors take into account the context within which a victim of domestic violence lives, and how it is their context that creates meaning in their everyday decisions to seek safety for themselves and their children. This context is different for every client and can vary dramatically from survivor to survivor. Rather than imposing options for survivors based on a clinician's or agency's timeline or goals, Goodman et al. (2016) suggest using a survivor-defined approach that takes into consideration the unique situation of clients and the complexity of their lives.

Using a survivor-defined approach considers clients within the context of their environments, encouraging providers to consider factors such as the client's cultural background, including their immigration status, their family situations, their financial status, their level of support outside the relationship, and so on. It's the unique complexity of survivors' lives that influences their individual goals and the path to achieve their goals (Goodman et al., 2009). Two clients can have the same goal of leaving an abusive relationship but depending on contextual factors in their lives their decision making may be quite different.

Consider the college-educated client who is in an abusive relationship with a husband of 3 years, has no children, has remained in the workforce, has a large support network, and has independent financial resources. Now consider the client who has been married for 15 years to an abusive partner, has three children under the age of 10, has been out of the workforce for over 10 years, did not graduate from high school, has few marketable skills, who is a Mexican immigrant with residency status dependent on her marital status, has very little family in the United States, comes from a family with intergenerational abuse, and has a history of substance abuse. Both women have the goal of leaving their abusive partners, but their paths will be quite different.

It's often tempting for clinicians, particularly those working in domestic violence agencies (such as transitional shelters) to push clients along, imposing timelines and enforcing goals (this is particularly common in transitional shelters). However, such a directive approach risks the clinician becoming just another external force exerting control in the client's life, which can have a devastating effect on the client's self-esteem and can also discourage continued engagement in the counseling process. Using a survivor-defined approach with the empowerment process model not only acknowledges (and in many respects honors) the unique circumstances of each client's life but also allows clients to take control of their lives, empowering them to take an active role in planning their future and their decision making, which increases their sense of autonomy, self-esteem, and self-efficacy.

Violence Against Women Act

In 1994 the federal government passed the Violence Against Women Act of 1994. The Violence Against Women Act (VAWA) established policies and mandates for how states were to handle cases of domestic violence, sexual assault, and dating violence (including stalking). The Act's policies and mandates included encouraging mandatory arrests, encouraging interstate enforcement of domestic violence laws, maintaining state databases on incidents of domestic violence, and establishing a national domestic violence database. This Act also provided for numerous grants for educational purposes (e.g., the education of police officers and judges), a domestic violence hotline, battered women's shelters, and improvements in the safety of public areas such as public transportation and parks.

The Violence Against Women Act spurred several states to pass similar legislation, which continues to change the nature of domestic violence prosecutions. With regard to current policies on the prosecution of domestic violence, it is important to note that, unlike a civil case, where a plaintiff brings an action and thus has the right to subsequently drop the case, in criminal cases the plaintiff is the state and the victims are witnesses. But in the past, prosecutors have allowed victims to drop a case (typically at the urgings of the batterer). Domestic violence legislation has for the most part put a stop to this practice. Instead, domestic violence is typically treated as any other crime where the victim is called as a witness and must appear at the trial to testify on behalf of the state. This can create emotional tension for victims, who may initially want court involvement immediately after experiencing violence, but then want to resist any intervention when the honeymoon phase begins and renewed hope for authentic change seems possible. Since the passage of the Violence Against Women Act, incidents of domestic violence have been cut by more than half, and the national hotline handles about 22,000 calls per month.

VAWA was reauthorized in 2000, in 2005 as the Violent Crime Control and Law Enforcement Act, and again, after a fierce bipartisan battle, in 2013, focusing on the expanded coverage of the legislation. Prior to the 2013 reauthorization, VAWA did not protect all women who were victims of domestic violence, sexual assault, and dating violence and stalking. The reauthorization, signed into law March 7, 2013, by then-President Obama, extended protection to Native women, immigrants (including undocumented immigrants), and same-sex couples (the source of the bipartisan controversy). VAWA was up for reauthorization in 2019 and the House introduced and passed H.R. 1585 in April 2019, which included some important changes and updates to the bill (Violence Against Women Reauthorization Act, 2019). H.R. 1585 was sent to the Senate for review and approval shortly thereafter, but to date, the bill has not put up for a vote; thus, VAWA has not been reauthorized. There are many reasons for this, but most notably, Senate Republicans (who were in the majority in 2020) note key areas of the reauthorization that they believe are controversial, despite bipartisan support in the House.

The sticking points center on a few key forms, including broadening the definition of domestic violence to include "boyfriends" and not just married or cohabiting couples; new provisions that would offer increased protections for Native American women, including increasing tribal access to national crime databases and increasing tribal authority over non-Native perpetrators of IPV (including sexual assault and trafficking) when the victim is a member of a federally recognized tribe (Agoyo, 2019); and increased protections for victims of bullying, with increased support for prevention education on college campuses, specifically campus health centers. Senate Republicans' concerns about these proposed changes are detailed in the conservative policy think tank, the Heritage Foundation's 2019 Backgrounder report, which reflect more traditional notions of gender roles and concerns that the changes in the reauthorization were just too significant (Jipping, 2019).

Intervention Strategies with Batterers

Strategies for reducing recidivism rates among batterers have varied through the years, with some approaches involving punishment via the criminal justice system and other strategies focusing on court-mandated psychological intervention. In the past the criminal justice system sought traditional forms of justice for those convicted of domestic violence in the form of incarceration. However, this approach was often unsuccessful because some judges were reluctant to break apart families and some victims of domestic violence were reluctant to testify against their partners or spouses, particularly if it meant the possibility of incarceration. In response, many states developed specialized domestic violence courts with the goal of incorporating mental health and **psychoeducational approaches**, such as empowerment theory anger management training, in lieu of jail. If defendants successfully completed a batterer intervention program (BIP), their sentences were vacated, but if they did not, or if they engaged in repeated violence, their sentences were reinstated.

Many BIPs are based upon the Duluth Model—a psychoeducational program drawn from feminist theory, which posits that domestic violence is caused by a patriarchal ideology that promotes the concept that men have the right to control their female partners. Many BIPs are also based upon group treatment using cognitive behavioral therapy (CBT) and anger management training, although anger management training alone is insufficient because it does not address the underlying values of **patriarchy** and control (anger is not the root of the problem, but rather a tool used by the batterer). Newer programs use a multifaceted treatment design, based on the premise that battering is a complex problem encompassing a deeply rooted belief system of power and control; thus, a combination of psychoeducation, CBT, and anger management in a group setting is more likely to be successful.

Programs range in duration from 6 weeks to 1 year and are often mandated by the court as a part of sentencing. Batterers are taught to respect personal boundaries, the difference between feelings and actions, the concept of personal rights, the nature of violence, conflict interruption techniques, communication skills, and the nature of egalitarian relationships. Dynamics of **social learning theory**, including modeling, are also explored so participants can discover how their violent behavior is likely patterned after a parent or some other influential person in their lives. Participants also learn how to identify their personal triggers and learn strategies for managing their anger, including how to control impulses and how to use "I" statements to avoid getting caught up in making accusations.

Most batterer treatment programs have similar goals, including increasing awareness of violent behavior and encouraging the batterer to take responsibility for violent behavior. Common program philosophies include the following beliefs:

- Violence is an intentional act
- Domestic violence uses physical force and intimidation as coercive methods to obtain and maintain control in the relationship
- Using violence is a learned behavior and as such can be unlearned.

Whether BIPs are effective overall is a question that remains for the most part unanswered, but there has been increasing clarity in more recent studies. A 2003 study commissioned by the U.S. Department of Justice found little support for the success of batterer intervention programs with regard to recidivism rates or attitudes toward domestic violence. The only significant difference found was in the recidivism rates of men who completed programs 26 weeks or longer. While these men had significantly lower recidivism rates, their attitudes about domestic violence did not appear to change much. For instance, men in the experimental group (the batterer intervention program) viewed their partners only slightly less responsible for the battering incident than men in the control group. A follow-up study on the Duluth Model in 2014 found that about one-third of participants eventually reoffended, and those who completed at least 24 weeks of treatment experienced the most positive outcomes among all participants, defined as decreases in physical and verbal aggression (Herman et al., 2014).

Other research on the effectiveness of BIPs found that a key factor in successfully completing the program (defined as authentic change and low recidivism rates) focused on participants' readiness to change—a batterer's personal motivation to effect a meaningful change in their attitudes and behaviors about violence and control in intimate relationships. Motivation to change was assessed through **motivational interviewing** assessments, as well as through the manner in which a participant entered a program (court-ordered vs. self-referral). The studies found that participants who were ready to change had far higher success rates after completing a batterer intervention program than those who had little motivation to change (Bowen & Gilchrist, 2010; Zalmanowitz et al., 2012). While these results may not seem surprising, they can be helpful for practitioners and other professionals working in the area of domestic violence in terms of assessing high-risk perpetrators, making sentencing decisions (based on assessments of who is most amenable to treatment), and exploring ways to increase clients' motivations and readiness to change.

More recent research examining differences in the traits of resistant participants versus responsive participants has been more definitive. For instance, a 2018 study found that certain factors tend to create barriers to responsiveness, such as having perpetrator attitudes about IPV, possessing hypermasculine attitudes, being exposed to violence as children, having co-occurring mental health issues, and denying or minimizing the abuse or blaming their partners for the abuse (Morrison et al., 2018). Another study found that perpetrators with an external locus of control (blaming others for their problems and having a "victim mentality") were far more resistant to change, but perpetrators who attended a program longer experienced more significant positive change (Carbajosa et al., 2017). The approach and style of BIP facilitators makes a big difference with participants as well, with a nonjudgmental attitude significantly reducing resistance among participants (Morrison et al., 2019). Thus, while the research on the effectiveness of BIP has been somewhat mixed, more recent research studies that dig a bit deeper into personality traits and attitudes of participants have yielded very useful information for human services providers working with male perpetrators of violence.

RAPE AND SEXUAL ASSAULT

Learning Outcome 11.2   Examine the complex nature of rape and sexual assault

Another form of violence against a person is the act of rape or sexual assault. Sexual assault involves forcing some form of sexual act on another person without his or her consent. Determining the rate of sexual assault in the United States is difficult due to dramatic variations in the way sexual assault is defined. Although both men and women can be raped, women are victims of rape far more often than men. Approximately 1 in 5 women in the United States have been raped sometime during their lifetime, and more than half of them were raped by intimate partners (Black et al., 2011).

For the first time since 1927, the legal definition of forcible rape has been changed. According to the Uniform Crime Reports, the former definition was "the carnal knowledge of a female, forcibly and against her will." That definition, unchanged since 1927, was outdated and narrow. It only included forcible male penile penetration of a female vagina. The new definition is "[t]he penetration, no matter how slight, of the vagina or anus with any body part or object, or oral penetration by a sex organ of another person, without the consent of the victim." This is an important victory for advocates since this expanded definition now includes rape of both genders, rape with an object, and sexual acts with anyone who cannot give consent due to mental or physical disability.

According to the National Crime Victimization Survey (NCVS), there were 150,420 victims of rape or sexual assault (attack or attempted attack, including unwanted sexual contact) in 2014 (compared to 173,610 in 2013 and 118,700 in 2012), of which only about one-third were reported to police (Truman & Langton, 2015). About 75% of all women who were raped were assaulted by perpetrators they knew, and about 25% were assaulted by strangers. Black women are raped at a higher rate (relative to the population) than White or Hispanic women, and indigenous populations (Native Americans, Alaskan Natives, Hawaiian Natives, and Pacific Islanders) are 2.5 times more likely to experience violent sexual assault in their lifetimes.

The Controversy Surrounding Rape

There is considerable controversy surrounding rape statistics, including the methodology used to collect data, how questions are phrased, and even how rape and sexual assault are defined. Consider, for example, that according to the Centers for Disease Control and Prevention's (CDC) National Intimate Partner and Sexual Violence Survey, about 2 million adult women were raped in 2011. Compare this statistic to the U.S. Department of Justice NCVS, which estimated that there were 238,000 rapes and sexual assaults reported in 2011 (U.S. Department of Justice, 2011). Why is there such a difference in estimates? First, the NCVS statistic includes only reported incidents of rape and sexual assault, and such incidents tend to be highly underreported. Second, critics cite some gender bias in the CDC survey such as questions designed to elicit an affirmative response from women but a negative response from men (Young, 2014).

Consider that the CDC definition for rape or sexual assault against women is quite broad, whereas for men, it is quite narrow. For instance, the CDC survey includes incapacitated sexual acts—defined as sexual activity when the respondent was too intoxicated to consent—for women only. Incapacitated sexual acts constituted two thirds of all reported rapes in the CDC survey, yet did not include instructions to rule out instances of voluntary sex while intoxicated. Further, the CDC defined rape of men as forcible sexual activity by another man, but did not include instances where men were too incapacitated to consent to sexual activity with women, or instances where men were forced to penetrate a woman or receive or give oral sex to a woman (rather, these were included as "other sexual violence").

In other words, if a man reports being forced to have sexual intercourse with a woman, the CDC classifies that not as rape, but as "sexual coercion" or "other sexual violence," but if a woman reports being forced to have sexual intercourse with a man, or having sex while intoxicated (voluntarily or involuntarily), that is considered rape. Are the differences in definitions fair? Do they factually represent qualitative differences in sexual experiences where men have more power in society than women? Or do they reflect gender-based stereotypes where men always want sex (regardless of who it is with) and women are not responsible for the choices they make, even the foolish ones?

Does presuming women are always victims and cannot be perpetrators of violence accurately capture the culture of rape and patriarchy in our society, or does it rob women of their free choice and agency? Some critics of the CDC approach believe that the latter is true, and that such an attitude trivializes the problem of female-perpetrated assaults on men (Young, 2014). Treating sexual assault in a gender-neutral manner may sound good on the surface, but, on the other hand, the question must be asked whether this approach trivializes the long-standing problem of violence against women in our society. If this is the case, then perhaps relying on gender-contextualized definitions of rape and sexual assault is the most effective way of reflecting longstanding and deeply rooted gender power disparities in society. What do you believe?

Sexual Assaults on College Campuses

The problem of sexual assault on college campuses, particularly **incapacitated sex**, has gained considerable attention and generated significant controversy, in the past few years, in large part due to several high-profile on-campus rape allegations. The attention was warranted because of the alarming rate of sexual assaults on college campuses across the country, particularly incapacitated sex, and the perceived general indifference on the part of many college administrators. According to a 2019 study by the American Association of Universities (AAU) of 181,752 students across 33 U.S. college campuses, 13% of all respondents had been sexually assaulted or had been subjected to nonconsensual sexual contact such as harassment or stalking. This study was a follow-up to a 2015 AAU study and showed that sexual assault and nonconsensual sexual contact, including incapacitated sex, is on the rise (Cantor & Fischer, 2015; Cantor et al., 2020).

According to the 2019 study, sexual assault is far more common among certain groups, such as undergraduate females and transgender, **genderqueer**, and nonconforming (TGQN) students, compared to students enrolled in graduate and professional programs. For instance, 59% of undergraduate females reported being sexually harassed on campus, 14% reported experiencing IPV, and 10% reported being stalked on campus. TGQN students reported even higher rates of sexual victimization, with 65% reporting being sexually harassed on campus, 21% reporting being a victim of IPV, and 15% reporting being stalked on campus. The study also found that while most students (65%) surveyed believed that campus administrators would take sexual assaults seriously, fewer than half (45%) believed administrators wouldn't take their complaints seriously (nonconsensual sexual contact or the inability to consent to sexual activity seriously) (Cantor et al., 2020).

Unfortunately, there have been a few high-profile cases involving false allegations, such as the *Rolling Stone* magazine story of "Jackie," the college student from the University of Virginia who alleged being gang raped by a group of fraternity members (Coronel et al., 2015a). Jackie's story did not stand up to scrutiny, and *Rolling Stone* ultimately recanted the story, leading to a flurry of accusations and counter-accusations and threatening to diminish the seriousness of college sexual assault (Coronel et al., 2015b). Despite the very few highly publicized and very damaging false allegations, as well as controversies related to how statistics are calculated, the nature of campus policies and their effectiveness, and the effectiveness and equity in universities' responses, the problem of rape and sexual assault in the United States, and particularly on college campuses, is very serious and in need of continued attention and scrutiny. One area of further examination is to evaluate what factors on college campuses may be contributing to increased assaults on campus, and how colleges can strike an equitable balance between ensuring accused students have an opportunity to defend themselves, while at the same time ensuring that survivors are treated with respect and dignity and are not subjected to further humiliation. Hiring highly trained human services providers who can provide on-campus trauma-informed counseling and advocacy is also vitally important.

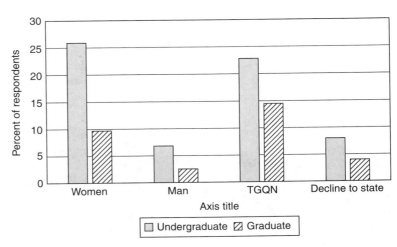

Figure 11.1 Percent reporting nonconsensual sexual contact involving physical force or inability to consent or stop what was happening since enrolling in the school by gender and affiliation.

Recognizing the role patriarchy has played in creating a culture that stigmatizes female victims and makes excuses for male offenders does not negate the existence or seriousness of female-on-male rape. Sexual assault is a complex social problem that involves an abuse of power, most often targeting members of the population that lack power within society. Thus, while all forms of sexual assault warrant a serious response, rape and sexual assault targeting populations that have historically lacked power in society, such as women, particularly women of color, is at the core of sexual assault advocacy for women. Online advocacy movements using social media have had a particularly powerful effect on patriarchal attitudes toward sex, gender roles, and what is now considered appropriate behavior in the workplace.

Consider the #MeToo movement that exploded on Twitter and other social media platforms in 2017. The #MeToo hashtag was originally created in 2006 by Tarana Burke, a social justice activist in Brooklyn, New York. Burke used the hashtag on MySpace, the social media predecessor to Facebook, to provide women of color a place to share their stories of sexual abuse. On October 15, 2017, in response to the widespread accusations

A marcher at the 2016 Women's March carries a sign with the popular hashtag #MeToo used to bring awareness to sexual harassment against women.

of sexual harassment and sexual assault against the famous and very powerful film producer Harvey Weinstein, actress and social justice activist Alyssa Milano tweeted a very simple request to her followers. She asked them to reply to her tweet with "me too" if they had ever been sexually harassed or assaulted.

The tweet went viral and to date over 60,000 women have responded to her, with thousands more posting original posts with #MeToo stories. The goal of the tweet, according to Milano, was to raise awareness of the magnitude of the problem of sexual harassment and sexual assault against women, particularly by powerful men. And the #MeToo social media movement did just that. One year later there were over 19 million social media posts from around the globe using the #MeToo hashtag (Anderson & Toor, 2018). This powerful social movement had and continues to have many positive outcomes. It's raised awareness about the extent of sexual misconduct in the workplace, and it brought down over 200 powerful men accused of sexual harassment, including comedian Louis C.K., television host Charlie Rose, network executives, and several Republican and Democratic politicians (Carlsen et al., 2018). And in March 2020 Harvey Weinstein was sentenced to 23 years on prison for sex crimes.

Why Men Rape Women

An important factor in prevention is understanding why men rape women, which includes being able to distinguish fact from myths. One of the more common myths of why rape occurs includes blaming the victim by asserting that the victim wanted it, liked it, or in some way deserved the sexual assault because she provoked the assailant (by dressing or acting provocatively, etc.). Myths about rapists include assertions that men just cannot control their sexual desires and thus are not responsible for sexually assaulting women (Burt, 1991). The damage done by the proliferation of these rape myths is plentiful because they blame the victim while exonerating the perpetrator, which undermines societal prohibitions against sexual violence. In fact, a 1998 study at University of Mannheim in Germany (Bohner et al., 1998) found that such myths actually encourage sexual assault by giving rapists a way of rationalizing their antisocial behavior. In other words, although Western social customs may claim to abhor rape, popular rape myths provide rapists a way around such social mores by encouraging the belief that victims in some way asked for it and that men simply cannot control themselves, and thus they really haven't done anything wrong, or at least nothing that many other men haven't done as well.

Exploring what influences men (and women) to accept rape myths is important because this information can inform providers working with both perpetrators and survivors. For instance, a 2018 study found that men who expressed the desire to join a fraternity were more likely to score higher on the "rape myth scale" compared to men who were not interested in Greek life (Seabrook et al., 2018). This information can influence education and training programs for both advisors and fraternity members.

Pearson eText

Video Example 11.2

This video explores the rate of rape on college campuses. What are three ways that human services professionals effectively address the stigma that often discourages women from reporting rape?

https://www.youtube.com/watch?v=4f9YnSr1U2M

Research has also shown that men who are heavy users of social media tend to more readily accept rape myths and have more patriarchal views on sexuality (McCoy, 2020). Attitudes about rape, including what "real" rape is and how a "real" rape victim should behave, have significant implications for survivors of assault. Consider how the attitudes of jury members serving on sexual assault trials might influence their judgments. Those who have more traditional attitudes about rape and sexuality (those who embrace rape myths) will undoubtedly base their decisions about the veracity of victim testimonies on those attitudes, which in turn can significantly impact the possibility of achieving justice for sexual assault survivors (Leverick, 2020).

Male Victims of Sexual Assault

Men are also victims of sexual assault, in the form of child sexual abuse, same-sex date rape, male-on-male stranger rape, prison rape, and female-on-male rape. Research on male-on-male sexual assault is sparse, with the exception of some early efforts to identify the nature and dynamics of male rape and some more recent studies that have examined perceptions of male-on-male rape. The reason for the lack of studies in this area may be related to the belief that male rape is rare, at least outside prison walls. In fact, historically, the legal definition of rape does not even account for the possibility of men being victims.

Due to the stigma associated with being a victim of male-on-male sexual assault, most incidences of rape go unreported, and thus it is impossible to accurately assess incidence rates. Even rapes that occur in prisons often go unreported, not only because of the fear of retaliation, but also because of the shame men feel in response to being victimized in this manner. Additionally, research shows that most people surveyed do not believe men can be raped because of the perception that most men are strong enough to resist (Ballman et al., 2016). Thus, while male-on-male rape may involve gay men or straight men, most people have very limited awareness of the nature of this type of sexual assault and may even assume the assault was a normative part of a same-sex relationship (Ioannou et al., 2017). But male-on-male rape does exist, and the incidence may be growing, particularly in prison settings and the military (Matthews et al., 2018). Overall male-on-male rape tends to be more violent than other types of sexual assault, frequently resulting in genital injury (Ioannou et al., 2017).

Treating men who have been sexually assaulted is similar in some respects to serving the female survivor population except that the shame men feel, although equal in intensity, tends to be more focused on their gender identity as males. Heterosexual men who were victims of male-on-male rape reported questioning their sexual identity and orientation because they were unable to fight off their attackers. Men also have a greater tendency to turn to alcohol and drugs in response to the rape. Men also experience sexual dysfunction and problems getting close to people, particularly in intimate relationships. In addition, as is the case with female victims, some male victims become sexually promiscuous after a sexual assault or abuse (Burgess & Carretta, 2016; Mezey & King, 1989).

More studies need to be conducted on both female-on-male rape and male-on-male rape, particularly on the differing dynamics of sexual assault in ethnic minority populations and contexts, such as military rapes, including differences in perceptions of male rape victims (Matthews et al., 2018). What research there is on ethnic minority populations seems to indicate that victims of sexual assault who are White and have higher levels of academic education tend to seek mental health counseling more often than victims of color or those with less education (Ullman & Brecklin, 2002; Vearnals &

Campbell, 2001). This certainly has practical implications for human services providers who through assessment or advocacy have the opportunity to reach out to survivors of sexual assault and abuse.

The Psychological Impact of Sexual Assault

The physical and psychological impact of sexual assault is serious and long lasting and may include PTSD, depression, increased anxiety (Carey et al., 2018), fear of risk taking, development of trust issues, increased physical problems including exposure to sexually transmitted diseases such as HIV/AIDS, chronic pelvic pain, gastrointestinal disorders, and unwanted pregnancy (CDC, 2005). Lynda Holmstrom and Ann Burgess (1975) coined the term "**rape trauma syndrome**" (RTS), a collection of emotions similar to PTSD and commonly experienced in response to forced violent sexual assault. RTS includes an initial phase where the survivor experiences both psychological and physical symptoms, such as feeling extreme fear, persistent crying, and sleep disturbances, as well as other reactions to the actual assault such as the common fear of being killed during the assault.

Survivors in subsequent phases avoid social interaction, experience a loss of self-esteem, feel inappropriate guilt, and in some cases develop clinical depression. Many survivors minimize their feelings and reactions to the assault and avoid seeking treatment because they do not want to be stigmatized, which can contribute to RTS. In fact, one of the primary reasons most rape crisis advocates refer to clients as "survivors" rather than as "victims" is to reduce this stigma by focusing on the strength it takes to survive sexual violence. The specialized nature of RTS is why it's important that any human services provider working with survivors use a trauma-informed approach, which recognizes the vast extent of impacts on survivors and their trauma adaptations (including the role of power within relationships and society) with a goal of increasing personal empowerment while decreasing opportunities for retraumatization (DePrince & Gagnon, 2018).

Rape Crisis Centers

Human services providers working in any practice setting will likely encounter a victim of sexual assault at some point in their careers. This might involve a recent victim seeking support services on the heels of an assault, but it is far more likely that rape victims will present for counseling at some point long after an assault, perhaps even years later, and might not even connect the problems they are currently experiencing with a past sexual assault.

Human services providers who work directly with victims of sexual assault usually do so at a rape crisis center or sexual assault advocacy organization. Many states require that each county have at least one rape crisis center that offers a wide range of services including a 24-hour hotline, around-the-clock on-site advocacy during medical examinations and investigative interviews, and crisis counseling, as well as long-term individual and group counseling.

Many human services providers who work with sexual assault victims receive from 40 to 50 hours of specialized training focusing on the history of the rape crisis movement, the nature of crisis counseling, the dynamics of RTS, rape myths, and the dangers of gender oppression. Training also includes information on normal child and adult developmental stages and how these stages are affected by sexual violence and trauma.

HATE CRIMES AGAINST LGBTQ PEOPLE

Learning Outcome 11.3   Explore the treatment of LGBTQ and gender nonconforming people in the United States

Historically, individuals (primarily men) who were "homosexual" were considered sinful and immoral, committing "unnatural acts," called either sodomy or buggery. Men who were suspected of engaging in "homosexual behavior" were often subjected to inhumane and unscientific examinations of their anuses in an attempt to determine whether sexual intercourse with another man had occurred (this type of examination is still occurring in some parts of the world). In fact, not only were same-sex relationships criminalized in the United States, they were considered a mental disorder by the American Psychiatric Association until 1973.

One of the most powerful legal mechanisms for criminalizing same-sex relationships is anti-sodomy laws, which typically prohibit oral and anal sex between consenting adults. The most common characterization of "sodomy" in the context of these laws and same-sex relationships is that sodomy is an "abomination and detestable crime against nature." The U.S. Supreme Court case *Lawrence v. Texas* challenged Texas' sodomy law and invalidated similar laws across the nation (*Lawrence* v. *Texas*, 2003). In 2020 there were 12 states that still had sodomy laws in place, despite the 2003 decision. These states include Alabama, Florida, Idaho, Kansas, Louisiana, Michigan, Mississippi, North Carolina, Oklahoma, South Carolina, Texas, and Utah, and according to advocates, these laws are still used as a mechanism to harass members of the LGBTQ communities (Villarreal, 2019).

Many of the hateful acts committed against members of LGBTQ people can be better understood if viewed through the lens of **homophobia**—the irrational dread of, hostility toward, and prejudice against members of **LGBTQ populations**. Although the term "homophobia" is now perceived as somewhat limiting in the sense that it does not capture the totality of oppression and discrimination that the LGBTQ community has experienced, considered in a broader context, it can be useful in better understanding anti-gay attitudes rooted in stigma and sexual prejudice (Herek, 2009). Acceptance and support of LGBTQ people has been on the rise in the United States for several years, but a national survey conducted in 2018 by the Gay and Lesbian Alliance Against Defamation (GLAAD) and the Harris Poll found that acceptance and support are declining, particularly among millennials, a group that previously had the largest number of allies.

The decline in acceptance and support of LGBTQ people began in 2016, continued in 2017, and seemed to have stabilized in 2018. Examples of some of the questions on the survey include asking respondents whether they would be uncomfortable if their child's teacher was LGBT, if their child came out as LGBT, seeing an LGBT co-worker's wedding photos, or learning that their physician was LGBT. Heterosexual males between the ages of 18 and 34 had the highest increase in discomfort and the most significant declines in being allies, compared to any other group (Harris Poll, 2019). Interestingly, according to a recent Gallup Poll, support for same-sex marriage has never been higher (67%), but clearly not among all groups (McCarthy, 2020).

GLAAD points out that incidents of discrimination against LGBTQ people (or those presumed to be LGBTQ) have increased during this same time period as well. Examples of recent hate crimes against LGBTQ people include physical attacks, for instance, when a same-sex couple is seen holding hands; verbal harassment, such as calling LGBTQ people derogatory names; sexual harassment and assault against lesbians and transgender

Dennis and Judy Shepard donated personal papers and objects from their son, Matthew Shepard, a young gay college student who was murdered in October 1998 in Wyoming to the Smithsonian National Museum of American History in Washington, DC.

© PATSY LYNCH/SHUTTERSTOCK

people, such as sexual groping; and destruction of personal property, such as destroying Pride flags (GLAAD, 2019). Crimes against the LGBTQ people are not limited to physical assault or harassment. There have been numerous incidents of LGBTQ people being murdered for no reason other than their sexual orientation and gender expression.

On October 6, 1998, at around 8:00 p.m., a 21-year-old gay Wyoming college student Matthew Shepard was kidnapped by two men, driven to a remote area, tied to a fence, beaten ruthlessly, and left for dead. The perpetrators, both 21-year-old locals, saw Shepard in a bar and pretended to be gay in order to gain Shepard's trust. They targeted him because he was gay and their attack and ultimate murder of him was an intentional act. The two men could not be charged with a hate crime because at the time, sexual orientation, gender, and gender identity were not protected classes in existing hate crimes legislation. In response to this heinous crime and the work of social justice advocates, in October 2009 then-President Obama signed into law the Matthew Shepard & James Byrd, Jr. Hate Crimes Prevention Act (Pub. L. No. 111- 84). This act makes it a federal crime to assault individuals because of their sexual orientation, gender, or gender identity. The passage of this somewhat contested legislation has been lauded by civil rights organizations as a significant step forward in the fight for equality and protection of LGBTQ people. However, far more must be done, particularly since hate crimes against LGBTQ people tend to be grossly underreported, particularly crimes that are extremely violent (Human Rights Campaign, 2013).

LGBTQ people are acutely aware of the risks they face, and even if they haven't personally been targeted, the high number of hate crimes targeting this population can lead to a sort of **vicarious trauma**. This dynamic is reflected in a 2019 Pride Poll, which found that 57% of LGBTQ people surveyed reported being concerned about becoming victims of a hate crime, and of these, 16% reported being very afraid (Whitman Insight Strategies and Buzzfeed News, 2019). These percentages become even more meaningful when compared to that of the general population, where only about 6% of people reported being concerned about becoming a victim of a hate crime, and over half of the general population reported no concerns at all about hate violence (Marzullo et al., 2009).

The vulnerability of LGBTQ people to be marginalized in society and experience injustice and violence due to their sexual orientation and gender identity expression is magnified considerably with increasing levels of vulnerability. The interaction between multiple aspects of identity, such as gender, race, class, and sexual orientation, and their impact on social inequality is often referred to as the intersectionality of vulnerability (Wallace & Santacruz, 2017). In the context of sexual orientation, the theory of intersectionality posits that incidents of societal oppression in the form of various types of social injustice, such as racism, sexism, **ableism**, **ageism**, and homophobia do not act independent of one another, and in fact interact, creating increasingly magnified forms of social oppression depending on the number of vulnerabilities an individual possesses.

While all women experience some form of gender bias, an economically disadvantaged Black woman will experience more social oppression than a middle-class White woman, because of the two identity categories of vulnerability (racial minority and poverty). However, add sexual orientation, a complex identity category, and the intersection of race, gender, sexual orientation, and perhaps gender identity expression, and gender nonconformance will significantly increase this individual's vulnerability to social oppression, injustice, and bias-based violence (Meyer, 2012). In fact, transgendered women of color are disproportionately targeted in hate crimes (Chestnut et al., 2013).

Human services providers working with a diverse population may not be aware of the sexual orientation or gender identity of their clients but can more effectively advocate for them if they remain open to disclosures and remain aware of the vulnerability of LGBTQ people to marginalization, **micro-aggressions**, and violence. Clients may or may not initially disclose orientation and gender identity due to fear of stigmatization; thus, developing cultural competence in working with these populations is vitally important, as a provider's awareness and sensitivity will increase the likelihood that clients will feel more at ease disclosing any negative experiences.

Hate crimes targeting populations perceived as different in some way remain a serious problem, despite attempts to stop them through awareness campaigns and legislation. LGBTQ people remain targets of hate crimes, which can have a lasting impact on those who are victimized, as well as their family and friends. Even if a member of the LGBTQ community is not personally a victim of bias-based violence, research shows that many within this population are afraid they will be; thus, the experience of vicarious trauma is common. Creating an accepting environment and incorporating trauma-informed therapies into the counseling of LGBTQ and **gender nonconforming populations** can have a positive effect on clients who have experienced hate crimes and other types of violence.

Pearson eText

Video Example 11.3

This video explores the increase hate crimes committed against transexual women of color. Identify the intersectionality experienced by this population?

https://www.youtube.com/watch?v=W-caWqO441I

WORKING WITH VICTIMS OF VIOLENT CRIME

Historically, victims of crime had virtually no rights in criminal proceedings because the U.S. criminal justice system is based on the presumption of innocence. Because defendants charged with a criminal offense are innocent until proven guilty, legally there can be no victims until after a verdict is rendered. If there are no victims prior to a defendant being convicted, then there are no rights to enforce. In addition, in criminal proceedings the case is considered an action committed against the state, and thus other than being a witness, historically, victims of crime have had no special status. This logic, which is consistent with the U.S. criminal justice system, is completely backward for most victims and victim advocates.

The victims' rights movement gained momentum in the 1980s when victims of crime came together along with advocates in the human services fields to secure both a voice within the criminal justice community and some basic rights in the criminal justice system. The victims' movement is based not on the desire to lessen the rights of criminal defendants, but rather on the desire to increase the rights of victims. Rights include being notified of court hearings, appearing at all legal proceedings, making a statement at sentencing, and being kept apprised of the incarceration status of the perpetrator. Most crime victims and victim advocates state that a primary goal of the victims' movement is to ensure that crime victims have a voice within the community, specifically within the criminal justice system (Mika et al., 2004). How that voice gets heard is certainly up for debate. Whether through direct face-to-face meetings with criminal justice officials or through the active involvement in victim-sensitive training of police personnel, prosecutors, and judges, victims advocacy groups continue to work toward a system that sees victims as a central aspect of the criminal justice process (Quinn, 1998).

In response to the victims' movement and subsequent federal legislation (42 U.S.C. § 10606[b]), all states now have a Victim's Bill of Rights ensuring certain basic rights to victims as well as protection for victims of violent crime. Although there is some variation from state to state, most states ensure that victims of violent crime be afforded the following rights:

- The right to be treated with dignity and fairness and with respect for the victim's dignity and privacy
- The right to be reasonably protected from the accused offender
- The right to be notified of court proceedings
- The right to be present at all public court proceedings related to the offense, unless the court determines that testimony by the victim would be materially affected if the victim heard other testimony at trial
- The right to confer with the attorney for the government in the case
- The right to restitution
- The right to information about the conviction, sentencing, imprisonment, and release of the offender (Victim's Rights Act of 1998).

Victim–Witness Assistance Programs

In response to federal legislation and Victim's Bill of Rights, state prosecution units within prosecutors' offices (state's attorney, district attorney, and attorney general offices) developed specialized units called Victim–Witness Assistance, designed to enforce victims' rights and provide support for victims through the criminal justice process. Human services providers working within these departments offer the following services:

- Crisis intervention counseling
- Referrals to coordinating human services agencies such as rape crisis centers, battered women's shelters, and crime victim support groups
- Referrals to advocacy organizations such as Mothers Against Drunk Driving (MADD), who have a presence in court to ensure enforcement of victims' rights
- Advocacy and accompaniment in court proceedings
- Special services or units for victims of domestic violence, child victims, older adults, and victims with disabilities
- Case status updates including notification of all public court proceedings
- Foreign language translation
- Assistance with obtaining compensation such as reimbursement for counseling and medical costs
- Assistance in preparing and writing victim impact statements to be read by the victim at the sentencing hearing.

Victim–witness advocates may have a master's degree in any of the applied social science disciplines (social work, psychology, general human services), but often work at the bachelor's level with some specialized training in the dynamics involved in violent crime victimization. Advocates must also be familiar with the inner workings of the criminal justice system because victims of violent crime often feel revictimized when they must endure the often confusing labyrinth of the prosecution system.

The average person may not be familiar with the differing duties of a local police department and a state prosecuting office, nor with how a criminal case proceeds toward prosecution. Those individuals who have become victims of a crime must be quick studies so they can be prepared for what is going to happen next. Victim–witness advocates can help crime victims understand the process of a criminal trial and the importance and value of each step within the prosecution process.

If a case goes to trial, the victim–witness advocate will work closely with the victims to help prepare them to testify. The clinical issues involved depend on the nature of the crime and victimization. For instance, if the defendant is the victim's spouse who is charged with domestic battery, the clinical issues will likely involve fear of retaliation and guilt in response to testifying against a spouse, particularly if there is a possibility that the defendant might have to serve time in jail or prison. If the defendant is charged with sexual assault, the victim will likely experience feelings of shame, embarrassment, and fear. A victim of home invasion might experience intense fear of retaliation once the defendant becomes aware of the victim's cooperation and testimony. In each instance the victim–witness advocate will work with community human services agencies and advocates to provide support and assistance to the victim in preparation for trial.

Once a defendant is found guilty, either through trial or a **plea arrangement**, a sentencing hearing is scheduled. In a sentencing hearing, both sides have an opportunity to advocate for a sentence they believe is appropriate. It is the responsibility of the victim–witness advocate to assist victims in writing their victim impact statements, which are often read in open court before the judge, jury, and defendant. Although the statements are written in the words of the victims, they have a dual purpose—giving victims a voice in court and assisting the prosecutor in obtaining the desired sentence. Thus, it is important that victims receive guidance in writing their statements. This also serves as another opportunity for victims to express and work through their pain, and thus it is often an effective clinical tool.

WORKING WITH PERPETRATORS OF CRIME

Learning Outcome 11.4   **Explore the role of the human services provider in working with perpetrators of violent crime**

The human services profession has a long history of association with the criminal justice system, most notably working in jails, prisons, government probation departments, police departments, and agencies offering services to recently released offenders. Human services providers working within the criminal justice system may be employed as prison or correctional psychologists who conduct psychological evaluations on recently charged defendants or who provide assessment or counseling to offenders within the prison system.

Human services providers working with perpetrators of crime may be licensed social workers who provide counseling and facilitate support groups focusing on various forms of violence designed to reduce recidivism. They may be probation officers charged with the responsibility of coordinating treatment and supervising the offender's compliance with the conditions of probation (e.g., entering a drug treatment program, obtaining counseling, attending an anger management program, or completing community service), or they may be bachelor's-level correctional treatment specialists or case managers who provide general counseling to the prison population, assisting them in preparing for release and reentry into society. They may also be aides or volunteers working with youth gang members in an after-school diversion program.

Human services providers may also work at the community level, advocating for prison reform such as the development of mental health courts, substance abuse treatment programs in prisons, or increased mental health services for mentally ill prisoners. Although this field of service is broad, the clinical issues are specialized, requiring training focusing on the common issues facing offenders both within prison and on release.

Mental Health Programs in Correctional Facilities

Pearson eText

Video Example 11.4

In this video a prison social worker collaborates with a prison official on a prisoner experiencing a mental health client. In what ways is the social worker advocating for the prisoner?

The issues confronting human services providers working within the criminal justice system, particularly within a correctional facility, will vary depending on the demographics of the population and type of crime committed by the defendant. A key goal of the criminal justice system is to reduce recidivism. Therefore, "success" in terms of treatment is often focused on whether a prisoner, once released, reoffends and returns to prison. Behavioral programs within prisons can focus on many clinical issues, some related to criminal behavior and some related to other issues the inmates might be experiencing. Programs related to criminal behavior typically focus on issues such as drug abuse, sexual violence, domestic violence, anger management, and the development of social skills (for prisoners with antisocial tendencies). Programs designed to address psychosocial issues not directly related to criminal behavior typically focus on grief and separation issues, sexual abuse victimization (particularly for female inmates because a large proportion of the female inmate population has been the victim of sexual violence at some point in their lives), self-esteem, and issues related to the impact of being incarcerated.

Female inmates are often incarcerated for non-violent offenses related to drug addictions, and while Black women are overrepresented in the female prison population, the number of White women who are incarcerated for drug offenses, often pharmaceutical drugs, is increasing at an alarming rate. Advocates are concerned about the long prison sentences many women are receiving for nonviolent offenses, as well as the high rate of prisoners who struggle with mental illness and have histories of domestic violence and sexual abuse.

Women who are pregnant or parenting when in prison often have to rely on the county foster care system for the care of their children during their incarceration, and the fact that women of color, particularly Black women, are disproportionately affected, has drawn attention from the human services and broader social justice community (Cross, 2020; Rodriguez, 2019; Siefert & Pimlott, 2001). Human services providers working in a female correctional facility will likely encounter women who are grieving over the loss of their children or are anticipating their loss once they give birth. One of the roles of human services providers is to work with outside agencies that can arrange to transport children to see their incarcerated mothers to maintain the mother–child bond. Parenting issues are often explored with the goal of maintaining close family ties and reducing the incidence of prenatal damage and infant mortality related to drug use during pregnancy.

Some prisons have grant-funded programs that provide intensive prenatal care, nutrition counseling, substance abuse treatment, and individual and group counseling. One such program is called Women and Infants at Risk, which helps mothers break intergenerational cycles of abuse, giving infants the best start in life possible. This is particularly important in light of how the "cards" are already stacked against infants who are born behind prison walls (Siefert & Pimlott, 2001). Research shows that when states fund prison nurseries so their mothers can remain with their infants, recidivism significantly declines (Carlson, 2018).

Another significant issue often confronting both inmates and human services providers involves the high rate of infectious diseases that exists within the prison population, made worse by the ongoing problem of sexual assaults. Diseases such as hepatitis B and hepatitis C are prevalent in some prisons, and HIV/AIDS remains a serious concern among prisoners and correctional staff alike. A 2002 report by the National Commission on Correctional Health Care indicated

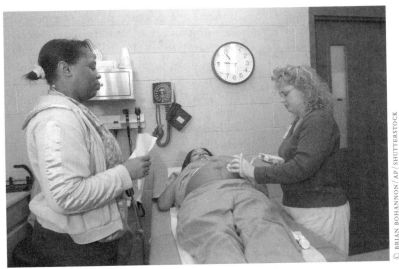

Babies Behind Bars Nurse's aide Shannon Gould, left, and Nurse Practioner Denise Burkett, right, listen to inmate Nikisha Robinson's unborn child's heartbeat, during a check-up at the Kentucky Correctional Institute for Women in Pewee Valley, Ky. Robinson, 22, is pregnant and serving a 15-year sentence for violating her probation on a charge of facilitation to commit robbery.

that the incidence of HIV in the U.S. prison population is five times that of the general population, and the primary method of transmission is sexual assault (Robertson, 2003), but the incidence has steadily declined in the last two decades (U.S. Department of Justice, 2017). There was considerable concern in 2020 about the spread of the novel coronavirus in prison settings, due to the highly contagious nature of the virus and the congested nature of most jails and prisons across the country. These concerns became a reality by June 2020 when prisons overtook nursing homes and meat processing plants as the biggest clusters of infection (Williams et al., 2020). Most states responded by facilitating early releases for thousands of inmates from overcrowded jails and prisons. Federal guidance stipulated that prisoners who had served at least 50% of their sentences and who had less than 18 months remaining on their sentences should be released. But later in the same week, new guidance was released reducing the recommended time served to 25% (Gerstein, 2020). Although the intention was to release only those defendants who committed misdemeanors and low-level felonies, some released prisoners had been convicted of violent offenses, angering and frightening many of their victims (Eligon, 2020).

A common complaint among mental health providers in correctional settings is the underfunding and understaffing of mental health programs experienced in many jails and prisons across the country. There is a disproportionate number of inmates with mental illness, and jails and prisons are legally mandated to provide these services. Developing effective and comprehensive mental health services within correctional facilities is an important aspect of efforts to reduce recidivism rates among the prison population. However, the U.S. criminal justice system is punitive in nature and not based on a rehabilitation model, so mental health programs are often not a priority within the criminal justice system, as evidenced by a consistent lack of funding, understaffing, and limited outreach.

Yet even in prisons that have sufficient mental health services, barriers still exist that often prevent prisoners from accessing these services. A 2004 study surveying prisoner attitudes about mental health services identified several perceived barriers to services, including uncertainty about how or when to access counseling, the lack of confidentiality, and a fear that other prisoners would believe they were a snitch (Morgan et al., 2004).

Pearson eText

Video Example 11.5

In this video a prison social worker educates a prison official about the prisoner's challenges. What theories is the social worker drawing on when providing context for the prisoner's problematic behavior?

Pearson eText

Video Example 11.6

In this video a prison so-cial worker collaborates with other prison officials educating them on new ways social workers could engage in prisoner pro-cesses. What other types of functions and roles might human services professionals participate in the mental health care of prisoners?

Almost 2 decades later, it doesn't appear much has changed. Prisoners and advocates still cite numerous barriers to prisoners receiving adequate mental health services, particu-larly for Black and Latina/o inmates, who have the lowest level of access (Kaba et al., 2014). Correctional facilities located in more rural areas and in conservative districts also tend to offer mentally ill prisoners the least access to mental health services (Helms et al., 2016). And then finally, inmates and mental health advocates note that despite the impor-tance of providing mental health services to inmates in need, a correctional facility is not really conducive to the development of positive therapeutic relationships. As referenced earlier, there is no confidentiality and it's difficult to establish interpersonal connections in an environment of deprivation (Jacobs & Giordano, 2018). Human services providers need to be aware of these barriers so that strategies can be designed to overcome both real and perceptual barriers to seeking mental health counseling in correctional facilities that extend beyond mere medication management.

CONCLUSION

Working in forensic human services offers rich opportunities for human services pro-viders at all education levels. The opportunity to interact with several other advocacy organizations and to coordinate services with agencies offering complementary services provides the human services professional with a broad range of professional experiences. Human services providers facilitate counseling and case management and advocate on behalf of victims and offenders, thus making a difference in the lives of the members of society most in need.

Victims of violent crime such as domestic violence, sexual assault, hate crimes, and other violent crimes need advocacy and counseling to turn tragedy into triumph and powerlessness into empowerment. Human services providers are on the front lines of bringing issues formerly kept in the dark out into the open, removing stigmas, and creat-ing change that is meaningful and long-lasting.

Criminal activity and subsequent incarceration leave long-lasting scars on the fam-ilies of offenders, often plunging them into a cycle of poverty and social isolation. This process significantly increases the likelihood of creating an intergenerational pattern of incarceration. Thus, some of the most important work that forensic human services pro-viders do involves working with the family members of prisoners, particularly children who not only feel abandoned by their incarcerated parents but often are forced to enter the foster care system if no family members are available to care for them.

Rehabilitation offers the most hope of lowering recidivism rates among the prison population, yet a correctional philosophy that incorporates rehabilitation is controver-sial because in the eyes of many in the general public, counseling and other mental health programs feel too much like a luxury, not deserved by those who have committed crimes. However, not only are prisoners not a heterogeneous group (i.e., many prisoners have been incarcerated for relatively minor offenses), but those who have committed the most serious offenses are in many cases those who need mental health services the most. Unfortunately, mental health programs are often the first to be cut from state and federal budgets because, on the whole, the prisoner population does not garner much sympathy within the general public. For this reason, it is imperative that human services providers advocate for the basic rights and needs of prisoners, as they do with all vulner-able populations.

SUMMARY

- The role of the human services provider in working with survivors of intimate partner violence is critically analyzed. The nature of intimate partner violence, including the cycle of violence, motivations to commit violent acts on intimate partners, and the impact on survivors and their children is discussed. The role of the human services provider working with survivors of IPV is explored, including an exploration of common practice settings and intervention strategies based on empowerment theory.
- The complex nature of rape and sexual assault is examined. Rape and sexual assault are explored within the context of patriarchy and other cultural factors that increase the vulnerability of women. Disparity in victimization among women of color, rape on college campuses, rape myths, and rape trauma syndrome are also explored within the context of the role and function of human services providers working with the survivor population.
- The ways in which LGBTQ and gender nonconforming populations respond to hate crimes are explored. The history and nature of hate crimes against LGBTQ and gender nonconforming populations are examined, with a particular focus on the intersectionality of vulnerability that render some populations at increased risk of violence. Hate crimes legislation as well as effective intervention strategies used by human services providers are explored.
- The role of the human services provider in working with perpetrators of violent crime is explored. The ways in which human services providers work with victims of violent crime, such as surviving victims of homicide, are examined. General crime victimization within the context of the role of human services providers working with victims of crime, such as survivors of homicide, is explored. The Victim's Bill of Rights is also explored in a broader discussion of the role of victims in the criminal justice process.

END-OF-CHAPTER QUESTIONS

1. Describe at least three dynamics involved in intimate partner violence that make it difficult for women to leave those relationships.
2. Describe key elements in the violence against women act and explain how this legislation has changed the way domestic violence cases are addressed.
3. Describe the rape myth and explain what elements within society support and promote this myth.
4. What are some key dynamics involved in the increasing number of hate crimes against LGBTQ people?
5. What do you believe are some strengths human services providers should possess when working with survivors of crime and/or perpetrators?

References

Agoyo, A. (2019). 'Political football': Protections for Native women caught up in partisan stalemate. *Indianz News.* https://www.indianz.com/News/2019/11/21/native-women-political-football-vawa-mmiw.asp.

Anderson, M., & Toor, S. (2018). *How social media users have discussed sexual harassment since #MeToo went viral.* Pew Research Center. https://www.pewresearch.org/fact-tank/2018/10/11/how-social-media-users-have-discussed-sexual-harassment-since-metoo-went-viral/?utm_source=Pew+Research+Center&utm_campaign=bc6a468ed2-EMAIL_CAMPAIGN_2018_10_11_05_08&utm_medium=email&utm_term=0_3e953b9b70-bc6a468ed2-400487317

Ballman, A. D., Leheney, E. K., Miller, K. E., Simmons, B. L., & Wilson, L. C. (2016). Bystander perceptions of same-gender versus mixed-gender rape: A pilot study. *Journal of Aggression, Maltreatment & Trauma, 25*(10), 1079–1096.

BBC. (2019). *America's gun culture in charts.* https://www.bbc.com/news/world-us-canada-41488081

Black, M. C., Basile, K. C., Breiding, M. J., Smith, S. G., Walters, M. L., Merrick, M. T., Chen, J., & Stevens, M. R. (2011). *The national intimate partner and sexual violence survey (NISVS): 2010 summary report.* Centers for Disease Control and Prevention, National Center for Injury Prevention and Control.

Blair, F., McFarlane, J., Nava, A., Gilroy, H., & Maddoux, J. (2015). Child witness to domestic abuse: baseline data analysis for a seven-year prospective study. *Pediatric Nursing, 41*(1), 23.

Bohner, G., Reinhard, M., Rutz, S., Sturm, S., Kerschbaum, B., & Effler, B. (1998). Rape myths as neutralizing cognitions: Evidence for a causal impact of anti-victim attitudes on men's self-reported likelihood of raping. *European Journal Social Psychology, 28*, 257–268.

Bowen, E., & Gilchrist, E. (2004). Do court- and self-referred domestic violence offenders share the same characteristics? A preliminary comparison of motivation to change, locus of control and anger. *Legal and Criminological Psychology, 9*(2), 279–294.

Breiding, M. J., Basile, K. C., Smith, S. G., Black, M. C., & Mahendra, R. R. (2015). *Intimate partner violence surveillance: Uniform definitions and recommended data elements*, Version 2.0. Centers for Disease Control and Prevention, National Center for Injury Prevention and Control.

Burgess, A. W., & Carretta, C. M. (2016). Rape and its impact on the victim. In R. R. Hazelwood & A. W. Burgess (Eds.), *Practical aspects of rape investigation: A multidisciplinary approach* (pp. 3–18). CRC Press.

Burt, M. R. (1991). Rape myths and acquaintance rape. In A. Parrot & L. Bechhofer (Eds.), *Acquaintance rape: The hidden crime* (pp. 26–40). Wiley.

Cantor, D., & Fisher, B. (2015). *Report on the AAU campus climate survey on sexual assault and sexual misconduct assault and sexual misconduct.* American Association of Universities. http://sexualassaulttaskforce.harvard.edu/files/taskforce/files/final_report_-harvard_9.21.15.pdf

Cantor, D., Fisher, B., Chibnall, S., Harps, S., Thomas, G., Lee, H., Kranz, V., Herbison, R., & Madden, K. (2020). *Report on the AAU Campus Climate Survey on Sexual Assault and Misconduct.* American Association of Universities. https://www.aau.edu/sites/default/files/AAU-Files/Key-Issues/Campus-Safety/Revised%20Aggregate%20report%20%20and%20appendices%201-7_(01-16-2020_FINAL).pdf

Carbajosa, P., Catalá-Miñana, A., Lila, M., Gracia, E., & Boira, S. (2017). Responsive versus treatment-resistant perpetrators in batterer intervention programs: Personal characteristics and stages of change. *Psychiatry, Psychology and Law, 24*(6), 936–950.

Carey, K. B., Norris, A. L., Durney, S. E., Shepardson, R. L., & Carey, M. P. (2018). Mental health consequences of sexual assault among first-year college women. *Journal of American College Health, 66*(6), 480–486.

Carlsen, U., Salam, M., Miller, C.C., Lu, D., Ngu, A., Patel, J. K., & Wichter, Z. (2018). #Metoo brought down 201 powerful men. Nearly half of their replacements are women. *New York Times.* https://www.nytimes.com/interactive/2018/10/23/us/metoo-replacements.html

Carlson, J. R. (2018). Prison nurseries: A way to reduce recidivism. *The Prison Journal, 98*(6), 760–775.

Carneiro, J. B., Gomes, N. P., Estrela, F. M., Santana, J. D. D., Mota, R. S., & Erdmann, A. L. (2017). Domestic violence: repercussions for women and children. *Escola Anna Nery, 21*(4).

Cattaneo, L. B., Calton, J. M., & Brodsky, A. E. (2014). Status quo versus status quake: Putting the power back in empowerment. *Journal of Community Psychology, 42*(4), 433–446.

Cattaneo, L. B., & Goodman, L. A. (2015). What is empowerment anyway? A model for domestic violence practice, research, and evaluation. *Psychology of Violence, 5*(1), 84.

Centers for Disease Control and Prevention [CDC]. (2005). *Sexual violence: Fact sheet.* National Center for Injury Prevention and Control. http://www.cdc.gov/ncipc/factsheets/svfacts.htm

Chestnut, S., Dixon, E., & Jindasurat, C. (2013). *Lesbian, gay, bisexual, transgender, queer, and HIV-affected hate violence in 2012. A report from the National Coalition of Anti-Violence Programs (NCAVP).*

Cooper, H. L. (2015). War on drugs policing and police brutality. *Substance use & misuse, 50*(8-9), 1188–1194.

Coronel, S., Coll, S., & Kravitz, D. (2015a). Rolling Stone and UVA: The Columbia University Graduate School of Journalism report. *Rolling Stone, 5.*

Coronel, S., Coll, S., & Kravitz, D. (2015b). Rolling Stone's investigation: A failure that was avoidable. *Colombia Journalism Review.* http://www.cjr.org/investigation/rolling_stone_-investigation.php

Crawford, K. L. (2016, March). Traumatized worldview: Children who witness domestic violence. In *3rd Annual Waldron College Interprofessional Symposium & Expo.*

Cross, J. (2020). Imprisoning pregnant and parenting women: A focus on social justice, equal rights, and equality. *Health & Social Work.* [Advance online publication]. https://doi.org/10.1093/hsw/hlaa008

Davis, K. C., Neilson, E. C., Wegner, R., Stappenbeck, C. A., George, W. H., & Norris, J. (2018). Women's sexual violence victimization and sexual health: Implications for risk reduction. In L. M. Orchowski & C. A. Gidycz (Eds.), *Sexual assault risk reduction and resistance: Theory, research, and practice* (pp. 379–406). Academic Press.

DePrince, A. P., & Gagnon, K. L. (2018). Understanding the consequences of sexual assault: What does it mean for prevention to be trauma informed? In L. M. Orchowski & C. A. Gidycz (Eds.), *Sexual assault risk reduction and resistance: Theory, research, and practice* (pp. 15–35). Academic Press.

Edwards, F., Lee, H., & Esposito, M. (2019). Risk of being killed by police use of force in the United States by age, race–ethnicity, and sex. *Proceedings of the National Academy of Sciences, 116*(34), 16793–16798.

Eligon, J. (2020). 'It's a slap in the face': Victims are angered as jails free inmates. *The New York Times.* https://www.nytimes.com/2020/04/24/us/coronavirus-jail-inmates-released.html

Gerstein, J. (2020). *Feds again shift guidance on prisoner releases due to coronavirus.* Politico. https://www.politico.com/news/2020/04/23/coronavirus-prisons-206155

GLAAD. (2019). *Incidents of anti-LGBTQ hate violence in 2019.* https://www.glaad.org/blog/incidents-anti-lgbtq-hate-violence-2019

Goodman, L. A., & Epstein, D. (2008). *The advocacy response.* American Psychological Association.

Goodman, L. A., Glenn, C., Bohlig, A., Banyard, V., & Borges, A. M. (2009). Feminist relational advocacy: Processes and outcomes from the perspective of low-income women with depression. *The Counseling Psychologist, 37*, 848–876.

Goodman, L. A., Thomas, K., Cattaneo, L. B., Heimel, D., Woulfe, J., & Chong, S. K. (2016). Survivor defined practice in domestic violence work measure development and preliminary evidence of link to empowerment. *Journal of Interpersonal Violence, 31*(1), 163–185.

Gordon, K. C., Burton, S., & Porter, L. (2004). Predicting the intentions of women in domestic violence shelters to return to partners: Does forgiveness play a role? *Journal of Family Psychology, 18*(2), 331–338.

Gun Violence Archive [GVA] 2020. (2020). *Six year review.* https://www.gunviolencearchive.org/

Harris Poll, The. (2019). *Accelerating acceptance: A survey of American acceptance and attitudes toward LGBTQ Americans.* https://www.glaad.org/sites/default/files/Accelerating%20Acceptance%202019.pdf

Heise, L. L. (1998). Violence against women: An integrated, ecological framework. *Violence against women, 4*(3), 262–290.

Helms, R., Gutierrez, R. S., & Reeves-Gutierrez, D. (2016). Jail mental health resourcing: A conceptual and empirical study of social determinants. *International Journal of Offender Therapy and Comparative Criminology, 60*(9), 1036–1063.

Herek, G. M. (2009). Sexual stigma and sexual prejudice in the United States: A conceptual framework. In D. A. Hope (Ed.), *Contemporary perspectives on lesbian, gay & bisexual identities: The 54th Nebraska Symposium on Motivation* (pp. 65–111). Springer.

Herman, K., Rotunda, R., Williamson, G., & Vodanovich, S. (2014). Outcomes from a Duluth model batterer intervention program at completion and long term follow-up. *Journal of Offender Rehabilitation, 53*(1), 1–18.

Holmstrom, L. L., & Burgess, A. W. (1975). Assessing trauma in the rape victim. *American Journal of Nursing, 75*(8), 1288–1291.

Holt, S., Buckley, H., & Whelan, S. (2008). The impact of exposure to domestic violence on children and young people: A review of the literature. *Child Abuse & Neglect, 32*(8), 797–810.

Human Rights Campaign. (2013). *LGBT cultural competence.* http://www.hrc.org/resources/entry/lgbt-cultural-competence.

Igielnik, R., & Brown, A. (2017). *Key takeaways on Americans' views of guns and gun ownership.* Pew Research Center. https://www.bbc.com/news/world-us-canada-41488081

Ioannou, M., Hammond, L., & Machin, L. (2017). Male on male sexual assault: Victim, offender and offence characteristics. *Journal of investigative psychology and offender profiling, 14*(2), 189–209.

Jacobs, L. A., & Giordano, S. N. (2018). "It's not like therapy": Patient-inmate perspectives on jail psychiatric services. *Administration and Policy in Mental Health and Mental Health Services Research, 45*(2), 265–275.

Jewkes, R., Flood, M., & Lang, J. (2015). From work with men and boys to changes of social norms and reduction of inequities in gender relations: A conceptual shift in prevention of violence against women and girls. *The Lancet, 385*(9977), 1580–1589.

Jipping, T. (2019). *Serious flaws in the Violence Against Women Act reauthorization bill.* The Heritage Foundation, Backgrounder. https://www.heritage.org/sites/default/files/2019-07/BG3428.pdf

Johnson, R. (2017). *Helping domestic violence victims: A research brief.* Dolan Consulting Group. https://www.dolanconsultinggroup.com/wp-content/uploads/2017/09/RB_Helping-Domestic-Violence-Victims_1.pdf

Kaba, F., Lewis, A., Glowa-Kollisch, S., Hadler, J., Lee, D., Alper, H., Selling, D., MacDonald, R., Solimo, A., Parsons, A., & Parsons, A. (2014). Solitary confinement and risk of self-harm among jail inmates. *American Journal of Public Health, 104*(3), 442–447.

Kapaya, M., Boulet, S. L., Warner, L., Harrison, L., & Fowler, D. (2019). Intimate partner violence before and during pregnancy, and prenatal counseling among women with a recent live birth, United States, 2009–2015. *Journal of Women's Health, 28*(11), 1476–1486.

Karakurt, G., & Cumbie, T. (2012). The relationship between egalitarianism, dominance, and violence in intimate relationships. *Journal of Family Violence, 27*(2), 115–122.

Karakurt, G., Smith, D., & Whiting, J. (2014). Impact of intimate partner violence on women's mental health. *Journal of Family Violence, 29*(7), 693–702.

Knickmeyer, N., Levitt, H., & Horne, S. G. (2010). Putting on Sunday best: The silencing of battered women within Christian faith communities. *Feminism & Psychology, 20*(1), 94–113.

Kunst, M. J., & van Bon-Martens, M. J. (2011). Examining the link between domestic violence victimization and loneliness in a Dutch community sample: A comparison between victims and nonvictims by Type D personality. *Journal of Family Violence, 26*(5), 403–410.

Launius, M. H., & Lindquist, C. U. (1988). Learned helplessness, external locus of control, and passivity in battered women. *Journal of Interpersonal Violence, 3*(3), 307–318.

Lawrence v. *Texas*, 539 U.S. 558 (2003).

Leverick, F. (2020). What do we know about rape myths and juror decision making? *The International Journal of Evidence & Proof*, 1365712720923157.

Mapping Police Violence. (2019). Database. https://mappingpoliceviolence.org/

Marzullo, A., Libman, A. J., Crimes, H., Lesbian, V. A., & Ruddell-Tabisola, J. G. (2009). *Research overview: Hate crimes and violence against lesbian, gay, bisexual and transgender people.* Human Rights Campaign. http://citeseerx.ist.psu.edu/viewdoc/download;jsessionid=3157FB57B30A89B8EAAF1F4C7A826B43?doi=10.1.1.296.4909&rep=rep1&type=pdf

Matthews, M., Farris, C., Tankard, M., & Dunbar, M. S. (2018). Needs of male sexual assault victims in the US Armed Forces. *Rand Health Quarterly, 8*(2).

McCarthy, J. (2020). *U.S. support for same-sex marriage matches record high.* Gallup. https://news.gallup.com/poll/311672/support-sex-marriage-matches-record-high.aspx

McCarthy, K. J., Mehta, R., & Haberland, N. A. (2018). Gender, power, and violence: A systematic review of measures and their association with male perpetration of IPV. *PloS one, 13*(11), e0207091.

McCoy, E. K. (2020). *The impact of social media use on the acceptance of rape myths and subsequent views on sexuality* [Doctoral dissertation]. Ohio Dominican University.

Meyer, D. (2012). An intersectional analysis of lesbian, gay, bisexual, and transgender (LGBT) people's evaluations of anti-queer violence. *Gender & Society, 26*(6), 849–873.

Mezey, G., & King, M. (1989). The effects of sexual assault on men: A survey of 22 victims. *Psychological Medicine, 19*, 205–209.

Mika, H., Achilles, M., Halbert, E., Amstutz, L., & Zehr, H. (2004). Listening to victims—A critique of restorative justice policy and practice in the United States. *Federal Probation, 68*(1), 32–39.

Morgan, R. D., Rozycki, A. T., & Wilson, S. (2004). Inmate perceptions of mental health services. *Professional Psychology: Research and Practice, 35*, 389–396.

Morrison, P. K., Cluss, P. A., Hawker, L., Miller, E., George, D., Bicehouse, T., Fleming, R., & Chang, J. C. (2019). Male IPV perpetrators' perspectives on facilitation of batterer intervention program: Results from a 2-year study. *Partner Abuse, 10*(4), 483–506.

Morrison, P. K., Hawker, L., Cluss, P. A., Miller, E., Fleming, R., Bicehouse, T., George, D., Burke, J., Wright, K., & Chang, J. C. (2018). The challenges of working with men who perpetrate partner violence: Perspectives and observations of experts who work with batterer intervention programs. *Journal of Interpersonal Violence* (Advance online publication). 0886260518778258.

Myhill, A. (2017). Measuring domestic violence: Context is everything. *Journal of Gender-Based Violence, 1*(1), 33–44.

Owusu-Bempah, A. (2017). Race and policing in historical context: Dehumanization and the policing of Black people in the 21st century. *Theoretical Criminology, 21*(1), 23–34.

Pape, K. T., & Arias, I. (2000). The role of attributions in battered women's intentions to permanently end their violent relationships. *Cognitive Therapy and Research, 24*, 201–214.

Power, C., Koch, T., Kralik, D., & Jackson, D. (2006). Lovestruck: Women, romantic love and intimate partner violence. *Contemporary Nurse: A Journal for the Australian Nursing Profession, 21*(2), 174–185.

Quinn, T. (1998). Restorative justice: An interview with former visiting fellow Thomas Quinn. *The National Institute of Justice Journal, 235*, 10–16.

Ridgeway, C. L., & Correll, S. J. (2004). Unpacking the gender system: A theoretical perspective on gender beliefs and social relations. *Gender & Society, 18*(4), 510–531.

Roberts, A., Gilman, S., Fitzmaurice, Decker, M., & Koenen, K. (2010). Witness of intimate partner violence in childhood and perpetration of intimate partner violence in adulthood. *Epidemiology, 21*(6), 809–816.

Robertson, J. E. (2003). Rape among incarcerated men: Sex, coercion and STDs. *AIDS Patient Care and STDs, 17*(8), 423–430.

Rodriguez, C. R. (2019). "Who's gonna take my baby?": Narratives of creating placement plans among formerly pregnant inmates. *Women & Criminal Justice, 29*(6), 385–407.

Seabrook, R. C., McMahon, S., & O'Connor, J. (2018). A longitudinal study of interest and membership in a fraternity, rape myth acceptance, and proclivity to perpetrate sexual assault. *Journal of American College Health, 66*(6), 510–518.

Siefert, K., & Pimlott, S. (2001). Involving pregnancy outcome during imprisonment: A model residential care program. *Social Work, 42*(2), 125–134.

Smith, M. E., & Randall, E. J. (2007). Batterer Intervention Program: The victim's hope in ending the abuse and maintaining the relationship. *Issues in Mental Health Nursing, 28*, 1045–1063.

Smith, S. G., Zhang, X., Basile, K. C., Merrick, M. T., Wang, J., Kresnow, M., & Chen, J. (2018). *The National Intimate Partner and Sexual Violence Survey (NISVS): 2015 Data Brief – Updated Release*. Centers for Disease Control and Prevention, National Center for Injury Prevention and Control.

Sultana, A. (2010). Patriarchy and Women s Subordination: A Theoretical Analysis. *Arts Faculty Journal*, 1–18.

Swan, S. C., Gambone, L. J., Caldwell, J. E., Sullivan, T. P., & Snow, D. L. (2008). A review of research on women's use of violence with male intimate partners. *Violence and Victims, 23*(3), 301–314.

Sweet, P. L. (2019). The sociology of gaslighting. *American Sociological Review, 84*(5), 851–875.

Tracy, N. (2012, July 24). *Gaslighting definition, techniques and being gaslighted*. HealthyPlace. https://www.healthyplace.com/abuse/emotional-psychological-abuse/gaslighting-definition-techniques-and-being-gaslighted

Truman, J. L., Langton, L., & Planty, M. (2015). *Criminal victimization, 2015*. U.S. Department of Justice, 1-20.

Truman-Schram, D. M., Cann, A., Calhoun, L., & Vanwallendael, L. (2000). Leaving an abusive dating relationship: An investment model comparison of women who stay versus women who leave. *Journal of Social and Clinical Psychology, 19*, 161–183.

Ullman, S. E., & Brecklin, L. R. (2002). Sexual assault history, PTSD, and mental health service seeking in a national sample of women. *Journal of Community Psychology, 30*(3), 261–279.

U.S. Department of Justice. (2011). *National crime victimization survey.* Office of Justice Programs, Bureau of Justice Statistics. http://bjs.ojp.usdoj.gov/content/pub/pdf/cv10.pdf

U.S. Department of Justice. (2017). *Number of state and federal prisoners who had HIV in 2015 was the lowest level in more than two decades.* Bureau of Justice Statistics. https://www.bjs.gov/content/pub/press/hIPV15stpr.cfm

Vearnals, S., & Campbell, T. (2001). Male victims of male sexual assault: A review of psychological consequences and treatment. *Sexual and Relationship Therapy, 16*(3), 279–286.

Victim's Rights Act of 1998, 42 U.S.C. § 10606(b) (West 1993).

Villarreal, D. (2019). *Sodomy laws are still being used to harass LGBTQ people.* LGBTQ Nation. https://www.lgbtqnation.com/2019/09/sodomy-laws-still-used-harass-lgbtq-people/

Violence Against Women Reauthorization Act. (2019). H.R.1585 — 116th Congress (2019–2020). https://www.congress.gov/bill/116th-congress/house-bill/1585/text.

Walker, L. E. (1979). *The battered woman.* Harper Collins Publishing.

Walker, L. E. (2016). *The battered woman syndrome.* Springer Publishing Company.

Wall, K. M., Haddad, L. B., Mehta, C. C., Golub, E. T., Rahangdale, L., Dionne-Odom, J., Karim, R., Wright, R. L., Minkoff, H., Cohen, M., Kassaye, S. G., Cohan, D., Ofotokun, I., & Cohn, S. E. (2019). Miscarriage among women in the United States Women's Interagency HIV Study, 1994–2017. *American Journal of Obstetrics and Gynecology, 221*(4), 347–e1.

Wallace, B. C., & Santacruz, E. (2017). LGBT psychology and ethnic minority perspectives: Intersectionality. *LGBT Psychology and Mental Health: Emerging Research and Advances,* 87–108.

Whitman Insight Strategies and Buzzfeed News. (2019). LGBTQ in America survey – Topline results. https://assets.documentcloud.org/documents/6175837/Whitman-Insight-Strategies-LGBTQ-in-America.pdf

Williams, T., Seline, L., & Griesbach, R. (2020, June 17). Coronavirus cases rise sharply in prisons even as they plateau nationwide. *The New York Times.*

Young, C. (2014). The CDC's rape numbers are misleading. *Time.* http://time.com/3393442/cdc-rape-numbers/

Zalmanowitz, S. J., Babins-Wagner, R., Rodger, S., Corbett, B. A., & Leschied, A. (2012). The association of readiness to change and motivational interviewing with treatment outcomes in males involved in domestic violence group therapy. *Journal of Interpersonal Violence, 28*(5). https://doi.org/10.1177/0886260512459381

12

Rural Human Services

© JIMMY ROONEY / SHUTTERSTOCK

Carrie Lynn lives in the small rural town of Booneville in eastern Kentucky—a part of central Appalachia. She has been struggling with alcoholism for most of her life and was recently referred for services with her community's itinerant counselor, Sandra, a licensed counselor who comes to town once or twice a month. Carrie Lynn has been drinking alcohol steadily since the 8th grade, quitting only during her pregnancies. Without any formal intervention, she resumed drinking once her babies stopped breastfeeding. Carrie Lynn's drink of choice is a homemade alcohol that her family and friends have been brewing for years because until recently her county had been dry, and though now it is legal to drink alcohol, one needs to drive a long distance to buy it. She isn't certain of the alcohol content of this homemade brew, but she is certain it is high. In addition, she adds the alcohol to just about everything she drinks, even her morning coffee. As a widowed mother of four young children, the pressure of trying to keep a roof over the heads of herself and her children is almost unbearable, and drinking helps her to manage the everyday grind. Despite her alcoholism, Carrie Lynn is a good mom, or at least she tries to be. She hung in after she and her husband lost the small farm that had been in her family for more than 100 years. She hung in after she lost one of her babies to "crib death." She hung in when she lost her two siblings to cirrhosis of the liver. She hung in when her husband lost his job in the coal mines, and when he died last year of lung cancer. She even hung in when she lost her part-time job at the local lumber mill, when it shut down a few months ago. Carrie Lynn now survives on government aid and the little bit of money she earns from babysitting some neighborhood kids.

Booneville, Kentucky, like many small towns in Appalachia (a large swath of land encompassing portions of 13 states, stretching from northern Mississippi to southern New York), is a community mired in deep poverty. Located in Owsley County, in the Eastern Coalfield region of Kentucky, Booneville is the county seat. Once a thriving boomtown for common folks working in the coalmines and lumber mills, today the town is home to about 81 people according to the last U.S. census. Owsley County has the highest rate of child poverty in the country and is considered the poorest county in the nation. The per capita income in Owsley County is just over $10,000 per year, and more than half of all families living in the county fall below the federal poverty line. Government benefits account for about 53% of personal income, and there is no indication that things will be turning around any time soon. Carrie Lynn is only 45, but she looks much older. A life of stress, loss, chronic back pain, obesity, and alcoholism has taken its toll on her body and her sense of well-being.

While she's somewhat open to receiving counseling services, she's concerned about the stigma. Everyone knows everyone in the small town of Booneville, and Carrie Lynn knows that if her car is seen in the counselor's office parking lot, then people will start to talk. Sandra, the counselor, agrees to meet Carrie at the local park to avoid suspicion, and it is during their first meeting that Carrie Lynn expresses concern that her neighbors may no longer trust her with their kids if they think she's "crazy." The counselor is sympathetic and understands Carrie Lynn's concerns. Gossip is a big issue in small towns, which lack the anonymity of urban and suburban communities. Sandra works for a human services agency in central Kentucky and spends several days a week driving to different rural communities to provide macro and micro services, including substance abuse counseling, well-being checks for older adults, and counseling for people dealing with domestic violence and child welfare issues. She is considered an outsider to those living in the communities she serves, and because she is responsible for such a large geographic area, she can only visit each community once or twice per month—certainly not enough time to develop meaningful relationships and, most important, trust. These challenges have required that she be creative in her approach to service delivery, meeting clients in places of their choosing, not keeping an eye on the clock, and accepting token gifts in exchange for payment, so that her clients, most of whom pride themselves on their self-sufficiency, don't feel as though they're a burden on her.

THE STATE OF RURAL COMMUNITIES

Learning Outcome 12.1   Identify current social and economic issues and trends in rural communities.

A practice area that has recently gained nationwide attention is rural human services—the provision of human services, on a micro and macro level, in rural communities (Martinez-Brawley, 2000). The reasons for the recent attention are many, but essentially, despite the historic glamorization of small-town life (think "Mayberry" of *The Andy Griffith*

Show fame), rural communities have been struggling for decades—economically, with social isolation, and with a number of other social problems. But before exploring the challenges facing many of America's small towns and rural communities, it's important to first clarify what we are talking about when we use the term *rural*.

Rural communities can be defined in several different ways—geographically, where people live in small isolated towns or farming and ranching communities; demographically, where population density is sparse; or functionally, where a community is characterized by its economy, rural identity, and social and community characteristics (Daley, 2020; Housing Assistance Council [HAC], 2011, 2012). While rural communities are often located in geographically remote areas, there are also **rural enclaves** located within larger cities. Rural enclaves can form when suburban communities encroach on formerly rural areas, or when people from rural towns move to the city for work, and therefore create a rural island in the midst of an urban area (Daley, 2020; Foulkes & Newbold, 2008). Rural enclaves are sometimes called "rural ghettos" if they are residentially bounded areas with high poverty, social isolation, and high unemployment. When rural ghettos are comprised primarily of ethnic minority or immigrant populations, then the community is often racially stigmatized in addition to being stigmatized for poverty and social disorganization (Burton et al., 2013).

According to government sources, 46.1 million people live in rural communities, equaling about 15% of the U.S. population (Pender et al., 2019), compared to 60 million in 2010. Many rural communities are suffering due to the decline of blue-collar work in the United States. Many rural communities were once thriving "boom towns," offering solid incomes and a safe lifestyle for working class families. But for the past 20 years at least, many of the industries that once thrived in rural communities—family farming, timber, mining, textile mills, coal, and auto manufacturing—have significantly declined or disappeared altogether. This trend is often referred to as *deindustrialization*, and when rural residents are forced to leave their communities and head to metropolitan areas to find employment (or go to college), the trend is called *depopulation*. Many rural communities have been experiencing deindustrialization and depopulation for a few decades now, and the residents who have remained in their rural communities are often angry at their growing challenging conditions and feel left behind (Ulrich-Schad & Duncan, 2018).

Many people who have remained in small towns in rural America have experienced tremendous difficulty. Ulrich-Schad and Duncan's 2018 survey of nearly 17,000 rural residents highlighted their struggles as residents watched working class jobs and "Main Street" stores disappear. And while the specific challenges facing rural communities vary depending on the local industries, demographics of the community, and geographic location, a relatively uniform response among the subjects was that their way of life was disappearing and along with it, their pride and identities—as farmers, coal miners, factory workers—were disappearing as well. Some of the challenges many of America's small towns face include low educational attainment, high infant mortality rates, poor-quality health care, social isolation, poor housing options, high unemployment rates, and limited formal services (Daley, 2020). People living in rural communities are more likely to smoke tobacco, abuse alcohol and other drugs without treatment options, and suffer from a range of chronic lifestyle-related health problems such as diabetes, high blood pressure, and heart disease. Yet they are less likely to receive regular health care due to lack of access to quality medical services, lack of money, and poor (or no) health insurance (Pender et al., 2019).

The lack of available formal services means that people living in rural communities must travel longer distances for medical and mental health care. This challenge is compounded by the fact that many people living in remote regions are struggling with poverty and do not have reliable transportation, if they have any transportation at all. Although rates of mental disorders and mental illnesses are not considerably different in rural communities compared to urban areas, there are far fewer treatment options available in small towns that are geographically isolated. In addition, with transportation challenges and higher stigmatization of mental health and substance abuse issues, many people in rural communities do not receive the help they need (Conway et al., 2011; Crumb et al., 2019; Pender et al., 2019).

Perople who are geographically isolated tend to also engage in unhealthy behaviors (compared to those living in urban and suburban communities), such as alcohol and drug abuse, sedentary lifestyles, and unhealthy eating, as people resort to informal ways of experiencing relief and comfort, which exacerbates existing issues (Gonzalez et al., 2018; Lichter & Johnson, 2007). In fact, rural communities have experienced significantly higher rates of drug and alcohol abuse compared to urban communities for the past several decades, particularly the abuse of opioids among those with lower levels of education (Pear et al., 2019; Van Gundy, 2006). These challenges are intensified in areas with a lot of land mass and high population dispersion, such as Alaska, Montana, New Mexico, and North Dakota. The economic, cultural, and social isolation many people in rural communities experience also fosters a sense of independence and local interconnectedness that can be a strength as it relates to resiliency, but also a deficit when assistance from outsiders is shunned (Daley, 2020).

Other challenges facing rural communities include higher rates of adolescent smoking, alcohol use, and bullying, and low adolescent educational attainment, with high rates of teens dropping out of high school. And while many small towns experience far lower rates of violence than urban communities, in some rural communities, violence is more tolerated by the community and law enforcement, including adolescent violence and acting out (Pear et al., 2019; Pender et al., 2019). Also, adolescents often engage in higher-risk behaviors in rural communities, often out of boredom (Daley, 2020; Moreland et al., 2013). Some examples include excessive drinking of alcohol and partying, as well as engaging in high-risk pranks. Further, some researchers have noted that violence against women, while not necessarily more prevalent in rural communities, does tend to be more tolerated by local law enforcement and the community in general due to more patriarchal beliefs (DeKeseredy & Schwartz, 2009; DuBois et al., 2019; Rennison et al., 2013b).

RURAL POVERTY

Learning Outcome 12.2   Compare and contrast urban and rural poverty among subpopulations

There are approximately 430 counties in the United States that experience persistent poverty, and most of these counties are almost entirely rural. Many people who live in rural communities experience deep poverty—living in a household with a total cash income below 50% of the poverty guidelines. Deep or persistent poverty is a chronic condition that often shows no signs of abating. The 2020 federal government poverty guideline for a family of four is $26,200, which means the guideline for deep poverty for a family of four is a mere $13,100 (U.S. Department of Health and Human Services, 2020). And while the cost of living in rural communities is often lower than in urban regions, the difference does not account for the fact that it is impossible to effectively raise a family well on just over $13,000 per year.

Imagine what it must be like to live in the United States, a country known for opportunity, social and economic mobility, and great excess, and yet you were born in poverty with little chance of escape. Can you imagine the sense of despair you might feel? Those who live in chronically poor rural communities, such as those in the **Appalachian region**, understand that they live in a different America than those living in more affluent metropolitan areas, one with far fewer opportunities for advancement.

Dental student Carl Leiner, left, checks Lisa Kantsos teeth at the Remote Area Medical clinic in Wise, Va. Kantsos and hundreds of other uninsured patients came to the rural clinic for free dental and medical care.

© AP / SHUTTERSTOCK

Persistent poverty counties are those that have a 21.3% or greater poverty rate for 30 years or longer. As of 2018, there were 443 counties experiencing persistent poverty, with poverty rates ranging from 21.3% (Nevada County, Arkansas; Albany County, Wyoming) to 54% (Oglala Lakota, South Dakota) (Dalaker, 2020). Most of these counties are in rural communities, and many are in areas with high concentrations of ethnic minorities, most notably Black, Native American, and migrant farm workers. Some of the most affected areas are central Appalachia, which impacts primarily White people; the lower Mississippi Delta and the "Southern Black Belt" in the American South, which impacts primarily members of the Black community; the "Colonias" region along the U.S.–Mexico border, which impacts primarily migrant farm workers; and what the federal government calls "Indian Country"—Native American reservations and federally designated protected Native lands (Institute for Research on Poverty, 2020).

Rural poverty in large part stems from a changing economic climate that has in many respects left rural communities behind. Deindustrialization, including the collapse of the auto manufacturing industry, the 1980s farming crisis, a move away from coal mining to clean energy, and economic globalization have all disproportionately impacted rural communities. Additionally, the **out-migration** of younger populations, many of whom leave their small towns for jobs or educational opportunities and never return, is outpacing natural population growth, resulting in many small towns experiencing depopulation—a slow and painful death. While these population trends are mediated somewhat by in-migration (the return of former residents), out-migration in many small towns is having a devastating effect on the vitality and growth of the community (Reichert et al., 2014).

Not only do people living in rural communities face more challenges across a range of life domains, but the rural poor fare far worse compared to those living in poverty in urban communities. Rural populations tend to have poorer health outcomes than those living in urban communities, and, as referenced earlier, many people in rural communities experience a higher-than-average rate of chronic diseases, many of which are directly related to

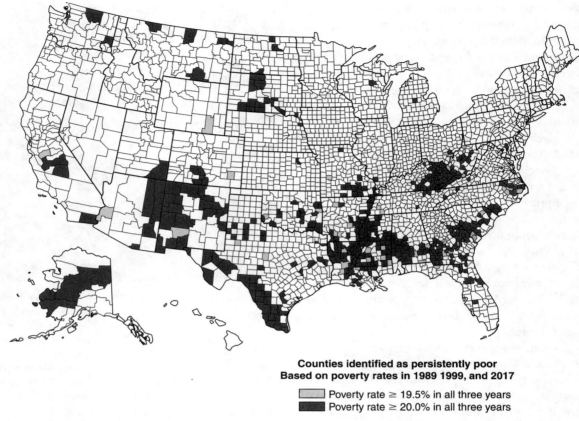

Counties identified as persistently poor
Based on poverty rates in 1989 1999, and 2017

☐ Poverty rate ≥ 19.5% in all three years
■ Poverty rate ≥ 20.0% in all three years

https://www.everycrsreport.com/files/20190327_R45100_32c312916f21fe28c866f0b1db2f8031c359c61e.html#_Toc4755057

Persistent Poverty Counties Using Two Rounding Methods, Based on 1990 Census, Census 2000, and 2017 Small Area Income and Poverty Estimates.

Source: Created by Congressional Research Service (CRS) using data from U.S. Census Bureau, 1990 Census, Census 2000, and 2017 Small Area Income and Poverty Estimates.

obesity and other lifestyle behaviors—consumption of unhealthy foods, a lack of exercise, tobacco use, and excessive alcohol consumption (Befort et al., 2012; Sriram et al., 2018).

But before we start blaming the rural poor for their eating habits, it's important to understand that for many people living in economically struggling rural communities, there may be no other choices. Many geographically isolated communities are located in what researchers call *food deserts*—regions where healthy food is a scarcity. Food deserts are quite common in rural communities where large grocery stores have either closed or never existed. A lack of reliable transportation (private and public) can also create barriers to accessing healthy foods (Canto et al., 2014; Rhone et al., 2019). Without access to healthy food options and education about what constitutes a healthy and nutritious diet, many people living in geographically isolated communities rely on junk food, which is cheap and filling but rarely nutritious (Rhone et al., 2019)

Many members of poor rural communities suffer in some manner, although various demographic groups are impacted differentially depending on the nature of the community and the impact of the various social problems on its residents. In many rural communities, women comprise about 52% of the full-time workforce and men comprise about

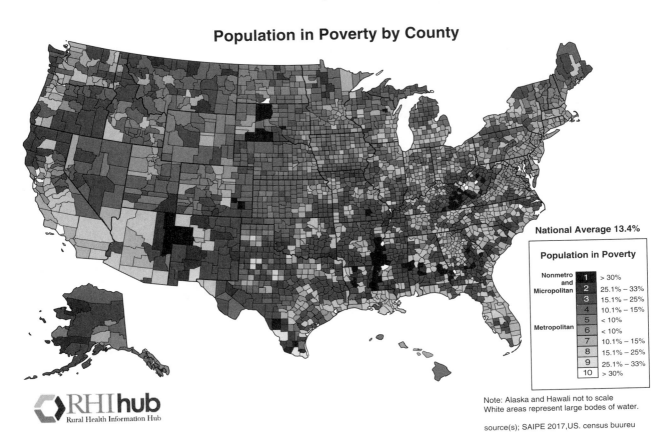

Population in Poverty by County

National Average 13.4%

		Population in Poverty
Nonmetro and Micropolitan	1	> 30%
	2	25.1% − 33%
	3	15.1% − 25%
	4	10.1% − 15%
	5	< 10%
Metropolitan	6	< 10%
	7	10.1% − 15%
	8	15.1% − 25%
	9	25.1% − 33%
	10	> 30%

Note: Alaska and Hawali not to scale
White areas represent large bodes of water.

source(s); SAIPE 2017,US. census buureu

https://www.ruralhealthinfo.org/rural-maps/mapfiles/population-in-poverty-all-ages.jpg?v=1

48%, but women, particularly women of color, are paid significantly lower wages (Gallagher Robbins et al., 2018). There has also been a steady rise in female single heads of households and **multi-partner fertility** (women with children with more than one partner) in rural areas, which increases social isolation and financial stress, and which has implications for the entire family structure, since rural communities are often geographically cut off from necessary resources such as prenatal care (Daley, 2020; U.S. Department of Agriculture, 2020). For instance, a 2015 study found that pregnant women living in rural communities had to travel very long distances for their prenatal care (1 to 2 hours each way), which was particularly challenging during the winter months (Gjesfjeld et al., 2015). The study also found that there were few childcare

Residents tour the New Dekalb County mobile farmer's market in Decatur Georgia. The bus which will make regular stops in 'food deserts ' is a converted prisoner transport bus.

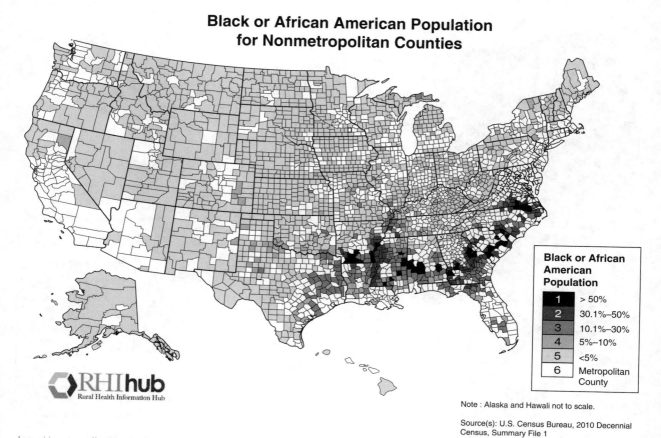

Black or African American Population for Nonmetropolitan Counties

Black or African American Population

1	> 50%
2	30.1%–50%
3	10.1%–30%
4	5%–10%
5	<5%
6	Metropolitan County

Note : Alaska and Hawaii not to scale.

Source(s): U.S. Census Bureau, 2010 Decennial Census, Summary File 1

https://www.ruralhealthinfo.org/rural-maps/mapfiles/black-african-american-population-nonmetro-counties.jpg

options in rural communities. This situation has been made worse by the decline of manufacturing jobs, which offered regular, set hours, and a move toward service sector jobs, which often involve erratic hours and little opportunity for advancement. As a consequence, many women believe they cannot afford to work outside the home, and thus rely on informal employment and government assistance.

Children are among the most vulnerable members of poor rural communities. More than half of all rural children live in low-income families, and more than one fourth live far below the federal poverty line (Rothwell & Thiede, 2018). The rate of child poverty in rural areas is not only higher than in urban communities, but it is also more persistent (Schaefer et al., 2016). The economic situations in many rural communities began to slowly improve in 2014, except for child poverty, which has increased by almost 25% since the 2007 recession, and continues to increase at a modest, but still concerning rate (Rothwell & Thiede, 2018). Research has shown strong links between child poverty and developmental delays, which can lead to low educational attainment, social skills deficits, and other challenges that can have long-lasting consequences for children and their families (Vernon-Feagans & Cox, 2013; Whiteside-Mansell et al., 2019).

The Poorest Regions in Rural America

Among the poorest rural regions noted earlier, the Mississippi Delta, the Southern Black Belt, and the Appalachia region rank among the poorest regions in the entire country

Pearson eText

Video Example 12.1

This video explores intergenerational poverty in rural Kentucky in the Appallachia region. What are some similarities and differences between rural and urban poverty?

https://www.youtube.com/watch?v=689_XLd2_JA

Table 12.1   ARC Economic Rating of Appalachian Counties

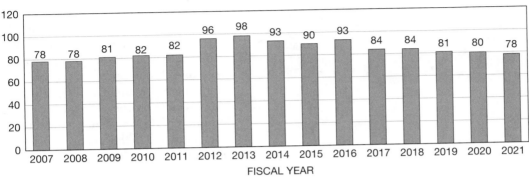

Number of Distressed Counties in Appalachia, FY 2007–FY 2021
(Years with Index-Based Methodology)

https://www.arc.gov/classifying-economic-distress-in-appalachian-counties/

(Institute for Research on Poverty, 2020; Ulrich-Schad & Staley, 2011). **The Mississippi Delta** is known for its serene and beautiful farmland as well as its shameful and violent history of slavery, long-standing racial segregation, and deep and chronic poverty, much of which is rooted in decades of institutionalized racism, such as post–slavery era **Jim Crow laws**. For instance, although **sharecropping**, which replaced slavery, permitted some Black people to purchase land, most later lost their land due to overt exploitation and inequity and because Jim Crow laws permitted no legal recourse for exploited Black families.

Today, the Mississippi Delta is considered the poorest area in the nation's poorest state and is an example of **rural depopulation**. The first wave of depopulation occurred during the height of the Civil Rights movement in the 1950s and 1960s, when Whites left the Delta in droves, a process that sociologists refer to as *White flight* (Munford, 1973). This was followed by a second wave of depopulation in the 1950s and 1960s, called *Black flight*, or the Great Black migration, when thousands of Black workers and their families migrated north to cities such as Chicago, Philadelphia, and Detroit in search of jobs and better economic opportunities (Heinicke, 1994). Those who have remained in the Delta are either too poor to leave, have no place to go, or don't want to leave their families behind.

Poverty remains high in the Delta, particularly in the lower Mississippi Delta, where infrastructure is poor, and, despite various discussions about community investment, very little economic restructuring has been accomplished. The remaining residents in this area either commute long distances for jobs in one of the few remaining factories or survive on government assistance and the charity of family and friends. Among the many social ills gripping the Delta, alcoholism has been a growing problem for the past few decades. As grocery stores and other industries have closed, liquor stores have opened, and alcoholism among the communities' remaining residents has taken hold (Goodman et al., 2020; Rodd, 2015).

The Southern Black Belt is an almost all rural region in the southern part of the United States, which includes 11 states that contain counties with high Black populations as well as extremely high poverty rates. The states included in the Southern Black Belt are Alabama, Arkansas, Florida, Georgia, Louisiana, Mississippi, North Carolina, South Carolina, Tennessee, Texas, and Virginia. The Southern Black Belt was originally named for the color of the fertile soil where slaves worked—a rich black velvet—but the term became known for the demographic makeup of the area when Booker T. Washington, an author and leader in the Black community, used the term in reference to states where

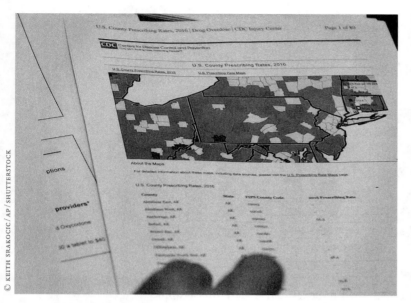

© KEITH SRAKOCIC / AP / SHUTTERSTOCK

Assistant U.S. Attorney Robert Cessar, shows a map illustrating the rates of opioid prescriptions by county during an interview in Pittsburgh. The Justice Department is giving federal prosecutors in 12 regions ravaged by the opioid abuse epidemic a trove of data officials say will help them stop overprescribing doctors. But some experts say doctors are just a small part of a problem that won't be cured without prevention and treatment.

the Black population was higher than the White population. The states of Louisiana and Mississippi have the highest rates of poverty (about 20%) (U.S. Census, 2019a), and Virginia has the lowest (about 11%) (U.S. Census, 2019b). The Southern Black Belt suffers from many of the same social problems as other poor rural regions—chronic and persistent poverty, high unemployment rates with poor employment prospects, low educational attainment, higher-than-average infant mortality, and higher-than-average government dependence (Chi et al., 2019; Harris, 2013; Zekeri, 2019).

One of the poorest areas in the United States is the Appalachian region, a large geographical area (about 205,000 square miles) extending through 13 states, from northern Mississippi to southern New York, along the Appalachian mountain range. There are about 25 million people who live in the Appalachian region, which includes all of West Virginia and parts of Mississippi, Alabama, Tennessee, Georgia, South Carolina, North Carolina, Kentucky, Virginia, Ohio, Maryland, Pennsylvania, and New York. Demographically, Appalachia is primarily White and older, and the region is mostly rural and mountainous. The economy is for the most part stagnant, having historically depended on coal mining, timber, agriculture, and manufacturing—industries that have been declining since the mid-1980s (Pollard & Jacobsen, 2019). The region is plagued by low educational attainment, chronic health problems, alcoholism, rampant opioid addictions, depression, and other health and mental health problems commonly associated with persistent poverty (Moody et al., 2017). Water supplies, in the form of streams and lakes, are often tainted in central Appalachia from years of coal mining (Cianciolo et al., 2020), and there has been a resurgence of black lung disease in many Appalachian coal miners (Potera, 2019).

Most regions throughout Appalachia have been left behind economically due to a lack of opportunity and the inability to engage in new educational and economic opportunities available online due to notorious low-quality or nonexistent broadband internet access. In fact, according to a 2019 report prepared by the Appalachia Regional Commission (ARC)—an economic development agency established by Congress—only about 60% of people living in Appalachia have residential Internet access and only about 42% have a smartphone (compared to the national average of 81%) (Pollard & Jacobsen, 2019). The lack of availability of fast and reliable residential broadband service in the Appalachia region, particularly in the more rural areas, impacts residents' access to telehealth services, education, job searches, and basic news (Khan et al., 2020).

ARC was established by Congress in 1965 as a part of President Lyndon Johnson's War on Poverty, to address the persistent poverty in this region. ARC ranks each county in the region by economic status with the goal of stimulating economic development through a range of economic activities and the investment in infrastructure.

Counties are ranked each fiscal year on a five-level ranking system, with *distressed* being the lowest ranking and *attainment* being the highest ranking. Many counties in the region gained transitional status by the mid-2000s, but progress was lost due to the 2007 recession, and most counties have not economically recovered more than a decade later. The counties with the most economic distress are located in central and eastern Kentucky, eastern Tennessee, West Virginia, southeastern Ohio, and northeastern Mississippi, right along the spine of the Appalachian mountain range (ARC, 2020).

Experts on this region urge caution though, in painting a holistically grim picture of the Appalachia region because far too often, it is outsiders telling the stories—people who do not really understand the area or the people who live there. Author Paul Nyhan reveals a different side of Appalachia, particularly of what is occurring in eastern Kentucky, one of the poorest regions in Appalachia. He shares stories of innovation, creativity, and entrepreneurship that are lifting people out of poverty and providing communities with a sense of hope. He notes how the dominant media narrative of regional coal miners, which is often politicized, renders other voices silent, such as the growing LGBTQ community and the stories of women, immigrants, and members of the Black community engaged in a range of economic activities. He cites examples of a community in transition as people leave coal mining careers to enter into the solar industry and the increasing number of farmers markets popping up in longtime food deserts. There is even a health care program, the Community Farm Alliance, which started an innovative program called "Farmacy," where physicians prescribe fruits and vegetables for residents' ailments, rather than opioids (Nyhan & Choi, 2019).

POPULATIONS WARRANTING SPECIAL ATTENTION

Learning Outcome 12.3   Identify the needs of populations warranting intervention in rural communities

While everyone who experiences poverty in rural communities warrants attention from human services professionals, there are certain longstanding and more recent trends among specific populations that warrant particular attention. Many ethnic minority populations in the United States have a long history of challenges, particularly in rural communities. For instance, rural minorities experience some of the highest rates of poverty in the entire nation, more than twice that of rural Whites, and tend to be highly segregated, even if they aren't living in poverty (ARC, 2020; Lichter et al., 2012).

The majority of Black people in the United States live in rural communities in the South, in high-poverty counties. While Whites have the highest rates of poverty in numbers, Black people have the highest rates of poverty relative to their proportion of the population. Poverty rates for rural Black children reached about 45% in 2007 and surpassed 50% in 2019, reflecting a concerning backward trend (USDA, 2020). Black people who live in rural communities also experience significantly higher rates of obesity, heart diseases, hypertension, and diabetes (Befort et al., 2012) and as a consequence have generally lower life expectancies than White prople living in rural Commuties and affluent Black people living in suburban and urban communities (Singh & Siahpush, 2014). Most ethnic minority populations experienced increased poverty rates during the 2007–2009 recession, but almost all have since returned to pre-recession rates, except members of the rural Black community (USDA, 2020).

Pearson eText

Video Example 12.2

In this video a single mother describes the despair she feels about the enduring poverty she and others in her community are experiencing. In what ways can human services professionals respond on a micro and macro level to address this type of hopelessness?

https://www.youtube.com/watch?v=1kyZD3wtnaw

Pearson eText

Video Example 12.3

This video explores the intersect between poverty in the Mississippi Delta and COVID-19. Using the ecological systems approach, what are some of the environmental factors at play in this situation?

https://www.youtube.com/watch?v=HDfk_BrVnv0

Another rural population warranting special attention is a rather surprising one to many social scientists—middle-aged White people particularly women (Davis & Francis, 2011). This is surprising because for generations members of the White community have experienced disproportionately better outcomes on virtually all indicators compared to other demographic groups—psychosocial, educational attainment, mental health, physical health, and life expectancy. Data revealing that this group in particular was struggling were discovered somewhat inadvertently, when two researchers, Anne Case and Angus Deaton, were reviewing census data and noted an unexpected trend: while all other demographic groups were experiencing gains in **longevity**, middle-aged White people were heading in the wrong direction—dying younger than in previous generations (Case & Deaton, 2015).

Case and Deaton wondered what could be causing this disturbing trend and after some further exploration, they discovered several alarming dynamics. Death rates for middle-aged White Americans had risen about 22%, but only for those with lower levels of education living in rural communities. As education levels rose, so did longevity. They also found that those with lower educational attainment (high school degree and lower) had more health problems, including higher rates of musculoskeletal diseases, chronic joint pain, sciatica, and mental health disabilities, including higher levels of anxiety and psychological distress. This group also experienced, on average, about a 20% drop in income in recent years. Case and Deaton noted that as this group's income and health declined, their rates of alcoholism and substance abuse rose, particularly the abuse of heroin and prescription **opioids**.

They also found an even more disturbing trend—an "epidemic" of suicides among middle-aged White people that corresponded with increasingly poor mental and physical health and worsening financial situations. Their research discovered that the mortality rate from alcohol and drug poisoning quadrupled for middle-aged White people with only a high school degree, and deaths from chronic liver disease, such as **cirrhosis of the liver** (caused by excessive alcohol consumption), rose by 50%. Case and Deaton noted that the spike in early deaths among middle-aged White people from alcoholism, drug abuse, and suicide was so dramatic that it was reminiscent of the AIDS epidemic just a few decades ago. They concluded this population may just be a "lost generation," and they called their premature mortality "deaths of despair" (Case & Deaton, 2020).

So how is this population doing now? Well, about the same, or slightly worse. Mortality rates increased again in 2016 and 2017. Case and Deaton have since written a book in an attempt to answer the question of why. Why are middle-aged White men and women without 4-year college degrees living in primarily rural communities dying of addictions and suicide? Case and Deaton note that a significant factor impacting this population is the breakdown of rural communities, which has led to increased stress and despair. They also attribute "deaths of despair" to the broken U.S. healthcare system, which makes it extremely difficult if not impossible for certain populations to access good preventative care (Case & Deaton, 2020).

While additional research in this area is important to help us better understand causal relationships and correlates, thus filling in the gaps, hearing from those who are living these realities is equally important. An April 2016 article in the *Washington Post* provides a personal glimpse into the lives of middle-aged White people living in rural Oklahoma (Saslow, 2016). The article explores the life of recently deceased Anna Marrie Jones. Anna died at the age of 54 of cirrhosis of the liver after years of alcohol abuse. The author writes a story of heartache and challenges, of never-ending financial hardship, and of multiple friends lost to an equally hard lifestyle, including Jones' best friend and fiancé, who also died during middle age of cirrhosis of the liver.

WORKING WITH RURAL POPULATIONS

Learning Outcome 12.4   Examine important factors associated with working with rural populations

There is a shortage of human services providers working in rural communities (Talebreza et al., 2017). There are many reasons for this shortage, including a lack of awareness of this practice area on the part of providers, as well as the fact that most educational programs are located in urban areas, which creates challenges for those living in rural communities wishing to enter the field. Many rural human services providers have limited education, with few opportunities to advance their educational status. Rural human services providers also face challenges with networking for themselves and their clients. The closest psychiatrist or treatment center may be hundreds of miles away. There may be no children's counseling center within a day's drive and the closest battered women's shelter may be several counties away. This can leave many rural human services providers feeling cut off from the broader profession, as there are few opportunities for referrals and collaboration and few opportunities for advancement (Daley, 2020). As with other professions, when rural youth desiring a career in the human services leave their communities to attend college, many fail to return, opting instead to seek positions with advancement opportunities in more urban areas.

Rural **itinerant human services providers** often have difficulty making strong connections to their clients because they are perceived as outsiders, and their services are often stigmatized (Daley, 2020). Domestic violence intervention in rural communities is an example of stigmatized services that not only place clients at risk of gossip, but also can place them in danger due to the lack of anonymity in many rural communities, as well as the tight-knit natures of these communities. In some rural communities, victims of domestic violence are hesitant to report violence or to seek services because they know their husbands or partners can rely on a network of other males, including members of law enforcement, for protection (DeKeseredy & Schwartz, 2008; Rennison et al., 2013). Agencies providing domestic violence services must be creative in how they conduct outreach, as well as how they provide counseling and advocacy, because exposing a victim's involvement with a human services agency can increase the risk of violence and marginalization within their extended families and community.

Technology can help with some of these challenges, particularly with a lack of access and anonymity. E-counseling, telephone sessions, and e-mail can increase the frequency of provider contact and enable clients to seek services without having their car spotted in the only counseling center in town, although in many rural communities, Internet access is still spotty, and low-income clients may not have Internet access in their homes. Additionally, while technology is a valuable tool for rural human services providers and their clients, it can also create additional challenges, especially in cases of violence, where abusive parents, partners, or classmates can use technology to inflict abuse on others, such as is the case with cyberbullying and cyberstalking.

The reality is that many of the human services professions, including counseling and social work, were developed within urban communities with urban problems in mind; thus, many of the treatment models that are taught in educational programs and relied on in field placement settings are urban based and will not necessarily work in a rural environment (Daley, 2020). This places rural human services providers in a position of having to be very creative, perhaps even engaging in community development to create the services that the community members need, rather than applying an urban template

Pearson eText

Video Example 12.4

In this video a Latina woman describes her mental health challenges and difficulty accessing care in her rural community. What are some of the most common challenges human services providers face working in rural communities?

https://www.youtube.com/watch?v=MVg8uNLQ6DI

to a rural environment. Rural human services may involve solely direct practice, but often there are elements of community development that occur right alongside counseling, focusing on the needs of the population being served. Examples of community development efforts include organizing health drives, school supply giveaways, educational programs, and parenting classes. Thus, rural human services providers must be able to wear many hats.

Rural Cultural Competence

There is a distinct culture that exists within rural communities that human services providers must be aware of to be effective in their service delivery. Sociologists refer to rural culture as **rurality**. According to Daley (2020), rural culture, while varied depending upon age cohort, race, and location, is often based on shared interests, social interaction, and behavior patterns. More specifically, people living in rural communities tend to have a stronger attachment to their land and community than their urban counterparts. There tends to be far less mobility in rural communities, and rural people will often cite the importance of remaining in a region where their families have been for generations. Rural communities also tend to be closely knit, and the lives of community residents are often highly intertwined. Rural people tend to have a more personal style of communication and social interaction, and they have more natural and informal helping networks.

© John Minchillo / AP / Shutterstock

Lumps of coal are sold as ornamental trinkets at the Winding Road Marketplace, a hub for selling the wares of local businesses, stands in his store, in Shawnee, Ohio. Communities across Appalachia are turning increasingly to the region's rich reserves in things other than coal, namely, history and rugged natural beauty, to frame a new tourist economy. Enjoying a drink, hike or overnight stay or in region infused with stories, sweat and strife is turning out to be a draw to aging baby boomers and millennials alike. Studies show these efforts are attracting tourists, new residents and a new sense of self-worth to the region.

Religious faith tends to be important to people living in rural communities, and rural populations tend to be more conservative and traditional in lifestyle and beliefs (Daley, 2020).

How these aspects of rural living manifest are often the foundation of many of the negative stereotypes associated with rural communities. For instance, Daley notes that couches and other living room furniture on porches or in yards are often perceived as trashy by urbanites, but when evaluated through the lens of rurality, such practices are seen as a way of extending the inside out, allowing residents to connect with their neighbors and friends. A couch in a yard is an invitation for someone to sit and visit, a core component of a rural way of life. In a similar vein, rural communities, particularly those in the southern part of the country, tend to be more collectivist in nature than individualistic. Extended "kin" is important, reflected in a form of **familism**, defined as family loyalty, interconnectedness, and interdependence. Family members are encouraged to rely on one another, and decisions are made with family in mind (Daley, 2020).

Human services providers working in rural communities must develop rural cultural competence, which begins with a willingness and ability to move beyond the myths and negative stereotypes often associated with a rural way of life. Unfortunately, there is a lack of information about the complexity of rural life, particularly what has happened in the wake of deindustrialization and depopulation. Human services professionals must be willing to invest in the rural communities they serve and take time in getting to know the broader and more contextual cultures, including similarities and differences between rural and urban societies.

Understanding that the lack of formal resources has caused many people within rural communities to resist outside help, or to turn to natural helpers (e.g., family, friends, paraprofessionals) (Waltman, 2011), can help human services professionals recognize the value of these informal resources rather than negate them. Taking a strengths-based approach can assist human services providers recognize that much of rural culture has evolved in response to generations of struggles, resulting in resiliency, independence, compromise, and ongoing adaptation (Daley, 2020).

Ethical Standards in a Rural Context

Rural human services providers often face challenges in adhering to some of the ethical standards foundational to the human services profession, particularly the admonition against having **dual relationships** with clients, and remaining detached and professional within the context of their work. Challenges are particularly common if rural human services providers live in the communities they serve (Walters et al., 2019). Brocious et al. (2013) refer to this as the *rural reality*—many rural communities are so small and interconnected that dual relationships are unavoidable.

In a study exploring the experiences of human services providers in rural and remote communities, providers expressed their experiences with attempting to maintain professional boundaries and personas, as well as avoiding dual relationships. Many of the providers expressed feeling personally isolated and at times going so far as to not engage in the community at all (i.e., avoiding going to bars or parties) in order to avoid dual relationships and appearing unprofessional. They also discussed the challenges associated with overlapping roles and relationships because their communities were so small. Some respondents noted how various friends, family, and others in the community would often ask them service-related questions, and that they felt it would be rude not to answer, as informality, friendliness, and helpful attitudes were so integral to rural culture. They also cited their difficulty with ethical mandates against accepting gifts, since gift-giving is a part of rural culture (Brownlee et al., 2015).

Several respondents also shared their struggles with how to handle thirdhand knowledge and community gossip, which they noted was very common in small towns and rural communities. They described how living in a rural community was like living in a fishbowl, and when they learned information about their clients from thirdhand sources, they weren't sure how to respond (Brownlee et al., 2015). According to Pugh (2007), gossip in rural communities creates unique ethical dilemmas not addressed in most professional ethical codes. Pugh questions whether at times it is more ethical to violate confidentiality to set the record straight and quash damaging rumors about clients that could significantly harm them.

Brocious et al. (2013) also question whether ethical standards developed with urban communities in mind are applicable to rural contexts. For instance, they note that some dual relationships can be beneficial to clients. They recommend using a strengths-based approach to this and similar challenges, balancing the establishment of good boundaries with rural realities. Brocious et al. assert that, with advanced training, rural human services providers can manage complex situations, such as negotiating dual relationships, in a way that does not harm clients, but enhances the provider–client relationship.

CONCLUSION

Rural human services have existed for decades or longer but recently have gained attention because of the increase in social problems plaguing many rural communities. Rural human services is a vibrant practice area providing human services providers with opportunities to engage in micro and macro practice with populations that are in dire need of assistance. Many of the challenges noted in the literature associated with reaching remote communities can be addressed through creative solutions such as the development of interagency coalitions, community development, and the integration of various types of technology into practice. Educational institutions can also play an active role in addressing many of these challenges by offering coursework in rural practice and developing field placement sites in much the same way they would develop international placements—with consistent outreach and flexible and creative placement options such as block placements with subsidized housing.

Although there are similarities between urban and rural human services, there are enough differences to warrant increased attention to rural practice and challenges facing human services providers. Increasing attention to researching rural communities, healthcare, and educational opportunities in rural communities is also important. Developing effective intervention strategies designed for rural contexts on a micro and macro level may provide some of the best opportunities for reversing many of the alarming trends currently experienced within rural populations.

SUMMARY

- Current issues and trends in rural communities are identified. The current state of rural communities, including many of the challenges facing rural populations, such as deindustrialization, high poverty, low educational attainment, high unemployment and underemployment, limited formal services, and geographic isolation, are examined.

- Urban and rural poverty are compared and contrasted. The nature of rural poverty, including an examination of ways that rural poverty differs from urban poverty, are discussed. Some of the poorest rural regions in the United States are explored, including the Mississippi Delta, the Southern Black Belt, and the Appalachia region, with an examination of the history of these areas, and the reasons why they are facing economic challenges.
- The needs warranting intervention in rural communities are identified. The nature of human services assistance for people living in rural communities who are in particular need, such as ethnic minority populations living in the South and middle-aged Whites, particularly women, is examined. Issues such as poor health, psychological distress, increasing alcohol and substance abuse, and increasing mortality rates, particularly among middle-aged Whites, are explored.
- Important factors associated with working with rural populations are examined. The nature of rural human services is explored. Issues such as rural culture and the importance of rural cultural competence are examined. Common ethical dilemmas, such as dual relationships and maintaining professional distance, are explored within a rural context.

END-OF-CHAPTER QUESTIONS

1. Describe four key dynamics that have contributed to enduring poverty unique to rural communities.
2. What are some challenges facing at-risk populations in U.S. rural communities?
3. Why has the opioid epidemic hit rural communities more than many urban or suburban communities?
4. What are some differences between cultural competence in urban practice and rural practice?

References

Appalachian Regional Commission. (2020). *County economic status in Appalachia, FY 2020.* https://www.arc.gov/research/MapsofAppalachia.asp?MAP_ID=149

Befort, C. A., Nazir, N., & Perri, M. G. (2012). Prevalence of obesity among adults from rural and urban areas of the United States: Findings from NHANES (2005–2008). *Journal of Rural Health, 28,* 392–397.

Brocious, H., Eisenberg, J., York, J., Shepard, H., Clayton, S., & Van Sickle, B. (2013). The strengths of rural social workers: Perspectives on managing dual relationships in small Alaskan communities. *Journal of Family Social Work, 16*(1), 4–19.

Brownlee, K., Halverson, G., & Chassie, A. (2015). Multiple relationships: Maintaining professional identity in rural social work practice. *Journal of Comparative Social Work, 7*(1).

Burton, L. M., Lichter, D. T., Baker, R. S., & Eason, J. M. (2013). Inequality, family processes, and health in the "new" rural America. *American Behavioral Scientist,* 0002764213487348.

Canto, A., Brown, L. E., & Deller, S. C. (2014). Rural poverty, food access, and public health outcomes. *Choices, 29*(2), 1–5.

Case, A., & Deaton, A. (2015). Rising morbidity and mortality in midlife among White non-Hispanic Americans in the 21st century. *Proceedings of the National Academy of Sciences, 112*(49), 15078–15083.

Case, A., & Deaton, A. (2020). *Deaths of despair and the future of capitalism.* Princeton University Press.

Chi, G., Shapley, D., Yang, T. C., & Wang, D. (2019). Lost in the Black Belt South: health outcomes and transportation infrastructure. *Environmental Monitoring and Assessment, 191*(2), 297.

Cianciolo, T. R., McLaughlin, D. L., Zipper, C. E., Timpano, A. J., Soucek, D. J., & Schoenholtz, S. H. (2020). Impacts to water quality and biota persist in mining-influenced Appalachian streams. *Science of The Total Environment, 717,* 137216.

Conway, P., BigFoot, D. S., & Sandler, E. P. (2011). Resiliency and behavioral health challenges among American Indians and Alaska natives in rural communities. In L. Ginsberg (Ed.), *Social work in rural communities* (5th ed., pp. 249–269). Council on Social Work Education.

Crumb, L., Mingo, T. M., & Crowe, A. (2019). "Get over it and move on": The impact of mental illness stigma in rural, low-income United States populations. *Mental Health & Prevention, 13,* 143–148.

Dalaker, J. (2020). *The 10-20-30 provision: Defining persistent poverty counties* (CRS Report No. R45100). https://crsreports.congress.gov/product/pdf/R/R45100

Daley, M. R. (2020). *Rural social work in the 21st century.* Lyceum Books.

Davis, L., & Francis, E. (2011, July 27). *"Most stressed out" in U.S.? Middle-aged women have lowest well-being, study finds.* http://abcnews.go.com/Health/MindMoodNews/stressed-us-middle-age-women-lowest-study-finds/story?id=14174138.

DeKeseredy, W. S., & Schwartz, M. D. (2008). Separation/divorce sexual assault in rural Ohio: Survivors' perceptions. *Journal of Prevention & Intervention in the Community, 36,* 105–120.

DeKeseredy, W., & Schwartz, M. (2009). *Dangerous exits: Escaping abusive relationships in rural America.* Rutgers University Press.

DuBois, K. O., Rennison, C. M., & DeKeseredy, W. S. (2019). Intimate partner violence in small towns, dispersed rural areas, and other locations: Estimates using a reconception of settlement type. *Rural Sociology, 84*(4), 826–852.

Foulkes, M., & Newbold, K. B. (2008). Poverty catchments: Migration, residential mobility, and population turnover in impoverished rural Illinois communities. *Rural Sociology, 60,* 181–201.

Gallagher Robbins, K., Frye, J., & McGrew, A. (2018). *The gender wage gap among rural workers.* Center for American Progress. https://www.americanprogress.org/issues/economy/news/2018/04/10/449284/gender-wage-gap-among-rural-workers/

Gjesfjeld, C. D., Weaver, A., & Schommer, K. (2015). Qualitative experiences of rural postpartum women and implications for rural social work. *Contemporary Rural Social Work, 7*(2), 115–126.

Gonzalez, K. M., Shaughnessy, M. J., Kabigting, E. N. R., Tomasulo West, D., Callari Robinson, J. F., Chen, Q., & Stewart Fahs, P. (2018). A systematic review of the health of vulnerable populations within US rural societies. *Online Journal of Rural Nursing and Health Care, 18*(1), 112–147.

Goodman, M., Thomson, J., & Landry, A. (2020). Food environment in the lower Mississippi Delta: Food deserts, food swamps and hot spots. *International Journal of Environmental Research and Public Health, 17*(10), 3354

Harris, R. (2013). Community-university partnerships for change in the Black Belt South. *Professional Agricultural Workers Journal, 1*(1), 4.

Heinicke, C. (1994). African-American migration and urban labor skills: 1950 and 1960. *Agricultural History, 68*(2), 185–198.

Housing Assistance Council [HAC]. (2011). *Rurality in America.* http://www.ruralhome.org/storage/research_notes/Rural_Research_Note_Rurality_web.pdf

Housing Assistance Council [HAC]. (2012). *Poverty in rural America* [Rural research brief]. http://www.ruralhome.org/storage/research_notes/rrn_poverty.pdf

Institute for Research on Poverty. (2020). *Many rural Americans are still "left behind"* [Fast Focus Research/Policy Brief No. 44–2020]. https://www.irp.wisc.edu/resource/many-rural-americans-are-still-left-behind/

Khan, M. L., Welser, H. T., Cisneros, C., Manatong, G., & Idris, I. K. (2020). Digital inequality in the Appalachian Ohio: Understanding how demographics, internet access, and skills can shape vital information use (VIU). *Telematics and Informatics,* 101380.

Lichter, D. T., & Johnson, K. M. (2007). The changing spatial concentration of America's rural poor population. *Rural Sociology, 72*(3), 331–358.

Lichter, D. T., Parisi, D., & Taquino, M. C. (2012). The geography of exclusion: Race, segregation, and concentrated poverty. *Social Problems, 59*(3), 364–388.

Martinez-Brawley, E. E. (2000). *Close to home: Human services and the small community.* NASW Press.

Moody, L. N., Satterwhite, E., & Bickel, W. K. (2017). Substance use in rural Central Appalachia: Current status and treatment considerations. *Journal of Rural Mental Health, 41*(2), 123.

Moreland, J. J., Raup-Krieger, J. L., Hecht, M. L., & Miller-Day, M. M. (2013). The conceptualization and communication of risk among rural Appalachian adolescents. *Journal of Health Communication, 18*(6), 668–685.

Munford, L. (1973). White flight from desegregation in Mississippi. *Integrated Education, 11*(3), 12–26.

Nyhan, P., & Choi, J. (2019). *Appalachia's story: How the national media gets it wrong.* Marguerite Casey Foundation. https://caseygrants.org/evn/appalachia-true-story-economic-development/

Pear, V. A., Ponicki, W. R., Gaidus, A., Keyes, K. M., Martins, S. S., Fink, D. S., Rivera-Aguirre, A., Gruenewald, P. J., & Cerdá, M. (2019). Urban-rural variation in the socioeconomic determinants of opioid overdose. *Drug and Alcohol Dependence, 195,* 66–73.

Pender, J., Hertz, T., Cromartie, J., & Farrigan, T. (2019). *Rural America at a Glance* [Economic Information Bulletin No. EIB-212]. U. S. Department of Agriculture.

Pollard, K., & Jacobsen, L. A. (2019). *The Appalachian region: A data overview from the 2013–2017 American Community Survey. Chartbook.* Appalachian Regional Commission.

Potera, C. (2019). Black lung disease resurges in Appalachian coal miners. *AJN The American Journal of Nursing, 119*(4), 14.

Pugh, R. (2007). Dual relationships: Personal and professional boundaries in rural social work. *British Journal of Social Work, 37*(8), 1405–1423.

Reichert, C., Cromartie, J. B., & Arthun, R. O. (2014). Impacts of return migration on rural US communities. *Rural Sociology, 79*(2), 200–226.

Rennison, C. M., DeKeseredy, W. S., & Dragiewicz, M. (2013). Intimate relationship status variations in violence against women urban, suburban, and rural differences. *Violence Against Women,* 1077801213514487.

Rennison, C. M., Dragiewicz, M., & DeKeseredy, W. S. (2013). Context matters: Violence against women and reporting to police in rural, suburban and urban areas. *American Journal of Criminal Justice, 38*(1), 141–159.

Rhone, A., Ver Ploeg, M., Williams, R., & Breneman, V. (2019). Understanding low-income and low-access census tracts across the nation: Subnational and subpopulation estimates of access to healthy food [Economic Information Bulletin No. EIB-209]. U. S. Department of Agriculture.

Rodd, S. (2015). *The depths of poverty in the Deep South.* Think Progress. http://thinkprogress.org/economy/2015/06/15/3669553/tchula-mississippi/

Rothwell, D. W., & Thiede, B. C. (2018). Child poverty in rural America. *IRP Focus, 34*(3). https://www.irp.wisc.edu/wp/wp-content/uploads/2019/02/Focus-34-3d.pdf

Saslow, E. (2016, April). We don't know why it came to this. *The Washington Post.* http://www.washingtonpost.com/sf/national/2016/04/08/we-dont-know-why-it-came-to-this/.

Schaefer, A., Mattingly, M. J., & Johnson, K. M. (2016). *Child poverty higher and more persistent in rural America* [National Issue Brief #97]. Carsey Research. https://scholars.unh.edu/cgi/viewcontent.cgi?article=1265&context=carsey

Singh, G. K., & Siahpush, M. (2014). Widening rural–urban disparities in life expectancy, US, 1969–2009. *American Journal of Preventive Medicine, 46*(2), e19–e29.

Sriram, U., Morgan, E. H., Graham, M. L., Folta, S. C., & Seguin, R. A. (2018). Support and sabotage: a qualitative study of social influences on health behaviors among rural adults. *The Journal of Rural Health, 34*(1), 88–97.

Talebreza-May, J. W., Jensen, R., & Shay, N. (2017). An assessment of the strengths and needs of rural social workers in the northwestern United States. *Contemporary Rural Social Work, 9*(1), 1.

U.S. Census. (2019a). *Quick facts, Persons in poverty, percent, Mississippi.* https://www.census.gov/quickfacts/fact/table/MS/INC110218

U.S. Census. (2019b). *Quick Facts, Persons in poverty, percent, Virginia.* https://www.census.gov/quickfacts/VA

U.S. Department of Agriculture [USDA]. (2020, February). *Rural poverty and well-being.* Economic Research Service. https://www.ers.usda.gov/topics/rural-economy-population/rural-poverty-well-being/#demographics

U.S. Department of Health and Human Services. (2020). *2020 poverty guidelines.* Office of the Assistant

Secretary for Planning and Evaluation. https://aspe.hhs.gov/2020-poverty-guidelines#guidelines

Ulrich-Schad, J. D., & Duncan, C. M. (2018). People and places left behind: Work, culture and politics in the rural United States. *The Journal of Peasant Studies, 45*(1), 59–79.

Ulrich-Schad, J. D., & Stanley, M. J. (2011). *Rural Americans in chronically poor places report less access to health services than other rural Americans* (Carsey Brief, Fall 2011). The Carsey Institute, University of New Hampshire.

Van Gundy, K. (2006). *Substance abuse in rural and small town America.* A Carsey Institute Report on Rural America. Carsey Institute.

Vernon-Feagans, L., & Cox, M. (2013). Poverty, rurality, parenting, and risk: An introduction. *Monographs of the Society for Research in Child Development, 78*(5), 1–23.

Walters, J. E., Jones, A. E., & Brown, A. R. (2019). Work experiences of rural social workers in the United States. *Journal of Social Service Research*, 1–19.

Waltman, G. (2011). Reflections on rural social work. *Families in Society: The Journal of Contemporary Social Services, 92*(2), 236–239.

Whiteside-Mansell, L., McKelvey, L., Saccente, J., & Selig, J. P. (2019). Adverse childhood experiences of urban and rural preschool children in poverty. *International Journal of Environmental Research and Public Health, 16*(14), 2623.

Zekeri, A. A. (2019). Food insecurity and maternal mental health among African American single mothers living with HIV/AIDS in the Alabama Black Belt. *Journal of Health Care for the Poor and Underserved, 30*(5), 151–159.

13

International Human Services

© HIKRCN / SHUTTERSTOCK

Samood Akter is an 18-year-old refugee who recently received political asylum in the United States and is seeking trauma counseling at a refugee resettlement agency. During Samood's initial intake, she explained that she had worked as a sewing operator in a garment factory in Bangladesh since she was 13 years old, making garments for many large stores in the United States and Europe. Most of the brands of clothing she sewed were very popular in the United States and include t-shirts, shorts, and athletic clothing. Samood's job was to attach collars to shirts, which she said was a very difficult job because she had to match the pattern of the fabric exactly. Samood sought asylum in the United States because she is a member of a religious minority and believed she was moving to the city for a better life but learned once she arrived that she had been sold to a garment factory as an indentured servant. Samood also shared that the garment factories hired only girls between the ages of 10 and 18 to work on the lines because they were more passive and did not have to be paid as much as men. All the supervisors were men, and they would often scream at the girls to make them work faster. She explained that if she finished 20 collars an hour, they would demand that she do 30, and if she did 30, they would demand that she do 40. But, she explained, that was impossible, although that did not stop the male supervisors from abusing and harassing the girls to compel them to work faster. Sadook described beatings she and the other girls had to endure, including having their faces and heads slapped, being grabbed by the hair, and being shoved. Samood explained the men would often use vulgar language toward the girls, calling them whores and telling them they were worthless. Samood also described how they would make the girls stand on benches for hours as punishment. Her hours were from 7:30 a.m. to 10:00 p.m. 7 days a week, but they often forced the girls to work until 3:00 a.m. with very few bathroom breaks, especially in the months leading up to the Christmas holidays. Most of the girls got only a handful of days off per year. When the girls worked until 3:00 a.m. they often slept in the factory near their sewing machines until the bells rang at 5:00 a.m. so they could get ready to start work again. Samood described how the supervisors would throw water on their faces and play loud music to keep them awake. They received no sick days or vacation, and Samood and the other girls were paid 18 cents an hour but often were paid for only 8 hours a day, since that was a requirement of the American and European businesses. Samood also talked about the food insecurity she and the other girls experienced. She described modest meals of rice with lentils and admitted that she weighs only 82 pounds despite being 5 feet, 3 inches tall.

WHAT IS INTERNATIONAL HUMAN SERVICES?

There is a movement for all professionals in the human services to become more engaged in global issues, even if they do not plan to travel internationally or directly engage in global practice. For instance, almost two decades ago Chi-Ying Chung (2005) made several recommendations to professional counselors to get involved in international human rights work, suggesting they apply their training in multicultural counseling and competencies to the international arena to combat human rights abuses. In fact, most, if not all of the human services professions are encouraging increased international awareness and engagement, at least on some level (Villarreal Sosa & Nuckolls, 2018). One of the most significant benefits of developing a more international lens for evaluating social problems is that human services providers, even those who do not travel internationally, will gain increased awareness of social justice on all levels (Coffey et al., 2020).

The human services profession exists worldwide, and there are many shared concerns among providers, regardless of the country in which they practice. Human services professionals in Central Africa and Asia are just as concerned about gender-based violence and children's rights as human services professionals in the United States and Great Britain. The nature of the social issues and the function and role of the human services professional may vary depending on the political and economic conditions unique to each country, but concerns about human rights, poverty, and other social problems are shared globally.

What has historically differed, though, are understandings of the underlying values of the human services profession, particularly in relation to the values of self-determination and freedom of individual choice. Consider the social work profession, for instance. In the United States, self-determination and freedom of choice are very highly valued, but in many countries that practice collectivism, such as some in Asia, Africa, and Eastern Europe, self-determination has not historically been perceived as an important core value of the profession because it's seen as detracting from the value of community and cooperation (Canda et al., 1993; Weiss, 2005). For instance, a 1971 cross-cultural study comparing social worker prioritization of professional values in the United States and Turkey found that U.S. social workers highly valued individuality, freedom, and diversity, while Turkish social workers more highly valued social control and uniformity (Feldman, 1971). This cultural divide has eased in the last decade or so, with more recent cross-cultural studies showing less of a difference in how social workers from individualistic and collectivist countries perceive self-determination and freedom of choice (Zhao et al., 2018).

Regardless of how the values of individuality and collectivism may be shifting in global societies, it is still very important for human services professionals to recognize and respect cultural tensions surrounding differences in how the concepts of individuality, self-determination, and autonomy are culturally interpreted from a professional values perspective. For far too long, "Western" values have dominated the mental health care fields, rendering more collectivist cultures' notions of community and cooperation as defective in some manner. In fact, a significant aspect of international work involves the process of "decolonizing" the professions by addressing professional attitudes and expectations that are influenced by predominantly White "Western" notions of normative behavior (Lewis et al., 2018; Moe et al., 2020; Sewpaul & Henrickson, 2019).

Human services professionals in essentially every country place a high value on the protection of human rights, social justice, and the end to human oppression in whatever form it might manifest within a particular region. In many regions of the world, certain groups of individuals are oppressed due to their ethnic background, religious heritage, or **caste system** level, and as a consequence they often have little to no political power and are subjected to mistreatment and exploitation. A primary concern of human services professionals in South Africa, for instance, relates to issues of racial inequities remaining from the country's former system of apartheid. South African school social workers are commonly used to teach positive race relations to the students in the South African public school system. Race issues may take on a different form in the United States, related to the country's history of slavery and mass immigration, but the point is that the similarities between the two regions is an overriding concern about human rights.

The Impact of Globalization

Many professionals working in the human services fields have long wanted to venture into the arena of international work but haven't had either the knowledge or opportunity. Without strong networking connections in the world of global advocacy, it has historically been very difficult to break into the field of international work. But the world is getting smaller, not in terms of population, but in terms of its interconnectedness. This is making it far easier to gain knowledge about what is going on in other parts of the world and to make worldwide connections with other practitioners and advocates. The increased international connectedness among all countries, and consequently, all people, is called *globalization*.

No longer are countries completely isolated in either their financial economies or political processes and activities. In the world's newest wave of globalization, countries throughout the world are connected through the development of a global economy (e.g., international financial interdependence, mutual trade, financial influence), increased international migration, and increased ease in communication. Consider how easy it is for anyone with a mobile device connected to WiFi to access anyone anywhere in the world using social media, such as Facebook or Twitter, or by using one of the many free communication apps, such as Apple's iMessenger or WhatsApp or video conferencing apps, such as Apple's FaceTime, Zoom, or Google Meets. All of these forces, driven in large part by technology, combine to create situations where the cultural, economic, and political states of one country influence the cultural, economic, and political states of others (Al-Rawi, 2020; Betoret & Betoret, 2020; Block, 2004).

One of the positive impacts of a shrinking world is increased awareness, communication, and cooperation among social advocates around the world. In fact, social reform on a global level is now more possible than ever before. Consider the impact the internet has had on the exchange of information between relatively remote communities, and especially oppressive countries with closed communication. Although limits can be placed on information exchange, the internet has made the global exchange of information about social issues as easy as pressing a few buttons. Of course, that is a somewhat simplistic statement, but the importance of the internet and computer-mediated communication cannot be understated.

Human rights organizations that track social issues around the globe have a far broader reach now that they are able to communicate so quickly and directly with their support base. Consider Amnesty International, a human rights and advocacy organization with a website that includes a comprehensive list of human rights abuses and concerns occurring throughout the world. With an internet connection and a few clicks, individuals can obtain detailed information about the types of abuses and targeted populations, as well as instructions on how to take steps to assist in the global campaign to address these concerns. We can also learn real-time information from the informational websites of **nongovernmental organizations** (**NGO**) and can watch documentaries for free and direct eyewitness reports on YouTube.

International Human Services Organizations

There are many human services-related organizations that have stressed the need for the profession to develop a more international perspective. The International Association for Counselling (IAC) is a United Nations (UN)-affiliated international NGO that works to advance the counseling profession worldwide through advocacy, education, and research. Founded in 1966, the IAC advocates for the practice of counseling globally to enhance people's lives, reduce suffering, and increase well-being. A chief goal of the IAC is to increase access to counseling, such as professional counseling associations, particularly in countries without counseling structures. One way that IAC meets its goal of promoting the counseling profession on an international level is to host annual international conferences in a different country each year. IAC conferences have been held in Turkey, Malta, Italy, and Canada.

About 40 professional counseling associations and universities with counseling programs around the world have institutional memberships with the IAC, including the American Counseling Association and the Association for Counselor Education and

Supervision, both based in the United States. Other professional and academic programs with institutional membership are from Singapore, India, Italy, Canada, Uruguay, Australia, China, Malawi, Ireland, Saudi Arabia, Belgium, the United Kingdom, and Malaysia, just to name a few. The IAC also works in collaboration with several national, regional, and international NGOs and institutes, including the World Health Organization (WHO), the International Labor Organization (ILO), and the National Board for Certified Counselors in the United States.

Other human services international organizations include the International Federation of Social Workers (IFSW), the International Association of Schools of Social Work (IASSW), the International Council on Social Welfare (ICSW), and the International Consortium for Social Development (ICSD). The IFSW, founded in 1956, works with a broad range of human services organizations and NGOs to encourage international cooperation and communication among human services professionals around the globe. The IFSW has members from 80 different countries in Africa, Asia, Europe, Latin America, and North America. The IASSW is a support organization and information clearinghouse that promotes high standards in education, research, and scholarship, with a focus on global well-being. The IASSW also supports an exchange of information and expertise between social work educational programs. Both the IFSW and the IASSW have ethical standards that set the bar for practice, knowledge, and cultural competence.

The ICSW is an independent organization founded in 1928 in Paris and committed to social development. The ICSW works with the United Nations on matters related to social development, social welfare, and social justice throughout the world. The work of the ICSW is an excellent example of community development, using networking and international liaisons with other organizations to achieve its goals.

The ICSD is dedicated to economic and social development facilitated by practitioners, scholars, and students in the human services. The ICSD's primary goal is to confront social and **economic injustice** by increasing individual and community capacity and sustainable economic structures. The ICSD provides opportunities for collaboration among professionals, academics, and researchers, as well as organizations such as the United Nations, the World Bank, and NGOs. It serves as an information clearinghouse and as a source for experts in a range of areas pertinent to economic and social development, and facilitates an annual symposium attended by academics and practitioners from around the world.

The work of all of these international organizations reflects how macro practice occurs through a comprehensive network of agencies and organizations on all levels of society to achieve the global mission of eliminating social injustice.

In the next several sections I will explore examples of international social issues, including human rights violations, as well as some strategies for combating social problems on a global level, including global poverty, female genital mutilation, child labor, human sex trafficking, global human rights violations—specifically against indigenous populations; lesbian, gay, bisexual, transgender, and queer/questioning (LGBTQ) populations; and refugees and migrants—rape as a weapon of war, and genocide. While this certainly is not an exhaustive list of international issues and targeted populations, my goal is to provide readers with a summary of some of the more serious global social problems while providing readers with some guidance and insights on how human services professionals work, either from home or abroad, to make the world a better, safer, and more equitable place.

GLOBAL POVERTY AND SOCIAL EXCLUSION

Learning Outcome 13.1 **Explore the nature of globalization and its impact on advocacy and global poverty**

A common theme underlying most types of disadvantage, often fueled by globalization, is poverty because it leads to and results from various types of oppression and injustice. Somewhere between one quarter and one half of the world's population suffers from poverty, meaning that they do not have enough money for their basic needs. While global poverty has been declining in recent years, determining actual progress across the globe is complex, with some countries' economies growing and others remaining stagnant.

The process of accurately framing the poverty condition is a challenging one due to its complex nature. There is no universally applied concept of poverty (Ghafoor, 2017; Lister, 2004). Perceptions of poverty (and its causes) are often framed ideologically and politically, which then often dictates how poverty is addressed, including the development of policy directing the societal distribution of goods and resources. Thus, arriving at a universally agreed-upon definition of poverty and method of measuring poverty is challenging due in part to the politically laden "call of action" such definitions often require. Any definition of poverty must effectively capture the full impact and manifestation of poverty, as well as accurately reflect the reciprocal relationship between the poverty condition and other related forms of disadvantage (Martin, 2014; Wagle, 2017).

Traditionally poverty has been defined (and then measured) in either absolute or relative terms. **Absolute poverty** uses a poverty threshold, such as a minimum standard of living, where individuals who fall below the established threshold are considered to be living in poverty (Gordon, 2000; Ravallion, 2016; Townsend, 1979). The World Bank's definition of extreme poverty of living on less than $1.90 per day, and moderate poverty as living on less than $3.10 per day, is another example of poverty being defined in absolute terms (World Bank, 2020). These narrower and more concrete definitions of poverty use income and resources as tools with which to define and describe poverty in absolute terms. Also, absolute poverty measures do not vary from country to country and do not take living standards into consideration (Ravallion, 2016; Simler & Arndt, 2007).

Poverty in developing countries is often reflected in absolute terms, primarily because poverty in many regions of the world, such as sub-Saharan Africa, is extreme, but absolute poverty measures are often criticized because they don't provide the full picture of global poverty and also make global comparisons difficult (Ravallion, 2016). Absolute poverty measures are also somewhat arbitrary in nature because the amount of money that is determined to be required to live "adequately" differs widely from community to community, yet the absolute poverty threshold is set at a static level and does not consider geographic differences or general standards of living for comparative purposes (Marx & van den Bosch, 2007; Townsend, 1979). For example, consider that many low-income programs (e.g., low-cost internet, supportive housing program) use the federal poverty guidelines for qualification purposes, which in 2020 was $21,720 for a family of three. Now, that salary is low no matter where one may live, but the money is going to stretch much further in a place like Brownsville, Texas, where the median home value in 2020 was $87,600 compared to San Francisco, California, where the median home value in 2020 was $1,009,500!

Another way of defining poverty is in relative terms, where the poverty threshold is set relative to the standard of living within a particular community (Mowafi, 2004; Simler & Arndt, 2007). Relative measures of poverty recognize that evaluating poverty in relation to a standard of living is more meaningful than using an arbitrary threshold. An advantage of considering poverty in relative terms is that inequality and the level of relative deprivation can be more easily explored, which more accurately reflects the complicated nature of poverty (Alcock, 2006; Lister, 2004; Mowafi, 2004). Additionally, when poverty is measured in relative terms and within context, complexities of differing financial markets, varying lifestyles, and the ease (or challenge) of social mobility are considered. Most European countries use **relative poverty** measures where poverty is measured based on economic distance from the median income level, whereas the United States still uses an absolute poverty measure (Mowafi, 2004; Ravallion, 2016).

Poverty is almost always considered along with the concept of **social exclusion**, a form of deprivation that involves the **marginalization** and consequent exclusion of vulnerable groups from various domains within society such as the labor market, education, and housing (Bernard et al., 2019; Griffin, 2000; Lessof & Jowell, 2000; Lee & Murie, 1999). Individuals can be said to be living in poverty when they lack the resources to eat sufficiently or participate in the mainstream activities (such as working and voting), and lack the living conditions and amenities customary for their culture (Townsend, 1979). In other words, poverty is not just a lack of money. Rather, poverty is a holistic condition that involves deprivation on multiple levels.

Global poverty is a multidimensional social problem with complex causes and manifestations. The roots of poverty in many countries, particularly countries with **developing economies** and **least-developed countries (LDCs)** (as defined by the United Nations), are deep, often rooted in histories of colonialism and a world economic order that favors some countries while crippling others with unfair labor practices and large debt (Polack, 2004). According to Oxfam, an international NGO, women bear the brunt of global poverty due to discrimination they face in multiple sectors of society, as well as the fact that they engage primarily in unpaid labor and low-paid service-sector jobs (Coffey et al., 2020).

© YAVUZ SARIYILDIZ/SHUTTERSTOCK

Pushkar, India, November 3, 2014: A poor women draws water from the well and takes it to her tent.

Additionally, in many parts of the world, women lack the ability to own and maintain control of their assets due to gender-based restrictive laws (Meinzen-Dick et al., 2019).

Poverty, particularly extreme poverty, is considered a human rights issue because it intersects with other social problems that make it difficult, if not impossible, to live optimal lives while remaining safe. Women living in extreme poverty often do not have access to clean drinking water, sufficient food, adequate health care (including family planning), education, and suitable sustainable employment, and often cannot protect themselves and their children from violence and other forms of exploitation (Dominelli, 2019; Martin, 2014).

Women living in LDCs are at increased risk of poverty because the majority of women live in rural areas and are dependent on agriculture for their livelihood. There are approximately 47 countries that are considered LDCs, many of which are located in Africa and Asia. Approximately 800 million people live in LDCs, which consists of 12% of the world's population (UN-OHRLLS, 2020). Over 70% of the population in all LDCs live in rural areas, where informal employment within the agriculture sector (often called the *grey economy*) is the main source of employment and food insecurity is a daily reality (Bonnet et al., 2019; United Nations Women, 2015). While both men and women experience food shortages in rural areas in LDCs, women who work in the agricultural sector are particularly vulnerable because they have less access than men to economic opportunities and resources, get paid less than men, are often excluded from the lending and credit market, and work in informal or undocumented work such as domestic work, which can be unstable and insecure (Bonnet et al., 2019).

Many global lending practices are an example of economic policies that can hit women hard. Many economic policies in LDCs are not designed with women in mind, and whether intended or unintended, women are often the most significantly affected by policies that are economically unjust and exclusive. For example, microfinancing in developing countries—loans by lending agencies in the **Global North** provided to individuals and small enterprises in the **Global South**—often require applicants to provide collateral to secure a loan, but in most countries in the Global South, women are legally and culturally barred from owning property or other types of collateral (Kende-Robb, 2019).

Polack (2004) discusses the impact of hundreds of billions of dollars in loans made to countries in the Global South (South America, South Asia, and Sub-Saharan Africa) by countries in the Global North (United Kingdom, France, Germany, the United States, etc.). The cumulative impact of these loans to some of the poorest countries in the world has been devastating to the most economically vulnerable members, many of whom are women. Additionally, very little if any of the loan money has benefited women in LDCs; in fact, in many cases it has harmed them by increasing the poverty within the already devastatingly poor regions. In an attempt to repay this debt, many countries in the Global South exploit their own workers, many of whom are women, forcing them to work long hours under extremely harsh conditions for very little pay. Although Polack's analysis is older, his insights remain on point even today.

The UN Millennium Development Goals and the Sustainable Development Goals

The remedies to global poverty are as complex as the problem. Many experts working with NGOs believe that community development programs coupled with humanitarian relief with the goal of reducing conflict are the best approaches to reducing poverty

Pearson eText

Video Example 13.1

This video explores the impact of COVID-19 on global poverty and progress toward meeting the goals of the UN Sustainable Development Goals. What roles have international human services workers taken to address this new global challenge? https://www.youtube.com/watch?v=SmhEhqLAn8A

(Boussquet, 2020). The United Nations and world leaders made a commitment in 2000 to significantly reduce extreme poverty by half and address related social problems by 2015. The result of this project was the development of eight goals, called the **Millennium Development Goals** (**MDG**):

1. Eradicate extreme hunger and poverty
2. Achieve universal primary education
3. Promote gender equality and empowerment
4. Reduce child mortality
5. Improve maternal health
6. Combat HIV / AIDS, malaria, and other diseases
7. Ensure environmental sustainability
8. Develop a global partnership for development

Each goal had a target(s), indicators reflecting progress and success. For instance, Target 1 for eradicating extreme poverty was to cut poverty in half between 1990 and 2015 for those people who earned less than $1 a day, as indicated by World Bank population statistics, the poverty gap ratio, and the percentage of the poorest quintile in national consumption. Target 2 for eradicating extreme hunger was to cut the proportion of people suffering from hunger by half from 1990 to 2015. The indicators for this target were the prevalence of underweight children under age 5 and the proportion of the population below the minimum level of dietary consumption (United Nations Development Programme, 2000).

The Millennium Project, an independent advisory board, was commissioned by the U.N. Secretary General in 2002 and charged with the responsibility of developing an action plan to help the United Nations and world leaders achieve the MDGs by 2015. The final report of the Millennium Project, *Investing in Development: A Practical Plan to Achieve the Millennium Development Goals* (2005), made 10 core recommendations for all country leaders, a summary of which included the following:

1. The development of bold MDG-based poverty reduction strategies in a transparent and inclusive process by 2006
2. Developed and developing countries jointly initiating a rapid response to crisis situations (called Quick Wins), including mass distribution of malaria bed-nets, increasing the availability of antiretroviral treatment for AIDS patients, and the massive training of community-based workers
3. Increased donor support for regional projects, such as the building of roads and railways
4. An increase in assistance from high-income governments (as defined by the United Nations)
5. And an increase in support for global scientific research and development addressing the needs of the poor.

United Nations Sustainable Development Goals

© DENI NANDAR SUKANWAR / SHUTTERSTOCK

While this summary provides only a brief synopsis of the comprehensive recommendations, it reflects the report's focus on development and governance (from the top down and bottom up) as key strategies for combating extreme poverty and its correlates (e.g., hunger, child mortality, health pandemics).

In 2015 the United Nations announced that significant progress was made in meeting the MDGs. In a summit held in September 2015, the U.N. General Assembly launched a post-MDG campaign, which focused on sustaining progress and achieving what wasn't achieved during the MDG campaign. The summit report, *Transforming Our World: The 2030 Agenda for Sustainable Development,* outlines 17 Sustainable Development Goals (SDGs) (see Table 13.1) and 169 indicators, which were adopted during the summit and came into full force in January 2016. World leaders agreed to take all necessary measures to achieve these goals by 2030. The SDGs build on the MDGs, focusing on strategies that encourage economic growth and address areas that are known to combat poverty and other social problems, such as education, health, peace, and job opportunities, while also addressing global problems related to climate change and environmental protection.

Table 13.1   Sustainable Development Goals

Goal 1	End poverty in all its forms everywhere
Goal 2	End hunger, achieve food security and improved nutrition, and promote sustainable agriculture
Goal 3	Ensure healthy lives and promote well-being for all at all ages
Goal 4	Ensure inclusive and equitable quality education and promote lifelong learning opportunities for all
Goal 5	Achieve gender equality and empower all women and girls
Goal 6	Ensure availability and sustainable management of water and sanitation for all
Goal 7	Ensure access to affordable, reliable, sustainable, and modern energy for all
Goal 8	Promote sustained, inclusive, and sustainable economic growth, full and productive employment, and decent work for all
Goal 9	Build resilient infrastructure, promote inclusive and sustainable industrialization, and foster innovation
Goal 10	Reduce inequality within and among countries
Goal 11	Make cities and human settlements inclusive, safe, resilient, and sustainable
Goal 12	Ensure sustainable consumption and production patterns
Goal 13	Take urgent action to combat climate change and its impacts
Goal 14	Conserve and sustainably use the oceans, seas, and marine resources for sustainable development
Goal 15	Protect, restore, and promote sustainable use of terrestrial ecosystems; sustainably manage forests; combat desertification; halt and reverse land degradation; and halt biodiversity loss
Goal 16	Promote peaceful and inclusive societies for sustainable development, provide access to justice for all, and build effective, accountable, and inclusive institutions at all levels
Goal 17	Strengthen the means of implementation and revitalize the global partnership for sustainable development

Source: http://www.un.org/sustainabledevelopment/ The United Nations Association United States (UNA-USA) is a U.S.-based NGO that exists to provide assistance to the United Nations at the local level. A chief responsibility of the UNA-USA is to advocate for local policies that will help the United States achieve the SDG goals by 2030. Many larger counties in the United States have a UNA-USA chapter and county residents can become members, including attending meetings and lobbying events sponsored by the UNA-USA chapter. Volunteering as an intern or board member is an excellent way to gain international experience and exposure to global human rights violations and UN responses.

GLOBAL ENVIRONMENTAL PROTECTION AND ENVIRONMENTAL JUSTICE

Learning Outcome 13.2 Explore mechanisms for global environmental protection

Many of the social problems experienced in the world right now have an environmental cause, such as people who are forced to flee their homes and communities due to a natural or human-made disaster. Additionally, many social problems are exacerbated by an environmental crisis, such as droughts exacerbating poverty and food insecurity. The United Nations Development Programme (UNDP) notes how mismanagement of ecological and environmental resources contributes to growing inequality in the world. Many of the world's poorest and most vulnerable populations, especially those living in the Global South, are disproportionately impacted by environmental crises such as the increase in natural disasters and floods due to climate change, air and water pollution, and the dumping of toxic waste. All of these environmental problems have significant impacts on people's health and well-being, their ability to maintain a livelihood, and even their ability to find sufficient shelter, food, and water (UNDP, 2014).

Human services professionals have worked to protect the earth's natural resources while advocating for those populations most vulnerable to environmental injustice for as long as the profession has been around. But the area of "eco-human services" has not yet evolved into a distinct practice setting. I've included content on environmental protection and environmental justice in this chapter because environmental crises and environmental activism are global concerns; environmental issues such as air pollution, ocean plastics, and climate change are not contained by national borders. In general, the human services field is concerned with any environmental issue or crisis that impacts people. That doesn't mean that we aren't concerned with environmental crises that impact animals, natural resources, or other environmental ecosystems, but the primary concern for the human services profession is to improve the quality of life of the clients they serve through generalist intervention strategies and prevention efforts (National Organization for Human Services, n.d.).

When providing services to those impacted by an environmental crisis, including environmental injustice, the focus of human services professionals is on the intersect between the "eco" issue and its negative impact on the client or client systems (Dominelli, 2012; Drolet et al., 2015). Broad examples of these impacts include the effect of the climate crisis on human populations; natural and human-made disasters, such as hurricanes and wildfires (natural) and oil spills (humanmade) (Elliott & Pais, 2006); human-made pollution in the air, land, and water; and the impact of ongoing urbanization, such as overcrowding and the lack of open spaces.

Human services professionals who acknowledge the importance of considering the natural environment in their evaluation of people and their problems are increasingly using an *eco-social lens* and an *environment-in-person approach* when evaluating social problems, both of which consider the ways in which the natural world (particularly its mismanagement) impacts human populations (Dewane, 2011; Dominelli, 2012; Muldoon, 2006). At the heart of using an eco-social lens is the fight for environmental justice, because although everyone may be affected by an environmental crisis, not everyone is impacted in the same way or to the same extent (Dominelli, 2018; UNDP, 2014). As referenced earlier, it is most often the disenfranchised and economically disadvantaged populations and

Pearson eText

Video Example 13.2

This video explores the impact of the climate change on the people of Kiribati, a remote nation in Pacific ocean, between the United States and Australia. In what ways can human services professionals help raise awareness of the plight of this nation? https://www.youtube.com/watch?v=46yvAKge3qQ

regions that are most at risk of being negatively impacted by environmental degradation and environmental exploitation (Besthorn & Meyer, 2010). Consider the plight of entire communities that have been displaced due to droughts caused by climate change (Podesta, 2019), or indigenous populations who have lost land and water rights due to mining and oil extraction activities (Boele et al., 2001), or the impact of forced urbanization due to flooding in many countries, such as Bangladesh, altering an entire way of living for formerly agrarian communities (Byomkesh et al., 2012).

Environmental activism tends to be very grassroots in nature, and, contrary to the stereotype of environmentalists being White, educated, and wealthy, research shows that those concerned about the environment are demographically diverse with regard to age, race, education level, and income (Pearson et al., 2018). What most environmental activists do have is a deep passion for the natural environment and the populations most impacted by environmental degradation and environmental exploitation, which the research consistently shows are economically disadvantaged communities of color and indigenous populations in the Global South (Desai, 2019; Schoenherr, 2019; Skelton & Miller, 2016).

The field of environmental protection and environmental justice also tends to be community based, focusing on social change, such as advocating for environmentally friendly and sustainable policies and pro-environmental legislative action (Dominelli, 2018). Human services professionals are ideally situated for global environmental activism (even if they never leave their home country) because human services is concerned with human rights, and environmental injustice almost always involves the destruction and exploitation of the environment and environmental resources (often for economic gain), which perpetuates structural inequalities (Dominelli, 2012, 2018).

There are several SDGs that pertain in some way to environmental protection, but these relate directly to the environment:

- Goal 13: Take urgent action to combat climate change and its impacts
- Goal 14: Conserve and sustainably use the oceans, seas, and marine resources for sustainable development
- Goal 15: Protect, restore, and promote sustainable use of terrestrial ecosystems; sustainably manage forests; combat desertification; halt and reverse land degradation, and halt biodiversity loss.

It's interesting to note that the MDGs, initiated in 2000, lacked any specific focus on environmental concerns. The SDGs' direct focus on the environmental reflects just how recently environmental protection matters have emerged as global priorities. Some examples of environmental crises in need of urgent attention include climate change (what is often referred to as the *climate crisis*) and the resulting impacts on human populations.

The Climate Crisis and the Impact on Human Populations

The consensus of the scientific community is that human activity has negatively impacted the climate (Oreskes, 2018). Since terms like "global warming" and "climate change" have become a part of the culture wars, and political polarization surrounding the legitimacy of the climate crisis has ensued, particularly in the United States (Hoffman, 2015). But it's important to note that these debates are primarily politically and economically motivated, and all one needs to do is consult the climate science literature to discern the scientific validity of the climate crisis. The evidence of what is technically referred to as *anthropo-*

genic climate change is overwhelming. Human activity is causing global temperatures to rise, impacting the temperature of both air and water (Oreskes, 2018). In fact, the Intergovernmental Panel on Climate Change (IPCC) released a report in 1995 suggesting there was strong evidence to support the link between human activity and the acceleration of climate change, and by 2001 the IPCC asserted that the evidence for such a connection was definitive (IPCC, 2001).

While climate change is a complex process, it essentially involves the release of greenhouse gases, such as carbon dioxide (CO_2) and methane (CH_4), into the atmosphere. Greenhouse gases absorb and radiate energy, and when released into the earth's atmosphere, they retain heat very effectively. Natural events can release greenhouse gases, such as when organic matter decomposes and release methane or when volcanos are active and release carbon dioxide. But almost 90% of the carbon dioxide released into the atmosphere from human activity is from the burning of fossil fuels such as natural gas, oil, and coal. Since the Industrial era, the burning of fossil fuels has skyrocketed, and as CO_2 levels have increased, the risk of the unnatural warming of our planet has increased as well (IPCC, 2014).

Human-made climate change occurs in a dangerous cycle, where unnatural warming causes the release of more greenhouse gases, which then causes increased unnatural warming, which then leads to other dynamics, that in turn increase the production of greenhouse gases. For instance, there are many places in the world that have permafrost—sections of land that are permanently frosted over. Places like Alaska, Greenland, Antarctica, and areas of Russia have permafrost, and it's important that they remain frosted because the ice holds in dangerous gases from decomposing material from millions of years ago. As more carbon dioxide is being released into the atmosphere, though, a considerable amount of the earth's permafrost is melting, revealing decomposed matter, which then releases methane into the atmosphere, causing an increase in global temperatures, which then leads to more permafrost melting. Glaciers and sea ice are also melting, which contributes to this destructive cycle. Glacier and sea ice are white and very reflective, so they reflect solar sunlight, which helps keep the planet cool. But when glacier and sea ice melt, darker ground and sea water are exposed, leading to the absorption of solar light. Once solar light is absorbed by the darker ground and ocean, heat is emitted, which is then retained by existing greenhouse gases in the atmosphere (Schuur et al., 2009).

It's important to note that climate is different than weather, so on a freezing cold day when someone professes "what about global warming?!" they're talking about the weather, not the climate. There is a connection between climate and weather, though, which explains recent trends of record temperature highs and lows. As global

The Greenland ice sheet, the second largest body of ice in the world which covers roughly 80 percent of the country, has been melting and its glaciers are retreating at an accelerated pace in recent years due to warmer temperatures.

© David Goldman/AP/Shutterstock

temperatures rise, oceans become warmer; permafrost, ice sheets, and glaciers melt; weather becomes increasingly unpredictable; and this unpredictability can lead to extreme weather events such as an increase in polar vortexes (Wuebbles, 2017). In other words, global warming is causing not just warmer weather, but colder weather as well.

One of the most reliable ways that climate scientists can determine historic climate patterns (called climate modeling) is by relying on data from the ice core studies—a series of studies conducted on ice cores obtained from places like Greenland and Antarctica (National Science Foundation, 2020; Raynaud et al., 2020; Thompson, 2000). The reason these studies are so valuable is that ancient ice obtained from drilling far into the earth in places with permafrost contains valuable data on what the climate was like thousands of years ago. With each snowstorm, particles of dust, pollen, and even sea salts are trapped in gas bubbles and preserved, leading to layer upon layer of ice that holds historic atmospheric data. When a core is drilled and removed, researchers can test the particles contained in the gas bubbles and compare them over a series of time dating back 800,000 years (Petit & Raynaud, 2020). Comparing levels of greenhouse gases through the years can then be compared to human activities and events, such as the onset of the Industrial Revolution and the development of the automobile, both of which involved the mass burning of fossil fuels.

In the last 800,000 years there have been eight cycles of increased CO_2, with peaks reaching between 260 and 300 parts per million (ppm). The modern climate era began approximately 11,700 years ago, which also marks the beginning of human civilization. According to the National Aeronautics and Space Administration (NASA), changes in climate temperatures prior to the modern climate era were primarily due to natural changes in the Earth's orbit, which then impacted solar energy levels (NASA, 2020). But then the Industrial Revolution began with the burning of fossil fuels, and evidence from the ice core studies reveals definitive evidence of the impact of human activity on CO_2 levels. In 1950 CO_2 levels reached an all-time high of just over 300 ppm, and as Figure 13.1 illustrates, current CO_2 levels have reached approximately 410 ppm, and there is no indication of levels declining.

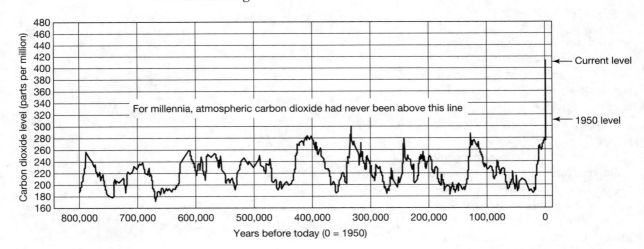

Figure 13.1   This graph, based on the comparison of atmospheric samples contained in ice cores and more recent measurements, provides evidence that atmospheric C02 has increased since the Industrial Revolution (Credit: NOAA Mauna CO2 record).

Extreme Weather Events

So, what are the impacts of climate change on human populations? There are several, including increases in extreme weather events such as hurricanes, cyclones, floods, and droughts. These events in turn impact the availability of safe water and food sources, which when scarce can have dangerous impacts on human health, livelihoods, and livestock (Kovats et al., 2005; Rojas-Downing et al., 2017). Marine life is also affected, with similar impacts (Barange, et al., 2014). Regions in the Global South are getting hit the hardest, including Central and South America, the Arabian Peninsula, Southeast Asia, and throughout the African continent (Samson et al., 2011).

Increases in air and water temperatures are "supercharging" storms, leading to increases in severity and duration, which in turn leads to increased natural disasters and increased devastation (Deschenes & Moretti, 2009; Doan, 2014; Eckstein et al., 2019). A "natural disaster" is defined most commonly as an unexpected event that is contained in time and space and that impacts the majority of people in an affected community (Fritz, 1961; Hossain, 2011). Natural disasters place people in extreme danger, causing significant loss (personal and environmental) and the disruption in essential societal functioning at a level beyond most affected communities' capacity to respond (Hossain, 2011). Natural disasters can cause millions of dollars in destroyed property and infrastructure (Gough et al., 2019; Yates et al, 2014). They also cause extreme collective stress because of the crisis nature of the event, which often leads to significant psychological harm and life disruption among those affected by the disaster (Hossain, 2011; Quarantelli, 1998).

According to Oxfam, an international NGO that engages in disaster relief, climate-related disasters have more than tripled in the last 30 years, displacing more than 20 million people per year (Oxfam 2020). As referenced earlier, countries in the Global South have been disproportionately impacted by natural disasters, both in occurrence and consequences. Regions that are already struggling with extreme poverty, civil unrest, and health pandemics are particularly vulnerable (United Nations General Assembly, 2019). Examples of natural disasters due to increases in extreme weather events include the dramatic increase in drought-related wildfires such as the 2019–2020 bush fire in Australia that burned over 27 million acres and took 28 lives, and the massive wildfires in California, which burned over 4 million acres in 8,834 incidents in just in 2020 (Cal Fire, 2020).

Additional examples of natural disasters include monsoon-related flooding in South Asia resulting in loss of life and the displacement of over 12 million people (Oxfam, 2020), and a series of cyclones that hit Zimbabwe, Malawi, and Mozambique in 2019, leading to massive flooding, crop destruction, the destruction of property and community infrastructure, and massive loss of life (MacClune et al., 2020). Cyclone Idai hit first, sweeping with intense force through the three countries, and within 6 weeks Mozambique was hit by another cyclone—Cyclone Kenneth, which led to a mass cholera outbreak that further overwhelmed the country's already fractured health care system (Cambaza, 2019).

Disaster Relief.

The International Federation of Red Cross and Red Crescent Societies [IFRC] (2011) defines disaster response and management as the facilitation and organization of all humanitarian-related activities involved in preparedness, response, and recovery, to reduce the devastating impact of disasters. According to the U.S. Federal Emergency Management Agency (FEMA), there are four phases of emergency relief:

1. **Mitigation:** Relief efforts focus on prevention efforts
2. **Preparedness:** Relief efforts focus on the development of disaster relief plans
3. **Response:** Relief efforts focus on emergency action during the disaster designed to save lives and protect individuals
4. **Recovery:** Relief efforts focus on actions to return life to normal (FEMA, 2007).

FEMA also notes the importance of all phases of emergency response efforts occurring within a framework that is comprehensive, progressive, integrated, collaborative, well-coordinated, flexible, and professional (FEMA, 2007).

Human services professionals are uniquely suited to respond to extreme weather events and crises, particularly those impacting vulnerable populations (Zakour & Harrell, 2004). Human services providers can assist in all phases of disaster relief, coordinating with other professionals and paraprofessionals while playing a key role in crisis response, emergency management, and case management, such as coordination of services, including providing trauma-informed counseling (McFadden, 2005). Many natural disasters result in large numbers of people being displaced either temporarily or permanently, and human services professionals can also provide housing relocation services, including securing temporary and long-term housing for those displaced by the crisis. They can also provide case management focused on finding necessary services for displaced populations in their new communities (Muskal, 2012).

Recovery work for survivors of natural disasters is a long-term prospect, reflected not only in the personal testimonies of impacted populations but also in research studies on survivor and community recovery (Bell, 2008; Cunningham, 2009; Dewan, 2008; Laska & Morrow, 2006; Mills et al., 2007). For instance, a study conducted by the Texas Health and Human Services Commission on Hurricane Katrina survivors living in Texas found that 2 years after the hurricane struck, almost 60% of survivors were still unemployed, almost 50% relied on housing subsidies, and between 37 and 40% of those surveyed reported that they had significant physical and mental health needs (Texas Health and Human Services Commission, 2006; as cited in Bell, 2008). Six years later, New Orleans reported a 70% post-Katrina rise in homelessness (Reckdahl, 2011). The impacts on populations in developing and least-developed countries is even more severe, but long-term assistance is often lacking (Asim et al., 2019; Lee et al., 2020; Panwar & Sen, 2019).

Environmental Injustice

The U.S. Environmental Protection Agency (EPA) defines environmental justice as the "fair treatment and meaningful involvement of all people regardless of race, color, national origin, or income, with respect to the development, implementation, and enforcement of environmental laws, regulations, and policies" (USEPA, 2018, para. 1). This is an important definition because it captures the values of equality and worth regardless of one's socioeconomic status, race, or geographic location. But what is "fair treatment," and what does "meaningful involvement" look like? These are important questions to answer because they are the primary focus of the environmental activism movement—ensuring that everyone receives fair treatment and has a say in what happens in their communities.

The EPA asserts that fair treatment means that the negative consequences of industrial, governmental, and commercial environmental practices and policies do not disproportionately impact particular populations and communities (para. 3). In other words, if a company decides to dump toxic waste in a waterway in an economically disadvantaged ethnic minority neighborhood, tainting their water supply, the company is engaging in environmental injustice because a vulnerable population will bear the brunt of the negative consequences associated with that company's actions. The EPA defines "meaningful involvement" as people and communities having "an opportunity to participate in decisions about activities that may affect their environment and/or health" (para. 3). Meaningful involvement of impacted communities is also an issue that environmental activities support because this type of engagement ensures that at-risk populations are provided with an opportunity to become involved in environmental matters that impact them. Unfortunately, many companies and governments actively attempt to circumvent the involvement of potentially impacted populations because if an impacted population has input, particularly in some formal setting with public knowledge, opportunities for environmental exploitation are limited. Environmental injustice flourishes in secrecy.

Environmental injustice occurs globally, impacting the economically disadvantaged and communities of color the most, including ethnic and racial minorities, immigrants, and indigenous populations (Cifuentes & Frumkin, 2007; Kelly-Reif & Wing, 2016; Pellow & Park, 2002; Whyte, 2017). Environmental injustice isn't always inflicted on people of color, but when it is, the term most often used is *environmental racism*. There are numerous examples of environmental injustice throughout the world, including lead poisoning in the tap water in Flint, Michigan (Masten et al., 2016), higher rates of asthma and cancer in Black communities in St. Louis, Missouri, due to environmental degradation and substandard housing (Schoenherr, 2019), mass environmental degradation of Ogani tribal lands in the Nigeria Delta caused by decades of oil drilling by Shell Oil Company (Boele et al., 2001), and illegal land-clearing fires on tribal lands in Brazil's Amazon rainforest for commercial farming purposes (Desai, 2019).

One of the most well-known and egregious cases of environmental injustice involves the installation of the Dakota Access Pipeline (DAPL) on protected tribal land adjacent to the Standing Rock Sioux Reservation. The tribe and environmental activists assert that the construction of an oil pipeline on tribal land was in violation of Article II of the Treaty of Fort Laramie of 1868, as well as other federal environmental legislation. While this example is one that occurred in the United States, it serves as a highly relevant example of global environmental injustice, since all indigenous peoples in the U.S. are considered internally displaced sovereign nations. In light of the recency of these events, their global implications, the surrounding advocacy, and court litigation, I believe Case Study 13.1 provides a very useful example of industry- and government-sponsored environmental injustice and environmental racism against a historically oppressed and vulnerable group.

Case 13.1 highlights the egregious, overt, and targeted nature of many instances of environmental injustice (meaning the injustice is often inflicted knowingly and purposefully against a population perceived as lacking political power). The environmental injustice inflicted on the Standing Rock Sioux Tribe has strong global implications, since environmental degradation and environmental exploitation of indigenous land is not limited to the United States. These global implications are what prompted the United Nations Permanent Forum on Indigenous Issues to weigh in on this case, urging the United States to fulfil its obligation to the Great Sioux Nation by honoring its legally binding treaty

Case Study 13.1

The DAPL carries about 500,000 gallons of crude oil every day from North Dakota to the Gulf of Mexico, crossing several waterways, including the Lake Oahe reservoir, which provides the tribe's drinking water and serves as a source for sacred religious practices (Indian Country Today, 2016). The pipeline also required the destruction of sacred tribal land containing cultural and religious artifacts (Indian Country Today, 2016; Martin & Quiroga-Menéndez, 2018). The DAPL was originally planned to be installed north of Bismarck, North Dakota, but was later rerouted to tribal land because the primarily White population in Bismarck strongly opposed the pipeline due to fears of oil leaks and water contamination (Dakota Access Pipeline Project, 2014; Thornbecke, 2016). The decision to reroute the pipeline to tribal land led to accusations of environmental racism and environmental injustice against DAPL developer, Energy Transfer Partners, and the U.S. government.

The U.S. Army Corps of Engineers was the federal agency responsible for issuing an easement permit to Energy Transfer Partners so that the pipeline could cross the Missouri River and tribal lands, but federal law required that the agency first conduct a comprehensive environmental impact statement (EIS) that would evaluate the impact on tribal lands. The Corps made the determination that the EIS was unnecessary and issued the permit in 2016, but the Obama administration intervened, halting pipeline construction pending the Corps' completion of the EIS and an analysis of the impact on tribal treaty rights. Yet, on President Trump's second day in office, he reversed Obama's order, instructing the Army to expedite the review and begin construction without the EIS. The Standing Rock Sioux Tribe and other affected tribes filed suit against the Corps, accusing the agency of violating the National Environmental Policy Act (NEPA) and the National Historic Preservation Act, and asked the court for an emergency order to prohibit the initiation of construction on tribal land. Energy Transfer Partners began construction anyway and not only unearthed a sacred burial ground, but failed to report the finding of sacred artifacts as required by law, prompting the North Dakota Public Service Commission to file legal action (Indianz, 2017).

Construction of the pipeline was completed in June 2017, despite the tribes' pending litigation. In October 2017, a federal judge ruled in favor of the tribes, stating that the Corps failed to meet its legal obligation to conduct a thorough EIS prior to granting Energy Transfer Partners an easement, but did not order the halting of pumping operations. Thus, Energy Transfer Partners was allowed to continue pumping thousands of gallons of crude oil through tribal lands and adjacent to their water source, while concurrently completing the EIS. The DAPL has leaked at least five times between 2017 and 2018 (Brown, 2018).

The Corps completed the EIS per court order, but the Corps refused to allow the tribes to have meaningful input and also refused to consider the environmental analyses conducted by two of the nation's top environmental experts working on behalf of the tribe (Earthjustice, 2020). In response, the tribes filed suit again in August 2019, alleging that the EIS was insufficient and accusing the Corps

Authorities clear Standing Rock protest camp, North Dakota, USA - 23 Feb 2017

© Daniel William McKnight / Shutterstock

of environmental racism. On March 25, 2020, a federal judge ruled that the Corps did in fact violate the NEPA by circumventing the tribes' involvement in the environmental analysis and also by failing to sufficiently evaluate several environmental threats. As a consequence, the court rescinded the permit (Earthjustice, 2020; *Standing Rock Sioux Tribe* v. *U.S. Army Corps of Engineers*, 2020). In May 2020, the Standing Rock Sioux Tribe asked the court to shut down the pipeline pending the Corps' completion of the EIS (which could take years), asserting that allowing it continue to pump oil placed the tribes in jeopardy and permitted the continuation of a 200-year pattern of government-sponsored trauma (Earth Justice 2020).

The Standing Rock Sioux Tribe's fight against the U.S. government is important, not only because of the dangers the pipeline poses to the tribe (and surrounding tribes), but because of the impact the mass demonstrations had on indigenous rights around the world. Native Americans (self-identified as "water protectors," not protestors) and non-Natives allies from around the world engaged in months-long environmental action to stop the pipeline construction (American Horse, 2016; Woolf, 2016). Thousands of grassroot activists camped out on tribal lands while the world watched on their televisions, computer screens, and smartphones, aided by social media

and the trending hashtags #StandwithStandingRock, #NoDAPL, and #RezpectOurWater. The water protectors' attempts to stop the DAPL culminated in a standoff with authorities on the night of November 21, 2016, when police in riot gear confronted thousands of water protectors with rubber bullets, tear gas, concussion grenades, and water cannons in subfreezing temperatures (Hawkins, 2016). That evening signaled the shift from grassroots environmental activism to the more formal legal activism by Earthjustice, a nonprofit public interest legal organization.

Prior to social media, the plight of the Standing Rock Sioux Tribe would have likely played out in secrecy, and the government's and oil industry's environmental injustice and racism would have likely transpired without public awareness and scrutiny. Social media enabled the affected tribes and their non-Native allies to highlight the environmental injustice involved in the U.S. government's actions toward an indigenous population—routing a pipeline onto tribal land rather than the originally planned route through a majority White community. Indigenous populations throughout the world face similar environmental injustices rooted in environmental racism, and the Standing Rock Sioux Tribe's response and social media's ability to effectively recruit allies can serve as a model for future activism.

(John, 2016). This case also highlights the many ways in which human services professionals can become involved, particularly on a macro level.

Many human services providers were actively involved in the advocacy of the impacted tribal communities, both online and offline. Many human services providers traveled to Standing Rock Sioux Reservation and engaged in nonviolent advocacy as allies, and some as tribal members. Many human services providers working in policies fields also advocated for increased awareness and policy action by lobbying local officials.

Human services providers will quite likely be engaged in providing face-to-face advocacy and trauma-informed counseling as well. Human services providers working outside of the country can use the advocacy model advanced in the Standing Rock demonstration, with its significant use of social media, in advocacy campaigns on behalf of other groups impacted by environmental injustice—pushing informational content and calls to action throughout multiple social media sites with the help of trending hashtags. For instance, when word got out that law enforcement was tracking the whereabouts of Native American activists by monitoring their "check-ins" on social media, a call to action was disseminated on Facebook and Twitter asking allies to check into Standing Rock on their social media accounts, regardless of their location. And thousands of allies did just that in a show of nonviolent civil disobedience, theoretically thwarting law enforcement's ability to discern who was actually at the Standing Rock site. This novel tactic can be replicated by allies globally in similar situations.

HEALTH PANDEMICS AND MAJOR PUBLIC HEALTH CONCERNS

Learning Outcome 13.3 Identify major global health pandemics and other public health concerns

The SDGs are a "call to action" that emphasizes leaving no country behind (a reference to LDCs), but there are many threats to achieving the SDGs by the target date of 2030, including health pandemics. Major **health pandemics** occur worldwide, but they have a disproportionate effect on people living in developing countries and LDCs. Among those most significantly affected by major health pandemics, women and children are impacted the most severely due to their vulnerable status in many parts of the world. HIV/AIDS, malaria, Ebola, and other health crises put everyone at risk, but those living in LDCs are impacted the most because of increased prevalence and often marginal health care.

Dice et al. discuss the role of human services professionals in responding to pandemics, which may include advocacy, case management, counseling, prevention, education, and interprofessional collaboration. They also engage in various stages of response, including preparedness, response, and recovery. Human services professionals are well situated to take leadership roles in community responses. Human services professionals can also provide services to first responders who are experiencing vicarious trauma. One of the greatest strengths of human services professionals is that because they primarily work with vulnerable populations, they are likely to have established relationships with members of the communities that are most significantly impacted during a pandemic (Dice et al., 2018).

The Novel Coronavirus Threat to Least-Developed Countries

The novel coronavirus pandemic, which broke out in late 2019 to early spring 2020, has had a devastating impact on several LDCs and particularly vulnerable populations in slums and refugee camps. Coronavirus, the novel virus that causes COVID-19, overwhelmed health care systems in developed countries, such as the United States and Italy, so imagine the impact on LDCs, which have drastically underdeveloped health care systems, large land masses with very little infrastructure, and a majority of the populations living in remote rural villages (United Nations Department of Economic and Social Affairs [UN/DESA], 2020). One of the best ways to avoid the spread of coronavirus is through handwashing, except that in most LDCs there is a lack of clean water and little to no soap, making regular handwashing impossible (Clayton, 2020). Overcrowding is an issue as well, particularly in many refugee camps and informal settlements (often called "slums"), where more than 200 million people reside, making social distancing challenging, if not impossible (Williams, 2020).

Kibera, a densely populated informal settlement in urban Nairobi, Kenya, with a population of between 500,000 and 700,000 people, is an example of a community that is at high risk for coronavirus transmission, or the transmission of any other health pandemic. Most families live in one-room houses with mud walls and no running water. Most are day laborers who cannot socially isolate or distance themselves from others without plummeting even further into extreme poverty. Although the African continent had relatively low numbers of coronavirus cases, the potential for devastation was there, as was the need for innovative solutions. Residents of Kibera were the ones who developed a COVID-19 response that included the locals making homemade masks for residents, local artists painting murals as public service reminders on public walls throughout the settlement, and local activists setting up food banks for people who lost their jobs due to the shutdown in Kenya (Jones, 2020). Local NGOs also stepped into help by setting up community handwashing and shower stations. The important takeaway from Kibera's response to the coronavirus threat is that they did not wait for outside assistance. Rather they worked with local advocates and developed responses they believe would work based on the unique nature and history of this settlement.

HIV/AIDS and Malaria in Sub-Saharan Africa

AIDS is a life-threatening disease that has had a devastating impact on families, particularly children, in many parts of the world, but especially in sub-Saharan Africa. The life expectancy in many African countries has dropped from 61 to 35 years of age, and resulted in millions of children losing one or both parents due to AIDS. For instance, as of 2015, of the approximately 17.8 million children estimated to have been orphaned by the AIDS epidemic, 85% percent lived in sub-Saharan Africa (U.S. Agency for International Development [USAID], 2016). Of the 2.8 million children living with the HIV virus in 2019, over 9 out of 10 lived in sub-Saharan Africa (UNICEF, 2019). But progress is being made, in large part due to the health programs and treatment protocols initiated in coordination with the work of the United Nations, specifically the goals of MDGs and the SDGs.

Another serious health concern impacting many countries in the Global South is malaria, a disease caused by a parasite transmitted by mosquitos. Humans can be infected if they are bitten by a female mosquito that has the parasite. It is a serious health problem that annually infects over 228 million people worldwide, killing over 400,000 victims. Sub-Saharan Africa bears the burden of most of these cases, with over 90% of infections and deaths occurring in the region (WHO, 2020b). Women and children under the age of five are at particular risk of fatality. When someone is bitten by an infected mosquito, they typically develop a fever, headache, and other flu-like symptoms within 10 to 15 days. If the treatment isn't implemented within 24 hours, the symptoms become far more severe and often lead to death.

Although visitors to high-risk regions can take antiviral medication (such as Malarone) to prevent malaria, long-term use carries certain health risks, leaving those who live in moderate and high-risk areas vulnerable to infection. Malaria deaths have decreased by about 50% in recent years in most regions, including in sub-Sarahan Africa, but malaria remains a very serious health risk, particularly for women and children living in rural areas, which tend to have higher malaria risks and lower prevention protocol and compliance (WHO, 2020b).

The Roll Back Malaria Partnership (RBM) to End Malaria is an example of a large human services response. The RBM Partnership to End Malaria is a consortium of NGOs, consisting of over 500 partners around the globe, initiated in 1998 by the WHO, the

United Nations Children's Fund (UNICEF), the UNDP, and the World Bank. The RBM Partnership to End Malaria operates in conjunction with the MDGs and SDGs, with the ultimate goal of reducing malaria by 90% by 2030. RBM's Global Malaria Action Plan for a malaria-free world was initiated in 2008 (2008–2015), with a recommitment in 2016 (2016–2030). The plan to reduce malaria involves a wide range of responses, including vector control, wide dissemination of insecticide-treated nets, rapid treatment using anti-viral drugs, and research (Whittaker et al., 2014).

The novel coronavirus pandemic has put the RBM Partnership to End Malaria some-what at risk by diverting funding and resources in already weak health care systems. This threat led to the CEO of the RBM Partnership to End Malaria to issue an urgent plea to the most at-risk countries in Africa and Asia not to divert funds and to continue support-ing the consortium so that the progress can continue and malaria relapse and resurgence (a condition where malaria returns in a formerly infected person) are avoided (RBM Part-nership, 2020). The continuation of malaria prevention programs is particularly important in light of new statistical modeling by the WHO predicting that if, during or in response to the pandemic, all malaria treatments were suspended due to lack of funding (e.g., insecticide-treated net campaigns, antimalarial medication), malaria deaths could double and infections could return to 2000 levels (WHO, 2020c). This crisis provides an exam-ple of the complexity of global health crises and how one crisis can jeopardize others by diverting funds and political attention.

HUMAN RIGHTS VIOLATIONS AGAINST AT-RISK POPULATIONS

Learning Outcome 13.4 **Explore the nature of human rights violations against women and girls, displaced populations, LGBTQ people, and survivors of genocide and rape as a weapon of war**

Gender-Based Violence Against Women And Girls

Pearson eText

Video Example 13.3

This video explores the impact of female genital mutilation on women and girls. How can human ser-vices professionals balance respect for culture with human rights and the right of women and girls to have body autonomy? https://www.youtube.com/watch?v=D_TMgAPNIGQ

Women and girls in developing countries are at particular risk for a range of human rights violations, especially if they are from rural communities, live in extreme poverty, live where more traditional patriarchal customs are practiced, are from marginalized groups such as religious minorities, or are experiencing displacement (United Nations Women, 2017). It would be impossible to provide an exhaustive list of human rights violations in this chapter, so I am including some of the more significant human rights violations pre-senting the most significant risks to women and girls around the globe.

Female Genital Mutilation

A human rights violation impacting many women and girls across sub-Saharan Africa, Asia, and the Middle East is female genital mutilation (FGM) (also called female circum-cision). FGM is a historical tradition dictating that a girl's external genitalia, typically her labia and clitoris, be cut away in a rite of passage ceremony marking her entry into womanhood (see Table 13.2). There are no health benefits to FGM but numerous health risks. The WHO estimates that among all girls alive today, more than 200 million have undergone FGM between infancy and 15 years of age (WHO, 2020a). The prevailing belief in cultures that practice FGM is that female circumcision is necessary to ensure a woman's chastity and purity, to control her sexual behavior, and to ensure her compliance and obedience while married.

The most serious type of FGM is Type 3, which includes the cutting away of the labia minora and the sewing together of the labia majora (the outer vaginal lips), which then creates a seal with only a small opening for the passing of menstrual blood and urine. The vaginal seal is intended to keep the women in the tribe from having sexual relations before marriage. It is literally torn open during the woman's first sexual encounter with her husband, which not only causes extreme pain but also has serious health consequences such as bleeding and possible infection. In some cultures, the torn pieces of labia are actually sewn together again if the woman becomes pregnant and are then torn open again during childbirth.

FGM can cause serious health risks, including lifelong pain, infertility, and death (WHO, 2020a). FGM is rarely performed by a physician but is frequently conducted by a village leader with no pain medication. Girls are often tied down and subjected to this surgery. Clitorectomies are most common in African countries, with infibulation being most popular in Islamic cultures, although most Muslim countries do not practice FGM (Schubert, 2016). The origins of FGM are difficult to trace, but there are some indications that this practice can be traced back to Arab and Ethiopian cultures in the 5th century BCE, or perhaps even earlier. There are indications that it was practiced in ancient Rome and Egypt as well (Lightfoot-Klein, 1991).

© ALEXANDRA ZAVIS/AP/SHUTTERSTOCK

Former circumciser Mariam Coulibaly displays the tools of her trade, a knife handed down to her by her mother and herbs to heal the wounds, at her home in Salemata, southeastern Senegal. Coulibaly says that she performed circumcisions on more than 1,000 girls during her 30-year career, but gave up the practice after surrounding villages decided the practice was dangerous. The piece of red cloth is part of one of the bright red robes she used to wear while performing the rites.

Table 13.2   Types of Female Genital Mutilation

Type	Name	Description
1	Clitoridectomy	The partial or total removal of the clitoris and, in very rare cases, only the prepuce (the fold of skin surrounding the clitoris).
2	Excision	The partial or total removal of the clitoris and the labia minora, with or without excision of the labia majora.
3	Infibulation	The scraping away of the inner labia (labia minora). The outer labia (labia majora) is then sewn together to cover the wound and create a vaginal "seal," leaving only a small opening for the passage of menstrual blood and urine. This "seal" is intended to keep the girl or woman from having sex prior to marriage. It is often torn open the first time the woman has sex with her husband. In some cultures, the torn pieces of labia are then sewn back together and must be torn open again for childbirth.
4	Other	All other harmful procedures to the female genitalia for nonmedical purposes such as pricking, piercing, stretching, incising, scraping, and cauterizing the genital area.

The reasons for FGM are similar but vary somewhat. Most cultures practicing FGM connect female circumcision to purity, cleanliness, modesty, and sexual restraint. Currently, FGM is practiced in several Central, Eastern, and Northern African countries, as well as countries in the Middle East and some Asian countries. Somalia is one of the worst offenders, with 98% of women having undergone FGM by the age of 12 (Mitike & Deressa, 2009). Although FGM is believed to be primarily culturally rooted, some people in Muslim countries cite the practice as a religious one (United Nations Population Fund, 2009).

In general, the practice has its origin in the cultural belief that the clitoris is dirty, is dangerous, and will lead to sexual promiscuity. Girls who refuse to undergo FGM are not considered marriageable and often are treated with scorn and experience social isolation. In a report on FGM prepared by Human Rights Watch (HRW) detailing the extent of FGM in Iraqi Kurdistan, advocates emphasized that most girls are forced to undergo FGM by loving mothers and aunts who believe this is the only way to ensure their daughters or loved ones are marriageable, and in a culture where there are few other options for girls, turning away from this long-practiced cultural tradition is not easy (HRW, 2010b). Iraq outlawed FGM in 2012, but a 2019 study found that it was still being widely practiced, particularly in rural regions such as Kurdistan (Abdulah et al., 2019).

Hanny Lightfoot-Klein, a noted expert on the practice of FGM, conducted field research in Sudan, Kenya, and Egypt and wrote four books based on her years of research within each of these countries. In her first book, published in 1989, she describes some common perceptions in Sudan of the woman's clitoris, which reflects why changing attitudes in traditional cultures are so challenging. She cites a prevalent belief in Sudan that if the clitoris is not cut, it will grow into a penis. Sudanese men are so anxious about this possibility that most would never marry a woman who wasn't circumcised, and those girls who refuse to undergo the procedure for whatever reason are considered "unclean" and are shunned from society.

FGM is typically conducted by a community or tribal healer, such as a midwife, in a non-medical setting. The instruments used include unsterilized razors or scalpels, and ashes are often used as a healing agent. Women and girls who have undergone FGM share stories of being told they are going to see a friend, then being held down, and beaten if they resist. With their legs forced open, they are then compelled to endure the cutting of their labia and/or clitoris without pain medication. Many girls have shared stories of being in immense pain, sometimes for more than a month, sometimes for life (HRW, 2010b).

In addition to pain, there are numerous health risks associated with FGM, including infection, scar tissue that interferes with sexual intercourse and childbirth, urinary problems, infertility, cysts, and reinjury. When women undergo infibulation and have sex the first time, their vaginal opening is torn open, and must be kept open so that the wound does not heal and close the vagina again. This practice is particularly painful, as the raw and bleeding remnants of the labia may take months to heal (World Health Organization, 2020a).

There has been a strong international response to the practice of FGM, starting in the early 1990s with numerous U.N. international treaties referencing FGM, calling it a human rights violation against women and girls and identifying the practice as a form of gender-based discrimination. For instance, in 1990 the Committee for the U.N. Treaty *The Convention on the Elimination of All Forms of Discrimination* adopted a general recommendation calling on all state parties to develop health policies that incorporate measures to eradicate the practice of FGM. In 2002, the United Nations General

Assembly (UNGA) passed a resolution urging all nation states to enact national legislation to abolish FGM. In 2008 numerous U.N. agencies, such as the WHO, UNICEF, United Nations Population Fund, UNAIDS, and the United Nations High Commissioner for Refugees (UNHCR) (to name a few), issued a joint statement on FGM in a report that included increased information about the extent of the practice and the severity of the consequences. Three of the U.N. MDGs also directly addressed FGM by focusing on women's health.

Community-based approaches that can build upon international pressure will have the greatest likelihood of successfully eradicating FGM (Ekundayo & Robinson, 2019; Lexow et al., 2009; Mwendwa et al., 2020; UNICEF, 2004). There has been a recent surge in grassroots efforts to eradicate FGM in response to a backlash among local women, particularly in African countries such as Kenya and Nigeria. Such grassroots efforts address FGM from multiple perspectives, including training tribal leaders about the true origins of FGM and highlighting the physical risks and the effect on girls' self-esteem. Educational campaigns also help men better understand the female anatomy, confronting myths (such as the clitoris becoming a penis if left uncut) and explaining how their marital relationships would likely improve if their wives experienced increased sexual pleasure (Martin, 2014).

In 2012 I had the opportunity to visit Dr. Sr. Ephigenia Gachiri, a Loreto sister in Nairobi, Kenya, who has been engaging in a grassroots effort to stamp out FGM in Kenya for decades, particularly in the Maasai tribe, through her organization Stop FGM. Dr. Gachiri explained to me that when a girl (or her family) refuses to undergo FGM, she isn't just risking her ability to marry, she's risking her entire future. Maasai culture promotes the belief that if a woman does not undergo FGM she will become promiscuous and will not remain faithful to her husband, choosing instead to have sex with many men.

The Maasai (like many other cultures) also believe that uncircumcised women not only bring shame on their families but also will cause their deaths. Uncircumcised women are treated as social outcasts and are not allowed to interact with others in their community, such as eating communally or even gathering water with the other women. They are not allowed to attend school and, of course, they are not permitted to marry. Since FGM is the rite of passage to womanhood, uncircumcised women have virtually no authority in their communities and are considered children, with less authority than a young girl who has had FGM.

Uncircumcised Maasai girls (and girls from other traditional tribes across Kenya) typically have only two options available to them—become a nun or a prostitute—and according to Dr. Gachiri, the latter is far more common. The irony of this dynamic is that a justification many village leaders use in support of FGM is that women will become promiscuous if they aren't circumcised. Yet the primary reason why uncircumcised women in the Maasai and other tribes in Kenya resort to prostitution is because they were shunned.

Dr. Gachiri works closely with Maasai leaders, because although Kenya outlawed FGM in 2011, the practice is entrenched in their culture and changing culture is a very slow process. Dr. Gachiri has developed a new ceremonial rite of passage that she hopes ultimately will replace FGM. She has also developed an educational curriculum that is shown in many schools, educating teachers and students on the nature and risks of FGM. She works directly with tribal chiefs and elders, educating them about the myths of FGM. While FGM is perceived as a human rights violation against women, Dr. Gachiri points out that it is often the women in the village who force girls to undergo the ritual,

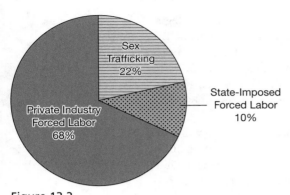

Figure 13.2
Trafficking in persons by type.
Source: International Labour Office [ILO], 2012

and women are often the circumcisers. In addition, sometimes uncircumcised women seek out FGM, despite their families' objections. Thus, Dr. Gachiri works with the women in the tribes as well, providing workshops and educational resources.

Dr. Gachiri's work is an example of the bottom-up approach—advocacy and community development initiated within communities by community members, where advocacy leaders have more legitimacy because they're seen as a part of the community, rather than as outsiders imposing change. Not only is Dr. Gachiri a native Kenyan (she is from the Kikuyu tribe), she also spent months getting to know the girls who had undergone FGM and sought permission from elders before doing so. She is perceived as having legitimacy because she is viewed as "one of them." She also collaborates with national and international partners who provide funding, technical support, and guidance when needed. Dr. Gachiri's approach to addressing FGM can be used as a model for similar advocacy efforts.

Human Trafficking

Trafficking in persons is a multi-billion-dollar criminal enterprise involving modern forced slavery, including sex trafficking, child sex trafficking, forced labor, forced child labor, domestic servitude and bonded labor, and unlawful recruitment and use of child soldiers. It's impossible to know how many people are victims of trafficking, but the latest estimate from International Labor Office (ILO) places the number at 40.3 million (adults and children)—24.9 million in forced labor, of which 16 million people are exploited in the private sector (e.g., agriculture, domestic work, sweatshops); 4 million in state-sanctioned forced labor (e.g., prisons); 15.4 million in forced marriage; and 4.8 million in forced sexual exploitation (commercial sex trafficking) (ILO, 2012). While men can be trafficked for sexual purposes, 99% of commercial sex trafficking victims are women or girls (ILO, 2017).

Forced Labor.

Forced labor involves compelling someone to work through coercion or manipulation. Labor traffickers may use physical threats or may use psychological coercion and deception to force someone to work for them. Examples include luring someone to work in a different country with promises of high pay and good working conditions, and then once they arrive, compelling them to work under harsh conditions for little or no money, and not allowing them to leave through threats of violence (ILO, 2017).

Forced labor can also include bonded debt, where an individual is either forced to work as repayment for a debt or inherits a family member's debt. The majority of victims of bonded labor are men. A common scenario involves a man who borrows money to support his family, with the agreement that he will work off the debt for a certain amount of time. But the terms of the work agreement always benefit the employer, and often the debt grows in time, rather than decreases. Bonded labor is particularly common in South Asian countries such as India and Pakistan. The industries where bonded labor is practiced the most include the agricultural sectors, bricklaying, mining, stonecutting, and carpet weaving (Premchander et al., 2015).

Forced Child Labor.

The ILO estimates that approximately 30% of forced labor involves children, totaling about 5.5 million children who are exploited in some form of forced labor: 21% in sex labor (sex trafficking), 27% in the private sector labor force (factories, agriculture, domestic servitude), and 33% in state-imposed labor (ILO, 2017). If children between 16 and 18 are included, the number of children forced into full-time labor jumps to 120 million: 61% in Asia, 32% in Africa, and 7% in Latin America.

Child labor is a social justice issue across the globe, but is a particular concern in Asian, African, and Latin American countries, where children as young as 4 years old are required to work up to 12 hours per day in jobs that put them in both physical and psychological danger. The opening vignette of Samood's life as a garment worker is a very loose adaptation of a story posted on an international labor advocacy group's website, and closely resembled the realities of children forced into labor through deception and manipulation, and the treatment they endure. Bangladesh and China are the largest garment and textile producing countries in the world, earning billions per year in exports to the United States and other countries in the Global North (World Trade Organization, 2019). Despite active and well-funded advocacy campaigns against sweatshops, they continue to prosper because Americans and Europeans love purchasing inexpensive clothing.

Child labor abuses occur in other parts of the world as well, including India, where young children are forced to plunge their hands into boiling water while making silk thread and children as young as 4 years in Asia are tied to rug looms for many hours a day and forced to make rugs. International human rights organizations such as HRW, Amnesty International, and UNICEF work diligently to protect children's rights, including lobbying for international policies and legislation that protect children and funding human rights efforts in specific countries to allow for intervention at the local level. But the problem of child labor, particularly in sweatshops in the Global South (Central and South America, Southeast Asia, India, and the Southern region of Africa), remains a serious problem impacting the entire world both socially and economically.

Polack (2004) discussed the impact of hundreds of billions of dollars in loans made to countries in the Global South by countries in the North (England, Spain, France, the United States, etc.) in the 1990s and early 2000s. Polack argued that the cumulative impact of these loans to some of the poorest countries in the world has been devastating to the poorest members of these countries because these loans (1) financed large-scale projects, such as hydroelectric plants, that either benefited the North or displaced literally millions of people, pushing them even further into poverty; (2) financed military armaments for government regimes that oppressed the countries' most vulnerable and poorest residents; or (3) lined the pockets of corrupt leaders of many countries in the Global South, resulting in increased oppression of the country's least-privileged members.

Very little if any of this loan money benefited the majority of the citizens of these countries; rather, it harmed them and in fact continues to harm them by increasing the poverty within these already devastatingly poor regions. In an attempt to repay this debt, many countries of the Global South exploit their own workers to make loan payments. For example, countries in South America have sold sections of rainforest formerly farmed by local residents to Northern timber companies, and other countries have been forced to privatize and then sell utility services formerly provided by the government, resulting in dramatic increases in the cost of utilities. These developments have resulted in many Northern companies making millions of dollars literally at the expense of the poorest residents of these debt-ridden countries.

One of the most devastating impacts of what has now evolved into trillions of dollars of debt for countries in the Global South is the evolution of the sweatshop industry, large-scale factories that develop goods exported to the North. Some of the poorest people in the world, including children, work in sweatshops throughout Asia, India, and Southern Africa, where horrific abuses abound. This occurs legally in many of these countries because in a desperate attempt to attract export contracts, many countries in Asia, including India, created "free trade" agreements or free-trade zones for Western corporations, allowing them to circumvent local trade regulations, such as minimum wage, working hour limits, and child labor laws, if they would open factories in their impoverished countries.

Polack (2004) suggested that literally every major retail supplier in the United States benefits from sweatshop conditions such as extremely low wages, extremely poor working conditions, physical and sexual exploitation without retribution, excessively long working hours (sometimes in excess of 12 hours per day with no days off for weeks at a time), and severe retribution such as immediate termination for complaints or requests for better working conditions. Child labor is the norm in these sweatshops, with most sweatshop owners preferring adolescent girls as employees because they tend to be more compliant and are more easily exploited.

Although local and international human services professionals work diligently to change these working conditions, at the root of the problem of child exploitation is economic injustice rooted in generations of intercountry exploitation. Thus, there is significant complexity not easily confronted without government involvement, which is often slow in coming when large corporations are making millions of dollars with the system as it currently operates. For instance, as labor unions became the norm in the United States, many companies such as Nike and Wal-Mart moved their factories to Asia and Central and South America, where millions of dollars can be saved in wages and benefits cuts. Addressing the issue of child labor and economic injustice will take the lobbying efforts of many international human rights organizations working with the media to create public awareness, where buying power is often the only tool powerful enough to influence sweatshop owners and large retail establishments.

Commercial Sex Trafficking.

While the gender breakdown in forced labor is about equal, the ILO estimates that 98% of sex trafficking involves female victims (ILO, 2017). In fact, younger women and girls are the most sought-after targets of large criminal organizations that are in the business of trafficking human beings. Human sex trafficking may comprise a smaller portion of all trafficking incidences per year, but its consequences are severe and long-lasting.

Girls are often sold into sex slavery by family members in need of money who are tricked into believing their girls will be employed as domestic workers in the city. Others are kidnapped or lured into the sex trade with promises of modeling contracts or domestic work in other countries. Many trafficked girls are kept in inhumane living conditions where they are forced to have sex with between 10 and 25 men a day. Many contract HIV/AIDS and are cast out onto the street once they become too sick to be useful (Martin, 2014; U.S. Department of State, 2019).

Much of the effort of human services professionals in countries with high rates of human trafficking, including India, Burma, Thailand, and Sri Lanka, is focused on rescuing these women and children and ensuring that they are delivered to safe communities where they will not be exploited again. Complicating intervention strategies is the fact that many government officials in many high-risk countries either look the other way when confronted with the illegal sex trade or openly contribute to it by protecting criminal organizations responsible for human trafficking. Human rights organizations have reported that many police officers, members of the military, and other government officials often arrest victims who attempt to flee, putting them in prison on charges of prostitution, a clear act of retaliation, rather than helping them to escape.

Efforts to confront trafficking are being fought on the legislative level as well. In 2000 the U.S. government passed the *Trafficking Victims Protection Act* (TVPA), which sets forth guidelines for how trafficking should be addressed on a national and global level. As a part of the legislation, the U.S. State Department releases an annual report entitled the *Trafficking in Persons Report*, which provides an update and analysis on the status of trafficking conditions worldwide. The report also ranks each country based on actions, such as the governments' actions in combating trafficking.

The ranking system—called the Watch List—consists of three tiers, with Tier 1 being the highest and reserved for those countries that are in compliance with the minimum standards set forth in the TVPA. Countries that are not in compliance with the TVPA but are making progress are ranked at Tier 2, and countries that do not meet the minimum standard and are not taking sufficient steps toward doing so are ranked at Tier 3. Summaries are included on the status of every country, including the country's tier, its annual accomplishments, and areas in need of improvement. Countries are assessed on their effectiveness in targeting and then prosecuting traffickers, as well as the level of services provided to victims.

Human services providers interested in advocating against commercial sex trafficking and on behalf of trafficking victims can get involved in this type of work in a number of different ways. They can work for a U.S.-based advocacy agency that works with women and girls trafficked into the United States. They can also work for an agency that advocates against commercial sex trafficking on a macro level, engaging in policy practice, education, and legislative advocacy. If they are interested in working abroad, many human services professionals can provide assistance to global advocacy organizations working around the world on prevention efforts. If one has language proficiency and expertise in a specific culture, it may be appropriate to work directly with survivors in another country, but most often U.S.-based human services professionals working abroad train locals to work more effectively with survivors.

MISTREATMENT OF DISPLACED PEOPLE

There are millions of displaced people in the world—those who are forced from their homes due to civil war, conflict, political and cultural persecution, natural disaster, ethnic cleansing, and genocide. Internally displaced people (IDPs) are those who are forced to flee their homes but remain in their home countries, whereas those who flee across an international border are referred to as refugees. Both IDPs and refugees are typically under the protection of a United Nations agency, depending on the country of origin and circumstances surrounding their forced migration. The United Nations estimates that there are approximately 70.8 million displaced persons worldwide, 41.3 million of whom are internally displaced, 25.9 million of whom are refugees, and 3.5 million of whom are asylum seekers—those who left their country of origin due to persecution (or fear of persecution) (UNHCR, 2019). Over half of the world's refugees are under the age of 18,

Pearson eText

Video Example 13.4

This video describes the realities of protracted refugees who are forced to live in limbo for decades. What are some key challenges protracted refugees face when resettled to a host country, such as the United States? https://www.youtube.com/watch?v=aiy_a_VAJh0

rendering this population one of the most vulnerable in the world.

Other displaced populations include indigenous peoples. As of 2020 there were an estimated 476 million indigenous people in 90 countries. Although five U.N. human rights treaties have been ratified to protect the world's indigenous populations, most indigenous populations remain highly vulnerable due to centuries of mass human rights violations, including land loss and extreme poverty resulting from generations of social exclusion and marginalization. Indigenous populations are also highly at risk for contracting COVID-19 due to communal living, social isolation, and a lack of infrastructure on tribal lands (The World Bank, 2020).

The Protection of Indigenous Peoples

Protecting the rights of **indigenous people** is a common concern of human services professionals practicing in countries such as the United States, Australia, and many Central and South American countries. Indigenous populations are often forced to engage in harsh and dangerous labor practices, such as working in fields sprayed with insecticides, transporting supplies on their person, or begging, in order to survive. They are also often victims of targeted state-sanctioned human rights violations, either to their person or through the taking of their land, similar to the plight of the Standing Rock Sioux Tribe discussed earlier in this chapter. .

The plight of the Australia Aborigines is similar in nature to those in the United States, where the historic immigration of Europeans displaced the indigenous tribal communities. In addition, both the United States and Australia engaged in an official campaign of mass discrimination, cultural annihilation, and outright slaughter for centuries (Brown & Brown, 2007; Elder, 2003; Weston, 2001). Indigenous tribes were forced off their lands and onto restricted areas where they were unable to practice traditional methods of self-support. Both indigenous populations in the United States and Australia were subject to the mass forced removal of children, who were mandated to attend schools where they were forced to abandon their cultural heritage and native language (Jacobs, 2006).

The 36-year civil war in Guatemala, which ended in 1996, involved what many human rights organizations consider the genocide of indigenous populations, or what is commonly referred to as the "disappearance" of indigenous peoples. The U.N. Truth and Reconciliation Committee estimates that up to 200,000 people were killed by government forces (HRW, 2008).

As a consequence of the intergenerational trauma that has resulted from physical and cultural genocide and forced migration, many indigenous people, including Native Americans, Native Hawaiians and Pacific Islanders, and Alaskan Natives, have experienced a decimation of their population, as well as extreme poverty and marginalization. These impacts often manifest in physical and mental health problems, family problems, and a range of other issues on a macro and micro level. Human services professionals may work with indigenous people in reconciliation efforts to restore them to a level of self-sufficiency and cultural pride. Several movements are underway within indigenous tribal communities intended to move them toward wholeness and a life without substance abuse, depression, and the brokenness in families that has so often been the result of social ills.

The *Healing Forest Model* is a community-based recovery approach rooted in the Native American "Wellbriety" movement. The program is based on the belief that everyone in a community is responsible for helping addicts recover, because if one member is impacted, all are. The ultimate focus of the Healing Forest Model is on restoration and healing. The Healing Forest Model was developed by a tribal member, Don Coyhis, who suffered from alcoholism for years and received inspiration and input from tribal elders who shared wisdom regarding traditional cultural laws for authentic change (Wolf, 2016).

The wisdom, or "laws of change," used in the Healing Forest Model is based on the philosophy of the medicine wheel, a Native American concept that addresses the interconnectedness of everything in life. According to the teachings of the medicine wheel, the pain of one person creates pain for the entire community, and thus there are no individual issues or concerns (Evans et al., 2013). This community concept of healing is very consistent with a model of macro practice, which posits that there are no such things as individual problems; instead, because people make up communities, all individual problems become community problems. This philosophy may be counterintuitive to North Americans, who as a society place an exceedingly high value on individuality, oftentimes at the cost of community. Yet, many believe that the key to reclaiming physical and mental health in indigenous culture is through such a community practice approach (Coyhis & Simonelli, 2005).

The Protection of Refugees and Internally Displaced Persons

Individuals may become refugees through a variety of circumstances such as natural disasters, health pandemics, climate change, religious or cultural persecution, and civil conflict. For instance, in the last two decades there have been between 17 and 33 armed civil conflicts at any one time, leading to civil unrest and instability in several developing countries and LCDs. In the midst of a civil war, innocent civilians are often forced to flee in search of safety, a phenomenon referred to as **forced migration**. As referenced earlier in this section, if civilians flee but do not cross international boundaries, they are referred to as internally displaced persons (IDPs), but if they are forced to flee into another country, then they often receive the legal designation of refugee.

When refugees live secretly in a country with closed borders, they are considered by the host country to be illegal immigrants. Life as an illegal immigrant is lived on the fringes, in constant fear of detection, detainment, and repatriation. In other situations, refugees are warehoused in refugee settlements or camps. In many refugee camps, refugees are not allowed to leave and are often considered a serious risk to the host country. Most refugee camps are established in border regions and may remain in close proximity to the conflict that caused the displacement in the first place. Many refugees remain in camps for decades, with no hope of resettlement or repatriation to their home country. **Protracted refugee situations** foster a sense of significant despair, as most protracted situations linger for generations. Those refugees fortunate enough to be selected for resettlement in the United States or another developed country often face years of challenges as they struggle to survive in a complex society, often underemployed and socially isolated (Hollenbach, 2008; Khan, 2019; Loescher et al., 2008; UNHCR, 2020).

Human services professionals often work with refugees in a variety of practice settings, including refugee resettlement agencies (contracted with the U.S. Department of State), schools, mental health agencies, international NGOs such as Oxfam, and even the United Nations. It is for this reason that human services providers should have awareness of global dynamics, even if they never intend to practice abroad. Many clients in need of human services have emigrated from countries where they were victims of oppression and human rights violations. Working with populations that have a history of oppression and marginalization requires an understanding of the wide range of global abuses related to social injustice and human rights violations, as well as a recognition of how these abuses have implications on direct practice with individual clients.

Human Rights Violations Against LGBTQ People

Pearson eText

Video Example 13.5

This video describes growing anti-LGBTQ sentiments in Poland and the fear members of this community are experiencing in response to growing human rights violations against the LGBTQ population. What factors most commonly influence anti-LGBTQ stances and what can advocates do to shift these negative perspectives? https://www.youtube.com/watch?v=EXurXvMAhxM

The plight of lesbian, gay, bisexual, transgender, and queer/questioning (LGBTQ) people and those who are gender nonconforming is quite bleak in many parts of the world. In many countries same-sex relationships are illegal, with punishments ranging from prison to death. Harassment and abuse of LGBTQ people, sometimes even by police or others in positions of power, are not uncommon. For instance, in Iran, having a same-sex relationship can result in anything from 100 lashes to a death sentence (HRW, 2010c; International Lesbian, Gay, Bisexual, Trans and Intersex Association [ILGA], 2019). In Senegal "homosexual conduct" is punishable by a minimum of 5 years in prison (HRW, 2010a; ILGA, 2019).

A report by HRW on crimes against the LGBTQ population in Iraq detailed the death squads that combed the country in 2009 searching for men who appeared gay. In what HRW describes as a "killing campaign," bands of armed men barged into private homes and abducted men who were perceived as gay, often for no reason other than they did not appear manly enough. Abducted men were murdered, and their dead bodies discarded, leaving evidence of gruesome torture, including having their genitals cut off and having glue injected into their anuses. HRW was informed that most of the death squads were from a militia group that espouses the threat of effeminate men and considers the killing of men perceived as gay as "social cleansing" (HRW, 2009, p. 4). Although the militia were from militant Islamic groups and may have been acting in response to a cleric's fatwa (order), neither the Iraqi government nor the Iraqi police investigated the killings or made any arrests, leading HRW and other advocacy organizations to believe that the Iraqi government is not concerned about these death squads, perhaps because they are targeting an undesirable and unsympathetic group (Martin, 2014).

South Africa is another country known for having high rates of violence, particularly against women. According to advocacy organizations, about half of all women in South Africa are victims of sexual assault (Doan-Minh, 2019; HRW, 2011). In fact, a U.N. Special Rapporteur report on gender-based violence in South Africa states that up to 75% of men have perpetrated sexual assault on a woman, and more than 50% of women have experienced gender-based violence (United Nations General Assembly, 2016). According to the report, many of these rapes were called "corrective rape," where lesbians, transgender women, and women whose gender expression is perceived as too masculine are raped to "correct their bodies." Often these rapes are particularly brutal, involving numerous men who beat the women while calling them derogatory names. These rapes are so brutal that many victims are killed as a result of the sexual assault. South African men who rape lesbians, trans women, or gender nonconforming women often do so with complete impunity, confident they will not be arrested.

Advocacy organizations around the world confront these injustices in a variety of ways, including through education and awareness, legal remedies, and U.N. remedies through the human rights treaty system. Advocacy on a legal level includes attempts to change U.S. asylum laws, making it easier for applications based on persecution due to sexual orientation to be accepted by immigration judges. Currently, despite the fact that many people around the globe are highly persecuted based on their sexual identity and/or sexual conduct, current

U.S. asylum laws make it difficult for LGBTQ people to be granted asylum because the legal test for persecution based on the membership in a social group does not allow for the contextual reality of sexual minorities who are forced to hide who they are, or risk imprisonment, physical assaults, or death (Mora, 2019; Sridharan, 2008).

Genocide and Rape as a Weapon of War

The 1948 U.N. Convention on the Prevention and Punishment of the Crime of Genocide defines genocide as any act committed with the intention to destroy, in whole or in part, a national ethnic, racial, or religious group: killing members of the group, causing serious bodily or mental harm to members of the group, deliberately inflicting on the group conditions of life calculated to bring about its physical destruction in whole or in part, imposing measures intended to prevent births within the group, and forcibly transferring children of the group to another group (U.N. General Assembly, 1948).

Genocides typically occur within a broader armed civil or international conflict. Thus, determining whether civilian deaths in conflict rise to the level of genocide can be challenging, highly influenced by politics. A determination of genocide can be made by any country that is a signatory of the 1948 U.N. Genocide Convention, as well as by the General Assembly of the United Nations. Yet it is important to note that even if the international community does not deem certain incidences of civilian killings as genocide, a genocide may still have occurred. There may be political reasons why the United Nations or a member country does not level charges of genocide against a particular government or group, such as a desire to avoid mandatory intervention.

There have been several genocides in the world's recent history, each one seemingly more gruesome than the next. The U.S. genocide of Native Americans during the 1700s through the 1800s and Turkey's genocide of the Armenians in 1917 are examples of genocides that have never been officially recognized by the international community. More recent genocides include the German Nazi Holocaust against the Jews in Europe during World War II, the Serbian genocide against the Bosnians in 1992 through 1994, and the Rwandan genocide against the Tutsi in 1994. Each of these genocides also involved **rape as a weapon of war**— the raping of women of the targeted ethnic or religious group in the midst of civil conflict.

Rape as a weapon of war is a systematic tactic used in armed conflict targeting the civilian population (primarily women and girls) that involves sexual violence in an officially orchestrated manner and as a purposeful policy to humiliate, intimidate, and instill fear in a community or ethnic group (Buss, 2009; Danjibo & Akinkuotu, 2019; HRW, 1996). Thus, rape during

Pearson eText

Video Example 13.6

This video describes how sexual violence is used as a weapon of war in the conflict in South Sudan. What is the role of culturally based stigma in survivor recovery? https://www.youtube.com/watch?v=veDZfz7QmT8

© Pete Muller/AP/Shutterstock

Judges in a military tribunal for eleven Congolese soldiers hear arguments during a court session in Baraka, Democratic Republic of the Congo (DRC). The accused are said to have raped nearly fifty women and looted shops in the town of Fizi on January 1-2, 2011. They face charges of crimes against humanity and rape. The trail was the first of its kind in which a ranking officer, Lt. Col. Kebibi Mutware, faced such significant charges. Mass rape has long been used as a weapon of war in eastern DRC.

wartime is not a byproduct of armed conflict but an instrument of it (Buss, 2009). For instance, in Rwanda, President Habyarimana's armed forces—government-sponsored militia groups called Interahamwe—and Hutu civilians not only used machetes to kill and maim almost a million Tutsi men, women, and children, but also subjected hundreds of thousands of Tutsi women to sexual violence with the goal of impregnating them as well as infecting them with HIV (Buss, 2009; Cohen et al., 2009; Des Forges, 1999; HRW, 1996).

In June 2008 the United Nations Security Council adopted Resolution 1820, which recognized rape as a weapon of war and established a commitment to addressing sexual violence in conflict, including punishing perpetrators (U.N. Security Council, 2008). This resolution became an important part of convictions by international criminal tribunals in response to genocides in former Yugoslavia, Rwanda, and in the United Nations–backed Special Court for Sierra Leone (UNDPKO, 2010).

In addition to international legal remedies, there are several advocacy and human services agencies that work with survivors of genocide and rape as a weapon of war. For survivors who have immigrated to a different country, culturally adapted trauma counseling can be very effective. For survivors remaining in their home country, indigenous healing approaches are often used based on a **restorative justice model**. Additionally, many human services professionals, such as social workers and psychologists from the United States and Europe, have partnered with agencies in Rwanda and other countries with histories of genocide. Using a *train-the-trainer* model, these professionals train counselors in Rwanda and Bosnia (for instance) to provide trauma-informed therapy to survivors, often merging Western approaches with indigenous ones.

CONCLUSION

As the world shrinks due to globalization, people are becoming more aware of human rights violations committed against vulnerable populations. Poverty is an underlying factor in virtually all global social problems, both with regard to who is affected and how governments and the international community respond. Human services professionals along with social justice advocates work on multiple levels to address a range of global social problems—health pandemics; human trafficking; the treatment of indigenous people, migrants, and refugees; mistreatment of LGBTQ populations; and genocide—using culturally adapted intervention strategies on micro and macro levels. Many human services providers may never practice abroad, but having knowledge of international dynamics, including the history of human rights violations targeting specific populations, is vitally important since the United States has a high percentage of immigrants and refugees, many of whom will likely be seeking treatment for themselves and or their children.

SUMMARY

- The nature of globalization and its impact on advocacy and global poverty are explored. The nature of globalization on various systems is explored, including how the globalization of communication, such as the internet, has made international human services more possible than it was in the past.
- Global poverty and social exclusion are also explored with a focus on how these conditions undercut the majority of social problems and human rights violations in the world, particularly those in developing economies and least-developed coun-

tries. Efforts to address poverty are explored, including the U.N. Millennium Development Goals and the Sustainable Development Goals.

- Environment protection and environmental justice are explored with a particular focus on the climate crisis and the impact on people of color and other disadvantaged and marginalized communities. The relationship between climate change and extreme weather events also is explored, with a focus on the role of human services professionals working with populations most impacted by earthquakes, hurricanes, wildfires, cyclones, and other destructive weather events. Environmental injustice and racism are also explored, including related factors and impacts on the most vulnerable populations.

- Major global health pandemics and other public health concerns, and the international community's response, are identified. Global health pandemics, such as HIV/AIDS, and other public health crises, such as malaria and COVID-19, are examined, with a particular focus on vulnerable populations.

- Human rights violations of several at-risk populations are explored, including the nature of gender-based violence on a global level, such as female genital mutilation, forced labor, and sex trafficking. Global initiatives focused on legal remedies as well as advocacy efforts on the micro and macro levels are explored, highlighting the role of human services providers facilitating direct services and macro-levels advocacy. The ways in which indigenous populations and refugees have been mistreated and marginalized and how human services professionals can respond are examined. Historic and current mistreatment of indigenous populations within the context of culturally adapted intervention strategies is explored. The plight of the world's refugees is also explored, including forced migration and protracted refugee situations. Advocacy efforts focusing on trauma, resettlement, and repatriation are also explored. The range of global human rights violations committed against lesbian, gay, bisexual, transgender, and queer/questioning populations, and ways that human services professionals can respond, are identified. The nature and types of human rights violations committed against LGBTQ people and those with nonconforming gender expression, including the nature of treatment of LGBTQ people in particular countries, are discussed. Advocacy efforts and challenges are explored, including the role of human services providers. The nature of genocide and rape as a weapon of war and the role of human services providers working with survivors are examined. The human impact of genocide on survivors and the path toward healing are explored. Rape as a weapon of war is explored, including the conditions under which it is committed, as well as ways that advocates and human services professionals can respond on a micro and macro level.

END-OF-CHAPTER QUESTIONS

1. How has the growth of internet-based communication apps impacted globalization?
2. Explain the factors involved in the disparate impact of environmental injustice on communities of color.
3. Describe the disparate impact of global pandemics such as the novel coronavirus, HIV/AIDS, and infectious diseases such as malaria.
4. What role can human services professionals take in advocating against global gender-based violence?

5. What are some examples of the long-term impacts of historic and current impacts of human rights violations against the world's indigenous people?
6. Provide three examples of human rights violations committed against LGBTQ people globally. How can human services professionals effectively advocate against global homophobia and gross mistreatment of sexual minorities?
7. What is the relationship between genocide and rape as a weapon of war? What are some models for human services providers from countries in the Global North working in support of survivors?

References

Abdulah, D. M., Sedo, B. A., & Dawson, A. (2019). Female genital mutilation in rural regions of Iraqi Kurdistan: A cross-sectional study. *Public Health Reports*, *134*(5), 514–521.

Alcock, P. (2006). *Understanding poverty*. Palgrave Macmillan.

Al-Rawi, A. (2020). Mobile news apps as sites of transnational ethnic mediascapes. *The Journal of International Communication*, *26*(1), 73–91.

American Horse, I. (2016, August 18). "We are protectors, not protesters": Why I'm fighting the North Dakota pipeline. *The Guardian*. https://www.theguardian.com/us-news/2016/aug/18/north-dakota-pipeline-activists-bakken-oil-fields

Asim, M., Mekkodathil, A., Sathian, B., Elayedath, R., Kumar, R., Simkhada, P., & Van Teijlingen, E. (2019). Post-traumatic stress disorder among the flood affected population in Indian Subcontinent. *Nepal Journal of Epidemiology*, *9*(1), 755.

Barange, M., Merino, G., Blanchard, J. L., Scholtens, J., Harle, J., Allison, E. H., Allen, I., Holt, J., & Jennings, S. (2014). Impacts of climate change on marine ecosystem production in societies dependent on fisheries. *Nature Climate Change*, *4*(3), 211–216.

Bell, H. (2008). Case management with displaced survivors of Hurricane Katrina: A case study of one host community. *Journal of Social Service Research*, *34*(3), 15–27.

Bernard, J., Contzen, S., Decker, A., & Shucksmith, M. (2019). Poverty and social exclusion in diversified rural contexts. *Sociologia Ruralis*, *59*(3), 353–368.

Besthorn, F. H., & Meyer, E. E. (2010). Environmentally displaced persons. *Critical Social Work*, *11*(3).

Betoret, E., & Betoret, N. (2020). Globalization of technologies: Pros and cons. In *Sustainability of the food system* (pp. 181–193). Academic Press.

Block, D. (2004). Globalization, transnational communication and the internet. *International Journal on Multicultural Societies*, *6*(1), 13–28.

Boele, R., Fabig, H., & Wheeler, D. (2001). Shell, Nigeria and the Ogoni. A study in unsustainable development: I. The story of Shell, Nigeria and the Ogoni people– Environment, economy, relationships: conflict and prospects for resolution 1. *Sustainable Development*, *9*(2), 74–86.

Bonnet, F., Vanek, J., & Chen, M. (2019). *Women and men in the informal economy: A statistical brief*. International Labor Office [ILO]. WIEGO.

Boussquet, F. (2020). *To end global poverty, invest in peace*. Brookings Institute. https://www.brookings.edu/blog/future-development/2020/03/18/to-end-global-poverty-invest-in-peace/

Brown, A. (2018). *Five spills, six months in operation: Dakota access track record highlights unavoidable reality– pipelines leak*. The Intercept. https://theintercept.com/2018/01/09/dakota-access-pipeline-leak-energy-transfer-partners/

Brown, D. A., & Brown, D. (2007). *Bury my heart at Wounded Knee: An Indian history of the American West*. Macmillan.

Buss, D. E. (2009). Rethinking "rape as a weapon of war". *Feminist Legal Studies*, *17*(2), 145–163.

Byomkesh, T., Nakagoshi, N., & Dewan, A. M. (2012). Urbanization and green space dynamics in Greater Dhaka, Bangladesh. *Landscape and Ecological Engineering*, *8*(1), 45–58.

Cal Fire. (2020). Current year statistics. https://www.fire.ca.gov/stats-events/.

Cambaza, E., Mongo, E., Anapakala, E., Nhambire, R., Singo, J., & Machava, E. (2019). Outbreak of cholera due to Cyclone Kenneth in northern Mozambique, 2019. *International Journal of Environmental Research and Public Health*, 16(16), 2925.

Canda, E. R., Shin, S. I., & Canda, H. J. (1993). Traditional philosophies of human service in Korea and contemporary social work implications. *Social Development Issues*, 15(3), 84–104.

Chi-Ying Chung, R. (2005). Women, human rights & counseling: Crossing international borders. *Journal of Counseling and Development*, 83, 262–268.

Cifuentes, E., & Frumkin, H. (2007). Environmental injustice: Case studies from the South. *Environmental Research Letters*, 2(4), 045034.

Clayton, J. (2020). *Q&A: Access to health services is key to halting COVID-19 and saving refugee lives* [Press Release]. United Nations High Commissioner for Refugees. https://www.unhcr.org/en-us/news/latest/2020/3/5e7dab2c4/qa-access-health-services-key-halting-covid-19-saving-refugee-lives.html

Coffey, C., Espinoza Revollo, P., Harvey, R., Lawson, M., Parvez Butt, A., Piaget, K., Sarosi, D., & Thekkudan, J. (2020). *Time to care: Unpaid and underpaid care work and the global inequality crisis* [Oxfam briefing paper.] https://ousweb-prodv2-shared-media.s3.amazonaws.com/media/documents/FINAL_bp-time-to-care-inequality-200120-en.pdf

Cohen, M. H., Fabri, M., Cai, X., Shi, Q., Hoover, D. R., Binagwaho, A., & Anastos, K. (2009). Prevalence and predictors of post-traumatic stress disorder and depression in HIV-infected and at-risk Rwandan women. *Journal of Women's Health*, 18(11), 1783–1791.

Coyhis, D., & Simonelli, R. (2005). Rebuilding Native American communities. *Child Welfare*, 84(2), 323–336.

Cunningham, M. (2009). *Preventing and ending homelessness: Next steps*. Urban Institute.

Dakota Access Pipeline Project. (2014). *North Dakota Public Service Commission combined application for certificate of corridor compatibility and route permit*. Dakota Access, LLC. https://psc.nd.gov/database/documents/14-0842/001-030.pdf

Danjibo, N., & Akinkuotu, A. (2019). Rape as a weapon of war against women and girls. *Gender and Behaviour*, 17(2), 13161–13173.

Desai, R. (2019). *The Amazon wildfires are a product of environmental racism*. The Swaddle. https://theswaddle.com/the-amazon-wildfires-are-a-product-of-environmental-racism/#:~:text=Because%20of%20environmental%20racism.,the%20communities%20that%20inhabit%20it

Deschenes, O., & Moretti, E. (2009). Extreme weather events, mortality, and migration. *The Review of Economics and Statistics*, 91(4), 659–681.

Des Forges, A. (1999). *Leave none to tell the story*. Human Rights Watch. http://www.hrw.org/legacy/reports/1999/rwanda/rwanda0399.htm

Dewan, S. (2008). Resources scarce, homelessness persists in New Orleans. *New York Times*. https://www.nytimes.com/2008/05/28/us/28tent.html

Dewane, C. J. (2011). Environmentalism and social work: The ultimate social justice issue. *Social Work Today, 11*(5), 20.

Dice, T. F., Simmons, J., & Wolfenden, O. (2018). Responding to epidemics and pandemics: The role of human services professionals. *Journal of Human Services*, 38(1).

Doan, M. D. (2014). Climate change and complacency. *Hypatia*, 29(3), 634–650.

Doan-Minh, S. (2019). Corrective rape: An extreme manifestation of discrimination and the State's complicity in sexual violence. *Hastings Women's Law Journal*, 30, 167.

Dominelli, L. (2012). *Green social work: From environmental crises to environmental justice*. Polity.

Dominelli, L. (Ed.). (2018). *The Routledge handbook of green social work*. Routledge.

Dominelli, L. (2019). *Women and community action: Local and global perspectives* (3rd ed.). Policy Press.

Drolet, J., Wu, H., Taylor, M., & Dennehy, A. (2015). Social work and sustainable social development: Teaching and learning strategies for 'green social work' curriculum. *Social Work Education*, 34(5), 528–543.

Earthjustice. (2020, March 25), *Standing Rock Sioux Tribe prevails as federal judge strikes down DAPL permits*. https://earthjustice.org/news/press/2020/standing-rock-sioux-tribe-prevails-as-federal-judge-strikes-down-dapl-permits.

Eckstein, D., Künzel, V., Schäfer, L., & Winges, M. (2019). *Global climate risk index 2020*. Germanwatch https://germanwatch.org/sites/germanwatch.org/files/20-2-01e%20Global, 20

Ekundayo, R., & Robinson, S. (2019). An evaluation of community-based interventions used on the prevention of female genital mutilation in West African countries. *European Scientific Journal*, 15(30).

Elder, B. (2003). *Blood on the wattle: Massacres and maltreatment of Aboriginal Australians since 1788*. New Holland.

Elliott, J. R., & Pais, J. (2006). Race, class, and Hurricane Katrina: Social differences in human responses to disaster. *Social Science Research, 35*(2), 295–321.

Evans, A. C., Lamb, R., & White, W. L. (2013). The community as patient: Recovery-focused community mobilization in Philadelphia, PA (USA), 2005–2012. *Alcoholism Treatment Quarterly, 31*(4), 450–465.

Feldman, R. A. (1971). Professionalization and professional values: A cross-cultural comparison. *International Review of Sociology, 1*(2), 85–97.

Fritz, C. E. (1961). Disasters. In R. K. Merton & R. A. Nisbet (Eds.), *Contemporary social problems* (pp. 156–191). Harcourt, Brace and World.

Ghafoor, S. (2017). *Can there be a universal definition of poverty?*. GRIN Verlag.

Gordon, D. (2000). *Breadline Europe: The measurement of poverty*. Policy Press.

Gough, K. V., Yankson, P. W. K., Wilby, R. L., Amankwaa, E. F., Abarike, M. A., Codjoe, S. N. A., Griffiths, P. L., Kasei, R., Kayaga, S., & Nabilse, C. K. (2019). Vulnerability to extreme weather events in cities: implications for infrastructure and livelihoods. *Journal of the British Academy, 27*, 155–181.

Griffin, K. (2000). Problems of poverty and marginalization. Political Economy Research Institute [PERI]. *Working Paper Series, 51*, 1–29.

Hawkins, D. (2016, November 21). Police defend use of water cannons on Dakota access protesters in freezing weather. *The Washington Post*. https://www.washingtonpost.com/news/morning-mix/wp/2016/11/21/police-citing-ongoing-riot-use-water-cannons-on-dakota-access-protesters-in-freezing-weather/?noredirect=on&utm_term=.20c2bfb75ee3

Hoffman, A. J. (2015). *How culture shapes the climate change debate*. Stanford University Press.

Hollenbach, D. (2008). *Refugee rights: Ethics, advocacy and Africa*. Georgetown University Press.

Hossain, S. M. N. (2011). *Addressing the natural disasters through physical planning: A case study of Manikganj Pourashava* [Unpublished MURP thesis]. Department of Urban and Regional Planning, Jahangirnagar University, Savar, Dhaka.

Human Rights Watch [HRW]. (1996). *Shattered lives: Sexual violence during the Rwandan genocide and its aftermath*. Human Rights Watch.

Human Rights Watch [HRW]. (2008). *Guatemala: World Report 2009*. http://www.hrw.org/en/node/79213

Human Rights Watch [HRW]. (2009). *Uganda: "Antihomosexuality" bill threatens liberties and human rights defenders: Proposed provisions illegal, ominous, and unnecessary*. http://www.hrw.org/en/news/2009/10/15/uganda-anti-homosexuality-bill-threatens-liberties-and-human-rights-defenders

Human Rights Watch [HRW]. (2010a, November 30). *Fear for life: Violence against gay men and men perceived as gay in Senegal*. http://www.hrw.org/reports/2010/11/30/fear-life.

Human Rights Watch [HRW]. (2010b). *"They took me and told me nothing" Female genital mutilation in Iraqi Kurdistan*. https://www.hrw.org/report/2010/06/16/they-took-me-and-told-me-nothing/female-genital-mutilation-iraqi-kurdistan

Human Rights Watch [HRW]. (2010c, December 15). *We are a buried generation: Discrimination and violence against sexual minorities in Iran*. http://www.hrw.org/node/94978.

Human Rights Watch [HRW]. (2011). *"We'll show you you're a woman": Violence and discrimination against Black lesbians and transgender men in South Africa*. https://www.hrw.org/sites/default/files/reports/southafrica1211.pdf

Indian Country Today. (2016). *Standing Rock Sioux Tribe condemns destruction and desecration of burial grounds by Energy Transfer Partners*. https://indiancountrytoday.com/archive/standing-rock-sioux-tribe-condemns-destruction-and-desecration-of-burial-grounds-tbGDUq4PW0aOVUZEiVIweA

Indianz. (2017). *Dakota Access enters settlement for "unanticipated discovery" of tribal artifacts*. indianz.com/News/2017/09/21/dakota-access-enters-settlement-for-unan.asp

Intergovernmental Panel on Climate Change [IPCC]. (2001). *Climate change 2001: Synthesis report*. In R. T. Watson & the Core Writing Team (Eds.), *Intergovernmental panel on climate change*. Cambridge University Press.

Intergovernmental Panel on Climate Change [IPCC]. (2014). *Climate change 2014: Synthesis report*. In Core Writing Team, R. K. Pachauri, & L. A. Meyer (Eds.). Author.

International Federation of Red Cross and Red Crescent Societies [IFRC]. (2011). *The Red Cross Red Crescent approach to disaster and crisis management.* https://www.ifrc.org/PageFiles/91314/1209600-DM-Position-Paper-EN.pdf

International Labor Office [ILO]. (2012). *ILO global estimate of forced labour: Results and methodology.* ILO Publications. https://www.ilo.org/wcmsp5/groups/public/—ed_norm/—declaration/documents/publication/wcms_181953.pdf

International Labor Office [ILO]. (2017). *Global estimates of modern slavery: Forced labor and forced marriage.* https://www.ilo.org/wcmsp5/groups/public/—dgreports/—dcomm/documents/publication/wcms_575479.pdf

International Lesbian, Gay, Bisexual, Trans and Intersex Association [IGLA]. (2019). *State-sponsored homophobia.* https://ilga.org/downloads/ILGA_State_Sponsored_Homophobia_2019.pdf

Jacobs, M. D. (2006). *Indian boarding schools in comparative perspective: The removal of Indigenous children in the United States and Australia, 1880–1940.* https://digitalcommons.unl.edu/historyfacpub/20/

John, E. (2016). *Report and statement from Chief Edward John, expert member of the United Nations Permanent Forum on Indigenous Issues: Firsthand observations of conditions surrounding the Dakota Access Pipeline (North Dakota, USA).* un.org/esa/socdev/unpfii/documents/2016/Docs-updates/Report-ChiefEdwardJohn-DAPL2016.pdf

Jones, R. (2020). In this sprawling city within a city fighting coronavirus requires solidarity. *National Geographic.* https://www.nationalgeographic.com/history/2020/06/kibera-sprawling-city-within-city-fighting-coronavirus-requires-solidarity/#close

Kelly-Reif, K., & Wing, S. (2016). Urban-rural exploitation: An underappreciated dimension of environmental injustice. *Journal of Rural Studies, 47,* 350–358.

Kende-Robb, C. (2019). *To improve women's access to finance stop asking them for collateral.* World Economic Forum. https://www.weforum.org/agenda/2019/06/women-finance-least-developed-countries-collateral/

Khan, F. (2019). In chronic exile: Rethinking the legal regime for refugees in protracted refugee situations. *Stellenbosch Law Review, 30*(2), 186–211.

Kovats, R. S., Campbell-Lendrum, D., & Matthies, F. (2005). Climate change and human health: Estimating avoidable deaths and disease. *Risk Analysis: An International Journal, 25*(6), 1409–1418.

Laska, S., & Morrow, B. H. (2006). Social vulnerabilities and Hurricane Katrina: An unnatural disaster in New Orleans. *Marine Technology Society Journal, 40*(4), 16–26.

Lee, J. Y., Kim, S. W., & Kim, J. M. (2020). The impact of community disaster trauma: A focus on emerging research of PTSD and other mental health outcomes. *Chonnam Medical Journal, 56*(2), 99.

Lee, P., & Murie, A. (1999). Spatial and social divisions within British cities: beyond residualisation. *Housing Studies, 14*(5), 635–640.

Lessof, C., and Jowell, R. (2000). *Measuring social exclusion* [Working paper, No. 84], Centre for Research into Elections and Social Trends (CREST), University of Oxford.

Lewis, M. E., Hartwell, E. E., & Myhra, L. L. (2018). Decolonizing mental health services for indigenous clients: A training program for mental health professionals. *American Journal of Community Psychology, 62*(3–4), 330–339.

Lexow, J., Berggrav, M., & Taraldsen, S. (2009). *Prevention and eradication of female genital mutilation (FGM) and other harmful traditional practices (HTPs).* Norad Collected Reviews. http://www.norad.no/en/Tools+and+publications/Publications/Publication+Page?key=125122

Lightfoot-Klein, H. (1991, April 30–May 3). *Prisoners of ritual: Some contemporary developments in the history of female genital mutilation* [Presentation]. Second International Symposium on Circumcision, San Francisco.

Lister, R. (2004). Poverty. Cambridge: Polity. *Applied Ethics and Social Problems,* 715–728.

Loescher, L., Milner, J., & Troeller, G. (2008). *Protracted refugee situations: Political, human rights and security implications.* United Nations University Press.

MacClune, K., Norton, R., & Szönyi, M. (2020). *When the unprecedented becomes precedented: Learning from Cyclones Idai and Kenneth.* http://repo.floodalliance.net/jspui/bitstream/44111/3478/1/PERC%20africa.PNG

Martin, M. E. (2014). *Advocacy for social justice: A global perspective.* Pearson Publishing.

Martin, M., & Quiroga Menéndez, P. (2018). Advocating for social and environmental justice and human rights: Listening to indigenous voices. In M. Rinkel & M. Powers (Eds.), *Social work promoting community and environmental sustainability: A workbook for global social workers and educators.* International Federation of Social Workers.

Marx, I., & K. van den Bosch. (2007, September). *How poverty differs from inequality. On poverty measurement in an enlarged EU context: Conventional and alternative approaches* [Presentation]. 34th CEIES Seminar, Helsinki.

Masten, S. J., Davies, S. H., & Mcelmurry, S. P. (2016). Flint water crisis: What happened and why? *Journal American Water Works Association*, 108(12), 22–34.

McFadden, R. (2005). New Orleans awash in corpses. *New York Times*. https://www.aspentimes.com/news/new-orleans-awash-in-corpses/

Meinzen-Dick, R., Quisumbing, A., Doss, C., & Theis, S. (2019). Women's land rights as a pathway to poverty reduction: Framework and review of available evidence. *Agricultural Systems*, 172, 72–82.

Millennium Project. (2005). *Investing in development: A practical plan to achieve the Millennium Development Goals.* Report to the UN Secretary General. http://www.un-millenniumproject.org/reports/index_overview.htm

Mills, M. A., Edmondson, D., & Park, C. L. (2007). Trauma and stress response among Hurricane Katrina evacuees. *American Journal of Public Health*, 97(Supplement_1), S116–S123.

Mitike, G., & Deressa, W. (2009). Prevalence and associated factors of female genital mutilation among Somali refugees in eastern Ethiopia: A cross-sectional study. *BMC Public Health*, 9(1), 1.

Moe, J., Carlisle, K., Augustine, B., & Pearce, J. (2020). De-colonizing international counseling for LGBTQ youth. *Journal of LGBT Issues in Counseling*, 14(2), 153–169.

Mora, C. (2019). Shoot them: The Trump administration's immigration policy and its effect on LGBTI migrants and asylum seekers. *Georgetown Immigration Law Journal*, 34, 121.

Mowafi, M. (2004). The meaning and measurement of poverty: A look into the global debate. *Development Gateway Foundation*, 1–53.

Muldoon, A. (2006). Environmental efforts: The next challenge for Social Work. *Critical Social Work,* 7(2),

Muskal, M. (2012). Last FEMA trailer leaves Louisiana 6 years after Katrina. *Los Angeles Times*. http://latimesblogs.latimes.com/nationnow/2012/02/last-fema-trailer-leaves-new-orleans-six-years-after-hurricane-katrina.html

Mwendwa, P., Mutea, N., Kaimuri, M. J., De Brún, A., & Kroll, T. (2020). "Promote locally led initiatives to fight female genital mutilation/cutting (FGM/C)" Lessons from anti-FGM/C advocates in rural Kenya. *Reproductive Health*, 17(1), 1–15.

National Aeronautics and Space Administration [NASA]. (2020). *Climate change: How do we know?* Global Climate Change. https://climate.nasa.gov/evidence/.

National Organization for Human Services [NOHS]. (n.d.). *What is human services?* http://www.nationalhumanservices.org/what-is-human-services

National Science Foundation. (2020). *About ice cores. NFS icecore facility.* https://icecores.org/about-ice-cores

Oreskes, N. (2018). The scientific consensus on climate change: How do we know we're not wrong? In E. A. Lloyd & E. Winsberg (Eds.), *Climate modelling: Philosophical and conceptual issues* (pp. 31–64). Springer Verlag.

Oxfam. (2020). *5 natural disasters that beg for climate action.* https://www.oxfam.org/en/5-natural-disasters-beg-for-climate-action

Panwar, V., & Sen, S. (2019). Economic impact of natural disasters: An empirical re-examination. *Margin: The Journal of Applied Economic Research*, 13(1), 109–139.

Pearson, A. R., Schuldt, J. P., Romero-Canyas, R., Ballew, M. T., & Larson-Konar, D. (2018). Diverse segments of the US public underestimate the environmental concerns of minority and low-income Americans. *Proceedings of the National Academy of Sciences*, 115(49), 12429–12434.

Pellow, D. N., & Park, L. S. H. (2002). *The silicon valley of dreams: Environmental injustice, immigrant workers, and the high-tech global economy* (Vol. 31). NYU Press.

Petit, J. R., & Raynaud, D. (2020). Forty years of ice-core records of CO 2. *Nature*. https://media.nature.com/original/magazine-assets/d41586-020-00809-8/d41586-020-00809-8.pdf

Podesta, J. (2019). The climate crisis, migration, and refugees. *Global economy and development at Brookings*. https://www.brookings.edu/wp-content/uploads/2019/07/Brookings_Blum_2019_climate.pdf

Polack, R. (2004). Social justice and the global economy: New challenges for social work in the 21st century. *Social Work*, 49(2), 281–290.

Premchander, S., Prameela, V., & Chidambaranathan, M. (2015). *Prevention and elimination of bonded labour: The potential and limits of microfinance-led approaches.* International Labor Organization [ILO]. http://www.ilo.org/wcmsp5/groups/public/—ed_norm/—declaration/documents/publication/wcms_334875.pdf

Quarantelli, E. L. (Ed.). (1998). *What is a disaster? Perspectives on the question.* Psychology Press.

Ravallion, M. (2016). Toward better global poverty measures. *The Journal of Economic Inequality*, 14(2), 227–248.

Raynaud, D., Beeman, J. C., Chappellaz, J., Parrenin, F., & Shin, J. (2020). Antarctic air bubbles and the long-term ice core record of CO2 and other greenhouse gases. In M. Oliva & J. Ruiz-Fernández (Eds.), *Past Antarctica* (pp. 27–50). Academic Press.

RBM Partnership. (2020). *Global malaria partnership urges countries to act during 'window of opportunity' to save lives from malaria and COVID-19.* https://endmalaria. org/news/global-malaria-partnership-urges-coun-tries-act-during-%E2%80%98window-opportuni-ty%E2%80%99-save-lives-malaria

Reckdahl, K. (2011). Homeless population in New Orleans rises 70 percent since Hurricane Katrina. *The Times-Picayuna.* http://www.nola.com/politics/index. ssf/2011/06/homeless_population_in_new_orl.html

Rojas-Downing, M. M., Nejadhashemi, A. P., Harrigan, T., & Woznicki, S. A. (2017). Climate change and livestock: Impacts, adaptation, and mitigation. *Climate Risk Management, 16,* 145–163.

Samson, J., Berteaux, D., McGill, B. J., & Humphries, M. M. (2011). Geographic disparities and moral hazards in the predicted impacts of climate change on human popula-tions. *Global Ecology and Biogeography, 20*(4), 532–544.

Schoenherr, N. (2019). *Environmental racism in St. Louis.* Washington University in St. Louis. https://source. wustl.edu/2019/09/environmental-racism-in-st-louis/

Schubert, K. A. (2016). Female circumcision. *Encyclopedia of Family Studies,* 1–12.

Schuur, E. A., Vogel, J. G., Crummer, K. G., Lee, H., Sickman, J. O., & Osterkamp, T. E. (2009). The effect of permafrost thaw on old carbon release and net carbon exchange from tundra. *Nature, 459*(7246), 556–559.

Sewpaul, V., & Henrickson, M. (2019). The (r)evolution and decolonization of social work ethics: The global social work statement of ethical principles. *International Social Work, 62*(6), 1469–1481.

Simler, K. R., & Arndt, C. (2007). *Poverty comparisons with absolute poverty lines estimated from survey data.* Review of Income and Wealth, Vol. 53, No. 2, pp. 275–294.

Skelton, R., & Miller, V. (2016). *The environmental justice movement.* The Natural Resources Defense Council [NRDC]. https://www.nrdc.org/stories/environmen-tal-justice-movement

Sridharan, S. (2008). *The difficulties of U.S. asylum claims based on sexual orientation.* Migration Information Source. http://www.migrationpolicy.org/article/diffi-culties-us-asylum-claims-based-sexual-orientation

Standing Rock Sioux Tribe v. U.S. Army Corps of Engineers, 205 F.Supp.3d 4, 2020.

Thompson, L. G. (2000). Ice core evidence for climate change in the Tropics: Implications for our future. *Qua-ternary Science Reviews, 19*(1–5), 19–35.

Thornbecke, C. (2016). *Why a previously proposed route for the Dakota Access Pipeline was rerouted.* ABC News. http://abcnews.go.com/US/previously-proposed-route-dako-ta-access-pipeline-rejected/story?id=43274356

Townsend, P. (1979). *Poverty in the United Kingdom: A survey of household resources and standards of living.* University of California Press.

UN-OHRLLS. (2020). *About LDCs.* http://unohrlls.org/about-ldcs/

United Nations Children's Fund [UNICEF], U.S. Agency for International Development. (2004). *Children on the brink 2004: A joint report of new orphan estimates and a framework for action.* The Joint United Nations Programme on HIV/AIDS. United Nations Children's Fund.

United Nations Children's Fund [UNICEF]. (2019). *Children, AIDS and HIV: Global and regional snapshots.* https://data.unicef.org/resources/children-hiv-and-aids-global-and-regional-snapshots-2019/.

United Nations Department of Economic and Social Affairs (UN/DESA). (2020). *COVID-19 and the least de-veloped countries* [UN/DESA Policy Brief #66]. https://www.un.org/development/desa/dpad/publication/un-desa-policy-brief-66-covid-19-and-the-least-developed-countries/

United Nations Department of Peacekeeping Operations [UNDPKO]. (2010). *Review of the sexual violence elements of the judgments of the international criminal tribunal for the former Yugoslavia, the International Criminal Tribunal for Rwanda, and the special court for Sierra Leone in the light of Security Council Resolution 1820.* http://www.unrol.org/files/32914_Review%20of%20the%20Sexual%20Vio-lence%20Elements%20in%20the%20Light%20of%20the%20Security-Council%20resolution%201820.pdf

United Nations Development Programme [UNDP]. (2000). *Millennium development goals.* http://www.undp.org/mdg/basics.shtml

United Nations Development Programme [UNDP]. (2014). *Environmental justice: Comparative experiences in legal empowerment.* https://www.undp.org/content/dam/undp/library/Democratic%2520Governance/Access%2520to%2520Justice%2520and%2520Rule%2520of%2520Law/Environmental-Justice-Comparative-Ex-periences.pdf

United Nations General Assembly. (1948, December 9). *Prevention and punishment of the crime of genocide* [A/RES/260]. http://www.unhcr.org/refworld/docid/3b00f0873.html

United Nations General Assembly. (2016). *Report of the special rapporteur on violence against women, its causes and consequences on her mission to South Africa* [A/HRC/32/42/Add.2]. Human Rights Council, Thirty-second session. https://www.ohchr.org/Documents/Issues/Women/SR/A.HRC.32.42.Add.2.pdf

United Nations General Assembly. (2019). *Unprecedented impacts of climate change disproportionately burdening developing countries, delegate stresses, as second committee concludes general debate* [GA/EF/3516]. https://www.un.org/press/en/2019/gaef3516.doc.htm

United Nations High Commissioner for Refugees [UNHCR]. (2019). *Figures at a glance.* https://www.unhcr.org/en-us/figures-at-a-glance.html

United Nations High Commissioner for Refugees [UNHCR]. (2020). *Protracted refugee situations explained.* https://www.unrefugees.org/news/protracted-refugee-situations-explained/

United Nations Population Fund [UNFPA]. (2009). *The end is in sight: Moving toward the abandonment of female genital mutilation/cutting. Annual Report 2009.* UNFPA/UNICEF Joint Programme.

United Nations Security Council, 5916th Meeting. (2008). Resolution 1820 [sexual violence as a war tactic] 19 June 2008. In *Resolutions and decisions of the security council 2008* (S/RES/1820) (pp. 51–52). Official Record.

United Nations Women. (2015). *Progress of the world's women 2015–2016: Transforming economies, realizing rights.* https://www.unwomen.org/-/media/headquarters/attachments/sections/library/publications/2015/poww-2015-2016-en.pdf?la=en&vs=0.

United Nations Women. (2017). *United Nations entity for gender equality and the empowerment of women (UN-Women): Strategic plan 2018–2021* [UNW/2017/6/Rev.1]. https://undocs.org/en/UNW/2017/6/Rev.1

U.S. Agency for International Development. (2016). *Orphans and other vulnerable children affected by HIV and AIDS.* https://www.usaid.gov/what-we-do/global-health/hiv-and-aids/technical-areas/orphans-and-vulnerable-children-affected-hiv#section2

U.S. Department of State. (2019). *Trafficking in persons report.* https://www.state.gov/wp-content/uploads/2019/06/2019-Trafficking-in-Persons-Report.pdf

U.S. Environmental Protection Agency [EPA] (2018). *What is retrieved from:* https://www.epa.gov/environmental-justice/learn-about-environmental-justice

U.S. Federal Emergency Management Agency [FEMA]. (2007). Principles of emergency management supplement. https://www.fema.gov/media-library-data/20130726-1822-25045-7625/principles_of_emergency_management.pdf.

Villarreal Sosa, L., & Nuckolls, R. (2018). School social workers: A call to action in support of human rights. *International Journal of School Social Work, 3*(1), 1.

Wagle, U. R. (2017). The politics of poverty measurement and social policies: Global observations. In R. White (Ed.), *Measuring multidimensional poverty and deprivation: Incidents and determinants in developed countries* (pp. 7–30). Palgrave Macmillan, Cham.

Weiss, I. (2005). Is there a global common core to social work? A cross-national comparative study of BSW graduate students. *Social Work, 50*(2), 102–110.

Weston, R. (2001). Facing the past, facing the future: Applying the Truth Commission model to the historic treatment of Native Americans in the United States. *Arizona Journal Of International & Comparative Law, 18,* 1017.

Whittaker, M. A., Dean, A. J., & Chancellor, A. (2014). Advocating for malaria elimination—Learning from the successes of other infectious disease elimination programmes. *Malaria Journal, 13,* 221.

Whyte, K. (2017). The Dakota access pipeline, environmental injustice, and US colonialism. *Red Ink: An International Journal of Indigenous Literature, Arts, & Humanities, 19,* 1.

Williams, W. (2020). *COVID-19 and Africa's displacement crisis.* Africa Center for Strategic Studies. https://africacenter.org/spotlight/covid-19-and-africas-displacement-crisis/

Woolf, N. (2016, August 29). North Dakota oil pipeline protesters stand their ground: "This is sacred land." *The Guardian.* https://www.theguardian.com/us-news/2016/aug/29/north-dakota-oil-pipeline-protest-standing-rock-sioux

Wolf, D. (2016). *What, exactly is a Healing Forest?* Medium. https://medium.com/growing-healing-forests/https-medium-com-derekw518-what-exactly-is-a-healing-forest-6c2b9be77c94

World Bank. (2020). *Indigenous peoples*. https://www.worldbank.org/en/topic/indigenouspeoples#:~:text=There%20are%20approximately%20476%20million,worldwide%2C%20in%20over%2090%20countries.

World Health Organization [WHO]. (2020a). *Female genital mutilation: Key facts*. https://www.who.int/news-room/fact-sheets/detail/female-genital-mutilation

World Health Organization [WHO]. (2020b). *Malaria: Key facts*. https://www.who.int/news-room/fact-sheets/detail/malaria.

World Health Organization [WHO]. (2020c). *The potential impact of health service disruptions on the burden of malaria: A modelling analysis for countries in sub-Saharan Africa*. https://www.who.int/publications/i/item/the-potential-impact-of-health-service-disruptions-on-the-burden-of-malaria.

World Trade Organization [WTO]. (2019). *World trade statistical review*. https://www.wto.org/english/res_e/statis_e/wts2019_e/wts2019_e.pdf

Wuebbles, D. J., Fahey, D. W., Hibbard, K. A., Dokken, D. J., Stewart, B. C., & Maycock, T. K. (Eds.). (2017). *Climate science special report: Fourth national climate assessment* [Vol. I] U.S. Global Change Research Program.

Yates, D., Luna, B. Q., Rasmussen, R., Bratcher, D., Garre, L., Chen, F., Tewari, M., & Friis-Hansen, P. (2014). Stormy weather: Assessing climate change hazards to electric power infrastructure: A Sandy case study. *IEEE Power and Energy Magazine, 12*(5), 66–75.

Zakour, M. J., & Harrell, E. B. (2004). Access to disaster services: Social work interventions for vulnerable populations. *Journal of Social Service Research, 30*(2), 27–54.

Zhao, F., Fu, F., & Yang, B. (2018). Social work value system in mainland China: Construction of a scale and value commitment assessment. *International Social Work, 61*(6), 917–929.

The Future of Human Services Is Now

The United States is in a time of significant conflict and chaos, politically and socially. While the roots of the current state of polarization run deep, there are several contemporary social dynamics that have added a new twist, one of the most significant being people's reliance on social media for connection, news, community engagement, political activism, and a range of other activities (Shearer, 2018; Tucker et al., 2018). Political activism is not new, but since political activism is dependent on the development of a sense of solidarity among like-minded people (Taylor & Van Dyke, 2003) and social media herds like-minded people together so effectively (Fullilove, 2008), sites such as Facebook and Twitter are a major contributor to an overall increase in political engagement and polarization (Bail et al., 2018). Social media has a number of positive uses—finding lost family members, reconnecting with old friends, professional networking, connecting with others with similar interests—but social media is also being used for nefarious purposes, most notably the dissemination of false propaganda, most of which is designed to invoke fear of the "other" (Bradshaw & Howard, 2017; Buchanan & Benson, 2019; Shu et al., 2020).

So, what are the consequential impacts of all this political and social polarization on social problems and the future provision of human services? Despite there being a change in presidential leadership in January 2021, there will likely be strong lingering effects of the current divisive political rhetoric, the spike in political and social polarization, the health and economic impact of COVID-19, and the impacts of many other recent dynamics explored in this book. Cross-border political asylum seekers may no longer be separated from their families, but the impacts of thousands of family separations will be felt for decades. Environmental regulatory protections may be restored, but the impact of increased mining and oil excavation on formerly protected lands will no doubt have long-term consequences. A vaccine for the novel coronavirus became available in 2021 but the impact of hundreds of thousands of lives lost and the economic consequences of enduring shutdowns will likely be experienced for years to come, particularly for the economically fragile and communities of color (Martin et al., 2020; Millett et al., 2020).

But hope is not lost! I have no intention of ending this book on such a negative note. Yes, many challenges lie ahead, but in many respects that is why the field of human services exists. It is a desire to address psychosocial and sociopolitical challenges that often draw people into this field in the first place. In other words, this is a great time to go into the human services field—there is certainly a need for more caring and compassionate human services professionals, and we also have more tools than ever to tackle social problems such as hate crimes, poverty, child maltreatment, aging, poverty, homelessness, behavioral health disorders, and violence, just to name a few. As a profession, there is every indication that human services will continue to grow—in response to growing need, but also in recognition that increased prevention efforts (in the form of social programs) save money and lives.

There are several trends forecast for the human services profession. First, in light of the probability that funding sources will continue to decline while human need will continue to increase, human services organizations are going to be increasingly tasked with doing more with less—finding creative ways to increase services provision with fewer funding sources (Isaacs et al., 2020; Van de Water, 2020). Another future trend relates to globalization and the shrinking world. Globalization can lead to challenges, such as escalating income inequality, but it can also lead to increased opportunities for U.S.-based human services professionals to work on a global level, made easier by the globalization of communication technologies. Telehealth services will continue to grow, even in the post-COVID world (Wosik et al., 2020), which will increase access to mental health services for some populations but may limit access to many people if they lack fast and stable residential broadband (Bauerly et al., 2019; Hirko et al., 2020). And this issue leads me to what I believe will be one of the biggest future trends in the human services—increased reliance on technology (Decker et al., 2019; Gil et al., 2014; Trahan et al., 2019).

Technology has been around for decades, but the human services field has been rather slow in adopting many existing technological tools for a variety of reasons, some related to concerns about confidentiality, some related to a perception that technology reduces meaningful human-to-human contact, and some related more to the personality styles of those drawn to this field (Ramsey & Montgomery, 2014). But as the rest of the world becomes less paper based and more dependent on technological tools, human services agencies are following suit. What this means in a practical sense is that clinical notes are increasingly submitted online, initial job interviews are increasingly facilitated via an online video platform such as Zoom or Skype, and more clients are being offered the option of accessing needed services via the internet. These growing trends have raised ethical concerns currently being addressed through updates of ethical codes and training opportunities, including an increase in technology training in human services educational programs (Curran et al., 2019; Wasik et al., 2019).

An increase in reliance on technology in all aspects of human services provision will provide more opportunities for the creative development of new partnerships, including global partnerships, which may also lead to new funding sources. An increase in reliance on technology will also provide more educational opportunities for those people who wish to enter the field of human services, but do not live near a college or university. And finally, an increase in reliance on technology will open up new frontiers in the human services field with increased reach and impact.

References

Bail, C. A., Argyle, L. P., Brown, T. W., Bumpus, J. P., Chen, H., Hunzaker, M. F., Lee, J., Mann, M., Merhout, F., & Volfovsky, A. (2018). Exposure to opposing views on social media can increase political polarization. *Proceedings of the National Academy of Sciences, 115*(37), 9216–9221.

Bauerly, B. C., McCord, R. F., Hulkower, R., & Pepin, D. (2019). Broadband access as a public health issue: The role of law in expanding broadband access and connecting underserved communities for better health outcomes. *The Journal of Law, Medicine & Ethics, 47*(Suppl. 2), 39–42.

Bradshaw, S., & Howard, P. (2017). Troops, trolls and troublemakers: A global inventory of organized social media manipulation. *Computational Propaganda Research Project.* Working Paper No. 2017–02. https://ora.ox.ac.uk/objects/uuid:cef7e8d9-27bf-4ea5-9fd6-855209b3e1f6/download_file?safe_file-name=Troops-Trolls-and-Troublemakers.pdf&file_for-

mat=application%2Fpdf&type_of_work=Report

Buchanan, T., & Benson, V. (2019). Spreading disinformation on Facebook: Do trust in message source, risk propensity, or personality affect the organic reach of "fake news"?. *Social Media+ Society*, *5*(4), 2056305119888654.

Curran, V., Fleet, L., Simmons, K., Lannon, H., Gustafson, D. L., Wang, C., Garmsiri, M., & Wetsch, L. (2019). Adoption and use of mobile learning in continuing professional development by health and human services professionals. *Journal of Continuing Education in the Health Professions*, *39*(2), 76–85.

Decker, V., Valenti, M., Montoya, V., Sikorskii, A., Given, C. W., & Given, B. A. (2019). Maximizing new technologies to treat depression. *Issues in Mental Health Nursing*, *40*(3), 200–207.

Fullilove, M. (2008). *World Wide Webs: Diasporas and the international system*. Lowy Institute Paper 22: Lowy Institute for International Policy. Double Bay, NSW, Longueville Media.

Gil, A., Dutta-Gupta, I., & Roach, B. (2014). *The technology opportunity for human services*. Data Smart City Solutions. https://datasmart.ash.harvard.edu/news/article/the-technology-opportunity-for-human-services-470#:~:text=Using%20technology%2C%20human%20services%20administrators,track%20and%20evaluate%20program%20performance

Hirko, K. A., Kerver, J. M., Ford, S., Szafranski, C., Beckett, J., Kitchen, C., & Wendling, A. L. (2020). Telehealth in response to the COVID-19 pandemic: Implications for rural health disparities. *Journal of the American Medical Informatics Association*. https://doi.org/10.1093/jamia/ocaa156

Isaacs, J. B., Lou, C., & Lauderback, E. (2020). *How would the president's proposed 2021 budget affect spending on children?* Urban Institute.

Martin, A., Markhvida, M., Hallegatte, S., & Walsh, B. (2020). Socio-economic impacts of COVID-19 on household consumption and poverty. *Economics of Disasters and Climate Change*, *4*, 473–479.

Millett, G. A., Jones, A. T., Benkeser, D., Baral, S., Mercer, L., Beyrer, C., Honermann, B., Lankiewicz, E., Mena, L., Crowley, J. S., Sherwood, J., & Sullivan, P. S. (2020). Assessing differential impacts of COVID-19 on Black communities. *Annals of Epidemiology*, *47*, 37–44.

Ramsey, A. T., & Montgomery, K. (2014). Technology-based interventions in social work practice: A systematic review of mental health interventions. *Social Work in Health Care*, *53*(9), 883–899.

Shearer, E. (2018). *Social media outpaces print newspapers in the U.S. as a news source*. Pew Research Center. pewresearch.org/fact-tank/2018/12/10/social-media-outpaces-print-newspapers-in-the-u-s-as-a-news-source/

Shu, K., Bhattacharjee, A., Alatawi, F., Nazer, T. H., Ding, K., Karami, M., & Liu, H. (2020). Combating disinformation in a social media age. *Wiley Interdisciplinary Reviews: Data Mining and Knowledge Discovery*. https://arxiv.org/abs/2007.07388

Taylor, V., & Van Dyke, N. (2003). Get up, stand up: Tactical repertoires of social movements. In D. Snow, S. Soule, & H. Kriesi (Eds.), *The Blackwell Companion to Social Movements Reader* (pp. 262–293). Blackwell.

Trahan, M. H., Smith, K. S., & Talbot, T. B. (2019). Past, present, and future: Editorial on virtual reality applications to human services. *Journal of Technology in Human Services*, *37*(1), 1–12.

Tucker, J. A., Guess, A., Barberá, P., Vaccari, C., Siegel, A., Sanovich, S., Stukal, D., & Nyhan, B. (2018). *Social media, political polarization, and political disinformation: A review of the scientific literature*. Hewlett Foundation. https://www.hewlett.org/wp-content/uploads/2018/03/Social-Media-Political-Polarization-and-Political-Disinformation-Literature-Review.pdf

Van de Water, P. (2020). *2021 Trump budget would increase hardship and inequality*. Center on Budget and Policy Priorities. https://www.cbpp.org/research/federal-budget/2021-trump-budget-would-increase-hardship-and-inequality.

Wasik, S., Barrow, J., Royal, C., Brooks, R., Dames, L., Corry, L., & Bird, C. (2019). Online counselor education: Creative approaches and best practices in online learning environments. *Research on Education and Psychology*, *3*(1), 43–52.

Wosik, J., Fudim, M., Cameron, B., Gellad, Z. F., Cho, A., Phinney, D., Curtis, S., Roman, M., Poon, E. G., Ferranti, J., Katz, J. N., & Tcheng, J. (2020). Telehealth transformation: COVID-19 and the rise of virtual care. *Journal of the American Medical Informatics Association*, *27*(6), 957–962.

Glossary

Ableism discrimination in favor of able-bodied people.

Abrahamic religions a religion whose people believe that Abraham and his descendants hold an important role in human spiritual development. Judaism, Christianity, and Islam are Abrahamic religions.

Absolute poverty a set standard that is the same in all countries and which does not change over time. An income-related example would be living on less than $X per day.

Abstinence-only program sex education programs that focus solely on encouraging students not to have sexual relations, compared to prevention programs that explore birth control, empowerment, and sexual health.

Abstract reasoning ability the ability to use critical thinking in cognitive processing.

Acting out behavior a term often used to describe rebellious behavior within the adolescent population.

Active aging potential, well-being, and active participation in all life has to offer within a range of domains, including social, economic, cultural, spiritual, and civic domains.

Active listening skills the ability to attend to the speaker fully, without distraction, without preconceived notions of what the speaker is saying, and without being distracted by thoughts of what one wants to say in response.

Activities of daily living daily self-care activities that healthy people can perform without assistance, such as walking, bathing, dressing, toileting, brushing teeth, and eating.

Administration on Aging the primary agency of the U.S Department of Health and Human Services designated to carry out the provisions of the Older Americans Act of 1965.

Adult Protective Services Agency agencies that provide services to abused, neglected, or exploited older adults and adults with disabilities. APS is typically administered by local or state departments and provide investigative services as well as other support services.

Advance directives a written statement of a person's wishes regarding medical treatment, often including a living will, made to ensure those wishes are carried out should the person be unable to communicate them to a doctor.

Affective flattening a lack of emotional expressiveness. Also called blunted emotions.

Affordable Care Act the Patient Protection and Affordable Care Act (ACA), commonly called Obamacare, is a U.S. federal statute signed into law on March 23, 2010, that significantly overhauled the U.S. health care system.

Affordable housing housing costs (including utility costs) that make up no more than 30 percent of a household's income.

Ageism discrimination based on age.

Aid to Families With Dependent Children an entitlement program passed as a part of the Social Security Act of 1935 that provided economic assistance to mothers and their children. AFDC was replaced with the passage of PRWORA 1996 and TANF.

AIDS cocktail a variety of antiretroviral drug therapies used to treat HIV-infected patients to prevent the virus from replicating. In many cases the combination of drugs can restore the patient's T-cell counts, thus improving quality and longevity of life.

Alaska Natives indigenous peoples of Alaska, United States, including the Iñupiat, Yupik, Aleut, Eyak, Tlingit, Haida, Tsimshian, and a number of Northern Athabaskan cultures.

Allah refers to the God in Abrahamic religions. A term used by Muslims to refer to their God.

Alzheimer's disease progressive, degenerative disorder that attacks the brain's nerve cells, or neurons, resulting in loss of memory, thinking and language skills, and behavioral changes.

Anger management a structured set of classes or program that focus on strategies designed to assist individuals in managing their anger more effectively.

Annual Homeless Assessment Reports (AHAR) uses collective Homeless Management Information System (HMIS) data from communities across the country, as well as the CoC applications, to produce an annual report presented to U.S. Congress on the extent and nature of homelessness. AHAR reports provide nationwide estimates of homelessness, including information about the demographic characteristics of homeless persons.

Appalachian Region a 205,000-square-mile region that follows the spine of the Appalachian Mountains from southern New York to northern Mississippi. Known for high rates of poverty, particularly among Caucasians.

Apprenticeship a labor system involving the legal binding of an individual, including children, through indenture to a master craftsman in order to learn a trade.

Area Agencies on Aging a nationwide network of programs created in response to the Older Americans Act of 1965, providing an array of services for the older adult population.

Atypical antipsychotic drugs second-generation antipsychotics used to treat psychiatric disorders.

Authorization to release information a signed voluntary agreement between a client and service provider granting permission to the provider to release certain privileged communication.

Baby boomers an age cohort of people born between 1946 (just after World War II) and 1964. The age cohort is important demographically because it was large and therefore has been a powerful lobby. The baby boomers are currently between the ages of about 56 and 74 years of age, and thus are an important factor in the growing older adult population.

Behaviorism a theory used to explain human behavior. Behaviorists believe that behavior is learned through conditioning (reward and punishment), and not due to feelings and emotions.

Best interest of the child doctrine a court's determinations involving child welfare cases that are determined to serve the best interest of the child.

Bias-based bullying harassment, intimidation, or bullying based on a person's gender, race, ethnicity, perceived sexual orientation, religion, age, familial status, or mental, physical, or sensory handicap.

Bind out a historic labor system that connected host families with poor children, usually boys, for the purposes of coerced labor.

Biopsychosocial model an approach that recognizes the reciprocal involvement of biological, psychological, and social factors in human functioning.

Black flight the large-scale out-migration of African Americans from black or mixed areas with the goal of seeking better economic opportunities, safer communities, newer housing, and better schools.

Bridge employment a job between full-time work and retirement. Many people will engage in bridge employment when they're approaching retirement age, but aren't quite ready to retire, either for emotional or financial reasons.

Caregiver respite a service provided for family caregivers (often spouses) of older adults with dementia, providing the family caregiver with a temporary break from caregiving responsibilities. Respite services can be provided in the home or in an adult day care setting.

Case management a collaborative process involving the coordination of services with a client's service providers, including assessment, planning, evaluation, and treatment to meet a client's psychosocial needs.

Caste system a class structure that is determined by birth. In some societies with little social mobility, an individual is destined to remain in the caste within which they are born throughout their life.

Catatonic behavior a symptom of psychosis involving repetitive behaviors or the lack of movement, such as remaining frozen for long periods of time.

Charity Organization Society a movement in the late 1800s that had as its goal the organization and centralizing of poor relief, based on the belief that outdoor relief created dependency, and that the poor were better helped through the diagnosis of the causes of poverty by friendly visitors, and the development of a case plan that focused on behavioral reform. The approach of the Charity Organization Society movement is considered the origin of case management.

Child bonded servants   children who were bonded out for labor in early America.

Child labor   children involved in the labor force, often on a coerced basis by the government or parents, often due to the child's orphan status and/or social position within society.

Child Protective Services   government agencies charged with the legal responsibility for the protection of minor children.

Christian right   a social and political movement espousing traditional values and a return to "traditional America," composed of a number of groups from various conservative Christian denominations, most principally evangelicalism and fundamentalism. Also referred to as the conservative right and the hard right.

Chronically homeless   an individual or family who has either been continuously homeless for a year or more or has had at least four episodes of homelessness in the past three years.

Cirrhosis of the liver   a slowly progressing disease in which healthy liver tissue is replaced with scar tissue, eventually preventing the liver from functioning properly. Caused by hepatitis C, a fatty liver from obesity and diabetes, and alcoholism.

Class conflict   the tension or antagonism that exists in society due to competing socioeconomic interests and desires between people of different socioeconomic classes. Also referred to as class warfare or class struggle.

Cognitive symptoms   a collection of symptoms associated with schizophrenia involving cognitive processes, including neurocognitive deficits, such as issues with memory, attention, and social skills.

Cognitive theory   a theory used to explain mental processing involving thinking and learning, often applied to human behavior. Cognitive theorists believe that behavior is influenced by an individual's thoughts.

Colonial America   a period of time in the history of the United States between 1492 and 1763 when it was still under the control of England, prior to independence.

Compulsory education laws   state laws that require children to attend school. The first state to pass a compulsory education law was Massachusetts in 1852, and the last state to pass a compulsory education law was Alaska in 1929. The majority of states passed laws between 1870 and 1915. The lower age limit for attendance ranges between 5 and 7 years of age, and the upper age limit ranges between 16 and 18 years of age.

Conservative Christians   a term used to describe identified Christians who tend to follow conservative values. Evangelicals, fundamentalists, and some Pentecostal faith traditions are considered conservative Christians. Also associated with the "Christian Right," a conservative religious movement that advocates for traditional family values.

Contemplative practice   practices that cultivate an accepting awareness and enhanced attention to present moment experiences, and a belief that with this experience, a sense of interconnectedness to everything else emerges on its own. Also referred to as the mindfulness movement.

Continuum of Care (CoC) program   an organization of service providers established by the Department of Housing and Urban Development (HUD) to oversee community planning around homelessness. Also refers to HUD's federal funding program.

Coronavirus   a family of related viruses. Many of them cause respiratory illnesses. Coronaviruses cause COVID-19, SARS, MERS, and some strains of influenza, or flu. The coronavirus that causes COVID-19 is officially called SARS-CoV-2, which stands for severe acute respiratory syndrome coronavirus 2.

COVID-19   the illness caused by the coronavirus SARS-CoV-2. COVID-19 stands for "coronavirus disease 2019."

Counter-transference   the alternate process associated with transference—the process of a client transferring his or her emotions onto a therapist. Countertransference involves the same process, but the therapist transfers emotions onto the client. The concepts of transference and countertransference were originally defined and explored by theorist and psychoanalyst Sigmund Freud.

Court-appointed special advocates   CASA workers are court-appointed volunteers who provide advocacy services for children involved in the child welfare system.

Cultural competence   the ability to work effectively with people of color and minority populations by being sensitive to their needs and recognizing their unique experiences within society, both historically and culturally.

Curative treatment   medical care focused on curing a patient's illness.

Cyberactivism   civic, social, and political advocacy that occurs online, particularly via social media.

Cyberbullying   the use of electronic communication to bully a person, typically by sending messages of an intimidating or threatening nature, usually via social media.

Cyberstalking   the repeated use of electronic communications to harass or frighten someone, for example, by sending threatening emails or stalking someone online.

Cycle of poverty   a phenomenon where poor families remain impoverished because they have no ancestors who can transmit the intellectual, social, and cultural resources necessary to lift them out of poverty.

Cycle of violence   drawn from the work of Lenore Walker, who theorized that domestic violence occurred most often in repeated cycles, beginning with a honeymooning phase, followed by a tension phase, and culminating in an explosion phase, which then led back to another honeymoon phase, repeating the cycle.

Deindustrialization   a process of economic change caused by the reduction of industry, such as manufacturing, in a geographical region.

Deinstitutionalization movement   the process of transitioning from an institutionalized system of mental health care to a community-based mental health model. Often criticized due to a lack of funding that resulted in erratic and inefficient care for the seriously mentally ill.

Delusions   strongly held false beliefs or misperceptions that are not consistent with the person's culture, many of which could not possibly be true.

Dementia   a chronic and degenerative brain disease, primarily experienced in old age, marked by memory disorders, personality changes, impaired reasoning, and the eventual shutting down of all bodily systems.

Developing economies   a term typically used to describe governments with capitalist societies and democratic governments. The term is criticized by some for implying that other types of economies are inferior to capitalistic ones.

Digital abuse   the use of technologies such as texting and social networking to bully, harass, stalk, or intimidate another person, most often a partner. Similar to cyberstalking.

Direct practice   counseling practice with individuals.

Discrimination   is the behavior or actions, usually negative, toward an individual or group of people, especially on the basis of a unique and defining characteristic, such as gender, race, nationality status, sexual orientation, ability status, social class, and age.

Disenfranchised populations   a group of people often considered to lack power in society, with no political voice. Examples include refugees, some immigrant groups, and other populations that have experienced social exclusion.

Disorganized speech   speech often reflects thinking that makes no sense, with frequent trailing off into incoherent talk.

Disproportionality (child welfare system)   a term used to describe the overrepresentation of children of color within the child welfare system.

Domestic sex trafficking   the process of forcing an individual to engage in sexual acts for payment against their will. Domestic trafficking involves activities that originate within the United States.

Domestic violence shelters   housing and support services for survivors leaving a domestic violence relationship. Services are typically provided to women and children.

Don't Ask, Don't Tell (DADT)   the official U.S. policy on service by gays and lesbians in the military. DADT was instituted by President Bill Clinton on February 28, 1994, in response to an attempt to lessen the punitive measures taken when a member of the military was determined to be gay or lesbian. DADT ended on September 20, 2011.

Do-not-resuscitate (DNR)   a medical order written by a doctor at a patient (or patient's family's) request instructing health care providers to not do cardiopulmonary resuscitation (CPR) if a patient's breathing stops or if the patient's heart stops beating. Usually used in cases where the patient is terminally ill.

Doubling-up   living with family and friends for economic reasons, also called "couch surfing." Considered a part of the hidden homeless.

Dual relationships   a term used in the mental health field to refer to multiple roles held by the mental health provider, such as counselor and friend, or counselor and teacher. Such relationships can lead to ethical dilemmas.

Duty-to-protect a mental health provider's legal obligation to determine that his or her client presents a serious danger of violence to himself or herself, or another human being, and to then take necessary and reasonable steps to protect the client or intended victim against danger.

Duty-to-warn a legal obligation of mental health providers to verbally tell a potential victim that there is a foreseeable danger of violence.

Eastern religious philosophies religions originating from Eastern and Southeastern Asian countries, such as India, China, and Japan. Some Eastern religious philosophies include Taoism.

Ecological model a theory in the social sciences that describes dynamic interrelations among and between personal and environmental factors, for example, Urie Bronfenbrenner's Ecological Framework for Human Development.

Economic injustice disparity within economic distribution with regard to individuals' economic positions, often related to certain characteristics, such as ethnic background, gender, geographic location, and family socioeconomic status.

Elizabethan Poor Laws of 1601 the Act for the Relief of the Poor 1601, popularly known as the Elizabethan Poor Law, was a collection of laws passed in 1601 creating a national poor law system for England and Wales. This legislation effectively formalized previous poor relief legislation and policies.

Emergency shelters supervised sheltering programs that provide beds, a hot meal, drinking water, and restroom facilities. Most emergency shelters include time limits for stays ranging from 30 to 120 days, and offer basic services, such as case management.

Emotional regulation the ability to control one's emotions.

Empowerment theory a multi-dimensional social process that helps people gain control over their own lives.

Empty nesting a stage in the family's life cycle when the children have grown up and moved out of the parental home. This stage can be particularly difficult for some parents, particularly women who may grieve the loss of their daily parenting responsibilities, compelling them to renegotiate their identity, and develop new interests.

Enmeshment a Western concept introduced by Salvador Minuchin to describe families where personal boundaries are undifferentiated, leading to a loss of autonomous development.

Environmental Injustice unfair treatment and exclusion in the development, implementation, and enforcement of environmental laws, regulations, and policies. Unequal protection from environmental and health hazards, with unequal access to the decision-making process resulting in exposure to an unhealthy environmental for living, learning, and working.

Ethical dilemmas refers to situations where there is a choice to be made between two or more options, where none of the options appear to clearly resolve the situation in an ethically acceptable fashion. No clear right or wrong answer, or an argument could be made for each option as being the moral one.

Ethical standards pertaining to conduct in accordance with the rules (or standards) of correct conduct, especially the standards of a profession.

Ethical values determine what is right and what is wrong, behaviorally. To behave ethically means to behave in a manner that is morally correct.

Ethics moral principles that govern an individual's or group's behavior.

Ethnic cleansing the mass expulsion or killing of members of an unwanted ethnic or religious group within a society.

Ethnicity cultural factors, including nationality, regional culture, ancestry, and language.

Euthanasia the practice of intentionally ending a life in order to relieve pain and suffering. Illegal in most countries due to ethical issues, including the active role a physician takes in ending a life.

Familism a social structure where the needs of the family are more important and take precedence over the needs of any of the family members.

Family continuity stability along various domains, such as emotional, psychological, and financial, within a family system.

Family genogram a pictorial representation of a person's family tree used in Murray Bowen's family systems theory, highlighting communication styles and other psychosocial dynamics, and focusing on the intergenerational transmission of relational patterns.

Family preservation programs a movement designed to keep children at home with their biological families rather than remove and place them in foster homes or institutions.

Family reunification the process of reunifying children who have been placed in foster care and returning them to their biological parent(s).

Feeble-minded an outdated term used during the visiting teacher movement in reference to children with intellectual and cognitive disabilities.

Feudalism the primary system structure in medieval Europe, where the nobility controlled the monarchy's land in exchange for military service, while the peasants or serfs worked the land in exchange for housing, a share of the produce, and protection.

Food deserts a low-income region where a substantial number of residents have limited access to a supermarket or large grocery store.

Forced migration the coerced movement of a person or persons away from their home or home region.

Forensic interviewing techniques an evidence-based and developmentally sensitive method of obtaining factual information in cases involving abuse or violence. Interviewing techniques involve open-ended questions and forced-choice questions that are not leading in nature.

Friendly visitor a volunteer working for a charity organization society who visited clients to assess the nature of their problems and offer support and guidance.

Gay-straight alliance clubs (GSAs) a gay-straight alliance (GSA) is a student-run club in a high school or middle school that brings together LGBTQ and straight students to support each other, provide a safe place to socialize, and create a platform for activism to fight homophobia and transphobia.

Gender nonconforming populations an umbrella term that refers to people who do not follow other people's ideas or stereotypes about how they should look or act based on the female or male sex they were assigned at birth.

Genderqueer a person who does not subscribe to conventional gender distinctions but identifies with neither, both, or a combination of male and female genders.

Generalist practice model a model of working with people in a helping capacity that focuses on basic skills involved in the helping process.

Generalist skill set the use of a wide range of professional roles, approaches, and skills in a planned change process in diverse settings.

Gerotranscendence the process of transcending the material aspects of life and moving toward a more existential existence.

Global North United States, Canada, Western Europe, and developed parts of East Asia. A preferred term to "Western." Typically references a socioeconomic and political divide.

Global South Africa, Latin America, and developing Asia including the Middle East. A preferred term to "eastern countries" or "non-Western" countries.

Globalization a process of increasingly interrelated interactions among people, organizations, governments, and systems, including communication that has essentially made the world smaller and more closely connected.

Graying of America a term used to describe the growing aging population.

Great Recession of 2007 one of the terms used to describe a major recession that began in December 2007 in response to the bursting of the real estate bubble, in large part due to predatory lending practices. The recession quickly became a global crisis because of the globalization of market economies, and although the recession officially ended in June 2009, many economists believe the country is still in recovery.

Great Society programs the poverty alleviation programs that were developed in response to President Lyndon B. Johnson's war on poverty legislation.

Grief an emotional reaction, such as deep sorrow, in response to a significant loss, such as a death.

Halakhah the totality of Jewish law.

Hallucinations sensations that are experienced as real, but are not, such as hearing voices, seeing things that are not there, smelling smells that do not exist, or feeling sensations when nothing is present.

Health insurance marketplace a resource (website) where individuals, families, and small businesses can learn about their health coverage options; compare health insurance plans based on costs, benefits, and other important features; choose a plan; and enroll in coverage. Also called the Exchange.

Health pandemic a global disease outbreak.

Hidden homeless   although there is not one definition of the hidden homeless, the term typically refers to those individuals who are homeless but not living in shelters or on the streets. Rather they may be "couch surfing," living temporarily with friends or family and not paying rent, or they may be institutionalized, or may be living in a motel not paid for by a government program. This population is considered "hidden" because they usually do not access homeless supports and services even though they are improperly or inadequately housed. Because they do not access services, they do not show up on standard statistics regarding homelessness.

Higher power   a term used to refer a deity. An alternate term used for God that doesn't refer to a specific denomination.

HIPAA Privacy Rule   the first national standards to protect patients' personal health information (PHI).

Historically oppressed and marginalized groups   groups of individuals who have experienced intergenerational oppression, often due to some defining characteristic because of race, gender, age, social status, and so forth and are then excluded from the activities and benefits of mainstream society.

HIV/AIDS   HIV stands for human immunodeficiency virus. If left untreated, HIV can lead to the disease AIDS (acquired immunodeficiency syndrome).

HIV-positive status   being diagnosed with HIV means that an individual has been infected with the human immunodeficiency virus (HIV) and that two HIV tests—a preliminary test and a confirmatory test— have both come back positive.

Holistic   interconnectedness, such as seeing an individual as a whole and not in a compartmentalized fashion.

Holistic health   an ancient approach to health that considers the whole person with an emphasis on the connection between mind, body, and spirit.

Homeless Emergency Assistance and Rapid Transition to Housing (HEARTH) Act   reauthorized HUD's McKinney-Vento Homeless Act Assistance programs under the Obama administration in 2009. The HEARTH Act consolidates three of the separate homeless assistance programs administered by HUD under the McKinney-Vento Homeless Assistance Act into a single grant program, and revises the Emergency Shelter Grants program and renames it the Emergency Solutions Grants (ESG) program. The HEARTH Act also codifies in law the Continuum of Care planning process. The HEARTH Act enhanced the definition of homelessness.

Homophobia   the irrational fear of, aversion to, or discrimination against "homosexuality" or "homosexuals." Note: the term homosexual and homosexuality is now considered an offensive term, which is why these terms are reflected in singular quotation marks.

Housing projects   a euphemism for 1960 congregated housing subsidized by the government through HUD. Also called "the projects."

Imam   a title of various Muslim leaders, including the person who leads prayers in a mosque.

Implicit bias   bias in judgment and/or behavior that results from subtle cognitive processes, such as attitudes and belief in stereotypes, that often occur below a conscious level of awareness.

Incapacitated sex   sexual activity engaged in when a party is too intoxicated on drugs and/or alcohol to consent.

Indentured servitude   a labor system commonly employed in the 18th century in North America, where people paid for their passage by working for an employer for a set amount of years. The system was often a source of exploitation of the poor, particularly immigrants.

Indigenous people   people defined in international or national legislation as having a set of specific rights based on their historical ties to a particular territory, and their cultural or historical distinctiveness from other populations that are often politically dominant.

Indigenous populations   groups with historical ties to a particular territory that are culturally distinct from other populations. Indigenous populations are often protected in international or national legislation.

Individualized Education Plan (IEP)   a plan or program developed to ensure that a child who has a disability identified under the law and is attending an elementary or secondary school receives necessary instruction specialized for the student.

Indoor relief   social welfare assistance under England's poor laws and later America's early social welfare system, consisting of recipients being required to enter a workhouse or poorhouse. Indoor relief was typically reserved for those deemed the unworthy poor.

Informed consent   a written document that informs clients of the purpose of the services, related risks, limits to services, and clients' right to refuse services or withdraw consent, and the time frame covered by the consent.

Institutionalized racism   a form of racism expressed in the practice of social and political institutions.

Interfaith   an organization that is comprised of different faith traditions working together for some cause.

Interparental violence   violence occurring between parents in a family structure.

Intersectionality   the interconnected nature of social categorizations such as race, class, and gender, as they apply to a given individual or group, regarded as creating overlapping and interdependent systems of discrimination or disadvantage.

Islam   the religious faith of Muslims, founded by the prophet Muhammad.

Islamophobia   dislike of or prejudice against Islam or Muslims, especially as a political force.

Itinerant human service providers   human service providers responsible for a large geographical area, who visit communities on a monthly or bimonthly basis.

Jim Crow laws   state and local laws enforcing racial segregation in the Southern United States until 1965. Among other restrictions, Jim Crow laws mandated the segregation of public schools, public places, and public transportation, including restrooms, restaurants, and drinking fountains for whites and blacks. Many believe that Jim Crow laws picked up where slavery left off, leaving African Americans with minimal protections and civil rights.

Judeo-Christian   refers to the common roots of the Jewish and Christian religions. Also refers to an ethical system.

Kaposi's sarcoma (KS)   a cancer that develops from the cells that line lymph or blood vessels. KS is considered an "AIDS defining" illness, thus when KS occurs in someone infected with HIV, that person officially has AIDS.

Learned helplessness   a condition in which a person suffers from a sense of powerlessness caused by repeated trauma where they initially have no possibility of escape (or perceive they have no control). Individuals who struggle with learned helplessness often continue to feel and act helpless long after their circumstances change and they have power to change their situation.

Least developed countries   a group of countries that have been classified by the UN as "least developed" in terms of their low gross national income (GNI), their weak human assets, and their high degree of economic vulnerability.

Least restricted environment   a requirement of federal law that students with disabilities must receive their education with nondisabled peers, to the maximum extent appropriate, and that special education students are not removed from regular classes unless, even with supplemental aids and services, education in regular classes cannot be achieved satisfactorily.

LGBTQ + populations   an acronym for lesbian, gay, bisexual, transgender, queer/questioning, and others, a population of people united by having gender identities or sexual orientations that differ from the heterosexual and the gender majority.

Licensed clinical social worker (LCSW)   the professional license obtained by social workers who have an MSW and complete 3,000 hours of practice work supervised by an LCSW.

Limits of confidentiality   legal limitations of clients' right to confidentiality, including a provider's duty to protect and duty to warn.

Linear stage theory   theories of development that posit that people proceed through a set of sequential stages, with earlier stages serving as a foundation for successive stages.

Living will   a written legal document that spells out medical treatments you would and would not want to be used to keep you alive, as well as other decisions such as pain management or organ donation.

Longevity   length of life.

Macro level   practice on a societal level.

Macro practice   practice on a broad level, with organizations, communities, or on a policy level.

Macrosystems   in ecological systems theory describing the culture in which individuals live.

Maladaptive behavior   behavior that interferes with an individual's functioning within a range of domains of life.

Mandated clients   clients who enter treatment under the coercion of a legal body such as a court order, a probation department, or child protective services. Also called involuntary clients.

Mandated reporters   the legal obligation of professionals who regularly engage with children to report cases of suspected abuse to the appropriate legal authorities.

Marginalization   a concept used to describe a contemporary form of social disadvantage and relegation to the fringe of society. Subpopulations with stigmatizing characteristics related to race, sexual orientation, gender, age, religion, immigration status, nationality, and socioeconomic status are often marginalized by more privileged and powerful members of society.

Mass urbanization   a population shift from rural to urban, often in response to a changing economy.

Medical power of attorney   a type of advance directive in which you name a person to make decisions for you when you are unable to do so. In some states this directive may also be called a durable power of attorney for health care or a health care proxy.

Men who have sex with men (MSM)   a term used to categorize males who engage in sexual activity with other males, regardless of whether they identify themselves as gay or straight.

Mental Health Courts Program   a Bureau of Justice Assistance (BJA) program designed as an alternative court system for adult mentally ill nonviolent felony defendants with the goal of diverting offenders with a diagnosed mental illness from the criminal justice system to the mental health system. Services include counseling, employment, housing, and support services.

Mental health parity   a term used to describe mental health conditions and substance use disorders being treated equally to physical health disorders by insurance companies.

Mezzo level   counseling practice with groups.

Mezzo practice   same as "mezzo level"

Micro-aggressions   everyday verbal and nonverbal slights, snubs, or insults, whether intentional or unintentional, which communicate hostile, derogatory, or negative messages to target persons based solely upon their marginalized group membership. Often used in reference to disparate treatment of certain ethnic minority populations and other marginalized groups.

Micro level   practice with individuals.

Micro practice   counseling practice with individuals, also called direct practice.

Microsystems   the institutions and groups that most immediately and directly impact the child's development, including family, school, religious institutions, neighborhood, and peers.

Middle Ages   the period of European history from the fall of the Roman Empire in the West (5th century) to the fall of Constantinople (1453), or, more narrowly, from circa 1100 to 1453.

Midlife crisis   a term used to describe an experience that some individuals have in middle age when they reach the midpoint in their lives and realize they have more time behind them than ahead of them. Although there is no empirical support for the uniformity of the midlife crisis, contemporary folklore posits that people in a midlife crisis are prone to behave irrationally in an attempt to regain their lost youth, such as buying a sports car, quitting their job, or having an extramarital affair.

Millennium Development Goals   eight international development goals designed to better the lives of the world's poorest people. They were established following the Millennium Summit of the United Nations in 2000.

Mindfulness Movement   a broad term used to describe a practice that helps individuals develop a sense of awareness and presence in their daily life.

Mission statement   a formal summary of the goals and values of a company or organization.

Mississippi Delta   a 200-mile long and 70-mile wide (at its widest point) of the northwest section of the state of Mississippi between the Mississippi and Yazoo Rivers. Known for its unique history, including its history of slavery, as well as for high rates of poverty.

Mood symptoms   a collection of symptoms associated with schizophrenia involving alterations in mood, typically including excessive happiness or sadness.

Moral treatment movement   an approach to mental disorder based on humane psychosocial care that emerged in the 18th and 19th centuries in response to systemic abuses of the mentally ill.

Morality   principles concerning the distinction between right and wrong or good and bad behavior.

Motivational interviewing (MI)   a method that works on facilitating and engaging intrinsic motivation within the client in order to change behavior.

Mourn the process one undertakes to psychologically deal with a significant loss, such as a death.

Multi-infarct dementia multiple strokes in the brain that cause memory loss and other cognitive impairments.

Multi-partner fertility parents who have children with more than one partner.

Muslims a follower of the religion of Islam.

Native American a member of any of the indigenous populations of America, but often excluding those of Hawaiian, Pacific Islander, or Alaskan origin, who have their own distinct designations.

Native-born born in a particular country. Often used in the context of native-born citizen, indicating that an individual gained citizenship by being born in a country, compared to naturalized citizenship granted to a foreign-born citizen.

Native Hawaiians and Other Pacific Islanders the indigenous peoples of Hawaii, Guam, Samoa, or other Pacific Islands.

Negative symptoms a collection of symptoms associated with schizophrenia involving a lack of feelings or behaviors that are present in the normal population. For example, the loss of interest in everyday activities. Associated with psychotic disorders, such as schizophrenia.

Neoliberal philosophies political philosophies that support laissez-faire economic liberalism, including privatization, deregulation, free trade and smaller government. There is considerable debate surrounding whether neoliberalism benefits all members of society or principally the more wealthy. The term has its origins in 1930s Europe but experienced a resurgence in the 1980s to reflect a more radical form of capitalism that advocates for a significant reduction in government involvement.

New Age spirituality a term applied to a range of spiritual or religious beliefs and practices that share a belief in a holistic and universal divinity. The New Age movement is comprised of a loose network of organizations that became popular in Western countries in the 1970s and 1980s that believe in mysticism and universalism, a holistic approach to the divine where all is one.

New Deal programs a series of domestic programs enacted by Congress and executive order by President Franklin D. Roosevelt in the United States between 1933 and 1938, in response to the Great Depression. The New Deal Programs focused on the "Three R's": Relief, Recovery, and Reform.

No Child Left Behind Act federal legislation focusing on standards-based educational reform. Reauthorized as the Every Student Succeeds Act, which, in response to intense criticism about NCLB's national mandates, returned primary control for curriculum development to the states.

Non-governmental organizations an organization or charity that is not a part of a government or a for-profit business.

Observation skills the ability of a counselor to observe all aspects of clients' demeanor during sessions, including their words, eyes, and body language.

Older Americans Act the first federal law, passed in 1965, that provided comprehensive services for older adults.

Open-ended questions questions that do not allow respondents to answer "yes" or "no" and permit them the scope to answer in a way they believe is appropriate.

Opioids opioids are medications that reduce pain by lowering the intensity of pain signals reaching the brain. Opioids also control emotion. Common opioids include Vicodin, OxyContin, Percocet, morphine, and codeine. Opioids can be highly addictive.

Orphan trains a movement in the late 19th and early 20th centuries started by Rev. Loring Brace that involved sending street orphans from New York and other large urban centers on trains to reside with farming families in the west who were willing to care for them.

Orphans a child with no parents, either through death or abandonment. May also include children with only one parent, or unaccompanied children.

Outdoor relief social welfare assistance under England's poor laws and later America's early social welfare system, consisting of money, food, clothing, or goods without the requirement that the recipient enter an institution.

Outlaw motorcycle gang (OMG) a group of motorcycle owners who band together and agree to disobey society's laws, typically for monetary gain and to increase power and terror. The Hells Angels is considered an outlaw motorcycle gang.

Out-migration　the process of leaving one community to settle in another. It is usually widespread, as seen in population movements that are economically driven.

Palliative care　specialized medical care for people with serious and/or life-threatening illnesses that focuses on providing patients with relief from the symptoms and stress of a serious illness, including pain. The goal is to improve quality of life for both the patient and the family.

Parachurch organizations　faith-based organizations that work outside of a specific church to engage in human services and evangelism.

Parenting classes　a structured set of classes or program that focus on parenting training, including normative child development and best practice in regard to parenting styles and techniques. Often required for biological parents involved in the child welfare system.

Patient Protection and Affordable Care Act　a U.S. federal statute signed into law by President Barack Obama on March 23, 2010. Also referred to as the Affordable Care Act (ACA) or colloquially Obamacare. Considered a significant overhaul of the U.S. health care system, with the goals of increasing the quality and affordability of health insurance, and reducing the costs of health care for individuals and the government.

Patriarchy　a hierarchical political and social system that privileged males, where men as a group have more power and control women as a group, both structurally and ideologically.

Permanency plan　a report prepared by child welfare workers involving a plan regarding children being removed from their homes and biological parents and placed in the custody of the child welfare system.

Permanent housing programs　supportive housing programs that offer subsidized housing on a permanent basis, typically government subsidized through HUD.

Person-in-environment approach　a practice-guiding principle in social work that highlights the importance of understanding an individual within the context of the environmental contexts in which that person lives and acts.

Personal Responsibility and Work Opportunity Act　social welfare legislation passed in 1996 that ended the former entitlement social welfare program, ushering in a welfare-to-work philosophy.

Physician aid-in-dying (PAD)　a practice in which a physician provides a competent, terminally ill patient with a prescription for a lethal dose of medication, upon the patient's request, which the patient intends to use to end his or her own life. This newer approach to assisted dying is believed to be easier for the physician ethically since the physician does not take as active an approach as with euthanasia.

Plea arrangement　an agreement in a criminal case between the prosecutor and defendant where the defendant agrees to plead guilty to a particular charge in return for some concession from the prosecutor. Also called a plea bargain and plea deal.

Pneumocystis carinii pneumonia (PCP)　a lung infection caused by the fungus *Pneumocystis jirovecii*. PCP occurs in people with weakened immune systems, including people with HIV. The first signs of infection are difficulty breathing, high fever, and dry cough.

Point-in-time (PIT) counts　(as defined by HUD) is a snapshot of the homeless population taken on a given day. It provides a count of sheltered and unsheltered homeless persons from either the last biennial count or a more recent annual count. This count includes a street count in addition to a count of all clients in emergency and transitional beds.

Policy advocacy　a form of macro advocacy that is facilitated on a policy level in an attempt to change government policies and legislation to benefit human services clients.

Positive symptoms　a collection of symptoms associated with schizophrenia involving a presence of thoughts, behaviors, and sensory perceptions, not present in the normal population.

Post-traumatic stress disorder (PTSD)　a clinical disorder that involves a collection of symptoms in response to the exposure of a traumatic event, including intrusive memories, hyperarousal, and efforts to avoid emotional triggers.

Prejudice　an unjustified or incorrect attitude (usually negative) toward an individual based solely on the individual's membership in a social group.

Privileged communication　a client's legal right barring having their disclosures to certain professionals revealed during legal proceedings or other communication, without their informed consent.

Proselytizing   the process of converting or attempting to convert (someone) from one religion, belief, or opinion to another.

Protestant work ethic   a term originally coined by Max Weber emphasizing that hard work and frugality are a result of a person's status of salvation in the Protestant faith, particularly in Calvinism (also referred to as the Puritan work ethic).

Protracted refugee situations   the Office of the United Nations High Commissioner for Refugees (UNHCR) defines protracted refugee situations as those "in which refugees find themselves in a long-lasting and intractable state of limbo. Their lives may not be at risk, but their basic rights and essential economic, social, and psychological needs remain unfulfilled after years in exile."

Psychoeducational approaches   an intervention strategy that combines counseling with education about psychosocial dynamics and other relevant phenomena.

Psychosocial assessment   a comprehensive evaluation prepared by many mental health providers upon intake of a client's mental health, social status, and functioning level and capacity.

Qur'an   the Islamic sacred book, believed to be the word of God as dictated to Muhammad by the archangel Gabriel and written down in Arabic. Also spelled Koran.

Race   a person's physical characteristics, such as bone structure and skin, hair, or eye color.

Rape as a weapon of war   wartime sexual violence involving rape, gang rape, and any type of sexual violence by combatants during armed conf lict.

Rape trauma syndrome   the psychological trauma experienced by a rape victim, which includes disruptions to normal physical, emotional, cognitive, and interpersonal thinking and behavior.

Rapid rehousing   Continuum of Care funds may provide supportive services, and/or short-term (up to three months) and/or medium-term (for 3 to 24 months) tenant-based rental assistance as necessary to help a homeless individual or family, with or without disabilities, move as quickly as possible into permanent housing and achieve stability in that housing. Assistance must include case management services.

Relative moral principles   the view that ethical standards and morality (principles of right or wrong) are culturally determined and thus subject to a person's individual perspectives, worldview, and choice. Also referred to as moral relativism.

Relative poverty   a standard for defining poverty in terms of the society in which an individual lives and which therefore differs between countries and over time.

Religion   a social or cultural experience grounded in a religious tradition.

Resilience   a person's ability to recover quickly from challenges and difficult times.

Restorative justice model   a model for handling crime that is based not on punitive measures, but on bringing the victim, offender, and community together, where all parties have equal parts in repairing the relationships destroyed by crime.

Restraint   physical restraint that immobilizes or reduces the ability of a student to move. Physical restraint does not include actions taken to break up a fight, comfort a student, or actions taken to prevent a student's impulsive act to injure him or herself.

At-risk populations   populations at increased risk for a range of social problems, including poverty and social, economic and political marginalization (also referred to as "vulnerable populations"). Including, but not limited to children, older adults, Black people, Latinas/os, the homeless, immigrants, veterans, the mentally ill, members of the LGBTQ population.

Rural depopulation   decreasing populations of remote and economically depressed rural communities.

Rural enclaves   rural areas within a larger geographic community.

Rurality   a sociological term defining what is rural.

Schizophrenia   an incurable and chronic brain disorder that impacts how people think, feel, and behave. Characterized by hallucinations, delusions in thinking, as well as other profoundly debilitating symptoms.

Seclusion   the involuntary isolation of a student in a room, enclosure, or space from which the student is isolated from others.

Section 8 Housing   a HUD subsidized housing program for the general population.

Section 811 Housing   a HUD subsidized housing program for adults with disabilities, including mental illness.

Self-efficacy a concept originally coined by social psychologist Albert Bandura referring to an individual's belief in his or her competence in completing tasks successfully.

Self-fulfilling prophecy a prediction that directly or indirectly causes itself to become true.

Serious mental illness any mental, behavioral, or emotional disorder that significantly interferes with life activities, such as relationships, employment, parenting, or personal life management skills.

Settlement house movement a reformist social movement (1880–1920) initiated in England and then the United States that established interdependent communities of middle class and poor (especially immigrants) with the goal of creating community through the sharing of knowledge and culture in order to alleviate poverty and social exclusion. The settlement houses provided advocacy, child care, housing, and classes.

Settlement houses social service residential organizations in large urban centers that provided a home and services to primarily newly arrived and non-English-speaking immigrants who were often exploited in factories. The settlement house movement was initiated in the United States by Jane Addams.

Sharecropping a system of agriculture in which a landowner allows a tenant to use the land in return for a share of the crops produced on their portion of land. Similar to feudalism in the Middle Ages. Sharecropping was practiced after the end of slavery, but few blacks had any legal protection because despite working a piece of land for generations, upon the sale of a property, or the whim of a landowner, black sharecropping families could be evicted from the land with little notice and no recourse.

Single room occupancy the SRO Program provides rental assistance for homeless persons in connection with the moderate rehabilitation of SRO dwellings. SRO housing contains units for occupancy by one person.

Social change change affected on a social level involving social justice and human rights.

Social Darwinism a concept referring to the application of the biological principles of natural selection and survival of the fittest to the social and political realms.

Social diagnosis a concept created by Mary Richmond, an early COS leader, involving the search for the cause of poverty by examining the interaction between the poor and their environment.

Social exclusion often considered in relation to poverty, referring to the overt or covert exclusion of segments of society from the benefits of mainstream society, including political activities (e.g., the limiting of voting rights), social activities (e.g., through the barring of church attendance or club memberships), and economic activities.

Social gospel a Protestant religious movement in the United States in the late 19th century that had the goal of compelling the Christian church to be more responsive to social problems, such as poverty and social reform.

Social learning theory explains how people learn new behaviors, values, and attitudes through watching others and modeling after their behavior.

Social mores acceptable customs, norms, and behaviors in a particular society or social group.

Social oppression a concept that describes a relationship of dominance and subordination between categories of people in which one benefits from the systematic abuse, exploitation, and injustice directed toward the other.

Social problems a social issue, such as poverty, that negatively impacts segments of society (often more vulnerable members of society).

Southern Black Belt a group of counties containing higher than average percentages of black residents, stretching through parts of Virginia, the Carolinas, Georgia, Florida, Alabama, Mississippi, Tennessee, Louisiana, Arkansas, and Texas. Known for high poverty rates, particularly among African Americans.

Spirituality the experience of having an independent relationship with a deity, involving a search for the sacred—a process that involves seeking out that which is considered holy or the divine.

Statement of faith a creed summarizing the core tenets of a religious community.

Strengths-based approach a practice perspective used initially in social work, developed by David Saleebey, that focuses on finding strengths in client and communities, rather than focusing on deficits. Saleebey believed that clients have the ability to be resourceful and resilient in the face of adversity, and that by using a strengths-based perspective with any counseling model, a social worker could tap into these strengths to assist clients and client systems in more effectively managing challenges.

Student services team a multidisciplinary team of professionals that support students in a range of ways. Most student services teams include school social workers, school counselors, school psychologists, as well as speech/language therapists, learning specialists, and school administrators.

Successful aging a term used to describe aging well psychologically, socially, and biologically.

Suicidal ideation the process of thinking about committing suicide, without actually doing so.

Survival of the fittest a term coined by Herbert Spencer, a British philosopher, referring to the application of the biological principles of natural selection to the social world. Survival of the fittest implies that only the stronger members of society are destined to survive, thus charity and other means to intervene in the natural order will only serve to weaken society.

Sweatshop conditions any working environment, but particularly factories, that does not employ labor laws and compels workers to work in harsh conditions, such as long hours, unsafe working conditions, and perhaps even emotional and physical abuse.

Systems perspective as applied to social work, this perspective is based on a theory that human behavior is influenced by a range of interactive factors, such as family, friends, economic class, religion, culture, and social dynamics (such as racism and gender bias).

Tanakh the Jewish scriptures, which consist of three divisions, the Torah, the Prophets, and the Writings.

Temporary Assistance for Needy Families (TANF) the public assistance program in the United States that replaced Aid to Families with Dependent Children (AFDC). The social welfare program developed in response to PRWORA of 1996 legislation.

Thanatologist an individual who practices the scientific study of death and the practices associated with it, including the study of the needs of the terminally ill and their families.

Therapeutic foster care intensive, individualized mental health services provided to children within specialized foster care placement.

Three-strikes law a law that significantly increases the prison sentences of persons convicted of a felony who have been previously convicted of two or more violent crimes or serious felonies. Three-strikes laws often result in individuals receiving an automatic sentence of life for their third qualifying felony. Often criticized by human rights advocates due to the harsh nature of the law, including what qualifies as a serious felony (e.g., drug offenses) and the age of those being charged (youth or young adults).

Torah the law of God as revealed to Moses and recorded in the first five books of the Hebrew scriptures, also called the Pentateuch.

Transitional housing programs temporary housing programs that offer housing and associated services for up to 24 months.

Transitional shelter a long-term shelter for female survivors of intimate partner violence focusing on gaining self-sufficiency and autonomy.

Trauma-informed therapy an organizational structure and treatment framework that involves understanding, recognizing, and responding to all types of traumatic experiences.

Treatment modalities a therapeutic approach including treatment intervention strategies used with individual clients or within a mental health program.

Tudor Poor Laws poor relief laws in England during the Tudor period (1485–1603). These laws were replaced with the passage of the Elizabethan Poor Laws of 1601.

Tzedakah the religious obligation to do what is right and just for the poor and needy.

U.S. Housing and Urban Development (HUD) the U.S. Department of Housing and Urban Development (HUD) is a department in the executive branch of the U.S. federal government. HUD's mission is to create strong, sustainable, inclusive communities and quality affordable homes for all.

Ungame a non-competitive learning and communication board game that fosters listening skills and pro-social communication skills.

Universal moral principles the view that ethics and morals are universal for all people in similar situations, regardless of culture, race, sex, religion, nationality, sexual orientation, or any other distinguishing feature. Also referred to as moral universalism.

Vagrancy a term used in early America and England to describe an idle homeless person, typically a man. The term was often used as a pejorative.

Vicarious trauma   the impact on a trauma worker or helper that results from empathic engagement with traumatized clients and their reports of traumatic experiences.

Visiting Teacher Movement (1906–1940)   visiting teachers were social workers who worked at settlement houses in large urban centers and volunteered to work in public schools to help immigrants, children with disabilities, and maladjusted children. The focus of the visiting teacher movement was on creating stronger connections between home and school and encouraging children to attend school.

War on Poverty   the unofficial name for legislation introduced by President Lyndon B. Johnson during his State of the Union address on January 8, 1964, in response to an unprecedentedly high national poverty rate.

Watergate scandal   a major political scandal that occurred in the United States in the 1970s following a break-in at the Democratic National Committee (DNC) headquarters at the Watergate office complex in Washington, D.C., and President Richard Nixon's administration's attempted cover-up of its involvement. President Nixon resigned in response to the scandal.

Welfare queen   a pejorative phrase used in the United States to refer to people, usually women of color, who are accused of fraudulently collecting welfare benefits because they do not want to work. Most historians and social policy experts now deem the welfare queen a myth created and used by politicians to manipulate the public into supporting reductions in social welfare spending.

White flight   the large-scale out-migration of middle-class Caucasians from racially mixed urban regions to more racially homogeneous suburban or exurban regions. Sociologists believe that when a neighborhood reaches approximately 30 percent racially mixed, Caucasians will begin to leave.

White privilege   societal privileges that benefit white people (often from European descent), unavailable to non-white people under the same social, political, or economic circumstances.

Women's shelter   a temporary shelter for women and their children escaping a domestic violence relationship. Also called a battered women's shelter.

Women's suffrage   women's right to vote.

Word salad   a symptom of schizophrenia involving disorganized speech and incoherent talk.

Worthy and the Unworthy Poor   under England's earliest poor laws the poor were categorized as either worthy or unworthy. Worthy poor included those dependent persons who were poor through no fault of their own—principally, orphans, widows, the handicapped, and older adults were considered the worthy poor. Dependent persons who were perceived as having caused their own poverty—principally those who were vagrants, drunkards, lazy and immoral, and refused to work—were considered the unworthy poor. Many social welfare experts believe that elements of these sentiments remain in contemporary social welfare policy.

Wraparound services   an approach to human services that provides intensive, individualized, and holistic care to individuals in need.

Xenophobia   an intense or irrational dislike or fear of people from other countries.

Index